KU-585-274

FROMMER'S

PORTUGAL, MADEIRA, AND THE AZORES

DARWIN PORTER

Assisted by
Danforth Prince
Margaret Foresman

11TH EDITION

Published by Prentice Hall Trade Division
A Division of Simon & Schuster Inc.
15 Columbus Circle
New York, NY 10023

ISBN 0-13-332470-2
ISSN 1044-2278

Manufactured in the United States of America

*Although every effort was made to ensure the accuracy
of price information appearing in this book,
it should be kept in mind that prices
can and do fluctuate in the course of time.*

CONTENTS

MAPS

A DISCLAIMER

Although every effort was made to ensure the accuracy of the prices and travel information appearing in this book, readers are advised that prices fluctuate in the course of time and travel information changes under the impact of the varied and volatile factors that affect the travel industry. The authors and publisher cannot be held responsible for the experiences of the reader while traveling. Readers are invited to write the publisher with ideas, comments, and suggestions for future editions.

Readers should also note that the establishments described under Reader's Selections or Suggestions have not in all cases been inspected by the authors and that opinions expressed there are those of the individual reader(s) only and do not in any way represent the opinions of the publisher or author of this guide.

WHEN A $ IS NOT A $

Portugal is one of the most inexpensive countries in which to travel in Europe. But first-time U.S. visitors often panic at price quotations, because Portugal uses the same $ sign to designate its currency. The **escudo** is written as 1$00. The dollar sign is written between the escudo and the **centavo,** of which there are 100 to the escudo, thus 1$50 is one escudo, 50 centavos.

There is no fixed rate of exchange between the escudo and the dollar. At press time, one escudo was worth approximately $.0065 (a little more than half a penny) in U.S. coinage, meaning you could buy 154 escudos with one dollar. There is no way to predict what the escudo will be worth when you arrive—so check with a banker, at home or in Portugal, for the latest information.

FROMMER'S PORTUGAL, MADEIRA, AND THE AZORES

1. THE REASON WHY
2. USING THIS GUIDE
3. FROMMER'S DOLLARWISE TRAVEL CLUB—HOW TO SAVE MONEY ON ALL YOUR TRAVELS

At the dawn of the Age of Exploration, mariners believed that two-headed, fork-tongued monsters big as houses lurked across the Sea of Darkness, waiting to gulp a caravel down their fire-lined throats. It was even feared that white men would turn black if they ventured near the equator.

In spite of these formidable problems, Portugal—in what has been called its "épopée of yesteryears"—launched legendary caravels on missions that became historic: Vasco da Gama to India, Ferdinand Magellan to circumnavigate the globe, Bartholomeu Dias to round the Cape of Good Hope. In time, Portuguese navigators explored two-thirds of the earth.

1. The Reason Why

Although the Iberian country was in the vanguard of world-wide exploration, it has never been as successful in attracting visitors to its own shores. Outside of Greater Lisbon, the Algarve, and Madeira, in the past Portugal was unknown to the main-line tourist, although it offers sandy beaches, art treasures, a respectable cuisine, unique Manueline architecture, inexpensive handcrafts, a mild climate, moderate hotel tariffs, and friendly people. The country may be small—roughly about the size of Maine—but like Mighty Mouse, it packs a powerful punch. Portugal measures only 136 miles at its widest point, and 350 miles at its longest span.

I have set myself the formidable task of seeking out the finest in Portugal, but the premise of this book is that the best need not necessarily be the most expensive. Hence my aim is not only to familiarize you with the offerings of Portugal, but also to stretch your dollar power, to show you that you need not always pay high prices for charm, top-grade comfort, and first-rate food.

In this guide I'll devote a great deal of attention to those old meccas—Lisbon, Estoril, Cascais, Sintra—focusing on both their obvious and hidden treasures. But important as they are, they do not fully reflect the diversity and complexity of Portugal. To discover that, you must venture deep into the provinces.

Unlike many nations in Europe, Portugal defies a clear, logical, coherent plan of sightseeing. It is a patchwork of treasures, with many of the choicest items tucked away in remote corners. To sample the best of Portugal, especially some of its most intriguing accommodations, you'll have to seek out a faraway country estate deep in the heartland, or perhaps a 14th-century monastery now converted into a *pousada* (tourist inn) in the old Roman city of Évora in Alentejo, or even an 18th-century palace in Seteais, where Lord Byron worked on *Childe Harold* in the front garden. Living outside of Lisbon whenever possible will, of course, give you a chance to get acquainted with the Portuguese, a more difficult task in most capital city hotels.

THE PEOPLE

The Portuguese have developed a decidedly different character from the people of Spain, their sister nation on the Iberian peninsula. Those who travel among and mingle with the Portuguese usually return home filled with a special warmth for the people. They are easily approachable, helpful, and you may find after you've left that you have made several lifetime friends and correspondents.

In Portugal, the family as an institution remains firmly entrenched, even in the aftermath of revolution and upheaval. Many of its people have no close friends outside the family unit. The Catholic church still enjoys strong power and prestige over many segments of society. It is rare to meet a Portuguese Protestant or other non-Catholic.

Although the people in the cities have become increasingly sophisticated, their counterparts down the economic and social scale, especially in the country, tend to retain their traditional social roles. Portuguese women work in the fields with their men, sowing seed, guiding oxen, carrying milk jugs, and harvesting. Children often labor in the fields alongside their parents. The wife of a fisherman may help repair nets and then sell the catch in the streets, returning in the evening to her cottage to do all the housework, cooking, and mending.

In Lisbon the people dress well, particularly in the business district. In the country you still see traditional garb; women still wear black shawls draped around their shoulders and carry baskets of produce balanced on their heads.

The Portuguese are a proud people. Life is more formal in the industrial north of Portugal, while in the south, in the Algarve, the approach to life seems more casual, and the people's attitude more relaxed and friendly.

WHY CHOOSE PORTUGAL?

It may be presumptuous to give you reasons why to go to Portugal. Dozens may have already occurred to you. If you're of Portuguese ancestry, you may want to trace your ancestors or relatives. I'll merely add a few that you may not have thought about.

To Learn the Meaning of *Saudade*

The word is hard to translate, evoking a mood of melancholy, a sense of sadness expressed most dramatically in Portuguese music. One scholar called it "the nostalgic memory of past greatness, the myth of a golden century, the deep sense of loss which has been called Atlantic melancholy." You'll want to listen to *saudade*'s most heart-throbbing and poignant expression, *fado*—Portugal's most authentic and absorbing art form. Classically beautiful singers will entertain you. Clutching a traditional black shawl around herself, the *fadista* raises her sensitive voice in a dimly lit tavern near the Alfama and the docks, singing the plaintive and poetic songs of her people. It doesn't matter whether you understand the words. The power and the dynamic quality of the lament transcends language, forming its own vocabulary, finding its own reality.

To Do Something Majestic

Atop the highest turret of the seemingly impregnable fortress of St. George in Lisbon, the sounds of the quays and streets are only a distant hum. A great eagle encaged within the fortress bewails its captivity. And whenever all sounds seem to have faded, the unnerving screams of one of the castle's white peacocks shatters the tranquility. Then you understand why the ancients trembled at the harsh, discordant shrieks of this bird—supposedly ill-omened harbingers of war, blood, and death.

Below, great ocean-going vessels trudge out of the custard-brown harbor toward the blue Atlantic. There before you are ancient façades and chipped slate backsides; teeming, narrow city streets and rolling hills; major religious monuments; and steel-and-glass testimonies to technology. You can sit straddled upon a giant cannon that once protected the wealthiest of maritime empires and which trembled through many an earthquake. In a glance you can view Roman occupation, Visigothic walls, Moorish remains, the conflict with Spain, the cradle of the Portuguese empire, the modern world—a continuum of time unbroken.

To Wander Back into the Middle Ages

Involve yourself in the rural life, the very soul of Portugal. To sample a way of life fast disappearing, go to, say, Entrocamento, in the bull-breeding province of Ribatejo. This village, like so many others in Portugal, exudes the simple rusticity and warmth of a people still connected spiritually to the land.

From any street, you can see the outskirts of vineyards, in which cork trees are abundantly interspersed. Streams flow swiftly through the vineyards on their way to the nearby Tagus. You can follow one up into the foothills; and if you possess or can borrow a string and hook, chances are that you'll be having fish for supper.

The men come in from the fields at dusk, heading directly for the taverns for many carafes of deep-purple wine topped with an inch of froth. An entire family—including the mother, father, and children, even friends—works behind the serving tables, drawing glasses from the damp, cool casks. Once inside one of these bustling taverns, an olive-skinned habitué will motion you toward a serving table, give a quick jerk on his earlobe, a wink of the eye from under a dark beret, and a repeated flip of his thumb toward his lips—the lever on the cask creaks.

To Build Bridges to Other People

As crusty as cork bark, as hard as an olive pit, yet as warm as life ought to be, the people of Portugal are the greatest experience in this still provincial country. Their bridges of giving are strong and sturdy. Those travelers accustomed to a smile or friendly gesture used to cover an ulterior motive may find themselves clumsy in dealing with the Portuguese. But once you let yourself go, venturing into the countryside and exposing yourself to the Portuguese way of life, you'll feel the organic kindness of a remarkable people.

For example, you might stop a white-bearded farmer in Alentejo and innocently inquire about directions. Don't be surprised if he invites you inside his family compound, where all the activity really takes place. It is here that he grows the produce that feeds his large family, barters with his neighbors, and generally carries on the business of living. He'll ask you to warm yourself at a hearthside fire, while he takes out a large loaf of bread, slicing it and spreading it with home-churned butter, then coating it with farm-grown honey kept in a large crock. Wine made from his own grapes will be offered in ceramic mugs.

When you leave, again don't be surprised if he tells you with conviction that the next time you pass through, you're to bed down as a guest of his family.

To Feel the Impact of the Sea

While the Portuguese fishermen are the challengers of the sea, the women are the guardians and sentinels. At Nazaré, Portugal's most colorful fishing village (north of Lisbon), the ritual of launching and bringing in those brightly painted Phoenician-inspired boats is as regular as the tidal rhythm of the sea. The bearded fishermen, in their long, tasseled stocking caps and plaid shirts, push out to the sea, paddling continuously, riding through the fury of the first breaker. When at sea, they search for the best fish-producing waters, letting down their nets and depositing their catch at the bottom of the boat. Perhaps they will return to shore early with smiles of victory; but too often their return is delayed. Tragically, an occasional storm may rise suddenly to strike them down.

As the sun sinks, the women of Nazaré, immobile as classical statues, wait on the beach for the return of their men. They have spent the first part of the day gossiping and repairing nets; but when it's time for the homecoming of the fleet, they gather quietly at the water's edge. Standing there in lonely vigil, they say not a word, a silent understanding among them. While the young girls wear seven bright petticoats, the older women are nearly always draped in black. There is no one who has not lost a father, a brother, or a son. Tightening their woolen black shawls around themselves, they gaze out to the now-darkening sea, squinting their eyes, searching for the first signs of the high-bowed seeing-eye boats. When the fleet appears, the women cross themselves many times in gratitude to their protector saint, then rush out to do their part in unloading the boats.

The sea gives life and takes it away.

---

2. Using This Guide

In brief, this is a guidebook giving specific details (including prices) about Portuguese hotels, restaurants, bars, sightseeing attractions, nightlife, and tours. Establishments in *all* price ranges have been documented and described.

About 10% of the recommendations include the luxury hotels such as the Palácio at Estoril, while 35% suggest inexpensive accommodations: budget hotels, guesthouses, or country inns, offering provincial-style bedrooms with private bath. The greatest number, 55%, fall in the middle price range.

In all cases, establishments have been judged by a strict yardstick of value. If they measured up, they were included, regardless of price classification. The uniqueness of this book, I think, lies in the fact that it can be used either by a society matron ("We always stay at the Ritz in Lisbon") or by an escudo-lean collegian ("There's this little restaurant in Lisbon where a prato do dia will cost about $6").

But the major focus of the book is centered on the average, middle-income-bracket voyager who'd like to patronize the almost wholly undocumented establishments in Portugal—that is, the first- and second-class hotels or some of the better, but less heralded, restaurants, where you can often get a superb dinner.

In Portugal, of course, a first-time visitor is often bewildered as to what to see. The country suffers from lack of publicity. People know of Lisbon, Estoril, Sintra, and the Algarve, and that's about it.

However, I've penetrated deep into remote villages, such as baroque Lamego in the provinces. Naturally, all the big-time attractions are explored as well, ranging from Byron's glorious Eden at Sintra, to the sunny beaches of the Algarve, to the coastal villages of the north.

A CALDEIRADA OF BARGAINS

Borrowing the title of this heading from the classic fish stew of Portugal, I'll preview some of the delectable establishments awaiting you. In my journeys through every province of the country, I have discovered charm and comfort offered for little cost, or establishments where the homemade or creative touch of their proprietors lifts them far above the ordinary. For an understanding of what I mean, I'll offer a few examples. You'll meet dozens more in the pages ahead, perhaps discover some all on your own when you actually go to Portugal.

□ In Lisbon's museumland, Belém, you can stay at a renovated inn with regional furnishings, Hotel da Torre, which has a handsome wood-paneled bar and a restaurant serving regional food. For a double room with a continental breakfast you pay only 6,800$ ($44.20) nightly.

□ Or perhaps a crow's nest, modern stone inn perched near the crest of a mountain of Caramulo. This government-owned pousada is a favorite retreat of in-the-know Portuguese who appreciate a blazing fire on an open hearth for after-dinner coffee, a panoramic view from the dining room, and immaculately kept and cozy bedrooms with private balconies and tile baths. You can stay in the pousada for 9,800$ ($63.70) in a double with a shower.

□ Or perhaps you'll be drawn to the splendid life in the historic Roman city of Évora, staying at a luxury pousada. In this converted 14th-century convent you'll pay only about 17,600$ ($114.40) per day for a double bedroom filled with antique reproductions, and a private tile bath, with breakfast. You can wander through a Manueline cloister, pause beside a gurgling marble fountain, and drink the local wine in the former dining hall.

□ Finally, you may want to become a guest in an ancient stately home (*quinta*) on the faraway island of Madeira, at a converted private estate with its own sun-pocket swimming pool. Two people can stay here in individualized bedrooms with antiques for 13,000$ ($84.50) daily. That figure includes breakfast served on a silver tray on the flagstone terrace overlooking the harbor.

What about restaurants?

□ In the kitchen of the former royal palace at Queluz, outside of Lisbon on the road to Sintra, you can enjoy a first-class meal in a regal setting. You dine seated on high ladder-backed chairs under a towering vaulted ceiling, with stone arches, a fireplace, and a 15-foot marble-topped chef's table laden with appetizing food. For 4,000$ ($26) and up, you can order a dinner, such as a regional soup, seafood bubbly with cheese, plus assorted cheeses from the neighboring countryside, as well as fresh fruit.

□ You can dine on some of the best-cooked fish dinners in the Lisbon area at a restaurant reached by ferryboat. As you watch the activity on the Tagus from its left bank, you can enjoy such dishes as turbot meunière or the fish stew, *caldeirada*, a meal in itself, followed by strawberries with sugar or manjor de príncipe, made of eggs and almonds. A meal costs from 1,800$ ($11.70) at this favorite restaurant of Portuguese families.

SOME DISCLAIMERS

No restaurant, inn, hotel, *pensão,* shop, or nightclub paid to be mentioned in this book. What you read are entirely personal recommendations—in many cases the proprietors never knew their establishments were being visited or investigated for inclusion in a travel guide.

A word of warning: Unfortunately, costs change, and they rarely go downward. The government virtually imposes rent control on its hotels, and many establishments have gone two or three years before changing their tariffs. Owing to sudden improvements or upgrading, prices in other places have skyrocketed.

Always, when checking into a hotel, inquire about the tariff. This policy can save much embarrassment and disappointment when the time comes to settle your bill. Unfortunately, you cannot ever insist on being charged the precise prices quoted in this book, although every effort has been made to secure the accurate tariffs as much as they were foreseeable.

THE ORGANIZATION OF THIS BOOK

Here's how Frommer's information is organized, chapter by chapter:

I. Directly ahead, this chapter deals with ways of flying to Portugal, and then with various modes of transportation within the country. Naturally, the focus is on the least expensive means of transport, on such items as excursion fares and off-season discounts.

II. The spotlight is turned on "The Scene in Portugal"; it's meant to fortify you for your plunge into the country by outlining its history, providing tips on food specialties and wine, and previewing the hotel outlook.

III–IX. These chapters take on a huge task—that of exploring the hotels, restaurants, shopping, attractions, and nightlife not only of **Lisbon,** but of the leading resorts along the Costa do Sol **(Estoril** and **Cascais),** and of **Sintra.** Documented first are the deluxe and first-class hotels, followed by those in the middle bracket and budget range. Beginning with the most expensive and elegant restaurants, such as Tagide and Aviz, the list continues downward to the lowly beer tavern serving an icy-cold stein and a juicy steak. Nightlife, especially fado, can be found in a wide variety of places, ranging from a rowdy sailors' bar in Lisbon to a posh disco in Cascais.

X–XI. We move outside of Lisbon for a trip south of the **Tagus** to the fishing port of **Setúbal** and the three-castle district, to the resort village of **Sesimbra,** and to the cove of **Portinho da Arrabida** at the foot of the Arrabida hills. Heading north, although still based in Lisbon, you can explore the fortress town of **Óbidos,** the 12th-century Cistercian monastery of **Alcobaça,** the 14th-century battle abbey at **Batalha,** the fishing village of **Nazaré,** the world-famed pilgrimage shrine at **Fáti-ma,** and the historic Templars city of **Tomar.**

XII. The **Algarve,** the African-looking, southernmost province of Portugal is described. Stretching along the coast from Sagres to Vila Real de Santo António, it spans a distance of about 94 miles. For those who like beaches and sunshine, it sends out a call, and the tariffs are moderate, although still among the highest in Portugal.

XIII. This chapter bites off a big hunk, **Alentejo** and **Ribatejo.** Ribatejo is a land of pastures, known for bull breeding. The chief attraction is Tomar. The Alentejo is a district of olive trees and cork, its major goal the old Roman city of **Évora.**

XIV. This chapter explores **Coimbra,** famous for its university dating from 1290, and the environs, especially the former royal palace and forest of **Buçaco** and the remains of a Roman settlement at **Conimbriga.**

XV–XVI. The same is done for Portugal's second city, **Porto** (where port wine is shipped out to the world), and for the **Minho** district in the northwestern corner of the country. Hotels, pousadas, sights, and so forth are detailed.

XVII. We pay a visit to **Trás-os-Montes,** which translates as "beyond the mountains," the far-northeastern plateau bordering Spain on the north and east of the province, a wild and rugged country of vineyards, deep ravines, and tiny villages clinging impossibly, it would appear, to steep cliffs.

XVIII. Now we head out into the Atlantic for the mountainous, vegetation-rich island of **Madeira,** centering at **Funchal.**

XIX. Our trip concludes in the remote **Azores,** referred to as the "daughters of the ocean" and discovered in the 15th century.

Finally, the appendix offers vital minutiae: menu translations, capsule vocabularies, and a currency conversion.

TIME OUT FOR A COMMERCIAL

The very fact that you have purchased a guide to a small country of Europe puts you into a special, sophisticated category of traveler—that is, one who wants to explore and get to know a single country or two, as opposed to the "Grand Tour" individual who wants to do not only Belgium on Tuesday, but Rome on Wednesday, and reach the North Cape by Friday.

Even so, on your tour of Portugal you will come several times to the doorstep of one of the great tourist countries of Europe—Spain, which occupies the Iberian Peninsula with Portugal. By the time you reach the Algarve, you may feel you're so close to North Africa you'll want to make the plunge into exotic Morocco. Also, after visiting Madeira, you may be interested in exploring some more Atlantic islands. Because a limitation had to be placed on the number of chapters in this one guide, the publisher also issues a companion guide, *Spain and Morocco on $40 a Day* which includes a chapter on the Canary Islands.

AN INVITATION TO READERS

Frommer's Portugal, Madeira, and the Azores hopes to maintain a continuing dialogue between its writer and its readers. All of us share a common aim—to travel as widely and as well as possible, at the best value for our money—and in achieving that aim, your comments and suggestions can be of aid to others. Therefore, if you come across an appealing hotel, restaurant, nightclub, even sightseeing attraction, please don't keep it to yourself. Your letters need not only apply to new establishments, but to hotels and restaurants already recommended in this guide. The fact that a listing appears in this edition doesn't give it squatter's rights in future publications. If its services have deteriorated, its chef grown stale, its prices risen unfairly, whatever, these failings need to be known. Even if you enjoyed every place and found every description accurate, a letter letting me know that, too, can cheer a gray day. Send your comments to Darwin Porter, c/o Prentice Hall Travel, 15 Columbus Circle, New York, NY 10023.

3. Frommer's™ Dollarwise® Travel Club—How to Save Money on All Your Travels

In this book we'll be looking at how to get your money's worth in Portugal, Madeira, and the Azores, but there is a "device" for saving money and determining value on *all* your trips. It's the popular, international Frommer's Dollarwise Travel Club, now in its 30th successful year of operation. The club was formed at the urging of numerous readers of the $-A-Day and Frommer Guides, who felt that such an organization could provide continuing travel information and a sense of community to value-minded travelers in all parts of the world. And so it does!

In keeping with the budget concept, the annual membership fee is low and is immediately exceeded by the value of your benefits. Upon receipt of $18 (U.S. residents), or $20 U.S. by check drawn on a U.S. bank or via international postal money order in U.S. funds (Canadian, Mexican, and other foreign residents) to cover one year's membership, we will send all new members the following items.

(1) Any *two* of the following books

Please designate in your letter which two you wish to receive:

Frommer $-A-Day® Guides
Europe on $40 a Day
Australia on $30 a Day
Eastern Europe on $25 a Day
England on $50 a Day
Greece on $35 a Day
Hawaii on $60 a Day
India on $25 a Day
Ireland on $35 a Day

Israel on $40 a Day
Mexico (plus Belize and Guatemala) on $35 a Day
New York on $60 a Day
New Zealand on $45 a Day
Scandinavia on $60 a Day
Scotland and Wales on $40 a Day
South America on $35 a Day
Spain and Morocco (plus the Canary Is.) on $40 a Day
Turkey on $30 a Day
Washington, D.C. & Historic Virginia on $40 a Day

($-A-Day Guides document hundreds of budget accommodations and facilities, helping you get the most for your travel dollars.)

Frommer Guides

Australia
Austria and Hungary
Belgium, Holland & Luxembourg
Bermuda and The Bahamas
Brazil
Canada
Caribbean
Egypt
England and Scotland
France
Germany
Italy
Japan and Hong Kong
Portugal, Madeira, and the Azores
South Pacific
Switzerland and Liechtenstein
Alaska
California and Las Vegas
Florida
Mid-Atlantic States
New England
New York State
Northwest
Skiing USA—East
Skiing USA—West
Southern Atlantic States
Southeast Asia
Southwest
Texas
USA

(Frommer Guides discuss accommodations and facilities in all price ranges, with emphasis on the medium-priced.)

Frommer Touring Guides

Australia
Brazil
Egypt
Florence
London
Paris
Scotland
Thailand
Venice

(These new, color illustrated guides include walking tours, cultural and historic sites, and other vital travel information.)

Gault Millau
Chicago
France
Italy
London
Los Angeles
New England
New York
San Francisco
Washington, D.C.

(Irreverent, savvy, and comprehensive, each of these renowned guides candidly reviews over 1,000 restaurants, hotels, shops, nightspots, museums, and sights.)

Serious Shopper's Guides
Italy
London
Los Angeles
Paris

(Practical and comprehensive, each of these handsomely illustrated guides lists hundreds of stores, selling everything from antiques to wine, conveniently organized alphabetically by category.)

A Shopper's Guide to the Caribbean
(Two experienced Caribbean hands guide you through this shopper's paradise, offering witty insights and helpful tips on the wares and emporia of more than 25 islands.)

Beat the High Cost of Travel
(This practical guide details how to save money on absolutely all travel items—accommodations, transportation, dining, sightseeing, shopping, taxes, and more. Includes special budget information for seniors, students, singles, and families.)

Bed & Breakfast—North America
(This guide contains a directory of over 150 organizations that offer bed and breakfast referrals and reservations throughout North America. The scenic attractions, and major schools and universities near the homes of each are also listed.)

California with Kids
(A must for parents traveling in California, providing key information on selecting the best accommodations, restaurants, and sightseeing attractions for the particular needs of the family, whether the kids are toddlers, school-age, pre-teens, or teens.)

The Candy Apple: New York with Kids
(A spirited guide to the wonders of the Big Apple by a savvy New York grandmother with a kid's-eye view to fun. Indispensable for visitors and residents alike.)

Caribbean Hideaways
(Well-known travel author Ian Keown describes the most romantic, alluring places to stay in the Caribbean, rating each establishment on romantic ambience, food, sports opportunities, and price.)

Frommer's Belgium
(Arthur Frommer unlocks the treasures of a country overlooked by most travelers to

Europe. Discover the medieval charm, modern sophistication, and natural beauty of this quintessentially European country.)

Frommer's Cruises
(This complete guide covers all the basics of cruising—ports of call, costs, fly-cruise package bargains, cabin selection booking, embarkation and debarkation and describes in detail more than 60 or so ships cruising the waters of Alaska, the Caribbean, Mexico, Hawaii, Panama, Canada, and the United States.)

Guide to Honeymoon Destinations
(A special guide for that most romantic trip of your life, with full details on planning and choosing the destination that will be just right in the U.S. [California, New England, Hawaii, Florida, New York, South Carolina, etc.], Canada, Mexico, and the Caribbean.)

Manhattan's Outdoor Sculpture
(A total guide, fully illustrated with black and white photos, to more than 300 sculptures and monuments that grace Manhattan's plazas, parks, and other public spaces.)

Marilyn Wood's Wonderful Weekends
(This very selective guide covers the best mini-vacation destinations within a 200-mile radius of New York City. It describes special country inns and other accommodations, restaurants, picnic spots, sights, and activities—all the information needed for a two- or three-day stay.)

Motorist's Phrase Book
(A practical phrase book in French, German, and Spanish designed specifically for the English-speaking motorist touring abroad.)

The New World of Travel
(From America's No. 1 travel expert, Arthur Frommer, an annual sourcebook with the hottest news and latest trends that's guaranteed to change the way you travel—and save you hundreds of dollars. Jam-packed with alternative new modes of travel that will lead you to vacations that cater to the mind, the spirit, and a sense of thrift.)

Paris Rendez-Vous
(An amusing and *au courant* guide to the best meeting places in Paris, organized for hour-to-hour use: from power breakfasts and fun brunches, through tea at four or cocktails at five, to romantic dinners and dancing 'til dawn.)

Skiing Europe
(Describes top ski resorts in Austria, France, Italy, and Switzerland. Illustrated with maps of each resort area. Includes supplement on Argentinian resorts.)

Swap and Go—Home Exchanging Made Easy
(Two veteran home exchangers explain in detail all the money-saving benefits of a home exchange, and then describe precisely how to do it. Also includes information on home rentals and many tips on low-cost travel.)

Travel Diary and Record Book
(A 96-page diary for personal travel notes plus a section for such vital data as passport and traveler's check numbers, itinerary, postcard list, special people and places to visit, and a reference section with temperature and conversion charts, and world maps with distance zones.)

Where to Stay USA
(By the Council on International Educational Exchange, this extraordinary guide is
the first to list accommodations in all 50 states that cost anywhere from $3 to $30
per night.)

(2) Any *one* of the Frommer City Guides
Amsterdam
Athens
Atlantic City and Cape May
Boston
Cancún, Cozumel, and the Yucatán
Chicago
Dublin and Ireland
Hawaii
Las Vegas
Lisbon, Madrid, and Costa del Sol
London
Los Angeles
Mexico City and Acapulco
Minneapolis and St. Paul
Montréal and Québec City
New Orleans
New York
Orlando, Disney World, and EPCOT
Paris
Philadelphia
Rio
Rome
San Francisco
Santa Fe, Taos, and Albuquerque
Sydney
Washington, D.C.
(Pocket-size guides to hotels, restaurants, nightspots, and sightseeing attractions
covering all price ranges.)

(3) A one-year subscription to *The Dollarwise Traveler*
This quarterly eight-page tabloid newspaper keeps you up to date on
fastbreaking developments in low-cost travel in all parts of the world bringing you
the latest money-saving information—the kind of information you'd have to pay
$35 a year to obtain elsewhere. This consumer-conscious publication also features
columns of special interest to readers: **Hospitality Exchange** (members all over the
world who are willing to provide hospitality to other members as they pass through
their home cities); **Share-a-Trip** (offers and requests from members for travel companions who can share costs and help avoid the burdensome single supplement);
and **Readers Ask . . . Readers Reply** (travel questions from members to which
other members reply with authentic firsthand information).

(4) Your personal membership card
Membership entitles you to purchase through the club all Frommer publications for a third to a half off their regular retail prices during the term of your membership.
So why not join this hardy band of international budgeteers and participate in
its exchange of travel information and hospitality? Simply send your name and address, together with your annual membership fee of $18 (U.S. residents) or $20
U.S. (Canadian, Mexican, and other foreign residents), by check drawn on a U.S.

bank or via international postal money order in U.S. funds to: Frommer's Dollarwise Travel Club, Inc., 15 Columbus Circle, New York, NY 10023. And please remember to specify which *two* of the books in section (1) and which *one* in section (2) you wish to receive in your initial package of members' benefits. Or, if you prefer, use the order form at the end of the book and enclose $18 or $20 in U.S. currency.

Once you are a member, there is no obligation to buy additional books. No books will be mailed to you without your specific order.

GETTING THERE

Although Lisbon is a major gateway city to Europe, in bygone days travelers went to France or England first and then began their Grand Tour, perhaps (but most likely not) stopping over in Portugal.

Air transportation has changed this habit, and more and more sun-seeking travelers are beginning their European adventure in Lisbon. Portugal is, in fact, one of the European countries closest to North America, and it costs less to fly from New York to Lisbon than from New York to Paris, Amsterdam, or Frankfurt.

In the paragraphs that follow I'll describe the basic structure of air fares, exploring various methods of cutting your air transportation costs, and then I'll deal with methods of traveling within Portugal once you arrive.

1. Plane Economics

Since deregulation, the airlines have competed fiercely with one another for traffic. To many destinations, an airline now proposes a fare structure; another airline then files a competing and perhaps different fare structure. The competition may or may not result in a uniform price structure for all airlines flying to that particular country.

It all adds up to chaos—but often *beneficial* chaos for the alert traveler willing to study and consider all the fares available. The key to bargain air fares is to shop around.

In what follows I'll point out the current options available for flying directly to Portugal—only two airlines do so and they are **TAP** (the Portuguese international airline) and **TWA**. If you don't want to fly directly to Portugal, then remember to check all the airlines to find the most inexpensive transatlantic fare that coincides with your itinerary and travel plans.

TAP TO LISBON
When it was established in 1946, the routes of TAP were limited to flights between Lisbon and the then-Portuguese colonies of Angola and Mozambique. Over the years the number of destinations have increased and the technical skill of the airline has improved. Today TAP flies to more than 50 destinations and has earned

the respect of the travel industry for its selection in 1987 by Federal Express to provide maintenance for that carrier's fleet.

Like the early Portuguese explorers, the airline goes to four continents, touching down in New York, Boston, Los Angeles, Toronto, and Montréal, plus nine destinations within Portugal. These include Lisbon, Porto, Faro, Funchal (Madeira), and Terceira (the Azores).

TAP's modern fleet, which includes L-1011s, A-310s, B737s, and B727s, benefits from an impressive record of punctuality, safety, and comfort. TAP flies frequently on much-used routes originating in most of the major cities of western Europe. Its routes to Lisbon from London are especially value-conscious, sometimes priced so attractively that a reader might combine a sojourn in England with an inexpensive side excursion to Portugal. What better way to celebrate the "Old Alliance" between the two countries than with an investigation of them both during the same itinerary?

Stopover Options

Although both TAP and TWA fly between North America and Lisbon, TAP gives passengers the option of stopping midway across the Atlantic in the Azores, and also makes baggage transfers and seat reservations on connecting flights within Portugal much easier.

Ticket Options

Several ticket options exist for transatlantic passengers eager to experience both Portugal and its national carrier. At press time, TAP offered a winter senior citizen fare from New York and Boston to Portugal. The round trip fare is as low as $469. The definition of a senior citizen is a traveler 60 years of age or older. An interesting feature in TAP's senior citizen fare is that an accompanying traveler pays the same fare as the senior citizen but doesn't have to be in that age category. The minimum stay is three months. Tickets must be purchased at least seven days before departure. This fare is of special interest to retirees who wish to escape winter, because spring arrives very early in Portugal. The almond trees are in full bloom in the Algarve in the last weeks of January, and in Lisbon the spring flowers are in bloom in early February.

Most passengers prefer to travel in Portugal in the spring, summer, and autumn. One of TAP's most popular tickets is called a midweek **APEX fare.** The cost differs with the season, but is competitive with similar fares carrying similar restrictions on other airlines. Its price varies, depending on the day of the week and the season of the year, from $492 to $685. Tickets must be purchased 14 days before departure. In some cases, a $100 penalty is imposed for any changes made after payment on either leg of a passenger's itinerary. Nevertheless, if your plans are flexible enough, and if you're aware of the intended date of return, this might be the ticket option for you. For families, one strong attraction is the fact that children under 12 traveling with a parent pay between 50% and 67% of the adult fare.

For the purpose of APEX tickets, TAP divides its calendar year into three seasons: basic, shoulder, and peak. The cheapest season stretches between November 1 and December 9 and from Christmas Day until March 31. The most expensive season, when passengers tend to book most transatlantic flights solidly, stretches between June 1 and August 15, at least for APEX travelers.

Clients who prefer not to specify when they will return home, or who can't purchase their tickets within 14 or 21 days prior to takeoff, usually opt for an **excursion fare.** Costing more than either of the APEX options, it requires that passengers stay from 10 to 180 days before jetting back to North America. On this ticket, peak season lasts from June 1 to August 15.

The most exclusive, and the most expensive, class of service available on TAP is named after the seafaring pioneers who spread Portugal's empire throughout the world. **Navigator Class** passengers benefit from better service, food, and drink.

Navigator Class is TAP's name for business class and is comparable to first class on other major carriers.

For exact departure dates and up-to-the-minute tariffs, you can phone a reservations clerk at TAP. In the continental U.S., dial toll free 800/221-7370. In New York City, dial 212/944-2100.

TWA TO LISBON

A more limited air service is offered by Trans World Airlines. It flies only to Lisbon from North America, and does so only from JFK Airport in New York. TWA flights are once a day except Sunday. Flights generally depart JFK at 6:45 p.m., arriving in Lisbon at 6:20 a.m. the next day. Because of this early arrival, many passengers reach their hotel rooms before the previous night's guests have checked out and the maids haven't had time to prepare the rooms. So plan accordingly, and perhaps take along an overnight bag for your comfort.

The least expensive tickets on TWA, as of this writing only, cost $732 round trip. This type of ticket requires a 14-day advance purchase and a delay of from 7 to 60 days before using the return portion of the ticket. This price is for high season transatlantic passage. In shoulder season, the cost is about $100 less. Travel in low season is even cheaper: about $200 less.

Connections can be made from most major points throughout North America on TWA's network. But if you live anywhere outside of New York, you must prepare yourself for an airline transfer at Kennedy.

Subject to change, TWA offers a youth fare of $268 each way in high season, about $240 one way in low season. However, this fare is available only to travelers age 25 or under, providing space is available. Tickets of this type can be purchased at the last minute, since they are booked *only* within 72 hours of departure. They cannot be mailed, and must be purchased in person at any TWA ticket counter.

CHARTER FLIGHTS

Strictly for reasons of economy, some travelers may wish to accept the numerous restrictions and possible uncertainties of a charter flight to Portugal. Charters require that passengers strictly specify departure and return dates, and full payment is required in advance. Any changes in flight dates are possible (if at all) upon payment of a stiff penalty. Any reputable travel agent can advise you about fares, cities of departure, and most important, the reputation of the charter company.

AIRPORT AND AIRLINES

Both foreign and domestic flights arrive at Lisbon's **Portela Airport,** which lies about four miles from the heart of the city. For all airport information, telephone 01/80-20-60. A green line bus, called *Ligne Verte,* carries passengers into the city for 95$ (60¢) for one zone. The bus goes as far as the Santa Apolónia Rail Station. There is no charge for luggage.

For ticket sales, flight reservations, information about the city and the country, you can get in touch with the polite and efficient personnel of **TAP Air Portugal** at 3A Praça Marquês de Pombal (tel. 01/57-50-20, the airline's reservation number).

---

2. Traveling Within Portugal

TRAINS IN PORTUGAL

The railway system seems underdeveloped when compared to the more industrialized nations of Western Europe. Still, the connections between the capital and more than 20 major towns are mainly electric and diesel. Express trains run between Lisbon and Coimbra (the university city), as well as Porto. Leaving from Lisbon's waterfront, electric trains travel along the Costa do Sol (Estorial and Cascais) and on to Queluz and Sintra.

At any rate, nobody complains about the prices charged: 13$ (8½¢) per kilometer in first class on the express trains or 7½$ (5¢) in second class. Regular trains cost 6$ (4¢) per kilometer in first class and 4$ (3¢) in second class. Discounts up to 20% are granted on Weekend Tickets, valid only from 5 p.m. on Friday till noon on Sunday. Parties of ten or more can apply at any Portuguese railway station for substantial reductions if the total combined rail miles exceeds 31.

In Lisbon at the **Apolónia Station,** connections can be made for international services and the Northern and Eastern Lines. **Rossio** serves Sintra and the Western Lines; and at the **Cais do Sodré** connections are made for the Costa do Sol resorts of Estoril and Cascais. Finally, trains leave from the **Sule Sueste** for the Alentejo and the Algarve. In addition, express trains connect Lisbon to all the major capitals of Western Europe, and there is a direct link with Seville.

Daily express trains in summer depart Lisbon for the Algarve (except on Sunday). These leave from the Barreiro Station (across the Tagus—take one of the ferries departing frequently). Off-season service is reduced to four times weekly.

For **information** about rail travel in Portugal, phone 01/87-60-25 in Lisbon.

Railway information and tickets on the **Portuguese National Railroad** may be obtained in North America from its representative, the **French National Railways, 610 Fifth Ave., New York, NY 10017** (tel. 212/582-2110); 360 Post St., San Francisco, CA 94108 (tel. 415/982-1993); 9465 Wilshire Blvd., Beverly Hills, CA 90212 (tel. 213/272-7967); 11 East Adams St., Chicago, IL 60603 (tel. 312/427-8691); 2121 Ponce de Leon Blvd., Coral Gables, FL 33134 (tel. 305/445-8648); or 1500 Stanley St., Montréal, Québec (tel. 514/288-8255).

If you plan to travel heavily on the European and/or British railroads, you will do well to secure the latest copy of the Thomas Cook European Timetable of European Railroads. This comprehensive, 500-plus-page timetable details all of Europe's passenger rail and ferry services with great detail and accuracy. It is available exclusively in North America from Forsyth Travel Library, P.O. Box 2975, Shawnee Mission, KS 66201 (tel. toll free 800/FORSYTH), at a cost of $19.95 including Priority postage.

If you're visiting the environs of Lisbon, such places as Cascais or Sintra, refer to the section in Chapter III, "Electric Trains," under "Transportation."

Senior Discounts

Those 65 years or older benefit from the 50% discount policy of the Portuguese Railway Company. These tickets are good all year.

Eurailpass

This ticket, sold only to people living outside of Europe or North Africa, gives unlimited first-class rail travel over the more than 100,000-mile national railroad networks of Western European countries (not including Great Britain). You travel first class on any train (subject to first-class availability, of course), making as many stops as you please en route at no extra fare. A Eurailpass also entitles you to free or reduced rate travel on many bus lines, lake and river steamers, and ferries. Reservation fees and sleeping accommodations are extra. The Eurailpass, together with the Eurail Saverpass and Eurail Youthpass (see below), must be purchased before you go to Europe. Half fare is charged for children 4 to 12 years of age.

Vacationers planning a trip can purchase a 15-day Eurailpass for $320; otherwise, prices are $398 for 21 days, $498 for one month, $698 for two months, and $860 for three months. A pass must be used within six months of its date of issuance. The first day of validity must be stamped at the railroad station where travel begins, and such validity expires at midnight on the last day of the period for which the pass was purchased.

Travel agents in all towns, and railway agents in major cities in the United States sell Eurailpasses. Readers who live elsewhere can write to: Eurailpass, P.O. Box 10383, Stamford, CT 06904.

EURAIL SAVERPASS This ticket offers 15 days of discounted travel, but only if groups of three people travel constantly and continuously together between April and September, or if two people travel constantly and continuously together between October and March. The price of a Saverpass, valid all over Europe, good for first class only, is $230.

EURAIL YOUTHPASS If you're under 26, you can purchase a Eurail Youthpass offering a true travel bargain. It gives you one or two months of unlimited second-class (coach) rail travel in the Eurailpass countries. Rates are $340 for one month, $470 for two months.

EURAIL FLEXIPASS A time-flexible Eurailpass ticket gives travelers nine days of rail travel that can be used either consecutively or otherwise in 16 countries within any one 21-day period. It costs $340 and assures nine days of travel of your choice without the feeling that you're losing travel days after you have validated your pass, if you elect to stay in one place a little longer.

CAR RENTALS

So many of the scenic parts of Portugal are so isolated from a train or bus station that it's almost indispensable to have a private car if you plan to do much serious touring. That way, you're your own free agent, unhindered by the somewhat fickle timetables of trains and buses, which often limit your excursions to places close to the beaten track.

There are few superhighways in Portugal, and the few that exist are often interrupted by lengthy stretches of traffic-clogged single-lane thoroughfares. The roads, however, provide access to hard-to-reach gems, undiscovered villages, mountain passes with panoramic views and waterfalls, rustic country inns, hidden beaches and sandy coves, all the charms of rural Iberia.

Most visitors opt for an auto-rental plan providing weekly rentals with unlimited kilometers included in the overall price. Four of North America's major car-rental companies maintain dozens of branches at each of Portugal's most popular commercial and tourist centers, at rates that are usually competitive.

Budget Rent-a-Car maintains offices in 12 locations within Portugal. The most central—and most used—of these are Lisbon, Faro (the heart of the Algarve), Porto, Praia da Rocha (also a popular Algarve destination), and Madeira. If you're searching for their rock-bottom rates, their least expensive car is a four-door Renault 4, which costs about $136 U.S. per week with unlimited mileage, plus 17% tax. This price requires a 48-hour advance notice before leaving the U.S. The Renault 4 has manual transmission and no air conditioning. Collision damage waivers cost an optional $6 extra per day. If you decline this option, you are responsible for the first $1,300 worth of damage to the vehicle. On more expensive car rentals at Budget, the insurance is an extra $9 per day, and renters without it are responsible for the first $2,000 worth of damage. Because Portugal has one of the highest accident rates in Europe, it is a good idea to buy this extra insurance.

Budget's least expensive car with automatic transmission is a mid-size vehicle at $400 per week, unlimited mileage, again without air conditioning. A car with air conditioning is a Ford Scorpio at $550 per week, unlimited mileage and with manual transmission. Call Budget toll free at 800/527-0700 for the latest prices and information.

Hertz (call toll free at 800/654-3001) has about 20 locations in Portugal and requires a two-day advance booking for its least expensive tariffs. An Opel Corsa (or similar car) with manual transmission and no air conditioning costs $160 a week with unlimited mileage. This is more expensive than Budget. Its collision damage

MILEAGE BETWEEN TOWNS AND CITIES
Distance in Miles

	Aveiro	Beja	Braga	Bragança	Castelo Branco	Coimbra	Évora	Faro	Fátima	Guarda	Leiria	LISBON	Porto	Santarém	Setúbal	Valença do Minho	Vila Real	Vila Real de St. António	Viseu
Aveiro																			
Beja	236																		
Braga	75	311																	
Bragança	199	365	143																
Castelo Branco	135	174	204	191															
Coimbra	36	206	105	193	99														
Évora	187	48	317	263	158	132													
Faro	311	94	449	287	282	238	132												
Fátima	86	159	249	258	104	56	223	223											
Guarda	112	240	163	66	104	110	324	324	171										
Leiria	71	164	235	104	192	42	240	171	14	146									
LISBON	151	119	315	160	122	116	86	86	146	226	80								
Porto	42	278	33	157	73	81	354	128	115	104	143	221							
Portalegre	184	130	241	50	148	93	213	92	104	143	194	221	158						
Quintanilha	151	161	19	210	232	335	468	268	144	254	334	176	297						
Santarém	119	227	315	160	122	93	185	86	135	114	194	31	176						
Setúbal	121	88	358	251	153	310	64	150	230	215	274	77	225	158					
Valença do Minho	88	326	30	218	120	277	401	176	182	161	241	44	72	205	213				
Viana do Castelo	88	377	66	218	128	289	422	184	97	169	249	72	213	249	280	122			
Vila Real	114	388	85	163	251	125	289	236	317	97	241	355	104	213	280	414			
Vila Real de St. António	313	77	442	251	283	238	125	32	115	53	101	181	355	198	165	435	414		
Viseu	59	293	115	147	118	60	238	376	115	53	101	181	83	145	212	162	68	370	

waivers range from $6 to $7.25 per day and are optional, but without them you're responsible for $1,200 to $1,500 in damages.

One often overlooked option for Portuguese car rentals is a rapidly emerging company based near New York City called **Kemwell**, 106 Calvert St., Harrison, NY 10528 (tel. 800/678-0678). It is the U.S. sales representative for a Portuguese rental company called **Mendes**. Typical of its business-promoting rates is an arrangement whereby a client pays one week in advance, prior to leaving the U.S. Under such a deal, a manual transmission Fiat Marbella two-door hatchback might cost as little as $119 per week. A slightly larger car might go for $189 per week. Of course, these rates will surely change in the lifetime of this edition—but they are likely to remain competitive. Kemwell, incidentally, offers no cars with either air conditioning or automatic transmission. Tax at 17% and insurance are extra.

Avis has an office at the airport in Lisbon, plus as many as ten convenient offices in Lisbon and Estoril. The main office is at Avenida Praia da Vitória in Lisbon (tel. 01/56-11-77). For reservations from the United States (made by calling toll free 800/331-2112), tariffs range from 16,380$ ($106.50) in low season and 27,370$ ($177.90) in high season for a car in Class A (Seat Marbella), up to 48,300$ ($313.95), low season, and 121,500$ ($790.35), high season, in Class L (Austin Rover 213 with automatic shift) per week with unlimited mileage. Ask for the Supervalue rate.

Gas

Lisbon is well provided with garages and gasoline pumps; some are open around the clock. If you're motoring in the provinces, best fill up, as in some parts of the country gasoline stations are few and far between.

HITCHHIKING

There's no law against it, but it isn't commonly practiced. If you decide to hitchhike, do so with discretion. Usually, Portuguese auto insurance doesn't cover hitchhikers.

---

3. Where to Go

Everybody heads for Lisbon, the gateway to Portugal. If you've flown over, you'll need the first day to recover from jet lag before plunging into the sights in and around the Portuguese capital. So count on losing the first day for rest time. On the second day, you can see the highlights of Lisbon, including St. George's Castle and the major attractions of Belém, such as Jerónimos Monastery. On the third day, while still based in Lisbon, I suggest that you do some exploring in the environs, heading first to Quelez Palace, 9½ miles from Lisbon, then going on to Sintra, 18 miles from Lisbon.

For a fourth and fifth day, I recommend leaving Lisbon behind and anchoring into one of the resorts along the Costa do Sol, principally Cascais and Estoril. This sun coast, also called the "coast of kings," is easily reached from Lisbon. You can relax in the sun or continue to take a number of excursions. The most interesting sights are at Guincho, near the westernmost point in continental Europe, and Mafra, which is Portugal's El Escorial.

On your sixth day, you can head south from Lisbon across the Tagus (see chapter X) to such intriguing destinations as Setúbal, 31 miles from Lisbon. After exploring the area, perhaps visiting Palmela Castle, you can continue south toward the Algarve. However, if it is running late, seek accommodations in and around Setúbal. Except for a pousada or two, the accommodations on the somewhat-barren route between Lisbon and the Algarve are sparse.

On your seventh day, you will have reached Sagres, the extreme southwestern corner of Europe, 183 miles south from Lisbon. For a description of what to see and where to stay in the Algarve, refer to chapter XII. My advice here is to settle in your favorite village, town, or resort, and explore the full length of the coast. For this, you must allow a minimum of three days and nights. For example, if you choose to stay at Faro, you will be roughly in the center of the Algarve and can branch out in either direction, east or west. The coastline stretches a distance of 100 miles, but know that it will be slow moving, regardless of which direction you select.

On the tenth day, if you must leave, I recommend that you return to Lisbon via a different route, heading first for Beja, the capital of Baixo Alentejo, 96 miles north from Faro. After a stopover there, you might continue north to Évora, 90 miles to the east of Lisbon, where you may want to spend the night. After exploring Évora the next morning, you can drive west to Lisbon.

From Lisbon, if you have the time, I suggest you fly to Madeira for a minimum of three days, spending time in the sun but also a full day exploring this island, one of the most beautiful in the world.

By now you may have run out of time. If not, the treasures in the north of Portugal beckon to you.

Heading north from Lisbon, most people have as their first goal a stopover at Óbidos, 59 miles away. After a visit, the next recommended stopover is at Alcobaça, 67 miles from Lisbon. This former Cistercian monastery was once the richest and most prestigious in Europe. Since accommodations in both these places are extremely limited, your target for the first night should be the well-known fishing village of Nazaré, 77 miles from Lisbon. (*Warning:* Hotel space is extremely tight in summer.)

After exploring this village, you might head out on your second day for Batalha, the spectacular "Battle Abbey" of Portugal, built in a Gothic-Manueline style. Its location is 73 miles north of Lisbon. From Batalha, you can drive east to Fátima, the world-famous pilgrimage site, which is 36 miles east of Nazaré and about 88 miles north of Lisbon. Instead of spending the night there, you might head instead to Tomar, lying in the east, 85 miles from Lisbon.

For your third day, I suggest that you drive north to Coimbra, whose university is among the oldest in the world. The town, 124 miles to the north of Lisbon, is rich in attractions and makes a suitable overnight stopover.

On your fourth day you can drive north to Porto, some 175 miles from Lisbon. This is Portugal's second city, home of port wine.

For a fifth day, I recommend that you at least "dip a toe" into the folkloric Minho district in the far-northern reaches of Portugal. Two stopovers are extremely worthy: Guimarães, called the "cradle" of Portugal, lying 31 miles from Porto; and Viana do Castelo, Portugal's northern city of folklore, lying 43 miles north of Porto.

After that, it's back to Lisbon if you wish. If you follow these suggestions, you will not have seen all of Portugal by any means, but you will have skimmed the highlights, and for many visitors that is all their time will allow.

TOURS

Many people never see anything of the Iberian peninsula except perhaps Spain. You may have wondered about Portugal—is it worth a visit, what is there to see and do, how to get around. One way to get a look at the country and dip briefly into its culture, is to take an organized tour. Consult a travel agent for the best ones currently offered.

Remember: The advantages of such tours are many. You need not be afraid of traveling alone or perhaps with timid companions. Everything is arranged for you —transportation in the countries visited, hotels, service, sightseeing trips, excursions, luggage handling, tips, taxes, and many of your meals. You're even given time to go shopping or to nose around on your own to find interesting attractions. And you may find that some members of your group have interests that are similar to your own, so you can chat and compare notes. Take a copy of this guide along with you, and you'll recognize many places to which you will probably want to return on your own someday.

---

4. Alternative and Special-Interest Travel

Mass tourism of the kind that has transported vast numbers of North Americans to the most obscure corners of the map has been a by-product of the affluence, technology, and democratization that only the last half of the 20th century was able to produce.

With the advent of the 1990s, and the changes they promise to bring, some of America's most respected travel visionaries have perceived a change in the needs of many of the world's most experienced (and sometimes jaded) travelers. There has emerged a demand for specialized travel experiences whose goals and objectives are clearly defined well in advance of an actual departure. There is also an increased demand for organizations that can provide like-minded companions to share and participate in increasingly esoteric travel plans.

This yearning for a special-interest vacation might be especially intense for a frequent traveler whose expectations have already been defined by earlier exposure to foreign cultures. With that in mind, the author of this guide hopes to enhance the quality of his readers' travel experiences by including the following section.

Caveat: Under no circumstances is the inclusion of an organization to be interpreted as a guarantee either of its creditworthiness or its competency. Information about the organizations listed below is presented only as a preliminary preview, to be followed by your own investigation should you be interested.

INTERNATIONAL UNDERSTANDING

About the only thing the following organizations have in common is reflected by the headline. These organizations not only promote trips to increase international understanding, but they often encourage and advocate what might be called "intelligent travel."

The Friendship Force was founded in Atlanta, Georgia, under the leadership of former President Jimmy Carter during his tenure as governor of that state. This nonprofit organization exists for the sole purpose of fostering and encouraging friendship among peoples around the world in a nonpolitical, nonreligious context of cooperation and good will.

Visits usually occur once a year. Because of group bookings by the Friendship Force, the price of air fare to the host country is usually less than an individual APEX ticket. Each participant is required to spend two weeks in the host country (host countries are primarily in Europe, but also throughout the world). One stringent requirement is that every participant must spend one full week in the home of a family as a guest, supposedly to further the potential for meaningful friendships between the host family and the participants. Most volunteers spend the second week traveling in the host country. It should be noted that no particular study regime or work program is expected of participants, but only a decorum and interest level which speaks well of America and its residents.

For more information, contact The Friendship Force, 575 South Tower, 1 CNN Center, Atlanta, GA 30303 (tel. 404/522-9490).

Servas, 11 John St., New York, NY 10038 (tel. 212/267-0252). Founded in 1948 by an American-born conscientious objector living in Denmark, this organization grew slowly from a collection of index cards kept in a friend's kitchen to one of the most prominent groups of people of goodwill in the world. Servas (translated from the Esperanto, it means "to serve") is a nonprofit, nongovernmental, international, interfaith network of travelers and hosts whose goal is to help build world peace, goodwill, and understanding.

Servas travelers are invited to share living space in a privately owned home within a community, normally staying without charge for visits lasting a maximum of two days. This is unquestionably geared to more thoughtful and peace-oriented travelers who want to share common experiences above and beyond what they might find in a typical bed-and-breakfast establishment. Visitors pay a $45 annual membership fee, fill out an application, and are interviewed for suitability by one of more than 200 Servas interviewers throughout the country. They then receive a Servas directory listing the names and addresses of Servas hosts who will allow (and encourage) visitors in their homes.

Visitors can also request simply a day visit or a shared meal instead of the actual overnight in the host home. What's amazing is that with all the potential problems that an organization this diverse might have, there seem to be surprisingly few trouble zones. Hosts eager to meet other members of Servas live throughout the world, including all the countries of Europe. This is, frankly, one of the best opportunities for a visiting North American to spend quality time in the homes of families on all six continents. The manager of the New York office is Alan Atkisson, who will probably be sympathetic to visions of world peace and global understanding.

International Visitors Information Service, 733 15th St. NW, Suite 300, Washington, DC 20005 (tel. 202/783-6540). For $4.95, this organization will mail anyone a booklet listing opportunities for contact with local residents in foreign countries. Europe is heavily featured. Checks should be made out to Meridian House/IVIS.

SENIOR CITIZEN VACATIONS

One of the most dynamic organizations in the world of postretirement studies for senior citizens is **Elderhostel,** 80 Boylston St., Boston, MA 02116 (tel. 617/426-7788). Established in 1975 by Martin Knowlton, a retired engineer and professor of political science, it is, quite simply, one of the most creative forces in the lives of senior citizens. During a four-year backpacking tour of Europe, which he began in his mid-50s, he noticed an inefficient summer use of college dormitories. He became inspired to try to fill them with crowds of what many universities consider their most avid students, senior citizens. Today, Elderhostel maintains a dazzling array of programs throughout the world, including England, Scotland, and all major countries on the continent. Most courses last around three weeks, representing remarkable value, considering that air fare, hotel accommodations in student dormitories or modest inns, all meals, and tuition are included. Currently, three weeks with all of these included cost a surprisingly low $1,992 for a program in England, for example. Courses involve no homework, are ungraded, and are especially centered on the liberal arts. Even field trips are related to the academic discipline being studied in the classroom.

In no way is this to be considered a luxury vacation, but rather an academic fulfillment of a type never possible for senior citizens until several years ago. Participants must be over the age of 60. However, if a pair of members goes as a couple, only one member needs to be older than 60. Meals are the kind of solid, no-frills fare most college undergraduates know only too well. But most graduates would consider gourmet cuisine of relatively unimportant merit because of the multiple additional benefits. A frequently unpublicized side benefit of this program is the safety in which many older single women can travel. Some 70% of the participants are women, who understandably prefer to travel with a goal, an orientation, amid like-minded individuals waiting for them at the end of their transatlantic airplane ride.

Anyone interested in participating in one of Elderhostel's programs should write for their free newsletter and a list of upcoming courses and destinations.

One company that has made a reputation exclusively because of its quality tours for senior citizens is **Saga International Holidays.** Established in the 1950s as a sensitive and highly appealing outlet for older tour participants, they prefer that joiners be at least 60 years of age or more. Insurance and air fare are included in the net price of any of their tours, all of which encompass dozens of locations in Europe and usually last for an average of 17 nights. For more information, get in touch with Saga International Holidays, 120 Boylston St., Boston, MA 02116 (tel. toll free 800/ 343-0273).

EDUCATIONAL AND STUDY TRAVEL

If you're interested in scientific discoveries in Europe, you might find out more about **Earthwatch,** P.O. Box 403N, Watertown, MA 02271 (tel. 617/926-8200). It organizes scientific projects throughout the world, including several in Europe. Most expeditions are organized into two-week work teams, where participants interested in a "hands-on study project" each contribute to its cost. Examples of studies include surveys of birds, glaciers, architectural history, and marine ecology, as well as archeological excavations.

Earthwatch is a nonprofit organization to which university professors from around the world apply for paying volunteers for their research projects. Payments that volunteers make are considered tax-deductible contributions to a scientific project. Only 7% of the volunteers are students. A work project with Earthwatch offers a "chance to pursue for a brief while the path not taken." It has also been defined as a "scientific short-term Peace Corps." About a third of the 350 college professors who apply yearly are accepted on the basis of the research merits of their projects. Tasks include everything from weighing a wolf pup to measuring turtle eggs to researching genealogical records. The organization publishes a magazine six times a year, listing the dozens of unusual opportunities.

A TRAVEL COMPANION

A recent American census showed that 77 million Americans over 15 years of age are single. However, the travel industry is far better geared for double occupancy of hotel rooms. One company that has made heroic efforts to match single travelers with like-minded companions is now the largest and best-listed company in the United States, thanks to a rash of acquisitions of its former competitors across the country. Jens Jurgen, the German-born founder, charges between $29 and $66 for a six-month listing in his well-publicized records. New applicants desiring a travel companion fill out a form stating their preferences and needs. They then receive a mini-listing of the kinds of potential partners who might be suitable for travel. Companions of the same or opposite sex can be requested. Because of the large number of listings, success is often a reality.

For an application and more information, get in touch with Jens Jurgen, **Travel Companion,** P.O. Box P-833, Amityville, NY 11701 (tel. 516/454-0880).

II

THE SCENE IN PORTUGAL

1. THE COUNTRY
2. DINING AND WINING
3. THE HOTEL OUTLOOK
4. THE ABCs OF PORTUGAL

In an increasingly mechanized age, there is still Portugal.

It is a land of gardens and natural produce, of abundant flowers, a place that still values the artful homemade touch. The wine you drink may be from your host's own casks, the tablecloth made by his wife, the bread fresh from the oven and baked by a daughter-in-law.

A long line of expatriates, including exiled royalty, knows what has long been called "the last foreign country of Europe." That the society has been termed "feudal" forms part of its medieval charm for many. But change is in the air. Even so, visitors are still rare in the more remote parts of Portugal. One Canadian couple were themselves the subjects of sight-seeing interest as they made their way through a village en route to a 14th century church.

You can divide your Portuguese holiday into four parts, spending the first part of your trip in **Lisbon** and at the Costa do Sol resorts of **Estoril** and **Cascais.** Perhaps you'll allow time for a series of day trips from the capital, going to **Sintra, Nazaré, Tomar, Fátima, Óbidos,** as well as the scenic spots south of the **Tagus.**

The second phase can be devoted to one of the hotels on the **Algarve** in the south, studded with sandy beaches. En route to the Algarve, you can detour through the **Alentejo** district, stopping at the old Roman city of **Évora.**

Before leaving continental Portugal, you should experience the relatively unknown north. Go there to see towns and monuments—**Coimbra, Porto** (home of port wine), **Viana do Castelo**—and some of the country's finest scenery. Before beginning your homeward trek, you can wind down in the islands, either **Madeira** or in the more remote **Azores.**

On your Portuguese holiday you should allow for recuperative days in the sun and at the sea, all of which will fortify you to drink from Lisbon's chalice: listening to fado songs, seeing its museums, attending a bullfight, an opera, dining in a palace, browsing through numerous handcraft shops.

When traveling through the countryside, it's best to plot your trips so that you'll stop over at the government-owned pousadas (tourist inns), ranging from restored castles on the Atlantic coast to mountain chalets.

SOUNDS, SMELLS, AND SIGHTS

Windmills clacking in the Atlantic wind . . . the plaintive sound of fado echoing through the narrow streets of Lisbon's Alfama . . . lonely *varinas* draped in black, waiting at the surf, their melancholy faces wrinkled by the harsh sea wind . . . purple wisteria cascading over the walls of mosaic courtyards . . . plodding oxen pulling carts along ribbon roads . . . sun-baked, grape-yielding slopes . . . the stark ruggedness of the seascape . . . sun-scorched, bull-breeding plains . . . houses bathed in birthday-cake colors with contrasting *azulejos* in ivory white, mustard gold, indigo blue, and emerald green.

Wicker baskets of eels steeped in the scent of the sea . . . terraced rice fields evoking the Orient . . . the pine groves of Leiria . . . bullock carts trundling across arched bridges . . . the ringing of a church bell in a mountain village . . . the singsong litany of a fish auction . . . lemons, snowy almonds, and cactus . . . richly embroidered regional costumes . . . horseback-riding *campinos* . . . the violent grandeur of the Mouth of Hell . . . pagan festivals . . . medieval monasteries . . . and some women still filling their jugs at fountains, as in biblical times.

THE SEASONS

"We didn't know we had an April," one Lisbon resident said, "until *that* song came out." "April in Portugal" is famous, both the song and the season. Summer may be the most popular season, but for the traveler who can chart his or her own course, spring and autumn are the delectable seasons.

For North Americans, the climate of Portugal most closely parallels that of California. The Portuguese consider their climate one of the most ideal in Europe, and it is. There are only slight fluctuations in temperature between summer and winter, the overall mean ranging from 77° Fahrenheit in summer to about 58° Fahrenheit in winter. However, the rainy season begins in November, usually lasting through January. The proximity of the Gulf Stream allows Portugal's northernmost province, the **Minho,** to enjoy mild, albeit very rainy, winters, even though it's at approximately the same latitude as New York.

Snow brings many skiing enthusiasts to the **Sêrra de Estrêla** in north-central Portugal; but, for the most part, winter entails only some rain and lower temperatures in the other provinces.

The **Algarve** and especially **Madeira** are the exceptions: they enjoy warm and temperate winters. Madeira, in fact, basks in its high season in winter. The Algarve, too, is somewhat of a winter Riviera, attracting sunworshippers from both North America and Europe. Summers in both tend to be long and hot, crystal clear and dry.

Lisbon and **Estoril** enjoy 46° to 65° Fahrenheit temperatures in winter, rising to between 60° and 82° Fahrenheit in summer.

Travelers have dubbed the country a "country for all seasons."

1. The Country

A CAPSULE HISTORY

In the 12th century the ancestors of today's Portuguese decided they didn't want to be associated with their Spanish neighbors in León and Castile. The split

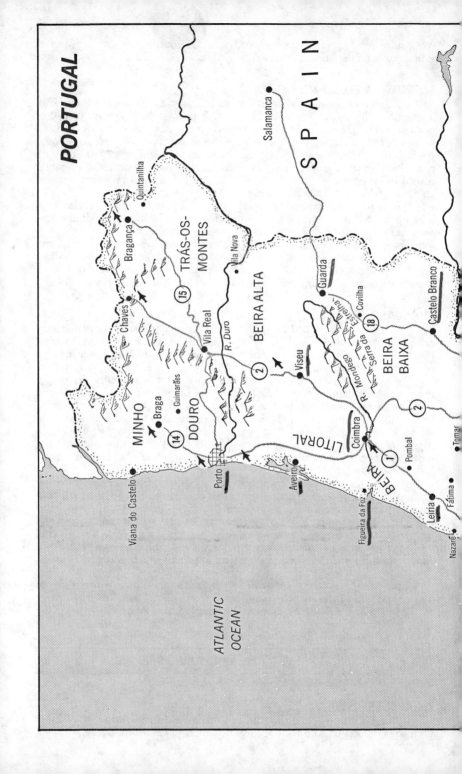

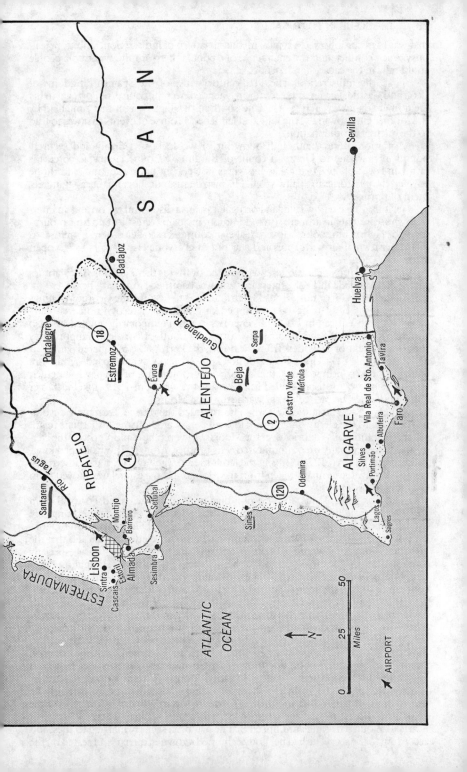

that was to occur followed a typical medieval pattern of indiscretion, ambition, jealousy, open conflict, and the emergence of a popular hero around whom the people could rally in the cause of independence.

First, the indiscretion. The 11th-century ruler of the Spanish kingdoms of León and Castile, Ferdinand I (the Great), handed over the county of Portugal to his illegitimate daughter, Teresa. The land south of the Tagus was at that time held by the Moors. Unknowingly, the king had launched a course of events that was to lead to the birth of another nation.

Ambition. Teresa, although born out of wedlock, was firmly and securely bound in marriage to Henry, a count of Burgundy. Count Henry accepted his father-in-law's gift of Portugal as his wife's dowry, but upon the king's death, he coveted the territories in Spain as well. His own demise cut short further aggrandizement of territory.

Jealousy. Teresa now ruled in Portugal, casting a disdainful eye on and an interfering nose into her legitimate sister's kingdom in Spain. Teresa lost no time mourning poor Henry, but took as a lover a Galician count, Fernão Peres. Teresa's refusal to guard her own affair with Peres and stay out of everyone else's affairs led to open strife with León.

Her son, Afonso Henriques, was incensed by his mother's actions. Their armies met at São Mamade in 1128. Teresa lost and was banished along with her lover.

Ungrateful son or not, Afonso Henriques was to become the George Washington of Portugal. In 1143 he was proclaimed king, and official recognition eventually came from the Vatican in 1178. His enemies in Spain temporarily quieted, Afonso turned his eye toward the Moorish territory in the south of Portugal. Supported by the armed might of Crusaders from the north, the Portuguese conquered Santarém and Lisbon in 1147. Upon his death in 1185, Afonso was succeeded by his son, Sancho I, who continued his father's work of consolidation of the newly emerged nation. His heir, Afonso II, ruled for 12 years, beginning in 1211. Like his father and grandfather, he carried on the war against the Moors.

Sancho II was an adolescent when he ascended the throne. Extremely devout, he returned to the clergy much that had been confiscated during his father's reign. He scored numerous victories over the Moors. However, he couldn't pacify the clergy and was eventually excommunicated. His brother, Afonso III, was named king, ruling from 1248 to 1279. During the latter's reign, the Algarve, the southern district of Portugal, was finally taken from the Moors, and the capital was moved from Coimbra to Lisbon.

The new king, Dinis, the son of a bigamous marriage, ruled Portugal from 1279 to 1325. He is sometimes known as the poet king or the farmer king. He founded the country's first university, in Lisbon, in 1290. Dinis married an Aragonese princess, Isabella, who was later canonized, although evidence indicates that the vigorous young king would have preferred a less saintly wife. Isabella was especially interested in the poor. A legend about her tells that once she was smuggling bread out of the palace to feed them when her husband spotted her and asked what she was concealing. When she showed him, the bread had miraculously turned into roses.

The son of these two famous monarchs, Afonso IV is remembered today for having had assassins murder his son's mistress, the legendary Inês de Castro. Early in life Afonso's son, who would later rule as Pedro I, was betrothed to a Spanish princess, but fell in love with her beautiful lady-in-waiting. Inês was deeply attracted to him, and their affair blossomed. Eventually Inês was banished from the country, although she returned upon the death of the Spanish princess to live openly with Pedro. Jealous sycophants in court persuaded Afonso IV to sanction her murder. Pedro never recovered from the shock of seeing his dead mistress. Patiently he waited until his father died and then he set out to seek revenge. Tracking two of the assassins to Spain, he had them returned by force to Portugal, where he had their hearts torn out. The king announced that he had been secretly married to Inês, and according to the story, he had her body exhumed, crowned queen, and seated on the throne, summoning the members of the court to pay her homage and kiss her hand. Inês, and later Pedro, were buried at Alcobaça, where their tombs are frequently visited today.

During Pedro's reign (1357–1367), the influential representative body, the Cortes (an assembly of clergy, nobility, and commoners), began to gain ascendancy, while the majority of the clergy, greedy for power, fought the sovereign's reform measures, thus allying the people more strongly with the crown. Pedro's son, Ferdinand I (1367–1373), saw Portugal invaded by Castilian forces, Lisbon besieged, and the demise of his dynasty.

In 1383, rather than submit to Spanish rule, the Portuguese people chose the illegitimate son of Pedro as regent. The house of Avís was thereby established. João de Avís (1383–1433) secured Portuguese independence by defeating Castilian forces at Aljubarrota in 1385. His union with Philippa, granddaughter of Edward III of England, produced a son who was to mark the emergence of Portugal as an empire—Prince Henry the Navigator.

Henry's demand for geographical accuracy, his ambition to possess the legendary wealth in gold and ivory, slaves, and spices of the East and his desire to promote Christianity by joining with the fabled Christian kingdom of Prester John and driving the Muslims out of North Africa all drove Henry to exploration. Facing him was a Sea of Darkness, where ships supposedly melted in the equatorial regions, sea serpents flourished, and strange beasts sought to destroy any interloper.

Henry established a community of scholars at Sagres on the south coast of Portugal to develop navigational and cartographical techniques. He infused the court with his zeal and brought his nation to face a destiny imminent from the time of their earliest contacts with Phoenician and Greek mariners. Henry was responsible for the discovery of Madeira, the Azores, Cape Verde, Senegal, and Sierra Leone, and he established the blueprint for continued exploration during the rest of the century. In 1482 Portuguese ships explored the mouth of the Congo; in 1488 Dias rounded the Cape of Good Hope; and in 1497, Vasco da Gama reached Calicut (Kozhikode) on India's west coast, clearing the way for trade in spices, porcelain, silks, ivory, and slaves. The original appellation of the Cape of Good Hope, the Cape of Storms, might have been a more prophetic one.

The Treaty of Tordesillas, negotiated by João II in 1494 for as yet undiscovered lands in the Western Hemisphere, ensured Portugal's possession of Brazil, not discovered until 1500. Utilizing the inflowing wealth of the whole empire, Manuel I (the Fortunate, 1495–1521) imprinted his imagination and name upon great monuments of art and architecture. His reign inspired Portugal's Golden Age. By 1521 the country had begun to tap the natural resources of Brazil and had broken the spice-trade monopoly formerly held by the Venetians. Portugal was mistress of nearly all accesses to the Indian Ocean. At her noontide, she stood as the first of the great maritime world empires.

João III (1527–1557) ushered in the Jesuits and the Inquisition. When his son Sebastião disappeared in battle in Morocco in 1578, leaving Portugal without an heir, the way was opened for Spanish control. Philip II of Spain claimed the Portuguese throne and began 60 years of Spanish domination. In the East, Portugal's strength had been undermined by Dutch and English traders.

A nationalist revolution in 1640 brought a descendant of João I to the throne as João IV. This began the house of Bragança, which lasted into the 20th century, as well as a long series of revolutions and intrigues. João IV arranged an English alliance, wedding his daughter to Charles II. For her dowry he "threw in" Bombay and Tangier. In 1668 the Treaty of Lisbon with Spain gave Portugal recognized independence.

All Saints Day, 1755. The great earthquake destroyed virtually all of Lisbon. In six minutes 15,000 people were killed, thousands while attending morning masses. The Marquês de Pombal, adviser to King José (1750–1777), met the emergency and later reconstructed Lisbon as a safer and more beautiful city. An exponent of absolutism, his expulsion of the Jesuits in 1759 earned him powerful enemies throughout Europe. His virtual dictatorship had its beneficial side, however; he curbed the power of the Inquisition and reorganized and expanded industry, agriculture, education, and the military. On the death of his patron, King José, he was exiled from court.

In 1793, Portugal joined a coalition with England and Spain against Napoleon. An insane queen, Maria I (1777–1816), plus an exiled royal family, made overthrow by a military junta easy. The Cortes was summoned, a constitution was drawn up, and Maria's son, João VI, accepted the position of constitutional monarch in 1821. João's son, Pedro, declared independence for Brazil in 1822 and became a champion of liberalism in Portugal.

The years 1853–1908 felt the rumble of republican movements that assaulted the very existence of the monarchists. In 1908 Carlos I, "the painter king" and the crown prince were assassinated at Praça do Comércio in Lisbon. His successor was overthrown in an outright revolution on October 5, 1910, which ended the Portuguese monarchy and made Portugal a republic.

Instability was the watchword of the newly proclaimed republic, with revolutions and uprisings occurring two or three times a year. An attempt to remain neutral in World War I failed when, influenced by her old ally, England, Portugal commandeered German ships in the Lisbon harbor, which promptly brought a declaration of war from Germany.

The precarious foundations of the republic collapsed in 1926 when a military revolt established a dictatorship, with Gomes da Costa as its head. He was followed by Fragoso da Carmona, who remained president until 1951, but only as a figurehead. António Salazar became his finance minister in 1928, rescuing the country from a morass of financial difficulties. He went on to become the first minister, acting as (but never officially) head of state. In World War II, he asserted his country's neutrality, although he allowed British and American troops to establish bases in the Azores in 1943.

In 1955 Portugal joined the United Nations. Salazar suffered a stroke in 1968 and died in 1970.

The old dictatorship was overthrown on April 25, 1974, in a coup dubbed "the flower revolution" because the soldiers wore red carnations instead of carrying guns. Change swept across the land, and Portugal drifted into near anarchy. Finally, after several years of turmoil and constant dissension between left and right, plus frequent failures of provisional governments (there were 16 from 1976 to 1983), a revised constitution is in force. Defining Portugal as a republic engaged in the formation of a classless society, the constitution calls for presidents to be elected by popular vote for five-year terms. The prime minister is appointed by the president, who also names other members of the government. A unicameral Legislative Assembly is made up of representatives elected by the people to four-year terms.

Of its once extensive territorial possessions, only the Madeira group and the Azores in the Atlantic, and Macao on the south China coast, are still under the flag of Portugal. The year 1976 marked great change for the country in the realm of rulership. In that year, the Azores and Madeira were granted partial autonomy. Macao received broad autonomy, and all the colonial territories in Africa became independent countries—Angola, the Cape Verde Islands, Portuguese Guinea, Mozambique, and São Tomé and Príncipe (islands in the Gulf of Guinea). The Portuguese colony of East Timor in the Indonesian archipelago was released by Portugal but immediately seized by Indonesia.

Portugal joined the European Common Market in 1986, but unemployment remains a serious problem. The country had to resettle some 700,000 refugees from its former colonies in Africa, including Angola. Emergency steps to improve agriculture and industry have been called "wrenching."

After a long slump in the 1970s and 1980s, tourism has been on the upswing in mainland Portugal, with visitors coming in by the thousands. Portugal is considered one of the safest countries of all Europe in which to travel.

THE PEOPLE

The Portuguese have a mixture of ethnic ancestry. The blood of the first Ibero-Celtic tribes (later called *Lusitani* by the Romans), Phoenicians, Carthaginians, Romans, Germans, Visigoths, Moors, Jews, Arabs, and Berbers flows in the veins of the Portuguese of today, making a description of the people as being of homogeneous Mediterranean stock perhaps the most accurate assessment. A small African minority has appeared in the country as a result of decolonization of Portugal's African territories. The provinces of the country present a diverse set of social structures; some are classless but impoverished, others have well-defined hierarchical parameters. Despite the declaration in the constitution that the republic is "engaged in the formation of a classless society," the nature of humankind makes social and economic divisions inevitable, especially when they are based on land ownership, urban or rural environment, and regional variation, to name only a few variables.

LANGUAGE

Portuguese is a Romance language, evolved mainly from a dialect spoken when it was a province of the Spanish kingdom of León and Castile. Portuguese has developed separately from other Romance dialects, such as those that evolved into the Spanish language. After Portugal became an independent country in the 11th century, its borders were pushed southward to the sea, taking in areas previously governed by Muslim Moors. The language called *Mozarabic*, spoken by the Christians living as Moorish subjects, was integrated into the Portuguese dialect, and the language of Portugal came into being. The basic language of today, both oral and written, was solidified and perfected in Lisbon, the capital, and Coimbra, the ancient university city. Of course, there are regional variations and pronunciations.

One writer suggested that Portuguese has "the hiss and rush of surf crashing against the bleak rocks of Sagres." If you don't speak it, you'll find French, Spanish, and English commonly spoken in Lisbon, along the Costa do Sol, and in Porto, as well as many parts of the Algarve. In small villages and towns, hotel staffs and guides usually speak English. The native tongue is difficult, but the Portuguese people are helpful and patient. Gestures often suffice.

THE CULTURE

Portugal cannot claim a high place in the scale of cultural impact on the world, but within the little country, there have been a few notable figures in arts and letters arising from time to time, even in the face of wars, poverty, and periods of suppression of ideas.

Literature

Manuscripts of song lyrics from the 12th century are the oldest written Portuguese literature. Many of them came from the oral poetry recited by the people of Iberia in ancient times. The oral lyrics were adopted and adapted by court troubadors, public entertainers, and even clerics and aristocrats. The *cantigas* (lyric songs) were mainly songs of the court. After the rule of King Dinis, the *romanceiro*, or Castilian ballad, replaced the lyric songs. Portuguese was used from the 14th century for telling historic tales in poetic form. The lyric tradition of the court troubadors continued off and on until the mid-16th century.

Meanwhile, Portuguese prose began to appear in the chronicles of court life, many with literary merit, like the work of **Fernão Lopes** in the 15th century. By the 16th century, chroniclers changed their focus to the global discoveries and Portugal's oceanic empire. The nation's India ventures led also to the writing of travel books. One of the most popular of these was the work of **Fernão Mendes Pinto,** known as "the Father of All Lies." His *Peregrinaçam* (Pilgrimage) and other writings were based more on his colorful imagination than on fact, but they read well.

High on the list of literary figures of Portugal is **Gil Vicente,** father of Portuguese theater. He lived in the late 15th and early 16th centuries and was acclaimed for his *autos* (religious dramas) and farces. His satirical, often ribald, wit might have signaled the birth of theatrical greatness in the country, but he fell out of favor with the court, and soon after his death his work was drastically censored and some of it destroyed by the Inquisition, which banned secular theater.

Luis Vaz de Camões (1524–1580) is Portugal's most famous poet and a national hero. Also an explorer in an age when that was the honored vocation, he was a kinsman of Vasco da Gama who discovered the sea route to India in 1497–1498. Da Gama's exploits were the subject of *Os Lusíadas,* an epic poem by Camões.

Many Portuguese writers preferred to use the Castilian language for their work during the Habsburg sovereignty over both their country and Spain from 1580 to 1640. However, the most widely circulated work attributed to a 17th-century Portuguese writer was the one that became the prototype of 18th-century epistolary novels. Published in French, *Lettres portugaises* (Portuguese Letters) contained five letters purportedly written by a nun from Beja, **Sister Marianna Alcoforado,** to her lover, the French Conde de Chamilly. The letters describe their passionate love affair with lyric clarity.

The Age of the Discoveries was a time of glory for Portugal, and since that time the people have tended always to look backward to that glory in their literature and their lives. Although some realism can be seen in more recent literary efforts, lyric poetry is still predominant. Romanticism was the only European intellectual movement whose effect is visible in Portuguese literature, as it fit the people's innate mood and their belief in Portuguese nationalism. This belief, blended with an uncertainty caused by growing unrest early in this century, resulted in a provincialism on the part of Portugal in general and its literature. Lyric poetry and historical novels and novellas are expressions of *saudade,* a nostalgia based on a fatalistic melancholy. One writer around the turn of the century described *saudade* as "the key to understanding the Portuguese soul" and concluded that "progress was not possible for a people whose past will always be more attractive than their futures."

A poet and dramatist who escaped this pall of *saudade* and broadened the scope of Portuguese literature was **Fernando Pessoa** (1888–1935), who has been called the country's greatest poet after Camões. Some writers who disagreed with Pessoa's metaphysical focus have turned to neorealism, but they are little known outside their own country.

An interesting Portuguese work that has achieved notoriety in recent years, probably only exceeded by that accorded the 17th-century *Portuguese Letters,* is *Nova Cartas Portuguesas* (New Portuguese Letters). It is the work of the **"Three Marias,"** Maria Isabel Bareno, Maria Teresa Horta, and Maria Fátima Velho da Costa. This women's lib volume has been widely circulated in Portugal.

Music

The *saudade* that has influenced the country's literature, is most clearly present in the **fado** songs, traditional expressions of the sad, romantic, nostalgic mood of Portugal. (See chapter IX for more about fado.)

Folk songs from ancient times and sacred and secular music from the church and courts have played their part in Portugal. Musical plays and choral pieces evolved eventually into opera, which is still the country's most popular form of classical music. A student of Franz Liszt, **Alfredo Keil** was successful as a composer of Romantic opera. Today he is remembered for his patriotic hymn, *A Portuguesa,* Portugal's national anthem. Lisbon's opera houses still draw devotees of serious music, although the fare offered is mainly of foreign origin.

The Lisbon Philharmonic, the National Radio System's Symphony Orchestra, and the Gulbenkian Orchestra and Chorus give frequent performances, especially in the capital.

Arts and Crafts

Two Portuguese artists who gained recognition outside their own country are **Nuno Gonçalves** and **Domingos António de Sequeira.** Gonçalves (1482–1552) was court painter to King Afonso V. He is especially known for the retable of St. Vincent, a six-paneled altarpiece representing 15th-century society and showing Lisbon's patron saint being given homage by the court and people of Portugal. Sequeira (1768–1837), also subsidized by the court, went from academic neoclassic painting to a later technique similar to Goya's. The charcoal drawings done late in his career are his finest works.

All the artistic trends have been tried in Portugal, but through the years of restlessness and oppression in this century, many promising painters left the country and have become more closely linked with foreign art.

Sculpture has not been an outstanding art form in Portugal, although there are a few noteworthy works in ecclesiastical and tomb ornamentation done in the Middle Ages. Except for the impressive work of sculptors and stonecarvers during the Manueline period in the early 16th century, the major departure from the ordinary was in the 18th century: **Machado de Castro** produced the equestrian statue of King José I in Praça do Comércio in Lisbon, plus statuary at Mafra where he lived and taught.

Later sculptures of merit are the *saudade* in stone done by **Soares dos Reis** and portrait busts of children by **Teixeira Lopes.** Considered the top 20th-century Portuguese sculptor is **Francisco Franco** (*not* the Spanish dictator). Not attributed to any individual stone sculptor are two well-known works: the huge *Christ in Majesty* stela overlooking the estuary of the Tagus River, and the *Padrão dos Descobrimentos* (Monument to the Discoveries) beside the Tagus commemorating the 500th anniversary of the death of Prince Henry the Navigator in 1460.

The Portuguese preferred working in wood rather than in stone, with some beautiful examples from the late Middle Ages. Fine, often exotic, wood from the East, Madeira, and Brazil were used to carve altarpieces, wall coverings, and ceilings of cathedrals and palaces. The 16th-century **Coelho family** retables are outstanding examples of woodcarving skill. Fine wood furniture was also turned out by skilled craftsmen.

A distinctive and important Portuguese craft is the making of ceramics called **azulejos.** Because of the decorative design of these tiles, a 15th-century import from Andalusia, they were adopted by the builders in Portugal. Change in fashion has taken this ceramic art from the Moorish polychromatic design to Dutch Delft blue and white (to compete with Dutch imports) back to muted colors. They were mass-produced to meet post-earthquake rebuilding needs in the 18th century and can be seen in the design of public structures, churches, and private houses put up under the direction of the Marquês de Pombal.

Another craft from early days still followed in Portugal is the weaving of **Arraiolas rugs.** In the 16th century, Moorish women in the Alentejo district produced the rugs, and they are still woven in Persian-inspired patterns.

ARCHITECTURE

Little ancient architecture has survived in Portugal, with mere traces of Roman, Byzantine, Visigothic, and Moorish building remaining. Castles dating from the 12th century can be seen, however, the Bragança citadel being the most outstanding. Fortifications dating from the 14th century are at Lisbon and Ameira, their architecture borrowed respectively from the city fortresses of Italy and the crusader castles of Syria.

Cathedrals and churches were built in styles ranging from Romanesque to Cistercian (a blend of Romanesque and Gothic), and true Gothic. An example of the latter type is the monastery at Batalha, which bears the stamp of the English stone-masons imported to build it. Most of the ecclesiastical structures today are a mixture of architecture and decoration, having been changed through the centuries to memorialize successive monarchs. Changes in ornamentation have therefore resulted in decoration in Manueline, Palladian, and baroque design, both of interiors and façades.

The style known as **Manueline** (named for Manuel I, 1495–1521) was a design unique to Portugal. It was mainly used as decorative architecture to change old structures rather than for new buildings (except for the Tower of Belém and the Jerónimos Monastery, also at Belém). It was used to construct portals, porches, and interiors. This architectural invention, sometimes called Atlantic Gothic, was flamboyant and exuberant, an expression of Portugal in the age when its seaborne empire flourished.

Since that time, Portuguese architecture has been mostly imitative, following such foreign styles as Renaissance, Palladian, Italianate, baroque, rococo, Spanish, and so forth. The use of new or original design has not been encouraged. True, azulejos (see above under "Arts and Crafts") have been used to some extent for embellishment even in modern times, giving a Portuguese flavor to borrowed architectural design. Examples of this can be seen at the João de Deus and Infanto Santo housing projects and the Gulbenkian Foundation complex and Exhibition Hall in Lisbon.

2. Dining and Wining

Portuguese food was summed up well by Mary Jean Kempner in her *Invitation to Portugal:* "The best Portuguese food is provincial, indigenous, eccentric, and proud—a reflection of the chauvinism of this complex people. It takes no sides, assumes no airs, makes no concessions or bows to Brillant-Savarin—and usually tastes wonderful."

Dining hours in Portugal are much earlier than they are in Spain. The best time for lunch is between 1 and 2:30 p.m.; for dinner from 7:30 to 9 p.m.

WHAT TO EXPECT

The first main dish you're likely to encounter on any menu is **bacalhau** (salted codfish), the *o fiel amigo* (faithful friend) to the Portuguese. As you drive through fishing villages in the north, you'll see racks and racks of the fish drying in the sun. Bacalhau has literally saved the lives of thousands from starvation, and the Portuguese not only are grateful to it, they like it as well.

Foreigners may not wax as rhapsodical about bacalhau, although it's prepared in imaginative ways, reportedly one for every day of the year. Common ways of serving it include *bacalhau cozido* (boiled with vegetables such as carrots, cabbage, and spinach, then baked together); *bacalhau à Bras* (fried in olive oil with onions and potatoes and flavored with garlic); *bacalhau à Gomes de Sá* (codfish that has been stewed with black olives, potatoes, onions, then baked and topped with a sliced boiled egg); and, finally, *bacalhau no churrasco* (barbecued).

A Kettle of Fruits of the Sea

Aside from codfish, the classic national dish is **caldeirada,** once described as the Portuguese version of a savory Mediterranean bouillabaisse. Prepared at home, it is a simple kettle of fish, with bits and pieces of the latest catch. From the kitchen of a competent chef, it is a pungent stew with choice bits and pieces of fruits of the sea.

Next on the platter is the Portuguese sardine, which many gastronomes have called elegant. This unassuming fish goes by the pompous Latin name of *Clupea pilchardus,* and is found off the Atlantic coasts of Iberia as well as France. Many of the sardines come from Setúbal, a city south of the Tagus, which is most often visited on a day trip from Lisbon. As you stroll through the alleys of the Alfama, or pass along the main streets of small villages throughout Portugal, you'll sometimes see women kneeling in front of braziers on their front doorsteps, grilling these large sardines left behind for domestic consumption. To have them grilled, order *sardinhas assadas.*

Shellfish is one of the great delicacies of the Portuguese table. Its scarcity and the demand of foreign markets have led to astronomical price tags. However, tourists devour them, many lamenting later when the bill is presented. The price of lobsters or crabs changes every day, depending on market quotations. Therefore the tariff doesn't appear on the menu. Rather, you'll see the abbreviation, "Preco V.," meaning variable price. When the waiter brings one of these crustaceans to your table, ask the price. That way you'll avoid shock when your sin is tallied up.

If you decide to splurge, make sure you get fresh shellfish. Many of these creatures from the deep, such as king-size crabs, are cooked, then displayed in restaurant windows. If they don't sell that day, I suspect the chef places them there tomorrow.

When fresh, *santola* (crab) is a delicacy. It's often served stuffed (*santola recheada),* although this specialty may be too pungent for unaccustomed Western palates. Amêijoas, the baby clams, are a reliable item of the Portuguese kitchen. Lagosta is translated as lobster; in fact, it's really a crayfish, best when served without adornment. If you see the words "piri-piri" on the menu following lobster, rush for the nearest exit. This is a sauce made of hot pepper from Angola. Jennings Parrott once wrote: "After tasting it you will understand why Angola wanted to get it out of the country." However, in fairness, many foreigners accustomed to hot, peppery food like this dish.

In Pursuit of an Incomparable Morsel

Many Portuguese begin their meals with *percébes,* roughly translated as goose barnacles. These little devils are the subject of much controversy. One local newspaper in Lisbon suggested to tourists that if they "can bear their repulsive appearance," they'll find "an incomparable morsel of delicious seafood" within. Others claim that all they taste from barnacles is brackish sea water.

There will be no controversy among those who are partial to **camarãoes** (shrimps). Most restaurants serve a heaping, delectable platter full.

A wide variety of good-tasting and inexpensive fish dishes are also available: *salmonete* (red mullet) from Setúbal; *robalo* (bass); *lenguado* (sole); and the sweet-tasting *pescada* (hake). Perhaps less appealing to the average diner, but preferred by many discriminating palates, are *eirós* (eels), *polvo* (octopus), and *lampreias* (lampreys), the latter a seasonal feature in the northern Minho district.

Of course, another way of beginning your repast is to select from the offerings of trays of *acepipes variados,* Portuguese hors d'oeuvres, which might include everything from a sea creature known as "knife" to the inevitable olives and tuna fish.

Meat, especially beef and veal, is less satisfying. Porto residents are known as "tripe eaters." The specialty is *dobrada,* tripe with beans, a favorite of the workers. The *cozido à Portuguesa,* is another dish much in demand: a stew often employing both beef and pork, along with fresh vegetables and sausages. The chief offering of the beer tavern is *bife na frigideira,* beef in a mustard sauce, usually served with a fried egg on top, all piping hot in a brown ceramic dish. Thinly sliced *iscas* (calves' livers) are usually well-prepared and sautéed with onion.

The best meat in Portugal is *porco* (pork), which is usually tender and juicy. In particular, order *porco Alentejano,* fried pork in a succulent sauce with baby clams, often cooked with herb-flavored onions and tomatoes. In the same province, *cabrito* (roast kid) is another treat, flavored with herbs and garlic. Chicken tends to be hit and miss, and is perhaps best when spit-roasted a golden brown (*frango no espeto).* In season, game is good, especially *perdiz* (partridge) and *codorniz estufada* (pan-roasted quail).

From the soup kitchen, the most popular broth is *caldo verde,* literally green broth. Made from cabbage, sausage, potatoes, and olive oil, it is commonly encountered in the north. Another ubiquitous soup is *sopa alentejana,* simmered with garlic and bread among other ingredients. The Portuguese housewife is canny, knowing how to gain every last morsel of nutrition from her fish, meat, and vegetables. The fishwives make a *sopa de mariscos* by boiling the shells from fish, then richly flavoring the stock and lacing it with white wine.

The Question of Olive Oil and Garlic

The basis of much Portuguese cooking is olive oil. However, the oil seems blander than that used in Spain. Furthermore, chefs in most Portuguese hotels, certainly first-class ones, offer routine international fare rather than regional cuisine. Garlic is used extensively and forms the basis of many dishes. However, if you select anything prepared to order you can request that it be *sem alho* (without garlic).

It's customary in most establishments to order soup (invariably a big bowl filled to the brim), then a fish and a meat course. Potatoes and/or rice are likely to accompany both the meat and fish platters.

In many restaurants, the chef features a *prato do dia*—that is, a plate of the day, which is actually several listings. These dishes are prepared fresh that day, and often are cheaper than the regular offerings.

The Sugaring of the Egg

Locked away in isolated and remote convents and monasteries, nuns and monks created wonderful and original sweet-tooth concoctions. Many of these delectable dessert specialties have been handed down over the years and are nowadays sold in little pastry shops throughout Portugal. In Lisbon or Porto, and a few other Portuguese cities, you can visit a *salão de chá* (tea salon) at four o'clock in the afternoon where you can sample these delicacies. Regrettably, too few restaurants feature regional desserts, many relying on caramel custard or fresh fruit.

Portugal doesn't offer many egg dishes, except for the omelet. However, eggs are used extensively in many of the sweets. Although egg yolks cooked in sugar may not appeal to you, you may want to try some of the more original offerings. Perhaps the best known are *ovos moles* (soft eggs sold in colorful barrels) that originate in Aveiro. From the same district capital comes *ovos de fio* (string eggs).

The most typical dessert is *arroz doce,* rice pudding flavored with cinnamon. As mentioned, flan, or caramel custard, appears on all menus. If you're in Portugal in summer, ask for a peach from Alcobaça. One of these juicy, succulent yellow fruits will spoil all other peaches for you forever. In first-class restaurants, the waiters go through an elaborate ritual of peeling it in front of you. Sintra is known for its strawberries, Setúbal for its orange groves, the Algarve for its almonds and figs, Elvas for its plums, the Azores for their pineapples, and Madeira for its passion fruit. Some people believe that if you eat too much of the latter, you'll be driven insane.

Cheese *(queijo)* is usually eaten separately and not with fruit, as in France. The most common varieties of Portuguese cheese are made from sheep or goat's milk. A popular variety is *queijo da sêrra* (literally, cheese from the hills). Another much-in-demand cheese is *queijo do Alentejo,* plus *queijo de Azeitão.* Many prefer *queijo Flamengo* (similar to the Dutch Gouda cheese).

The Pleasures of Port

One of the joys of dining in Portugal is to discover its regional wines. With the exception of port and madeira, they remain little known in Europe.

Port wine is produced in a region on the arid slopes of the Douro. Only vineyards within this area are recognized as yielding genuine port wine. The wine is shipped from Portugal's second-largest city, Porto, which the English have dubbed Oporto. Drunk in tulip-shaped glasses, it comes in many different colors and flavors. The pale dry port makes an ideal apéritif, and you can request it at a time when you might normally order dry sherry. The ruby or tawny port is sweet or medium dry, usually drunk as a liqueur after dessert. The most valuable port is either vintage or crusted wine. Crusted port does not mean vintage—rather, it takes its name from the decanting of its crust. Vintage port is the very best wine. In a period of a decade, only three years may be declared vintage.

Port is blended to assure a consistency of taste. Cyril Ray called it "one of the heartiest and handsomest of wines." Matured in wooden casks, the wood ports are either white, tawny, or ruby red. At first the wine is a deep ruby color, turning more like the color of straw as it ages.

Port wine had "perpetuated and glorified the fame of Porto," as one citizen put it. The first foreigners to be won over by it were the English in the 17th century. In more recent times, however, the French import more of the wine than the British. The grapes are still crushed by barefoot men; but this shouldn't alarm you as the wine is purified before it's bottled.

Falstaff's Soul for a Glass of Madeira

Its greatest chic was in times gone by, but madeira wine remains popular. It was highly favored by the early American colonists. Made with grapes grown in volcanic soil, it is fortified with brandy before it's shipped out.

The major types of madeira are Sercial (a dry wine, drunk as an apéritif, once a favorite with characters in Galsworthy novels); Malmsey (the dessert wine that the Duke of Clarence allegedly asked to drown in to escape torture at the hands of his brother); and Boal (a heady wine used on many different occasions, from a banquet following a hunt to a private tête-à-tête). Perhaps one of the finest statements ever made about madeira wine is the following: "It gives vivacity to a social gathering, profundity to a solitary meditation, helps a man to think well of his friends and to forgive his enemies. . . ."

Feminine, but Virile

Among the table wines, my personal favorites are from the mountainous wine district known as Dão. Its red wines are ruby-colored, their taste often described as velvety, whereas the white wines are light and delicate enough to make a fit accompaniment to Portuguese shellfish. From the sandy dunes of the Colares wine district, near Sintra, emerges a full-bodied wine made from Ramisco grapes (this wine is served at the Palácio de Seteais hotel). Of Colares wine, a Portuguese writer once noted that it has "a feminine complexion, but a virile energy."

The *vinhos verdes* (green wines) have many adherents. These light wines, low in alcoholic content, come from the northwestern corner of Portugal, the Minho district. The wine is gaseous, as it's made from grapes not fully matured. Near Estoril, the Carcavelos district produces an esoteric wine, commonly served as an apéritif or with dessert. As it mellows, its bouquet is more powerful. Finally, the Bucelas district, near Lisbon, makes a wine from the Arinto grape, among others. Its best-known wine is white, with a bit of an acid taste.

Water and Beer

Drinking water is safe in Lisbon, along the Costa do Sol (Estoril and Cascais), and in Porto. In less-visited towns and villages, you may want to order bottled water. You can ask for it to be with or without "gas."

Beer *(cerveja)* is gaining new followers yearly. One of the best of the home brews is sold under the name of Sagres, honoring the town in the Algarve that enjoyed associations with Henry the Navigator.

3. The Hotel Outlook

The government-sponsored **pousadas,** similar to Spain's paradores, were originally created for Portuguese holiday-seekers in remote sections of the country. The Portuguese government has fashioned these inns in historic buildings, such as convents, palaces, and castles. Often they stand in beautiful physical settings. Generally (but not always) the pousadas are in regions that do not have too many suitable hotels: everywhere from Henry the Navigator's Sagres to a feudal castle in the walled city of Óbidos. The tariffs are moderate, but a guest can't stay more than five days, as there is usually a waiting line of other visitors. Special terms are granted to honeymoon couples.

A more recent addition to the accommodations scene in Portugal are the **solares,** mostly spacious country manor houses of the Portuguese aristocracy that are now being restored and opened as guesthouses. Many date from the days of the Discoveries, when navigators brought riches back from all over the world and established lavish homes that have passed down to their heirs. Most of these are along the Costa Verde, between Ponte de Lima and Viana do Castelo, although they are found all over the country, from the coastal area that was the seat of ship-building and sailing power to the Alentejo plains.

Information on the solares program is available from the **Portuguese National Tourist Office,** 590 Fifth Ave., New York, NY 10036 (tel. 212/354-4403). For a tour of the solares or to make reservations, get in touch with **Direcção Geral do Turismo,** Divisão do Turismo no Espaço Rural, 86 Avenida António de Aguiar, 1099 Lisboa Codex (tel. 01/57-50-15). If you prefer to stay on the Costa Verde, you can receive information and assistance from Central Reservations for the Houses (manor houses) of **Delegação de Turismo** de Ponte de Lima, Praça da República, 4990 Ponte de Lima (tel. 058/94-23-35). You can arrange to go from one solar to the next through this office.

One of the best associations for arranging for stays in private homes is the **Associação das Casas em Turismo,** Torre D2-8A, Alto da Pampilheira, 2750 Cascais (tel. 01/284-44-64). It has both manor houses and country homes where accommodations can be arranged in all the major tourist districts of the country. Two persons in a comfortable but simple room pay from 6,000$ ($39) to 8,000$ ($52). However, for accommodations rated "very comfortable," the charge for two is from 9,000$ ($58.50) to 13,000$ ($84.50).

ADVANCE RESERVATIONS

Advance reservations for peak-season travel in Portugal are essential, especially since many of the country's hotels are filled to the seams every summer with vacationing Europeans. Unless you're incurably spontaneous, you'll probably be better off in Portugal, even in low season, with some idea of where you'll spend each night.

4. The ABCs of Portugal

It's maddening to have your trip marred by an incident that could have been avoided if you'd been tipped off previously. Hocking your watch, renting a fur, seeking medical care, getting your hair cut, and ferreting out the nearest toilet can at times become paramount problems. Although I don't promise to answer all these needs, there are a variety of services, especially in Lisbon, that can ease your adjustment to Portugal.

The concierge in your hotel is usually a reliable dispenser of information, including the location of the nearest pharmacy or advice on transportation problems, as well as bullfight tickets. However, should you desire more immediate or more detailed answers to your questions, the following brief summary of some of Portugal's facts of life may prove helpful.

For more specific data about Lisbon, see "Practical Facts" in chapter III, "Settling into Lisbon."

BABYSITTING: Check with the staff of your hotel for arrangements. Most first-class hotels can provide competent women or girls for babysitting from lists that the concierge keeps. At smaller establishments, the girl is likely to be the daughter of the proprietor. Rates are low. Remember to request a babysitter no later than in the morning if you're going out that evening.

BEACHES: Portugal has more than 500 miles of sandy beaches. They range from those at the cosmopolitan resort centers close to Lisbon and along the Algarve to remote wild stretches at sleepy fishing villages. You can find swimming, waterskiing, skindiving, surfing, sailing, fishing, and rowing at many places either along the west or the south coasts on the Atlantic Ocean. Starting in the north at Costa Verde, you can explore Costa de Prata, Costa de Lisboa, Costa Dourada, and the Algarve, and you're sure to find a lot of favorites among the little sandy coves, peninsulas, and wide strips of sand.

CAMPING AND CARAVANS: Portugal provides parks for campers and house trailers (caravans) near beaches and in wooded areas all over the country. Some have swimming pools, athletic fields, markets, and restaurants among other facilities, while many are simply convenient sites with water and toilets away from the hustle and bustle of cities and towns. For a guide to such parks, their classification, equipment, and capacity, get in touch with **Federação Portuguesa de Campismo e Caravanismo,** 15 Avenida de Outubro, 1000 Lisboa (tel. 01/52-33-08), or ask your travel agent.

CIGARETTES: The price of American-brand cigarettes (which varies) is always lethal. Bring in at least 200 cigarettes as allowed by Customs. If you're saving money, try one of the Portuguese brands as an adventure. Many smokers have found Portuguese tobacco excellent.

CLOTHING SIZES: For the most part, Portugal uses the same sizes as other European countries. The sizes of women's stockings and men's socks are international.

FOR WOMEN

Juniors		Misses		Shoes	
U.S.	Portugal	U.S.	Portugal	U.S.	Portugal
5	34	10	40	5	36
7	36	12	42	5½	36½
9	38	14	44	6½	37½
11	40	16	46	7½	38½
		18	48	8	39
		20	50	8½	39½
				9	40

FOR MEN

Shirts		Slacks		Shoes	
U.S.	**Portugal**	**U.S.**	**Portugal**	**U.S.**	**Portugal**
14	36	32	42	5	36
14½	37	34	44	6	37
15	38	36	46	7	38
15½	39	38	48	7½	39
15¾	40	40	50	8	40
16	41			9	41
16½	42			10	42
17	43			10½	43
				11	44
				12	45

Warning: This chart should be followed only for general outline, as in the same country there are big differences in sizes. If possible, try on all clothing or shoes before making a purchase. You'll be glad you did.

CRIME: Whenever you're traveling in an unfamiliar city or country, stay alert. Be aware of your immediate surroundings. Wear a moneybelt and don't sling your camera or purse over your shoulder; wear the strap diagonally across your body. This will minimize the possibility of your becoming a victim of crime. Every society has its criminals. It's your responsibility to be aware and be alert even in the most heavily touristed areas.

CURRENCY: The exchange rate is approximately 154 escudos (154$) to the U.S. dollar, but that is subject to change at any minute.

It's a good idea to buy a small amount of escudos to take with you when you go to Portugal—say, about $50 worth—in small bills to take care of paying for transportation, tips, and other matters upon arrival. You can get this currency at many banks or at the foreign-exchange counter at large airports. Taking some escudos with you will prevent delays and possible embarrassment if the exchange offices happen to be closed at the airport at which you arrive, so that you have to wait until you can cash your traveler's checks.

CUSTOMS: You may be asked how much tobacco you're bringing in: the limit is 200 cigarettes or 50 cigars. One still camera with five unexposed rolls of film is allowed duty free; also a small movie camera with two reels, a portable tape recorder, a portable record player, a portable musical instrument, and a bicycle (not motor bikes). Campers and sporting types are allowed to bring in one tent and camping accessories (including a kayak not exceeding 18 feet), a pair of skis, two tennis racquets, a tackle set, and a small firearm (for hunting only) with 50 bullets. A normal-size bottle of wine and a half pint of hard alcohol are permitted, as are a "small quantity" of perfume and a half pint of toilet water.

Upon leaving Portugal, citizens of the United States who have been outside the U.S. for 48 hours or more are allowed to bring in $400 worth of merchandise duty free—that is, if they have claimed no similar exemption within the past 30 days. Beyond this free allowance, the next $1,000 worth of merchandise is assessed at a flat rate of 10% duty. If you make purchases in Portugal, it's important to keep your receipts. On gifts, the duty-free limit is $50.

DOCUMENTS FOR ENTRY: Canadians and Americans need only a valid passport to enter Portugal.

ELECTRIC CURRENT: Many North Americans find that their plugs will not fit into the sockets in Portugal, where the voltage is 220 volts AC, 50 cycles. Adapters and transformers should be purchased before you go. It's always best to check at your hotel desk before plugging in any electrical equipment. In some remote districts, the voltage is 100 volts DC.

EMBASSIES: For information on this important topic, see "Practical Facts" in chapter III, as the foreign embassies are in Lisbon.

FILM: This is expensive so I suggest you bring in all that Customs will allow. There are no special restrictions on photographs, except in certain museums.

GOLF: Portugal offers a wide range of golf courses from the north, with the century-old Porto Golf Club (second oldest on the continent), to splendid championship courses on the Algarve in the south. Many of them are laid out on promontories overlooking the sea and the ubiquitous vineyards, with fairways bordering on woodlands. For information on courses, their locations, and their facilities, get in touch with the Portuguese National Tourist Office (see "Tourist Information," in "Practical Facts," chapter III) at its offices in Lisbon or in the United States before you travel.

HOLIDAYS AND FESTIVALS: Watch out for holidays and adjust your banking needs, or whatever, accordingly. Aside from the regular holidays such as Christmas, Portugal has a few all its own: Universal Brotherhood Day on January 1; a Memorial Day to the country's greatest poet, Camões, June 10; Assumption Day, August 15; the Anniversary of the Republic, October 5; All Saints' Day on November 1; Independence Day on December 1; and the Feast of the Immaculate Conception on December 8. Good Friday and the Feast of Corpus Christi are also holidays, but their dates differ every year.

LAUNDRY: Most hotels in this guide provide laundry services, but if you want your garment returned on the same day, you'll often have to pay from 25% to 40% more than the regular price. Simply present your maid or valet with your laundry or dry cleaning (usually lists are provided). Note: Materials needing special treatment (such as certain synthetics) should be called to the attention of the person handling your laundry. Some establishments I've dealt with in the past treated every fabric as if it were cotton.

LIQUOR LAWS: You have to be 18 years of age to drink liquor in the bars of Portugal. Liquor is sold in most markets, as opposed to package stores in the United States. In Lisbon you can drink till dawn. There's always some bar or some fado club open serving alcoholic beverages.

MAIL DELIVERY: While in Portugal you may have your mail directed to your hotel (or hotels), to the American Express representative (providing you are a client), or the General Delivery *(poste restante)* in Lisbon. Your passport must be presented for mail pickups. In Portugal, a letter to the United States (or any country outside Europe) costs 87$ (60¢) for up to 20 grams. A postcard to the U.S. and other non-European countries goes for 82$ (55¢). An airmail or regular letter to anywhere in Portugal and Spain costs 29$ (20¢), the same price for a postcard.

MEDICAL CARE: Portugal does not have free medical service. The concierge of your hotel can usually put you in touch with the house doctor, or summon him or her in case of emergencies.

METRIC CONVERSION CHART: In Portugal, you face a whole new way of measuring. Even the temperature will be expressed in centigrade. This chart will show you how to convert kilometers into miles, grams into pounds, meters into yards, and liters into ounces. Once you get the hang of it, it isn't as hard as it first appears.

Length
    1 millimeter = 0.04 inches (*or* less than ⅟₁₆ in)
    1 centimeter = 0.39 inches (*or* just under ½ in)
    1 meter   = 1.09 yards (*or* about 39 inches)
    1 kilometer = 0.62 mile (*or* about ⅔ mile)

To convert kilometers to miles, take the number of kilometers and multiply by .62 (for example, 25 km × .62 = 15.5 mi).

To convert miles to kilometers, take the number of miles and multiply by 1.61 (for example, 50 mi × 1.61 = 80.5 km).

Capacity
    1 liter = 33.92 ounces
          = 1.06 quarts
          = 0.26 gallons

To convert liters to gallons, take the number of liters and multiply by .26 (for example, 50 l × .26 = 13 gallons).

To convert gallons to liters, take the number of gallons and multiply by 3.79 (for example, 10 gal × 3.79 = 37.9 l).

Weight
    1 gram   = 0.04 ounces (*or* about a paperclip's weight)
    1 kilogram = 2.2 pounds

To convert kilograms to pounds, take the number of kilos and multiply by 2.2 (for example, 75 kg × 2.2 = 165 pounds).

To convert pounds to kilograms, take the number of pounds and multiply by .45 (for example, 90 lb × .45 = 40.5 kg).

Area
    1 hectare (100m²) = 2.47 acres

To convert hectares to acres, take the number of hectares and multiply by 2.47 (for example, 20 ha × 2.47 = 49.4 acres).

To convert acres to hectares, take the number of acres and multiply by .41 (for example, 40 acres × .41 = 16.4 hectares).

Temperature

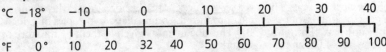

To *convert* degrees C to degrees F, multiply degrees C by 9, divide by 5, then add 32 (for example, $9/5 \times 20°C + 32 = 68°F$).

To *convert* degrees F to degrees C, subtract 32 from degrees F, then multiply by 5, and divide by 9 (for example, $85°F - 32 \times 5/9 = 29°C$).

NEWSPAPERS: The *International Herald Tribune* is sold at most newsstands in Lisbon, either in major hotels or along the street. The Trib is also sold at leading newsstands throughout the country, including Porto and the Algarve.

OFFICE HOURS: Hours in general are 9 a.m. to 5 or 5:30 p.m., with a break for lunch sometime from 1 to 3 p.m.

PETS: Pets brought into Portugal must have the okay of the local veterinarian and a health certificate from the home country.

PHARMACIES: The Portuguese government requires selected pharmacies *(farmácias)* to stay open at all times of the day and night. This is effected by means of a rotation system. So check with your concierge for locations and hours of the nearest drugstores, called *farmácias de servico*. In general, pharmacies in Portugal are open from 9 a.m. to 1 p.m. and 3 to 7 p.m. Monday to Saturday.

POLITICS: The dust of the revolution has long settled. Portugal, as mentioned, is one of the safest countries in which to travel in Western Europe. The Portuguese Republic, after years of dictatorship, is a democratic state, and tourists can travel without restriction in every province of the land.

RADIO AND TV: In Lisbon there are two major TV channels—**Channel I (VHF)** and **Channel II (UHF).** Many foreign films are shown, often in English with Portuguese subtitles.

RELIGIOUS SERVICES: Portugal is a Catholic country, and there are places of worship in every city, town, and village.

RESTROOMS: All major terminals (airports and railways) have such facilities, and Lisbon has several public ones. However, you can often use the restroom at a café or tavern, as there is one on practically every block. It is considered polite to purchase something, however—perhaps a small glass of wine or whatever.

TAXES: Portugal is now a member of the European Common Market, so it imposes a Value Added Tax, called **IVA.** The tax ranges from 8% to 30% and, as prescribed by law, is included in your bills, such as hotel and restaurant tabs as well as for purchases of particular items, including medicine. Tourists resident in foreign countries can now benefit from duty-free purchases, except for the following items: foodstuff (other than alcoholic drinks), tobacco, works of art, collectors' items and antiques whose value exceeds 20,000$ ($130), unset gems, goods for the fueling and provisioning of private means of transport, and certain purchases "of a commercial nature" such as those made in bulk amounts. The minimum amount of purchase required for American tourists to claim a duty-free exemption is 10,000$ ($65), exclusive of tax. There is a service desk at the Lisbon airport where tourists can get tax refunds, but they must produce the original and two copies of a document known as "Form Mod. B." This document is given to them by the store or vendor who sold them the merchandise.

TELEGRAMS: At most hotels, the receptionist will help you send a cable or telegram.

TELEPHONES: Calling from **pay-phone booths** in Portugal, providing you have the right change, will allow you to avoid high hotel surcharges. Most booths take 2$5, 5$, and 25$ coins. Put the coins in a slot at the top of the box while you hold the receiver, then dial your number after you hear the dial tone. Once a connection is made, the necessary coins will automatically drop. If enough coins are not available, your connection will be broken. A warning tone will sound and a light over the dial will go on in case more coins are needed. For **long-distance** (trunk) calls within the country, dial the right trunk code, followed by the number you want.

Telephone calls can also be made at all post offices, which will also send telegrams. Calls to Europe are made by dialing 00, followed by the country code, the area code (not prefaced by 0), then the phone number. Calls outside Europe are made by dialing 097, followed by the country code, the area code, and the phone number. For example, the country code for the United States and Canada is 1.

The national emergency number in Portugal is 115.

TELEX: Ask your hotel for assistance.

TIME: Portugal is six hours ahead of the United States (Eastern Standard Time). For the local time in Lisbon, phone 15.

TIPPING: Portugal has now caught up with the rest of Western Europe. Most service personnel expect a good tip rather than a small one, as in former times.

Hotels: The hotels add a service charge (known as *serviço*), which is divided among the entire staff. But individual tipping is also the rule of the day: 50$ (35¢) to the bellhop for errands run, 50$ to the doorman who calls you a cab, 100$ (65¢) to the porter for each piece of luggage carried, 500$ ($3.25) to the wine steward if you've dined often at your hotel, and 300$ ($1.95) to the chambermaid for stays of less than a week.

In first-class or deluxe hotels the concierge will present you with a separate bill, outlining your little or big extras, such as charges for bullfight tickets, etc. A gratuity is expected in addition to the charge, the amount depending entirely on the number of requests you've put to him or her.

Hairdressers: For a normal haircut, you should leave 50$ (35¢) behind as a tip to the barber. But if your hair is cut at the Ritz, don't dare leave less than 100$ (65¢). Beauticians get 150$ ($1); a manicurist, around 150$ also.

Taxis: Figure on about 20% of the regular fare for short runs. For longer treks —for example, from the airport to Cascais—15% is adequate.

Restaurants: Restaurants and nightclubs include a service charge and government taxes. As in hotels, this service is distributed among the entire staff, including the waiter's mistress and the owner's grandfather—so extra tipping is customary. Add about 5% to the bill in a moderately priced restaurant, up to 10% in a deluxe or first-class establishment.

Services: Hatcheck women in fado houses, restaurants, and nightclubs expect at least 50$ (35¢). The women who stand on sentinel duty in washrooms usually get no more than 25$ (15¢). The shoeshine boys of Portugal are the most undertipped creatures in society. Here I recommend greater generosity, providing the shine was good.

TOURIST INFORMATION: For travel information before you go to Portugal, get in touch with the **Portuguese National Tourist Office,** 590 Fifth Ave., New York, NY 10036 (tel. 212/354-4403). For information on the tourist board's facilities in Lisbon, see "Practical Facts," chapter III.

III

SETTLING INTO LISBON

1. ORIENTATION
2. PUBLIC TRANSPORTATION
3. PRACTICAL FACTS

In its golden age it was called the eighth wonder of the world. Travelers returning from a trip to Lisbon reported that its riches rivaled those of Venice.

As one of the greatest maritime centers in history, the Portuguese capital has enjoyed exotic riches from the far-flung corners of its empire. Aside from the wealth of cultural influences, Lisbon stockpiled goods, beginning with its earliest contacts with the Calicut and Malabar coasts. Treasures from the Orient brought in on Chinese junks to Indian seaports eventually found their way back to Lisbon: porcelain, luxurious silks, rubies, pearls, and other rare gems. The abundance and variety of spices from the East—tea, indigo, turmeric, ginger, pepper, coconut, cumin, betel —were to rival even Keats's vision of "silken Samarkand."

From the wilds of the Americas came red dye-wood (Brazil-wood), coffee, gold (discovered in 1698), diamonds (unearthed in 1729), and gemstones. All this extensive contact signaled a new era in world trade, with Lisbon sitting as the grande dame of maritime empires, the hub of commerce between Europe, Africa, and Asia. And then came . . .

THE GREAT EARTHQUAKE

"From Scotland to Asia Minor, people ran out of doors and looked at the sky, and fearfully waited. It was, of course, an earthquake," as once chronicled a *Holiday* article. Tidal waves, 50 feet high, swept over Algeciras, Spain. The capitals of Europe shook.

It was 9:40 on the morning of All Saints Day, November 1, 1755. The churches were packed to overflowing; smoky tapers and incense burned upon the altars. After the initial shock, 22 spasms followed. Roofs caved in; hospitals (with more than 1,000 patients), prisons, public buildings, royal palaces, aristocratic town houses, fishermen's cottages, churches, and houses of prostitution—all were toppled. Overturned candles helped ignite a fire that would consume the once-proud capital in six days, leaving her a gutted, charred shambles. Voltaire described the destruction in *Candide:* "The sea boiled up in the harbor and smashed the vessels lying at anchor. Whirlwinds of flame and ashes covered the streets and squares, houses collapsed, roofs were thrown onto foundations and the foundations crumbled." All told, 30,000 inhabitants were crushed beneath the tumbling debris.

When the survivors of the initial shocks ran from their burning homes toward the mighty Tagus, they were met with walls of water 40 feet high. Estimates vary, but the final tally of all who died in drownings and the six-day holocaust that followed is put at around 60,000.

Voltaire cynically commented on the aftermath of the disaster, particularly the *auto-da-fé* that followed: "It was decided by the University of Coimbra that the sight of several people being slowly burned with great ceremony was an infallible means of preventing the earth from quaking."

PLAYING THE COQUETTE GAME

Today, the "new" Lisbon is distinctly feminine. In fact, she was once called a coquette. Under a stark blue sky, her medley of pastel-washed houses dazzles, like a city in North Africa. The Tagus has been called her eternal lover.

Sea gulls take flight from her harbor, where trawlers from Africa unload their freight. Pigeons sweep down on Praça do Comércio, also known as Black Horse Square. From the Bairro Alto (upper city), cable cars carry Lisbon's denizens down to the waterfront. The sidewalks are characteristic black and white mosaics forming arabesques. Streets bear colorful names or designations, such as the Rua do Açúcar (Street of Sugar). Fountains abound: one, the Samaritan, dates from the 16th century. Wide, symmetrical boulevards split through the city to new high-rise apartment houses, while in other quarters laundry hanging from 18th-century houses laps the wind.

It is a city that gives nicknames to everything from its districts (the Chiado, named after a poet) to its kings. Fernando, who built one of the most characteristic walls around Lisbon, was honored with the appellation "The Beautiful."

THE LEGEND OF ULYSSES

Lisboans have always known they are special. Regardless of how fanciful, every legend has its adherents. In the Alfama, many of the residents claim unabashedly that Ulysses founded their city. Others, more scholarly, maintain that the Phoenicians or the Carthaginians were the original settlers. The body of the country's patron saint, Vincent, is said to have arrived in Portugal on an abandoned boat, with only two ravens to guide it. It is further alleged that the birds lived in the cathedral tower until as late as the 19th century.

The Romans settled in Lisbon in the 1st century B.C., building a fortification on what is now St. George's Castle. The city was captured by the Visigoths in the 5th century A.D., a conquest later followed by long centuries of Moorish domination beginning in A.D. 714. The first king of Portugal, Afonso Henriques, captured Lisbon in 1147. But it wasn't until 1256 that King Afonso III moved the capital there, deserting Coimbra, the major university city of Portugal.

Now in its seventh century as the center of the Portuguese nation, Lisbon is the westernmost capital of continental Europe. Part of its legend is that it spreads across seven hills, like Rome. If that statement were ever true, it has long since become historical, as Lisbon now sprawls across more hills than that. Most of it lies on the right bank of the Tagus.

1. Orientation

No one ever claimed that getting around Lisbon was easy. Streets rise and fall across the legendary seven hills, at times dwindling into mere alleyways. But exploring it is well worth the effort.

Lisbon is best approached through its gateway, the **Praça do Comércio**, bordering the Tagus. Like a formal parlor, it is one of the most perfectly planned squares in Europe, rivaled perhaps only by the Piazza dell' Unità d'Italia in Trieste, Italy

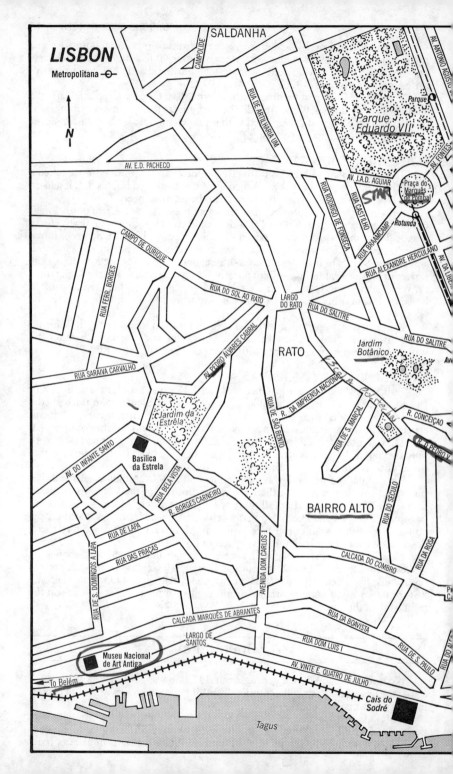

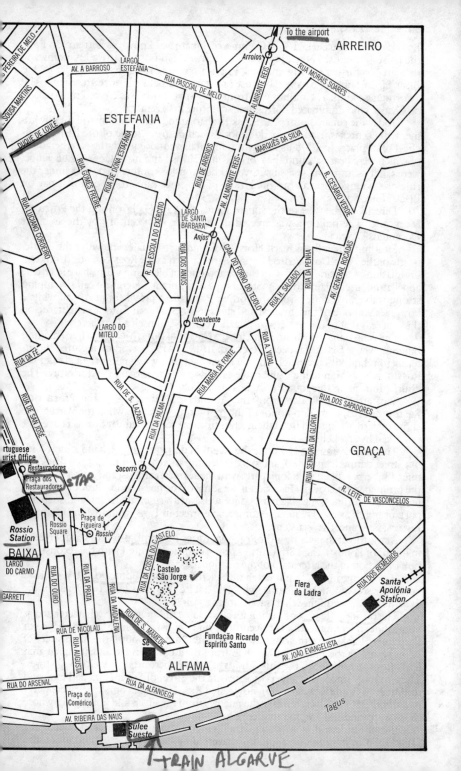

Before the earthquake of 1755, Commerce Square was known as Terreiro do Paço, the palace grounds, as the king and his court lived in now-destroyed buildings on that site. To further confuse matters, English-speaking residents often refer to it as Black Horse Square, so named because of a statue (actually a bronze green) of José I, a Portuguese king. The monument from the 18th century was created by Machado de Castro, who dominated Portuguese sculpture in his era.

Today the square houses the Stock Exchange and various ministries of government. Its center is used as a parking lot, which destroys some of the harmonious effect of its praça. In 1908 its most monumental event occurred, the reverberations of which were heard around the world. King Carlos I and his elder son, Luís Filipe, were fatally shot by an assassin. It would hold on for another two years under the rule of a younger prince, but the House of Bragança came to an end that day on Black Horse Square.

Directly to the west of the square stands the City Hall fronting the **Praça do Município.** The building was erected in the latter 19th century by the architect Domingos Parente.

Heading north from Black Horse or Commerce Square, you enter the hustle-bustle of the Praça Dom Pedro IV, popularly known as the **Rossio.** The "drunken" undulation of the sidewalks, with their arabesques of black and white, have led to the appellation, used mainly by tourists, of "the dizzy praça." Here you can sit, sipping strong unblended coffee from the former Portuguese provinces in Africa, while a boy gives you one of the cheapest and slickest shoeshines in Europe. The statue on the square is that of the emperor of Brazil, Pedro IV, himself a Portuguese.

Opening onto the Rossio is the **Teatro Nacional Dona Maria II,** a free-standing building whose façade has been preserved. In 1967–1970, workmen gutted the interior to rebuild it completely. If you arrive by train, you'll enter the **Estação do Rossio,** whose Manueline exuberance offends those sensitive to architecture. The Tourist Bureau on this square is in the Palácio Foz.

Separating the Rossio from the Avenida da Liberdade is the **Praça dos Restauradores,** named in honor of the restoration—that is, when the Portuguese chose their own king and freed themselves from 60 years of rule by Spain. That event is marked by an obelisk.

The main avenue of Lisbon is the **Avenida da Liberdade,** a handsomely laid-out street dating from 1880, and once called the antechamber of Lisbon. The Avenue of Liberty is like a mile-long park, with shade trees, gardens, and center walks for the promenading crowds. Flanking it are some of the finest shops, headquarters for many major airlines, travel agents, coffeehouses with sidewalk tables, and such important hotels as the Tivoli. The comparable street in Paris would be the Champs-Élysées; in Rome, the Via Veneto.

At the top of the avenue is the **Praça Marquês de Pombal,** with a statue erected in honor of Pombal, the 18th-century prime minister credited with the reconstruction of Lisbon in the aftermath of the earthquake.

Proceeding north, you'll enter the splendid **Parque Eduardo VII,** named to honor the son of Queen Victoria, who paid a state visit to Lisbon. In the park is the **Estufa Fria,** a greenhouse that is well worth a visit.

The business district of Lisbon is called **Baixa,** its architecture characterized as Pombaline, referring to the 18th-century prime minister again. Many of the major Portuguese banks have their headquarters here. Running south, the main street of Baixa separates the Praça do Comércio from the Rossio. In fact, a triumphal arch leads from the square to the **Rua Augusta,** where there are many clothing stores. The two most important streets of Baixa are the Street of Silver (Rua da Prata) and the Street of Gold (Rua da Ouro), now called Rua Aurea. Of course they were never paved with gold or silver, but take their names from the silver- and goldsmiths whose shops were (and still are) found there.

If you head west from Baixa, you'll enter a shopping district known as the **Chiado.** From its perch on a hill, it is traversed by the **Rua Garrett,** honoring the

Portuguese poet and dandy of the 19th century. Many of the finest shops in the city, such as the Vista Alegre, a china and porcelain house, are here. One coffeehouse, in particular, A Brasileira, has been a traditional gathering spot for the Portuguese literati.

Continuing your ascent, you arrive at the **Bairro Alto** (the upper city). This sector, reached by trolley car, occupies one of the legendary seven hills of Lisbon. Many of its buildings were left fairly intact by the 1755 earthquake. Containing much of the charm and color of the Alfama, it is of interest mainly because it is the center of some of the finest fado cafés in Lisbon, including A Severa and Lisboa a Noite. In addition, some of the best restaurants in the city are found here, as well as unpretentious taverns featuring hearty Portuguese cuisine.

To the east of the Praça do Comércio lies the oldest district of Lisbon, the **Alfama.** For a more detailed description of this section, refer to chapter VI, "The Sights of Lisbon." Saved only in part from the devastation of the earthquake, the Alfama was the Moorish sector of the capital. Centuries later, before the earthquake struck, it was the residential district of aristocrats. Nowadays it is occupied mainly by stevedores, plus fishermen and their barefoot *varinas* (fishwives).

Overlooking the Alfama is **St. George's Castle,** once a Visigothic fortification, and later used by the Romans. Destroyed and rebuilt so many times that its history is a jumble, the present castle dates from the 12th century.

On the way to the Alfama, on the Rua dos Bacalheiros, stands the **Casa dos Bicos** (the House of the Pointed Stones). This early 16th-century town house, not open to the public, is graced with a façade studded with diamond-shaped stones. And while it was partially demolished by the earthquake, it remains an impressive sight.

In the west, on the coastal road to Estoril, is the suburb of **Belém** (Bethlehem). It contains some of the finest monuments in Portugal, a few of which were built during the Age of Discovery, near the point where the caravels set out to conquer new worlds (at Belém, the Tagus reaches the sea). At one time, before the earthquake, Belém was an aristocratic sector filled with elegant town houses.

Two of the principal attractions in all of Portugal stand here: the **Jerónimos Monastery,** erected in the 16th century in the Manueline style, and the **National Coach Museum,** the finest of its kind in the world. Actually, Belém is Lisbon's museumland, containing the **Museum of Popular Art,** the **Ethnological Museum,** and the galley-stuffed **Naval Museum.**

On the south side of the Tagus, where puce-colored smoke billows out from the factories, is the left-bank settlement of **Cacilhas.** It is inhabited mainly by the working class, yet visited by right-bank denizens for its seafood restaurants, such as the Floresta (see my dining recommendations). You can reach the settlement by way of a bridge or by taking a ferryboat across, leaving from Praça do Comércio.

Of course the most dramatic way to cross the Tagus is on the **Ponte 25 de Abril,** the longest and most expensive suspension bridge ever erected in Europe, the total outlay exceeding $75 million. The bridge opened up that sector of Portugal lying south of the Tagus. Its towers peaking at 625 feet, the bridge is 7,473 feet long. Standing guard on the left bank is a monumental statue of Christ with his arms outstretched.

---

2. Public Transportation

Public transport is inexpensive but inadequate at times. Yet considering the hilly terrain of the city and the fact that many of the streets were designed for donkey carts, the Portuguese manage very well. However, even the most skilled chauffeurs have been known to scrape the fenders of their clients' rented limousines while maneuvering through the narrow alleyways.

A lot of the city can be walked, especially by those adept at hill climbing. However, to get from one point to the other—say, from the Alfama to the suburb of Belém—you'll need public transport or your own car.

Evamarie Doering of Belmont, Calif., writes: "In the 15 years since my last visit there, Lisbon has become one of the noisiest cities I've ever visited. Traffic is outrageous; driving is difficult because of the speed and the tendency of the natives to ride six inches from your rear bumper. The buses, of which there are a great many, are *very* noisy, and produce volumes of smoke. Honking of car horns seems to be a national pastime."

TAXIS

Taxis in Lisbon tend to be cheap and are a popular means of transport for all but the most economy minded of tourists. The taxis usually are diesel-engined Mercedes, charging a basic fare of 80$ (50¢) for the first 400 yards. After that, you'll be assessed another 6$ (4¢) for each additional 180 yards, with 20% additional for night fare from 10 p.m. to 6 a.m. The driver is allowed by law to tack on another 50% to your bill if your luggage weighs more than 66 pounds. If you travel outside Lisbon, the driver is allowed to charge you 34$50 (25¢) per kilometer. Most Portuguese tip about 20% of an already-modest fare.

Many visitors stay at one of the Costa do Sol resort hotels, such as the Palácio in Estoril and the Cidadela in Cascais. If that is your situation, then you'll probably find taxi connections from Lisbon prohibitively expensive. Far preferable for Costa do Sol visitors is the electric train system (see below).

TRAMS AND BUSES

These are among the cheapest in Europe. The trolley cars, such as those that make the steep run up to the Bairro Alto, are usually painted a rich Roman gold. The double-decker buses, on the other hand, come from London and look as if they need Big Ben in the background to complete the picture. If you're trying to stand on the platform at the back of a jammed bus, by the way, you'll need both hands free to hold on.

At the foot of the Santa Justa elevator, lying on the Rua Aurea, a stand will give you a schedule pinpointing the zigzagging route of these trams and buses. Your hotel concierge should be of help to you also.

You will pay a flat fare of 100$ (65¢) on a bus if you buy the ticket from the driver. The transportation system within the city limits is divided into zones ranging from one to five. The price of your fare depends upon how many zones you traverse. You can purchase a block of 20 tickets called *modulos*. If so, depending on the number of zones traveled, your fare will range from 23$ (15¢) to 69$ (45¢).

On a streetcar a ticket purchased from a driver costs 85$ (55¢). However, prepurchased modulos mean rides ranging from 23$ (15¢) to 46$ (30¢), depending on the number of zones traveled. On express buses, you either pay 100$ (65¢) if you buy the ticket from the driver or else use three modulos costing 69$ (45¢).

SUBWAYS

Lisbon's Metro stations are designated by large *M* signs. A single ticket costs 35$ (25¢) per ride if you purchase it from a vending machine, 45$ (30¢) if purchased from a toll booth. One of the most popular trips, and likely to be jam-packed on *corrida* (bullfight) days, is from the Avenida da Liberdade to the Campo Pequeno, the brick bullring away from the center of the city.

FERRYBOATS

Long before the Ponte 25 de Abril was built, reliable ferryboats chugged across the Tagus, connecting the left bank with the right. They still do, and are as popular as ever, as many Portuguese find the bridge too expensive to cross with their automobiles. Therefore they leave their cars at home and take the ferryboat to work.

Most of the boats leave from the Praça do Comércio, heading for Barreiro and Cacilhas. On the Lisbon-Cacilhas ferryboat, the single fare is 60$ (40¢) one way. However, if you purchase your ticket from a vending machine, the cost is reduced to 55$ (35¢). If you plan to make several trips back and forth across the river, you can buy a block of 20 modulos. Using two modulos on each trip, the cost of the fare is reduced to 46$ (30¢) per one-way passage.

PONTE 25 DE ABRIL

As mentioned, this suspension bridge, the largest ever built in Europe, connects Lisbon with its left bank and the district south of the Tagus. For a small car, the toll charge is 40$ (25¢), increasing to 80$ (50¢) for a larger automobile. A van pays 130$ (85¢). Not only can you take the bridge to reach Cacilhas, but you can use it for such cities as Setúbal in the south, and Évora, the old Roman city in the east.

Finally, the most important means of transport are the:

ELECTRIC TRAINS

Lisbon is connected with all the towns and villages along the Portuguese Riviera by a smooth-running electric train system. You can board the train at the waterfront **Cais do Sodré** station in Lisbon, heading up the coast all the way to Cascais.

Only one class of seat is offered, and the rides are cheap. Sintra, that third major destination in the environs, is not reached by the electric train. You must go to the **Estação do Rossio** station, opening onto the Praça Dom Pedro IV or the Rossio, where frequent connections can be made. The one-way fare is one class only. On the Lisbon-Cascais, Lisbon-Estoril, or Lisbon-Sintra run, the one-way fare is 110$ (70¢) per person.

---

3. Practical Facts

AMERICAN EXPRESS: STAR is the representative of **American Express** in Portugal, and it will hold or forward mail for you, providing you are a client. There, too, you can buy tickets for tours, exchange currency, and, of course, cash American Express traveler's checks. Its offices are at 4-A Avenida Sidónio Pais (tel. 01/53-98-71). It's open daily from 9 a.m. until 12:30 p.m. and 2 to 6 p.m. weekdays; closed Saturday and Sunday. The main office is near Pombal Square and easily reached by bus.

BANKS: What bank to use? Check with your home bank before your departure, as many banks in Canada and the United States have affiliates in Lisbon. The majority of the banks open at 8:30 a.m., closing at 3 p.m. Monday to Friday. A trio of major banks include **Banco Português do Atlântico,** 112 Rua Aurea (tel. 01/36-64-15); the **Banco Expírito Santo e Comercial de Lisboa,** 195 Avenida da Liberdade (tel. 01/54-12-18); and at the airport a branch of **Banco Totta & Açores** (tel. 01/88-40-11), which is open at all hours of the day and night, including holidays. More banks in Lisbon offer night service. For example, the **Banco Borges & Irmão,** 9-A Avenida do Liberdade (tel. 01/32-10-68), is open Monday to Friday from 6 to 11 p.m., and the **Banco Pinto & Sotto Mayor,** Praça dos Restauradores (tel. 01/32-10-83), is open Monday to Friday from 5 to 8 p.m.

CABLES: There is a **cable dispatch** service in Lisbon. A 24-hour service is at Marconi, 20 Rua D. Luís I. You can call 3298 (gratis). Another Marconi service, this one closer to the center, is at 36 Rua da Madalena. But they do not accept cables by phone. You have to appear in person. Cables are delivered from 10 a.m. to noon and 1 to 6 p.m. daily.

DENTAL CARE: If it's dental attention you need, place a call to Centro de Medicina Dentaria, 1 Calçada Bento da Rocha Cabral (tel. 01/68-41-91). Some of the dentists there speak English.

DRUGSTORE: A popular drugstore in Lisbon is **Farmácia Azevedo, 31** Rossio (tel. 01/32-74-78).

EMBASSIES: If you lose your passport, or have some other pressing problem, you'll need to get in touch with the **American Embassy,** on the Avenida das Forças Armadas (à Sete Rios), 1600 Lisbon (tel. 01/726-66-00). Hours are 8:30 a.m. to 12:30 p.m. and 1:30 to 4:30 p.m. Monday to Friday. If you've lost a passport, a photographer will be recommended who can provide the proper-size photos for American passports. The **Canadian Embassy** is at 2 Rua Rosa Araujo, 1200 Lisbon (tel. 01/56-38-21); the **British Embassy** is at 37 Rua São Domingos à Lapa, 1200 Lisbon (tel. 01/66-11-91); and the **Australian Embassy,** 244 Avenida da Liberdade, 1200 Lisbon (tel. 01/53-91-08).

EMERGENCIES: To call the **police** (or for an **ambulance**) in Lisbon, telephone 115. In case of **fire,** call 01/32-22-22. The **Portuguese Red Cross** is reached at 01/61-77-77.

HAIR CARE: If your hair needs attention, men are advised to go to any of the big **barbershops** in the deluxe hotels, such as the Ritz in Lisbon. For women, three **hairdressers** in Lisbon are particularly recommended: Cabeleireiro Martins, 31-1° Dt. Avenida Defensores de Chaves (tel. 01/54-89-33); Cabeleireiro Isabel Queiroz do Vale, 35-1° Avenida Fontes Pereira de Melo (tel. 01/54-82-38); and Lúcia Piloto, 12 Avenida da Liberdade (tel. 01/32-05-35).

LAUNDRY: Keeping your clothes clean can be a problem if you're not staying long in Lisbon. Do-it-yourselfers may want to take their clothes to a self-service laundry, **Lavimpa,** 22-A Avenida de Paris (tel. 01/89-03-88) (Metro: Alvalade). It's part of a chain that has three other branches in Lisbon, one at Estoril, and one at Cascais.

LIBRARY: If you're looking for a library for research or whatever, the **Biblioteca Nacional (Lisboa),** 83 Campo Grande (tel. 01/76-77-86), near University City, contains more than two million volumes (books, periodicals, nonbook material) and is open from 9:45 a.m. to 8 p.m. Monday to Friday mid-July to mid-September, from 9:45 a.m. to 7:30 p.m. Monday to Saturday in winter. In addition, the **American Cultural Center** at 22-B Avenida Duque de Loule (tel. 01/57-01-02) has a library of some 8,000 volumes and 132 periodicals. It's open from 2 to 6 p.m. on Tuesday, Wednesday, and Friday, 2 to 7 p.m. on Monday and Thursday.

MEDICAL CARE: In case of a medical emergency, you can ask at your hotel or else call the American Embassy (see above) and ask the staff there to recommend a physician who speaks English; or try the **British Hospital,** 49 Rua Savaiva Carvalho (tel. 01/60-20-20), where the telephone operator, staff, and doctors all speak English, of course.

POST OFFICE: In Lisbon, the general post office is at Praça dos Restauradores (tel. 01/37-00-51), open from 8 a.m. to 8 p.m. daily except Sunday.

RELIGIOUS SERVICES: As mentioned earlier, Roman Catholicism is the leading religion in Portugal, and you find churches everywhere. If you're a Protestant, a Baptist evangelical church exists in Lisbon. It's the **Igreja Evangélica Baptista de Lisboa**, 36-B Rua Filipe Folque (tel. 01/53-53-62), with Sunday services in Portuguese at 11 a.m. and 7:30 p.m. (also at 7:30 p.m. on Wednesday). For Jewish readers, services are held at the **Shaare Tikua Synagogue**, 59 Rua Alexandre Herculano (tel. 01/68-15-92). From April to October, service is at 8:15 p.m. Friday. However, in other months, the service is at 7 p.m. Friday.

TELEPHONES: The area code for Lisbon and environs is 01. To make a telephone call locally in Lisbon, you can use one of the many telephone booths. However, you'll need some coins. You can talk for three minutes for 10$ (7¢). For most long-distance telephoning, particularly transatlantic calls, go to the central post office in Lisbon at the Praça dos Restauradores (tel. 01/37-00-51). Give an assistant there the number you wish, and he or she will make the call for you, billing you at the end.

TOURIST INFORMATION: Headquarters for the **Portuguese National Tourist Board** is at 86 Avenida António Augusto de Aguiar in Lisbon (tel. 01/57-50-15). The entity responsible for promotion is the Portuguese Council for Tourism Promotion, 51-2° Rua Alexandre Herculano in Lisbon (tel. 01/68-11-74). The public information section of this council is housed at the Palácio Foz at Praça dos Restauradores (tel. 01/36-33-14), and at the Lisbon airport (tel. 01/89-36-89).

For information about Portugal before heading there, you can make contact with the **Portuguese National Tourist Office,** 590 Fifth Ave., New York, NY 10036 (tel. 212/354-4403).

WEATHER: To find out about the weather, if you don't speak Portuguese, ask someone at your hotel desk to translate one of the weather reports that appear daily in the leading newspapers of Lisbon.

LISBON: AVERAGE MONTHLY TEMPERATURES

	High	Low		High	Low
January	56	46	July	81	63
February	59	47	August	82	64
March	62	50	September	78	62
April	66	53	October	72	58
May	69	55	November	63	52
June	76	60	December	57	47

THE HOTELS OF LISBON

When you check into a hotel, you'll see the official tariffs posted in the main lobby as well as somewhere in your room, perhaps at the bottom of the closet. These rates are dictated by the Directorate of Tourism and are strictly regulated. They are really a form of rent control. They include the 13.1% service charge, IVA, and a tourist tax.

Most hotels will allow you to keep your room or deposit your luggage there until noon. From that point on, the manager can add the cost of an additional full day's rent to your bill.

When checking into a hotel, clear up the all-important question of how many meals, if any, you plan to take in the dining room. Full pension (board) means a room and three meals a day; half board means a room, breakfast, and at least one other meal. It is proper for the hotel clerk to ask which of those main meals, either lunch or dinner, you'll be taking. Those on the half- or full-board plans must pay for a meal even if they miss it. It saves you money to take full or half board, as you are granted a reduction in the overall rate, as opposed to staying at a hotel and taking your meals there on an à la carte basis. But the manager is not obliged to grant you a discount on a pension plan unless you are staying at his establishment two full days and nights.

Should an infraction such as overcharging occur, you may demand to be given the Official Complaints Book. In this tome you can write your allegations. The hotel manager is then obligated to turn your comments over to the Directorate of Tourism, where they are reviewed by a staff to see if any punitive action should be taken against the establishment.

Hotels in Portugal are rated from five stars to one star. The difference between a five-star hotel and a four-star hotel will not always be apparent to the casual visitor. Often the distinction is based on square footage of bathrooms and other technical differences.

When you go below this level, you enter the realm of the second-class hotel and the third-class, the latter comprising the most raw-boned and least-recommended hotels in Portugal. However, some can be good.

Tourist inns, not government run, are known as **estalagems.** Often these offer some of the finest accommodations in Portugal, many decorated in the native or *típico* style and representing top-notch bargains.

The **residências** are a form of boarding house, except without board. Only a room and breakfast are offered at these establishments. The **pensão** is a Portuguese boarding house that charges the lowest tariffs in the country. The deluxe pensão is a misnomer. The term simply means that the pensão enjoys the highest rating in its category. The accommodation is decidedly not luxurious. A luxury pensão is generally the equivalent of a second-class hotel. The boarding houses are finds for the budget hunter. Many of them prepare a good local cuisine with generous helpings. For bottom-of-the-barrel type of living, there are both first-class and second-class boarding houses.

Coastal hotels, especially those in the Algarve, are required to grant off-season (November to February) visitors a 15% reduction on the regular tariff. To attract more off-season business, a number of establishments extend this, starting the reduced rates in mid-October and granting them until April 1.

1. Deluxe Accommodations

THE TOP CHOICE

Now a landmark, **The Ritz,** 88 Rua Rodrigo da Fonseca, 1200 Lisboa (tel. 01/69-20-20), was built in the late 1950s. Its suites have the finest decoration of all the first-class Portuguese hotels. Slender mahogany canopied beds with fringed swags, marquetry desks, satinwood dressing tables with tip-mirrors, plush carpeting—no wonder the Ritz has been traditionally the preferred choice of celebrated guests. The modern rooms facing the avenue are cheaper; the more expensive ones have terraces opening onto Edward VII Park. All are air-conditioned and soundproof, with marble baths with double basins, local and satellite TV, radio, and mini-bar. For a double, the tariff ranges from 28,000$ ($182) to 34,000$ ($221) daily. In a single the rate goes from 25,000$ ($162.50) to 30,000$ ($195). All prices include service, taxes, and a continental breakfast.

The main dining room, Veranda, is dignified and pleasant, and from May to October you can take meals outdoors on the attractive Veranda Terrace. The Grill Room is traditionally decorated (see my restaurant recommendations in the next chapter). The Ritz Bar is a magnet. Lodged in a corner of the hotel, overlooking the terrace and park, it offers everything from a Pimm's No. 1 Cup to a mint julep. The Ritz is operated by Intercontinental Hotels.

OTHER DELUXE HOTELS

Many seasoned travelers choose the **Hotel Tivoli,** 185 Avenida da Liberdade, 1298 Lisboa CODEX (tel. 01/53-01-81), because of its enticing features. First, its location is choice, right on the main boulevard of Lisbon. Second, it's large enough to accommodate more than 600 guests—hence, its public facilities are bountiful. Third, its prices are not extravagant, considering its amenities. The two-story-high reception lobby has an encircling mezzanine lounge that is almost arena-size, with comfortable islands of furniture arranged on Oriental rugs. The wood-paneled O Zodiaco restaurant offers a buffet for both lunch and dinner. Meals are all à la carte. On the top floor, O Terraço offers a view of Lisbon. Here, à la carte meals are provided, with the emphasis on steaks and chops, which you select yourself and have cooked on a tile charcoal grill. Adjoining the restaurant is a home-like salon with a wood-burning fireplace, Oriental rugs, and restrained decor.

The regular room prices are scaled according to position—the larger and more expensive ones facing the boulevard. Singles with breakfast are 17,000$ ($110.50) to 21,000$ ($136.30) daily, and doubles are 19,000$ ($123.50) to 22,000$ ($143). The air-conditioned rooms contain a mixture of modern and traditional furniture. All have private bath, and taxes and service are included in the tariffs. Guests have access to the Tivoli Club, surrounded by a lovely garden, with a swimming pool that can be heated when necessary, a tennis court, a solarium, a bar, and a restaurant where you can order light snacks.

Le Meridien, 149 Rua Castilho, 1000 Lisboa (tel. 01/69-09-00), one of the most dramatic major hotels in Lisbon, opened in 1985. Each of the bedrooms has a wrap-around window that overlooks the Edward VII Park and lets in the bright Iberian sunshine. The air-conditioned lobby glitters with white marble, polished chromium, and mirrors. A symmetrical entranceway frames the tile-bottomed fountains whose splashing rises to the top of the sunlit atrium.

You'll find lots of attractive and interesting public rooms, including a tea room with Portuguese tiles, a ground-floor brasserie with a view of the park and the adjacent boulevard, and a formally glamorous upstairs Restaurant Atlantic. There's a piano bar, upholstered in maroon velvet, and a health club is also on the premises. The facilities are operated by a competent staff. Depending on the season, the 331 handsomely furnished bedrooms rent for 30,000$ ($195) to 32,000$ ($208) daily in a single, 34,000$ ($221) to 36,000$ ($234) in a double, all tariffs including a continental breakfast, service, and taxes.

Lisboa Sheraton Hotel & Towers, 1 Rua Latino Coelho, 1097 Lisboa (tel. 01/57-57-57), the tallest hotel and one of the tallest buildings in Lisbon, is easy to spot from most of the major parks and gardens of the city. The hotel contains nearly 400 rooms, two restaurants, a health club, and one of the more enviable outdoor swimming pools in Lisbon. Originally built in 1972, but renovated several times since, it has its most desirable rooms in the tower. From there, views open onto either the longest bridge in Europe and the Tagus or the cityscape. In peak season, singles, depending on the view and amenities, range from 18,000$ ($117) to 34,000$ ($221) daily, with doubles costing from 21,000$ ($136.50) to 37,000$ ($240.50). Breakfast is included in these rates. Each room contains a private marble bath, phone, TV, and mini-bar. Amenities vary widely from room to room. On the premises are two restaurants and three bars, one of which is noted for its 26th-floor panoramic view.

Hotel Alfa Lisboa, Avenida Columbano Bordalo Pinheiro, 1000 Lisboa (tel. 01/72-21-21), removed from the commercial center of Lisbon, is a five-star hotel that has gained popularity with business travelers since it opened. The staff works hard to make visitors comfortable. Someone at the imposing reception desk in the marble-floored lobby will quote singles at 13,000$ ($84.50) to 17,000$ ($110.50) daily and twins and doubles at 15,500$ ($100.75) to 21,000$ ($136.50), with breakfast included.

The occupants of the hotel's 355 well-furnished rooms and junior suites can enjoy an array of drinking and dining facilities. The most formal is the Pombalino Restaurant, with an 18th-century Portuguese palatial decor and an international cuisine. The most popular and least expensive selection is A Aldeia, a coffeeshop and restaurant decorated in regional Portuguese style. The Labirinto Bar with a piano player nightly is the most popular drinking spot.

Hotel Altis, 11 Rua Castilho, 1200 Lisboa (tel. 01/52-24-96), is a luxurious modern hotel, with 307 attractively furnished bedrooms and suites, right in the commercial and cultural center of Lisbon. The Portuguese hospitality offered by the staff and management, together with the refurnishing of the lobby, public areas, restaurants, and bars makes for an enjoyable five-star hotel. For example, you can order a drink or a meal night or day. Many services are provided, as befits a big-city hotel, and that includes a laundry and dry-cleaning service right in the hotel. Bedrooms are well-equipped, with air conditioning, baths, color TV with eight channels via satellite, radios, and mini-bars, and are fitted with warm contemporary furnishings. A twin-bedded room rents for 22,000$ ($143) daily, and a single goes for 20,000$ ($130). Breakfast is served in the Girassol Restaurant, and for lunch or dinner a guest can choose either the Don Fernando Grill overlooking the city or the spacious Girassol. Continental dishes are featured along with Portuguese regional food. The Piano Bar has live music for dancing, and if you want to see the Lisbon skyline, you can take the elevator to the São Jorge Bar on the top floor. The indoor heated pool and health club are other facilities offered by the hotel.

2. Leading First-Class Hotels

Avenida Palace, 123 Rua 1 de Dezembro, 1200 Lisboa (tel. 01/346-01-54), is Lisbon's leading hotel link to the past, a world reflected in crystal and antiques. The second-floor drawing room attracts those partial to the age of silk-brocaded wall paneling, fringed velvet draperies, crystal chandeliers, marquetry tables, consoles, and hand-woven Portuguese carpets. Five tall windows in the dining room overlook the avenue. The location is noisy, right at the Rossio, minutes from fado clubs, restaurants, and some of Lisbon's major shops.

Major renovations have prevented the Avenida Palace from slipping into disrepair and deterioration. Most of the rooms have been redone. The redecorated bedrooms are furnished in a traditional manner, with 18th-century antiques or artwork and are air conditioned and centrally heated, with TVs, mini-bars, and music. The spacious bathrooms are faced in Portuguese marble. A single room rents for 18,480$ ($120) daily, with a continental breakfast, rising to 22,330$ ($145) in a double room.

Tivoli Jardim, 7-9 Rua Julio Cesar Machado, 1200 Lisboa (tel. 01/53-99-71), is the sister to the previously recommended Hotel Tivoli. Set in back of its namesake, avoiding the traffic noises from the Avenida da Liberdade, it features a free parking area for guests. The air-conditioned structure is adorned with cliff-hanging balconies, two shafts of elevators, and well-styled bedrooms. The walls are white plaster, the furnishings basic built-in, with color TV, mini-bar, reading lights, maid-summoning bells, and channel music, as well as comfortable armchairs, and a glass wall (curtained off at night) leading to the balcony. The baths have patterned tile, with a bidet, shower, and tub. For a room and breakfast, a single person is charged 12,000$ ($78) daily in high season; a double costs 14,500$ ($94.25).

There are adequate public lounges. Portuguese business people have found the Jardim ideal for meeting clients in the cathedral-high lobby, with its wall of glass through which the Iberian sun pours in. Dominating everything is a ceiling-high tapestry in sunburst colors. The tile and marble floors are peacock blue and emerald green, the staircase leading to the mezzanine a blood red. The dining room is tasteful, with its white brick walls and green tables, its wall niches filled with Portuguese ceramics. Guests can use the facilities of the Tivoli Club in the Hotel Tivoli.

Hotel Lisboa Plaza, 7 Travessa do Salitre, Avenida Liberdade, 1200 Lisboa (tel. 01/36-39-22), is a charmer, right in the heart of the city. A family-owned and operated four-star hotel, the Plaza has many appealing art nouveau touches, including its façade. My favorite rendezvous point is the 1900s-style bar, with its soothing olive colors and tufted leather chairs. Through another art nouveau entrance you enter the restaurant with its selection of Portuguese dishes. The rooms—100 in all—have marble baths, air conditioning, direct-dial phones, color TVs, and in-house videos. They are all well styled and comfortable. Singles cost from 11,000$ ($71.50) to 16,000$ ($104) daily; doubles, 11,000$ ($71.50) to 20,000$ ($130).

Hotel Diplomático, 74 Rua Castilho, 1200 Lisboa (tel. 01/56-20-41), is a first-class hotel near the Ritz and the Edward VII Park. The two-story-high lobby and lounge is dominated by a mural by George Bramdeiro. Spread among the 11 floors are the tasteful bedrooms, which often have small balconies and air conditioning if required. A single rents for 10,000$ ($65) nightly, with twins costing 11,500$ ($74.75) and triples 13,500$ ($87.75). The hotel also offers the Park Restaurante, serving an array of international dishes along with Portuguese regional specialties.

Príncipe Real, 53 Rua de Alegria, 1200 Lisboa (tel. 01/36-01-16), is a modern hotel, reached after a long, very steep climb from Avenida da Liberdade. Behind its rather impersonal façade lies a small world of fine living. Guests get acquainted in the bar. Selectivity and care are shown in the individualized bedrooms, which are small but tasteful. The beds are reproductions of fine antiques, with excellent mattresses. Each room is color coordinated, a happy blending of floral fabrics. You'll be charged 13,500$ ($87.75) daily in a single room, 16,000$ ($104) in a double, these tariffs including a continental breakfast, taxes, and service. Meals are served in a glassed-in rooftop room.

Hotel Rex, 169 Rua Castilho, 1000 Lisboa (tel. 01/68-21-61). Sandwiched between its neighbors in a desirable location a few steps from the Hotel Ritz and the Hotel Meridien, this retreat offers accommodations and a helpful staff at prices far below those of its more prestigious competitors. Many of the rooms have spacious balconies, whose panoramic vistas include views of Edward VII Park and the lushly baroque Manueline church on its far edge. The cozy bedrooms have mini-bars, TVs, radios, tile baths, and built-in beds whose wide edges are covered in full-grain lengths of well-rubbed Iberian leather. If you're lucky enough to be lodged in one of the pleasant suites, you'll enjoy a cozy sitting room with its own breeze-swept terrace, in addition to the comfortable bedroom. The rent is 15,000$ ($97.50) daily in a double, 12,500$ ($81.25) in a single. From the large front windows of the elegant lobby with its high coffered wood and plaster ceiling, an unusual bronze statue of women bearing baskets is visible. On the ground floor, a darkly intimate restaurant, Cozinha d'El-Rey, has two levels lined with provincial artifacts. The Panoramic Restaurant on the top floor offers a sweeping view of one of Lisbon's most beautiful parks, as well as of the city far below.

Dom Carlos, 121 Avenida Duque de Loulé, 1000 Lisboa (tel. 01/53-90-71), just off the Praça Marquês de Pombal, faces its own triangular park, dedicated to the partially blind Camilo Castelo Branco, a 19th-century "eternity poet." The curvy façade of the hotel is all glass, giving guests an indoor-outdoor feeling, reinforced by green trees and beds of orange and red canna. In summer, there is air conditioning; in winter, central heating. The hotel offers 73 bedrooms, including 17 suites. The bedrooms, all with private baths and TVs, are paneled in reddish Portuguese wood. The Nordic-inspired furnishings are softened by an occasional hand-carved cherub or collage. The single rate is 7,000$ ($40) daily, increasing to 8,500$ ($55.25) in a double. The lobby-lounge is satisfactory, but even more inviting is the mezzanine salon, where sofas and chairs face the park. In addition, there's a miniature drinking bar, with leather chairs, ideal for a tête-à-tête.

Hotel Fenix, 8 Praça Marquês de Pombal, 1200 Lisboa (tel. 01/53-51-21), enjoys a front-row position on the circular plaza dedicated to the 18th-century prime minister of Portugal. From most of its bedrooms you can view the trees on the avenue and in Edward VII Park. A modern hotel, the Fenix is run by the HUSA chain. The hotel is favored by many clients who return repeatedly. All its 125 bedrooms and suites are equipped with private bath, air conditioning, phone, radio, TV, and mini-bar. In a double or twin-bedded room, the daily rate is 11,200$ ($72.80), 9,800$ ($63.70) in a single, including a continental breakfast. The brightly furnished and air-conditioned two-floor reception lounge, with a cozy bar-lounge on the mezzanine, is much favored. Another plus is the grill room in the hotel, the Bodegón, worthy of a separate recommendation as a restaurant.

Hotel Lutécia, 52 Avenida Frei Miguel Contreiras, 1700 Lisboa (tel. 01/80-31-21), is in a shopping center, five minutes by subway from old Lisbon, toward the airport, offering 143 air-conditioned rooms, plus eight suites, that have distilled beauty and space and are without excessive adornment. The rooms are furnished with leather-and-wood armchairs, a desk and dressing table, a room-wide headboard, and walnut and leather paneling complete with pushbuttons, reading lights, and phones. The baths are tiled, with a tub and shower combination, and large wraparound towels on heated rods. Breakfast is available either on your private balcony or from the buffet in the roof restaurant. The tariff for one person is 10,500$ ($68.25) per day, increasing to 12,000$ ($78) for a double, taxes and services included. All rooms are air-conditioned and have eight-channel satellite color TV and mini-bar.

Its 12 stories are set back from a busy thoroughfare, with a formal driveway entrance. The public lounges consume most of the first two floors, although you must take an elevator to the top for the open-view dining room. In the lobby, the Concorde Bar, with French decoration based on a picture of the Place de la Concorde in Paris at the beginning of the 20th century, is ideal for a drink. In the snackbar, a good meal costs around 1,600$ ($10.40), including taxes. You can order a three-course menu in the restaurant for 2,400$ ($15.60) and up.

Mundial Hotel, 4 Rua Dom Duarte, 1100 Lisboa (tel. 01/86-31-01), is right in the heart of everything. The top-floor restaurant offers a view of St. George's Castle and the Alfama, and is a short walk from the Rossio, theaters, and shops. The staff is efficient, everything is properly manicured and polished, and the hotel is high on the preference list of European business people. The 150 rooms, all with private bath, are comfortable, spacious, and restrained in decor. The tiled baths have bidets, shower/tub combinations, and plenty of mirrors and shelf space for toilet articles. Singles are 9,500$ ($61.75) daily, doubles are 11,600$ ($75.40) to 14,200$ ($92.30), and triples are 13,500$ ($87.75) to 17,500$ ($113.75). All tariffs include a continental breakfast.

The sky-view dining room provides both indoor and outdoor meals, according to the weather. You can get a better-than-average four-course table de'hôte meal here.

3. Middle-Bracket Hotels

Hotel Albergaría da Senhora do Monte, 39 Calçada do Monte, 1100 Lisboa (tel. 01/86-28-46), is a special little hilltop hotel with a unique character. It's perched near a belvedere, the Miradouro Senhorado Monte, in the Graça district, a spot where a knowing Lisboan takes his favorite person for a memorable nighttime view of the city, the Castle of St. George, and the Tagus. Built originally as an apartment house, the hotel has been converted into a club-like establishment, with lots of lavish touches for those seeking an unusual atmosphere. The living room is intimate, with large tufted sofas and oversized tables and lamps. Many-leveled corridors lead to the excellent bedrooms, all 27 of which contain private baths and verandas. The rooms reveal the touch of the decorator, especially the gilt-edged door panels, the grass-cloth walls, and the tile baths with bronze fixtures. A single with bath rents for 7,500$ ($48.75) daily, a double with bath for 8,800$ ($57.20). The tariffs include a continental breakfast, service, and taxes. In a suite for two, the rate is 10,500$ ($68.25). The inn has no restaurant.

Dom Manuel, 189 Avenida Duque d'Ávila, 1000 Lisboa (tel. 01/57-61-60), may be a small hotel, but its style is high, and for such an atmosphere the rates are low. It's a short distance from the very heart of Lisbon, on a tree-lined avenue. Its guest lounge, with an open fireplace, is like a private home in an estate. Flanking white sofas are set on an Oriental area rug. On one wall is an Aubusson tapestry, and a picture window looks out onto an interior planter with subtropical greenery. On a mezzanine there is an intimate little cocktail lounge. You dine on the lower level which is very Portuguese, with formal leather armchairs and elegant floor torchères. Each of the bedrooms is in a restrained modern style, with muted color coordination, built-in headboards, a desk and armchair, bed lights, and all-tile baths. Charges are 8,200$ ($53.30) daily in singles, 8,900$ ($57.85) in doubles, and 9,700$ ($63.40) in triples. These tariffs include a continental breakfast.

Hotel Eduardo VII, 5 Avenida Fontes Pereira de Melo, 1000 Lisboa (tel. 01/ 53-01-41), is a completely renovated 121-room hotel in a desirable location in the commercial and cultural center of Lisbon. It offers many amenities and much comfort. Each bedroom has air-conditioning, a mini-bar, TV, and a private bath. Depending on the accommodation, single rooms range from 6,900$ ($44.85) to 8,900$ ($57.85) daily, while doubles cost 8,300$ ($53.95) to 10,900$ ($70.85), with a continental breakfast included. A lovely terrace-style restaurant with a greenhouse wall of windows offers good food and a sweeping view over the city. Nearby, a posh bar offers relaxing end-of-the-day drinks.

Jorge V Hotel, 3 Rua Mouzinho da Silveira, 1200 Lisboa (tel. 01/56-25-25), is a neat little hotel of modern design, with amenities, moderate prices, and a choice location a block off the Avenida da Liberdade. Its façade contains rows of cellular balconies, roomy enough for guests to have breakfast or afternoon "coolers." A tiny elevator takes you to a variety of rooms at different price levels. The rooms aren't generous in size, but are comfortable in a compact way. All have small tile bathrooms, phones, and radios. Singles cost from 7,500$ ($48.75) daily, including a continental breakfast, and doubles rent for 9,000$ ($58.50). The reception lounge shares space with a bar. Most favored by guests is a regional-style combination drinking bar and breakfast room of nicely melded aggregate stone and wood paneling.

Presidente Hotel, 13 Rua Alexandre Herculano, 1200 Lisboa (tel. 01/53-95-01), is a small-scale establishment near Avenida da Liberdade on a busy street corner. It's recommended for families, as children under nine are granted a 50% reduction; babysitting can be arranged. There's a laundry on the premises, and medical service. The general atmosphere, including the furnishings, is of good taste. The 59 bedrooms are small and nicely laid out, with chestnut built-in headboards including radios, bed lights, and phones. There are double-view windows, a small entry with two closets, bath tiled in bright colors, and even a valet stand. The high-season rate, with breakfast, for a double is 8,300$ ($53.95) daily; in a single, 6,700$ ($43.55). In the wood-paneled mezzanine lounge, only breakfast is served. The public rooms, all the suites, and the bedrooms are air-conditioned. The modest-size reception lounges are on three levels, connected by wide marble steps.

Hotel do Reno, 195-197 Avenida Duque d'Avila, 1000 Lisboa (tel. 01/54-81-81), opened in 1959, lies only about a ten-minute taxi ride from the heart of Lisbon. A three-star hotel, it enjoys heavy patronage by Germans and Scandinavians, but it also attracts English and American visitors. There is a large sitting room, and a pleasant bar is near the main entrance. The bedrooms are contemporary, each with a small sitting area that includes a desk and an armchair, a private bath, radio, phone, and central heating. Most of the 56 rooms have balconies. Singles cost 5,500$ ($42.25) daily; doubles, 6,500$ ($42.25); and triples, 7,500$ ($48.75). All tariffs include a continental breakfast. Children up to 8 years of age are granted a substantial reduction on the rates.

Hotel Príncipe, 201 Avenida Duque d'Ávila, 1000 Lisboa (tel. 01/53-61-51), an establishment over a quarter of a century old, is a favorite with visiting Spanish and Portuguese matadors. All of its large bedrooms have private baths, and most of them open onto their own balconies. The hotel's eight floors are accessible by two elevators. Rooms contain TV with music (three channels), and half of them are air-conditioned. A single costs 6,500$ ($42.25) daily, and a double- or twin-bedded room goes for 8,000$ ($52), all rates including a continental breakfast. Children up to 8 years of age are given a 50% reduction on the rates. The matadors do seem to like the Príncipe's dining room and bar. Don't confuse this hotel with the first-class Príncipe Real, recommended previously.

Miraparque, 12 Avenida Sidónio Pais, 1000 Lisboa (tel. 01/57-80-70), is a first-class modern hotel on a secluded quiet street, opposite Edward VII Park. The lounges are furnished in simulated brown leather with wood-paneled walls. The tiny bar, with stools and lounge chairs, has a neat and comfortable ambience. The dining room, also wood-paneled with contemporary chairs, has a wall-wide mural. Bedrooms have the same modified contemporary styling, with pastel colors. All units have private baths. For bed and a continental breakfast, the rate is 5,600$ ($36.40) daily in a single, rising to 6,400$ ($41.60) in a double. Dinner is another 2,200$ ($14.30).

Capitol Hotel, 24 Ruà Éça de Queirós, 1000 Lisboa (tel. 01/53-68-11), is a fine little hostelry, just minutes from the top of the Avenida da Liberdade and the Praça Marquês de Pombal. It nestles on a quiet street, away from busy boulevards, and opens onto a wedge-shaped park with weeping willows and oaks. The Capitol places the emphasis on good, roomy chambers with private bath, all of which are simply furnished. The more desirable rooms open onto private balconies. Singles pay 8,700$ ($56.55) nightly; doubles, 10,000$ ($65). A continental breakfast is included. On the premises are a bar, snackbar, and restaurant.

Hotel Roma, 33 Avenida de Roma, 1700 Lisboa (tel. 01/76-77-61), one of the capital's largest reasonably priced hotels, is popular with commercial travelers. It is on a traffic-clogged boulevard on the northeast side of town. It has a turquoise and white tile façade, and recessed balconies extend out from the air-conditioned bedrooms. Each of these is comfortably filled with contemporary furnishings, sometimes with a gauzy curtain that coyly separates the sleeping alcove from the living room. The 265 rooms rent for 6,000$ ($39) daily in a single, 8,000$ ($52) to 9,000$ ($58.50) in a twin-bedded room, and 10,000$ ($65) in a triple. The more expensive accommodations are spacious. Any last-minute shopping can be done in the array of shops that fill the marble-floored arcade near the reception desk. There's a swimming pool in the basement, plus a sauna and massage facilities. The hotel has restaurants on the ground floor and the tenth floor.

---

4. Old-World Inns

York House, 32 Rua das Janelas Verdes, 1200 Lisboa (tel. 01/66-25-44), provides the drama of the past with the conveniences of the 20th century. York House was once a 16th-century convent and is outside the center of traffic-filled Lisbon, attracting those who want peace and tranquility. Long known to the English and embassy personnel, it is almost opposite the National Art Gallery, sitting high on a hillside street overlooking the Tagus.

You go past an old iron gate and ascend a flight of stone steps past trailing ivy and rugged walls and enter through a garden cloister, where guests congregate under gnarled trees. Owned and run by José Telles, York House was tastefully furnished by one of the most distinguished designers for theater, opera, and villas in Lisbon. Each bedroom has antique beds, soft mattresses, and 18th- and 19th-century bric-a-brac. Almost all of the bedrooms have private baths. The charge is 16,000$ ($104) daily in a double. Singles with bath go for 12,000$ ($78) to 14,000$ ($91). Lunch and dinner cost 2,500$ ($16.25) each.

The guest book reveals that York House is favored by embassy staffs, artists, writers, poets, and professors.

In the public rooms are inlaid chests, coats of armor, carved ecclesiastical figures, paintings, and ornate ceramics. The former monks' dining hall has deepset windows, large niches for antiques, and best of all, a combined French and Portuguese cuisine. Guests gather in the two-level lounge for before- or after-dinner drinks.

Mr. Telles has acquired a former town house at no. 47 (tel. 01/66-81-43), down the street, adjacent to the museum. Here you can book larger, more luxurious rooms, with abundant closet space and large, tiled bathrooms. Only breakfast is served here, and main meals are provided at the convent. The lounge is Victorian, predominantly red, turn-of-the-century Lisbon. Over the fireplace is a grotesque portrait of Alfonso, the former king of Spain, as a child. Breakfast is brought on a tray to your room, to the lounge, or to the rear walled-in terrace which has an antique iron staircase whose steps are filled with potted flowering plants.

Estalagem do Cavalo Branco (The White Horse Inn), 146 Avenida do Almirante Gago Coutinho, 1700 Lisboa (tel. 01/88-61-21). To stay here requires a sense of adventure, humor, and a love of the fantastic. This former villa on a residential boulevard leading to the airport is run by the Leal family, who collect Iberian antiques. The bedrooms are individually decorated in a theatrical way, using bright colors and occasional antiques. A group of rooms on the lower level is for use in an emergency only, but generally the better rooms, up and down short flights of steps, are quite comfortable and never boring. One person is charged 6,200$ ($40.30) daily, and the price for a double is 8,000$ ($52). A continental breakfast, taxes, and service are included in the tariffs. All the rooms have private baths with tubs or showers, TVs, and radios. The inn is under the flight path of approaching jets, so be warned.

---

5. Budget-Range Hotels

Hotel da Torre, 8 Rua dos Jerónimos, 1400 Lisboa (tel. 01/63-62-62), is in Belém, a suburb of Lisbon, near an estuary of the Tagus. As such, it is suitable primarily for those who want to be in the belt of Lisbon's museumland. The renovated inn rises three stories, and is furnished in a regional style. Doubles with a continental breakfast peak at 6,800$ ($44.20) daily, and singles are charged 5,200$ ($33.80). The air-conditioning is confined to the public rooms and the wood-paneled bar. The modern lobby contains sunken seating areas, overhead balconies, and large front windows. A wood-paneled bar serves drinks in air-conditioned comfort. Regional food is served in the provincial restaurant.

Hotel Excelsior, 172 Rua Rodrigues Sampaio, 1100 Lisboa (tel. 01/53-71-51), enjoys a setting one block from Marquês de Pombal Square, at the entrance to Edward VII Park. Right off the upper regions of Lisbon's major boulevard, it contains 90 good-size bedrooms, each with its own private bath. Most of the rooms have a small sitting area, with a combination desk and dressing table. For a single, the maximum rate is 6,775$ ($44) daily, increasing to 10,000$ ($65) for the most expensive double. A continental breakfast and taxes are included in the tariffs. In a room with shower, but no tub, the tariffs are reduced. Most of the units contain TVs and radios. In addition to the air-conditioned bar and cocktail lounge with color TV, the hotel has a spacious breakfast room which has large-view windows.

Borges Hotel, 108 Rua Garrett, 1200 Lisboa (tel. 01/36-19-51), has a beehive reception area as crowded as the 19th-century coffeehouse next door, A Brasileira, the traditional gathering spot for the Portuguese literati. On the second floor of the Borges, the dining room partially escaped modernization, its paneled walls and crystal chandeliers intact. The 93 bedrooms and 12 suites have been refurnished in a semi-contemporary manner, with traditional draperies and counterpanes. All the rooms have private bath or shower, the doubles ranging from 6,500$ ($42.25) to 7,500$ ($48.75) daily, the singles going for anywhere from 5,500$ ($65.75) to 6,500$ ($42.25). A continental breakfast, taxes, and service are included. The location is persuasive, in the Chiado district, minutes from some of Lisbon's best-known restaurants and fado clubs, as well as the shops of Baixa.

Lis Hotel, 180 Avenida da Liberdade, 1200 Lisboa (tel. 01/56-34-34). The richly ornate art nouveau façade occupies only a narrow storefront on the busy boulevard, but the cream and buff sides stretch far back from the street. Inside you'll find beautifully molded plasterwork in the lobby, a pleasant, multilingual receptionist, and 63 simple but comfortable bedrooms with private baths, each reasonably priced and well located. Singles cost from 6,000$ ($39) daily, doubles run from 6,500$ ($42.25), and triples cost from 8,000$ ($52). There's an elevator to take you to your floor, and a continental breakfast and taxes are included in the price of the room.

Hotel Botânico, 16-20 Rua Mãe d'Água, 1200 Lisboa (tel. 01/32-02-41), perches near a hilltop in a neighborhood dotted with parks and cafés, not far from the Botanical Gardens. A modern cement building with a tasteful wood-accented lobby, it was renovated recently. The rooms, although small, are clean and convenient, and each contains a private bath, phone, and radio. Thirty in all, the rooms cost 6,900$ ($44.85) daily in a single, 8,900$ ($57.85) in a double, and 10,500$ ($68.25) in a triple. No meals other than breakfast are served.

Residencia Alicante, 20 Avenida Duque de Loulé, 1000 Lisboa (tel. 01/53-05-14). Its burnt orange postwar façade curves around a quiet residential street corner in an undistinguished neighborhood. This hotel is nonetheless clean, welcoming, and safe. You register on the street level, with a kindly staff who speak little or no English, then take a small elevator to one of the four upper floors. There, 36 rooms with bath (and 16 without) are available. Furnishings and size vary, but most budget-minded visitors find the Alicante an acceptable and reasonable headquarters for a stay in Lisbon. With breakfast included, rooms with private bath cost 3,200$ ($20.80) daily in a single and 4,300$ ($27.95) in a double. Without bath, the price is 2,100$ ($13.65) in a single, 3,000$ ($19.50) in a double, and 3,900$ ($25.35) in a triple. The quieter rooms overlook an interior courtyard.

6. The Best of the Pensions

Residência Horizonte, 42 Avenida António Agusto de Aguiar, 1000 Lisboa (tel. 01/53-95-26). When it was built as an apartment house, the architect designed an impressively proportioned flight of stone steps leading up from the busy tree-lined boulevard outside. As you enter, the lower-level reception area is at the bottom of a short flight of stairs. What used to be an elegant lobby is a bit grim today. Nonetheless, the 52 rooms upstairs are clean, and unpretentiously comfortable. A few have balconies. The units in the back are slightly less sunny than those at the front, but are much quieter. With breakfast included, singles rent for 5,200$ ($33.80) daily, while doubles go for 5,800$ ($37.70). Metro: Parque.

Residência Imperador, 55 Avenida 5 de Outubro, 1000 Lisboa (tel. 01/57-48-84), not far from the center, provides rooms with private baths or showers costing 5,000$ ($32.50) daily in a single, 6,000$ ($39) in a double. The front entranceway, designed in Portuguese pine wood, is barely large enough to set down one's suitcase. However, the bedrooms and upper lounge are adequate in size. Opening onto balconies, the front bedrooms face a tiny private garden. The units are neatly planned with built-in beds and simple lines. Muted colors are used on the walls and in the fabrics. On the top floor is an airy public room and terrace with a glass front, where breakfast is served. Tram 1 or 21 and the Metro (Saldanha station) can whisk you into the city center.

Residência América, 47 Rua Tomás Ribeiro, 1000 Lisboa (tel. 01/53-67-12), was built as a bank nearly 40 years ago and became a comfortable, unpretentious hotel through later renovation. Each of the 56 bedrooms contains a private bath. The 1950s-style accommodations all differ in floor layout and size. The quiet rooms are in back, and they tend to be slightly smaller and darker than those in front. Prices quoted by the young and friendly staff in the tiny lobby are 4,000$ ($26) daily in a single, 4,920$ ($32) in a double, and 5,540$ ($36) in a triple, with a continental breakfast included. No visitor to the América should leave without checking out the seventh-floor bar, whose leatherette furniture has been there so long that it is by now right in style. Having a drink in this eyrie can be a lot of fun, adding a note of nostalgia to a stay here. The América has no restaurant.

Residencial O Paradouro, 106 Avenida Almirante Reis, 1100 Lisboa (tel. 01/82-23-44), occupies a somewhat inconvenient location on a busy traffic artery on the east side of town. Once you find it, amid a cluster of commercial and residential buildings, you'll take an elevator to the seventh-floor reception area. The 27 clean rooms are scattered over two floors of the building. Bathless singles cost 3,000$ ($19.50) daily. With bath, the cost of a single is 4,400$ ($28.60). Doubles without bath rent for 4,800$ ($31.20), going up to 5,000$ ($32.50) with bath. In July, August, and September, prices go up about 10%. You'll be served breakfast while seated in a wrought-iron garden chair near a big window with a view over a 19th-century villa far below. A bar offers drinks throughout the afternoon. Parking is available in the basement. Metro: Arroios.

Residência Nazareth, 25 Avenida António Agusto de Aguiar, 1000 Lisboa (tel. 01/54-20-16). You'll recognize it by its dusty pink façade, some of the windows of which are surrounded with decorative arches raised in low relief. Take an elevator to the fourth-floor landing. There, far from the beauticians, hair stylists, and offices below, someone has re-created the look of the medieval vaulting you might find in a romanticized version of a Portuguese fortress. The distressed plaster and wrought-iron lanterns are obvious facsimiles, yet their undeniable charm somehow works wonders on a tired sightseer after a full day of exploring the capital. Even the spacious bar and TV lounge look like a vaulted cellar. Light floods in from the windows. Some of the simple bedrooms contain platforms, requiring guests to step up or down to the bathroom or to the comfortable bed. Each of the 32 units has a private tile bath, and a continental breakfast is included in the room prices. Singles cost from 4,500$ ($29.25) daily, with doubles priced from 5,500$ ($35.75) and triples from 6,800$ ($44.20).

Casa de São Mamede, 159 Rua da Escola Politécnica, 1200 Lisboa (tel. 01/66-31-66). A blue and white tile mural on this establishment's façade depicts St. Mamede (a 12-year-old martyr in the early Christian church) between a lion and a bull. Originally built in the 1800s as a private villa for the count of Coruche, it was transformed into a hotel in 1945. Today, its 28 bedrooms are managed by the Marqués family. Breakfast is served in a sunny second-floor dining room decorated with antique yellow and blue tiles. Although renovated, the rooms retain an aura of their original high-ceilinged and slightly dowdy charm. Each has a phone, air-conditioning, and a bath. In high season, singles cost 3,300$ ($21.45) daily, with doubles at 5,000$ ($32.50) and triples at 6,000$ ($39). A suite for two is reasonably priced at 7,000$ ($45.50). Breakfast is extra.

THE RESTAURANTS
OF LISBON

Lisbon offers a wide range of dining places, headed by such places as Aviz and Tágide. The cuisine in these establishments is of a high standard, ranking with Europe's leading restaurants. Here, you'll encounter the best of Portuguese dishes, intermixed with classics from the continental repertoire. In such establishments, a knowledgeable maître d'hôtel and a wine steward are at your elbow to guide your culinary decisions.

But you needn't pay high prices for top-quality food in Lisbon and its environs. There are many noteworthy regional restaurants offering Portuguese cooking, even foreign viands, at all price levels, from a simple beer and steak tavern to a formal town-house-style dining room, to a cliffside restaurant with a panoramic view. Aside from the recommendations found in this chapter, you may also want to consider having your evening meal at one of the fado cafés (see my nightlife suggestions).

Portuguese friends often confide that it takes two hours for people of their country to dine—"one hour to talk, another to eat."

1. Deluxe Restaurants

Restaurante Aviz, 12-B Rua Serpa Pinto (tel. 32-83-91), is Portugal's poshest restaurant, a visual reminder of the city's past. Known for its top-notch gourmet cuisine the Aviz is a treasure. What is now the Aviz was saved from the demolition of the famed hotel of the same name, once (in pre-Ritz days) the only deluxe hotel in

Lisbon. You ascend a staircase into an elegant foyer lounge. While drinks are served, menu selections are made. Mahogany paneling, tufted black leather chairs, green marble columns, and crystal create the ambience of a private club. The former hotel staff brought not only parts of the torn-down establishment with them, including all the silver, a meat trolley, and the wall torchères, but the secrets of the kitchen as well.

Aviz turns out many specialties, so making decisions is difficult. For a beginning, try mushroom caps stuffed with snails in herbed garlic butter. An alternative might be vichyssoise Rothschild, based on creamed prawns blended with the other ingredients of that delectable inspiration. A bevy of superb main dishes includes perdreau mode d'Alcantara, about which Bonaparte's Marshal Junot wrote, "It is the only positive factor that emerged from our ill-fated Iberian invasion campaign." Desserts are profuse, but do not miss Aviz crêpes, exquisitely flavored and flamed in kirsch at the table. A dinner costs from 5,000$ ($32.50) and up, with the emphasis on up. Your table must be reserved in one of the trio of intimate dining rooms, preferably the larger green and gold chamber, with its ornate bronze, frosted-glass and globed chandelier. The Aviz is open from 1 to 3 p.m. and 8 to 10:30 p.m.; closed at lunchtime Saturday and all day Sunday.

Tágide, 18-20 Academia National de Belas Artes (tel. 32-07-20), has had a prestigious past. Once the town house of a diplomat, then a major nightclub, it now is one of Lisbon's leading restaurants. Its situation is colorful—up from the docks, on a steep hill on a ledge overlooking the old part of Lisbon and the Tagus. The dining room has view windows overlooking moored ships and the port. Set into the white plaster walls are large figures made of blue and white tiles, each depicting a famous queen; glittering above are crystal chandeliers.

Both Portuguese dishes and selections from the international repertoire are featured and are beautifully served. For an appetizer, I suggest the salmon pâté, cold stuffed crab, or smoked swordfish. Other specialties include suprême of halibut with coriander, pork with clams and coriander, and grilled baby goat with herbs. For dessert, I recommend the stuffed crêpes Tágide. Expect to spend from 5,000$ ($32.50), plus the cost of your wine. Food is served from noon to 2:30 p.m. and 7:30 to 10:30 p.m. The restaurant is closed on Saturday night and Sunday. Always call for a reservation.

António Clara, 38 Avenida da República (tel. 76-63-80). Even if it weren't one of the capital's best restaurants, this exquisitely crafted turn-of-the-century villa would still be famous as the former private home of one of Portugal's most revered architects. It was built in 1890 by Miguel Ventura Terra (1866–1918), whose photograph hangs amid polished antiques and gilded mirrors. The angled and tiled wings of the villa seem to embrace visitors as they approach the vaguely Moorish façade. The soaring height of the curved staircase and the elegant moldings serve as attractive backdrops for 17th-century wood carvings and belle époque porcelain. You might enjoy a before-dinner drink in the 19th-century saloon, where griffins snarl down from the pink-shaded chandelier. Even the service areas of this house, the ones rarely seen by visitors, contain ceiling frescoes. The dining room is one of the loveliest in Lisbon.

Full meals, priced from 4,500$ ($29.25), include such specialties as smoked swordfish, paella for two, châteaubriand béarnaise, codfish Clara style, and beef Wellington. A well-coordinated group of wine stewards, headwaiters, and attendants make wine tasting a ceremony. The restaurant is open every day except Sunday. Lunch is served from noon to 3 p.m. and dinner from 7 p.m. to midnight. Reservations are suggested. There's a ground-floor bar, accessible through its own entrance, for an after-dinner drink if you're interested. The bar contains an art gallery with frequent special shows.

Gambrinus, 25 Rua das Potas de Santo Antão (tel. 32-14-66), is one of the premier restaurants of Lisbon, perhaps the finest choice for fish and shellfish. The location is in the congested heart of the city, off the Rossio near the rail station on a little square in back of the National Theater. You can arrive early (providing you made a reservation) and enjoy an apéritif at the bar in front while munching on "sea crea-tures." Later you are shown to a table in one of the paneled dining rooms.

There is a diversified à la carte menu, and you can also peruse the specialties of the day. The soups are good, especially the bisque of shellfish. The most expensive items on the menu are shrimp and lobster dishes. However, you might prefer conch with shellfish Thermidor or seabass minhota. If you don't fancy fish, and you like your dishes *hot*, ask for chicken piri-piri. The restaurant also offers elaborate desserts. Coffee with a 30-year-old brandy complements the meal perfectly. Expect to spend from 3,500$ ($22.75) to 6,500$ ($42.25). The restaurant is open daily from noon to 2 a.m.

Restaurante Clara, 49 Campo dos Mártires da Pátria (tel. 57-04-34). In a hill-side location amid decaying villas and city squares, this green-tile house contains an elegant hideaway. You might enjoy a drink under the ornate ceiling of the bar, whose locale has functioned over the years as an antiques store, the living room of a private apartment, and the foyer of a palatial house. A piano plays softly at dinner. During lunch, however, you might prefer a seat near the plants and fountain of the garden terrace. At night, an indoor seat—perhaps near the large marble fireplace—is more appealing. Menu specialties include tournedos Clara, stuffed rabbit with red wine sauce, four different kinds of pasta, codfish Clara, filet of sole with orange pheasant with grapes, and Valencian paella. Full meals, costing from 5,500$ ($35.75), are served daily except Sunday throughout the year. Hours are noon to 3:30 p.m. and 7 p.m. to midnight.

Ritz Grill Room, 88 Rua Rodrigo da Fonseca (tel. 69-20-20), is in the Ritz Ho-tel, overlooking the terrace and Edward VII Park, but fortunately set apart from the main hotel lobby. This restaurant features a sophisticated menu of French and inter-national cuisine. Each dish is prepared with the freshest ingredients. The crème de crustaces (lobster soup) is a velvety opening, and the petit feuilleté de scampi (king prawns with saffron on puff pastry) is prepared with consummate skill. Among meat specialties, you can have mignons of boeuf with chicken liver and mushrooms or entrecôte au vin de colares with green peppercorns. The fish selections feature such specialties as sole Prince Albert au Noilly or escalope de turbot en papillote. For des-sert, a large variety of pastry is available from the trolley. For a finish, try filtered coffee. Service and taxes are included in the price, which is likely to be from 4,000$ ($26), plus the cost of your wine. Hours are daily from noon to 3 p.m. and 7:30 to 10:30 p.m.

Restaurante Tavares, 37 Rua de Misericórdia (tel. 37-09-06), is a gilt and crys-tal world under a glass bell. This slice of the past offers a palace-style setting and fine cuisine. White and gold paneled walls, three chandeliers, and Louis XV armchairs all keep intact the spirit of the 18th century. Actually, Tavares was originally a café founded in 1784. When the two Tavares brothers died in the 19th century, half a dozen waiters formed a partnership and took over the restaurant. It is still owned by a group of waiters, who continue its high standards. It is the oldest restaurant in Lisbon, attracting many diplomatic and government heads, as well as the literati. However, its reputation as an exclusive bastion of Portuguese society faded with the revolution. Drinks are served in the petite front salon, where you can plan your meal. The wine steward aids you in your selection (he tries to provide a pleasant wine and does not push the most expensive bottles).

A beginning might be crêpes de marisco. A main-course selection might be the sole in champagne, a real delicacy, or tournedos Grand Duc. Many continental dishes are scattered throughout the menu, including the classic scallops of veal Viennoise. However, the restaurant nearly always serves sardines and salted codfish, so secure is it in its reputation. Expect to spend from 5,300$ ($34.45). For a wine, perhaps you'll try Cepa da Sêrra 1975. To complete your meal, why not try the chef's dessert specialty, a high-rise soufflé, followed by a café filtro? The restaurant is open from 1 to 3 p.m. and 8 to 10:30 p.m. It's closed Saturday and for lunch on Sunday.

2. Middle-Bracket Restaurants

Sua Excelência, 40-42 Rua do Conde (tel. 60-36-14), is the creation of Francisco Queiroz, who was a travel agent in Angola before he settled in Portugal. In Lisbon, he has created his little dream restaurant, with a refined, sedate atmosphere, attracting a discerning clientele. Outside you'll see no sign. Just ring the bell to announce your arrival and the patron will greet you. The atmosphere he has created is somewhat like a fashionable drawing room, with colorful tables placed in an intimate Portuguese provincial decor, made cool by the terracotta floor and high painted ceiling.

Some dishes served are uncommon in Portugal. Specialties include prawns piri-piri (not unreasonably hot), roll-mop sardines, what he proclaims as the "best smoked swordfish in Portugal," and clams in at least five different recipes. One unusual specialty is "little jacks," a small fish eaten whole: heads, tails, everything. It's served with a well-flavored "paste" made from two-day-old bread. Meals cost 2,800$ ($18.20) and up. Hours are 1 to 3 p.m. and 8 to 10:30 p.m. The place is closed on Wednesday, on Saturday and Sunday at lunchtime in July and August, and for the entire month of September. The restaurant is just a block up the hill from the entrance to the National Art Gallery, so it could be visited on a tie-in museum/luncheon adventure, although its ambience is more charming in the evening.

Bachus, 9 Largo da Trindade (tel. 32-12-60). Amusing murals cover the wood-paneled façade of this deluxe restaurant, and inside, the decor is both elaborate and sophisticated. The ambience feels like something between a private salon in a Russian palace, a turn-of-the-century English club, and a stylized Manhattan bistro. You can drop in for a drink or mount the brass staircase that winds around a column of illuminated glass to the dining room. Menu specialties include a frequently changing array of dishes based on the market availability of their ingredients. Full meals, priced from 4,000$ ($26) per person, might include a mixed grill Bachus, châteaubriand with béarnaise sauce, mountain goat, beef Stroganoff, shrimp Bachus, or other daily special. The wine list is extensive. Food is served daily from noon to 2 a.m.

Chester, 87 Rua Rodrigo da Fonseca (tel. 65-73-47), near the Ritz Hotel, is an attractive restaurant and bar, with a good cellar. Its specialty is grilled steaks. The pepper steak is tempting, as is the rib steak for two. Entrecôte with whisky sauce is hearty, and the fondue bourguignonne is prepared only for two persons. You might begin with a crab cocktail, finishing with flambéed pineapple. The tab is likely to range from 3,000$ ($19.50) to 4,000$ ($26) for a complete meal. Service is efficient, and reservations are suggested. Open daily except Sunday from 12:30 to 3 p.m. and 8:30 to 10:30 p.m., the restaurant is upstairs, and the cozy little bar lies below.

Bodegón, Hotel Fenix, 8 Praça Marquês de Pombal (tel. 53-51-21), is a first-class grill room attached to this previously recommended hotel. A marble staircase descends to it from street level. After stopping for an apéritif in the bar, you dine in a tavern setting with beamed ceiling, tile floors, and wood-paneled pillars. Depending on availability you might enjoy quail, partridge, or fresh salmon from the north of Portugal. You can also order cultivated oysters, which are at their best after October. Among à la carte selections are fried squid, Valencian paella, and some Italian dishes. For dessert, try, if featured, the delectable fresh strawberries from Sintra. Expect to spend from 3,500$ ($22.75) for a meal which is offered daily from 12:30 to 3 p.m. and 8 to 10:30 p.m.

Conventual, 45 Praça de Flores (tel. 60-91-96). In many ways this is one of my favorite Lisbon restaurants. That's due in large part to the taste and sensitivity of its gracious owner, Mrs. Dina Marques. It's on one of the loveliest residential squares in town, behind a discreetly plain wooden door. Once inside, you'll be treated to a display of old panels from baroque churches, religious statues, and bric-a-brac from Mrs. Marques's private collection in an attractively austere environment whose temperature is kept gratifyingly cool by the building's very old, thick stone walls and terracotta floor. If you select this place, you'll be in good company, since the prime minister of Portugal comes here. Lunch is served from 12:30 to 3:30 p.m. and dinner from 7:30 to 11:30 p.m. As is appropriate in any establishment even resembling a convent, work stops on Sunday.

Many of the delectably flavored recipes were invented by the owner. They include a creamy coriander soup, stewed partridge in port, ox tongue in egg sauce, and a tempting form of grilled monkfish in a herb-flavored cream sauce, along with osso buco, frogs' legs in buttery garlic, and stewed clams in a sauce of red peppers, onions, and cream. Meals begin at 3,000$ ($19.50), and reservations are suggested.

Casa do Leão, Castelo de São Jorge (tel. 87-59-62). My idea of the perfect way to visit the charmingly located Castle of St. George is to combine a trip to it with a midday meal at this restaurant. It's in a low-slung stone building within the castle walls. You'll pass between a pair of ancient cannons before entering a sun-flooded vestibule where the splashing from a dolphin-shaped fountain and the welcoming voice of the uniformed maître d' provide the only sounds. Once seated in the spacious blue-tile dining room, beneath soaring brick vaulting, you'll enjoy a panoramic view of the Alfama and the legendary hills of Lisbon. There's even a baronial fireplace, which in cold weather provides an intimate retreat for an apéritif.

Regrettably, this establishment is open only for lunch, which it serves daily from 12:30 to 6 p.m. Full meals, which range upward from 4,500$ ($29.25), include roast duck with orange or grapes, pork chops St. George style, codfish with cream, smoked swordfish from Sesimbra, and an array of the chef's daily specials. Reservations are suggested.

Casa da Comida, 1 Travessa de Amoreiras (tel. 68-53-76), is recognized by local gourmets as having some of the finest food in Lisbon. If you're in the city on one of the gray, rainy days that often occur December through March, this is an excellent choice for dining, with a roaring fire greeting and warming you. At any time of year, however, you will find the food good and the atmosphere pleasant. The dining room is handsomely decorated, the bar is done in period style, and there's a charming walled garden. Specialties include roast kid with herbs, a medley of shellfish Casa da Comida, and pregado with green pepper. French cuisine is also offered. An excellent selection of wines is available from the cellar. Meals cost from 5,000$ ($32.50) up. The restaurant is open from 12:30 to 3:30 p.m. and 7:30 p.m. to 1 a.m. It's important to make a reservation here. The place is closed Saturday at lunchtime and on Sunday.

Pabe, 27A Rua Duque de Palmela (tel. 53-56-75), is the Portuguese name for pub, and that's what this cozy English-style place is. Convenient to the Praça do Pombal, the pub has done its best to emulate English establishments. There's a soft carpet on the floor, mugs hanging over the long bar, a beamed ceiling, coats-of-arms, and engravings of hunting scenes around the walls. Two saloon-type doors lead into a wood-paneled dining room, where you can sup on meat specially imported from the U.S. A chateaubriand for two is about the most expensive dish. If you prefer local fare, start off with a shrimp cocktail, then Portuguese veal liver, or a supremo de galinha (chicken breast with mushrooms). Finish with sherbet. Meals cost from 3,000$ ($19.50) and up per person, plus drinks. The crowd tends to be a well-groomed Portuguese set as well as resident Yanks and Britons. The Pabe is open daily from noon to 1 a.m.

Sancho, 14 Travessa dos Glória (tel. 36-97-80), is a cozy, rustic style restaurant just off the Avenida da Liberdade, close to Praça dos Restauradores. The decor is in a classic Iberian style, with a beamed ceiling, a fireplace, and leather and wood chairs. The walls are stuccoed. In summer there is air conditioning. A fish gratinée soup is the classic opener. Shellfish is the specialty, and it's always expensive. Main dishes are likely to include the chef's special hake or pan-broiled Portuguese steak. If your palate is made of asbestos, order churrasco de cabrito (goat) au piri-piri. For dessert, try the crêpes suzette or perhaps a chocolate mousse. Meals cost from 2,500$ ($16.25), and service is daily except Sunday from noon to 3 p.m. and 7 to 10 p.m.

Restaurant 33, 33A Rua Alexandre Herculano (tel. 54-60-79), is a little discovery. Decorated in a style evocative of an English hunting lodge, it lies in the vicinity of many of the hotels previously recommended, including the Altis. It specializes in an array of Portuguese and international dishes, including shellfish rice served in a crab shell. You can also order smoked salmon or lobster Tour d'Argent, as well as peppersteak. Service is daily except Sunday from 12:30 a.m. to 3 p.m. and 8 to 10 p.m. On Saturday, only dinner is served. You can enjoy a glass of port as an apéritif in the small bar at the entrance while you peruse the menu. A full meal costs from 2,000$ ($13).

Telheiro, 10A Rua Latíno Coelho (tel. 53-40-07), means "The Roof" in Portuguese, and it's a bistro-like place not far from the Sheraton Hotel. The ceilings are beamed, and you sit on wooden chairs with heart shapes carved out of their backs. The waiters are clad in scarlet waistcoats. Peppers hang from the chandeliers. Pâté, butter, and rolls are placed on your table before you even order. Specialties are the gazpacho, a cabbage and potato soup, mussels, suckling pig, grilled fresh sea bass or sole, and seafood with rice in a casserole. For dessert, try the fresh Portuguese fruit. At the presentation of your bill, be prepared to pay 1,500$ ($9.75) to 2,000$ ($13). Hours are daily from 12:15 to 3 p.m. and 7 to 11 p.m.

Escorial, 47 Rua das Portas de Santo Antão (tel. 36-44-29). You can dine here with Spanish flair. Right in the heart of Lisbon's restaurant district, this Spanish-owned establishment combines classic Spanish dishes with an inviting ambience. The dining room walls are paneled in rosewood, with frosted-globe lighting. Before dinner you can have a drink in a cocktail lounge called the Art Room that exhibits contemporary Portuguese artists. A menu is printed in English (always look for the course of the day). Your most expensive selection would be from the lobster tank. You might enjoy a sampling of Portuguese oysters or squid on a skewer. A selection of the chef's specialties is likely to include barbecued baby goat, beef Stroganoff, or partridge casserole. A dinner begins at 4,000$ ($26), and service is from noon to midnight daily.

Au Chalet d'Isabelle, 138 Rua do Seculo (tel. 37-22-19), is a bar with a snack service and a restaurant with limited dinner service. It is owned by Isabel Ferrão, a former actress. It's a special place, one of those "secret addresses" so beloved by the Portuguese. From 4 p.m. to 2 a.m., it serves regional and international dishes, including grilled steaks. On Saturday, its hours are from 6 p.m. to 2 a.m. The door of the main entrance is painted in black with golden hardware, and the whole façade is brightly illuminated in the evening. Meals cost about 3,000$ ($19.50).

Restaurante O Faz Figura, 15-B Rua do Paraíso (tel. 86-89-81), is one of the best and most attractively decorated dining rooms in Lisbon. When reserving a table, ask to be seated on the veranda, where you can order both lunch and dinner overlooking the Tagus. The restaurant lies in the heart of the Alfama, and it offers faultless service and typical Portuguese food along with international specialties. A complete meal will cost from 3,000$ ($19.50) to 4,000$ ($26). You are given a warm reception and then shown to your table unless you want to stop first for a before-dinner drink in the "international cocktail bar." The restaurant serves daily from 12:30 to 3 p.m. and 8 p.m. to midnight. It is closed on Sunday.

 ## 3. Budget Restaurants

António Restaurante, 63 Rua Tomás Ribeiro (tel. 53-87-80), was created especially for Portuguese business people who want a relaxing ambience and good food. A corner establishment, just a bit away from the din of central traffic, it is a refreshing oasis. The color scheme of blue and white prevails, with blue and white glazed earthenware tiles, a blue free-form ceiling, blue linen tops over white cloths, even crisp blue jackets on waiters. The menu is in English. You can start with shell-fish soup. Orders of fish, garnished with vegetables, include filets with tomato sauce and baked sole. Arroz de marisco (rice with shellfish) is a specialty. Among the fowl and meat dishes, try an order of breaded chicken with spaghetti or pork with clams, in the Alentejana style. The owner-manager of the restaurant, António Oliveira, recommends his acorda de marisco, a stew-like, breaded dish of shellfish and eggs, which is a treat. The dessert list is extensive, with even a banana split. A full meal comes to 2,800$ ($18.20). Food is served daily from noon to 4 p.m. and 7 to 10:30 p.m.

Restaurante Leão d'Ouro, 93 Rua 1 de Dezembro (tel. 36-94-95), stands beside the Estação do Rossio, the railway station best described as Victorian Gothic. The atmosphere of a large, old tavern prevails—high brick arches, a beamed ceiling, and a pictorial tile, depicting Portugal's liberation from Spain in 1640. In the late 1980s, this restaurant once more became the fine dining room it was once reputed to be. The waiters are again clad in formal black clothing with black bow ties. You can start your meal with a rich-tasting soup, such as *crème de camarão* (cream of shrimp) or *sopa à alentejana* (made with bread and garlic, among other ingredients). Among the meat dishes, try pork chops prepared in the Alentejana way or filet mignon. A fowl specialty is *frango de churrasco* (barbecued chicken). For dessert try the *pêssegos* (peaches). The average cost of a meal, including wine, is from 2,000$ ($13). Service is from 11 a.m. to midnight daily except Sunday.

Bonjardim, 10 Traverssa de Santo Antão (tel. 32-74-24), quite rightly deserves the enthusiastic approval of a Boston traveler: "I was given the names of eight inexpensive restaurants, including Bonjardim, to try out in Lisbon during my five-day stay. I ended up trying only two of them, as I took the rest of my meals at Bonjardim, sampling a different dish for lunch and dinner every day." Manuel Castanheira, who owns and manages the restaurant, caters mostly to families, providing wholesome meals that fit most budgets. So successful has been the operation that he has taken over a building across the street, where the same menu is offered.

In the main restaurant, the second-floor air-conditioned dining room is in the rustic Portuguese style, with a beamed ceiling and a tile mural depicting farm creatures. The noonday sun pours in through seven windows. The street-floor dining room, with an adjoining bar for before-meal drinks, has walls of decorative tiles. During your dinner the aroma of fat chickens roasting to a golden brown on the charcoal spit can only persuade you to try one. An order of this house specialty, frango no espeto, is adequate for two persons, with a side dish of french fries. The cook also bakes hake in the Portuguese style. An alternative dish is pork fried with clams. For dessert, you can order a cassate. You can dine well here for less than 1,800$ ($11.70). The Bonjardim is open seven days a week from noon to 11:30 p.m.

O Funil (The Funnel), 82A Avenida Elias García (tel. 76-60-07), specializes in *cozinha portuguese* (Portuguese cuisine) and does the cooking so well and so inexpensively that a line forms at the door, and it's often hard to get a table. You enter a street-floor tavern with crowded tables. But chances are you'll be directed to the lower level, where you can wait at a tiny bar while a table is made ready for you. The owners serve their own *vinho da casa* (wine of the house). Try their red Alijó. The kitchen buys good quality meat and fresh fish daily. The most successful fish dishes are boiled codfish with a sauce made with eggs, flour, olive oil, milk, and cream, and eels stewed with a sausage of pickled pork, smoked ham, and slices of toast. The most favored meat dish is mutton stew with boiled potatoes, as well as a chicken stuffed with smoked ham. For dessert, try the chocolate pyramid and nut tart. Meals cost from 1,800$ ($11.70), and service is from noon to 3:30 p.m. and 7 to 10:30 p.m. It is closed Sunday evening and Monday.

Toni dos Bifes, 50-E Avenida Praia da Vitória (tel. 53-60-80), is an old Lisbon standby where hungry Portuguese and foreigners have been going for years to get a good, inexpensive, and copious meal. Near the Monumental cinema, the restaurant has a plain but pleasant decor, with a counter on one side of the dining room and small tables on the other. Some tables and chairs are placed outdoors as well, in French café style, with a glass enclosure. You begin with small portions of pâté, along with butter and toast, bread and roll, and then you can launch into the home-made tomato soup or perhaps a seafood omelet, followed by a Toni special beefsteak. Other specialties include Toni calamares (squid), grilled or meunière sole, pork Alentejana style, and roast duck. Finish with a melon with ham or a peach Melba. The final tab is a modest 1,800$ ($11.70). It is open daily from noon to 10:30 p.m.

Frei Papinhas, 32 Rua Don Francisco Manuel de Melo (tel. 65-87-57), near Edward VII Park, lying off the Rua Castilho, is within an easy walk of the Ritz and Meridian Hotels. The restaurant was created by a group of writers and intellectuals who wanted a place where they could meet for really good food and enjoy vigorous conversation at their leisure. They ended up with their own attractive, cozy eating place, offering excellent service. The interior is done in sophisticated country style, relying on natural elements such as a wall of exposed stone, old brick behind the front bar, heavy black beams, and whitewashed walls. The ceiling is coved.

In air-conditioned comfort, you can enjoy an array of international cookery, including fresh fish and game dishes. You might begin with one of the chef's soups such as vichyssoise or gazpacho, followed by filet of swordfish or pork Alentejo. Racks of the best Portuguese wines are available. Meals cost from 3,000$ ($19.50). Hours are daily from 12:30 to 3 p.m. and 7 p.m. to midnight.

Tia Matilde, 12-B Rua Doutor Alvaro de Castro (tel. 77-21-72), is a very large busy place in the Praça de Espanha area. The service here is often hectic, and tourists are rare, but the Portuguese love this one. Here you can sample home cookery and the savory specialties of Ribatejo, that region of fighting bulls previewed in chapter XIII. Specialties include cabrito assado (roast mountain goat), arroz de frango (chicken with rice), bacalhau (codfish) à Tia Matilde, plus many other à la carte items. Chefs also make a pungent caldeirada, or fish stew. The restaurant is open from noon to 4 p.m. and 7 p.m. to midnight daily except Sunday. Meals cost from 2,500$ ($16.25).

Choupal, 9 Rua do Salitre (tel. 54-29-63), is a stylized taverna, one minute from Avenida da Liberdade, where regional dishes are served family style. Its walls have aqua and olive tiles, combined with wood paneling, and the ceiling is in a warm brown cork. There is an English menu. The waiter brings a loaf of crusty bread and a little ceramic jar of mildly seasoned pâté with sweet butter to begin your meal. You might start with a shellfish soup or savory Spanish-style clams. Two main-dish specialties are roast chicken and lampreys, those tiny eel-like creatures from the north of Portugal. The chef also does a special beef dish. A meal here will cost from 2,000$ ($13). The restaurant is open every day except Saturday from 9 a.m. to midnight.

Bonjardim, the previously mentioned restaurant, has a nearby self-service cafe-teria at 41 Rua do Jardim do Regedor (tel. 36-12-72). Sample dishes: seafood soup, always a good choice; half a roast chicken with trimmings, traditional and reliable; garoupa fish à Bretone, the chef's specialty; and mousse, a velvety finish. A meal costs around 1,200$ ($7.80), excluding your drink. The decor is simple, plastic, and efficient. The cafeteria is near the Rossio. It's open daily from noon to 10 p.m.

Bota Alta, 35 Travessa da Queimada (tel. 32-79-59). This Bairro Alto restau-rant, very tied into the neighborhood life around it, is little more than a hole in the wall. However, savory food and lots of local color are offered in generous quantities. It contains cramped tables, tile walls, lots of country implements hanging from its smoke-stained walls and ceiling. At night the street outside teems with nightlife. At lunch the neighborhood is more relaxed. Typical Portuguese meals are served for 2,000$ ($13). You might enjoy beefsteak Bota Alta, several preparations of codfish, including bacalhau real (royal), along with a frequently changing array of daily spe-cials. When I was last there, patrons were enjoying the chef's Hungarian goulash.

The establishment is open from noon to 2:30 p.m. and 7 to 10:30 p.m. every day but Sunday.

---

4. Seafood on the Left Bank

Floresta do Ginjal, 7 Ginjal (tel. 275-00-87), overlooks the waterfront on the left bank of the Tagus in Cacilhas. Floresta is reached by ferryboat, from Praça do Comércio or from Cais do Sodré. You can buy tickets right on the boat.

You dine on some of the best-cooked fish dinners in the area, while overlooking the river life and the hills of Lisbon. The restaurant draws a thriving family trade from right-bank Lisbon families, especially on Sunday afternoon. While there is a complete menu of meat and fowl dishes, the fish sets the pace. The fishermen's stew, or caldeirada, is a meal in itself. Another main course might be fried eels or turbot meunière. A dessert favorite is manjor de príncipe, made of eggs and almonds. You can also order strawberries with sugar. The average meal will cost from 1,800$ ($11.70). Food is served daily from noon to 3 p.m. and 7 to 10:30 p.m.

A few steps farther down the quay in Gingal are two restaurants for those on a tighter budget. Both are simple family places, with no frills.

---

5. The Foreign Colony

Michel, 5 Largo de Santa Cruz do Castelo (tel. 86-43-38), is a good French bistro with plenty of atmosphere and a hard-to-beat location right on the corner of a pocket-size plaza near St. George's Castle. It is considered one of the best restaurants in Lisbon. The restaurant is made up of three buildings: a barbershop, blacksmith's shop, and a wine tavern, all renovated and decorated in a tastefully rustic manner. Antique wood chests are used for coffee tables in the tavern portion, and a refectory table holding desserts stands in the walk-in fireplace. On the walls hangs everything from zithers to stirrups to ceramics. The chef-owner, Michel da Costa, an energetic host with a keen eye for food preparation and service, was trained in southern France. His restaurant provides gourmet food with cuisine moderne overtones. The menu includes such items as French onion soup—crusty with freshly baked cheese on top. Specialties include blinis with smoked swordfish, sole cooked in port and served with a mousse of fresh spinach, and roast duck cooked with three exotic peppers. A number of grilled meats are offered. An interesting selection of Portuguese cheeses is always ready to be brought out. However, most diners head immediately for the dessert list, called *sobremesas* in Portuguese, loaded concoctions such as a parfait made with almonds from the Algarve with a hot chocolate sauce. The fresh fruit of the season is also presented, but I personally gravitate to the sorbet with champagne, the most soothing finish to such rich fare, which is likely to cost from 3,800$ ($24.70) to 5,000$ ($32.50). The restaurant is closed on Sunday and for lunch Saturday but open otherwise from 12:30 to 3 p.m. and 8 to 11 p.m.

A Gondola, 64 Avenida de Berna (tel. 77-04-26), is Lisbon's "Little Italy," serving what are perhaps the finest Italian specialties in town. The restaurant offers indoor dining as well as al fresco meals in the courtyard. Although the decor isn't inspired, the food makes the restaurant worth the trip out of the city center. It's best reached by taxi (the street on which it sits crosses the Avenida da República). A full dinner is offered for about 2,500$ ($16.25) and up. This is quite a buy when you realize what you get. A first-course selection might be Chaves ham with melon and figs, followed by filet of sole meunière or grilled sardines with pimientos. This is followed by yet another course, ravioli or cannelloni in the Roman style, perhaps veal cutlet Milanese. The banquet is topped off by fruit or dessert. The restaurant is open from 12:45 to 3 p.m. and 7:45 to 10 p.m., closed Saturday for lunch and Sunday. This is a convenient choice if you're visiting the Gulbenkian Museum in the area.

Lychee, 37 Rua Barata Salgueiro (tel. 55-88-88), is a basement-level restaurant, with a decor inspired by the Portuguese colony of Macau. It is one of the finest Chinese restaurants in the city, serving daily from noon to 3 p.m. and 7 to 11 p.m. Meals cost from 1,800$ ($11.70), and an array of specialties are presented for your selection. Typical dishes include shrimp in a hot pepper sauce, fish with black bean sauce, honey garlic chicken wings, and deep-fried banana chicken. Reservations are rarely needed.

Velha-Goa, 41-B Rua Tomás de Anunciação (tel. 60-04-46), evokes memories of the Portuguese empire. The Portuguese colony of Goa was forcibly annexed by India in 1961, but the aura still lingers in this restaurant. The background is Oriental, and the cuisine is Goanese. All dishes are prepared according to the taste of the diners—that is mild, pungent, and *very* pungent. The meal begins with the appetizer, samuchas. House specialties include curries—prawns, chicken, Madrasta—but the chef also serves beef and pork chops in case you're dining with someone who doesn't like Indian food. Expect to pay 1,600$ ($10.40) to 1,800$ ($11.70) for a meal in the dining hall. At an adjoining pub you can enjoy a drink and listen to Indian music on weekends. The restaurant is open from noon to midnight, and you must arrive before 10:30 p.m. Closed Monday.

6. Dining in Belém

Restaurant S. Jerónimo, 12 Rua dos Jerónimos (tel. 64-87-97). A visit to this light-hearted and elegant restaurant could be combined with a trip to the famous monastery of the same name. The restaurant sits directly on the east side of the monastery, behind a big-windowed façade that floods the interior with sunlight. It takes its inspiration from the roaring '20s, with a French-style decoration; chairs are by Philip Stark, and armchairs in the bar by Carbusier. The waiters wear striped shirts, gray waistcoats, and gray aprons. Hours are from 12:30 to 3 p.m. and 7:30 to 11 p.m. daily except Sunday. The average price of a meal of Portuguese regional dishes or international specialties ranges from 3,000$ ($19.50) to 4,000$ ($26).

Dionysos', 124 Rua Belém (tel. 64-06-32), is a good Greek restaurant out in the suburb of Belém, an ideal place for lunch if you're visiting the Coach Museum or the monastery nearby. Of course, it's also open for dinner. At the latter, while ensconced at a crowded table under a beamed ceiling on the second floor, you can dine by candlelight, enjoying good service. You might begin with a Greek salad for two. The popular souvlaki is featured, and you can also select from a varied menu of fish and meat dishes, finishing with a homemade dessert. Meals cost from 2,500$ ($16.25). The restaurant is open daily from 12:30 to 3 p.m. and 7 to 10 p.m.

7. Special Dining Spots

SHELLFISH, STEAKS, AND BEEF

The "Number One" steakhouse of Lisbon is **Numero Um,** 44-A Rua Dom Francisco de Melo (tel. 68-43-26). The location, on a somewhat hard-to-find street, is off the Rua Castilho, near Edward VII Park. English is spoken. The atmosphere and English decor are relatively subdued, but the platters sizzle. Gourmets often fault Portuguese beef, but this special restaurant imports its beef from Brazil. The main menu is filet steak, T-bone, rumpsteak, and kebab. Naturally, you can order it well done, medium, or rare. Most guests order a mixed salad to accompany their meat platter, finishing with a fruit salad. Every day the kitchen prepares a meal of Portuguese regional cooking, costing from 2,000$ ($13). On Friday a Brazilian meal is offered, usually a feijoada, at the same price. Otherwise, à la carte meals cost from 2,500$ ($16.25) to 3,500$ ($22.75). Hours are from 12:30 to 3 p.m. and 7 p.m. to midnight. The restaurant is closed for dinner on Saturday and all day Sunday.

Cervejaria Ribadoura, 155 Avenida da Liberdade (tel. 54-94-11), is one of the typical shellfish and beer emporiums in central Lisbon, midway along the city's major boulevard at the corner of the Rua do Salitre. There's a minimum of decor in this tavern-style restaurant. The emphasis is on the varieties of fish: there are more than 50 fish and meat dishes, highlighted by the crustaceans and "sea fruit" recommendations. Try the bacalhau (codfish) à braz. You can dine lightly as well, particularly at lunch, on such plates as shrimp omelet. Many diners often follow fish with a meat dish. However, only those who've been trained for at least 25 years on the most mouth-wilting Indian curries should try the sautéed pork cutlets with piri-piri, the latter made with red hot peppers from Angola. A wedge of Portuguese cheese "from the hills" finishes off the meal nicely. Expect to spend from 1,500$ ($9.75). The place is open from noon to midnight daily.

Cervejaria da Trindade, 20-B Rua Nova de Trindade (tel. 32-35-06), is a combination of a German beer hall and a Portuguese tavern—the oldest of them all, owned by the brewers of Sagres beer. Here you can order tasty little steaks and heaps of crisp french-fried potatoes. Many of the Portuguese prefer bife na frigideira—that is, steak with a mustard sauce and a fried egg accompaniment, all in a clay frying pan. The tavern also features shellfish, which come from private fish ponds, and the house specialties are ameijoas (clams) à Trindade and the giant prawns. To go with your main course, a small stein of beer does nicely. For dessert, a good selection is a slice of queijo da sêrra (cheese from the mountains) and coffee. This restaurant was formerly a convent and later on a brewery. Its walls, which resisted the 1755 earthquake, are tiled with Portuguese scenes. Meals are served in the inner courtyard on sunny days and are likely to cost around 1,350$ ($8.80). Hours are daily from noon to 2 a.m.

Cervejaria Brilhante, 105 Rua dos Portas de Santo Antão (tel. 36-14-07), is where to go if you enjoy seafood with beer. Lisboans from every walk of life stop off for a stein of beer and mariscos. Opposite the Coliseu, the tavern is decorated with stone arches, wood-paneled walls, and pictorial tiles of sea life. You can dine either at the bar or at marble tables. The front window is packed with an appetizing array of king crab, oysters, lobster, baby clams, shrimps, even barnacles. And they aren't cheap. The price changes every day, depending on market quotations, and you pay by the kilo. A meal might cost 2,000$ ($13), unless you order some of the more expensive shellfish. Open daily from 9 a.m. to 1 a.m.

VEGETARIAN AND MACROBIOTIC

A center of healthy eating and living is **Restaurante A Colmeia,** 110 Rua da Emenda (tel. 37-05-00). On the top floor of this corner building are two entirely separate kitchens and cuisines, both vegetarian and macrobiotic. In addition, you'll find a miniature shop where you can purchase such natural ingredients as nuts, raisins, herbs, even pastries and black breads. You enter on the street floor through an old hall with a stone floor, then ascend scrubbed wooden steps, with an old Portuguese tile dado. The top floor has a narrow hallway lined with shelves of books dealing with metaphysics as well as healthful living. At your left is a reception room where you can ask for the dishes of the day and learn the prices. Meals cost from 600$ ($3.90) to 800$ ($5.20). Through the open doors of the two kitchens you'll see the aromatic pastries. Three dining rooms, each with large windows, are decorated differently. The restaurant is open from 12:30 to 3 p.m. and 6 to 8:30 p.m. On Saturday it closes after the 3 p.m. lunch and remains so on Sunday. English is spoken.

THE COFFEEHOUSES OF LISBON

How can one go to Lisbon without visiting one of the traditional coffeehouses? It's like a trip to England without four o'clock tea, or to Munich without a stein in a beer hall. To the Portuguese, the coffeehouse is an institution, a democratic parlor where they can drop in for their favorite beverage, abandon their worries, relax, smoke a cigarette, read the paper, write a letter, or chat with friends about tomorrow's football match or last night's lover.

The coffeehouse in Portugal is no longer revered as it once was. The older and more colorful ones with their turn-of-the-century charm are rapidly being replaced by the 20th-century world of chrome and plastic.

One of the oldest coffeehouses in Lisbon is **A Brasileira,** 120 Rua Garrett (tel. 36-87-92), in the Chiado district. Behind an art nouveau façade, it's a 19th-century emporium, once a favorite gathering place of the literati. Today, the atmosphere has grown seedier, but it still remains a favorite of some diehard devotees. Guests sit at small tables on chairs made of tooled leather, while taking in the mirrored walls and marble pilasters. Aside from the architectural adornments, there is also a collection of paintings to admire. The café has the great Portuguese poet, Fernando Pessoa—or rather his statue—sitting on a chair side by side with the customers. You can order a glass of Imperial beer and join him for 70$ (45¢). A demitasse costs 35$ (25¢) at the counter, 40$ (25¢) at a table, and 110$ (70¢) at the more recently created section on the sidewalk. The café is open daily from 9 a.m. to 2 p.m.

Outside, the street speaks of past associations with men of letters. Garrett, a romantic dandy of the 19th century, was one of Portugal's leading poets (the street is named after him). The district itself, the Chiado, was named for another poet. On the square near the café a statue honors António Ribeiro, a 16th-century poet. Yet another poet, Bocage of Setúbal, used to frequent this coffeehouse. When once accosted by a bandit, he is said to have replied, "I am going to the Brasileira, but if you shoot me I am going to another world."

SNACKS AND BURGERS

Within the Ritz Hotel, **Ritz Snack Bar,** 77-C Rua Castilho (tel. 56-14-44), is a three-level dining establishment with a separate entrance facing Edward VII Park. A menu enticingly presents a variety of Portuguese and international specialties, including grilled fish and meats. Special emphasis is given to regional Portuguese dishes, which change on a daily basis. As a happy ending, the snackbar offers a goodly assortment of tarts, cakes, ice cream "coupes," and cheeses. Meals begin at 1,500$ ($9.75). The menu includes an English version. The snackbar is open daily from noon until 1:30 a.m.

The Big Apple, 19B Avenida Elias García (tel. 77-55-75). Dozens of tongue-in-cheek accessories adorn the walls and menu of this American-style eatery on a tree-lined boulevard of a residential neighborhood. You'll find a Texan's map of the U.S. (Amarillo appears just south of the Canadian border), and a red, white, and blue checkerboard awning out front. It's simple, pleasant, and clean, and you can order any one of 18 variations of hamburgers, many constituting a meal in themselves. You can also select five kinds of dinner crêpes along with five kinds of temptingly sweet dessert crêpes. A meal costs from 1,800$ ($11.70), and the Apple is open daily from noon to 3 p.m. and 7 to 11 p.m. Metro: Camp Pequeno.

THE ENJOYMENT OF PORT

A bar devoted exclusively to the drinking and enjoyment of port in all its known types is **Solar do Vinho do Porto,** 45 Rua de São Pedro de Alcántara (tel. 69-77-93). The Solar is near the Bairro Alto, with its fado houses. You enter what appears to be a private living room. In the rear of a large building, it offers a relaxing atmosphere, the feeling enhanced by an open stone fireplace.

Owned and sponsored by the Port Wine Institute, it displays many artifacts related to the industry. But the real reason for dropping in here during the day is for its *lista de vinhos*—there are nearly 150 wines to choose from. You can have a glass *(cálice)* for anywhere from 70$ (45¢) to 700$ ($4.55). Hours are from 10 a.m. to 11:30 p.m. Monday to Friday, from 11 a.m. to 10:30 p.m. Saturday. Closed Sunday. The location is about 50 feet from the upper terminus of the Glória funicular.

THE SIGHTS OF LISBON

In Lisbon it's still a case of the frame competing with the picture. The Portuguese capital offers many worthwhile attractions, yet its Lorelei environs echo a siren call that few can resist. Many guests end by using Lisbon only as a base, while venturing forth during the day to Lord Byron's "variegated maze of mount and glen" at Sintra, to the sandy beaches along the Portuguese Riviera (Estoril and Cascais), to the monastery and royal palace at Mafra, even as far north as the fishing village of Nazaré or perhaps Fátima, where three shepherd children claimed to have seen a vision of the Virgin Mary.

One reason Lisbon gets overlooked is that enough time isn't budgeted for it. One or two days simply isn't adequate for Lisbon and the environs. A minimum of five days is needed. A second reason is that the attractions of Lisbon remain relatively unknown. Seemingly, every stone in Rome has been documented or recorded by someone. But in talks with literally dozens of visitors, the question most often asked is: "What does one do in Lisbon?"

This chapter hopes to answer that question, specifically with regard to sightseeing. If your time is limited, and you can cope only with the most important, then you should explore: the **Coach Museum, Jerónimos Monastery,** and the **Alfama** and the **Castle of St. George.** At least two art museums, although not of the caliber of Madrid's Prado, merit attention: the **National Art Gallery** and the **Gulbenkian Center for Arts and Culture.**

Readers who enjoy more leisure time can visit the **Fundação Ricardo do Espírito Santa Silva** and watch reproductions of antiques being made, or books being gold-leafed; or you can see the gilded royal galleys at the **Naval Museum;** or wander through the **fish market;** or explore the arts and crafts of a **Belém folk museum,** and lots more.

More important, the Lisbon voyager will discover, just by walking its streets, a city unique in the world, a capital that extended its power across continents.

SIGHTSEEING TOURS

Lisbon travel agents will book you on organized tours. One of the most popular agencies is STAR, the representative of American Express for Portugal at 4-A Avenida Sidónio Pais (main office, tel. 53-98-71), close to Eduardo VII Park-South (Marqués de Pombal Square), the starting point of the tours. It also has a downtown branch office at 14 Restauradores Square (tel. 36-25-01). At the height of the season, from April 1 to October 31, most of the major tours are operated on a daily basis, excluding Monday and holidays. St. George's Castle, Belém's Jerónimos monastery, the National Art Gallery—all are highlighted by different city tours which stress cultural, historical, or scenic attractions.

Panorama Lisbon and Artistic Lisbon are popular morning tours, departing at 9:30 a.m. Touristic Lisbon is an afternoon trip, leaving at 2:30. The Lisbon-Mafra-Sintra-Estoril special departs daily at 9:30 a.m., and lunch is included.

You can journey north on a 12-hour trip to the walled city of Óbidos, the fishing village of Nazaré, and Fátima. The jaunt departs daily at 8:30 a.m.

Transtejo (Transportes Tejo), 181-4 Rua Aurea (tel. 87-50-58), offers trips on the river from April 1 to October 31, departing at 3 p.m. and returning at 5 p.m., costing 2,500$ ($16.25). A night cruise sails from 10 p.m. to midnight on Friday and Saturday from May 1 to September 30, costing 3,500$ ($22.75). The boats have bars, and there is entertainment. Transtejo's fleet includes 19 passenger ships and five ferryboats.

---

1. The Alfama

Lisbon of old lives on in the most typical quarter of the city. The wall built by the Visigoths and incorporated into some of the old houses is mute testimony to its ancient past. In East Lisbon, the Alfama was the Saracen sector of the city centuries before its conquest by the Christians.

Some of the buildings were spared from the earthquake of 1755, and the Alfama has retained much of its original charm, characterized by narrow cobblestone streets; cages of canaries chirping in the afternoon sun; fish in baskets balanced on the heads of *varinas;* strings of garlic and pepper inviting you inside a *típico* tavern; old street markets; and charming balconies.

The 19th-century Lisbon historian Norberto de Araújo wrote of "its perpetual resigned human tragedy from the habit of living it." In a colorful description he pointed up some of its elements: "labyrinth, confused, heaped up, multicolored; twisted and retwisted, lots of embracing narrow streets and kissing eaves; archways, backyards, blind alleys, stairways and terraces; commons and courtyards . . ."

The houses are so close together that in many places it's impossible to stretch your arms to their fullest length. That proximity was dramatically expressed by the poet Frederico de Brito: "Your house is so close to mine! In the starry night's bliss, to exchange a tender kiss, our lips easily meet, high across the narrow street."

Stevedores, fishmongers, and sailors occupy the Alfama. From the smallest houses that virtually hold hands, streamers of laundry protrude. The fishwives make early-morning appearances on their iron balconies, where they water their pots of geraniums.

But perhaps the most exciting sight is a little boy racing down a stone stairway in his droopy underwear (or wearing nothing at all) to hug his sailor father. The boy's mother will be preparing a steaming pot of caldeirada, the traditional fishermen's stew, for her family. When that same boy isn't racing to greet his father or isn't on an errand for his mother, he'll likely join one of Norberto de Araújo's "waves of little truants" who like to attach themselves to visitors. These children appear in ripples, always with an alert eye for a lost tourist. With hands outstretched and eyes soulfully pleading, they beg you to let them lead you to an open street market. Once there, you can wander in a maze of stacks of brightly colored vegetables from the country, bananas from Madeira, pineapple from the Azores, and fish from the sea.

Much of the charm of the Alfama lies in its armies of cats roaming the streets at will, asserting their unique rights. It is said that without these cats the sector would be rat infested. Occasionally, a black-shawled old woman, stooping over a brazier grilling sardines in front of her house, will toss one of these felines a fish head.

Once aristocrats lived in the Alfama, their memory perpetuated by the coats-of-arms of noble families slowly decaying on the fronts of some of the 16th-century houses. Some still do live there. One of the surviving members of an old family refuses to move, despite the pleadings of her relatives. "I will always live here," she said. "When I die, then you can remove my body." The best known aristocratic mansion is the one once occupied by the Count of Arcos, the last viceroy of Brazil. Constructed in the 16th century and spared, in part, from the earthquake, it lies on Largo da Salvador.

On your exploration, you'll suddenly come upon a belvedere and be rewarded with an overall perspective of the contrasting styles of the Alfama, from a simple tile-roofed fishmonger's abode to a gaily decorated baroque church. One of the best views is from the belvedere of **Largo das Portas do Sol,** near the Museum of Decorative Art. It's a balcony opening onto the sea, overlooking the typical houses as they sweep down to the Tagus.

One of the oldest churches is that of **St. Estevão** (St. Stephen), at the Largo de Santo Estevão. It was originally constructed in the 13th century. The present marble structure dates from the 18th century. Also of medieval origin is the **Church of São Miguel** (St. Michael), at Largo São Miguel, deep in the Alfama on a palm-tree-shaded square. The interior is richly decorated, with 18th-century gilt and trompe l'oeil walls. The church was reconstructed after the earthquake.

Rua da Judiaria (The Street of Jews) is yet another reminder of the past. It was settled largely by refugees fleeing Spain to escape the Inquisition.

At night the spirit changes. Although the Bairro Alto is the traditional fado quarter of Lisbon, the Alfama also reverberates to the plaintive sound of the fadista. Amália and Celeste Rodrigues, two celebrated fadistas, got their start in the vicinity of the dockland, selling flowers to tourists arriving on boats.

The Alfama was well summed up by another Portuguese writer who called it ". . . a sort of old curiosity shop, under a veil of humility here and there, ever inclined to be romantic and childish."

A WALKING TOUR

Allow at least two hours for your walking tour of the Alfama, more if you can afford the sightseeing time. The streets are rarely suitable for a car; at times you must walk up steep stone stairs. A good point to begin your tour is **Largo do Salvador** (a taxi can take you to this point). Here you'll see a 16th-century mansion that once belonged to the count of Arcos.

From there, turn down Rua da Regueira, leading to **Beco do Carneiro,** the "cul-de-sac of rams." The lane couldn't be narrower. Families live in houses four feet (if that much) apart.

At the end of the alley, circle back via a flight of steps to your left to **Largo de Santo Estevão** named after the church on the site. Round the church and from the back proceed to the **Patio das Flores,** via a flight of steps, where you can see some of the most delightful little houses fronted with characteristic Portuguese tiles (azulejos). Walk down the steps to the Rua dos Remédios, cutting right to **Largo do Chafariz de Dentro,** where you're bound to see Alfama housewives busily gossiping in front of an old fountain.

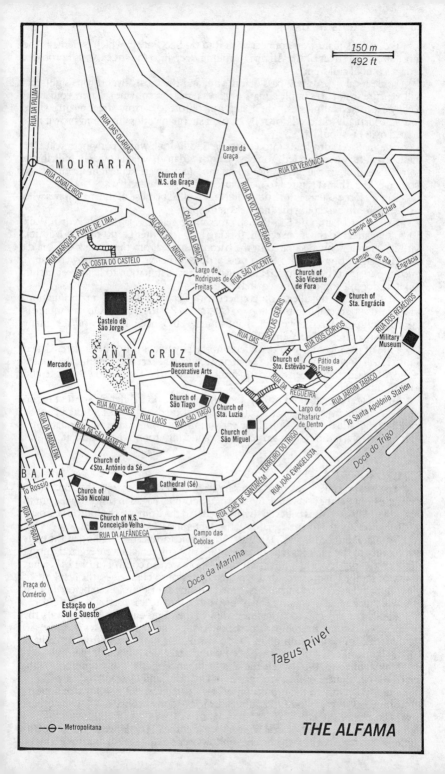

150 m
492 ft

RUA DA PALMA

RUA DAS OLARIAS

MOURARIA

RUA CAVALEIROS

RUA MARQUÊS PONTE DE LIMA

CALÇADA STO. ANDRÉ

RUA DA COSTA DO CASTELO

Largo da
Graça

RUA DA VERÓNICA

Church of
N.S. de Graça

CALÇADA DA GRAÇA

RUA (VOZ) DO OPERÁRIO

Campo de Sta. Clara

Campo de Sta. Engrácia

RUA SÃO VICENTE

Largo de
Rodrigues de
Freitas

Church of São Vicente
de Fora

Church of
Sta. Engrácia

RUA DOS REMÉDIOS

Castelo de
São Jorge

RUA DAS ESCOLAS GERAIS

RUA DOS CORVOS

Military
Museum

SANTA CRUZ

Mercado

Museum of
Decorative Arts

Church of
Sto. Estêvão

Pátio da
Flores

RUA JARDIM TABACO

RUA MILAGRES

Church of
São Tiago

RUA DA REGUEIRA

To Santa Apolónia Station

RUA DA SÃO MAMEDE

RUA LÓIOS

RUA SÃO TIAGO

Church of
Sta. Luzia

Largo do
Chafariz
de Dentro

Doca do Trigo

RUA DA MADALENA

Church of
São Miguel

Church of
Sto. António da Sé

RUA CAIS DE SANTARÉM

TERREIRO DO TRIGO

RUA JOÃO EVANGELISTA

BAIXA

To Rossio

Church of
São Nicolau

Cathedral (Sé)

RUA DA PRATA

Church of N.S.
Conceição Velha

RUA DA ALFÂNDEGA

Campo das
Cebolas

Doca da Marinha

Praça do
Comércio

Estação do
Sul e Sueste

Tagus River

—⊖— Metropolitana

THE ALFAMA

From the square, you connect with **Rua de São Pedro,** which is perhaps the most animated street of the Alfama. Strolling deep into the street, you'll probably attract a trail of children.

Some local taverns will pass before you, and the most adventurous sightseers will venture inside to sample a glass of *vinho verde* (green wine). Later, your head reeling from several glasses, you'll step out onto the narrow street again, where you'll be virtually knocked down by an old fisherman with saffron and brown nets draped over his shoulder.

Rua de São Pedro leads into **Largo de São Rafael,** which convinces you that the 17th century never ended. You pass a *leitaria* (dairy), which now sells milk in the bottle instead of via the old-fashioned method (cows were kept right inside, as the women of the Alfama wanted to make sure their milk was fresh).

Right off the square is **Rua da Judiaria,** so called because of the many Jews who settled there after escaping the Inquisition in Spain.

Go back to Largo de São Rafael, crossing to rejoin Rua de São Pedro. Walk down that street to the intersection, forking left. You enter **Largo de São Miguel,** with its church richly decorated in the baroque style. From there, walk up Rua da São Miguel, cutting left into **Beco de Cardosa,** where from some flower-draped balcony a varina is bound to scream down hell and damnation to her street urchin son if he doesn't come up immediately.

At the end of the alley, you connect with Beco Sta. Helena, a continuation, which leads up several flights of steps to **Largo das Portas do Sol.** On this square is the Museum of Decorative Art, handsomely ensconced in one of the many mansions that used to grace the Alfama.

One of the most favored belvederes in the city opens onto this square. Called **Santa Luzia Belvedere,** it's really a balcony to view the sea, overlooking the houses of the Alfama, as they sweep down in a jumbled pile to the Tagus. How fitting to end your tour here.

Although best explored by day, the Alfama takes on a different spirit at night, when street lanterns cast ghostly patterns against medieval walls and the plaintive sound of the fadista is heard until the early-morning hours in the traditional cafés. But, regrettably, it can be dangerous to go wandering around the Alfama at night.

ST. GEORGE'S CASTLE

The local people speak of it as the cradle of their city. **Castelo São Jorge** may well have been the spot on which the Portuguese capital began in times too distant to be known. Although it is believed to have predated the Romans, the hilltop was used by these warriors as a fortress guarding the Tagus and its settlement below.

From the 5th century A.D. it was a Visigothic fortification, falling in the early 8th century to the Saracens. Many of the walls that still remain were erected during the centuries of Moorish domination. The Moors were in control until 1147, a historic year for the Portuguese, for it was then that Afonso Henriques, the first king of the country, chased them out and extended his kingdom south. Even before Lisbon was made the capital of a newly emerging nation, the site was used as a royal palace.

For what many consider the finest view of the Tagus and the Alfama, walk the esplanades and climb the ramparts of the old castle. The structure takes its name, St. George, in commemoration of an Anglo-Portuguese pact dating from as early as 1371. (Portugal and England have been traditional allies, although their relationship was strained in 1961 when India, a member of the British Commonwealth, seized the Portuguese overseas territories of Goa, Diu, and Damão.)

Huddling close to the protection of the moated castle is a sector that appears almost medieval (many houses still retain their Moorish courtyards, while others have been greatly altered).

At the entrance to the castle, visitors pause at the Castle Belvedere. The Portuguese refer to this spot as their ancient window overlooking the Alfama, the Sêrras of

Monsanto and of Sintra, Ponte 25 de Abril spanning the Tagus, Praça do Comércio, and the tile roofs of the Portuguese capital. In the square stands a heroic statue—sword in one hand, shield in the other—of the first king, Afonso Henriques.

Inside the castle grounds, you can stroll through a setting of olive, pine, and cork trees, all graced by the appearance of a flamingo. In bad weather when rain is sweeping the city, you'll focus on a cannon and think of the massacres that must have occurred on this blood-soaked hill. On a fair day, you'll perhaps notice that only the willows weep or that the oleander dazzles. Swans with white bodies and black necks glide in a silence shattered by the bloodcurdling scream of the rare white peacock. Open every day from 9 a.m. till sunset, the castle may be visited without charge.

THE CATHEDRAL (SÉ)

Even the tourist literature admits that the cathedral is not very rich. Characterized by twin towers flanking its entrance, it represents an architectural wedding of Romanesque and Gothic. The façade is severe enough for a medieval fortress, and like many European cathedrals it has had many different architectural fathers. The devastation caused by the earthquakes of 1344 and 1755 didn't help either. At one point in its history the site of the present Sé was allegedly used by the Saracens as a holy mosque. When the city was captured by Christian Crusaders, led by Portugal's first king, Afonso Henriques, the structure was rebuilt. That early date in the 12th century makes the Sé the oldest church in Lisbon.

Inside are many treasures, such as the font where St. Anthony of Padua is said to have been christened in 1195. A notable feature is the Gothic chapel of Bartolomeu Joanes, constructed in the 14th century. Other things of interest are a crib by Machado de Castro (the 18th century Portuguese sculptor who did the equestrian statue on Praça do Comércio); the sarcophagus of Lopo Fernandes Pacheco, dating from the 14th century; and the original nave and aisles.

To visit the sacristy and cloister requires a guide. The cloister, built in the 14th century by King Dinis, is of ogival construction, with garlands, a Romanesque wrought-iron grille, and tombs with inscription stones. In the sacristy are housed marbles, relics, valuable images, and pieces of ecclesiastical treasure from the 15th and 16th centuries.

Whether you're Catholic or not, you may want to attend a service here. If seen in the morning, the stained-glass reflections on the floor evoke a Monet painting.

At Largo da Sé, the cathedral can be reached by taking streetcar 28 (Estrêla) or 11 (Graça). Hours are from 9 a.m. to 7:30 p.m. Monday, Wednesday, and Saturday. On other days, hours are from 9 a.m. to 5 p.m. It closes for lunch from noon to 2 p.m. For information, call 86-67-52 in the morning.

SANTO ANTÓNIO DA SÉ

St. Anthony of Padua was born in 1195 in a house that stood on this spot at Largo de Santo António da Sé. In the crypt, a guide will show you the spot where the saint was allegedly born.

Buried at Padua, Italy, this itinerant Franciscan monk remains the patron saint of Portugal. The devout come to this little church to light candles under his picture. He is known as a protector of young brides. He also has a special connection with the children of Lisbon. To raise money to erect the altar at the church, the children of the Alfama built miniature altars with a representation of the patron saint on them. June 12 of every year is designated as St. Anthony's Day, a time of merrymaking, heavy eating, and drinking. In the morning there are street fires and singing, climaxed by St. Anthony's Feast on the following day.

The original church was destroyed by the earthquake of 1755, and the present building was designed by Mateus Vicente in the 18th century. Hours are daily from 8:30 a.m. to noon and from 3 to 6 p.m. For information, call 86-91-45.

2. Belém

At Belém, where the Tagus (*Tejo* in Portuguese) meets the sea, the caravels were launched on their missions: Vasco da Gama to India, Ferdinand Magellan to circumnavigate the globe, Dias to round the Cape of Good Hope.

Belém emerged from the Restelo, that point or strand of land from which the ships set sail across the so-called Sea of Darkness. As riches, especially spices, poured back into Portugal, Belém flourished. Great monuments, such as the Belém Tower and Jerónimos Monastery, were built and embellished in the Manueline style.

In time the royal family established a summer palace here. Much of the character of the district came about when wealthy Lisboans began moving out and erecting town houses. For many years Belém was a separate municipality. Eventually, however, it became incorporated into Lisbon as a parish.

Nowadays it's a major target for sightseers, as it's a virtual monument-studded museumland.

For most visitors, the first sight is the Torre de Belém.

THE TOWER OF BELÉM

This quadrangular tower on the Avenida Marginal is a monument to Portugal's Age of Discovery. Erected between 1515 and 1520, the tower is Portugal's classic landmark, often used on documents and brochures as a symbol of the country. A monument to Portugal's great military and naval past, the tower stands on or near the spot where the caravels once set out.

In the Manueline style, its architect, Francisco de Arruda, blended Gothic and Moorish elements using such characteristic devices as twisting ropes carved of stone. The coat-of-arms of Manuel I rests above the loggia, and balconies grace three sides of the monument. Along the balustrade of the loggias, stone crosses symbolize the Portuguese Crusaders.

However, the richness of the façade fades once you cross the drawbridge and enter the Renaissance-style doorway. Gothic severity reigns; there are a few antiques, including a 16th-century throne graced with finials, and an inset paneled with pierced Gothic Tracery. If you scale the steps leading to the ramparts, you'll be rewarded with a panorama of boats along the Tagus and pastel-washed, tile-roofed old villas in the hills beyond.

Hours are daily June 1 to September 30 from 10 a.m. to 6:30 p.m. when admission is 400$ ($2.60). October 1 to May 31, it is open from 10 a.m. to 5 p.m. when admission is 250$ ($1.65). On Sunday year round its hours are from 10 a.m. to 2 p.m. when it is free. It is closed on Monday.

Facing the Tower of Belém stands a monument in commemoration of the first Portuguese to cross the Atlantic by airplane (not nonstop). The date was March 30, 1922, and the flight took pilot Gago Coutinho and navigator Sacadura Cabral from Lisbon to Rio de Janeiro.

At the center of the Praça do Império at Belém is the **Fonte Luminosa,** the Luminous Fountain. The patterns of the water jets, estimated at more than 70 original designs, make an evening show lasting nearly an hour if you want to see all of them.

MEMORIAL TO THE DISCOVERIES

Like a prow of one of the Age of Discovery caravels, this memorial at Praça da Boa Esperança stands on the Tagus, looking as if it's ready at any moment to strike out across the Sea of Darkness. The Portuguese call it **Padrão dos Descobrimentos.** Memorable explorers, chiefly Vasco da Gama, are immortalized in stone along the ramps.

At this point where the two ramps meet stands a replica of Henry the Navigator, whose genius opened up new worlds. The memorial was unveiled in 1960, and one of the figures in stone is that of a kneeling Philippa of Lancaster, the English mother of Henry the Navigator. Other figures in the frieze symbolize the Crusaders (represented by a man holding a flag with a cross), navigators, monks, cartographers, and cosmographers. At the top of the prow is the coat-of-arms of Portugal at the time of Manuel the Fortunate. The space in front of the memorial is floored with a map of the world in multicolored marble, with the dates of the discoveries set in metal. The continents are in red marble, the oceans a gray-blue, and the caravels are in still another color marble.

JERÓNIMOS MONASTERY

"Here, frozen forever in stone, is the blazing noontide of empire. Stylized hawsers writhe in the arches. Shells and coral and fish entwine in every column. Sanctuary lamps glow red above carved African lions." Or so wrote Howard La Fay.

In an expansive mood of celebration, Manuel I, the Fortunate, ordered this monastery built to commemorate the sailing of Vasco da Gama to India and to give thanks to the Lady Mary for its success. The style of architecture to which the king contributed his name, Manueline, combines flamboyant Gothic and Moorish influences with the dawn of the Renaissance in Portugal.

Opening onto Praça do Império in Belém, the monastery was founded in 1502, partially financed by the spice trade that was to grow following the discovery of the route to India. Originally, a small chapel dedicated to St. Mary had been built on this spot by Henry the Navigator, and although the earthquake of 1755 damaged the monastery, it didn't destroy it. Extensive restoration, some of it ill-conceived, was carried out.

The decorated southern doorway is outstanding. Inside, the most interesting architecture is to be seen in the cloister. Every pillar is different, as each craftsman vied with the others in exuberance of motifs. From the cloister, doors lead to cells where the monks lived in a confined area about seven feet long and four feet wide. You walk across the unmarked tombs of unnamed ghosts; other bodies were buried in the walls. The second tier of the cloister is approached by a stairway, where monks of old walked in meditation.

The interior of the church is divided into a trio of naves, noted for their fragile-looking pillars. Some of the ceilings, like those in the monks' refectory, have a ribbed barrel-vault ceiling. The "palm tree" in the sacristy is also exceptional.

Many of the greatest names in Portuguese history are said to be entombed at the monastery, but none is more famous than Vasco da Gama. The Portuguese also maintain that Luís Vas de Camões is buried here. Both tombs rest on the backs of lions. Camões, of course, was the national poet of Portugal, author of *Os Lusíadas* (The Portuguese), in which he glorified the triumphs of his compatriots.

Camões' epic poetry is said to have inspired a young Portuguese king, Sebastião, to dreams of glory. The foolish king—devoutly, even fanatically, religious—was killed at Alcácer-Kibir, Morocco, in a crusade against the Muslims in 1578. Those refusing to believe that the king was dead formed a cult. Known as Sebastianism, it rose to minor influence, and four men tried to assert their claim to the Portuguese throne. Each maintained steadfastly, even to death, that he was King Sebastião. Sebastião's remains were allegedly entombed in a marble shrine built in the 16th century in the Mannerist style.

Finally, the romantic poet Herculano (1800–1854) is buried at Jerónimos, as is Fernando Pessoa.

Open daily from 10 a.m. to 6:30 p.m. from June 1 to September 30 and from 10 a.m. to 5 p.m. from October 1 to May 31. The monastery charges no entrance fee to the church, but admission to the cloisters costs 400$ ($2.60) in summer, 250$ ($1.65) in winter. On Sunday year round, hours are from 10 a.m. to 2 p.m. and admission is free. It is closed on Monday. Take bus 43 from Praça de Figueira or 27 or 43 from Praça Marquês de Pombal.

THE NAVAL MUSEUM

The pageant and the glory that was Portugal on the high seas is evoked for posterity in this maritime museum, **Museu de Marinha** (tel. 61-47-41), one of the most important in Europe. Appropriately, it is installed in the west wing of the Monastery of Jerónimos.

These royal galleys re-create an age of opulence that never feared excess. Dragon heads drip with gilt; sea monsters coil with abandon; and, of course, assembling a large crew was no problem for kings and queens in those days. Surely Cleopatra sailing down the Nile on her barge would have recoiled with jealousy at the sight of the galley Queen Maria I ordered built for the marriage of her son and successor, Crown Prince João, to the Spanish Princess Carlota Joaquine Bourbon in 1784. Eighty dummy oarsmen, elaborately attired in scarlet- and mustard-colored waistcoats, represent the crew.

The museum contains hundreds of models of 15th- to 19th-century sailing ships, the transition from sail to steam, 20th-century warships, merchant marine vessels, fishing boats, river craft, and pleasure boats. In a section devoted to the East is a pearl inlay replica of a Dragon Boat used in maritime and fluvial corteges. Other models include a large reproduction of the frigate *Ulysses,* dating from December 15, 1792, and an early 20th-century destroyer with two torpedo tubes.

A full range of Portuguese naval uniforms is displayed, from one worn at a military outpost in Mozambique in 1896 to a model worn as recently as 1961. In a special room can be seen the queen's stateroom as it was on the royal yacht of Carlos I, the Bragança king who was assassinated at Praça do Comércio in 1908. It was on this craft that his son, King Manuel II, and his wife, the queen mother, Amélia, escaped to Gibraltar following the collapse of the Portuguese monarchy in 1910.

Historical exhibits include a letter from Lord Nelson dated October 24, 1799. A large map traces the trail of Brito Capelo and Roberto Ivens through the African continent in 1884–1885.

The Naval Museum also honors some of the early Portuguese aviators. On display is the aquaplane *Santa Cruz,* the first aircraft to cross the South Atlantic. The date was March 30, 1922 ("Aventura magnifica" hailed the press), and the captain was Commander Sacadura Cabral and the navigator Admiral Gago Coutinho, who invented a new sextant for use by airmen. The flight was from Lisbon to Rio de Janeiro, with stopovers en route. Also displayed is a 1917 airplane, the first one used by Portuguese aviators.

The museum charges 150$ ($1) (children 10 to 18 pay half price) for admission every day except Wednesday when it's free. It is open daily, except Monday and holidays, from 10 a.m. to 5 p.m.

Annexed to the Naval Museum, the **Calouste Gulbenkian Planetarium** (Planetário Calouste Gulbenkian; tel. 61-01-92) is open to the public April 1 to September 30 for sessions at 4, 5, and 6 p.m. on Saturday and Sunday; October 1 to March 31, at 4 and 5 p.m. Sessions are held in Portuguese unless a previous request has been made for a special session in English. Admission is 150$ ($1) for adults, 75¢ (50¢) for children aged 6 and above. (Those under 6 are not allowed.) The planetarium is free on Wednesday.

THE COACH MUSEUM

Visited by more tourists than any other attraction in Lisbon, the **Museu Nacional dos Coches** at Belém's Praça Afonso de Albuquerque (tel. 63-81-64), is considered the finest of its type in the world. Founded by Queen Amélia, wife of Carlos I, it's housed in what was originally an 18th-century riding academy connected to the Belém Royal Palace.

The coaches stand in a former horse ring, and most of them date from the 17th to the 19th centuries. Drawing the most interest is an opulently decorated trio of gilded baroque carriages once used by the Portuguese ambassador to the Vatican at the time of Pope Clement XI (1716). Also displayed is a 17th-century coach in which the Spanish Hapsburg king, Phillip II, journeyed from Madrid to Lisbon to see his new possession.

Other coaches include the processional chariot of "Our Lady of Cabo," the coach of King João V, of Queen Maria Ana de Austria, as well as Queen Maria's berlinda. Portuguese and foreign harnesses and trappings, all the gala livery, are exhibited on the second floor.

The portrait gallery belonged to the House of Bragança, which ended in 1910. Pictured are such notables as Maria I and also a host of minor royalty.

The museum is open from 10 a.m. to 5 p.m. daily except Monday and holidays. It charges 150$ ($1) admission.

FOLK ART MUSEUM

Nowhere are the folk arts and customs of the Portuguese displayed more dramatically than here at the **Museu de Arte Popular,** Avenida de Brasilia (tel. 61-12-82). The walls of the building, which previously housed the Regional Center during the 1940 Portuguese World's Exhibition, are painted by contemporary artists, some of the best in Portugal, including Carlos Botelho, Eduardo Anahory, Estrela Faria, Manuel Lapa, Paulo Ferreira, and Tomás de Melo (Tom). Their work is supplemented by enlarged photographs of the people of the provinces. The establishment of the Folk Art Museum in 1948 was a result of a campaign for ethnic revival directed by António Ferro. The collections, including ceramics, furniture, wickerwork, clothes, farm implements, and painting, are displayed in five rooms that correspond more or less to the provinces, each of which maintains its regional personality.

Entre-Douro and Minho: This room comprises examples of various objects related to different features of that area. There are flowers, musical instruments, goldsmith pieces, Barcelos painted pottery, and Vila Nova de Gaia painted earthenware dolls. Elaborate harnesses used for oxen are on display, along with farm implements. You can see models of regional boats, fishing tools, embroidered sweaters, Azurara stockings, rugs, a Viana do Castelo weaver's loom, and various items for the preparation of linen, for spinning, and for knitting. Bilros laces are also on exhibit.

The exhibition from Trás-os-Montes gives a survey of the activities of the northeast area. You'll see straw *escrinhos* (baskets), a Vila Real oxcart and a harrow for threshing corn, kitchen items (*transfogueiro* and a piece of furniture, *escano*), black earthenware, and a collection of bedspreads. *Chocalheiros,* the masks worn by men called by the same name who appear on feast days, are interesting displays.

The Algarve, well known to tourists, is represented by palm mats and baskets, a water cart, horse trappings, fishing nets, and a manually operated millstone, plus line-cut chimneys.

The room devoted to the Beiras contains a reproduction of the interior of a Monsanto country house, as well as a variety of wicker and straw baskets, fine Molelos black earthenware items, bedspreads, and rugs. Here too is a set of tools used in salt making from Aveiro. Of special interest is a *moliço* catcher's boat. Moliço is seaweed dredged up and used as fertilizer.

The fifth room, containing displays from Estremadura and Alentejo, holds a variety of objects, such as glazed pottery pieces from Leiria and Mafra; Nazaré fishing and clothing items, sculpture, and saints' registries; and a wax dummy modeling the garb of the *campino,* a herdsman who looks after the bulls on the plains. From Alentejo, you'll see a replica of a kitchen, glazed Redondo earthenware, Nisa earthenware, Estremoz polished and striped pottery, and earthenware painted dolls, together with items of shepherds' art and votive paintings.

The museum is open daily except Monday and holidays from 10 a.m. to 12:30 p.m. and 2 to 5 p.m. Admission is 150$ ($1). Buses 12 and 14 go there.

OTHER SIGHTS

If you have a car, drive up to **Restélo Chapel** before heading back to Lisbon. It was here that priests held masses, praying for the success of such epic voyages as that of Vasco da Gama. A chapel in the Manueline style stands on the spot. A belvedere overlooks the Tagus, offering good views of Belém Tower and Jerónimos Monastery.

Palácio Nacional de Ajuda, near Belém (tel. 63-70-95), built in the early 19th century, contains rooms that have not been changed since the days of royal supremacy in Portugal. The palace collection is extensive and of particular note are the Germain silver, the Sormani furniture, and the tapestries. The palace is open daily except Monday and public holidays from 10 a.m. to 5 p.m. Admission is 150$ ($1).

---

3. Museums and Galleries

Most of the major museums of Lisbon are at Belém, but two major attractions are found in the city: the National Art Gallery and the Gulbenkian Center for Arts and Culture, described below. For a survey of yet two more museums, the St. Roque gallery of ecclesiastical art and the Archeological Museum in the ruins of the Carmo Church, refer to "The Churches of Lisbon," following.

NATIONAL MUSEUM OF ANCIENT ART

The country's greatest collection of paintings is housed in this **Museu Nacional de Arte Antiga,** 95 Rua das Janelas Verdes or Jardim 9 de Abril (tel. 66-41-51). The museum occupies two connected buildings—an ancient palace from the 17th century and an added edifice which was built on the former site of the old Carmelite Convent of St. Alberto. The chapel of the convent was preserved and is a good example of the integration of ornamental arts, with gilt carved wood, glazed tiles (azulejos), and sculpture of the 16th, 17th, and 18th centuries.

The museum has many notable paintings, including the famous polyptych from St. Vincent's alter, *Veneração a São Vicente.* Painted by Nuno Gonçalves between 1460 and 1470 it contains sixty portraits of leading figures of Portuguese history. Other outstanding works are Hieronymus Bosch's triptych, *The Temptation of St. Anthony,* Hans Memling's *Mother and Child,* Albrecht Dürer's *St. Jerome,* and paintings by Velásquez, Zurbarán, Poussin, and Courbet. Paintings from the 15th through the 19th century by Portuguese artists trace the development of Portuguese art.

The museum also exhibits a remarkable collection of gold- and silver-smiths' work, both Portuguese and foreign. Among these is the cross from Alcobaça and the monstrance of Belém, constructed with the first gold brought from India by Vasco da Gama. Another exceptional example is the French silver tableware from the 18th century, ordered by King José I. Diverse objects from Benin, India, Persia, China, and Japan, reflect Portuguese expansion overseas. Two excellent pairs of screens depict the Portuguese relationship with Japan in the 17th century. Flemish tapestries, a rich assemblage of church vestments, Italian polychrome ceramics, and sculptures are also on display.

The museum is open daily except Monday from 10 a.m. to 5 p.m. Admission is 200$ ($1.30); free on Sunday morning.

CALOUSTE GULBENKIAN MUSEUM

Opened in the autumn of 1969, this museum, part of the Fundacão Calouste Gulbenkian, houses what one critic called "one of the world's finest private art collections." It was deeded to the state by the Armenian oil tycoon, Calouste Gulbenkian, who died in 1955. The multi-million-dollar modern center, at 45

Avenida de Berna (tel. 73-51-31), is in a former private estate that belonged to the Count of Vilalva.

From July to October it is open on Tuesday, Thursday, Friday, and Sunday from 10 a.m. to 5 p.m.; on Wednesday and Saturday from 2 to 7:30 p.m. (closed Monday and holidays). During other months of the year, it is open daily except Monday and holidays from 10 a.m. to 5 p.m., charging an admission of 40$ (25¢) except on Sunday when it's free.

The collections cover Egyptian, Greek, and Roman antiquities; a remarkable set of Islamic art including ceramics and textiles of Turkey and Persia; Syrian glass, books, bindings, and miniatures, along with Chinese vases, Japanese prints, and lacquer work. The European displays include medieval illuminated manuscripts and ivories, 15th- to 19th-century paintings and sculpture, Renaissance tapestries and medals, important collections of 18th-century French decorative works, French impressionist painting, René Lalique jewelry, and glassware.

In a move requiring great skill in negotiation, Gulbenkian managed to make purchases of art from the Hermitage at Leningrad. Among his most notable acquisitions are two Rembrandts: *Pallas Athène* and *Alexander the Great*. Two other well-known paintings are a *Portrait of Hélène Fourment* by Peter Paul Rubens and Renoir's *Portrait of Madame Claude Monet*. In addition, I'd suggest you seek out Mary Cassatt's *The Stocking*. The French sculptor Jean-Antoine Houdon is represented by a statue of *Diana*. Silver made by François-Thomas Germain, once used by Catherine the Great, is here, as well as one piece by Thomas Germain, the father.

As a cultural center, the Gulbenkian Foundation sponsors plays, films, ballet, and musical concerts, as well as a rotating exhibition of works by leading modern Portuguese and foreign artists.

CENTER FOR MODERN ART

Around the corner from the entrance to the Gulbenkian Museum, **Centro de Arte Moderna,** Rua Dr. Nicholau de Bettencourt (tel. 73-51-31), is the first major permanent exhibition center of modern Portuguese artists to open in Lisbon. The center shares park-like grounds with the Gulbenkian Foundation and was, in fact, a gift left in the legacy of the late Armenian oil magnate.

It is housed in a British-designed complex of clean lines and dramatically proportioned geometric forms, with a Henry Moore sculpture in front. The museum owns some 5,000 works of art. It displays the work of many modern Portuguese artists, some of whom enjoy world fame. These include Souza-Cardoso, Almada, Paula Rego, João Cutileiro, Costa Pinheiro, and Vieira da Silva.

Hours are from 2 to 7:30 p.m. on Wednesday and Saturday, from 10 a.m. to 5 p.m. Sunday, Tuesday, Thursday, and Friday from July to October. From November to June, the museum is open from 10 a.m. to 5 p.m. Tuesday to Sunday. It is closed year round on Monday and holidays.

MUSEUM OF DECORATIVE ART

The decorative arts school museum, **Fundaçao Ricardo do Espirito Santo Silva,** 2 Largo des Porta do Sol (tel. 86-21-83), is a foundation established in 1953 through the vision and generosity of Dr. Ricardo do Espirito Santo Silva, who endowed it with items belonging to his personal collection and set up workshops of handcrafts in which nearly all activities related to the decorative arts are represented. The handsomely furnished museum is in one of the many aristocratic mansions that used to grace the Alfama. The principal aim of the foundation is the preservation and furtherance of the decorative arts by maintaining the traditional character of the handicrafts while developing the craftspersons' skills and culture. In the workshops you can see how perfect reproductions of furniture and other objects are made in the purest styles. The foundation also restores furniture, books, and Arraiolos rugs. The workshops may be visited on Wednesday.

The museum has been given the appearance of an inhabited palace by placing objects in appropriate surroundings. Visitors can have a fairly accurate picture of what might have been the interior of an upper-class Lisbon home in the 18th and 19th centuries. There are outstanding displays of furniture, Portuguese silver, and Arraiolos rugs, all from the 17th through the 19th centuries, with 16th-century silver included.

The museum is open daily except Sunday and Monday from 10 a.m. to 1 p.m. and 2:30 to 5 p.m. Admission is 500$ ($3.25).

Close to the museum is a bar where visitors may have a rest, snacks, or a drink. To reach the museum, take tram 28 or bus 37.

NATIONAL MUSEUM OF CONTEMPORARY ART

Founded in 1911, the **Museu Nacional de Arte Contemporânea,** 6 Rua Serpa Pinto (tel. 346-80-28), has collections of paintings and sculptures going back to 1850. The romantic and naturalistic schools of the 19th century, and modern styles from the beginning of the 20th century—surrealism, neorealism, abstractionism, and neofigurative works—are represented. This is perhaps the most important collection of Portuguese painting and sculpture from those centuries, consisting of more than 2,500 works of art.

The collection is displayed in rooms of the old Monastery of Saint Francis, where the Lisbon Royal Academy of Arts opened in 1836, the first school and art gallery in the capital. The first three directors, famous painters Carlos Reis (1863–1940), Columbano (1857–1920), and Sousa Lopes (1879–1944), organized and exhibited the initial grouping. At that time, the museum was mainly an artistic workshop.

It is open from 10 a.m. to 6:30 p.m. daily except Monday from June 1 to September 30. Admission then is 400$ ($2.60). From October 1 to May 31, it is open from 10 a.m. to 5 p.m., charging 250$ ($1.65). On Sunday year round, hours are from 10 a.m. to 2 p.m. and admission is free.

Before going, check to see if the museum has reopened after remodeling.

MUSEU MILITAR (NATIONAL MILITARY MUSEUM)

This museum, in the Largo de Sta. Apolónia (tel. 86-71-31), in front of the International Railways Station, not far from Terreiro do Paco and São Jorge (St. George's) Castle, is on the site of a shipyard built during the reign of King Manuel I (1495–1521). Later, in the reign of King João III, a new foundry for artillery was erected which was also used for making gunpowder and to store arms to equip the Portuguese fleet. A fire damaged the buildings in 1726, and the 1755 earthquake destroyed them completely. Rebuilt at the order of King José I, the complex was designated as the Royal Army Arsenal. The museum, originally called the Artillery Museum, was created in 1851. Today the facility exhibits not only arms but also paintings, sculpture, tiles, and specimens of architecture.

The museum has one of the world's best collections of historical artillery. There are bronze cannons of various periods; one of these is from Diu, weighs 20 tons, and bears Arabic inscriptions. Some iron pieces date from the 14th century. Light weapons, such as guns, pistols, and swords, are displayed in cases. One of the prize exhibits is a gorget worn by Francis I, king of France. Other exhibits include the swords of King John I and Nuño Alvares Pereira, both of the late 14th century, and a two-handed sword, once belonging to Vasco da Gama. The museum is open Tuesday to Sunday from 10 a.m. to 4 p.m. Admission is 100$ (65¢).

THE NATIONAL COSTUME MUSEUM

A treasury of materials and clothing is contained within the **Museu Nacional do Traje,** Largo Júlio de Castilho, Lumiar (tel. 759-03-18). Some of the fabric is from medieval times, and there is Oriental finery and a wide selection of wearing apparel from different parts of the world. As the textiles cannot be kept on constant display, different exhibits of costumes, modern tapestries, jewelry, and other collections are shown at various times. A part of the museum depicts various processes required to produce materials, including weaving, spinning, and hand-printing. The museum is open from 10 a.m. to 1 p.m. and 2:30 to 5 p.m. except on Monday and public holidays. Admission is 150$ ($1).

Connected with the museum is the **Parque do Monteiro-Mor,** one of Lisbon's most beautiful botanical gardens, where you'll find a restaurant (tel. 758-58-52). The park and restaurant are open daily from 10 a.m. to 7 p.m. from May to October and from 10 a.m. to 5 p.m. the rest of the year. Closed Monday and on public holidays.

RAFAEL BORDALO PINHEIRO MUSEUM

Rafael Bordalo Pinheiro was a ceramicist and caricaturist in the 19th century, and this museum at 382 Campo Grande honors his memory. Actually, it's one of the most esoteric museums in Lisbon and is of little interest to the average North American visitor, unless he or she knows something about Bordalo Pinheiro's day —that is, 19th-century Portuguese life and the scandals of the literati. In his caricatures he poked fun at some of the most distinguished people of his day.

Bordalo Pinheiro's crustacean and reptilian ceramics are marvelous caricatures. Search out the portrait of Bordalo Pinheiro, by Columbano, the outstanding Portuguese painter who died in 1929.

The museum is open from 10 a.m. to 1 p.m. and 2 to 6 p.m. daily except Monday. Admission is 119$ (75¢); free to children up to 19 years of age.

---

4. The Bairro Alto

Like the Alfama, the Bairro Alto (the upper city) preserves the characteristics of the Lisbon of yore. It once was called the heart of the city, probably both for its location and its houses, streets, and inhabitants. Many of its buildings were left intact during the 1755 earthquake. Today it is the home of some of the finest fado cafés in Lisbon, making it a center of nightlife, but it is also a fascinating place to visit during the day, when its lasting charm of narrow, cobblestone streets and alleys, lined with ancient buildings can be enjoyed.

The Bairro Alto, originally called Vila Nova de Andrade, was started in 1513, when part of the huge Santa Catarina farm was sold to the Andrade family, who sold the land as plots for construction. Early buyers were carpenters, merchants, ship caulkers, who must have been astute businessmen: at least some of them immediately resold their newly acquired land to aristocrats, and little by little noble families moved to the quarter. The Jesuits followed, moving from their modest College of Mouraria to new headquarters at the Monastery of São Roque, where the *Misericórdia* (social assistance to the poor) of Lisbon is still carried on today. As often happens, the Bairro Alto gradually became a working-class quarter. Today the quarter is also the domain of journalists, since most of the big newspapers have their plants here. Writers and artists have been drawn here to live and work, attracted by the ambience and the good cuisine of local restaurants.

The area is a colorful one. From the windows and balconies, streamers of laundry hang out to dry, and here and there are cages of canaries, parrots, parakeets, and other birds. In the morning the street scene is made up of housewives coming out from their homes to shop for food, probably attracted by the cries of the varinas (fishmongers) and other vendors, some pushing creaky, heavily laden carts, and some, usually women, trudging by with baskets of fresh vegetables. Women lounge in doorways or lean on windowsills to watch the world go by.

The Bairro Alto blooms at night, luring with fado, food, discos, and small bars. Lisbon's budget restaurants, the tascas, proliferate here, together with more deluxe eateries. Victoria lanterns light the streets, where people stroll leisurely along.

5. The Churches of Lisbon

"If you want to see all of the churches of Lisbon, you'd better be prepared to stay here for a few months," the guide told a tourist. What follows is a selection of the most interesting churches.

PANTHEON CHURCH OF ST. ENGRÁCIA

When a builder starts to work on a Portuguese house, the owner often chides him, "Don't take as long as St. Engrácia." Construction on this Portuguese baroque church with its quartet of square towers began in the 17th century, and it resisted the earthquake. Nevertheless, it was not completed until 1966. The church is so well planned and built that relief and architectural idiosyncrasies would have been welcomed. The completed building appears pristine and cold, and the state has fittingly turned it into a neoclassic National pantheon, containing memorial tombs to Portuguese heads of state and other greats.

Memorials honor Henry the Navigator; Luís Vaz de Camões, the country's greatest poet; Pedro Álvares Cabral, discoverer of Brazil; Afonso de Albuquerque, viceroy of India; Nuño Álvares Pereira, warrior and saint; and Vasco da Gama, of course. Entombed in the National Pantheon are presidents of Portugal and several writers; Almeida Garrett, the outstanding 19th century literary figure; João de Deus, lyric poet, and Guerra Junquiero, also a poet.

The National Pantheon is closed on Monday and holidays. Otherwise, it is open to the public from 10 a.m. to 5 p.m. Admission is 150$ ($1). Ask the guards to take you to the terrace for a beautiful view over the river.

A visit to the Pantheon can be combined with a shopping trip to the Flea Market (walk down the Campo de Santa Clara, heading toward the river).

CARMO CHURCH (THE ARCHEOLOGICAL MUSEUM)

Standing in its ruins today, you can only imagine the glory of this former 14th century church. On the morning of November 1, 1755, the church was crowded for All Saints Day. The roof cracked and buckled. It was the Lisbon earthquake. When the debris was cleared, only a Gothic skeleton remained. For some reason, the Carmo Church was never reconstructed.

Silhouetted against the Lisbon sky are the chancel, apse, and the Great Door, a section of which has been converted into the **Museum Arqueológico da Associação dos Arqueológos Portugueses** (Archeological Museum; tel. 36-04-73). This museum contains collections of prehistoric weapons and implements, Roman and Visigothic pieces, pottery, statues, azulejos, and South American mummies, among other treasures. There are a great number of stone inscriptions in Latin, Hebrew, Arabic, and Portuguese.

The museum is at Largo do Carmo, best reached by taking the Santa Justa elevator from the Rua do Ouro below. The hours are 10 a.m. to 1 p.m. and 2 to 5 p.m. daily except Sunday and national holidays. Admission is 150$ ($1).

ST. ROQUE CHURCH AND MUSEUM

The St. Roque Church (tel. 346-03-61) was founded in the closing years of the 16th century by the Jesuits. To reach it, head for the Largo Trindade Coelho.

The church, with its painted wood ceiling, contains a celebrated chapel honoring John the Baptist by Luigi Vanvitelli. The chapel was assembled in Rome in the 18th century with such precious materials as alabaster and lapis lazuli, then dismantled and shipped to Lisbon, where it was reassembled. It was ordered by the Bragança king, João V, nine years before the end of his reign in 1750. The marble mosaics look like a painting. You can also visit the sacristy, rich in paintings illustrating scenes from the lives of the Society of Jesus saints. The Jesuits held great power in Portugal, at one time virtually governing the country for the king.

The St. Roque Museum is visited chiefly for its collection of baroque jewelry. A pair of gold and silver torch-holders, weighing about 840 pounds, is considered among the most elaborate in Europe. The gold embroidery from the 18th century is a rare treasure, as are the vestments. The paintings are mainly from the 16th century, including one of a double-chinned Catherine of Austria, another of the wedding ceremony of King Manuel. Look for a remarkable 16th-century *Virgin (with Child) of the Plague* and a polished conch shell from the 18th century that served as a baptismal font.

Hours for the museum are from 10 a.m. to 5 p.m. daily except Monday . The church is open during the same hours, except that it remains open Monday, closing at 4 p.m. Admission is 25$ (15¢), free on Sunday. Take bus 37 from the Rossio.

ST. VINCENT OUTSIDE THE WALLS

In this Renaissance church, **S. Vicente de Fora** (tel. 86-25-44), the greatest names and some forgotten wives of the House of Bragança were placed to rest. It's really a pantheon. Originally a convent from the 12th century, the church was erected between 1582 and 1627. At that time it was outside the walls of Lisbon. On the morning of the earthquake of 1755, the cupola fell in.

The Braganças assumed power in 1640 and ruled until 1910, when the Portuguese monarchy collapsed and King Manuel II and the queen mother, Amélia, fled to England. The body of Manuel II was subsequently returned to Portugal for burial. Amélia, the last queen of Portugal, died in 1951 and was also entombed here, as are her husband, Carlos I, the painter king, and her son, Prince Luís Felipe, both killed by an assassin at Praça do Comércio in 1908.

Aside from the royal tombs, one of the most important reasons for visiting St. Vincent is to see its azulejos (the glazed earthenware tiles), some of them illustrating the fables of La Fontaine. I suspect no one's officially counted them, but their number is placed at one million. Look for a curious ivory statue of Christ, carved in the former Portuguese province of Goa in the 18th century.

The church, at Largo de S. Vicente, may be visited from 10 a.m. to 1 p.m. and 3 to 6 p.m. for 75$ (50¢) admission. Closed Monday.

CHURCH OF MADRE DE DEUS

An outstanding characteristic of Portuguese churches is the architectural device of lining the walls with azulejos. Dutch blue and white usually predominate in the color scheme. Some of the finest azulejos decoration is found in this former convent founded by Queen Leonor in 1509. There is also a rich collection of 17th- and 18th-century oil paintings. The small sacristy of the church is lined with polychrome azulejos (Portuguese work), and there you can also see the retable of Sta. Auta, of the 16th-century Flemish school.

Near the riverside, at 4 Rua Madre de Deus (tel. 814-77-47), it is open from 10 a.m. to 5 p.m. except Monday and on public holidays. Admission is 200$ ($1.30). It is free on Sunday when it is open from 10 a.m. to 2 p.m.

6. A Bullfight Spectacle

Bullfighting in Portugal was once the sport of noblemen. In Portuguese bullfights, the bull is not killed, a prohibition instituted in the 18th century by the prime minister, Marques de Pombal, after the son of the Duke of Arcos was killed in the sport. The Portuguese bullfight differs in other respects from the Spanish version. The drama is attended with much ceremony and pageantry, and the major actors are the elegantly costumed *cavaleiros,* who charge the bull on horseback, and the *macos de forcado,* who grapple with the bull in face-to-face combat—for many, the most exciting event.

Warning: The bullfight is not for everyone. Even though the animal is not killed, many readers find the spectacle nauseating and take strong objection to the idea that it is beautiful, or an art form. The spears that jab the neck of the bull produce blood, of course, making the unfortunate animal visibly weaker. The so-called fight has been labeled "no contest!" One reader wrote, "The animals are frightened, confused, and badgered before they are mercifully allowed to exit. What sport!"

The season is from Easter until around mid-October. The 8,500-seat **Campo Pequeno** (reached on the Metro) in Lisbon is the largest ring in the country, and usually presents fights on Thursday and Sunday afternoons in season. These *touradas* and the names of the stars are announced well in advance, so your hotel concierge can be of help to you (many arrange tickets).

Another major bullring is the **Monumental de Cascais,** at Cascais (tel. 73-66-01), the resort lying west of Estoril on the Costa do Sol. The electric train from Lisbon ends its run in Cascais; from the station, an inexpensive taxi will take you to the bullring itself, just outside the center of town. The best place to buy tickets is, of course, right at the ticket office at the arenas. However, for the best seats, it is perhaps advisable to pay the usual 10% commission to an agency. The best ones are Agencia de Bilhetes Para Espectaculos Publicos, whose offices are at 140 Avenida da Liberdade (tel. 32-75-24), Praça dos Restauradores (tel. 36-95-00), and Parque Mayer (tel. 37-25-94).

7. Other Sights

Those sights in and around Lisbon that could not be categorically listed elsewhere are highlighted below. Some reveal much about the nation's natural resources, geography, climate, inhabitants, and lifestyle, and it is the knowledge of these things that makes you far more than just a tourist passing through.

THE SPECTACLE OF THE MARKET

The big market of **Ribeira Nova** is as close as you can get to the heart of Lisbon. Near the Cais do Sodré, where trains are boarded for the Costa do Sol, an enormous roof shelters a collection of produce stalls, where you'll see the produce you'll be eating later at one of Lisbon's fine restaurants. Foodstuffs are brought in each morning in bulging wicker baskets filled with oversize carrots, cabbages big enough for shrubbery, and stalks of bananas. Some of the produce arrives by donkey; some by truck; some balanced on the heads of Lisboan women in Mediterranean fashion— all from yesterday's field. The rich soil produces the juiciest of peaches, the most aromatic tomatoes.

"Seeing-eye" fishing boats, many believed to have been based on Phoenician designs, tie up at the dock at dawn with their catch. The fish are deposited on long marble counters: cod, squid, bass, hake, swordfish. Soon the varinas take wicker baskets of the fresh catch, balancing them on their heads, and climb the cobbled streets of the Alfama or the Bairro Alto to sell fish from door to door.

At the market, the mounds of vegetables, fruit, and fish are presided over by hearty, outgoing Portuguese women gaily clad in voluminous skirts and calico aprons. On cue the vendors begin howling out the value of their wares, stopping only to pose for an occasional snapshot.

Adjoining the market, away from the river, cut-stone streets are flanked with shops selling inexpensive Portuguese clothing. The best buy, if you can locate one, is a distinctively styled cape from the Alentejo district. In three tiers, these capes are often capped with red-fox collars.

THE GREENHOUSE

The Portuguese call it their **Estufa Fria**. It's in the handsomely laid out Edward VII Park, named after Queen Victoria's son to commemorate his three trips to Lisbon. Against a background of streams and rocks, tropical plants grow in such profusion that some writers have called it a "sylvan glade"; so luxuriant is its growth that it evokes a rain forest.

The park lies at the top of the Avenida da Liberdade, crowned by a statue of the Marquês de Pombal, with his "house pet," a lion. There's a 48$ (30¢) admission charge to the greenhouse, which is open from 9 a.m. to 6 p.m. in summer, from 9 a.m. to 5 p.m. in winter.

JARDIM ZOOLOGICO

The **Zoological Garden,** with a collection of some 2,000 animals, enjoys a flower-filled setting in the 65-acre Park of Laranjeiras, about a ten-minute subway ride from the Rossio, on the Estrada de Benefica. The Children's Zoo, with its miniature houses in small gardens, is exceptional. There are also a small train, rowboats, a roller skating rink, elephant and pony rides, films, and puppet shows presented on Sunday. It's open from 9 a.m. to 8 p.m. daily from April to October. In winter, hours are from 9 a.m. to 6 p.m. Admission is 300$ ($1.95) for adults, 175$ (1.15) for children aged 3 to 8. For information, phone 726-80-41. You can reach it on the Metropolitan or else take bus 15, 31, or 46, leaving from the Rossio.

BRITISH CEMETERY

Up the Rua da Estrêla at one end of the Estrêla Gardens lies the British Cemetery. It's famous as the burial place of Henry Fielding, the English novelist (*Tom Jones*) and dramatist. A sick man, Fielding went to Lisbon in 1754 for his health, and the story of that trip is narrated in the posthumous tract *Journal of a Voyage to Lisbon*. Reaching Lisbon in August, he died two months later. A monument honoring him was erected in 1830.

AN AQUARIUM

With a museum in addition, the **Vasco da Gama Aquarium,** Dâfundo (tel. 419-63-37), on the N6, near Algés on the Cascais railway line, has been in operation since 1898. Live exhibits include a pavilion containing eared seals, plus a vast number of tanks for fish and other sea creatures from all over the world. A large portion of the exhibits in the museum consists of zoological material brought back by King Carlos I on oceanographic expeditions. They include preserved marine invertebrates, water birds, fish, and some of the king's laboratory equipment. The aquarium is open daily from 10 a.m. to 6 p.m. Admission is 150$ ($1). Take tram 15 from the Praça do Comercio or a taxi.

THE AQUEDUCT

An outstanding baroque monument, the **Aguas Livres Aqueduct** runs from the Aguas Livres River in Caneças to the Casa da Agua reservoir in Amoreiras. The aqueduct, built under King João V in the early 18th century, runs for about 11 miles. Part of it is underground, but the above-ground section allows some of the 109 stone arches to be seen. For the best view, visitors can see the 14 arches stretching across the valley of Alcântara from Serafina to the Campolide hills.

SANTA JUSTA ELEVATOR

For a splendid rooftop view of Lisbon, take the Santa Justa elevator, an ornate concoction often attributed to the man who built that tower in Paris, the French engineer, Alexandre Gustave Eiffel. However, the elevator was actually built by a Portuguese engineer, Raoul Mesnier de Ponsard, born in Porto in 1849, son of French immigrants. He graduated in mathematics and philosophy at Coimbra, then studied in France, Germany, and Switzerland. The elevator goes from Rua Aurea, in the center of the shopping district near Rossio Square, up to the Carmo Church. It operates daily from 7 a.m. to 11 p.m. A ticket costs 22$50 ($1.45).

SHOPPING IN PORTUGAL

Portuguese handcrafts often have exotic influences because of the versatility of the Portuguese and their skill in absorbing other styles. The best showing of their work is in Lisbon. The shopkeepers and their buyers hunt out unusual items in the Madeira Islands and the Azores as well as in their own country. But there are also good buys throughout Portugal, especially in Porto, Barcelos, and the Madeira Islands.

If you want to bargain it is still possible in Lisbon, although it is not looked on kindly in the more prestigious shops. Use both your sixth sense and common sense. A good yardstick is whether or not a store is owner managed, as smaller ones usually are. In owner-managed stores you might work out a deal.

Baixia is the major area for browsing, but shops are spread all over the city. Baixia is the district forming downtown Lisbon. *Rua do Ouro* (Street of Gold, where the major jewelry shops can be found), *Rua da Prata* (Street of Silver), and Rua Augusta are Lisbon's three principal streets for shopping.

Especially good handcrafts buys from the Azores and Madeira Islands can be found in Portugal, including handmade embroideries, such as blouses, napkins, tablecloths, and handkerchiefs; products made of cork, from placemats to cigarette boxes; and *azulejos* (decorative glazed tiles). From Vista Alegre there is porcelain and china; there are fishermen's sweaters from Nazaré; filigree jewelry in gold and silver; Arraiolos carpets; local pottery; and, of course, fado records.

1. The Best Buys in Lisbon

Most stores open at 9 a.m., closing at noon for lunch. They reopen at 2 p.m., closing for the day at 7 p.m. However, many shopkeepers like to take lunch from 1 to 3 p.m., so check before making the trip. On Saturday, most stores in Lisbon, and elsewhere in Portugal for that matter, are often closed.

EMBROIDERY FROM THE ISLANDS

A good place to shop is **Madeira Superbia,** with a branch at the Ritz Hotel and a somewhat larger store at 75-A Duque de Loulé (tel. 01/53-79-68), an outlet for one of the best embroidery factories on the Madeira Islands. The exquisite craft they display, not inexpensive, includes tapestries, linens, and women's apparel, such as petit-point handbags and blouses. Often, high-quality fabrics are imported from Switzerland and Ireland, then embroidered on the islands. The collection of hand-embroidered napkins, tea cloths, pillowcases, and sheets is exceptional. Beautiful placemats often come in organdy with a linen appliqué (some are double-edged with shadow work embroidery). One of the most popular items is monogrammed linen handkerchiefs.

Madeira House, 131-135 Rua Augusta (tel. 01/32-68-13), a competitor, also specializes in a good selection of high-quality cottons, linens, and small gift items, and does so equally well. Its other locations in Lisbon are at 246 Rua Aurea, 44 Rossio, and 159 Avenida da Liberdade, and there is a shop at 2 Rua das Padarias in Sintra. At one of these shops you can purchase a hand-embroidered top sheet with two matching pillowcases in linen or cotton. The store also stocks wheat-colored six-by eight-foot linen tablecloths from the Minho district in north Portugal.

Casa Regional da Ilha Verde, 4 Rua Paiva de Andrade (tel. 01/32-59-74), specializes in handmade items, especially embroideries from the Azores. That's why it's called the Regional House of the Green Island. Each piece carries a made-by-hand guarantee. Some of the designs used on the linen placemats with napkins have been in use for centuries. You can get some good buys here.

Príncipe Real, 12-14 Rua da Escola Politécnica (tel. 01/36-59-45), specializes in linens elegant enough to grace the tables of monarchs, including, in days gone by, Princess Grace of Monaco. This family-run store produces some of Europe's finest tablecloths and sheets in cotton, linen, and organdy. Although the Rockefellers have purchased items here from its owner and designer, the merchandise (especially with beneficial escudo exchange rates) is not beyond the means of a middle-class tourist. About two dozen staff members can execute either a linen pattern to match a client's favorite porcelain, or else the owner can create one of her own designs.

CHINA AND GLASSWARE

Unparalleled for china and glassware, **Vista Alegre,** 18 Largo do Chiado (tel. 01/34-61-40), numbers royalty and diplomats, or whoever demands the very best, among its clientele. The colorful porcelain from Ilhavo, with many of the figurines depicting regional costumes, is of special interest to the casual shopper. Professional and do-it-yourself decorators are drawn to the porcelain figures and birds. They are amazingly lifelike, but also alarmingly high-priced. If you're bargain hunting, you'd do better buying a fruit bowl or a set of dishes. Prices for figurines begin at 20,000$ ($130), but could easily go much higher for the more complicated pieces.

SILVER, GOLD, AND FILIGREE

Considered a good buy in Portugal, gold is strictly regulated by the government, which requires jewelers to put a minimum of 19¼ karats in jewelry made of this expensive metal. Filigree jewelry in gold and silver is all the rage not only in Lisbon but elsewhere in Portugal. This art of ornamental openwork made of fine gold or silver wire, dates back to ancient times. The most expensive items—often objets d'art—are fashioned from 19¼-karat gold. Depictions of caravels are one of the forms this art expression takes. However, less expensive trinkets are often made of sterling silver, perhaps sterling silver that has been dipped in 24-karat gold.

At the foot of the Santa Justa elevator, **W. A. Sarmento,** 251 Rua Aurea (tel.

01/32-67-74), has been in the hands of the family that owns it for well over a century. The shop has been the favorite place for Lisboans to buy treasured confirmation and graduation gifts, and it has customers among the Costa do Sol aristocracy as well as movie stars and diplomats. They are the most distinguished silver- and gold-smiths in Portugal, specializing in lacy filigree jewelry. For additions to your charm bracelet, Sarmento is the place to go. There are literally dozens of choices. The shop is a member of the tax-free-for-tourists system.

Well on its way to being a century old, **Joalharia do Carmo,** 87b Rua do Carmo (tel. 01/32-30-50), is the best place in Lisbon to shop for filigree work. Some of the gold pieces here have been further adorned with either precious or semiprecious stones.

Lisbon is also known for its silver antique reproductions.

GLAZED PORTUGUESE TILES

Founded in 1741, **Sant'Anna,** 95-97 Rua do Alecrim (tel. 01/32-25-37), is Portugal's leading ceramic center. Famous for its *azulejos* (glazed tiles), Sant'Anna is in the Chiado section. The showroom is at the Rua do Alecrim location, but you can also visit the factory at 96 Calçada da Boa Hora; however, you must telephone ahead to make an appointment. Some of the designs that decorate the tiles are created by artisans who are among the finest in Europe, and many of them employ designs in use since the Middle Ages. Bargains I bought recently include a group of framed scenic azulejos, a two-holder candelabrum, an hors d'oeuvres tray (tiled), and a ceramic umbrella stand that is three feet high.

A rival to Sant'Anna, **Fábrica Cerâmica Viúva Lamego,** 25 Largo do Intendente (tel. 01/57-59-29), sells contemporary tiles, mostly reproductions of old Portuguese motifs, and also pottery, including an interesting selection of planters and umbrella stands. When you reach the address, you'll know you're at the right place: its façade is decorated with these colorful azulejos with figures in their rich plumage and dress.

TOYS

Parents seeking new and unusual toys for their children will find the best selection at **Biagio Flora,** 136 Rua do Ouro (tel. 01/36-06-91). Thousands of toys are displayed at this location in the center of town. Their specialty is electric trains.

HOUSE OF SUEDE

Diagonally across from the Ritz Hotel, **Caprice,** 67-B Rua Joaquim António de Aguiar (tel. 01/65-78-93), sells a fine line of suede items, such as long coats, suits, and skirts. It is owned by Philippe L. Gaulier, whose mother was a Lanvin stylist. He apparently inherited her good taste. Both he and his wife are English-speaking and will offer you an assortment of Alcantara suede (an acrylic called "ultrasuede," which is machine-washable) in both dresses, two-piece suits, and coats as well as men's safari shirts. The suede comes in a wide assortment of interesting colors, including pink, dark chocolate, navy, aqua, and caramel. In addition, the Gauliers present a selection of hand-crocheted suits and dresses, but, unfortunately, these items are so expensive to produce that they don't fall within the average person's price range.

THE THIEVES MARKET

Here is a place where you can haggle and enjoy the fun of getting a bargain. Called the **Feira da Ladra,** this open-air street market is like the flea markets of Madrid and Paris. Nearly every possible item that can be purchased is seen here in the street stalls. For the finest pickings it's best to go in the morning. The vendors peddle their wares on Tuesday and Saturday.

About a five-minute walk from the waterfront, in the Alfama district, the market sits in back of the Military Museum adjoining the Pantheon of São Vicente. Start your browsing at the Campo de Santa Clara. Portable stalls and individual displays are lined up on this hilly street with its tree-lined center.

You can often pick up a bargain here, but you must search diligently through masses of cheap clothing and lots of junk to find it. Everything from brass scales, oil lamps, portable bidets, cow bells, and old coins, to Macau china, antique watches, and Angola woodcarvings is on display.

ANTIQUE ALLEY

Along both sides of the narrow street Rua de S. José are treasure troves—shops packed with antiques from all over the world. Antique dealers from America come here to survey the wares. You'll find ornate spool and carved beds, high-back chairs, tables, wardrobes with ornate carving or time-seasoned woods, brass plaques, copper pans, silver candelabra, crystal sconces, and chandeliers, plus a wide selection of old wooden figures, silver boxes, porcelain plates, and bowls. But don't count on super bargains.

Rua Dom Pedro V is another street of antique shops, of which my personal favorite is **Solar,** 68-70 Rua Dom Pedro V (tel. 01/36-55-22). It is stocked with antique tiles salvaged from some of Portugal's historic buildings and manor houses. The condition of the tiles varies, of course. Many go back as far as the 15th century. Some 18th-century tiles cost from 2,000$ ($13) to 3,500$ ($22.75) apiece. The store also sells antique furniture and pewterware.

ARRAIOLOS CARPETS

Later when we explore Alentejo and Ribatejo, you can actually visit the little town of Arraiolos where these fine woolen rugs, which have earned an international reputation, are sold. Legend says these rugs were first made by Moorish craftsmen expelled from Lisbon in the early 16th century. The designs were said to be in imitation of those from Persia. Some of these carpets eventually find their way into museums.

In Lisbon the showcase for the Arraiolos carpet is **Casa Quintão,** 30-34 Rua Ivens (tel. 01/36-58-37). Rugs here are priced by the square foot, according to the density of the stitching. Casa Quintão can reproduce intricate Oriental or medieval designs in rugs or tapestries, and create any custom pattern specified by a client. The shop also sells materials and gives instructions on how to make your own carpets and tapestry-covered pillows. The staff seems genuinely willing to help.

HOUSE OF CORK

For something typically Portuguese, try **Casa das Corticas,** 4 Rua Escola Politécnica (tel. 01/32-58-58). "Mr. Cork" became somewhat of a legend in Lisbon for offering "everything conceivable" that could be made of cork, of which Portugal controls a hefty part of the world market. Mr. Cork is gone now, but the store carries on. You'll be surprised at the number of items that can be made from cork, including a chess set or a checkerboard. Perhaps a set of six placemats in a two-tone checkerboard style will interest you. For souvenirs, the cork caravels are immensely popular. Other items include a natural cutting board and ice bucket.

BOOKS

A corner bookstore, **Libraria Bertrand do Chiado,** 73-75 Rua Garrett (tel. 01/32-00-81), in the Chiado district, has a large selection of titles in English. They also have travel material such as good maps of Portugal.

ART GALLERIES

The leading art gallery of Lisbon is **Galeria Sesimbra,** 77 Rua Castilho (tel. 01/56-02-91), near the Ritz Hotel. It is operated by one of the most distinguished art dealers of Iberia. Mainly Portuguese artists are displayed here, but foreign artists "who have lived in Portugal long enough to get a feeling for the country" are also exhibited. The finest of Portuguese paintings, sculpture, and ceramics are sold here. Its best known works for sale, however, are Agulha tapestries. The Agulha tapestry is composed of a controlled variation of stitching, giving it an advantage over those made on looms. Many artists have turned to this new medium for depth and movement in their work. Size can range from 10 square feet to the "longest tapestry in the world."

Galeria 111, 113a Campo Grande (tel. 01/77-74-18), is recognized as one of the major art galleries of Lisbon, a distinction it has shared since 1964. Some of the leading contemporary artists of Portugal are on display here in a wide-ranging exhibition of sculpture, paintings, and graphics.

ROSSIO RAILWAY STATION SHOPPING MALL

There are some 150 boutiques, shops, and snackbars installed in four of the five floors of the Rossio Railway Station, in the heart of downtown Lisbon. The fifth floor is where the trains arrive and depart. Banks of escalators whisk you from floor to floor, and shopping in the maze of small shops is easier than walking on the congested streets. Conveniently, the shops are open every day of the year from 9 in the morning to midnight. The street floor is deceptively shabby—ignore it and take the escalator to the boutiques. You'll find apparel for men, women, and children, shops specializing in jewelry, fado records, and so forth. There's a pharmacy for "naturalists," beauty parlors, hairdressers, bookstores, leather goods, sweaters, and Portuguese handcrafts.

MODERN SHOPPING COMPLEXES

The most spectacular shopping complex in Lisbon is the **Amoreiras Shopping Center de Lisboa,** the largest in Iberia and the fourth biggest in Europe. You can wander through this Oriental fantasy, exploring the contents of more than 300 shops and boutiques. A huge array of merchandise is offered for sale, including Portuguese fashion, leather goods, crystal, and souvenirs. In addition to several restaurants and snackbars, there is also a health center. The location is on a hill at the entrance to Lisbon, lying in back of the old reservoir called Aguas Livres. The blue-and-pink towers rise 19 stories and have already changed the skyline of Lisbon. The mall is open daily from 10 a.m. to midnight.

Apolo 70, 10 Avenida Julio Dinis (tel. 01/77-15-94), near the bull ring, is a self-contained unit that includes everything from an interior sidewalk café to a cinema and a leather shop. Wander for an hour or two among the 38 shops, making purchases at a teenage boutique, getting your photograph blown up to poster size, or having your hair styled by experts, after which you can stop in the cozy bar for a cooling drink, on the lower level. Also on the lower level is a restaurant that vaguely evokes a merry-go-round.

2. Porto

The capital of the north boasts some of the finest gold- and silversmiths in Portugal. You'll find dozens of shops, especially along **Rua das Flores,** offering displays in their window cases. The most outstanding one is . . .

Pedro A. Baptista, 235 Rua das Flores (tel. 02/251-42), which offers an unusual collection of antique as well as new jewelry (often based on traditional designs), plus several upper floors of decorator items. In the ground-floor jewelry section you'll find intricate and delicate lace-like filigree pins, brooches, pillboxes, and bracelets, in both solid gold (19¼ karats) or gold-plated silver, plus an exquisite silver collection, including elaborately decorated tea services.

Antique watches are sold, antique pearl brooches, tie pins, or gold rings, even jeweled opera glasses and a gold-headed cane. The owner buys rare and beautiful antique jewelry which he "offers first to my wife." The decorative bric-a-brac collection upstairs features many ornate gilt pieces, such as a three-foot-high carved-wood church candelabrum and a trestle dining table.

Fábrica de Loica de Sacavem, 40 Rua das Carmelitas (tel. 02/220-33), across from the Clerigos Church, is Porto's leading outlet for ceramics and china. Long established, it is important enough to have wares made especially for it. Generally the china selections are sophisticated, but regional motifs are offered as well. Worth considering are some of its decorative vases, based on old designs, along with a wide assortment of mugs, tureens, platters, cups, saucers, and glasses. Of course, pastel-colored china comes in many different arrangements at widely varying prices.

Shopping Center Brasília, 113 Praça Mouzinho de Albuquerque (tel. 02/69-74-25). Its bustle, its multilevel attractions, and its omnipresent marble floors evoke an upscale shopping complex in South America. But the merchandise and patrons are pure Portuguese. Its main entrance faces the snarling lion and bloodied eagle atop the column of the Praça Mouzinho de Albuquerque, one of the city's busiest commercial centers. This is the most important shopping complex in Porto, laden with all kinds of goods and services such as shoes, casual wear, sportswear, haute couture, furs, jewelry, electronic gadgets, libraries, toys, ceramics, furniture, supermarket, exchange, and unusual bars and restaurants. In fact, spread before you will be the flashiest array of merchandise in the north of Portugal. It's open until midnight.

There's a place for everybody's taste, including **Gôgô,** Galeria 51, Loja 51-D (tel. 02/69-85-12), which sells upscale gift items, many of them organic, from around the world. You'll also see sophisticated silver or ivory baubles from Zaire, China, and the Philippines. If you've ever yearned for a basket of preserved ostrich eggs, or perhaps a stuffed viper in attack position, this is the place.

---

3. Nazaré

Even if they aren't worn by the actual fishermen of Nazaré, Portuguese fishermen's sweaters have become attractive and fashionable garments in the United States. These bulky, hand-knit pullovers are usually wheat-colored wool, with elaborate chain-stitching on the front, back, and sides. Aficionados of Portuguese lore claim that the regional origin of each sweater can be determined by the designs knitted into it.

Fishermen's sweaters are also available cardigan style, at dozens of stores in Nazaré. Watch out for acrylic blends, as even Portugal is becoming more industrialized. Because of irregular sizes, try on anything you fancy before buying it. Also for sale in Nazaré are wool tartan shirts (which the fishermen do wear), woolen caps and scarves, all bargains at dozens of shops throughout the town. At all shops feel free to bargain. I've always managed to get discounts ranging from 20% to 35% (on one winter day when business was bad, 65%).

For an all-around preview of the merchandise offered in Nazaré, visit **Pérola da Nazaré,** 49 Avenida da República (tel. 062/516-49), along the waterfront, opening onto the beach. At this English-speaking shop, you'll come across a wide range of fishermen's sweaters, along with handcrafts made not only in the environs but throughout Portugal. They also sell embroidery from the island of Madeira and lace from the Azores. It's open to midnight in winter.

---

4. Barcelos

Centro do Artesanato de Barcelos, Torre da Porta Nova (tel. 831-35), is a unique shopping center tucked away in a provincial town. But it displays some of the best regional handcrafts at the most compelling prices of any shop I've encountered in the north. It's in an age-old stone tower, opposite the Church of S. da Cruz. On its street level and upper floor is found a wide display of goods.

Outstanding (and worth the trip to Barcelos) is the collection of witty and sophisticated ceramics from the heirs of Rosa Ramalho, who was known as the Grandma Moses of Portuguese ceramics. Some of these figures were influenced by Picasso. Ms. Ramalho created figures depicting eerie people, some looking as if they stepped out of a painting by Hieronymus Bosch. She put the heads of wolves on nuns, gave goats six legs, and so forth, all in her muted forest green or butterscotch brown.

In addition, there is a good selection of the ceramic red-combed Barcelos cockerels, with many variations on the traditional motif in red and black. Local wares include black ceramic candlesticks, earthenware bowls traditionally used for caldo verde, hand-knitted pillows, handmade rugs in bold stripes, and hand-loomed bedspreads. As a novelty, the rugs and pillows made from flamboyantly dyed chicken feathers may attract you.

---

5. Viana do Castelo

The old city of the Minho district, Viana do Castelo should also be considered if you're on a shopping tour of the north of Portugal. Its regional costumes, for example, are the most intricate and colorful in the country. The women are known for their embroidery, and many of their items, such as tablecloths, make ideal gifts. The region also turns out an array of colorful rugs, ceramics, and filigree work.

In Viana do Castelo, the handcrafts of the local artisans can best be viewed by walking along **Avenida dos Combatentes da Grande Guerra** near the water. Here handcraft shops line the street, and you can walk along inspecting the merchandise both inside and out of doors.

A specific shop that merits inspection if you're an antique collector is **O Coche,** Largo Vasco da Gama (tel. 058/237-17). Owned by members of the Coelho family, this jumbled and dusty shop attracts professional antique dealers from as far away as Lisbon and Porto. It stands near the Hotel Viana Sol, and it's considered the most interesting antique store in town. The trio of showrooms usually contains several good-quality reproductions, but most of the pieces are 19th-century originals. The rustic farmhouse implements, such as intricately carved ox yokes, are rapidly becoming collector's items.

---

6. Madeira

Casa do Turista, 2 Rua do Conselheiro José Silvestre Ribeiro (tel. 091/249-07), near the waterfront, Funchal, is one of the best places on the island at which to purchase handcrafts of Madeira. Privately managed, it has a policy of clearly labeled and "firm" prices, unlike many of the bazaars which pick up added business by paying to have cruise-ship passengers directed to their establishments, or else having employees chase you down the street quoting lower tariffs after you've nixed their higher tabs. The setting of the Tourist House is beguiling, in an old quinta, once inhabited by a distinguished local family. Its elegant rooms are a natural setting to show off the beautiful handmade items. You're treated as a guest in a private home.

In the patio, with a fountain and semitropical greenery, is a miniature village, with small-scale typical rooms furnished in the local style. Among the merchandise offered are handmade embroideries in linen or cotton (the fabric is often imported from Switzerland and Ireland), tapestries, wickerwork, Portuguese pottery and ceramics, Madeira wines, fruit, and flowers. You'll find all types of embroidery and appliqué, as well as "shadow work," the tariffs determined by the number of stitches.

Specific merchandise includes embroidered Irish linen handkerchiefs for men (some with monograms); handbags made of banana skins, in different sizes; the characteristic goatskin boots; 12-string guitars; 15-piece embroidered placemat and napkin sets; appliquéd tray cloths in shadow work; old Madeira-style tablecloths; and embroidered bridge cloths with four napkins.

In one of the rooms is a display of old wines, with ceramic jugs. Old wines (*velho*) are sold in their original bottles, some costing very little. In addition, a half pint of sugarcane brandy is for sale in souvenir packages of five miniature varieties.

Other shops include the following:

Casa Oliveira, 1-B Rua da Alfandega (tel. 091/293-40), which has an embroidery factory right on the premises.

Likewise, **Jabara,** 59 Rua Dr. Fernão Ornelas (tel. 091/295-00), has its own embroidery factory, and specializes in regional articles.

Madeira Gobelins, 194 Rua da Carreira (tel. 091/220-73), is a specialist in art needlework, and you can visit its showroom and factory. In addition to needlework, it specializes in the production of Portuguese rugs, hand-stitched, as well as monogrammed linens and other items. It also has a second outlet in Funchal, the Savoy Boutique No. 2 on the Avenida do Infante. Although there is no factory in Lisbon, you can see Madeira Gobelins products in the shop they own at 40 Rua Castilho (corner of Rua Braamcamp).

Madeira Superbia, 27 Rua do Carmo (tel. 091/240-23), is known for its fine embroidery (of excellent quality) and is a specialist in tapestries.

Lino and Araujo Ltd., 15 Rua Dos Murcas (tel. 091/207-36), specializes in hand-embroideries and knitted goods. This shop is frequented by many non-Portuguese residents of Madeira.

Cayres Department Store, 56A-56B Rua Dr. Fernão Ornelas (tel. 091/249-54), is a good tourist shopping center, where you can find a variety of items personally selected by the store owner, who is also an art specialist. Regional art includes embroidery, tapestry, glass, crystal, pewter, porcelain, ceramics, and the famous Arraillos carpets. Women's fashions are in the Boutique, and there are sections of the store dealing in antiques, paintings, furniture, and Chinese porcelain.

ESTORIL, CASCAIS, AND SINTRA

The environs of Lisbon are so intriguing that many fail to see the capital itself, lured by the siren call of **Guincho** (near the western-most point in continental Europe), the roar from the **Mouth of Hell,** the muted song from Lord Byron's "glorious Eden" at **Sintra.** A day could be spent drinking in the wonders of the library at the monastery-palace of **Mafra** (Portugal's El Escorial), dining in the pretty pink rococo palace at **Queluz,** or enjoying seafood at the Atlantic beach resort of **Ericeira.**

However, the chief magnet remains the **Costa do Sol,** that string of beach resorts, such as **Estoril** and **Cascais,** that form the Portuguese Riviera on the northern banks of the mouth of the Tagus. In fact, if you arrive in Lisbon when the sun is shining and the air balmy, you should consider seeking lodgings along this cabaña-studded shoreline. So near to Lisbon is Estoril that it's easy to dart in and out of the capital on sightseeing jaunts or fado sprees, while ensconced at a base in a hotel by the sea. An inexpensive electric train leaving from the Cais do Sodré in Lisbon makes the trip frequently throughout the day and evening, ending its run in Cascais.

The sun coast is sometimes known as A Costa dos Reis, the coast of kings, because of all the deposed royalty who have settled there—everybody from exiled kings to pretenders, marquesses from Italy, princesses from Russia, and baronesses from Germany. These people may live simply as did a virtual recluse in an unpretentious villa, the late Princess Elena of Rumania (Magda Lupescu); or they may insist on rigid court ambience, as did Umberto, the 1946 one-month-king of Italy, who was forced into exile when a plebiscite went against the monarchy. Tending his cows in "baggy trousers and muddy boots" in Sintra is the Count of Paris, the pretender to the throne of France; a descendant of Louis Philippe, he was the son of the Duke of Guise. In 1969 another pretender, Don Juan, Count of Barcelona, was short-changed the Spanish throne when his son, Don Juan Carlos, was named successor by the late Generalisimo Franco. The count was once an officer in the British navy and is now a noted yachtsman. Other nobility include Joanna, the former queen of Bulgaria, and the Infanta Dona Maria Adelaide de Bragança, sister of the Portuguese pretender.

The Riviera is a microcosm of Portugal. Ride out on the train, even if you don't plan to lodge there. Along the way you'll pass pastel-washed houses, with red tile roofs and façades of antique blue and white tiles; miles of modern apartment dwellings; rows of canna, pines, mimosa, and eucalyptus; swimming pools; and in the background green hills studded with villas, chalets, and new homes.

1. Carcavelos

On the road between Lisbon and Estoril, this seaside town boasts the longest stretch of beach along the Costa do Sol. Often considered its gateway, it commands a view of the white Manueline-style Tower of Belém farther back. Carcavelos was noted for its fortress, **São Julião,** which once held prisoner left-wing radicals during the Miguelite wars. The fortress, with its pale-yellow walls and unusual turrets, is of a unique design that is attributed to the theories of Sebastien Le Prestre de Vauban, a French engineer.

The resort lies about 13½ miles outside of Lisbon and is easily reached on the electric train from the Cais do Sodré. Even if you don't go to Carcavelos, you may want to sample some of its full-bodied wine, praised by the Duke of Wellington.

A medium-priced accommodation here is provided by **Hotel Praia-Mar,** 16 Rua do Gurué, Carcavelos, 2775 Parede (tel. 01/247-31-31). You'll recognize this modern palace from a distance because of its angular design and dramatically recessed balconies. When you get closer, you'll appreciate the private world that unfolds behind the plant-bordered walls separating the elliptical swimming pool from the street outside. Unlike some of the other hotels on the coast, Praia-Mar is in a quiet neighborhood a few blocks away from the four-lane highway cutting alongside the coastline.

The lobby has large windows leading toward the sun-flooded swimming pool. There's a bar near the roof and another blue and white version in a remote corner of the lobby, graced with an imposing statue of an Amazon brandishing a ferocious-looking infant. Each of the 158 bedrooms contains a balcony, usually with a view toward the sea, along with a combination of contemporary and Iberian-inspired furniture. The in-house restaurant on the eighth floor serves well-prepared meals costing from 2,800$ ($18.20). Singles cost from 10,000$ ($65) daily, while doubles rent for 11,500$ ($74.75), with a continental breakfast included.

2. Estoril

This chic resort along the Portuguese Riviera has long basked in its reputation as a playground of kings. Fading countesses arrive at the railway station, monarchs in exile drop in at the Palácio Hotel for dinner, the sons of assassinated dictators sunbathe by the pool—and an international joie de vivre pervades the air.

Once Estoril was a figment of the imagination of Fausto Figueiredo, the founding father of the deluxe Palácio and the Casino. Before the First World War, Fausto Figueiredo envisioned hundreds of people strolling through the marble corridors and down mosaic sidewalks to the ocean as he gazed out over scrub pines and sandy hills. Before the Second World War, Estoril was firmly entrenched in the resort

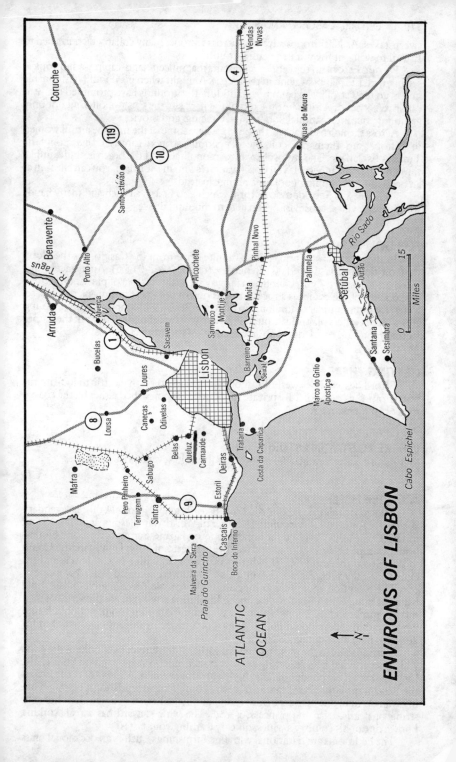

ENVIRONS OF LISBON

sweepstakes. As Nazi troops advanced across Europe, many collapsed courts fled to Estoril to wait out the war in a neutral country.

Parque Estoril, in the center, represents magnificent landscaping, a subtropical setting with the plants swaying in the breeze. At night when it's floodlit, fashionable guests go for a stroll. The palm trees studding the grounds have prompted many to call it "a corner of Africa." At the top of the park sits the **Casino,** offering not only gambling, but international floor shows, dancing, and movies.

Across the railroad tracks is the beach, where some of the most beautiful women in Europe sun themselves on the peppermint-striped canvas chairs along the Tamariz Esplanade. The atmosphere is cosmopolitan, and the beach is sandy, unlike the pebbly strand at Nice. If you don't want to swim in the ocean, you can check in at an oceanfront swimming pool for a plunge instead.

To the east is **São João do Estoril,** which also boasts a beach and many handsome private villas. Most visitors go here to dine and dance.

FOR GOLFERS

In the foothills of Sintra, a three-minute drive from the Casino, lies the **Clube de Golf do Estoril,** Avenida da República (tel. 01/268-01-76). An attraction for international sports figures, it offers a fairway set against a vista of pine and mimosa. The quality of the course is so acclaimed as one of the finest in Europe that it is selected for international championship matches. Both a 9-hole and an 18-hole course are offered. Golfers play from around 7:30 a.m. till sunset daily. Guests of the Estoril Palácio Hotel are entitled to a 50% reduction on the greens fees.

GETTING THERE

Estoril lies 15 miles west of Lisbon and is reached by an electric train from the waterfront Cais do Sodré. By private car, Estoril is approached either by the coastal road or an inland route.

WHERE TO STAY IN ESTORIL

Estoril has recommended accommodations in several price categories.

A Deluxe Hotel

Palácio Hotel, Parque Estoril, 2765 Estoril (tel. 01/268-04-00), is legendary as a retreat for exiled royalty and as a center of World War II espionage. At its debut in 1930, the Palácio received the honeymooning Japanese crown prince and his new bride. In time other royalty would follow: Umberto of Italy; Don Juan, the Count of Barcelona. In World War II, when people escaped with a case of jewels and the clothes on their back, diamonds, rubies, and gold were accepted instead of money.

The reception rooms are Pompeian, with sienna-colored marble pillars, bold bands of orange, and handmade carpets. Ideal for a tête-à-tête are the series of intimate communicating salons. In the classic central drawing room, with black-and-white marble checkerboard floors, groups of antique furnishings are arranged for guests to have after-dinner coffee.

Starting early in the morning, guests gather at the terrace overlooking the pool, which is encircled by a reflecting pool. A buffet luncheon is served on your chaise longue or at a table beside a garland hedge of bougainvillea. An asset of the Palácio is the Restaurant-Grill Four Seasons (see my dining recommendations, below). Dining is an event in one of the stateliest rooms along the Riviera. The jeweled choker or string of pearls, even the princess, is real. The wine steward has a real working knowledge of his country's wines, quickly learning your tastes.

The bedrooms are traditional with fine furnishings, such as an occasional brass bed, always a desk, a marble-topped chest, and twin wardrobes, plus baths with bidets and heated towel racks. In high season, the single rate is 17,600$ ($114.40) to 20,300$ ($133.90) daily, and a double costs 20,000$ ($130) to 22,100$ ($143.65). Low-season prices are 12,700$ ($82.55) to 14,300$ ($92.95) in a single, 14,300$ ($92.95) to 15,400$ ($100.10) in a double.

The hotel opens onto the side of Estoril Park, capped by the casino. The beach is only a short walk away. Seven clay surface championship tennis courts are right next door to the hotel, with three courts floodlit for night play. Guests of the hotel are offered special privileges at its own international championship golf course.

The Medium-Priced Range

Hotel Alvorada, 3 Rua de Lisboa, 2765 Estoril (tel. 01/268-00-70), opened its doors late in 1969 to provide Iberian pousada-style living on a small scale, opposite the casino and the formally styled Estoril Parque. Just a three-minute trek from the sands, it is recommended to those desiring well-styled bedrooms, which rent for 8,500$ ($55.25) daily in a double, 5,200$ ($33.80) in a single. There are 55 rooms in all, each with private bath and balcony. The public rooms are personalized and well conceived. Off the reception area, the drinking lounge is decorated with modern Portuguese paintings and provincial-style furnishings. The top-floor solarium offers a panoramic view of the sea.

Hotel Estoril-Anka, Estrada Marginal, 2765 Estoril (tel. 01/268-18-11), was built next door to its glamorous neighbor, the Palácio. Its seven floors with walls of glass soar high, about half the rooms boasting good-size balconies overlooking a view of the water and the casino with its formal gardens. Only a minute or so from the seafront and the electric train station, it is in the center of Estoril's boutique district. The upper-floor dining room provides unobstructed vistas of the sea and the nearby hills studded with villas. On many evenings a white-capped chef stands proudly in front of his specialty display table. In the marble-floored lounge and drinking bar, good contemporary design prevails, with plenty of museum-like space. Soft tufted leather chairs are gathered around marble-topped tables. Live music is played in the Bar Estoril every night from 6 p.m. to midnight, and there is also a disco in the hotel. A hairdressing salon is among the facilities offered.

The bedrooms are not only trim, utilitarian, and uncluttered, but many have sitting areas, with wood-grained pieces. French doors open onto balconies in most of the rooms. All have shiny tile private baths with a shower. Singles rent for 12,000$ ($78) daily, and doubles go for 14,000$ ($91), the prices including breakfast.

Lennox Country Club, 5 Rua Eng. Alvaro Pedro Sousa (tel. 01/268-04-24). Partially because of its emphasis on golf, this hillside hotel is a lot like a corner of Scotland. As you complete the steep climb to the reception desk you'll notice a series of Portuguese tiles depicting bekilted bagpipers and plaid-covered "bairns" playing golf, in almost a tongue-in-cheek comment on the juxtaposition of the two cultures. There's even a map of the golf course at St. Andrews near the bar, close to the autographed photos of the many championship golfers who have stayed here. The hydrangeas and the herbaceous borders in the gardens outside, coupled with the sunshine, make this place a potent attraction. Some of its comfortably attractive accommodations are scattered among a collection of buildings a short walk from the reception area. The most desirable are contained within the main building, which was formerly a private home. Self-caterers might be interested in one of the suites, each of which is equipped with a kitchenette. In high season, the charge is 12,500$ ($81.25) daily in a single, 17,500$ ($113.75) in a double.

The hotel provides free transport to the collection of golf courses lying a short distance away, as well as to the area's riding stables. For nearby relaxation, there's a kidney-shaped pool, adorned with intricate mosaics, terraced into a hillside near the main villa.

Hotel Lido, 12 Rua do Alentejo, 2765 Estoril (tel. 01/268-41-23), is a five-story white concrete cube set into a residential neighborhood on a hill above town. Each of its functional and comfortable bedrooms, 62 in all, benefits from a recessed balcony. In season, the half-board rate ranges from 10,000$ ($65) daily in a single to 15,000$ ($97.50) for two. The decor of the public rooms, whose floors are covered with slabs of gray-and-white marble, is extremely modern and just a bit sterile. The hotel's large, plant-ringed swimming pool is one of its most attractive features.

Estalagem Belvedere, 8 Rua Dr. António Martins, 2765 Estoril (tel. 01/268-91-63). Built as a private villa during the Edwardian age, and converted into a charming hotel some 25 years ago, this English-owned establishment offers two dozen bedrooms, each with private bath. Singles cost 5,700$ ($37.05) daily, and doubles go for 9,000$ ($58.50), with breakfast included. It sits in a gracious neighborhood of faded 19th-century residences, among century-old trees and gardens. Inside, the comfortable public rooms contain Iberian furnishings, a cozy bar filled with rustic bric-a-brac, and a dining room serving dinner only, from 7:15 to 10 p.m. daily. The hotel has a swimming pool.

The Budget Range

Hotel de Inglaterra, 2 Avenida de Portugal, 2765 Estoril (tel. 01/268-44-61). The rooms in this hotel provide only the minimum levels of comfort and accessories, but its façade is about as grand as any you'll see in Estoril. Although now it has stripped-down decor and inexpensive furnishings, it was built originally by a wealthy Portuguese industrialist at the turn of the century (his family occupied it up until it was sold for conversion into a hotel). The location is about a five-minute walk to the beach in a quiet residential section near the casino. A swimming pool fills most of the triangular front garden. The hotel has 38 rooms with private baths and 11 bathless accommodations. A few of the units have private balconies. Singles range from 4,500$ ($29.25) to 8,500$ ($55.25) daily, with doubles costing 5,000$ ($32.50) to 10,000$ ($65). The lower rates are for off-season only. Breakfast is included in the price. The basement contains a large and convivial bar where guests, sometimes members of tour groups who check in en masse, can socialize.

Residential Smart, 3 Rua José Viana, 2765 Estoril (tel. 01/268-21-64). Set on a hillside, in a grandly faded neighborhood of 19th-century villas, this 14-room hotel offers well-scrubbed accommodations and plenty of quiet. Don't expect opulent furnishings or glamour. What you get is a low-key welcome and unpretentious solitude. Depending on the season, and with breakfast included, singles range from 2,750$ ($17.90) to 4,500$ ($29.25) daily; doubles 3,000$ ($19.50) to 5,000$ ($32.50).

STAYING IN MONTE ESTORIL

A satellite of Estoril, Monte Estoril lies directly to the west on the road to Cascais, half a mile away. Built across the slope of a hill and containing many moderately priced hotels, it opens onto a vista of Cascais Bay and the Atlantic beyond.

The Leading Hotels

Estoril Eden, 209 Avenida Sabóia, Monte Estoril, 2765 Estoril (tel. 01/267-05-73), is a four-star suite hotel open all year. Built in 1985, this white-walled tower sits on a rocky knoll above the road paralleling the edge of the sea. A beautiful swimming pool, protected from the noise of the coastal road by its altitude and the wall, is one of the establishment's main attractions. There is also an indoor swimming pool. Other facilities include a health club. The apartments, ranging from one-bedroom units to a two-bedroom penthouse suite, are sound proof, air-conditioned, and elegantly decorated. Each accommodation has a kitchenette, private bath, direct-dial phone, radio, TV, in-house video, and a balcony opening onto a view of the sea. In the studio apartments, the beds are "in-wall," allowing larger living space during the v. High season rates in a double or twin studio suite range from 11,000$ ($71.70) y to 13,000$ ($84.50), a remarkable bargain in resort living. Dining facilities include The Garden Patio, offering both a regional and international cuisine either à la carte or buffet, and a poolside café bar, Le Bistrot. The Stella Maris sees disco action nightly, and you can stock up on food supplies in a mini-market.

Hotel Atlântico, 7 Estrada Marginal, Monte Estoril, 2765 Estoril (tel. 01/268-02-70), is a self-contained playground, almost directly on the sandy beach, that charges moderate tariffs. The hotel's separated from the beach by the electric train tracks from Lisbon. Its disadvantages are the whizzing coastal-road traffic in front, the clatter of the train in the rear. However, if you get a room high enough up facing the sea, you can be assured of quiet. Between the lower floor of the hotel and the tracks is a wide sun terrace, with a seawater swimming pool. The dining room, built cave-like under the width of the hotel, has a view through an all-glass wall overlooking the pool and the sea. One TV lounge has video; another lounge offers live music in the evening.

The bedrooms are medium size and moderately well furnished, with built-in headboards, reading lights, telephones, Swedish-style desks and armchairs, and tile baths and showers. Accommodations are priced according to the view. In high season, doubles peak at 18,500$ ($120) daily, with off-season reductions. The price includes a continental breakfast, service, and taxes.

Grande Hotel, Avenida Sabóia, Monte Estoril, 2765 Estoril (tel. 01/268-46-09), is a modern, 71-bedroom compound, just a few minutes up from the beach. It offers seven floors of spacious rooms with private bath, about half of which have balconies large enough for breakfast and sunbathing. Guests relax and swim in its covered pool opening off a cocktail terrace, with a view of eucalyptus and palm trees. The air-conditioned main dining room is undistinguished, yet still serves adequate meals. The large sitting room is popular, with a fireplace and groupings of comfortable furniture. An international collection of visitors wanders into the open wood-paneled lobby and into the chestnut-fronted drinking lounge.

The bedrooms are furnished in blond moderno (bedside tables, chest-desk combinations), the severity lightened by simple color schemes. The hotel charges 11,250$ ($73.15) daily in singles, 14,000$ ($91) in doubles in high season, with lower tariffs quoted off-season. Children under 8 are given a 50% reduction if they share a room with their parents. A few rooms have sitting areas, for which you'll pay more, of course. The better rooms open onto sea views.

Hotel Zenith, 1 Rua Belmonte, Monte Estoril, 2765 Estoril (tel. 01/268-02-02). You'll find comfortable modern accommodations inside this white and moss-green tower jutting skyward from a neighborhood of 19th-century villas above town. The ground-floor bar, encased in burnished tones of hardwood, offers a big-windowed rendezvous point to relax in air-conditioned comfort. Each of the 48 bedrooms contains a phone, radio, and private bath, plus access to the rectangular swimming pool whose waterside plants are sheltered from the wind by the bulk of the hotel itself. Singles rent for 11,000$ ($71.50) daily, and doubles go for 13,000$ ($84.50). There's a TV lounge with a fireplace, along with a basement-level snackbar and restaurant.

Aparthotel Vale do Sol, Rua do Viveiro, Monte Estoril, 2765 Estoril (tel. 01/268-33-85), is a modern apartment-house complex with accommodations for two or four persons. All are fully equipped with kitchenette, bath, terrace, TV, radio, and air conditioning. Cleaning service is available, and there are a supermarket, hairdresser, and restaurant on the premises. An apartment for two costs 5,000$ ($32.50) to 11,000$ ($71.50) daily. An apartment for four guests rents for 7,500$ ($48.75) to 13,000$ ($84.50). The prices depend on the time of year.

WHERE TO DINE IN ESTORIL

For fine food, go to the **Four Seasons,** Hotel Palácio (tel. 268-04-00). Its connection with one of Portugal's most famous hotels adds a vivid cachet to this restaurant. But even if it were independently operated, it would still be one of the finest—and also one of the most expensive—restaurants in the country.

The menus and the service of the Four Seasons depend on just that—the seasons. Dishes, uniforms, linen, china, and glasses are changed four times a year. Other than the handful of intimate tables set imperially on the upper mezzanine, each of the elaborately decorated tables is grouped around a beautiful but purely decorative Iberian kitchen, whose copper pots and blue tiles provide an appealingly rustic touch to an otherwise sophisticated decor. The hushed quiet, the candles, and the rich colors almost invite comparison to an elegant home in 19th-century Russia. However, the discreet charm and polite manners of the well-trained staff are distinctively Portuguese.

The cuisine is superb. For example, you might select the three-cheese crêpes as an appetizer. Or you might be tempted by lobster bisque or chilled mussel soup, following with chateaubriand, mussels in cream sauce, grilled beef and monkfish on a skewer, shrimps in garlic butter, or roast duckling with orange sauce. Reservations are necessary for full dinners, served daily from 8 to 11 p.m. and costing from 5,000$ ($32.50). You can enter this place either directly from the street or from the hotel lobby after enjoying a drink among the international clientele at the bar.

English Bar, Estrada Marginal (tel. 268-12-54). Many couples come here just to watch the sunsets over the Bay of Cascais. Its mock Elizabethan façade may lead you to think of steak-and-kidney pie and tankards of ale, yet the food is essentially Portuguese, and it's well prepared.

Try for a window seat in the handsome dining room, with its wide-plank floors, comfortable wood and leather-backed chairs. There are numerous English-style decorations: heraldic symbols, horsey prints, and bric-a-brac. From the à la carte menu, you can sample such highly recommended dishes as a savory *crème de mariscos* (cream of shellfish soup). The chef's specialty is *cherne na canoa,* a turbot dish served with baby clams and a succulent sauce. In season you can order *perdiz Sêrra Morena* (roast partridge). An excellent dessert is a mousse made with nuts. For a complete meal, expect to spend from 2,000$ ($13). Food is served daily from noon to 4 p.m. and 7:30 to 10:30 p.m.; closed Sunday.

Pak Yun, 5 Centro Comercial Estoril Parque (tel. 267-06-91), is one of the best Oriental restaurants along the Costa do Sol. Across from the main entrance to the casino, it lies right off Praça José Teódoro dos Santos in the heart of Estoril. One of its best bargains is a delectable Chinese meal for two, costing 3,500$ ($22.75). The chef is skilled at preparing such fare as shark-fin soup, Peking duck, steamed fresh fish, along with steamed seasonal vegetables in oyster sauce. The Oriental decor is attractively modern, and hours are daily except Monday from noon to 3 p.m. and 7 p.m. to midnight.

Tamariz, on Estoril Beach (tel. 268-16-65), is the most popular gathering spot on the beach. Bathing attire is not only permitted but encouraged. Some of the most attractive visitors on the Estoril coast fill some of the most imaginative bathing suits from the boutiques of Europe. They sit for hours at canopied tables on a terrace projecting out toward the beach. Light fare and snacks are the order of the day, including a hamburger, combination plates, coffee, and a milkshake. Meals, served daily from 9 a.m. to 6 p.m., cost from 1,500$ ($9.75). Shower facilities and lockers adjoin, and the swimming pool is open from April to October. Service may be a bit slow, but who's in a hurry?

BETWEEN SINTRA AND ESTORIL

At Alcabideche, **Sintra Estoril Hotel,** No. 9 ão km. 6 (Junto ão Autodromo), 2765 Alcabideche (tel. 01/269-07-21), is a crescent-shaped hotel at a triangle of Sintra, Cascais, and Estoril. On the outside it looks like a stadium, with encircling balconies. It's not unlike a modern museum inside, with its bedroom balconies opening onto a large playground area and Olympic-size swimming pool, tennis and volleyball courts. Its lounges are varied, lofty, and warmly colored. A few public rooms have drama, with shimmering mirrored walls, circular sofas, or a wall of abstract sculpture. Even the bedrooms have their own contemporary character, with built-in headboards, phones, radios, and piped-in music. All have two double beds, air conditioning, a terrace, and tile bath. In high season, a single rents for 8,500$ ($55.25) daily, rising to 10,500$ ($68.25) in a double or twin. From mid-September until the end of March, reductions are granted.

3. Cascais

In the 1930s Cascais was a tiny fishing village, attracting artists and writers to its little cottages. But its history as a resort is old. In fact, it was once known as a royal village, because it enjoyed the patronage of Portugal's royal family. When the monarchy died, the military moved in. Gen. António de Fragoso Carmona, president of Portugal until 1951, the man responsible for naming Dr. Salazar as minister of finance, once occupied the 17th-century fort guarding the Portuguese Riviera.

That Cascais is growing is an understatement. It's leapfrogging! At one entrance to the resort, someone penciled in the word "City" after Cascais. Even if not officially recognized as such, it is well on its way. Apartment houses, new hotels, and the finest restaurants along the Costa do Sol draw a never-ending stream of visitors every year.

However, the life of the simple fisherman still goes on. Auctions, called *lotas,* at which the latest catch is sold, still take place on the main square, except a modern hotel has sprouted up in the background. In the small harbor, rainbow-colored fishing boats must share space with pleasure craft owned by an international set that flocks to Cascais from early spring until autumn.

The tie that Cascais has with the sea is old. If you speak Portuguese, any of the local fishermen, with their weather-beaten faces, could tell you that one of their own, Afonso Sanches, discovered America in 1482, that Columbus learned of his accidental find, stole the secret, and enjoyed the subsequent acclaim.

Cascais lies only four miles west of Estoril, 18 miles from Lisbon proper. It's reached by the electric train that begins its run at the Cais do Sodré waterfront station, ending it in the center of town. Trains leave every 15 minutes.

Many visitors, both foreign and domestic, drive out to Cascais on a road-clogged summer Sunday to attend the bullfights at the **Monumental de Cascais,** a ring outside the "city" center.

The most popular excursion outside of Cascais is to the **Boca de Inferno** (Mouth of Hell). Reached by heading out the highway to Guincho, then turning left toward the sea, the Boca deserves its ferocious reputation. At their peak, thundering waves sweep in with such power and fury that they have long ago carved a wide hole, or boca, in the cliffs. However, if you should arrive when the sea is calm, you'll wonder why it's called a caldron. The Mouth of Hell can be a windswept roar if you don't stumble over too many souvenir hawkers.

WHERE TO STAY

Cascais has a number of accommodations in all price ranges. Reservations are vital in July and August.

The Top Hotels

Hotel Albatroz, 100 Rua Frederico Arouca, 2750 Cascais (tel. 01/28-28-21). The wandering albatross, of course, is a bird noted as a master of gliding flight, capable of staying airborne on motionless wings for hours on end. What an appropriate symbol for this treasure along the Costa do Sol. Whether you're seeking rooms or food, the hotel is your "good luck" choice. Positioned on a ledge of rocks just above the ocean, it is centered around a neoclassic villa which was originally built as a luxurious holiday retreat for the Duke of Loulé. It was later acquired in the 19th century by the count and countess de Foz. Sometime in this century it was converted into an inn, and in time received such guests as Anthony Eden, Cary Grant, Chief Justice Warren Burger, the duke and duchess of Bedford, Claudette Colbert, William Holden, Amy Vanderbilt, and the former queen of Bulgaria. Prince Rainier and the late Princess Grace visited on more than one occasion.

Today the hotel has benefitted from a tastefully elegant refurbishing which incorporates a lavish use of intricately painted tiles in garlanded patterns of blue and yellow, acres of white latticework, and sweeping expanses of panoramic glass. The stone-trimmed 19th-century core has been expanded with a terraced series of balconied additions, each of which contains some of the 37 pristinely elegant bedrooms. Depending on the season and the exposure of the accommodation, doubles range from 15,000$ ($97.50) to 32,000$ ($208) daily, while singles cost 12,000$ ($78) to 26,000$ ($169). An oval swimming pool nestles alongside the sun terrace midway between the new wing and the old. Dining here can provide one of your finest eating experiences along the Costa do Sol.

Estoril Sol, Parque Palmela, 2750 Cascais (tel. 01/28-28-31), is a luxury high-rise holiday world, perched on a ledge, with the coastal highway and electric train tracks separating it from the beach. It represents a dream come true for its late owner, José Teodoro dos Santos, a self-made man, who originally arrived in Lisbon with less than a dollar in his pocket. A modern land of resort living has been created: a gymnasium, an Olympic-size pool for adults, a smaller one for children, a complete sauna, a health club with squash courts, facilities for horseback riding, waterskiing, a shopping arcade, a garage and service station, and public rooms large enough for a great invasion of sun-seeking visitors.

The result was that the air-conditioned Estoril Sol ended up as one of the largest hotels in Portugal, with bedrooms and suites overlooking the sea or the hills beyond. It boasts the largest dining room on the Costa do Sol, the most spacious main lounge (a traffic cop would be helpful here), the greatest number of bars (five in all), the most expansive veranda on the peninsula, and a beach reached by an underground passageway. Savory specialties are served in a Grill Room. The designers have furnished the public rooms and bedrooms in a modified Miami Beach style. The more expensive rooms have sea views and balconies. Naturally, every room has a complete tile bath with gadgets. Single rooms cost 18,000$ ($117) daily, and doubles go for 22,000$ ($143).

Hotel Cidadela, Avenida 25 de Abril, 2750 Cascais (tel. 01/28-29-21). Architecturally and decoratively, this hotel is a citadel of high taste. Elegantly furnished in a restrained way, spacious in concept both in its private and public rooms, and gracious in its reception and amenities, it is emerging as the sleeper of the Sun Coast. Many Riviera-bound guests have deserted their old favorites for this holiday rendezvous.

You can reserve a first-class room, built into the central block with balconies, or else the Cidadela will place you in womb-like comfort in one of its twin-bedded, terraced suites or one of its apartment-like duplexes, the latter usually sheltering a menage of anywhere from three to six persons. Priced from 17,000$ ($110.50) daily during peak season, a regular double is tastefully furnished, the white walls becoming foils for the vibrant colors. Singles cost from 15,000$ ($97.50). The rear rooms, sheltered from the noise of traffic, are preferable. Two wings of rooms and duplexes face a garden with a large open swimming pool.

The duplexes are as complete as an apartment: a living room, dining room, and a fully equipped kitchenette on the lower floor, with a staircase leading to the upstairs bedrooms, two or three each, with private bath. Each floor opens onto verandas with garden furniture. A suite for four persons in high season costs 28,000$ ($182) daily. Service and taxes are included.

The three major public rooms are pleasantly decorated, the main living room with low modern groups of furniture in warm colors. In the good-size dining room, the sturdy armchairs, upholstered with Portuguese fabric, seat many diners desiring top-quality cooking. You can take lunch or dinner here for 2,500$ ($16.25) extra per person. However, nearby is a supermarket for those wanting to whip up their own concoctions. The intimate bar is done in blue and gray with "medievalesque" helmets and breast plates. On the premises are a garage, a boutique, a hairdresser, plus a concierge skilled at arranging boating and fishing trips, tennis games, a day at the golf course, horseback riding, or a ticket for the bullfight. The hotel divorces itself from the hustle-bustle of summering Cascais, and is reached by heading out on a tree-shaded avenue, past restaurants, boutiques, and nightclubs.

The Medium-Priced Range

Estalagem Senhora da Guia, Estrada do Guincho, 2750 Cascais (tel. 01/28-92-39). One of the loveliest hotels in the region was opened only a few years ago by the Ornelas family, who returned to their native Portugal after a sojourn in Brazil. Looking for a property to develop, they settled on the former country villa of one of the most famous fortunes of Portugal. The house was originally built as recently as 1970, but its thick walls, high ceilings, and elaborately crafted moldings give the impression of a much older building. Shortly after its construction it was abandoned by the heirs of the Sagres brewery when they fled to Brazil and the house fell into ruin.

Happily, a trio of blond, blue-eyed, multilingual siblings embarked on the backbreaking task of restoring the house to its former glory. Today each of the 28 elegant bedrooms is tastefully outfitted with reproductions of 18th-century Portuguese antiques, thick carpets, louvered shutters, spacious modern bathrooms, and many of extras. You'll be greeted by either Carlos, Maria, or Bernardo, who have to an increasing degree taken over the management of the property from their semi-retired parents. A polite member of the staff will usher you up an elegantly crafted wood, wrought-iron, and crystal staircase to your immaculate bedroom. Even the unvarnished floors of the place are frequently scrubbed with sand, Portuguese style, giving them the warm patina that would otherwise take years to achieve. The sun-washed bar is one of the more alluring rooms in the house. It's filled with some of the family antiques, many of them English and acquired during their years in Madeira. Upholstered sofas provide quiet corners, and there is a fireplace for cold weather.

The hotel, named after the patron saint of lighthouses, fishermen, and the surrounding region, serves as a focal point for repeat guests who have begun to make this their preferred stopover outside Lisbon. Sports lovers receive a 20% discount at a nearby golf and tennis club, while horseback riding can be arranged on short notice. In high season, singles rent for $130 (U.S.) daily, doubles run $145 and triples cost $152, with a continental breakfast included. In low season, charges are lowered to 8,740$ ($55) daily in a single, 10,000$ ($65) in a double, and 11,088$ ($72) in a triple. Because of the villa's position on a bluff above the sea, the views are excellent. Breakfast is served buffet style under parasols at the edge of the swimming pool. Lunches and dinners are offered beneath a ceiling of African hardwood in a formal dining room which remains cool even on the hottest days.

Estalagem Farol, 7 Estrada da Boca do Inferno, 2750 Cascais (tel. 01/28-01-73). When it was built in the late 19th century, its stone walls housed the entourage of the count of Cabral. Today its once-aristocratic interior has been converted into an inn whose allure is only slightly dimmed by the dozens of Portuguese families who make it the center of their vacation holidays. Today's owners have converted the gardens in back into a stone-ringed concrete slab with a small swimming pool in the center, a few steps from the sea.

One of the favorite places is the richly masculine bar area, where a water view and the handcrafted paneling create an elegant rendezvous point. The restaurant is tastefully outfitted with Iberian charm. There's a tennis court on the premises, shielded by a hedge from both the hotel and the busy highway. Rates for double occupancy vary with the season. Highest prices are charged between July and September, when doubles cost 9,000$ ($58.50) to 13,000$ ($84.50) daily. In winter, the double rate is reduced to 6,000$ ($39) to 9,000$ ($58.50).

The Budget Range

Casa Pergola, 13 Avenida Valbom, 2750 Cascais (tel. 01/284-00-40). Originally built in the 18th century behind a deep and well-planted garden, this elegant villa offers some of the most charming interiors in Cascais. In the center of town, it stands in a neighborhood filled with apartment houses and shops. Inside, the wall surrounding its flowers and hanging vines provides a calm from the hectic life and traffic outside. This is the domain of Maria de Luz, whose genteel Portuguese staff proudly displays a collection of antique furniture and blue-glazed tiles which surround the elegant second-floor sitting room. Eight of the establishment's dozen well-furnished bedrooms contain a private bath. Depending on the season, rooms with bath rent for 6,000$ ($39) to 9,500$ ($61.75), whereas units without bath cost 2,800$ ($18.20) to 6,000$ ($39). Each accommodation is suitable for one or two persons, and comes with breakfast included in the price.

Albergaría Valbom, 14 Avenida Valbom, 2750 Cascais (tel. 01/286-58-01). The white concrete façade with its evenly spaced rows of recessed balconies doesn't offer anything architecturally distinctive. Nonetheless, the interior is warmly and comfortably decorated, and the staff is helpful and polite. You'll find a spacious sienna-colored bar on the premises, along with a sun-washed TV lounge ringed with engravings of fish, and 40 conservatively decorated bedrooms, each with private bath. The quieter accommodations look out over the back. A continental breakfast is included in the price, which ranges from 4,000$ ($26) to 4,500$ ($29.25) daily in a single, 6,000$ ($39) to 7,500$ ($48.75) in a double. The Valbom lies on a commercial-residential street close to the center of Cascais, near the rail station.

Hotel Nau, 14 Rua Dr. Iracy Doyle, 2750 Cascais (tel. 01/28-28-61). The hotel's 56 rooms are popular with Europeans on a budget holiday and consequently there might be a tour bus pulled up near the concrete front. You'll find this place behind a balconied façade, a few steps from the town's rail station. A bar is on the second floor, and other facilities include a sun terrace on the roof and a dining room. The simple and functional bedrooms, which tend to be quieter in the back, offer balconies, phones, private bathrooms, and a well-scrubbed look. High-season rates are 12,000$ ($78) daily in a single and 14,000$ ($91) in a double. All tariffs include a continental breakfast. The hotel is next to one of the biggest garages in town.

WHERE TO DINE

Outside of Lisbon, this sprawling resort offers the heaviest concentration of high-quality restaurants in all of Portugal. Even if you're based in the capital, you should trek out to Cascais to sample the viands—both Portuguese and international dishes. Once you've tasted cognac-simmered lobster, mint-flavored shellfish soup, stuffed cuttlefish, shrimp pâté, even baked Virginia ham and southern fried chicken, you may become a total refugee from your hotel dining room.

Regrettably, from the customer's—not the owner's—point of view, many of the restaurants in Cascais tend to be overcrowded in summer, as they are so popular and quite reasonably priced. However, since many are excellent, press on to the next recommendation if you can't find a seat at your first choice. What follows is a wide-ranging survey of the best of the lot, in all price ranges.

The Top Choices

Restaurant Albatroz, 100 Rua Frederico Arouca (tel. 28-28-21). One of the finest dining experiences along the Costa do Sol can be found at this elegantly decorated restaurant, part of the most famous hotel along the coast (see my previous recommendation). Its summer-style decor is inviting year round. It's best to begin with an apéritif on the covered terrace high above the sea.

Afterward you'll be ushered into a glistening dining room. There, between walls pierced by large sheets of glass, under an alternately beamed and lattice-covered ceiling, you can enjoy some of the finest cuisine in Portugal. Your repast might include poached salmon, partridge stew, steak Albatroz, or a savory version of stuffed crab. For dessert, your choice will range from crêpes suzette to an iced soufflé. Accompanying your meal will be a wide selection of Portuguese and international wines. Full meals cost from 5,500$ ($35.75) per person, and reservations are necessary. Hours are daily from 12:30 to 3 p.m. and 7:30 to 10 p.m.

Restaurante O Pescador, 9 Rua das Flores (tel. 28-20-54). The name (the Fisherman), the lane (the Street of Flowers), and the proximity to the fish market may lead you to expect a simple café. Pescador is, however, considered the best restaurant in Cascais for fish. Its *caldeirada de lagosta com frango,* on which the tab fluctuates daily, is made with fresh lobster and tender chicken, simmered in a base sauce of cognac and rum with the natural juices, then served in a crockery pot. Even if you decide to forgo the house specialty, you may not want to pass up *sopa marisco* (shellfish soup), which is prepared with a savory tomato base and flavored with a sprig of mint. One appealing recommendation is *bacalhau* (codfish) *à pescador.* Finally, another Portuguese dish is *espeteda de lulas com gambas* (shrimp). If you forgo the high-priced lobster, your tab is likely to range in price from 4,000$ ($26) to 5,000$ ($32.50). Food is served from noon to 3 p.m. and 7:30 to 11 p.m.

The decor is tavern style, with hand-hewn beams, iron lanterns, cork and wood paneling, lobster baskets, ships' models, smoked fish and meats, and strings of garlic, red pepper, and onions. An appetizing table in the front displays a selection of prepared foods, fruit, wines, and cheeses.

Other Well-Known Restaurants

Reijos Restaurant, 35 Rua Frederico Arouca (tel. 28-03-11). First, you should be warned that it's likely to be crowded, and that you'll either have to wait for a table or abandon all hope in high season. This intimate, informal bistro is that good. The fine foods of two countries, the United States and Portugal, are combined on the menu, and the result is altogether pleasing. An American citizen, Ray Ettinger, long ago teamed up with a Portuguese, Tony Brito, pooling their talents in the running of this successful enterprise.

At times, to the homesick Mr. Ettinger, nothing is more delectable than roast beef à l'inglese or baked Virginia ham. Other popular items include lobster thermidor, peppersteak, and shrimp curry. From Macão, two Chinese dishes are prepared at your table: beef with garden peppers, and shrimp and cucumbers. Fresh seafood includes sole, sea bass, garoup, and fresh salmon, as well as the famous *bacalhau à Reijos* (dry codfish baked in the oven with a cheese sauce). Unlike many European restaurants, Reijos serves fresh vegetables at no extra cost with its main dishes. In addition, it has an outstanding selection of desserts made on the premises by Mr. Ettinger from fresh seasonal ingredients. Be prepared to spend from 2,500$ ($16.25) per person for dinner. Lunch is served daily from 12:30 to 3:30 p.m.; dinner, 7 to 11 p.m. (telephone first). The service is excellent.

O Pipas, 1-B Rua das Flores (tel. 286-45-01). If you order shellfish here, a meal can be very expensive. Otherwise, this popular restaurant offers well-prepared food at acceptable prices. Many diners consider it the finest independent (outside the hotels) restaurant at the resort. It stands on a teeming street of restaurants whose pavement is covered with black and white mosaics. The decor is Portuguese bistro style, with racks of exposed wine bottles, and big picture windows letting in sunlight and views of the busy street outside. Menu items include lobster, clams, shellfish of all kinds (including oysters), and several preparations of sole, along with a few meat dishes, especially beef O Pipas. Full meals begin at 2,800$ ($18.20). Hours are daily from noon to 3:30 p.m. and 7 to 11:30 p.m.

Restaurante O Batel, 4 Travessa das Flores (tel. 28-02-15), fronts the fish market. Styled as a country inn, it doesn't overdo with touristy gimmicks. The atmosphere is semirustic, with rough white walls and beamed ceilings. A display indicates the ingenuity of the chef, his wares enhanced by a basket of figs, plums, peaches, and fresh flowers. The prices are reasonable, and that, balanced with the superb viands, explains why the tiny tables are usually filled at every meal. Lobster Thermidor and lobster stewed in cognac are the house specialties, but the price on these items changes daily. For something less expensive, I recommend Cascais sole with banana, a savory dish of clams with cream, and mixed shellfish with rice. For an appetizer, you can try prawn cocktail. To complete your meal, such desserts as pineapple with madeira wine are offered. *Wine tip:* Order a Casal Mendes rosé, a cool choice. Tabs begin at 2,500$ ($16.25). The restaurant serves daily from noon to 3 p.m. and 7 to 10:30 p.m.

Restaurante Gil Vicente, 22-30 Rua dos Navegantes (tel. 28-20-32). This is the kind of bistro you usually find on a back street in a town along the Côte d'Azur. Set on the rise of a hill above the harbor, it was converted from a fisherman's cottage. Both the cuisine and the ambience reflect the mood of its owner, who sees to it that excellent meals are served. Hours are from 12:30 to 3 p.m. and 7:30 to 11 p.m. except on Monday. The name of the tavern, Gil Vicente, honors the 16th-century father of Portuguese drama, virtually the Iberian Shakespeare, if you will. The decor of the restaurant is simple—a setting of plaster walls, an old stone fireplace, windows recessed with pots of greenery. An ornate iron washstand has been adapted for condiments, and the walls contain heads of old iron bedsteads, gaily painted.

You may be won over by the cooking (pâté, crêpes, shellfish, or grilled chicken and steaks)—and the reasonable tariffs. To whet your appetite, try the assortment of hors d'oeuvres, the pâté maison, or the bisque of shellfish. At least three main dishes hit the mark every night: sole Colbert, sole delicia, and grilled steak with mushrooms. Among the desserts, you can order a fruit salad or a chocolate mousse, or a banana flambé. You can dine well for 2,200$ ($14.50) and up.

John Bull (Britannia Restaurant), 4-A Largo Luís de Camões (tel. 28-01-54). With its black-and-white timbered Elizabethan façade, this centrally located pub and restaurant is a wedge of England. In the street-floor pub, the John Bull, you can order an iced pint of lager. The setting is appropriate—wood paneling, oak beams, a fireplace, crude tavern stools and tables, pewter pots, and ceramic jugs. The meals at the second-floor Britannia Restaurant feature a medley of English and Portuguese, even American dishes. American southern fried chicken and T-bone steak are familiar Yankee favorites. For English tastes, specialties include cottage pie. An average meal here will cost from 2,200$ ($14.50). Hours are daily from 12:30 to 3:30 p.m. and 7:30 to 11:30 p.m.

Restaurant Baluarte, Avenida Dom Carlos I (tel. 286-54-71). This airy and contemporary restaurant often attracts a chic clientele, who understand that a meal here can be expensive, but is usually worth the escudos. It stands across the street from the waters of the port, behind a glass-fronted façade whose windows are separated from the sidewalk by a small but well-maintained cluster of flowerbeds. Inside you can enjoy a drink on one of the white barrel-shaped chairs of the bar before heading for the dining room. Full meals, priced from 4,000$ ($26), might include sea bass Ribatejo style, sole with almonds, Florentine-style snapper, ravioli carbonara, lobster bisque, and a large variety of shellfish dishes, including mixed seafood au gratin. Good service and fresh ingredients are the norm here, to be experienced daily from noon to 3 p.m. and 7:30 to 11 p.m.

Visconde da Luz, Jardim Visconde da Luz (tel. 286-68-48). The location of this well-known restaurant is one of its most appealing features. It sits within a low-slung bungalow at the edge of a park in the center of Cascais. The view from the windows encompasses rows of lime trees and towering sycamores where flocks of birds congregate at dusk (so be duly warned if you're walking under these trees). Inside, the decor is a modernized form of art nouveau, complete with mirrors, touches of scarlet, and a polite, uniformed staff eager to cater to your wishes. Before you enter, you might be interested in looking at the blue-and-white-tile kitchen. The food is well prepared with fresh ingredients. A meal, costing from 4,000$ ($26) to 5,000$ ($32.50), might include fried sole, shellfish, pork with clams, seafood curry, and clams in garlic sauce, finished off with an almond cake for dessert. Open from noon to 4 p.m. and 7 p.m. to midnight. Closed Monday.

Os Doze, 71 Rua Frederico Arouca (tel. 28-11-58), is an intimate tavern restaurant behind a stone façade and a thick wooden door on a busy pedestrian street in the center of town. The heart and soul of the place rest in the attentions of its owner, who will happily compose a menu selection for you if you are at all undecided about what to order. Within his small enclave, you can enjoy a seafood curry, avocado with shrimp, Portuguese oysters, chicken piri-piri (it's hot), or entrecôte bordelaise. He always has a wide selection of fresh fish, and you might try his delectable grilled sole or whiting sautéed in breadcrumbs. Full meals, costing from 2,500$ ($16.25), are served from noon to 2:30 p.m. and 7 to 10:30 p.m.; closed Tuesday evening and all day Wednesday.

Restaurante Alaúde, 8 Largo Luís de Camões (tel. 28-02-87). The blue tile façade of this convivial restaurant opens onto a statue-centered square teeming with vacationing Europeans. Its famous neighbor, the John Bull, frequently serves as the cocktail lounge for clients who eventually stroll over to Alaúde for dinner. The square onto which it opens is sometimes so crowded that it's referred to as "the living room of Cascais," offering plenty to see from the vantage point at one of this restaurant's outdoor tables. If you prefer, you can select a seat inside, enjoying one of several well-prepared Portuguese specialties. These include such dishes as sardines in olive oil with tomatoes, several preparations of scampi, clams of the house, and a grilled melange of shellfish. Full meals cost upward from 2,100$ ($13.65). The establishment is open from 10 a.m. to midnight seven days a week.

The Budget Range

Eduardo, 3 Largo das Grutas (tel. 28-19-01), is a rustic restaurant that offers good value. It's named for its French owner, Edouard de Beaulear, who turns out a selection of savory Gallic meals. The food is well-prepared, especially the French dishes. The average meal costs from 2,000$ ($13). Eduardo is open from noon to 3 p.m. and 7 p.m. to midnight daily except Wednesday.

Grande Tasca, 3 Rua Sebastião José de Carvalho e Melo (tel. 28-11-40), is operated by Cristina de Araújo, who speaks English fluently. If you don't order expensive shellfish platters, you'll find a large variety of specialties at reasonable prices. These are likely to include chicken surprise, steak Bali-Bali, shrimp on the spit, and several other dishes. The average meal in this rustic tavern costs from 1,500$ ($9.75). The restaurant is open daily from noon to 4 p.m. and from 7 p.m. to midnight. The bar, however, remains open throughout the day, and its summer hours are daily from 9 a.m. to midnight.

---

4. Guincho

Guincho means caterwaul, screech, shriek, yell, the cry that swallows make while darting among the air currents over the wild sea. These swallows at Guincho are to be seen all year, unlike their fickle fair-weather counterparts at San Juan Capistrano,

California. Sometimes at night the sea, driven into a frenzy, howls like a wailing banshee, and that too is guincho. The settlement is near the westernmost point on the European continent, known to the Portuguese as **Cabo da Roca**. The beaches are spacious and sandy; the sunshine, incandescent; the nearby promontories, jutting out amid white-tipped Atlantic waves, spectacular. The windswept dunes are backed by wooded hills, and to the east the Sêrra de Sintra is silhouetted upon the distant horizon.

Praia do Guincho draws large beach crowds each season. The undertow is treacherous—be forewarned. It's wise to keep in mind the advice of Jennings Parrott, writing in the *International Herald Tribune:* "If you are caught up by the current, don't fight it. Don't panic. The wind forces it to circle, so you will be brought back to shore." A local fisherman, however, advises that you take a box lunch along. "Sometimes it takes several days to make this circle."

Guincho lies about four miles from Cascais, about six from Estoril. To reach it, you have to either drive or take a bus from Cascais. One of the primary reasons for coming to Guincho is to sample its seafood restaurants, described below. You can try, for example, the crayfish-size, box-jaw lobsters known as *bruxas,* which in Portuguese means sorcerer, wizard, witch doctor, even a nocturnal moth. To be totally Portuguese, you must also sample the barnacles, called *percêbes,* meaning to perceive, to understand, to comprehend. After devouring these creatures, many foreign visitors fail to comprehend or perceive their popularity with the Portuguese. The fresh lobsters and crabs are cultivated in nearby shellfish beds, a fascinating sight.

If you're staying over at one of the recommendations described below, the night calls of the "sirens" may enrapture you.

FOOD AND LODGING

A fine choice is the **Hotel do Guincho,** Guincho, 2750 Cascais (tel. 01/285-04-91). In the 17th century an army of local masons built one of the most forbidding fortresses along the coast, within a few hundred feet of the most westerly point in Europe. The twin towers that flank the vaguely Moorish-looking façade still stand sentinel amid a sun-bleached terrain of sand and rock. Today, however, the inhabitants are more likely to be well-heeled representatives of a more glamorous world. In the past they've included Orson Welles, who was reportedly fascinated by the mist and the surging roar of the waves as they dashed upon the nearby cliffs. The late Princess Grace also found the place fascinating, as have prime ministers of both Italy and Portugal.

You'll enter through an enclosed courtyard, in the center of which sits the well that used to provide water for the garrison. The public rooms are filled with all the antique trappings of an aristocratic private home. In cold weather a fire might be blazing in one of the granite-framed fireplaces, illuminating the thick carpets and the century-old furniture. Each of the small but comfortable bedrooms is sheltered behind a thick pine door, heavily banded with iron. Each room has a vaulted stone ceiling, the keystone of which is carved into one of the 36 different heraldic shields. In addition to the wealth of 17th-century trappings, every room contains a color TV, mini-bar, private bath, and phone. Depending on the season and the accommodation, singles cost 11,400$ ($74.10) to 17,600$ ($114.40) daily, while doubles rent for 12,300$ ($79.95) to 20,300$ ($131.95). A few small but elegant suites, some with their own fireplaces, cost from 17,000$ ($110.50) to 25,000$ ($162.50), depending on the season. Half-board is priced at another 3,200$ ($20.80) per person daily.

If you're exploring the coast, the hotel also makes an ideal luncheon or dinner stop. Some celebrities have declared that many of their most perfect meals in Portugal were served here on a sunny afternoon, within sight of the surf a short distance away. The chef prepares such specialties as pâté of pheasant with morels, seafood salad, lobster newburg, grilled black grouper with tartare sauce, and roast suckling pig Portuguese style. Full à la carte meals begin at 4,000$ ($26) and are served every day of the week from 12:30 to 2:30 p.m. and 7:30 to 9:30 p.m.

Estalagem Muchaxo, Praia do Guincho, 2750 Cascais (tel. 01/285-02-21), was begun some four decades ago as a simple straw hut set up on rugged wave-dashed rocks, with the founding father selling brandy and coffee to the fishermen. Gradually, the senior Muchaxo started to cook for them. In time, beach-loving Germans discovered the place, and eventually even royalty arrived wanting to be fed. Nowadays the new has absorbed the old, yet the straw shack remains to please traditionalists. The Muchaxo family operates this overblown hacienda, placing emphasis on the rustic blended with a mild dose of the contemporary. The Estalagem is rectangular in shape, with windows of bedrooms overlooking either the courtyard or the nearby coast and hills. At one side, thrust out onto rock walls, is a swimming pool with terraces and diving boards. After a day of swimming, guests gather in the chalet living room to warm themselves at the huge raised stone fireplace.

There's a choice of two dining rooms, one modern, the other with bamboo ceiling, staccato black and white covered tables, and hand-painted provincial furniture. People drive from miles around just to sample the Muchaxo cuisine, highly praised by such discriminating Iberian travelers as author James A. Michener. The adventurous will begin their meals with barnacles, described previously. The house specialty is lobster, Barraca style, but the price is likely to change daily. An order of grilled sea bass is decidedly less expensive. A dish worth recommending is the chateaubriand. However, unless your throat is lined with asbestos, avoid ordering the chicken with piri-piri sauce made with hot pepper from Angola. One diner is said to have fainted after tasting this concoction. An excellent finish to a meal would be banana fritters. A typical meal here will cost 4,500$ ($29.25) to 5,500$ ($35.75).

Those who want to stay for the night will find a choice of 24 rooms—the most expensive directly overlooking the sea, the middle-price group with side views of the ocean, and the cheapest facing the blue-green hills on the horizon. Depending on the season, a single costs from 6,000$ ($39) to 11,400$ ($74.10) nightly. Two persons can stay here for 6,500$ ($42.25) to 12,000$ ($78). All rooms have private baths, phones, and central heating. Each unit is unique, although most of them have basic stark-white walls with beamed ceilings.

Mar do Guincho Estalagem, Praia do Guincho, Ghincho, 2750 Cascais (tel. 01/285-02-51). While this inn contains relatively inexpensive bedrooms, its success stems from its superb kitchen. The stone inn is simple, uncluttered, set on a low cliff, with its bedrooms facing the pounding surf. From the dining room and bar, decorated with hanging plants and flowers, you have a view of the beach below. Shellfish is the house specialty, and you may want to try the shrimp soup. You can select barnacles, mussels, or stuffed crab from the à la carte menu. Although its price is beyond the means of many diners, you can also enjoy a fresh and tasty broiled or grilled lobster if you want to splurge. The sweet-tasting, freshly caught clams served in their natural state are tempting. Prawns Mar do Guincho, roasted in madeira wine, are one of the specialties of the house. Meat eaters will find another specialty particularly attractive, an excellent roast lamb, and you can also order grilled steak au poivre. A wide range of Portuguese fruits is offered for dessert, or you might prefer almond cake. A regular meal will cost from 2,000$ ($13). Food is served daily from 1 to 3 p.m. and 8 to 11:30 p.m.

Sea-view double bedrooms cost 8,500$ ($55.25), with a continental breakfast included. Slightly cheaper rooms are available sans sea view. The bedrooms contain private baths and balconies. If you're tempted to stay here, you'll dine well, live informally in casual attire, sunbathe, play in the surf, and fall asleep listening to the constant rhythm of the waves breaking on the rocks below your balcony.

Restaurante Porto de Santa Maria, Estrada do Guincho (tel. 01/285-02-40). If you decide to drive to the isolated stretch of roadside where this restaurant is located, you won't be alone. Hundreds of vacationing Europeans and Portuguese might decide to join you, especially in summer. This restaurant is one of the most appealing of its type along the coast, and it also serves some of the best seafood. A doorman will usher you into the low-lying seafront building, where large windows take in views of the sometimes-treacherous surf.

The beige-and-white decor is highlighted with an enormous aquarium made from white marble and thick sheets of glass, within which trapped crustaceans such as lobsters wave their claws. A central serving table is laden with fruits and flowers. The polite staff serves every conceivable form of shellfish, priced by the gram, as well as such house specialties as grilled sole. Shellfish rice, known as *arroz de mariscos,* is the most popular specialty, and it's usually served to two persons. Full meals cost from 3,000$ ($19.50). You'll probably want to taste the rondelles of pungent sheep's-milk cheese that await the arrival of guests at each table. Hours are daily from 12:15 to 3:30 p.m. and 7 to 10:30 p.m.

5. Queluz ~~Passed~~

Back in Lisbon, we strike out this time on quite a different excursion. On the highway to Sintra, 9½ miles from the capital, **Palácio de Quelez,** 2745 Lisboa (tel. 01/95-00-39), shimmers in the sunlight, a brilliant example of the rococo in Portugal, inspired in part by Versailles.

Pedro III ordered its construction in 1747, and the work dragged on until 1787. The architect Mateus Vicente de Oliveira was later joined by French decorator and designer Jean-Baptiste Robillon. The latter was largely responsible for the planning of the garden and lakeland setting, through which the promiscuous queen, Carlotta Joaquina, raced to her next indiscretion.

Pedro III had actually adapted an old hunting pavilion that had belonged to the Marquis Castelo Rodrigo. Later the pavilion came into the possession of the Portuguese royal family. Pedro III liked it so much that he decided to make it his summer residence. What the visitor of today sees is not exactly what it was in 1787. Queluz suffered a lot during the French invasions, and almost all of its belongings were transported to Brazil when the royal family went into exile.

A fire in 1934 destroyed a great deal of Queluz, but tasteful and sensitive reconstruction has restored the light-hearted aura of the 18th century.

The topiary effects, with closely trimmed vines and sculptured boxhedges, are highlighted by blossoming mauve petunias and red geraniums. Fountain pools on which lilies float are lined with blue azulejos and reflect the muted facade, the statuary, and the finely cut balustrades.

Inside, you can wander through the dressing room of the queen, lined with painted panels depicting a children's romp; stroll through the Don Quixote Chamber (Dom Pedro was born here and returned from Brazil to die in the same bed); pause in the Music Room, complete with a French grande piano-forte and an 18th-century English harpischord; and stand in the mirrored throne room adorned with crystal chandeliers. The Portuguese still hold state banquets here.

Festooning the palace are all the eclectic props of the romantic era—the inevitable chinoiserie panels (these from the Portuguese overseas province of Macão), Florentine marbles from quarries once worked by Michelangelo, Iberian and Flemish tapestries, Empire antiques, indigo blue ceramics from Delft, 18th-century Hepplewhite armchairs, porcelains from Austria, carpets from Rabat, Portuguese Chippendale furnishings, and wood pieces (jacaranda) from Brazil—all of which are of exquisite quality. When they visited Portugal, Presidents Eisenhower, Carter, and Reagan were housed in the 30-chambered Pavilion of D. Maria I, as was Queen Elizabeth II on two occasions, and the Prince and Princess of Wales. These storybook chambers, refurbished by the Portuguese government, are said to have reverberated with the rantings of the grief-stricken monarch Maria I, who, it is alleged, had to be strapped to her bed at times. Before becoming mentally ill, she was a bright, intelligent, and brave woman who did a great job as ruler of her country in a troubled time.

The palace is open daily except Tuesday and holidays from 10 a.m. to 1 p.m. and 2 to 5 p.m. From June 1 to September 30, admission is 400$ ($2.60). During other months, the charge is 200$ ($1.30). It is free Sunday morning. It costs only 50$ (35¢) if you wish to visit only the gardens. From Lisbon, you can visit Queluz by a train departing from the central station at the Rossio, costing 60$ (40¢) for a one-way ride.

DINING IN AN 18TH-CENTURY KITCHEN

If you have only two or three meals in all of Portugal, take one of them at **Cozinha Velha** (Old Kitchen), Palácio Nacional de Queluz (tel. 95-02-32). Once it was the kitchen of the palace, built in the grand style; now it has been converted into a colorful dining room that finds favor with gourmets, royalty, and the average visitor seeking a romantic setting for a fine dinner.

The entrance is through a garden patio. The dining room is like a small chapel, with high stone arches, a walk-in free-standing fireplace, marble columns, and the original spits. Along one side is a 20-foot marble chef's table that's a virtual still life of the culinary skill of the chef, augmented by baskets of fruit and vases of flowers. You sit on ladderback chairs in a setting of shiny copper, oil paintings, and torchères. And the trained waitresses are costumed in regional dress.

Fortunately, meals are served seven days a week (luncheon, noon to 3 p.m.; dinner, 7:30 to 10 p.m.). I suggest the hors d'oeuvres for two persons, followed by such main courses as filet steak, poached sea bass, grilled pork on a spit, or whiting with capers. To finish, you might try the island cheese or a vanilla soufflé for two. Expect to spend from 4,000$ ($26), including your drink, for a complete meal.

---

6. Sintra ✓

"It is indeed a fairytale setting and gives one the feeling that this is where Sleeping Beauty must have rested all those years." These were the words of a publicist singing the praises of Sintra. Writers have been doing that ever since Portugal's greatest poet Luís Vas de Camões proclaimed its glory in *Os Lusíadas* (The Portuguese). Lord Byron called it "glorious Eden" when he and John Cam Hobhouse included Sintra in their grand tour of 1809. English romantics thrilled to its description in the poet's autobiographical *Childe Harold's Pilgrimage*.

Picture a town on a hillside, decaying birthday-cake villas covered with azulejos coming loose in the damp mist hovering like a veil over Sleeping Beauty. What would Sintra be without its luxuriant vegetation? It's all here: camellias for melancholic romantics, ferns behind which lizards dart, pink and purple bougainvillaea over garden trelliswork, red geraniums on wrought-iron balconies, eucalyptus branches fluttering in the wind, lemon trees studding the groves, and honey-sweet mimosa scenting the air. Be duly warned: there are those who visit Sintra, fall under its spell, and stay forever.

Sintra is one of the oldest towns in the country. When the Crusaders captured it in 1147, they fought bitterly against the Moors firmly entrenched in their hilltop castle, the ruins of which remain today.

The town, 18 miles from Lisbon, is on the northern slope of the granite Sintra Range. A 45-minute train ride from the neo-Manueline railway station at the Rossio in Lisbon will deposit you here. Visitors staying in the Costa do Sol hotels can make bus connections at both Cascais and Estoril. Sintra is also visited on many organized tours departing from Lisbon. But this latter method allows no time for personal discovery, which is essentially what Sintra is all about.

THE SIGHTS

The specific sights of Sintra are set forth below, but the task of selection is difficult. Byron put it well: "Ah me! What hand can pencil guide, or pen, to follow half on which the eye dilates."

National Palace of Sintra

Palácio Nacional de Sintra (tel. 923-00-85) was a royal palace until 1910. Its last royal inhabitant was Queen Maria Pía, the Italian grandmother of Manuel II, the last king of Portugal. Much of the palace was constructed in the days of the first Manuel, the Fortunate.

The palace opens onto the central square of the town. Outside, two conically shaped chimney towers form the most distinctive landmark on the Sintra skyline. Long before the arrival of the Crusaders under Afonso Henriques, this was a summer palace of Moorish sultans, filled with dancing harem girls who performed in front of bubbling fountains. The original was torn down, and the Moorish style of architecture was incorporated in latter-day versions of the palace. The entire effect is rather a conglomeration of styles, with Gothic and the Manueline predominant. The glazed earthenware tiles, or azulejos, lining many of the chambers are among the best you'll find in Portugal.

The Swan Room was a favorite of João I, one of the founding kings, father of Henry the Navigator, and husband of Philippa of Lancaster. It is said that one day the English queen came upon her king embracing one of the ladies of the court. Apparently she did not hold a grudge against him for this one indiscretion, but it grew into a court scandal of which the king became painfully aware. Hoping to end speculation and save his wife further embarrassment, he called in his decorators and gave them a secret mission. The room was locked. When the doors were finally opened to the ladies of the court, they marched in, only to discover that the ceiling was covered with magpies. The symbol of the chattering birds scored a point, and a new subject of gossip was discovered. Guides now call the salon the Chamber of the Magpies.

The Room of the Sirens or Mermaids is one of the most elegant in the palace. In the Heraldic or Stag Room, coats-of-arms of aristocratic Portuguese families and hunting scenes are depicted. From most of these rooms, wide windows look out onto attractive vistas of the Sintra mountain range. Tile-fronted stoves are found in the Old Kitchen, where the feasts of yore were held, especially game banquets in the reign of Carlos I, the king assassinated in 1908.

The palace is rich in paintings and Iberian and Flemish tapestries. But it is at its best when you wander into a tree- and plant-shaded patio and listen to the water of a fountain. Perhaps the young king Sebastião sat here lost in the dreams of glory that would one day take him and his country on an ill-fated mission to North Africa, a mission that would cost him his life.

As you approach the palace, you can buy a ticket at the kiosk on your left. The cost is 150$ ($1), one of the best investments you'll make in all of Portugal. Visiting hours are daily from 10 a.m. to 4:30 p.m., except on Wednesday when it is closed.

The Pena Palace

Towering over Sintra, the **Palácio Nacional da Pena** (tel. 923-02-27) appeals to special tastes. From its perch on a plateau about 1,500 feet above sea level, it stands like a medieval fortress on one peak, looking at the ruins of the old Moorish castle on the opposite hill. Part of the fun of visiting it is the ride up the verdant winding road, through the Parque das Merendas.

At the top you come upon a castle that was called a "soaring agglomeration of towers, cupolas, and battlemented walls" by *National Geographic*. The inspiration behind this castle in the sky was Ferdinand of Saxe-Coburg-Gotha, the husband of Maria II.

Of course, Ferdinand needed a German to help him build this fantasy. While dreams of the Middle Ages danced in his head, Baron Eschwege arrived. You can still see a sculptured likeness of the baron by looking out from the Pena at a huge rock across the way. Romantically, the architect fancied himself a soldier, armed with a halberd.

In the early 16th century Manuel the Fortunate had ordered a monastery built on these lofty grounds for the Jerónimos monks. Even today you can visit a cloister and a small ogival chapel that the latter-day builders decided to preserve.

Crossing over a drawbridge, you'll enter the palace proper, whose last royal occupant was Queen Amélia. On a long-ago morning in 1910, she clearly saw that monarchy in Portugal was drawing to an end. Having already lost her husband and her soldier son two years before, she was determined not to lose her second offspring, King Manuel II. Gathering her most precious possessions and only the small family heirlooms that could be packed quickly, she fled to Mafra where her son waited. Behind she left Pena Palace, not to see it again until 1945 when she returned to Portugal under much more favorable conditions. Pena has remained much as Amélia left it, and that is part of its fascination; it emerges as a rare record of European royal life in the halcyon days preceding World War I.

For an entrance fee of 300$ ($1.95), you can visit the palace daily from 10 a.m. until 4:45 p.m., except on Monday when it is closed.

Pena Park was designed and planted in a four-year span beginning in 1846. Again, Ferdinand was the controlling factor behind the landscaping. What he achieved was one of the most spectacular parks in Portugal, known for the scope of its plant and tree life. For an eye-opening vista of the park and the palace, you can make the ascent to **Cruz Alta.**

If you're not driving, you can take a taxi or the bus that departs from the main square of Sintra from May to September, heading for the palace, a 20-minute run. If you choose to walk, be warned that it's an arduous trip from the square, taking about two hours even if you're in good walking condition.

The Moorish Castle

The fortification, **Castelo dos Mouros,** had been around for a long time when Scandinavian crusaders in 1147 besieged and successfully captured it from its Moorish occupants. It was built sometime between the 8th and 9th centuries at a position 1,350 feet above sea level. The consort of Maria II, Ferdinand, the German responsible for Pena Palace, attempted restoration in the 19th century, but was relatively unsuccessful.

To reach its decaying ramparts, you take a path that's a ten-minute walk. The path branches off from the road Parque das Merendas (a small sign points the way). There's a parking area for your car, and a guide will send you in the right direction. From the royal tower, the view of Sintra, its palace and castle, and of the Atlantic coast is spectacular. Go between 8 a.m. and sunset daily.

Monserrate

An Englishman, Sir Francis Cook, set out between 1846 and 1850 to make Lord Byron's dream of a glorious Eden a reality. Bringing in landscape artists and flora from everywhere from Africa to Norway, he planned a botanical garden, the rival of which is not to be found either in Spain or Portugal.

The garden scales the slope of a hill—paths cut through to hidden oases—and you need to give it the better part of the afternoon. Walking back is rough for all but seasoned hill scalers. However, it's worth the descent.

At the bottom, Cook built his **Palácio de Monserrate.** It seemed that in his Eden, only a Moorish temple would do. But when Cook died, Monserrate faced a troubled future. An English manufacturer purchased the property and set out virtually to destroy Cook's dreams. He began by selling the antiques in the palácio, and it's said that he made so much money on the sale that he was paid back for all the cash he sank into Monserrate. He wasn't satisfied. When news leaked out to Lisbon that he was going to subdivide the park and turn it into a housing development of villas, the government belatedly intervened, and well that it did. When you see Monserrate, you'll surely agree that it belongs to all the people, preserved and well-maintained.

Lilies float on cool fountains, flowers scent the air, ferns scale the hillside, northern spruce grows tall, and flora from Africa thrives as if it were in its native habitat. Admission is free. The park is open daily from 10 a.m. to 6 p.m.

One final stopover, lying outside of Sintra, merits exploration.

Convento de Santa Cruz dos Capuchos

Dom Alvaro de Castro ordered that this unusually structured convent be built for the Capuchins in 1560. Cork was used so extensively in its construction that it is sometimes known as the cork monastery.

You walk up a moss-covered path, like a wayfarer of old approaching for his dole. Ring the bell, and a guide (not a monk) will appear to show you in and out of the miniature cells. The convent is in a secluded area, 4½ miles from Sintra.

It appears forlorn, forgotten. Even when it was in use, it probably wasn't too lively. The Capuchins who lived here, perhaps eight in all, had a penchant for the most painstaking of detailed work. For example, they lined the walls of their monastery with cork-bark tiles and seashells. They also carved a chapel out of rock, using cork for insulation.

When making toilets or "refrigerators," they displayed ingenuity. A hospital was even installed into the most cramped of quarters. Their monastery is perhaps the coziest in the world. Outside, one of them found time to fresco an altar in honor of St. Francis of Assisi.

In 1834, they left suddenly; but fortunately the monastery they left behind wasn't destroyed by vandals. From April to October, it is open daily from 9 a.m. to 6 p.m. The rest of the year, it is open from 9 a.m. to 5 p.m. Admission is 50$ (35¢). For information, phone 923-01-37.

UPPER-BRACKET LIVING AND DINING

I especially like the **Hotel Palácio de Seteais,** 8 Avenida Bocage, Seteais, 2710 Sintra (tel. 01/923-32-00), a palace converted into a hotel. Lord Byron worked on *Childe Harold* in the front garden. The palace is approached via a long private encircling driveway, past shade trees, a wide expanse of lawn, and yew hedges. The stone architecture is formal, dominated by an arched entryway. Seteais looks older than it is, having been built in the late 18th century by a Dutch Gildmeester. It was subsequently taken over and restored by the fifth Marquês de Marialva, who sponsored many receptions and galas for the aristocrats of his day.

The palácio is on the crest of a hill, with most of its drawing rooms, galleries, and chambers overlooking the formal terraces, flower garden, and vista toward the sea. Upon entering there is a long galleried hall, a dramatic staircase, with white and gilt balustrades and columns, leading to the lower-level dining room, drinking lounge, and garden terraces. Along the corridor are tapestries, groupings of formal

European furniture, and hand-woven decorative carpets. On the left is a library and an adjoining music room, furnished with period pieces. The main drawing room is decorated with antiques and a fine mural extending around the cove and onto the ceiling. Large bronze chandeliers with crystal add to the luster. The guest book reads like a Who's Who.

Don't just drive up to the entrance and expect to be given shelter. There are only 18 rooms (all with private bath), so advance reservations are definitely needed. Housed in a beautiful room furnished with antiques or reproductions, you'll pay from 21,500$ ($139.75) daily for one person to 23,000$ ($149.50) for two. A continental breakfast, service, and taxes are included. The hotel has a swimming pool and two tennis courts.

Lunch or dinner is special, and it's possible to come here just for your meal. In summer, the tables are graced with clusters of pink or blue hydrangea from the garden, and each is set with stemware and silver. The set meal for 4,500$ ($29.25) consists of four courses, with continental and regional dishes. The hors d'oeuvres are among the best, especially the crayfish and fish mousse. The dessert trolley is intriguing—pastries with light rich cream blended with a flaky crust and fruits. After-dinner coffee is taken on the adjoining terrace and loggia or in the dining room. Food is served daily from 12:30 to 2:30 p.m. and 7:30 to 9:30 p.m.

A FOUR-STAR HOTEL

The finest hotel in Sintra is the modern, airy **Hotel Tivoli Sintra,** Praça da República, 2710 Sintra (tel. 01/923-35-05), opened in 1981. It lies only a few doors to the right of the Central Hotel (recommended below) and the National Palace. The hotel offers an abundance of modern conveniences, including a garage (most important in Sintra). However, the decorator stuck to the typical Portuguese style, and the combination of modern with traditional is successful. In the cavernous lobby the floors are of marble. Brass lamps are used, and many earth tones are among the colors chosen. The air-conditioned bedrooms are spacious and comfortably furnished, with complete bath, phone, color TV, video, radio, large beds, and big easy chairs for relaxation. The balconies and the public rooms look out onto a wooded hill, with views of some of Sintra's *quintas* (manor houses). The sight, according to readers Peter and Cynthia Hecker, of Berkeley, California, "could have inspired mad Ludwig of Bavaria or at least Walt Disney." In high season two persons can stay here for 13,800$ ($89.70) daily, the price including a continental breakfast. Singles cost 11,800$ ($76.70). The hotel has a panoramic restaurant and bar, a beauty parlor, and a travel agency.

BUDGET HOTELS

A discreetly elegant place to stay is **Estalagem Quinta da Capela,** Monserrate, 2710 Sintra (tel. 01/929-01-70). The Latin motto carved above one of the entrances says it all. *Et in Arcadia Ego,* roughly translated, means "I'm in a country of dreams." The duc de Cadaval built this quinta of two-story stone buildings in the 16th century as a private home. Much later, the American ambassador to Portugal used it as his weekend house before being recalled from his assignment. The buyers of the estate were Marc Zürcher and Arturo Pereira, who began the backbreaking labor of turning it into a hotel just a few years ago.

Today the long expanses of sun-flooded hallways look much as they did when the granite and marble slabs were first laid. The furnishings in the antique-laden public rooms remind guests of a private home. The only concession to modernity is the array of lithographs created by Arturo, a basement-level health club and sauna, and an honor-system bar set out thoughtfully on a spinet piano beside an antique model of an 18th-century schooner under full sail. For additional diversion, a spring-fed swimming pool, with a view over the faraway hills, is at the edge of the property. The beach is ten minutes away for bathers who prefer salt water.

A pair of outlying cottages each contains a kitchenette. Even so, you may still want to ask for one of the seven beautifully furnished accommodations in the main house. No meals are served other than breakfast. Prices, with a continental breakfast included, run from 13,000$ ($84.50) daily in a double and from 11,000$ ($71.50) in a single. A cottage, suitable for up to four persons, rents for 20,000$ ($130) a day.

The romantically baroque castle of the gardens of Monserrate is visible from the sun-washed breakfast room. However, the best view of the sea is from one of the arches that pierce the wall surrounding the formal gardens. There, an outlying chapel sits serenely on a nearby hillock, near the still waters of a stone basin. These waters irrigate the gardens and are fed by a Renaissance-style fountain. The hotel is somewhat remote and difficult to find. Follow the signs toward Seteais from Sintra, passing both the hamlet and gardens of Monserrate, after which you'll detect the imposing stone columns and the sign marking the quinta's entrance.

Quinta de São Thiago, 2710 Sintra (tel. 01/923-29-23) is one of the most desirable places to stay in the Sintra area. Reached along a difficult road, it edges up a side of Sintra mountain. Its origins as a quinta go back to some time in the 1500s, and it's always been a private home. Now, in its role as an inn, it's been refurbished and handsomely furnished with antiques by its proprietors, British-born Nicholas Braddell and his Spanish wife, María Teresa. Visited by Lord Byron in 1809, it enjoys a tranquil woodland setting. Many of the rooms open onto views of the Valley of Colares and the water beyond. All through the 1980s, guests who stayed here enjoyed the many thoughtful touches of the Braddells, who often create a house-party atmosphere. On a hot day, a special delight is the swimming pool, with its views of Monserrate and the coastline along the Atlantic.

In the finest British tradition, tea is offered in the parlor which was transformed from the original kitchen. Dances are held in summer in the music room, and summertime buffets are a feature. Dinner is like eating in the private home of a Portuguese family. The cuisine is both regional and continental. Modern plumbing has been installed, and the quinta bedrooms are comfortably furnished and attractively decorated. Rates range from 13,000$ ($84.50) to 18,000$ ($117) a night for a twin-bedded room, including breakfast. It's also recommended that you book for a satisfying dinner in a lovely setting, at a cost of 4,000$ ($26), including your wine.

Central Hotel, 35 Largo da Rainha D. Amélia, 2710 Sintra (tel. 01/923-09-63), should be given a heavy check with your pencil if you prefer a charming family-owned and -operated village inn offering personalized accommodations and good food. The hotel opens onto the main square of Sintra, facing the National Palace. Because of its location, accommodations facing the square are noisy. The owner, Laura de Jesus Raio, along with her son and daughter-in-law, have created a homelike inn. The façade is inviting, with decorative blue and white tiles and an awning-covered front veranda with dining tables. The interior, especially the bedrooms, reflects the English background of the owners (they lived in Surrey, near London, for seven years and have accumulated some antiques). Each room is furnished individually, with a reliance on fine old pieces—polished woods, inlaid desks. The baths, one to nearly every room, are well designed, with tiles and cheerful colors. The cost for one person in a room with bath is 8,100$ ($52.65) nightly, increasing to 8,500$ ($55.25) for two. A continental breakfast is included. Complete board for two costs 15,700$ ($102.05).

The restaurant of the Central offers a choice of dining on the veranda overlooking the village, or in one of the large interior rooms. The cooking is primarily Portuguese, with such main courses as escalopes of veal in a madeira sauce, veal cutlet Milanese, beef Portuguese, and chateaubriand for two. A traditional dessert, homemade caramel pudding, makes a smooth finish. You can enjoy a complete dinner for 2,000$ ($13) and up. Food is served from 12:30 to 3 p.m. and 8 to 9 p.m. daily.

Estalagem da Raposa, 3 Rua Alfredo Costa, 2710 Sintra (tel. 01/923-04-

65), formerly was a private home that belonged to an old Sintra family. It's been run as an inn for 40 years, and is centrally located, within walking distance of the railroad station. The house is set back from the street in a fenced and flowered yard. The inn is owned by a Lisbon family who make you feel at home immediately. They keep a careful eye on the housekeeping and upkeep of the eight high-ceilinged rental units. Rooms all have tile baths, and they're furnished with old-fashioned pieces that are homey and comfortable. A double room with a continental breakfast rents for 5,300$ ($34.45) in winter, 6,700$ ($43.55) in summer. The maid who keeps the rooms in spotless condition is polite, and she runs right up with a ring of keys to open your door the moment she hears you on the carpeted stairs. You can enjoy regional specialties in the tea room.

WHERE TO DINE

The most reliable choice is the **Hotel Tivoli Sintra,** Praça da República (tel. 923-35-05). Because of its concealment within the concrete-and-glass walls of the town center's most desirable hotel, many visitors might overlook its impressive possibilities as a dining spot. Actually, it serves some of the finest food in town, priding itself on its associations with two hotels of note in nearby Lisbon. Staffed by a battalion of uniformed waiters, the place is capped with a shimmering metallic ceiling, ringed with dark paneling, and illuminated along one side with floor-to-ceiling panoramic windows. Full meals, priced from 5,000$ ($32.50), are served daily from 12:30 to 2:30 p.m. and 7:30 to 9:30 p.m. Specialties include tournedos Rossini, a delectable version of fish soup, filet of turbot elegantly prepared house style with mushrooms and garlic, and seafood.

Galeria Real, Rua Tude de Sousa, in São Pedro de Sintra (tel. 923-16-61), is a unique mixture of antique galleries and an 18th-century-style restaurant. The Galeria Real is one of the most impressive-looking places in Portugal. On the ground floor is a cocktail lounge as well as eight shops crammed with antiques, busts, and paintings. Going up a balustraded staircase, you come to further antique shops and a sumptuous restaurant. The main dining room has a hand-painted beamed ceiling, tile floors, small wooden frame windows, candles and flowers on each table. All this is a perfect setting for gracious dining. Lunch and dinner might start with a melon cocktail, followed by a filet of sole or a *queijada de bacalhau* (a codfish soufflé, which is a specialty of the house). The final course might be veal cutlets or a steak, topped by assorted desserts. On the à la carte menu, expect to spend 3,500$ ($22.75) to 4,500$ ($29.25). Food is served from 12:30 to 4 p.m. and 7:30 to 11 p.m.; closed Monday night.

Restaurante Solar S. Pedro, 12 Praça Don Fernando II, off the Largo da Feira in São Pedro de Sintra (tel. 923-18-60), is run by the helpful and hospitable Francisco Freitas, who speaks English. His place is a popular rendezvous, as diners are drawn not only to his personality but to his good selection of Portuguese cuisine, as well as Italian and French specialties. The lobster crêpes are a favorite, and another specialty is a flavorsome filet of sole. Trout with cream and toasted almonds is perfectly balanced. Also excellent is the steak Café Paris. Many of the beef specialties are distinguished as well, including the peppersteak and the entrecôte with mushrooms. Dinners cost 2,000$ ($13) to 4,000$ ($26). Hours are noon to 3 p.m. and 7:30 to 10 p.m. A lovely windowless room, the restaurant is decorated with tiles, wrought-iron and regional artifacts. It's closed Wednesday.

Tacho Real, 4 Rua da Ferraria (tel. 923-52-77). Sometimes Portuguese diners come all the way from Lisbon to enjoy a well-prepared meal at this restaurant. Fish and meat dishes are deftly handled in the kitchen, which turns out an array of Portuguese regional food and international specialties. Service is efficient and polite. It is open daily except Wednesday from 12:30 to 3 p.m. and 7:30 to 10 p.m. An average meal costs from 3,500$ ($22.75). Reservations are advised.

A Tiborna, 6 Largo Rainha D. Amélia (tel. 923-48-03), is one of the most popular cafés in Sintra (it's also a small restaurant), in an easy-to-find location on the main square, Praça da República. There's a well-stocked bar against one wall, but most drinkers try to secure one of the tables that spill out onto the sidewalk, where you can watch the eternal international parade. Or else you can retreat to the rear to enjoy the chef's array of dishes for the day. The bill of fare is likely to include roast veal Sintra style, escalope of veal with mushrooms, or filet of fish with a shellfish sauce. Expect to spend from 1,400$ ($9.10) for a complete meal. Hours are 8 a.m. to 11:30 p.m. daily except Monday.

Restaurant Alcobaça, 7 Rua dos Padarias (tel. 923-16-51). Popular with English visitors, this shop-size restaurant occupies two floors of a centrally located building on a steep and narrow pedestrian street. The place is *very* local, and consequently provides one of the cheapest meals in town. As you'd expect, Alcobaça serves typical Portuguese cuisine, including roast sardines, caldo verde, hake filet with rice, octopus, Alcobaça chicken, and many other dishes. Meals cost from 1,500$ ($9.75). It is open daily from noon to 4 p.m. and 7 to 10 p.m. It is closed on Wednesday.

7. Colares

At the end of the Sêrra de Sintra toward the sea is Colares, a small town with winding streets, old quintas, bright flowers, and vineyards. It is known for its white and red wines produced from grapes grown on the surrounding sandy soil. The good soil and sea breezes help assure the fundamental ingredient for some of the best wine of the country.

Colares lies 22 miles from Lisbon and five miles from Sintra. Many visitors drive here just to see the wineries, but others seek accommodations, preferring the quiet town to more crowded Sintra.

FOOD AND LODGING

About a mile and a quarter outside Colares stands the **Hotel Miramonte,** Praia das Maçãs, Colares, 2710 Sintra (tel. 01/929-12-30). What a visitor sees from the road appears to be an attractively maintained modern hotel, with an accommodating front porch and a screen of flowers and vines. You'll soon discover that this well-directed hotel stretches almost endlessly through a series of flower-ringed patios, pine-shaded terraces, and one of the most beautifully landscaped swimming pools in the region; there's even a Japanese garden. The well-organized bedrooms are usually inhabited by a quiet, often British, group of vacationers eager to take in the beauty of the surrounding countryside. Since the hotel is relatively isolated, most guests sign up for half board. In high season, a double on this basis goes for 9,000$ ($58.50) to 11,000$ ($71.50) daily, depending on the season. There's mini-golf on the property, plus disco dancing at the hotel three times a week.

Estalagem do Conde, Colares, 2710 Sintra (tel. 01/929-16-52), was originally built as a farmhouse in 1737. In the 1950s it was greatly expanded by a German family as their vacation home. Set on a cul-de-sac in the upper reaches of Colares, it lies just north of the center. It sports two acres of garden, a flagstone-covered terrace, and a sophisticated ownership by Yorkshire-born Dave and Jean Tinsley. It is decorated in a rustic style with a fireplace and regional furniture. The property opens onto a view of the faraway sea, lemon groves, and the hilltops of Sintra. It rents ten bedrooms, including a garden cottage with its own bath. It is open all year except in November, December, and January. The inn charges from 5,000$ ($32.50) to 7,000$ ($45.50) daily in a single and 5,500$ ($35.75) to 8,000$ ($52) in a double. Included in the price is an elegant continental breakfast. Each room contains a private bath, but TVs and radios are deliberately not included to achieve tranquility for guests.

Bistro, 2 Largo Dr. Carlos França (tel. 929-00-16). The best restaurant in all of

Colares is this bistro run by a sophisticated collection of young entrepreneurs. It's located in what used to be the town apothecary shop in a desirably romantic location on the square just to the side of one of the landmark churches. The part owners and managers of this place are German-born Gregor Hill and his Portuguese friend, Amélia Viegas da Silva. A full meal, costing from 2,200$ ($14.30), might include a selection of such dishes as beef Stroganoff, steak filet with potatoes, fried local fish garnished with fresh tomatoes, and an array of both Portuguese or continental specialties. The restaurant is open daily in summer for dinner only, from 7 to 10 p.m. November to March, it is open on Friday for dinner and from noon to 2:30 p.m. and 7 to 10 p.m. on Saturday and Sunday.

---

8. Mafra Palace

Palácio Nacional de Mafra, 2640 Mafra (tel. 523-32), baroque chef d'oeuvre of precision craftsmanship, is an ensemble of discipline, grandeur, and majesty. At the peak of its construction, it is said to have employed a working force of 50,000 Portuguese men. A small town was built just to house the workers. Its master model was El Escorial, that Daedalian maze constructed by Philip II outside Madrid. Mafra's corridors and complex immurements may not be as impressive, nor as labyrinthine, but the diversity of its contents is amazing. The end product was 880 rooms, housing 300 friars, who could look through 4,500 doorways and windows.

That devout king of "peace and prosperity," João V, seemingly couldn't sire an heir, and court gossips openly speculated that he was sterile. One day he casually mentioned to a Franciscan that if he were rewarded with an heir, he would erect a monastery to the order. Apparently the Franciscans, through what the king considered "divine intervention," came through. João produced his heir and Mafra was born, the work beginning in 1717. Originally it was to house 13 friars, but that figure rapidly mushroomed into 300.

It is said that Mafra, 13 years in the making, was built with gold and diamonds pouring in from the new colony of Brazil. Seeing it now, and considering building methods in those days, one wonders how such a task was ever completed in so short a time.

Its more than 110 chimes, made in Antwerp, can be heard from a distance of 12 to 15 miles when they are played at Sunday recital. Holding the chimes are two towers which flank a basilica, capped by a dome that has been compared to that of St. Paul's in London. The inside of the church is a varied assortment of chapels, 11 in all, expertly crafted with detailed jasper reredos, bas-reliefs, and marble statues from Italy. In the monastery is the pride of Mafra, a 40,000-volume library with tomes 200 and 300 years old, many gold-leafed. Viewed by some more favorably than the world-famed library at Coimbra, the room is a study in gilded light, decorated in what has been called grisaille rococo. In the Museum of Religious Art, the collection of elaborately decorated vestments is outstanding.

Following the omnipresent red Sintra marble, you enter the monks' pharmacy, hospital, and infirmary, the beds without mattresses. Later you can explore the spacious kitchens and the penitents' cells, with the flagellation devices used by the monks.

The summer residence of kings, Mafra was home to such members of Portuguese royalty as the banished Queen Carlotta Joaquina. In addition to his love of painting, Carlos I, the Bragança king assassinated at Praça do Comércio in 1908, was also an avid hunter. In one room, he had chandeliers made out of antlers and upholstery of animal skins. His son, who ruled for two years as Manuel II, spent his last night on Portuguese soil at Mafra before fleeing with his mother, Amélia, to England.

You can wander through the trompe l'oeil-ceilinged audience room, the sewing room of Maria I, and the music room of Carlos. Throughout the apartments hang decaying tapestries, taking their place among antiques, ceramics, and silverware.

The charge for admission is 150$ ($1), the hours, 10 a.m. to 5 p.m. From Sintra, you can make bus connections to Mafra, about 25 miles from Lisbon.

FOOD AND LODGING

For good accommodations, I recommend the **Albergaría Castelão,** Avenida 25 de Abril, 2640 Mafra (tel. 061/526-96), which has 34 comfortable rooms furnished with easy chairs, reading lamps, and carpeted floors, all having complete baths, TVs, radios, mini-bars, and phones. Guests can relax in a reading room. Singles cost from 6,000$ ($39) daily and doubles run from 7,300$ ($47.45). The hotel has four bars and a typical wine cellar. The panoramic restaurant, where meals cost from 1,200$ ($7.80), looks over the main street of the village. The food is well prepared. The location of the hotel is excellent, right in the heart of Mafra.

9. Ericeira

Some 32 miles from Lisbon and a quick 13 miles across the countryside from Sintra, this fishing village nestles on the Atlantic shore. Its narrow streets are lined with whitewashed houses, accented by pastel-painted corners and window frames. To the east, the mountains of Sintra appear.

The sea has been giving life to Ericeira for 700 years and continues to do so today. Not only do the fishermen pluck their food from it, but it is the sea, especially the beach, that lures streams of visitors every summer, adding a much-needed shot in the arm to the local economy. Along the coast lobsters are bred in cliffside nursuries, *sêrração*. Anyplace in Ericeira, lagosta is la specialité de la maison.

In 1584 Mateus Alvares arrived in Ericeira from the Azores, claiming to be King Sebastião (The Desired One), who was killed (some say disappeared) on the battlefields of North Africa. Álvares and about two dozen of his chief supporters were finally executed after their defeat by the soldiers of Philip II of Spain; but he is today remembered as the king of Ericeira. It wasn't until an October day in 1910 that the second monumental event occurred at Ericeira. From the harbor, the fleeing Manuel II and his mother, Amélia, set sail on their yacht to a life of exile in England.

For such a small place, there are quite a few sights of religious and historic interest. The **Church of São Pedro** (St. Peter) and the **Misericórdia** (charitable institution) both contain rare 17th- and 18th-century paintings. The **Hermitage of St. Sebastião,** with its Moorish designs, would seem more fitting in North Africa. There is one more hermitage honoring **St. Anthony.**

The chloride-rich spring waters of **Santa Maria** attract health-spa enthusiasts. But it is the crescent-shaped sandy **Praia do Sol** that is the favorite of Portuguese and foreign visitors alike. Ericeira maintains bus connections with both Sintra and Lisbon (you can also take the train from Lisbon to Mafra, where connections can be made).

WHERE TO DINE

If you're passing through for the day, a good restaurant stopover is **Parreirinha,** 12 Rua Dr. Miguel Bombarda (tel. 621-48). Lots of seafood dishes, as expected, appear on the menu, but I always gravitate to their tender pork cooked with baby clams. Steak, which is the most expensive item on the menu, is cooked with a special hot sauce, the recipe for which is known only to the chef. The service is accommodating. You'll want to stick around for supper. Everything tastes better when washed down with a bottle of vinho verde. Meals cost from 2,000$ ($13), and the restaurant is closed on Tuesday and in November. Hours are noon to 3 p.m. and 7 to 10 p.m. daily.

O Cantinho Madeirense, 10 Calçada da Baleia (tel. 636-69), is another good place to eat. You are served a wide range of cookery, with Portuguese specialties, especially seafood, predominating. Some 50 diners can pack in here, taking a table overlooking the esplanade and paying from 1,500$ ($9.75) for a good and filling meal. Food is served daily from noon to 4 p.m. and 7 to 10 p.m. The restaurant is closed on Wednesday in winter.

NIGHTLIFE IN AND AROUND LISBON

1. THE FADO CLUBS
2. THE CAPITAL AFTER DARK
3. ESTORIL BY NIGHT
4. THE CLUBS OF CASCAIS

Unless you have experienced the nostalgic sounds of fado, the songs of sorrow, you do not know Portugal. Certainly not its soul. The fado is Portugal's most vivid art form; and no visit to Lisbon should be planned without at least one night spent in a local tavern, where this traditional folk music is heard.

Originating in the lowly dock area, fado was embraced by the hearts of the Portuguese people. A rough translation of *fado* is fate, from the Latin *fatum,* meaning prophecy. The quintessence of saudade, fado usually tells of unrequited love, jealousy, a longing for days gone by. As one expert put it, it speaks of "life commanded by the Oracle, which nothing can change."

Fado found its earliest fame in the 19th century with Maria Severa, the beautiful daughter of a gypsy who took Lisbon by storm, singing her way into the hearts of the people, and especially the heart of the Count of Vimioso, an outstanding bullfighter of his day. Legend has it that she is honored by present-day *fadistas* who wear a black-fringed shawl in her memory.

In this century the most famous exponent of fado has been Amália Rodrigues, introduced to American audiences in the 1950s at the New York club, La Vie en Rose. She was discovered while walking barefoot and selling flowers on the Lisbon docks, near the Alfama. Fado is also sung by men, who are called fadistas as well.

Clutching black shawls around themselves, the female fadistas pour out their emotions, from the tenderest whisper of hope to a wailing lament of life's tragedies. As they sing, accompanied by a guitar and a viola, they seem to lose all contact with the surrounding world, standing against a black gas street lamp, without benefit of backdrops or makeup—just standing there. They seemingly outdo the Rhine's Lorelei in drawing you into their world of tenderness and fire. Though much enjoyment can be derived from understanding the poetic imagery, a knowledge of Portuguese is not essential. The lyric power, the warmth of the voices, and the personality of the singer communicate a great deal.

Don't go to hear fado and plan to carry on a private conversation. It's considered very bad form. Most of the authentic fado clubs are clustered near each other in either the Bairro Alto or in the Alfama, between St. George's Castle and the docks, and you can "fado hop" between these two typical quarters. Alfama-bound hoppers can ask the taxi driver to deliver them to **Largo do Chafariz,** a small plaza a block from the harbor, and Bairro Alto devotees can get off at **Largo do S. Roque.** Most of my recommendations lie only a short walk from either of these squares.

1. The Fado Clubs

In the clubs listed below, it isn't necessary always to have dinner. You can always go later and order just a drink. However, you often have to pay a minimum consumption charge. The music begins between 9 and 10 p.m., but it's better to arrive after 11 p.m. Many of the clubs stay open till 3 a.m.; others, till dawn.

Lisboa à Noite, 69 Rua das Gáveas (tel. 36-85-57). Electricity fills the air—the tempestuous Fernanda Maria is about to make her first appearance of the evening. Tossing down a shot of whisky offered by a waiter, she stands quietly, tensely clutching her black shawl. Then she comes forward, pauses, scans the audience, and pours forth all the fiery intensity of fado. You too may fall under her spell. Success has come to Fernanda—she owns the club.

The 17th-century-style setting is rustic, yet luxurious (once this Bairro Alto club was a stable). Creating its present ambience are thick stone-edged arches, heavy hand-hewn beams, blue and white tile walls, a round well with its original bucket, a collection of old engravings, antique guns, and pewter and copper. When it's cold, scented eucalyptus logs crackle in a high fireplace. In the rear is an open kitchen and charcoal grill, with an assemblage of spices, sausages, garlic pigtails, and onions hanging from the beams. It's customary to go here for dinner, enjoying such house specialties as dry codfish Fernanda Maria, named after the owner, or steak Lisboa à Noite flambé, named after the club. If you spend an evening here enjoying some of the chef's specialties, your tab is likely to begin at 5,000$ ($32.50), going up to 6,000$ ($39). The club is open from 8 p.m. to 2:30 a.m. daily except Sunday.

Cota D'Armas, 7 Beco de São Miguel (tel. 86-86-82). Nightclub cookery isn't always the best in Lisbon (is it anywhere?), but there is one restaurant that would rank among the top ten in Lisbon, even if it didn't present a nightly program of "fado and folklore." The elegantly decorated Cota D'Armas is one of the leading attractions on the nighttime circuit for those wishing to venture into the Alfama at night. You can arrive early for dinner, enjoying drinks in the bar decorated in the style of a regional stable. The dining room is upstairs, and it's graced with a hand-painted ceiling. The coat-of-arms (the English translation of the restaurant's name) is depicted on the export china of the East India Company. In winter this setting is made even more inviting by an open fireplace. During dinner, a well-seasoned group of fadistas and guitar players entertain you with Portuguese songs and music. You can also go for lunch, except on Sunday when it's closed all day. Dinner is served Monday to Saturday. Hours are 12:30 to 3 p.m. and 7 to 11 p.m. Meals begin at 4,000$ ($26).

A Severa, 49-57 Rua das Gáveas (tel. 346-40-06). Good food and careful selection of fadistas make this the perennial favorite. Before he became president, Richard Nixon selected it for a night on the town with his wife, leading a congalike line between tables, warbling the refrain, "Severa . . . Severa . . . Severa." Every night top singers, both male and female, appear at the Bairro Alto nightspot, accompanied by guitar and viola music, alternating with folk dancers. In a niche you'll spot a statue honoring the club's namesake, Maria Severa, the legendary gypsy fadista of the 19th century. After midnight tourists seem to recede a bit in favor of loyal Lisbon habitués, who request and sometimes join in on their favorite fado number.

The kitchen turns out regional dishes based on recipes from the north of Portugal. For dinner, the favorite main-dish selection is chicken cooked in a clay pot. Before that, you might like to order *caldo verde,* a green cabbage soup. Another house specialty, which may sound uninviting to some but is really tasty, is stuffed squid. Those less experimental may request the steak of the house, fried in a clay dish. Expect to spend from 5,000$ ($32.50) to 6,000$ ($39). The place is open daily except Thursday from 8 p.m. to 3 a.m.

Adega Machado, 91 Rua do Norte (tel. 346-00-95), has passed the test of time and is today one of the favored fado clubs of Portugal. Formerly you could perhaps spot Edward G. Robinson or Vittorio de Sica listening to the incomparable Amália Rodrigues. Alternating with its fadistas are folk dancers, whirling, clapping, singing their native songs in colorful costumes. The evening dinner hour starts at 8 p.m. and the doors don't close till 3 a.m. when the last fadista aficionado trails out humming his or her favorite song. The club is open daily except from November to March when it is closed on Monday.

Dinner is à la carte, and the cuisine is mostly Portuguese, with any number of regional dishes. House specialties include chicken in a pot, stuffed squid, steak Machado, roasted baby goat, and pork with clams. For dessert, I'd suggest almond cake made with nuts from the Algarve. Expect to spend 4,000$ ($26) to 5,000$ ($32.50) for a complete meal. Guests often join the singers and folk dancers, carrying arched garlands of flowers, as they parade around the crowded tables, singing the "Marcha do Machado."

Parreirinha da Alfama, 1 Beco do Espírito Santo (tel. 86-82-09). Seemingly, every fadista worth her shawl has sung at this oldtime café, just a one-minute walk from the dockside of the Alfama. It's fado and fado only that enthralls here, not folk dancing. You can order a good regional dinner beginning early, but it's suggested that you go toward the end of the evening and stay late. It's open from 8 p.m. to 3 a.m. daily. In the first part of the program, fadistas get all the popular songs out of the way, then settle in to their own more classic favorites.

You can order a filling dinner for 3,000$ ($19.50) to 3,500$ ($22.75), and the menu includes specialties from nearly every region of Portugal. The atmosphere is self-consciously taverna, and the walls are hung with all sorts of Portuguese provincial oddities along with photos of famous people who've been here. The singers selected by the management are first rate.

Luso, 10 Travessa da Queimada (tel. 32-22-81), has long been one of the most famous and enduring fado and folkloric clubs of the Bairro Alto. On a crowded street—often filled with waiting taxis and the sound of honking horns—the entertainment and the regional food are presented nightly except Sunday to some 160 patrons. Most guests come here for the fado and the entertainment. But full dinners are served, costing from 3,500$ ($22.75) and likely to include such specialties as *vieiras de peixe* (fish stuffed in a scallop shell) and *frango na Púcara* (chicken in a casserole). In air-conditioned comfort, guests can enjoy the dinner and music nightly from 8 p.m. to 3 a.m.

---

2. The Capital After Dark

Fado outshines other nighttime entertainment in Lisbon. However, for a change of pace, I've included suggestions for most tastes: vaudeville houses, nightclubs for conventional drinking and dancing, and disco for those of limber limb.

On a more cultural note, opera, and ballet buffs may want to attend a performance at the **Teatro Nacional de São Carlos,** 9 Rua Serpa Pinto (tel. 36-86-10), built in the 18th century and booking top companies from different countries. The season begins in mid-December, extending through May. In addition, there are several theaters presenting plays from autumn through spring, but only in Portuguese. The most famous theater is the **Teatro Nacional de D. Maria II,** Praça Dom Pedro IV (tel. 37-10-78). Seats cost 250$ ($1.65) to 400$ ($2.60).

Recitals and concerts are held at various places in Lisbon, especially the Greenhouse in Edward VII Park and the Gulbenkian Arts Center, 45 Avenida de Berna (tel. 77-91-31). Motion pictures are shown in their original language.

To obtain **information** on any of the above, consult a copy of *What's On in Lisbon,* available at most newsstands. Your hotel concierge is also a good bet for information, since one of his or her duties is reserving seats.

MUSICAL REVUES—PORTUGUESE STYLE

Just off the Avenida da Liberdade, in the Parque Mayer, is a cluster of vaudeville and music halls, each offering a *revista,* a Portuguese revue similar in some respects to a Spanish zarzuela. In the park are a few restaurants and Coney Island-style fun-and-chance stalls, where Lisboans throw darts and win dubious prizes. Here you can feel the entertainment pulse of the people, seeing everything from popular singers to fadistas to acrobats to ballet dancers. Sometimes you're treated to dancing girls and toe-tapping. Matinees are staged on Sunday at 4 p.m., and show time is nightly at 9:45 p.m. Tickets range from a low of 500$ ($3.25) for the worst seats in the house (definitely not recommended) to 1,100$ ($7.15) for a grand perch. One reader warns, "Ticket buyers should make sure they're seeking the vaudeville entertainment, and not something else. We were at first misdirected to one of the pornographic skin flicks in the same area."

THE DISCOS

Among disco devotees in Lisbon, **Banana Power,** 53 Rua Cascais (tel. 63-18-15), generates a lot of youthful enthusiasm. An old warehouse was converted into a disco in the Alcantara section, lying between the heart of the city and the suburb of Belém. Hundreds of Lisboans, all young, pour in here to enjoy the bands, paying a minimum of 1,000$ ($6.50) per person. Go late, as it doesn't open until 11 p.m. and rarely gets jumping until midnight. But once the action begins, it lasts until 4 a.m. Take tram 17 from Praça do Comércio (Black Horse Square). Actually, since taxis are inexpensive, it's best to take one to the entrance, which has only a small sign announcing itself.

Ad Lib, 28 Rua Barata Salgueiro (tel. 56-17-17), is a posh disco dreamed up by a clique of chaps who wanted an elegant place to have a bash. On the top floor of a modern building, it doesn't call attention to itself with a sign outside. A uniformed attendant at the formal entrance checks on the intercom system to weed out undesirables. If you're well groomed and not drunk or drugged, you stand a good chance of scaling the citadel; even so, it's wise to telephone in advance.

Upstairs, you'll enter a penthouse with a bar on one level, tables and a dancing area on another. A plant-filled terrace provides a view of Lisbon by night. The decor is oriental, with fine stone Buddhas from Macão, mirrors, and candles in red bowls. A disc jockey plays the newest continental and American records. There's a minimum charge of 7,000$ ($45.50), with a whisky costing from 700$ ($4.55). Hours are 11 p.m. to 4:30 a.m.

Springfellows, 8B Avenida Oscar Monteiro Torres (tel. 73-29-44), is one of the most elegant discos in Lisbon. Entrance is 1,200$ ($7.80), and a beer costs from 350$ ($2.30). A disc jockey rides between a trio of floors while encased in a glass cage. It is open nightly except Sunday from 11 p.m. to 4 a.m.

Whispers, Edificio Aviz, 35 Avenida Fontes Pereira de Melo (tel. 57-54-89), next to the Sheraton Hotel, is run by the R. R. Club, or Rolls-Royce, in Cascais. So successful was the Costa do Sol version of this chic disco, that its managers brought it to Lisbon as well. The cover charge is 5,000$ ($32.50). Whispers is open from 11 p.m. to 4:30 a.m. daily.

Elefante Branco, 83-A Rua Luciano Cordeiro (tel. 57-98-11), is a luxurious disco with a piano bar and restaurant. Hours for the restaurant are from 8:30 to 11 p.m. and for the disco from 11 p.m. to 4 a.m. The price of a meal costs from 4,000$ ($26), and the cover charge at the disco is 3,000$ ($19.50).

NIGHTCLUBS

In its nightly cabaret, **O Porão da Nau,** 1 Rua Pinheiro Chagas (tel. 57-15-01), a disco-nightclub, features Brazilian music, fado, and sometimes a drag show. The action takes place in the hold of a simulated Portuguese man-of-war of the 15th century. You descend to the lower levels at the centrally located Residência A Ponte and get the feeling that the gangplank will be lifted, the sails hoisted.

Around a circular marble dance floor, tables are set on different levels. The main beams are time-aged, the wall planked, and there are rope railings, a gun collection, an early map charting Portuguese possessions, a finely carved wooden figure used on the bow of a sailing vessel, and a spherical globe. A minimum of 1,000$ ($6.50) is charged, including service. Go only on Friday, Saturday, and Sunday after 11:30 p.m. At 4:30 a.m., the club closes.

Gafiera, 8 Calçada do Tijolo (tel. 32-59-53), is a Brazilian night spot featuring Brazilian music. You can sing and dance the samba, the bossa, even the xarado. The cover charge of 1,000$ ($6.50) can be spent by ordering two special Brazilian drinks. Hours are daily except Sunday from 10 p.m. to 3:30 a.m.

BARS IN LISBON

In addition to its role as a restaurant, **Bachus,** 9 Largo da Trindade (tel. 32-12-60), offers one of the capital's most convivial watering spots. In an environment filled with oriental carpets, fine hardwoods, bronze statues, intimate lighting, and uniformed, very polite waiters, you can hobnob with some of the most glamorous names in Lisbon. Late-night suppers are served in the bar by candlelight. The array of drinks is international, costing from 500$ ($1.30), and the spot is a good one in which to unwind in privileged circumstances. Open from noon to 2 a.m. daily.

Metro e Meio, 174 Avenida 5 de Outubro (tel. 77-59-97), is spotted easily. A giant yellow ruler forms its façade. In renovating, the management discovered several grotto-like rooms that had been hidden for decades. Now guests have a choice of a maze of rooms, with a central fireplace. The decor is formed by hand-loomed wall hangings, gilt mirrors, statues, hanging lamps, Victorian fringed shades, and contemporary paintings. Recordings are piped in. Whiskies begin at 400$ ($2.60), and you can order an omelet for 400$ also. A taxi ride from the center of Lisbon, the bar stands near the Gulbenkian Museum. Hours are daily from 6 p.m. to 2 a.m.

Procópio Bar, 21-A Alto de San Francisco (tel. 65-28-51), could easily become your favorite watering hole in Lisbon—that is, if you can find it. The street it lies on rarely appears on Lisbon maps. However, the location is just off Rua de João Penha, which itself is off the landmark Praça das Amoreiras. The café is a social center for many politicians and journalists. In a turn-of-the-century atmosphere, it leans heavily on nostalgia. Guests sit on red tufted velvet, enjoying the atmosphere of stained and painted glass, ornate brass hardware—and a piano awaiting an amateur player. It's like being in an intimate living room where the guests know each other. Long drinks cost from 450$ ($2.95).

Passport, 33 Rua Nova do Carvalho (tel. 347-15-07). The flashing neon sign in front promises bright lights and dancing. Once you're inside, the lights are cooler and the furniture more Iberian than you might have expected. In many ways the leather, wood, and masonry accents imply a Portuguese village, and there's always the chance to make new friends of one kind or another. The place opens every day at 9:30 a.m., closing much later, at 3:30 a.m. A whisky costs from 500$ ($3.25).

Bora-Bora, 201 Rua da Madalena (tel. 87-20-43). A Polynesian bar might seem out of context in Lisbon, but its concept is all the rage in Iberia these days. If, therefore, you have a yearning for the kind of fruited, flaming, and rum-laced drinks you thought you'd left behind on the West Coast, you'll find imaginative variations here. The couches are comfortable and inviting, and you can take in the Polynesian art on the walls. Hamburgers and other fare are available to accompany your Pacific Ocean nectars as well. Snacks cost from 450$ ($2.95). Hours are daily from 6 p.m. to 2 a.m.

A BAWDY CRAWL ALONG THE DOCKLAND

Remember those movies of port cities, showing red neon lights flashing, drunken sailors staggering down labyrinthine narrow streets, a mixed bag of human flotsam unmatched since Jean Genêt wrote of his "whores, thieves, pimps, and beggars." These rip-roaring scenes live on in Lisbon, in the little streets near the dock area, where sailors hang out at bars named after western American states: Arizona, California, Texas.

The most popular, occasionally drawing some of the slumming Ritz and Palácio crowd, is the **Texas Bar,** 24 Rua Nova do Carvalho (tel. 36-36-83), a gutsy tavern under a bridge. A singer usually warbles a Portuguese version of an old country and western hit. It's open day and night.

If you're a man alone (if you're a woman alone, stay away), you'll be surrounded on entering by the wildest assemblage of Gravel Gertie look-alikes this side of Barcelona or Marseilles. "Speak English?" is the typical query. One young man trying to escape answered a resounding, "No, Svenska," but a girl was found who spoke lilting Swedish. The Texas Bar accommodates all. When the fleet's in, and some fleet from some port is likely to be in all the time, this waterfront hotspot can be very rowdy. Open from 11:30 a.m. to 3:30 a.m., sometimes later.

For much tamer fare, we strike out for nighttime fun along the Costa do Sol.

3. Estoril by Night

GAMBLING

The glamor hub for international society is the **Casino** (tel. 268-45-21) at Estoril. Occupying a position on the rise of a hill, it opens onto the formal gardens of the Parque Estoril which sweep toward the water. The glass walls suggest an international museum of modern art, and enclose an inner courtyard, with tile paths, a fountain and pool, and borders of lilac-colored petunias and red carnations.

Off the main lobby are various bars, a motion-picture theater, an art gallery, and groups of boutiques. The five-star magnet, of course, is the Casino, which accepts your mad money daily from 3 p.m. to 3 a.m. (passport required). An adjoining salon is for one-armed bandits. In the main room you can take your chance at roulette, French banque, chemin de fer, baccarat, blackjack/21, craps, and slot machines. A nonresident pass is given for 400$ ($2.60).

Other diversions include the **Grand Salon Restaurant,** really a supper club offering Portuguese and international cuisine, beginning at 9 nightly. There's a cover charge of 2,000$ ($13), plus another 4,500$ ($29.25) to 6,000$ ($39) charged if you want dinner. Specialties include smoked swordfish, pâté, grilled prawns, calves' kidneys flambéed with cognac, and pressed duck. A tea dance is staged every Sunday afternoon at 5. The extravaganza stage show commences at 11:15 p.m. and 1 a.m. On the arena stage, leggy, feathered, and bejeweled showgirls strut their wares to good advantage in billowing trains and bespangled bras.

A small movie theater shows films daily. It's the same on weekends and holidays. There's also an art gallery selling contemporary paintings, and a few boutiques offering apparel and souvenirs.

DINING AND DANCING

On the coastal road, **A Choupana,** Estrada Marginal, São João do Estoril (tel. 268-30-99), is the best supper club along the Costa do Sol. It offers a good sound for dancing nightly in a setting on the edge of a cliff, with views of the sunset and the lights from fishing boats and ocean liners as well as the sounds of the surf. *Choupana* means hut or shack in Portuguese.

The main room is on two levels, with enough waterside window space to provide everyone with a good seat. On the bill of fare, you can order such dishes as partridge stewed in a casserole, duck with orange sauce, and a mixed grill Choupana. One exceptional fish dish is lampreys Portuguese style (only in season), and other Portuguese specialties and international cuisine are offered. In season, strawberries from Sintra make an exciting finish. Your tab will probably be 4,000$ ($26) or more. Last but not least is the top-notch trio. Music for dining begins at 9:30 p.m., for dancing at 10 p.m., and continues until closing at 2 a.m.

A FORTRESS DISCO

The very young meet in a very old setting at **Forte Velho** (Old Fort), Estrada Marginal, São Pedro Cadaveira, São João do Estoril (tel. 268-13-37). The disco was ingeniously conceived, capturing a 17th-century fortress on a cliff above the ocean. It's built of solid rock and offers a central room with fireplace.

Dancing is to records only, and there's an adjoining bar with stools and cozy banquettes, ideal for hand-holding couples. For a change of pace, drinks are carried out on the terrace to the parapet, where imbibers gasp at the steep drop to the surf below. The fun commences at 10 p.m., yet it doesn't really warm up till around midnight. The Old Fort rides the crest until closing at 3 a.m. every night. You pay a minimum charge of 1,000$ ($6.50) nightly, including two drinks.

A BAR IN ESTORIL

The most popular bar is the **Pickwick Pub,** 3 Avenida Biarritz (tel. 268-67-26). The Pickwick is decorated like an old English pub, complete with carpeted floor, mugs hanging over the bar, and plenty of cozy nooks and crannies where you sit in subdued lighting. Soft music is provided from a disc jockey sitting in an adjoining room. You can play darts, have light meals, and while away a couple of hours chatting with the locals and foreigners. It's open daily from noon to 2 a.m. Port and foreign beers cost 200$ ($1.30) to 275$ ($1.80).

BARS IN MONTE ESTORIL

An interesting watering spot, **Ray's Cocktail Bar & Lounge,** 425 Avenida Sabóia (tel. 268-01-06), in Monte Estoril, is popular with American expatriates, many of whom make it their private club, including the original Ray now that he's retired and has turned it over to Rafael Neves. It's a souped-up decorator extravaganza. Inside you're likely to find a completely catholic assemblage of elements—a fátima hand from Tangier, a glass ruby-colored newel post finial, chandeliers dripping with crystal, an ostrich fan (in black, no less), antique benches, provincial chairs, plus a heterogeneous mixture of modern art. Everyone seemingly enjoys the drinks (many enjoy quite a few of them). Most strong drinks cost 300$ ($1.95) to 500$ ($3.25). The bar is open daily from 6 p.m. to 2 a.m.

Mr. Busby's Bar and Pub, 3A Avenida Sabóia (tel. 268-09-75). The place is fun, a bit rowdy, and popular with a fickle crowd of pop music lovers. You'll find it on a steep hillside street a short distance above town. Illuminated through large sheets of plate glass, the high ceilings are covered with beer banners. Few of them get noticed when video movies are screened. In addition to drinks and beer, sandwiches are served. Hot dishes begin at 250$ ($1.65). The establishment is open from 4 p.m. to around 2:30 a.m. every day.

4. The Clubs of Cascais

Van Gogo, 9 Travessa Alfarrobeira (tel. 28-33-78), is a chic playground. Modestly hidden in a corner stone building, it was transformed from a simple fisherman's cottage into a disco. A doorman carefully evaluates those who would cross the threshold, using some inner radar I don't understand. Behind its façade, you'll encounter a young crowd similar to the one at Juan-Les-Pins. A seductive atmosphere is created by the black glass walls, and the customers can rock and roll. You pay a steep 3,000$ ($19.50) as an entrance minimum, unless they know you. The Van Gogo opens its doors year round at 11 p.m., closing at 4 a.m.

Palm Beach, Praia da Conceição (tel. 28-08-51), is a hillside disco and restaurant with a rather swank atmosphere—again with a doorman to weed out undesirables. It rides the crest of the wave along the Costa do Sol, drawing a young, fun-loving crowd that's well mannered enough to please the management. The club is positioned below the coastal road, its wide windows overlooking the bay at Cascais. You lounge comfortably on banquettes and chairs when not dancing on the mini-size floor. The atmosphere is informal, not dressy, and only records are played. The minimum charge at the disco is 1,000$ ($6.50), with beer going for 300$ ($1.95) and hard drinks from 400$ ($2.60). The restaurant, which has a maritime decor and a profusion of plants, overlooks the bay. Here you can order excellent shellfish and local fish dishes. The Palm Beach also has a pub-cocktail lounge, set up to look like the bridge of a steamboat. Hours are daily from 10:30 p.m. to 4 a.m.

Spirits Piano Bar, 3 Rua Alexandre Herculano (tel. 28-38-64). When you ring the doorbell of this chic rendezvous, a tuxedoed employee will open the speakeasy door if you look appropriate. Once inside, you descend a flight of stairs into a slightly cramped, but very intimate hideaway accented with ceiling beams, black mosaic floors, and thick stucco walls. Live music is presented on Saturday and Sunday. Otherwise the bar is open from 6 p.m. to 3 a.m. every night. Somewhat difficult to find, the bar is on a terrace a few feet above a street running into one of the corners of the triangular Jardim Visconde da Luz. A whisky costs 450$ ($2.95).

Rodrigo, Forte Dom Rodrigo (tel. 285-1373). Amália Rodrigues is still the leading fadista of Portugal, but since she doesn't sing that much any more, one of the most popular young fadistas in the country today is a singer known only as "Rodrigo." His club lies just outside the resort of Cascais, along Rua de Birre. Some of the most fashionable people in Lisbon drive out here just to hear Rodrigo sing—he's that good. His voice is haunting and melancholy. The nightclub opens at 8:30 p.m. for dinner, costing from 3,500$ ($22.75), but that is much too early to go, as Rodrigo himself rarely appears before 10 p.m. Closing time is 3 or 4 a.m. A minimum of 1,500$ ($9.75) is imposed, and be prepared to pay in cash, as credit cards aren't accepted. Closed Monday.

SOUTH OF THE TAGUS

The widow and the spinster, the rheumatic and those plagued with the "vapors"—the bulwark of Victorian England's 19th-century continental travelers—crossed the Tagus by boat and headed for the scenic wonders on the left bank of Lisbon.

Chances are, under one arm they carried a gold-leafed copy of a work by Robert Southey, England's poet laureate. After all, this Lake poet, a much-traveled gentleman, did more than anyone to publicize the glories that awaited his compatriots on the other bank. He virtually made the trek famous when he wrote: "I have never seen such a sublime panorama as the Arrábida Mountains afford, which, constantly changing as we go our way, offer us new beauties at every turn."

Nowadays the narrow isthmus south of the Tagus is fast booming into a major attraction. Behind the upsurge of interest is the Ponte 25 de Abril, the longest suspension bridge in Europe. It has speeded traffic and development to the area, and now it is possible to cross the Tagus in minutes, then head rapidly across good roads through pine groves to the vertices of the triangle known as "The Land of the Three Castles": Sesimbra, Setúbal, and Palmela. Of course, traditionalists still prefer taking the ferry from Praça do Comércio (Black Horse Square) in Lisbon, docking in Cacilhas.

The isthmus, long cut off from the Portuguese capital, is wild, rugged, lush, and productive. The strip of land plummets toward the sea, stretches along for miles of sandy beaches, and rolls through groves heavy with the odors of ripening oranges and vineyards of grapes used to make muscatel. With craggy cliffs and coves in the background, the crystalline waters of the Atlantic are ideal for swimming and skindiving, or for fishing for tuna, swordfish, and bass.

Sandy beaches double as the sites of fish auctions and leisurely sunbathing (some of the skimpy suits worn by north European beauties make aging black-shawled Portuguese varinas cross themselves). Farther up from the sardine-canning center of Setúbal, the coastline roughens where the Sêrra of Arrábida meets the sea, resulting in an abundance of caves, grottos, and precipitous crags.

The land possesses vivid reminders of its past, reflected in Moorish architectural influences, Roman ruins and roads, traces of the Phoenicians, and Spanish fortresses. Mighty castles and humble fishermen's cottages alike shook on a November day in 1755 when the earthquake brought Lisbon to her knees. Signs of that catastrophe are still evidenced in the ruins of the hamlet of Palmela, and the lonely walls of Coina Castle.

Its proximity to Lisbon (Setúbal is only 25 miles from the capital) makes it possible for a one-day excursion. But its unusual inns and moderate tariffs mark it as a place where the budget-minded reader will want to linger.

1. Azeitão

This sleepy village lies in the heart of quinta country. In Portuguese, a *quinta* means a farm, villa, or country house. At its most meager, it is a simple farmhouse surrounded by lands. At its best, it is a mansion of great architectural style filled with art decorations. Azeitão boasts the best.

It is said that King Manuel I started the concept of quintas in the early 16th century when he built the **Quinta de Bacalhoa** at Vila Fresca de Azeitão (tel. 208-00-11). The king's mother once lived there. In time it was taken over by the son of Afonso de Albuquerque. At one point in its history the building was owned by the Braganças, eventually falling into disrepair, as many of its decorations, specifically its antique tiles, were carted off by vandals.

Before World War II the mansion was purchased by an American woman who worked for years restoring it as much as possible to its original condition. The architecture is characterized by loggias, pavilions, half-moon domes that suggest a Moorish influence, and a trio of pyramided towers. One of the panels of 16th-century azulejos (tiles) depicts an innocent Susanna being hotly pursued by lecherous Elders. Some architectural critics have suggested that the palace is the first sign of the Renaissance in Portugal. Bacalhoa is a private villa, but its gardens are open to the public upon request from 1 to 5 p.m., except on Sunday and holidays. Admission is 25$ (15¢).

The farmland of the quinta is devoted to vineyards, owned by J. M. da Fonseca, International-Vinhos, Lda., makers of Lancers wine. There are two J.M. da Fonseca wineries half a mile apart: the "mother house," as it is called, and a newer plant characterized by white domes. The original winery and warehouses are in the center of Azeitão, as is the classic 19th-century house that was the Fonseca family home. A little museum and public reception room can be visited on the ground floor of the house. The century-old Fonseca wineries have made their product from grapes grown on the slopes of the Arrábida Mountains since the early 19th century, and the fine muscatel for which they have long been known is used in the flavoring and sweetening of white Lancers. Of course, the Fonseca vintners produce other wines you might like to try besides the popular Lancers, much of which is exported. Their top product is a muscatel called Setúbal, rarely sent abroad but delicious.

Another 16th-century mansion, **Quinta das Torres,** can not only be visited, but you can stop for a meal or even spend the night (see below). The third palace was erected at Vila Nogueira de Azeitão by the dukes of Aveiro in a classically Renaissance style.

Azeitão makes a good base for trekkers, especially those who want to scale the limestone Sêrra of Arrábida by foot. Others settle for long walks through scented pine woods or silvery olive groves. To cap your day, you can order some Azeitão cheese and a bottle of local muscatel. The village lies 9½ miles north of Setúbal, 15½ miles south of Lisbon.

FOOD AND LODGING

A 16th-century baronial mansion of deteriorating elegance, **Quinta das Torres,** 5 Estrada Nacional, Azeitão, 2900 Setúbal (tel. 065/208-00-01), has been kept intact on purpose for those desiring to live quietly, stepping back in time. It has been owned by the same family for many generations. The estate is approached through large gates and along a tree-lined driveway. Gradually, a pair of square peaked towers framing the entrance terrace comes into view. Ten bedrooms, all with private bath, have been set aside for paying guests. Each is quite different, ranging from smaller chambers to a ballroom-size suite dominated by princess-style brass beds, with a high tester and soft, flouncy ruffles. Some of the rooms have high shuttered windows, time-mellowed tile floors, antique furnishings, vases of fresh flowers, oil lamps, and niches with saints or madonnas. A single room, with breakfast, goes for 6,000$ ($39) daily, a double for 9,000$ ($58.50), and a suite for 10,000$ ($65).

The dining room of the Quinta has a covered ceiling, a tall stone fireplace where log fires are lit on chilly evenings, plus elaborate scenic tiles depicting "The Rape of the Sabine Women" and "The Siege of Troy." The rich-tasting, heavy cuisine is well recommended, and a meal will cost around 2,500$ ($16.25). The bill of fare is likely to include smoked filet of pork, steak au poivre, and giant prawns. Food is served daily from 1 to 3 p.m. and 7 to 9 p.m.

2. Sesimbra

Among the Portuguese, Sesimbra used to be a closely guarded secret. With justification, it was considered one of the most unspoiled fishing villages in the country. The varinas and fishermen still go about their time-honored task of plucking their livelihood from the Atlantic. Against a backdrop of rocky cliffs, sardines, shellfish, whiting, and the scabbard fish, with its whip-shaped body and dagger-like teeth, lie stretched out in the sun. When the fleet comes in, the day's catch is auctioned at a lota at the harbor (Porto Abrigo). However, Sesimbra today has been discovered with a vengeance, and high-rise buildings may one day engulf its old life.

Far down the beach, beyond the boat-clogged harbor, is the 17th-century **Fortress of St. Teodosio,** built to fortify the region against the pirates who plagued and plundered, carting off the most beautiful women and young girls.

A walk along the ruined battlements of the five-towered **Castle of Sesimbra** reduces the village to a nearly immobile miniature. The castle was captured from the Moors in 1165 and rebuilt following the 1755 earthquake, which sent sections of its crenelated walls tumbling to the ground. Enclosed within is a church and a meager archeological display of artifacts removed from the ruins.

Sesimbra also enjoys popularity as an angling center, attracting swordfish hunters. The resort lies about 19 miles south of Lisbon, 17 miles west of Setúbal. Sesimbra is connected by bus to Lisbon. You can also get to Sesimbra by taking the ferry from Praça do Comércio wharf, then a bus from Cacilhas.

From Sesimbra, you can head east to the headland of **Cape Espichel,** with its arcaded pilgrim hospices dating from the 1700s. Often violently wind-swept with sea gulls circling overhead, this strip of land has been called the "Land's End of Portugal." A pilgrimage church, Santuario Nossa Senhora do Cabo, in a state of disrepair, occupies space in this melancholy atmosphere. You can go inside, inspecting its baroque interior with gilded wood and sculpture. Later, you can walk to the edge of the cliffs in back of the church for a spectacular view. Beware: there's no guard rail, and it's a sheer drop of 350 feet to the ocean waters. Modern sculpture is inappropriately placed about in this forlorn setting. At the southern end of the Arrábida chain, this pilgrimage site has been popular since the 13th century. It was here in 1180 that Fuas Roupinho routed the Moors at sea, his forces capturing several ships of the enemy.

WHERE TO STAY

One of the most unusual self-contained beach-resort hotels south of the Tagus, **Hotel do Mar,** 10 Rua Combatentes do Ultramar, 2970 Sesimbra (tel. 01/223-33-26), is a beehive construction of units spreading from a high cliff to the water below. The passageways are like continuous art galleries, with contemporary paintings and ceramic plaques and sculpture, and the main lobby houses a glassed-in aviary with tropical birds. Special features include an "undersea" boîte beneath the pool, a haven for snug disco life. During the day one can soak up sun at the beach or at the circular swimming pool. The 120 bedrooms are stacked adobe fashion, each with its own bath and private terrace, with a view of the ocean and gardens sweeping down the hillside. Furnishings are streamlined and well selected; the rooms are airy, with breakfast being served on a flower-filled terrace. Singles cost from 9,200$ ($59.80) daily and doubles, from about 14,700$ ($95).

There are two dining rooms: one circular self-service, operating in summer; the other, on an upper ledge, warmed with wood-grain paneling and overlooking the sea. If you're stopping off on a day trip from Lisbon, you can order a meal for 2,800$ ($18.20) and up. The before-dinner gathering point is a rustically styled bar; after-dinner guests congregate in a living room, with a fireplace. The concierge will arrange for everything from fishing to hairdressing appointments to excursions by private boats. There are two tennis courts on the premises. The hotel operates transfer services.

Hotel Espadarte, Avenida 25 de Abril, 2970 Sesimbra (tel. 01/22-33-189), is named after the swordfish. The five-floor hotel is right on the esplanade, and below the incline ramp are boats and seamen mending their nets. Open all year, the hotel receives guests in its 80 bedrooms, each with private bath or shower and phone. Most of the accommodations also have private balconies overlooking the sea. Room furnishings, a sort of 1960s decor, are simple but comfortable. Including a continental breakfast, singles in high season rent for 6,000$ ($39) daily, with doubles costing 8,000$ ($52). Some of the hotel's facilities include a restaurant, Concha do Mar, specializing in seafood, as well as a self-service section. In the Bar Miami, guests can dance or watch a movie. There is also a solarium, along with laundry facilities and individual safes.

WHERE TO DINE

In the square near the town hall, **Chez Nous,** 11-13 Largo do Municipio (tel. 223-01-41), is an attractive restaurant behind a handful of sidewalk tables. When the owner, José P. Costa, founded it, he brought back to Portugal some of the culinary techniques he had learned during his stay in Mozambique. The walls of the interior are covered with dark green lattice, creating a garden effect around the bistro-style tables that sit close to one another with a view of the exposed kitchen. There, an array of employees concoct such specialties as grilled prawns, rice with seafood, mussels Chez Nous, kebabs of squid, filet of catfish, and peppersteak , which cost from 3,000$ ($19.50). The restaurant serves food from noon to 3 p.m. and 7 to 11 p.m. daily. It is generally closed on Tuesday, but in summer it is closed Tuesday only for lunch.

Restaurante Ribamar, Avenida dos Naufragos (tel. 223-31-07), serves some of the best Portuguese cookery in the area, specializing in fish and shellfish, most of it freshly caught off local waters. Its location is in front of the sea, a short stroll from the beach, with a view of the bay. There is space for about 60 seats outside and 80 inside. The chef's specialty is a platter of mixed fish and shellfish (served for two persons). Downstairs are two large aquariums where guests can "catch" their own lobster, crayfish, or crab. A typical meal here averages 2,500$ ($16.25), and service is daily from noon to 3 p.m. and 7 to 10:30 p.m.

3. Portinho da Arrábida

The limestone Arrábida Mountains stretch for about 22 miles, beginning at Palmela and rolling to a dramatic end at Cape Espichel on the Atlantic. At times the cliffs and bluffs are so high that it seems you have to peer through the clouds to see the purple waters of the Atlantic below.

A Swiss botanist once said the mountain range contained "the most amazing flora to be seen in Europe." The foliage that rims the cliffs and the surrounding areas is lush, subtropical, and wide ranging, with everything from holm oaks, sweet bay, pines, laurel, juniper, cypress, araucaria, magnolia, lavender, myrtle, and pimpernels. A riot of color and fragrance carpets the mountains.

The sêrra is riddled with numerous caves and grottos, the best known of which is the **Lapa de Santa Margarida.** Of it, Hans Christian Andersen wrote: "It is a veritable church hewn out of the living rock, with a fantastic vault, organ pipes, columns, and altars."

Perched on a hillside like a tiara over Portinho da Arrábida, the **New Convent** dates from the 16th century. You can go to the gate and ring for the caretaker, who may or may not show you around the precincts.

Plummeting down to the sea, you arrive at Portinho da Arrábida, at the foot of the sêrra. This is a favorite oasis with many families from Lisbon who rent little multicolored cottages on the beach. If you take a car down here in July and August, you do so at your own risk. There is virtually no parking space, and the road should be one way but isn't. You can be stranded for hours trying to get back up the hill. The other problem is this: to walk down and back could qualify you for the Olympics. Portinho da Arrábida, which can be approached from either Setúbal or Sesimbra, lies about 23 miles south of Lisbon. By public transportation, you must make bus connections in Sesimbra.

WHERE TO EAT

In summer, as mentioned, it is both frustrating and dangerous to take a car down the narrow, winding road whose edges are jammed with cars. More knowing visitors try to park on a wider road above the port, and then negotiate the hordes of summer visitors on foot. The walk back is steep and only for the hearty. However, a meal at **Restaurante Beira-Mar** (tel. 208-05-44) can be your reward for the trek. The most sought-after warm-weather tables at this airy restaurant are set out on a concrete balcony, a few feet above the still waters of the port, near the many fishing vessels. White paper usually serves as the napery for the savory but unpretentiously informal meals that are the rule here. Full meals, costing from 2,500$ ($16.25) each, include pork with clams, roast chicken, fish stew, grilled sardines, several preparations of codfish, grilled sole, shellfish rice, and several regional wines. Food is served daily from noon to 9 p.m. except Wednesday from October to April.

4. Setúbal

On the right bank of the Sado River, 25 miles south of Lisbon, lies one of Portugal's largest and most ancient cities, said to have been founded by the grandson of Noah. Motorists often include it on their itineraries because of an exceptional inn, the **Pousada de São Filipe,** installed in a late-16th-century fort overlooking the sea (see below).

Setúbal is known as the center of Portugal's sardine industry and for the production of the most exquisite muscatel wine in the world. As far back as the days of the Romans and the Visigoths, the aromatic and hearty grapes of this region were praised by connoisseurs.

Orange groves (a jam is made from the fruit), orchards, vineyards, and outstanding beaches (a popular one, **Praia da Figueirinha**) compose the environs of Setúbal. And the white pyramidal mounds you see dotting the landscape are deposits of sea salt drying in the sun, another major commercial asset of this seaside community.

Many artists and writers have come from Setúbal, none more notable than the 18th-century Portuguese poet Manuel Maria Barbosa du Bocage, a forerunner of romanticism. At Praça do Bocage, a monument honors him.

In Setúbal is the late-15th-century **Church of Jesus,** an example of the Manueline style of architecture. Of particular interest are the ornate decorations on the main doorway and the Arrábida marble columns. Each of the latter is actually three columns twisted together like taffy to form a cable or root-like effect. Somehow they don't seem to hold up the vaulted ceiling, but give the illusion of appendages grown down to the floor. Raymond Postgate wrote that the columns "look as if they had been twisted and wrung by a washerwoman," and Hans Christian Andersen recorded that the monument was "one of the most beautiful small churches that I have ever seen." The church has been heavily restored, the latest wholesale renovation in 1969–1970. Adjoining is the unpretentious **Museu da Cidade** (Town Museum) housing some early-16th-century Portuguese paintings, as well as some Spanish and Flemish works, coins, shards, and other artifacts from the sandy pit of Tróia. The church-museum is at the Praça Miguel Bombarda, off Avenida 22 de Dezembro. The museum is open daily except Monday from 9 a.m. to 12:30 p.m. and 2 to 5 p.m.

To reach this port, where windmills still clack in the countryside, roosters crow, and the "girls of the sardines" seem to speak Portuguese with Arabic accent, take the ferry from Lisbon to Barreiro. There, you can board a train for the rest of the way.

WHERE TO STAY
Interesting accommodations are offered at **Pousada de São Filipe,** Castelo de São Filipe, 2900 Setúbal (tel. 065-238-44). This fortress-castle, dating back to 1590, was built by an Italian architect who came to Portugal during the ill-fated reign of the young king Sebastião. The builder perched it on a hilltop overlooking the town and the harbor. You wind your way up a curving mountain road, passing through a stone arch, by towers to the belvedere. Rooms that once were for the soldiers and the governor have been tastefully and richly furnished with antiques and reproductions. In earlier days there were guns and ammunition, but they have given way to soft beds and ornate Portuguese crafted headboards. The walls of the chapel and the public rooms contain tile dados, depicting scenes from the life of São Filipe and the life of the Virgin Mary. Nearby there is a small chapel decorated with tiles that depict the life of São Filipe. They are dated 1736 and signed by Policarpo de Oliveira Bernardes.

The bedrooms are individually decorated. They are reached via what seems like miles of plant-filled corridors, up wide, worn stone steps. To stay here on a bed-and-breakfast basis costs 15,400$ ($100.10) daily in a double room, 13,600$ ($88.40) in a single.

Dining is pleasant, sitting in Windsor-style armchairs. Six alcoved windows open onto a panoramic view. Against a background of tile dado, a primitive tapestry, and photostated engravings, a luncheon or dinner, including many fish specialties, is served. Most guests take this meal when they stop over on a day trip from Lisbon, paying from 2,200$ ($14.30) to 2,800$ ($18.20). The clients seem to gravitate to the medieval-style drinking lounge, with its coved and arched ceiling, pierced-copper hanging lanterns, tile bar, and husky brass-studded armchairs. The sitting rooms are also intimate, with tile walls, antiques, bowls, engravings, chests, and copper artifacts in the niches.

Esperança Hotel, 220 Avenida Luisa Todi (tel. 065/251-51), stands in the heart of Setúbal, on the main inner street. It's a modern six-story hotel, with basic amenities, a clean-cut lounge, plus a reception area with streamlined furnishings, all in a restrained design. Each bedroom is done in pastel colors and has built-in headboards, a dressing table, bedside lighting, and all-tile bath. Singles run 6,500$ ($42.25) daily; doubles, 7,500$ ($48.75). There is a dining room on the top floor that provides a panoramic view of the area, including the Sado River. The hotel also has a bar and nightclub.

WHERE TO DINE

In the center of town, **O Beco,** 24 Largo da Misericórdia (tel. 246-17), is entered through a narrow passageway that leads to two dining rooms, decorated in a typical style with old ovens, regional artifacts, and a fireplace. The service is efficient, the food excellent. The quantities could be smaller and nobody would leave hungry. Shellfish soup is the classic opener. Pork chops are from the acorn-sweetened variety in Alentejo, and a special beefsteak is offered. *Cabrito* (goat) is also good. Two more recommendable regional dishes include a Portuguese stew, *cozido,* and paella. More adventurous seafaring palates will order the grilled squid. A typical dessert is the rice pudding. Count on spending 1,300$ ($8.45) to 1,900$ ($12.35). Food is served from noon to 3:30 p.m. and 7:15 to 10:30 p.m.; closed Tuesday.

Restaurante Bocage, 8-10 Rua da Marqueza do Faial (tel. 225-13). Old Portugal comes alive to visitors who approach the faded façade of this pink-walled town house, whose doors open onto a corner of the traffic-free main square of town. Inside you'll find a no-nonsense decor of 1950s-era ceiling fans, a coffered white ceiling, and a green-and-white terrazzo floor. Most patrons order a fruity muscatel to accompany the array of fresh fish served here. In deference to their almost exclusively local clientele, regional Portuguese cookery is emphasized. A meal is traditionally topped off with a taste of muscatel brandy, and full dinners cost from 2,800$ ($18.20). Hours are 12:15 to 3:30 p.m. and 7:15 to 10:30 p.m. daily. The restaurant is closed every Monday night and all day Tuesday.

5. Tróia

Tróia is a long, sandy peninsula across the Sado River estuary from Setúbal. The pine-studded strip of land is the site of one of Portugal's largest tourist enterprises, featuring the Torralta tourist complex with high-rise apartment hotels and a par-72, 6,970-yard, 18-hole golf course designed by Robert Trent Jones.

At **Cetóbriga,** ruins of a thriving Roman port have been discovered, with excavations beginning in the mid-19th century. The city, dating from the 3rd and 4th centuries, was destroyed by the ocean, but traces have been unearthed of villas, bathing pools, a temple decorated with frescoes, and a place for salt preservation of fish. There is also evidence that those long-ago seafarers, the Phoenicians, inhabited the peninsula at one time. Cetóbriga's ruins are about 1½ miles from the site of the present development of Tróia. Come here to enjoy the resort. Don't come looking for the ruins, as they are fenced off and not open at present for viewing by tourists. However, conditions may change.

You can reach Tróia by road, traveling on the N10 and the N120, turning toward the ocean in the vicinity of Comporta. Watch for the signs.

The best way to get there, however, is to go from Setúbal by car-ferry. The car-ferry leaves from near the commercial port in Setúbal every half hour in season, every hour the rest of the year, taking about 20 minutes to cross.

FOOD AND LODGING

An island resort, **Aparthotel Tróia,** Tróia 2900 Setúbal (tel. 065/44-221), is a tourist development that's part of the Torralta golf course and high-rise complex, with contemporary rooms and apartments. Against a white background, most of the rooms have strong colors, wide, low white couches and lounge chairs, white globe lights, large paintings, dining room areas, and complete kitchens. Bedrooms are stark but attractive. Each apartment will house two to four persons. In off-season, an apartment for two or three persons rents for 4,200$ ($27.30) daily. However, in July and September, charges are raised to 7,000$ ($45.50) daily. Highest prices are charged in August when the same apartment rents for 8,000$ ($52). The view of the coastline is special, and there are encircling sandy beaches. It's complete with all the resort amenities.

Torralta has several other apartment hotels in the complex, including **Rosamar and Magnóliamar,** Tróia 2900 Setúbal (tel. 065/44-151), both in magnificent settings of sea and sand with the golf course close by. Like the Tróia, they are furnished in contemporary style, with many amenities to make a complete resort vacation. In off-season, Rosamar charges from 6,500$ ($42.25) daily for an apartment suitable for two to four persons. That same apartment rents for 9,500$ ($61.75) in July and August, peaking at 11,500$ ($74.75) in August. In off-season, Magnoliamar charges 7,600$ ($49.40) for an apartment for two to four persons, the cost rising to 14,800$ ($96.20) from the first of July to the end of September.

---

6. Palmela

The village of Palmela lies in the heart of a wine-producing region, in the foothills of the Arrábida Mountains. It is famous for its fortress, from which, at a vantage point of 1,200 feet, you'll be rewarded with one of the most extensive and varied views in all of Portugal. Over sienna-hued valleys and vineyards heavy with grapes, one sees the capital to the north, the estuary of the Sado to the south.

The position of **Palmela Castle** has long been a strategic point in securing control of the lands south of the Tagus. It was from Palmela that Afonso Henriques, the first king of Portugal, drove out the Moors and established his new nation's domination of the district. The fortress was built in the 12th century, and was, in its day, a splendid example of medieval military architecture. It is further believed that the Celts founded a castle on this spot in 300 B.C.

Of special interest is the Roman road discovered behind the castle by archeologists. It is the only such road to be unearthed in Portugal, and makes for speculation as to its relationship with the Roman beach colonies of Tróia, off Setúbal. You can scale the hill to the castle any time of the day.

FOOD AND LODGING IN A POUSADA

One of the last remaining segments of the 12th-century castle is the **Pousada do Castelo de Palmela,** 2950 Palmela (tel. 01/235-12-26). It was built as a monastery within the castle walls in 1482 on orders of King João I and dedicated to St. James. The change to use as a pousada kept it from falling into complete ruin. The conversion was done skillfully and unobtrusively, so that the classic look and feel of a cloister has been preserved. It is located on the high crest of a hill, overlooking the valley and sea in the distance. It's traditional in design, a huge, square building opening into a large courtyard. The lower-level arches have been glassed in and furnished with lounge chairs.

Each of the bedroom cells has been opened up, enlarged, and given a glamorous up-to-date ambience. The rooms are furnished in the Portuguese manner, with hand-carved pieces, fine fabrics, and tile baths. Most of them open onto views. Rates in high season are 13,900$ ($90.35) daily in a single and 15,600$ ($101.40) in a double. There is a comfortable drawing room near the dining room, with a noteworthy washbasin once used by the monks for their ablutions.

The dining room, once the refectory of the monastery, is stately yet informal. The pulpit used for the reading of prayers during meals is still standing. The room is large and long, with terracotta tile floors, and large windows. The effect is beautiful, light, and elegant. The service is efficient. A three-course meal goes for 3,100$ ($20.15). Food is served daily from 12:30 to 2:30 p.m. and 7:30 to 9:30 p.m.

ESTREMADURA

The black-shawled women of Nazaré traced against the darkening sea . . . the phenomenon of Fátima . . . the sedate charm of the antique town of Óbidos . . . the curative waters of Caldas da Rainha . . . the jagged granite island of Berlenga . . . the rolling plains near Alcobaça . . . the sandy beaches along the way. The first flowers of empire bloomed in these lands north of Lisbon hundreds of years ago, and the beauty has not been diminished by time. Like the once-white limestone of Battle Abbey (Batalha), this land has been gilded in the sunlight of the passing years.

Estremadura is a land of contrasts. Stories, apocryphal and real, still inspire the burial hall of kings, empty niches never filled, and broad squares and green plains where faith has been restored and fate decided. Deaths and royal intrigues, castles rising in the air, all are woven together, the warp and woof inextricably bound up in the whole fabric.

The Atlantic smashes the coast of Guincho, while farther up it can hardly muster a ripple in the snug cove of São Martinho do Pôrto. These coastal regions are teeming with seafood: nursery-bred lobster, shrimp, crabs, squid, tuna, barnacles, and albacore. The sea is never far from any spot in Estremadura. From many a village's bastion, its shimmer can be seen, a reminder of the source of the land's bounty. In the many examples of Manueline architecture, especially at Batalha, the tie with the sea remains unbroken. The basic nautical designs—ropes, cables, armillary spheres, seascape effects—acknowledge the debt.

If it is impossible for you to spend several days exploring Estremadura, you can dip into it on one-day trips from Lisbon: first to Óbidos, 58 miles from Lisbon; then to Alcobaça, 67 miles from Lisbon; on to Nazaré, 81 miles from Lisbon; back to

Batalha, 73 miles from Lisbon; and finally a stop at Fátima, 87 miles from the capital. Traveling to these five major places will take you through the heartland of Estremadura.

---

1. Óbidos

Years after Afonso Henriques drove the Moors out of Óbidos, the poet king, Dinis, and his saintly wife, Isabella of Aragón, passed by the battlemented walls of this medieval borough and were struck by its beauty. The queen likened the village, with its extended walls and gleaming plaster-faced houses, to a jewel-studded crown. Anxious to please, Dinis made her a present of this gem-like village ribboned by a defensive wall. A tradition was established. Instead of giving precious stones, Portuguese royal bridegrooms presented Óbidos to their spouses—and it didn't cost them a penny. And what queen could complain at getting such a gift?

Entered through a tile-coated gatehouse, Óbidos rises on a sugarloaf hill, above a valley of vineyards. Its golden towers, its ramparts (rebuilt in the 12th century and subsequently restored), and its crenellated battlements contrast with bright white houses and the rolling countryside where windmills clack in the breeze. Inside its confines, you will have traveled back hundreds of years. The narrow streets are either cobbled or made of roughly hewn flagstones. Green shoots lodge in the crannies of the walls, and vines climb the sides of tile-roofed houses. A loom hums in a candlelit vaulted workshop. It's a living piece of history.

In the baroque **Parish Church of Santa Maria,** Afonso V, at the age of ten, exchanged marriage vows with his cousin, only eight. Inside, the church is lined with blue and white azulejos. Pause long enough to admire a Renaissance tomb and the paintings of Josefa of Óbidos, a 17th-century artist. In the Chapel of St. Lawrence are contained relics of saints' hands.

The castle has been converted into a tourist inn (*povsada*). From its ramparts you can bask in views of Estremadura, the scene so unspoiled one can imagine Afonso Henriques' retinue marching over the hills.

Save some time for browsing through the shops, searching out thick-woven fabrics, regional rugs (both hand- and machine-made), raffia and handmade bags, and the local lace.

This well-preserved national monument village lies 59 miles north of Lisbon. Trains leave the Rossio station in Lisbon.

WHERE TO STAY

For excellent accommodations, I recommend **Pousada do Castelo,** 2510 Óbidos (tel. 062/951-05). This Manueline-trimmed stone palace lodged on the ramparts of the walls of Óbidos is firmly rooted in Portugal's history, and today, with the supervision of the government, it is one of the best pousadas in the country. Reached via twisting cobblestone streets through the village, the entrance is through a thick Gothic archway. You ascend farther, into a wide sunny forecourt, and up a grand stone stairway to the main hall. Through the Manueline door, you can go to Foz do Arelho beach, a pleasant resort where the British writer, Graham Greene, used to spend his vacations.

There are several well-furnished lounges, but regrettably, only six double bedrooms, plus three suites. The fortunate few who snare the rooms enjoy the character of the bedchambers, furnished with antiques or fool-the-eye reproductions. Deeply set windows have tiny monk ledges, where you can squat to enjoy the view of the surrounding countryside. Home-like cretonne fabrics cover the beds, and a few rooms contain desks with brass church lamps, armchairs, and ecclesiastical wall plaques. Doubles cost from 16,600$ ($107.90). Fellow guests gather in one of two drinking lounges for sundown libations.

Most wayfarers stop off just for the day, partaking of the 2,500$ ($16.25) to 3,300$ ($21.45) luncheon or dinner. I particularly recommend the roast suckling pig and the chicken cooked in an earthenware pot with a red wine sauce. Try for a table near one of the view windows. The dining room is in the Portuguese quinta style, almost grand, yet nicely provincial, with old oak beams, tile dado, a fireplace, wrought-iron chandeliers, and leather chairs. If you're not staying at the pousada, call ahead for summertime dining reservations. Food is served daily from 12:30 to 3 p.m. and 7:30 to 9:30 p.m.

Estalagem do Convento, Rua Dom João de Ornelas, 2510 Óbidos (tel. 062/ 952-17), is an old village nunnery turned inn. Outside the town walls, it is owned by a chemist, Luís de Sousa Garcia. The reception lounge is surely the tiniest on the Iberian peninsula, with a fireplace, 17th-century chest, torchères, and a pair of gilt angels. The 24 rooms have furniture to complement the structure. Although the beds are old, the mattresses are more recent, and tile bathrooms have been sneaked in. The bed-chambers open off rambling corridors with chests and benches large enough to hold the trousseaux of a dozen brides. The cost for one person is 8,000$ ($52) daily with breakfast; a double, with sitting room and breakfast, is 9,000$ ($58.50).

Since this is primarily an inn and the food is good, it's wisest to pay the extra 4,200$ ($27.30) for two meals a day. Guests from outside are welcomed as well, and can order a 2,000$ ($13) table d'hôte or else specialties from the à la carte menu, including French onion soup, peppersteak, and crêpes suzette. The dining room decor consists of heavy black beams, an open corner stone fireplace, and a brick oven. On sunny days guests dine on the rear patio, in a garden with a moldy stone wall and tangerine and orange trees. Food is served from 12:30 to 2:30 p.m. and 7:30 to 9:30 p.m. daily. In addition to a bar with hand-hewn beams, there's a living room with leather armchairs, old paintings, an 18th-century desk, and a brass-studded chest dated 1827. A former wine cellar has been turned into a typical pub.

Albergaría Josefa d'Óbidos, Rua Dom João de Ornelas, 2510 Óbidos (tel. 062/952-28), is of recent construction although it looks much older. It is placed just outside the fortifications of the old town. Each of its 40 bedrooms contains a private bath, radio, and phone; some have wall-to-wall carpeting. Depending on the season, singles rent for 2,750$ ($17.90) to 4,000$ ($26) daily, with a twin or double going for 4,000$ ($26) to 6,000$ ($39), including a continental breakfast. There is a disco on the ground floor. Because the inn is set on a hillside, it is entered through two separate main doors. It also has a typical restaurant with a private terrace, which you may want to patronize even if you're not staying there. Service is daily from 12:30 to 3 p.m. and 7:30 to 10 p.m. You can have an apéritif in the bar, which is decorated with reproductions of the work of the artist who is the namesake of this albergaría.

Albergaría Rainha Santa Isabel, Rua Direita, 2510 Óbidos (tel. 062/951-15). Except for the necessity of negotiating a parking space, many visitors prefer this above many of the other hostelries in town. It's on a narrow cobblestone-covered street running through the center of town. It opened as a hotel in 1985, but the building itself, once a private home, is many centuries old. The high-ceilinged lobby is covered with blue, white, and yellow tiles. There's a comfortable and sunny bar area filled with leather-covered sofas and Victorian-style chairs. An elevator carries you to one of the 20 bedrooms, each of which is equipped with a private bath, TV, and phone. Singles cost from 5,000$ ($32.50) daily and doubles from 6,500$ ($42.25). In August, prices are 500$ ($3.25) more per room. Most guests drive through the town, and deposit their luggage at the reception desk before moving on to park on the square in front of the village church, about 100 feet away.

Pensão Martim de Freitas, Arrabalde, 2510 Óbidos (tel. 062/951-85), is outside the walls on the road that leads to Alcobaça and Caldas da Rainha. The accommodating hosts rent six simply furnished rooms at prices ranging from 4,500$ ($29.25) daily for two persons without bath to 6,000$ ($39) for a double with bath.

Everything is spotless in this establishment, which is generally cited by the tourist office to those seeking low-cost accommodations. Breakfast is the only meal served.

WHERE TO DINE

Most visitors to Óbidos like to dine at the pousada, previously recommended. However, you get far better value, less formality, and more local color at one of the typical little restaurants that exist either inside or outside the walls.

My favorite within the walls is the **Restaurant Alcaide,** Rua Direita (tel. 952-20). On a narrow street leading up to the pousada, this little restaurant is known for its local cookery and good and inexpensively priced wines. Decorated in a Portuguese tavern style, it opens onto a balcony where the lucky few quickly fill up the tables. Meals cost from 1,300$ ($8.45), and as many as 50 guests can be seated at one time. The restaurant serves daily except Monday. In the afternoon, you can drop in for either tea or a drink. Hours are 12:30 to 3:30 p.m. and 7:30 to 9:30 p.m. The restaurant takes a holiday in November.

Restaurant Dom João V, Largo da Igreja Senhor da Pedra (tel. 951-34), just outside Óbidos, specializes in the regional cuisine of Estremadura, accompanied by good Portuguese wines. The dining room is spacious and clean, and you're invited to look into the kitchen, so that you can make your own selection if you find the menu confusing. The helpful staff adds to the enjoyment of dining here, where the food is not fancy but tasty and good value for your money. A complete meal will cost from 1,800$ ($11.70). The restaurant serves from noon to 4 p.m. and 7 to 11 p.m. daily. Parking is possible, an important item in Óbidos.

AFTER DARK IN ÓBIDOS

You can spend a pleasant, Portuguese evening at **Bar Abrigo da Biquinha** (tel. 95-11-18), a little bar on the Rua Biquinho just outside the city walls. The building, which dates from the 15th century, has whitewashed walls and several floor levels. One has a bar with stools and houses the liquor supply and refrigerator; another is equipped with a balcony for fado entertainers and is furnished with tables and chairs; and still another has a large table made from an old millstone, surrounded by stools of padded kegs. The bar has a fireplace, two fountains built into the walls, and a little courtyard where you can enjoy your drinks in summer. The greeting here is warm, and the local people don't mind sharing their enjoyment with visitors. Hours are 9 p.m. to 2 or 3 a.m. A beer costs 100$ (65¢), and you can order sandwiches for 100$ (65¢) to 150$ ($1).

2. Caldas da Rainha

After a bad night's sleep, the sister-queen of Manuel the Fortunate one day set out from Óbidos to Batalha. Passing through a small village en route, the rheumatic Leonor is said to have seen peasants bathing in fetid pools off to the side of the road. When told of the therapeutic value of these springs, she had her ladies-in-waiting clear the area to protect her modesty. A screen of fabric was draped around her, and she descended partially dressed into a foul sulfur bath.

So great was her relief from her ailment that she returned to Caldas da Rainha again and again—in fact, she pawned her personal wealth in rubies and gold jewelry (many gems given to her by her deceased husband, the Perfect Prince, João II) to construct a hospital and an adjoining church. The chapel, **Nossa Senhora do Pópulo,** was built at the dawn of the 16th century in the Manueline style, then at its apex, and is graced with a well-executed landmark belfry. Inside are handsome 300-year-old glazed earthenware tiles in buttercup yellow and marine blue. Today a classic green bronze statue of Leonor stands at Largo do Conde de Fontalva; and the town has been a spa ever since, enjoying a particular chic in the 19th century.

The spa park is studded with palm trees, weeping willows, flowers, and statues on its green lawns, with lagoons breaking the patterns. In the park, you can visit the **Malhoa Museum** (tel. 319-84), which contains the painting of the popular artist, José Malhoa, portraits by Columbano, art pottery and the *Passion Christ* statues by Bordalo Pinheiro, as well as works by other painters and sculptors. Malhoa, Columbano, Bortalo worked in the latter 19th and early 20th centuries. The museum is open from 10 a.m. to 12:30 p.m. and 2 to 5 p.m. daily except Monday and holidays. Admission is 150$ ($1).

Caldas da Rainha is also noted for its ceramics, especially the cabbage-leaf designs on soup tureens and accompanying bowls. Inside the town and outside along the road to Alcobaça you can stop at many roadside stands and purchase these ceramics at far cheaper prices than you'd pay in Lisbon. However, you'll have to carry them back to the capital with you and arrange shipment there. These primitively painted reproductions of cabbage, fruit, shellfish, and lizards are made from the local clay, and many of them, especially the reptilian and crustacean specialties, evoke the designs of the ceramist and caricaturist Rafael Bordalo Pinheiro. He had a studio at Caldas da Rainha during its heyday as a 19th-century resort.

Caldas da Rainha is also a thriving market town, the activity centering on the Praça da República where you'll see what surely must be the world's largest cabbages. Women with weather-beaten faces sell wild hares in the shop stalls, and at day's end, trudge wearily home. In winter, men in fur-trimmed coats walk around clutching red hens, much to the pleasure of camera-snapping tourists. The town is some 60 miles north of Lisbon, and is usually visited after Óbidos, four miles away.

FOOD AND LODGING

A good choice is the **Hotel Malhoa,** 31 Rua António Sérgio, 2500 Caldas da Rainha (tel. 062/350-11). The curved façade of this hotel is widely acknowledged as belonging to both the newest and most dramatic modern building in town. Behind its eight-story bulk, an elliptically shaped swimming pool offers an encircling terrace to hotel guests. You'll find an attractive series of tiled and polished rooms: a bar, a restaurant, a sauna, a bingo room, and a disco. The unpretentiously comfortable bedrooms each contain a radio, air conditioning, and phone. There's a parking garage on the premises. The 100 rooms rent for 4,800$ ($21.20) daily in a single, 6,500$ ($42.25) in a double, with a continental breakfast included. Lunch or dinner costs from 1,500$ ($9.75).

Convívio, 1 Praça da República (tel. 230-74), is a simple restaurant in the center of town. It offers specialties from Estremadura, with an emphasis on fresh produce from the fields. Good-tasting meals with regional wines cost from 1,800$ ($11.70) to 2,500$ ($16.25) and are served daily except Sunday from 8 a.m. to midnight.

---

3. Peniche

The town of Peniche, 57 miles from Lisbon, stands on a high peninsula, also called Peniche, with wide, sandy beaches at the foot of the rocky cliffs. It is an important fishing port, where fish canning and packing, plus a dockyard, are the economic backbone of the community. The making of bobbin laced by hand was once an important cottage industry here, and efforts have been made to revive the method and quality of the traditional product through a school for apprentices at the **Industrial and Commercial School,** Avenida 25 de Abril. You can visit the school and see a display of samples of the beautiful lacework. The making of lace can be viewed at the **Work House of the Daughters of Fishermen** on Rua do Calvario, and the product can be purchased at a shop on Avenida do Mar.

Originally an island, Peniche and the mainland were connected when a channel was filled in with silt by the 15th century. There are traces of an ancient fortress at a point called Peniche-de-Cima, as well as indications that the Phoenicians landed here, founding a commercial outpost across the channel from the then-existing island. Greeks, Lusitanians, and Romans also landed and settled here.

A strong fortress begun in 1557 and finished in 1570, was built to defend Peniche, and became part of a coastline defense network. Today the warlike aspects have faded into history, and **Peniche harbor** is a striking place to visit, with its view of high peaked rocks and the activity of fishermen putting out to sea and returning with their loads of fish.

The **citadel,** intended to prevent landings by enemy troops and pirates that ravaged Peniche, was ordered constructed by King João I. It underwent many modifications, being used as a prison until 1974 and then as a temporary haven for people forced to flee Angola. You can see the water hole in the courtyard, the casemates, and the air grilles of the dungeons, as well as engraved stones and inscriptions.

The largest church in Peniche, the **Church of St. Pedro,** is a 16th-century building extensively altered through the centuries. The interior, with three naves, is still worth seeing, particularly the chancel with four enormous paintings depicting stages in the life of St. Peter.

Another house of worship worth visiting in the area is the Roman-Gothic **Church of St. Leonardo** at Atouguia da Baleia, on the coast just north of Peniche. Of great historical and architectural interest, it dates from the 13th century. The three naves are formed by ogival arches and covered with wood, while the chancel has a stone-ridged vault. Five paintings on wood on the lateral wall of one of the naves are from the 16th century. One of the two chapels is decorated with colorful 17th-century tiles. A 14th-century bas-relief sculpture in limestone, depicting the Nativity, is of interest for its naïve realism.

Perhaps the major reason most visitors go to Peniche is to explore **Cabo** (Cape) **Carvoeiro** on the peninsula, about three miles east of the town, which offers breathtaking views of the surf smashing into the wild rock formations hundreds of feet below the road. A *farol* (lighthouse), built in 1779, is some 80 feet high and affords a magnificent panorama over the archipelago of the Berlengas and Nau dos Corvos. The lighthouse stands at the end of the Cabo road. One reader, Robert M. Levine of Long Island, N.Y., says that "in many ways, the view ranks with that at the Grand Canyon."

DINING AT THE LIGHTHOUSE

For a dining room with a view, go to the **Restaurant Nau Dos Corvos** (tel. 724-10), at Cabo Carvoeiro. It's difficult to miss this glass-walled restaurant, since it's one of the few buildings at the end of the tip of land overlooking the rocks of Peniche. To some observers the handful of towering rocks isolated in the offshore surf look like petrified giants who didn't quite make it to shore before being turned to stone. Many Portuguese travel for miles for a view of the seascape, then later enjoy a meal in this four-star restaurant, seating 122 patrons. Service is daily except Tuesday from 11:30 a.m. to 3:30 p.m. and 7 to 10 p.m. Menu items feature both continental and regional specialties, including an array of fish and shellfish, plus several pork and beef dishes. Everything is accompanied by a good selection of Portuguese wines, both red and white, which the waiter or steward will be happy to recommend. Meals cost from 2,500$ ($16.25). There is space for parking, and the restaurant can at times get quite busy on a summer day.

4. Berlenga Island

Berlenga, a granite rock set in the Atlantic, is an island hideaway. Seven miles out in the ocean from Peniche, a medieval fortress once stood sentinel over the Portuguese coastline. The reddish granite mass of Berlenga is the largest island in a little archipelago made up of three groups of rocky rises known as the Farilhões, the Estelas, and the Forcades. Berlenga draws skindivers and fishermen, intrigued by the undersea fauna, the long-finned tunny (albacore), jackfish, and varieties of marine crustaceans. It has numerous coves and underwater caves.

The medieval fortress was destroyed in 1666 when 28 Portuguese tried to with-stand some 1,500 Spaniards who bombarded it from 15 ships. Rebuilt toward the end of the 17th century, it now houses a hostel. You can take a stairway from the fortress to the lighthouse, stopping along the way to look over the panorama of the archipelago. A cobblestone walk from the top of the lighthouse site takes you down to a little bay with fishermen's cottages along a beach.

You can arrange a boat trip around the island. On the way, to the south of the hostel, you can see the **Furado Grande,** a long marine tunnel that leads to a creek walled in by the granite cliffs. Under the fortress is a cave the locals call the **blue grotto,** except that its pool is more emerald green in color.

Between June and September there is regular boat service to Berlenga Island from the Peniche peninsula, operated by the Viamar Company, whose office is on the Peniche harbor. The crossing takes about an hour and costs 600$ ($3.90) per person round trip. The boat makes one round trip a day in June and September, three round trips a day in July and August (two in the morning and one in the after-noon). You can also rent equipment for underwater fishing and skindiving at Peniche, which is 57 miles north of Lisbon, jutting out into the Atlantic.

WHERE TO STAY

If you'd like to live in an offshore fortress, you can try for an accommodation at the already-mentioned hostel. It's the **Casa Abrigo São João Batista,** Berlenga Is-land 2520 Peniche (tel. 062/720-21). Before heading for Berlenga, if you plan to spend the night, you should make arrangements at the Tourist Office in Peniche on Rua Alexandre Herculano, 2520 Peniche (tel. 062/992-71). To stay here at this for-tress, which rises on an islet separated from the main body of land, you have to love the sea and savor the thrill in your bones of living in a converted fortress from the Middle Ages. Its stone walls, towers, and turrets rise up sturdily on its own rocky islet. Open only from June 1 to September 20, it was built as a far-out bulwark in the coastal defense of Portugal.

Still standing firmly on its granite foundation, it is prepared for a different inva-sion today—the romantic tourist thrilling to ocean waves lashing and spraying be-low his or her windows. The fortress turns its outer stone walls against the elements, opening its interior courtyards to those who relax in the sun. Umbrella tables are set on stone pavements. Individual rooms are very basic, and some dorm accommoda-tions are available as well. Lodgers take care of themselves, as there is no maid serv-ice. Guests must bring in their food and linen, cook their meals, make their beds, even clean the place. Requests for reservations at the Peniche Tourist Office start at the beginning of May. A deposit of 50% of the total cost of the stay must be sent in with the application for a reservation. A boarder can't stay at the hostel for more than seven days. The rates per person are from 400$ ($2.60) daily, and the place can ac-commodate about 50 travelers.

---

5. Alcobaça

At the apex of its power in the Middle Ages, this Cistercian monastery was one of the richest and most prestigious in Europe. Begun around 1152, it was founded to honor a vow made by Portugal's first king, Afonso Henriques, should he be victorious over the Moors at Santarém. Alcobaça, at the confluence of the Alcoa and Baça Rivers, was built to show his spiritual indebtedness to St. Bernard of Clairvaux, who inspired (others say goaded) many crusaders into battle against the infidel.

Today the monastery, in spite of its baroque façade and latter-day overlay, is a monument to simplicity and majesty. Somehow a sense of other-worldliness pervades as you walk down the 350-foot-long nave. Tall chalk-white clustered columns, like trees, hold up a vaulted ceiling nearly 70 feet high. The transept of Alcobaça shelters the Gothic tombs of two star-crossed lovers, the Romeo and Juliet of Portuguese history. They were Pedro the Cruel and the ill-fated Spanish beauty, Inês de Castro, his mistress and (later perhaps) his wife. The work of an unknown sculptor, their sarcophagi (although damaged) are considered the greatest pieces of sculpture from 14th-century Portugal.

The oval-faced Inês is guarded and protected by angels hovering over her. Her tomb rests on sculpted animals with human faces, said to represent the assassins who slit her throat. Inês was buried at Alcobaça following a ghoulish ceremony in which the king had her decaying body exhumed and forced his courtiers to kiss her rotted hand and honor her as "the queen of the realm." Around the tomb are panels depicting scenes from the Last Judgment.

Pedro hoped to rise on that day of Resurrection to greet Inês emerging from her sleep of centuries. On a wheel of fortune at his tomb, a sculptor, following his mandate, carved the words *ate o fim do mundo,* meaning "until the end of the world." Guarded by angels, his feet nestled on a dog, Pedro lies in a tomb supported by lions, symbols of his timeless rage and vengeance.

There is much to see at Alcobaça, certainly the Cloisters of Silence, with their delicate arches, favored by Dinis, the poet king. He sparked a thriving literary colony at the monastery, the monks busily engaged in translating ecclesiastical writings. But aside from the tombs and cloisters, the curiosity is the kitchen, through which a branch of the Alcoa River was routed. As in most Cistercian monasteries, the reason for a flowing brook was one of sanitation. Chroniclers have suggested that the friars fished for their dinner in the brook, later washing their dishes in it. In the huge chimneyed pit, five or six steers or oxen were roasted at the same time. A six-ton marble table resting here would probably have accommodated Gargantua and Pantagruel.

In the dining room are found niches where the monks prayed while the hierarchy ate. In honor of an old tradition, Queen Elizabeth II was feted at a luncheon here. In front of the dining room is a fountain, where Portuguese girls wet their fingers, putting the water to their cheeks. The old women of the village predict that by so doing the young girls will soon get married.

Finally, in the 18th-century Salon of Kings are niches with sculptures of some of the rulers of Portugal (many fell from their resting places and were damaged in the 1755 earthquake). An air of melancholy is lent to the scene by the empty niches left waiting for the rulers who were never sculpted. The tiles in the room depict, in part, Afonso Henriques' triumph over the Moors.

After your visit, you can explore the nearby market, said to sell the best fruit in all of Portugal, especially succulent peaches grown in surrounding orchards originally planted by the Cistercian monks. Many stalls also sell the blue and white pottery of Alcobaça.

Trains depart from Lisbon's Rossio station, 67 miles away.

FOOD AND LODGING

The most attractive modern hotel in town, **Hotel Santa Maria,** Rua Francisco Zagalo, 2460 Alcobaça (tel. 062/432-95), is on a sloping street just above the flower-dotted plaza in front of the monastery. Its position in a quiet but central part of the historic city is ideal. The combination TV salon, bar, and breakfast room are interconnected on the ground floor. Each is filled with paneling cut into well-polished geometrical shapes and comfortable contemporary chairs, some of which look out over the monastery. If parking is a problem, the hotel will open its garage. With a continental breakfast included, singles rent for 5,000$ ($32.50) daily, while doubles cost 8,000$ ($52). Each contains a private bath, phone, and radio. Some chambers contain balconies looking out over the square.

Trindade, 22 Praça Dom Afonso Henriques (tel. 423-97), is the most popular restaurant in town. It opens onto a side of the monastery, fronting a tree-shaded square. In fair weather, tables are placed on this square, and harried waiters rush back and forth across the street carrying cooling drinks. Trindade has both a full restaurant service and snackbar facilities. If you're dining here, count on spending from 1,500$ ($9.75) to 2,000$ ($13) for a complete meal, likely to include such dishes as shellfish soup, roast rabbit, and the fresh fish of the day. Roast chicken is also available. Hours are noon to 3:30 p.m. and 8 to 10 p.m. daily. It is closed on Saturday in winter.

---

6. Aljubarrota

Against a backdrop of mountain scenery, the extensive green fields on the Aljubarrota plateau are considered "the birthplace of Portugal." Between Alcobaça and Batalha, on August 14, 1385, near the village of Aljubarrota, Portuguese independence was secured. João I, the founder of the Aviz dynasty, and his young captain, Nuño Álvares—fortified by scythe- and shovel-bearing peasants and some English archers—defeated the Castilian soldiers.

A story of the battle relates how during the heat of conflict the king and his army were consumed by thirst under a blazing sun. He vowed that never would a voyager pass this way again without access to water. Today, outside the village, a small chapel offers a pitcher of fresh water in a niche in honor of that ancient commitment.

FOOD AND LODGING

A comfortable hacienda, **Casa de Padeira,** Rte. N8, Aljubarrota 2460 Alcobaça (tel. 062/482-72), is the private domain of a local professor of philosophy, Figueiredo Ventura, who with his charming wife and three children create an extension of their private home in each of the establishment's well-furnished modern bedrooms, eight in all. Each of the units contains some form of antique bed, as well as a scattering of family heirlooms. Some of them are Portuguese spool beds; others are well-rubbed art nouveau fantasies. Regardless of their style, they dominate each of the attractive rooms with their well-oiled beauty. The bedrooms each contain a private bath. From July to September, the charge is 7,000$ ($45.50) for two persons and 5,000$ ($32.50) for one guest on a daily basis. During the rest of the year rates are 5,500$ ($35.75) daily for two and 4,000$ ($26) for one. Breakfast is served at a Sheraton dining table between 8 and 10 p.m. daily. It's most generous, including a fruit gâteau, eggs, and an array of local fruits. Meals other than breakfast are prepared on request for 1,500$ ($9.75) per person.

The casa has a swimming pool and another room where guests can play snooker, table tennis, or watch some videos and slides about the Aljubarrota plateau. The Venturas will distribute handmade maps of the region, with multilingual descriptions of the nearby beaches, monuments, and places of interest. In winter, a fire is likely to be blazing in the stone fireplace of the guest lounge.

The Casa da Padeira was named after a local heroine who in 1385 is said to have single-handedly killed seven marauding Spanish soldiers with a baker's shovel. The legend is grisly, but a humorous version of it is displayed in blue and white tiles on the bar of the Ventura's comfortable salon and breakfast room.

7. São Martinho do Pôrto

This seaside village nestles between pine-covered foothills and the ocean. Its main attraction is an almost landlocked sandy beach, brightly scalloped into the terrain. The waters are calm and clear, the days gently descending from May to October.

For many, São Martinho do Pôrto makes a good base for touring: Óbidos is 12½ miles away; Alcobaça, 11; Fátima, 28; Batalha, 22; and Caldas da Rainha, 9½. It is 72 miles by rail from Lisbon, and only a short run north to the fishing village of Nazaré. A coastal road skirts the village, and buses run regularly into Nazaré.

FOOD AND LODGING

Old-fashioned and gracious, **Parque Hotel,** 3 Avenida Maréchal Carmona, 2465 São Martinho do Porto (tel. 062/985-05), is set in its own small private garden. Ideal for families who want to live pleasantly and inexpensively near the beach, it is surrounded by trees, with summer furniture set out for periods of relaxation. It's especially favored by economy-minded English tourists who like an atmosphere of large-size bedrooms and homelike furniture.

Open only from the first of July to the first of October, it has installed private baths in its 36 bedrooms. They cost from 4,500$ ($29.25) daily in a single, from 8,000$ ($52) in a double. A continental breakfast is included. You breakfast in a turn-of-the-century hall, with an elaborate ceiling and an old chandelier. In all, the hotel is a world of polished floors and well-scrubbed rooms. On the grounds are two tennis courts.

Since the hotel doesn't serve meals, you may want to go instead to the **Apartamentos Turísticos São Martinho** (tel. 062/983-35), which does. It offers both continental and regional cuisine. Service is efficient and polite, and full meals cost from 1,800$ ($11.70). Try for a shellfish and rice dish, or any of the grilled catches of the day. Service is daily from 12:30 to 2:30 p.m. and 7:30 to 10 p.m. This popular tourist complex also has a bar and disco.

8. Nazaré   Seat Mate

What strikes one immediately about the people of Nazaré is their self-containedness. The inhabitants of Portugal's most famous fishing village live in a unique, tradition-bound, ageless world. Many have never been to Lisbon; indeed, many have never left their village, except perhaps to make the pilgrimage to nearby Fátima.

The people remain insular, even though their village blossoms into a resort in summer. White tents filled with international visitors dot the crescent-shaped beach. Yet the natives go about their time-honored tasks, perhaps pausing to pose for cameras. Nazaré was originally discovered by writers and painters; but in the 1960s seemingly everyone arrived. For that reason, the young who have grown up in a tourist-oriented economy will probably not follow the time-honored folkways of their forebears.

Nazaré is best viewed in winter, because, chances are, you won't get to see it in summer. You'll be too busy looking for a parking place (virtually impossible to find) or else fighting for a place on the beach in a seething mass of humanity. The problem was that Nazaré was advertised as "the most picturesque" and "the most quaint" fishing village of Portugal. With advertising like that, the hordes arrived and now have almost engulfed the village itself. That, coupled with high-rise construction on every foot of available land, has made people wonder what happened to the fishing village. It's still there. You just have to look harder for it.

Don't expect stunning architectural styles or historic sights. The big attraction is its people and their boats. Claiming descent from Carthaginian and Phoenician ancestors, many of the natives are characterized by aquiline noses and dark brows. They are a gentle, hard-working folk whose classical features are marked and lined by sad, yet noble, countenances.

The clothes of the villagers are patch quilts of sun-faded colors. The rugged-looking men appear in rough woolen shirts and trousers, patched in kaleidoscopic rainbow hues, resembling Scottish plaid. Although the origin of this apparel remains unknown, one explanation ventured is that the fishermen picked up the designs from Wellington's troops who passed this way during the Napoleonic wars. On their heads the men wear long woolen stocking caps, in the dangling ends of which they keep their valuables—a favorite pipe, even a crucifix.

The women are mostly barefoot, wearing embroidered handmade blouses and pleated skirts also made of plaid woolens patched many times. It is customary for married women to don black as a traditional sign of mourning—black tasseled shawls, black capes or cowls; whereas the unmarried girls of the village are traditionally attired in seven petticoats. The government has made it illegal to count these petticoats, as many tourists were fond of doing in the 1950s.

The boats of the fishermen are Phoenician in design, elongated, slender, and decorated in bold colors. Crudely shaped eyes often appear on the high knife-like prows, eyes supposedly imbued with the magical power to search the deep for fish and to avert storms. Powered by oars, the boats contain lanterns for the dangerous job of fishing after dark. During the gusty days of winter, or at high tide, the boats are hauled in and lined up along the waterfront promenade.

While the men are at sea, the women wait, passing their time mending nets, drying sardines on the beach, perhaps nursing children, darning socks, or sewing patches on articles of clothing. At sundown they squat in circles, waiting on the somber shore. When their men come in, the business of sorting out the fish begins. The women trudge up toward the shoreline with heavy baskets balanced precariously on their heads. Some hang nets to dry in the night air; some slice entrails from the silver bodies upon the beach; others chase away pestering children . . . and some wait.

Nazaré is divided into two sections, the fishing quarter and the Sítio, the latter being the upper town which is almost exclusively residential. Near the beach, you'll find handcraft shops, the markets, restaurants, hotels, and boarding houses. The main square opens directly onto the sea, and narrow streets lead to the smaller squares, evoking a Medina in a Moorish village. Simple shops hang objects outside their doors, indicating what they sell (for example, a carved wooden cow head indicates the butcher shop). At the farthest point from the cliff and square are the vegetable and fish markets, where auctions are held.

Jutting out over the sea, the promontory of the Sítio is a sheer drop to the ocean and the beach below. It is reached either by a funicular or by a goat-steep cobblestone pathway. At the Sítio the Virgin Mary supposedly appeared in 1182. A young horseback-riding nobleman, Faus Roupinho, was pursuing a wild deer dangerously near the precipice, shrouded in mist. The fog lifted suddenly to reveal the Virgin and the chasm below. In honor of this miracle, the nobleman built the **Chapel of Memory.** Today, near the spot, you can go inside the 18th-century structure honoring that long-ago event.

About eight miles from Alcobaça, Nazaré lies 82 miles north of Lisbon. From the capital, take the three-hour train ride to the nearest station of Valado, where bus connections into Nazaré can be made. Coaches depart from Lisbon's Rossio station.

WHERE TO STAY

The leading hotel of town (where the competition is not keen) is **Hotel Praia,** 39 Avenida Vieira Guimarães, 2450 Nazaré (tel. 062/514-23). Built at the end of the 1960s, just when Nazaré was being put on the tourist maps of the world, the hotel is a 41-bedroom structure, rising six floors and decorated in a modern style. All rooms are equipped with private bath, and the location is about a three-minute walk to the sandy beach where the fishing boats and bathing cabins lie. In high season, a single with a continental breakfast rents for 8,880$ ($57.70) per day, with a double going for 9,250$ ($60.15) and a triple for 11,725$ ($76.20). Otherwise, reductions are granted (inquire when making a reservation). The hotel doesn't have a restaurant on the premises, but guests can patronize the Mar Bravo (see below), which it owns. The hotel remains closed for most of December.

Hotel Da Nazaré, Largo Afonso Zuquete, 2450 Nazaré (tel. 062/513-11), is the runner-up. This hotel will not please everybody (and hasn't in the past), yet many patrons count themselves lucky if they can get a room here on a hot summer day. The location is on a busy street set back from the water, about a three-minute walk from the promenade. The hotel opens onto a tiny plaza, and many of its front bedrooms have private balconies. Open all year, it rents 52 small bedrooms which are very simply furnished. With room and a continental breakfast, the single rate is 4,800$ ($21.20) per day, going up to 6,500$ ($42.25) in a double. A rooftop terrace for sun-lounging puts Nazaré and the clifftop Sítio in perspective. Frankly, the best feature of this hotel is its fourth and fifth floors, which contain dining and restaurant facilities. The dining room opens onto window walls peering out over the village housetops, the rugged cliffs, and the harbor where tomorrow's sardines are being hauled in. Specializing in fish dishes, this dining room is open to the general public. Featured dishes include lobster Thermidor, grilled crab, shrimps, and clams in a savory sauce.

Pensão-Restaurante Ribamar, 9 Rua Gomes Freire, 2450 Nazaré (tel. 062/511-58), is a genuine old-fashioned village inn, with a traditionally styled dining room where candlelit meals are served at night. It's right on the water, with most of its rooms opening onto balconies from which guests watch the beaching of the sardine-filled boats. Or you can watch (without being caught staring) the multipetticoated women or the tasseled stocking caps of the men. Even if you're passing through just for the day, you may want to try a regional meal in the oak-beamed dining room. A meal is offered for 1,500$ ($9.75) and includes specialties such as cream of shellfish soup, fish stew (*caldeirada*) in the Nazaré style, and roast kid. The atmosphere is genial, with ornate tiles, brown chairs and draperies, and stark-white cloths. Food is served daily from 12:30 to 3 p.m. and 7 to 10 p.m.

A twisting stairway in the rear leads to the old-style bedrooms, with rattan baskets of pine cones on each landing. Each bedroom is individually decorated, comfortable, and immaculately maintained. All 23 rooms have private bath. Singles rent for 5,500$ ($35.75) daily, with doubles costing 7,500$ ($48.75). Taxes are included in the tariffs.

Hotel Maré, 8 Rua Mouzinho de Albuquerque, 2450 Nazaré (tel. 062/511-22), has a modern lobby sheathed in vertical planks of wood, with black-and-white photographs of the fishermen of Nazaré. The hotel is right in the heart of the fishing port, and its 36 rooms are furnished simply. The site is a block from the beach. Including a continental breakfast, a double room costs 10,000$ ($65) daily, and a single goes for 8,500$ ($55.25). Usually the person at the desk speaks some English. The hotel's sun-flooded restaurant is on the fourth floor, offering a panoramic view. From 12:30 to 3 p.m. and 7 to 10 p.m. daily, guests enjoy meals for 1,300$ ($8.45), including such fare as steak in a cream sauce, escalopes of veal in madeira, and sea bass prepared fisherman's style. On the fifth floor is a bar with comfortable tables. At least half of the floor space is devoted to an outdoor sun terrace.

A three-star boarding house, the **Pensão Madeira,** 2450 Nazaré (tel. 062/511-80), is simple but adequate. Its 11 bedrooms, each with private bath, face the sea. A single with bath and breakfast costs 7,000$ ($45.50) daily, a double with the same amenities going for 9,000$ ($58.50).

WHERE TO DINE

One of the most frequented of the dozens of restaurants in this bustling village is **Mar Bravo,** 75 Praça Sousa Oliveira (tel. 511-80), on the corner of the town's busy square overlooking the ocean. The decor is tile, with a huge photo of the Nazaré beach covering the back wall. A complete meal costs 1,800$ ($11.70) and consists of soup, followed by a fish or meat dish, and bread. There's a menu in English. À la carte specialties are bass caprice, fish stew Nazarena, and grilled pork. Dessert might be a soufflé, a fruit salad, or a pudding. Hours are daily from noon to 4 p.m. and 7 to 10 p.m. Upstairs is a second dining room, with an oceanside view.

Beira-Mar, 40 Avenida da República, 2450 Nazaré (tel. 514-58), is one of the best restaurants in the port. In a modern building, it offers typical Portuguese dishes, including the "day's catch." Meat dishes are also available, along with regional soups, but Neptune is king. Meals cost 1,200$ ($7.80) and up, and are served daily from noon to 3 p.m. and 7 to 10 p.m. More than 75 diners can crowd in here on a busy day in summer. Opening onto the beach, this popular place is also one of the more reasonable inns in town if you're seeking modest accommodations at modest prices: from 8,000$ ($52) daily for one of the 15 simply furnished double rooms. Guests are received only from March through November.

Restaurante Maresia, Avenida Manuel Remigio (tel. 512-01), is one of the special restaurants of Nazaré. Maria José Conde Sousa and her daughter run this place, specializing in lobster which is displayed in a tank at the entrance. Overlooking the beach and the waterfront promenade, the restaurant serves excellently prepared food with a natural emphasis on the sea. Try any of their dishes such as shellfish rice, fish stew, roasted sardines, or codfish prepared in a number of ways. Meals cost from 1,500$ ($9.75) and can be enjoyed at one of the sidewalk tables in fair weather. Food is served daily from noon to 3 p.m. and 6:30 p.m. to midnight.

On the outskirts, try **Casinha Velha,** Valado dos Frades (tel. 474-13), which lies on the Nazaré-Alcobaça road, less than two miles east of Nazaré. On the first floor is a cozy bar, with the restaurant lying below. Manuel de Bragança installed the restaurant in a century-old Portuguese house, where he also set up a children's playground with horses to rent as well. He brought to his new venture his experience as a hotel manager in Madeira and the Algarve. Today his restaurant is widely recognized in the area for its food, which includes mussels gratinée and various salads as appetizers, followed by a selection of fresh fish and shellfish. Fish is often preferred grilled on a spit, and you can also order filet steaks. Clients oversee the preparation of their dishes through an exposed kitchen. Count on spending 1,800$ ($11.70) to 2,200$ ($14.30) for a meal here. The decoration is in the rustic style, with old farmers' tools. The establishment is open seven days a week from 12:30 to 3 p.m. and 7:30 to 10 p.m.

SHOPPING

For information about what to buy in Nazaré, refer to "Shopping in Portugal," chapter VII.

9. Batalha

The founder of the House of Aviz, João I, vowed on the plains of Aljubarrota in 1385 that if his underequipped and outnumbered army defeated the powerful invading Castilians, he would commemorate his spiritual indebtedness to the Virgin Mary. The result is the magnificent Battle Abbey, Batalha. Designed in the splendid Gothic-Manueline style, it appears as an imposing mass of steeples, buttresses, and parapets when approached from its western façade. Much restored, it is a jewel case of fine cut gems in stone, bearing the stamp of the English masons who built it.

The western porch, ornamented by a tangled mass of Gothic sculpture of saints and other figures, is capped by a stained-glass window of blue, mauve, and amber. The hue of the limestone has supposedly changed through the ages; today it is a light burnished beige, similar to the color of the façade of the Convent of Christ at Tomar. Napoleon's irreverent army used the stained-glass windows for target practice, turning the nave into both a latrine and a bordello.

In the Founder's Chapel, completed in 1435, João I and his English queen, Philippa of Lancaster, daughter of John of Gaunt, lie in peaceful repose, their hands entwined. Near that of his parents is the tomb of Prince Henry the Navigator, whose fame eclipsed their own even though he never sat on the throne but spent a great part of his life at the School of Navigation at Sagres, on the southern coast of Portugal. Henry's sculpted hands are clasped in prayer. Three of the other princes are also entombed here under a ceiling resembling snow crystals. The Royal Cloister is attributed to Afonso Domingues. These cloisters reveal the beginnings of the nautically oriented Manueline architecture. (Still a second cloister, called the Meditation Cloister, dates from the 15th century.)

The magnum opus of the monastery is the Chapter House, a square chamber whose vaulting is an unparalleled example of the Gothic style, bare of supporting pillars. When originally built by a French architect it collapsed, but a Portuguese redesigned it and slept under it for eight days to prove its soundness. The two tombs of Portugal's Unknown Soldiers from World War I are guarded by sentinels and the glow of an eternal flame. In one part of the quadrangle is the Unknown Soldiers Museum, housing gifts to the fallen warriors from the people of Portugal and from other countries, including a presentation from Maréchal Joffre. Beyond the crypt are the remains of the old wine cellars.

The filigree designs ornamenting the coral-stone entrance to the seven unfinished chapels is stunning. The *capelas,* under an inconstant "sky ceiling," are part of one of the finest examples of the Manueline style of architecture, a true extravaganza in stone. It seems a pity that construction was abandoned here so that workers and architects for Manuel I could help build his Monastery at Belém. Originally, the chapels were ordered by Dom Duarte, the son of João I, but he died before they could be completed.

Outside in the forecourt, a heroic statue was unveiled in 1968 to Nuño Álvares, who fought with João I on the plains of Aljubarrota. Batalha stands 73 miles north of Lisbon, reached by taking a train to Valado where bus connections are made to Batalha.

FOOD AND LODGING

Filling a big accommodation gap in this part of the country is **Pousada do Mestre Afonso Domingues,** Largo Mestre Afonso Domingues, 2440 Batalha (tel. 044/962-61). It stands right across the square from the Batalha, accommodating guests in good comfort. The hotel is extremely well kept, and everything is modern. Rooms are of good size, and all contain a well-equipped private bath. The manager has wisely employed a helpful staff. In high season, a double rents for 12,500$ ($81.25) daily, with singles costing from 11,300$ ($73.45). Some suites for two persons are also rented, costing 16,200$ ($105.30). Even if you're not staying overnight in Batalha, you can patronize the first-class dining room, enjoying typically Portuguese fare for 1,850$ ($12.05) to 2,500$ ($16.25) for a complete meal. Food is served daily from 12:30 to 3 p.m. and 7:30 to 10 p.m.

10. Fátima

This is a world-famous pilgrimage site. Thorny bushes, dwarfed holly, gnarled and twisted olive trees, a stray oak—the terrain around Fátima is wild, almost primitive, with an aura of barren desolation hanging over the countryside. But if you should go on the 13th of May or the 13th of October, the drama that unfolds is remarkable. Beginning on the 12th of each of those months, the roads leading to Fátima are choked with pilgrims traveling in donkey-pulled carts, on bicycles, or in automobiles. Usually, however, they go on foot, some even walking on their knees in penance. They camp out till day breaks. In the central square, larger than St. Peter's in Rome, a statue of the Madonna passes through the crowd. In the breeze 75,000 handkerchiefs flutter, like thousands of peace doves taking flight.

Then, as many as are able crowd in to visit a small slanted-roof shed known as the Chapel of the Apparitions. Inside stands a single white column marking the spot where a small holm oak once grew. It is alleged that an image of the Virgin Mary appeared over this oak on May 13, 1917, when she is said to have spoken to three shepherd children. The oak has long ago disappeared, torn to pieces by souvenir collectors. The oak that now stands near the chapel existed in 1917, but was not connected with the apparition. The original chapel constructed here was dynamited on the night of March 6, 1922, by skeptics who suspected the church of staging the so-called miracle.

While World War I dragged on in Europe, the trio of devoutly faithful children —Lúcia de Jesus and her cousins, Jacinto Marto and Francisco—claimed they saw the first appearance of "a lady" on the tableland of Cova da Iria. Her coming had been foreshadowed in 1916 by what they would later cite as "an angel of peace," who is said to have appeared before them.

Attempts were made to suppress their story, but news of it spread quickly, eventually generating worldwide enthusiasm, disbelief, and intense controversy. During the July appearance, the lady was reported to have revealed three secrets to them, one of which prefigured the coming of World War II, another connected with Russia's "rejection of God." The final secret, recorded by Lúcia, was opened by church officials in 1960, but they have refused to divulge its contents.

Acting on orders from the Portuguese government of the time, the mayor of a nearby town threw the children into jail and threatened them with torture, even death in burning oil. Still, they would not be intimidated, sticking to their original story. The lady was reported to have made six appearances, the final one on October 13, 1917, when the children were joined by an estimated 70,000 people who witnessed the famous Miracle of the Sun. The day of October 13 had broken to pouring rain and driving winds. Observers from all over the world testified that at noon "the sky opened up" and the sun seemed to spin out of its axis and hurtle toward the earth. Many at the site feared that the Last Judgment was upon them. Others later reported that they thought the scorching sun was crashing into the earth and would consume it in flames. Many authorities, and certainly the faithful pilgrims, agreed that a major miracle of modern times had occurred. Only the children reported seeing "Our Lady," however.

In the influenza epidemic that swept over Europe after World War I, both Francisco and Jacinto died. Lúcia became a Carmelite nun in a convent at the university city of Coimbra. She returned to Fátima to mark the 50th anniversary of the apparition, when the pope flew in from Rome.

A cold, white, pristine basilica in the neoclassic style was erected at one end of the wide square. If you want to go inside, you may be stopped by a guard if you're not suitably dressed. A sign posted outside reads: "The Blessed Virgin Mary, Mother of God, appeared in this place. Therefore, women are asked not to enter the sanctuary in slacks or other masculine attire." Men wearing shorts are also excluded.

Fátima lies 36 miles east of Nazaré and about 88 miles north of Lisbon. A train from the capital arrives near Fátima. From the rail station, coaches connect with the pilgrimage site. Outside of Fátima, in the simple and poor village of Aljustrel, you can still see the houses of the three shepherd children.

When you arrive, everything at first seems to be either a souvenir shop, a pension, or a hotel. But in accommodations, Fátima is disastrously equipped. On the days of the major pilgrimages, it's virtually impossible to secure a room unless you've reserved months in advance. Those visiting at other times of the year may find the following recommendations suitable.

LODGINGS

Rated three stars by the government, **Hotel de Fátima,** Rua João Paulo II, 2495 Fátima (tel. 049/523-51), is a leading accommodation. Many of its 122 rooms and nine suites overlook the sanctuary. The ever-increasing invasion of pilgrims to the shrine forced the hotel to enlarge. All rooms have natural wood furnishings in the provincial Portuguese style, with private bath, central heating, and phone. The building has three floors, serviced by two elevators. For half board, the price for two persons is 10,500$ ($68.25) daily, taxes included. On the main floor is a cozy little sitting room with a brick fireplace, a reception lounge, a large sitting room, plus a dining room where you can order a two-course table d'hôte luncheon or dinner for 1,750$ ($11.40).

Hotel Três Pastorinhos, Rua João Paulo II, 2495 Fátima (tel. 049/524-29), is translated as the Hotel of the Three Shepherd Children. The three-star facility is designed in a holiday style, with its most recently added bedrooms opening onto private balconies overlooking the sanctuary. All rooms have modern facilities, including a private bath. One person pays from 5,800$ ($37.70) daily for a room with bath; two persons are charged from 8,500$ ($55.25). Breakfast is included. If you're just passing through, you can come in for a multicourse meal costing 1,800$ ($11.70). The breakfast room opens onto raised sun terraces, edged with pots of flowering plants.

Estalagem Dom Gonçalo, 100 Rua Jacinto Marto, 2495 Fátima (tel. 049/522-62), is a modern, clean, 43-room hotel set in a large garden at the entrance to town and serving some of the best food in Fátima, with the biggest portions. Once it was known as the Pensão Zéca, but it has been considerably remodeled and improved upon. Rooms are comfortably and attractively furnished, costing from 4,200$ ($27.30) daily in a single, from 5,200$ ($33.80) in a double, these tariffs including a continental breakfast. The restaurant has an à la carte menu, a typical repast going for around 1,800$ ($11.70). You can order the usual selection of fish and meat dishes along with a mixed salad or perhaps a tasty omelet. Food is served daily from noon to 3 p.m. and 7:30 to 9:30 p.m.

Hotel Santa Maria, Rua de Santo António, 2495 Fátima (tel. 049/510-15), is a comfortable modern hotel set on a quiet side street just a few steps east of the park surrounding the sanctuary. Inside you'll find a lobby floored with gray and white marble, lots of exposed wood, and a sunny lounge area with plants that thrive in the light streaming through stained-glass windows. The well-trained staff charges 4,600$ ($29.90) daily in a single, 6,200$ ($40.30) in a double, and 8,500$ ($55.25) in a triple, with a continental breakfast included. Each of the 56 modern rooms contains a private bath, balcony, phone, and radio. Meals cost 1,800$ ($11.70).

Hotel Dom José, Avenida Dom José Alves Correia da Silva, 2495 Fátima (tel. 049/522-15). Set beside one of the busiest streets in Fátima, within walking distance of the sanctuary, this modern balconied hotel is large and urban, with 63 bedrooms. A uniformed staff will register you in the marble-floored lobby, after which you proceed by elevator to a comfortable room. Much that this hotel offers, including its bar and dining room, seems to have a bit more style than some of the other more spartan hotels in town. Each room has a private bath, phone, radio, and central heating. There's also a parking garage. Singles cost from 4,800$ ($21.20) daily, while doubles go for 6,200$ ($42.25) and triples for 8,500$ ($55.25), including a continental breakfast. Lunch or dinner is another 1,800$ ($11.70), per person.

Hotel Regina, Rua Dr. Gonego Manuel Formigão, 2495 Fátima (tel. 049/

523-03), is a good bet for a conservative, relatively unexciting, yet perfectly adequate hotel. It sits just east of the street bordering the sanctuary. Many of your fellow guests are likely to be elderly Portuguese pilgrims spending a slow-paced holiday. There's a very clean lobby, with an adjacent bar and TV room, which is popular just before bedtime. Many guests stay here on the half-board plan, enjoying their simple meals in the hotel's dining room. Each of the 87 comfortably outfitted bedrooms contains a private bath, air conditioning, and phone. Rates are 4,000$ ($26) daily in a single, 6,500$ ($42.25) in a double, and 7,800$ ($50.70) in a triple. Tariffs include a continental breakfast.

Hotel Cinquentenário, 175 Rua Francisco Marto, 2495 Fátima (tel. 049/ 521-41), is built onto a corner lot, a short walk east of the sanctuary. This balconied structure offers comfortable accommodations throughout the year. Inside, a heavily patterned series of carpets and wallpapers provide a warmly agreeable, slightly angular decor. Each of the 115 bedrooms contains a private bath, radio, phone, and central heating. There's a bar on the premises, plus a dining room serving typical Portuguese food. In high season, full board costs from 6,000$ ($39) per person daily. For bed and breakfast, the charge is from 3,500$ ($22.75) in a single, from 5,000$ ($32.50) in a double.

WHERE TO EAT

Fátima has many reliable hotels but few independent restaurants, mainly because those hotels have garnered most of the business. If you'd like an independent eatery, however, try **Grelha,** 76 Rua Jacinto Marto (tel. 516-33), which is one of the best in town. It offers not only regional specialties, but is known for its grills, and you can enjoy meals for about 1,800$ ($11.70). In the cooler months the fireplace is an attraction, and the bar is kept busy year round. Meals are served daily except Thursday from noon to 3 p.m. and 7 to 10:30 p.m.

THE FOUR CAVES CIRCUIT

Just eight miles from Fátima, the caverns in and near the village of Mira de Aire offer visitors a glimpse at another kind of miracle: the miracle of nature. The first of these subterranean marvels are the **Alvados Caves,** which are a series of caverns naturally segmented into many smaller caves dotted with lakes. The favorite of these is the Lake of Pearls, with rock formations unique in Europe, including even the remains of an ancient stag preserved in stone.

Mira de Aire Caves, opened in 1974, boast the only Portuguese cavern with an underground river, the Rio Negro, which forms the *Grande Lago* (Great Lake). Fountains and lighting add to the beauty of the underground wonderland, with its sparkling jewel room, the great hall, the red room, and the majestic Dome of the Second Shaft. Various formations have been given such names as jellyfish, Martian, the crib, and the Chinese hat. The return to the surface from the Great Lake is via a modern elevator.

Saint Anthony's Cave, Sêrra de St. António, opened in 1969, was the first Portuguese cave to become a tourist attraction. Its main feature is a single chamber about the size of a football field whose walls, ceiling, and floor are covered with unusual rock formations. Sound and light equipment are used here as in the other caverns to make the tour both enjoyable and educational. Atop the cave is a restaurant whose windows offer a panorama of the rolling hillsides around Mira de Aire.

Fourth in the cave circuit are the **Grutas da Moeda** (Coin Caves) of São Mamede, discovered in 1971 by two hunters searching for a fox that had gone underground. In their exploration, they found the Shepherd's Hall, as they named it, full of fantastic limestone formations. Other sections of the caves since opened to the public are the waterfall, the crib, the red cupola, the unfinished chapel, and the wedding cake, among others. The caves took the name "Coin Caves" from an old legend of a wealthy man who was the victim of robbers. The story goes that he was murdered but when he fell into a steep declivity in the earth, his coins fell with him, to the dismay of the thieves.

The caves are open from 9 a.m. daily, closing at 6 p.m. in January, February, March, October, November, and December; at 7 p.m. in April, May, and June; and at 8 p.m. in July, August, and September. Admission to St. Anthony's Cave is 225$ ($1.45). You can visit these caves and those of Alvados for 400$ ($2.60) admission. To visit both Mira d'Aire and Moeda costs 200$ ($1.30) each.

THE ALGARVE

In the ancient moorish town of Xelb (today called Silves), a handsome and sensitive vizier is said to have once lived. During one of his sojourns into northern lands, he fell in love with and won the hand of a beautiful blond-haired Nordic princess. Marrying her, he brought her back to the Algarve. Soon the young princess began to pine, finding no solace in the Moor's rose castle. Her young husband finally learned that his new bride's melancholy came from her longing for the snow-covered hills and valleys of her native land. Issuing a decree, the vizier demanded that thousands of almond trees be planted throughout his realm. From that day on, pale white almond blossoms have blanketed the Algarve in late January and early

February. The sight acted as an anodyne to the heart of the young princess. On see-ing the blossoms, she found she could finally fulfill her marital duties and lived hap-pily ever after in her vizier's sun-drenched kingdom with its sweet-smelling artificial winters . . . or so the story goes.

The maritime province of the Algarve, often called the Garden of Portugal, is the southwesternmost part of Europe, its coastline stretching a distance of 100 miles, all the way from Henry the Navigator's Cape St. Vincent to the border town of Vila Real de Santo António, fronting a once-hostile Spain.

Called Al-Gharb by the Moors, the land south of the *sêrras* (hills) of Monchique and Caldeirão remains a spectacular anomaly that seems more like a transplanted section of the North African coastline. The temperature in winter aver-ages around 60° Fahrenheit, increasing to an average of 74° in summer. During the day the sky is a pale blue, deepening in the evening to a rich cerulean. The country-side abounds with vegetation: almonds, lemons, oranges, carobs, pomegranates, and figs, the latter sending their branches across the ground like the tentacles of an octopus.

Expanses of sun-drenched golden sands contrast harmoniously with sinuous scored rock passageways that open up into high-ceilinged grottos and sea caves with natural pillars supporting ponderous arches above inrushing waters. The variety of the coastline provokes wonder: sluggish estuaries, sheltered lagoons, low-lying areas where the cluck of the marsh hen can be heard, long sandy spits, the pounding surf breaking upon pine woods, and promontories jutting out into the white-capped aq-uamarine foam.

Even though most of the towns and villages of the Algarve are more than 150 miles from Lisbon, the great earthquake of 1755 was felt here as well. Entire com-munities were wiped out; however, there remain many Moorish (even Roman) ruins. In the character of its fret-cut chimneys, mosque-like cupolas, and cubist houses, a distinct oriental flavor prevails. However, much of that flavor is gone forev-er, swallowed by a sea of dreary high-rise apartment blocks surrounding most towns. Years ago Portuguese officials, looking in horror at what happened to Spain's Costa del Sol, promised more limited and controlled development so they wouldn't make "Spain's mistake." That promise, in my opinion, was not kept.

The marketplaces in the shaded arcades of Algarvian villages sell esparto mats, copper work, pottery, and almond and fig sweets, sometimes shaped like birds and fish. Through the narrow streets comes the fast sound of little accordions pumping out the rhythmical corridinho.

Many small fishing villages dot the Algarvian coast, their names tongue twist-ing: Carvoeiro, Albufeira, Olhão, Portimão. The black dress of the varinas (with em-broidery on their apparel, flower-studded hats on their heads), the healthy ruddy faces of the "bullfighters of the sea," the fishing-craft—all create a living bridge with tradition in a land known to Phoenicians, Greeks, Romans, Visigoths, Moors, Christians, and now foreign visitors of every hue, who have changed the old land-scape forever.

Sports activities can be pursued year round in the Algarve, and the six champi-onship golf courses between Faro and Lagos lure players from all over the world. Near Almansil is the 27-hole Quinta do Lago course, which is acknowledged to be one of Europe's top ten. Hotels have tennis courts, and horseback riding can be ar-ranged with any of a number of stables quite near the beaches and in wooded moun-tain areas. Deep-sea fishing in the ocean waters, beach activities, and surfing attract thousands of vacationers to the Algarvian coast.

A NEW RIVIERA

Clearly a new Riviera has come to be.

Excellent accommodations are provided in nearly all price levels, the list topped by luxury hotels (some of which have their own championship golf course).

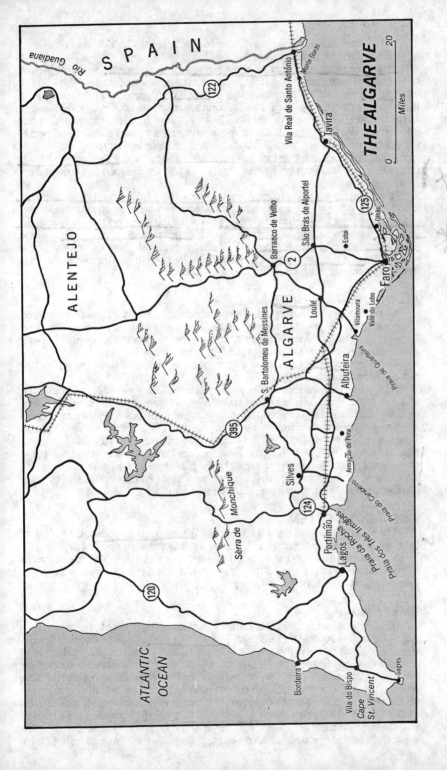

The hotels scattered along the coast from Monte Alvor to the Vale do Lobo often have reciprocal meal arrangements.

Budgeteers seek out bargains in the pensions and estalagems, some of them in converted mansions and villas. The government owns two pousadas—one on the sea at Sagres, the other in the mountains (São Brás de Alportel). In July and August the Algarve peaks in popularity, and accommodations without reservations made far in advance are difficult to obtain. The population of the Algarve in summer jumps from 300,000 to 800,000 and above, which causes strain almost to the breaking point on water and electrical supplies—and on traffic and tempers.

I find the area much more inviting in the low season, with February and March especially attractive, both because of the scenery and the cheaper, less crowded accommodations.

The flight from Lisbon to the Algarvian airport at Faro takes about 30 minutes. There are daily flights all year leaving Lisbon, with two daily return flights also. You can also go by one of the three daily trains. Take the ferryboat at Praça do Comércio in Lisbon, disembarking at Barreiro on the opposite bank of the Tagus, where Algarve-bound trains can be boarded. Three times a week there's a first-class-only special run. A daily motorcoach also leaves from Barreiro to the Algarve, and a drive in your own rented car takes about five or six hours.

ALONG THE WAY—SINES

On the somewhat barren route from Lisbon to the Algarve, attractions are rare. However, 99 miles south of the capital, almost exactly midway between there and Cape St. Vincent, sits Sines. The side road to the promontory of Sines runs through a land swept by sea breezes. Along the 11-mile route from the cutoff point at Santiago do Cacém, pine forests rise along the horizon, the scent from the resin-filled barrels permeating the air.

The origin of Sines is lost. Many of the natives, like those at Nazaré, trace their ancestry to the Phoenicians. The town sits upon the crest of a high inclined surface, its little houses trimmed in cobalt blue blending into the sky. Below the residential district, a natural rock looms over the tiny harbor. Off the coast is a small island, Pessegueiro, on which the crumbled ruins of a fortress remain. Vasco da Gama was born at Sines in 1469, and his house, long ago torn down, has been reconstructed in the original style. Anglers are attracted to Sines because of the bass and swordfish. Sand dunes rise along the extensive beaches, which are private, remote, seldom sharing their tranquil beauty with the Algarve-bound motorist.

SANTIAGO DO CACÉM

On the main road to the Algarve, about 60 miles from Setúbal, the village of Santiago do Cacém, dedicated to St. James, is crowned by the ruins of a castle built by medieval knights upon the foundation of a Moorish fortress. At the castle walls there is a fine view of the sea and the cypress-studded countryside, from which a low hum and clack of windmills can be heard.

Two Pousadas

Algarve-bound vacationers or returning suntanned tourists like to stop off for a luncheon at the **Pousada de Saõtiago**, Estrada de Lisboa, 7540 Santiago do Cacém (tel. 069/224-59). This salmon-pink hilltop villa is approached via a climbing road through pine and fir trees, seemingly like a private estate. Guests walk around the terraced garden or take a dip in a pool surrounded by lawns and rows of cypress trees, plus a classic piece of sculpture in a coved niche. In the chalet-style dining room (or on a wide terrace where tables are set under an arbor of magenta bougainvillea), you can order table d'hôte two-course luncheons at 2,400$ ($15.60). You get a bowl of soup from the tureen, fish caught that day at Sines, meat with vegetables, then seasonal fruit. Sinking into the sofa, you can take coffee in the lounge in front of a 15-

foot inglenook. This combination lounge and dining room is decorated in the provincial style, with a collection of handmade ceramic figures and jugs. Food is served daily from 12:30 to 2:30 p.m. and 7:30 to 9:30 p.m.

Seven bedrooms are furnished comfortably with antiques or good reproductions. Each accommodation contains a private bath. Guests are assigned rooms in both the main building and the annex. Rates range from 9,000$ ($58.50) daily in a double. Singles cost 8,700$ ($56.55).

Continuing south, we come upon the **Pousada Santa Clara,** at Barragem Marcello Caetano, 7665 Santa Clara-a-Velha (tel. 083/522-50), overlooking the large lake and dam of the Rio Mira. The charming pousada is a most convenient stopover on the Lisbon-Sagres road to the Algarve. There are six pleasant double rooms with bath. A twin-bedded room with private bath and breakfast included rents for 9,500$ ($61.75) daily, and a single goes for 8,500$ ($55.25). If you stop for just a meal, the tab is 1,800$ ($11.70) to 2,500$ ($16.25), served daily from 12:30 to 2:30 p.m. and 7:30 to 9:30 p.m. An ideal place for swimming and fishing, the inn has spacious lounges and good food, such as roast kid done to a turn or fish freshly caught from the lake. *We pAID 48 FOR (2) 24 eA.*

1. Sagres

At the extreme southwestern corner of Europe, Sagres is a rocky escarpment jutting out into the Atlantic, the ocean beating itself into an aquamarine froth upon the steep cliffs. It was here that Henry the Navigator, the Infante of Sagres, "dreamed dreams no mortal ever dared to dream before." He also proved that they could come true, launching Portugal and the modern world upon the seas of explorations. At Sagres, Henry, son of João I and Philippa of Lancaster, established his School of Navigation.

He died (1460) before the great discoveries of Columbus and Vasco da Gama, but those explorers owed a debt to him. A virtual ascetic, he assembled the best navigators, cartographers, geographers, scholars, sailors, and builders he could muster, infusing them with his rigorous devotion and methodically setting Portuguese caravels upon the Sea of Darkness.

Today, at the reconstructed site of his windswept fortress upon Europe's Land's End (nicknamed that after the narrowing westernmost tip of Cornwall, England), you can see a huge stone compass dial that he is alleged to have used in the naval studies pursued at Sagres.

At a simple chapel here, restored in 1960, sailors are said to have prayed for help before setting out into uncharted waters. To the left of the chapel is the villa where Henry lived (inquire at the Tourist Office nearby if you want to visit the interior). On what is believed to have been the site of the School of Navigation, a youth hostel has been installed. In the Auditorium of Sagres, a film is shown daily depicting the story of Henry the Navigator.

Three miles away is the promontory of **Cape St. Vincent.** The cape is so named because, according to legend, the body of St. Vincent arrived mysteriously here on a boat guided by ravens. Others claim that the body of the patron saint, murdered at Valencia, Spain, washed up upon the shores of Lisbon. A lighthouse stands here. Sea gulls glide upon the air currents; and on the approach, a few goats graze on a hill where once the trees are bent from the gusty wind.

Both the cape and Sagres (especially from the terrace of the pousada), offer a view of the sunset. To the ancient world, the cape was the last explored point, although in time the Phoenicians pushed beyond it. Many mariners thought that when the sun sank beyond the cape, it plunged over the edge of the world. To venture around the promontory was to face the demons of the unknown.

Sagres lies 174 miles south of Lisbon; from Lisbon's Praça do Comério you can take a ferry across the Tagus to Barreiro. From there, it's possible to make connections with the Southern Line Railway on its run to Lagos. At Lagos, buses go back and forth between that town and Sagres. The accommodations at Sagres are limited, but good.

WHERE TO STAY

In a ship's-bow position, **Hotel da Baleeira,** Sagres, 8650 Vila do Bispo (tel. 082/642-12) is a first-class whaleboat (its name in Portuguese), spread out above the fishing port with boats tied up in the harbor, it affords a view of the shoreline. Even its angular saltwater swimming pool is thrust out on a ledge, surrounded by a flagstone terrace. It's almost like swimming in the ocean, only you're perched high on a cliff. The largest hotel on this land projection, it offers 118 bedrooms, all with private bath and sea-view balcony. The hotel has nearly doubled the number of its bedrooms in recent years, although the older ones are quite small, as are the baths. The bedrooms are on the lower level. In high season, you pay from 9,000$ ($58.50) daily in a single, 10,000$ ($65) in a double.

If you're exploring the Algarve and are in Sagres just for the day, you can stop off and order a 2,000$ ($13) luncheon or dinner in a dining room cantilevered toward the sea, where everyone gets a view seat. The chef has his own private lobster tanks (no frozen lagosta here), and the meals are well prepared and served in an efficient manner.

The atmosphere is that of a private world, as the hotel has its own sandy beach, car park, cocktail lounge, and nearby hairdresser.

Pousada do Infante, Ponta da Atalaia, 8650 Sagres (tel. 082/642-22), seems like a monastery once built by ascetic monks who wanted to commune with nature —the rugged beauty of the rocky cliffs, the pounding surf, the sense of the infinity of the ocean. The glistening white-painted government-owned tourist inn with a tile roof is spread along the edge of a cliff, protruding rather daringly over the sea. It boasts a long colonnade of arches with an extended stone terrace set with garden furniture, plus a second floor of accommodations with private balconies. There are 23 bedrooms, and each has a private tile bath and is furnished with traditional pieces. All rooms have a direct-dial phone, and most of them also have a mini-bar and satellite TV. You pay 17,000$ ($110.50) daily for a double.

The public rooms are generously proportioned, gleaming with marble and decorated with fine tapestries depicting the exploits of Henry the Navigator. Large velvet couches flank the fireplace with tall brass floor lamps. In the dining room, the walls are lined with azulejos, and in the corner rests a cone-shaped fireplace with a mounted ship's model. Sitting in Portuguese provincial chairs, guests can order the traditional bargain luncheon or dinner of the pousadas, costing 3,000$ ($21.45) and including homemade bread, homemade soup, a fish course, meat with vegetables, and dessert. Have a before-dinner drink on the terrace, and watch the ocean-going vessels make their way around the point, heading for faraway ports of call. Other facilities include an outdoor saltwater swimming pool and a tennis court.

Residência Dom Henrique, Sítio Da Mareta, 8650 Sagres (tel. 082/641-33), is a sun-pocket, two- and three-story hotel with a restaurant, situated dramatically on the *promontorio,* the viewpoint above the beach. The view of the cliffs, beach, and sea from this hotel is so magnificent that it's featured on postcards sold in the area. More like a country house, it is a white stucco building stretched along a small garden. Each room has a sun balcony. There are regular rooms, and also apartments with three rooms, a balcony, two baths, plus a living room and kitchen. A single room with a private bath goes for 3,000$ ($19.50) to 5,500$ ($35.75) daily, depending on the season, and doubles with private bath cost 4,500$ ($29.25) to 8,500$ ($55.25). The most expensive doubles open onto the water. Lunch or dinner is another 2,000$ ($13) per person. Owner Maria Teresa Tavares Castro can arrange for boats, waterskiing, and bike rentals. It's also an informal place for afternoon tea, where you can sample some of the regional cakes.

LIVING ON THE OUTSKIRTS

A hospitable place, **Motel and Restaurant Gambozinos,** Praia do Martinhal, 8650 Vila do Bispo (tel. 082/643-18), has large, well-furnished rooms, modern baths, and an excellent restaurant. The Dutch touch by the management of Jacqueline Vermeer and Jan Willem and Frank Okhuijzen Mulder is evident in the well-run establishment. The room charges depend on the view: sea, land, or none to speak of. The rent for a room for two persons is 3,900$ ($25.35) to 9,500$ ($61.75) per night. The restaurant is charming and the food is tasty, with the sea platter (a lobster salad with other assorted seafood) a specialty. Other dishes include grilled fish, which are good to have with the gazpacho. You can dine inside or on the sea terrace. Meals cost from 1,200$ ($7.80) up. The restaurant is closed Wednesday. The beach is lovely and secluded, and is used almost exclusively by hotel guests. To find Gambozinos, turn off the road from Lagos to Sagres about two miles east of Sagres where a sign says "Martinhal—1 kilometer," where you'll also see a sign for the motel.

Restaurante Cabo de S. Vicente, Fortaleza do Beliche, Vila do Bispo, 8650 Sagres (tel. 082/641-24), stands in the vicinity of the lighthouse on the road to the cape. It rents a few modestly priced rooms, but it is primarily a restaurant and tea house. The restaurant is in the middle of the ancient fort, right close to the cliff's edge, and it offers a complete menu—soup, fish, meat, and dessert—for 2,500$ ($16.25). You can order à la carte as well. Hours are daily from 12:30 to 2:30 p.m. and 7:30 to 9:30 p.m. The hotel has only four bedrooms to rent, costing from 9,500$ ($61.75) daily in a double.

For those who want an escapist retreat, **Estalagem Infante do Mar,** Praia da Salema, 8650 Vila do Bispo (tel. 042/651-37), lies about 11 miles east of Sagres, set back from the main coastal road along the Algarve. A four-star accommodation, it was built on the crest of a hill, looking down onto the fishing village of Praia da Salema. It is bright and immaculately kept, and the welcome is gracious. A spacious double room with twin beds (good mattresses) is well furnished, and many rooms contain private balconies that overlook the fishing village and the sea beyond. In high season, one person can stay here paying, for room and breakfast, 7,500$ ($48.75) daily, the tariff rising to 8,000$ ($52) in a double. The hotel has a bar, TV, swimming pool, and a private car park. Even if you're just driving along the Algarve coast, you might want to drop in for a meal, as the food is well prepared and served in bountiful portions. Expect to spend around 1,800$ ($11.70) to dine here.

2. Lagos ✓ TOUR

What the Lusitanians and Romans called Locobriga, and the Moors knew as Zawaia, was to become, under Henry the Navigator, a private experimental shipyard of caravels. Edged by the *Costa do Ouro* (Golden Coast), the Bay of Sagres at one point in its epic history was big enough to allow 407 warships to maneuver with ease.

An ancient port city (one historian traced its origins back to the Carthaginians three centuries before the birth of Christ), Lagos was well known by the sailors of Nelson's fleet. From Liverpool to Manchester to Plymouth, the sailors spoke wistfully of the beautiful, green-eyed, olive-skinned women of the Algarve. Eagerly they sailed into port, looking forward to drinking the heady Portuguese wine and to carousing.

Actually, not that much has changed since Nelson's day, and few go to Lagos wanting to know of its history. Rather, the mission is to drink deeply of the pleasures of table and beach. In winter, the almond blossoms match the whitecaps on the water, and the climate is often warm enough for sunbathing. In town, the flea market sprawls through narrow streets, the vendors selling such articles as rattan baskets, earthenware pottery, fruits, vegetables, crude furniture, cutlery, knitted shawls, and leather boots.

Less than a mile down the coast, the hustle-bustle of market day is forgotten as the rocky headland of the **Ponta da Piedade** (Point of Piety) appears. This beautiful spot is considered by many the best on the entire coast. Dotted among the colorful cliffs and secret grottos carved by the waves are the most flamboyant examples of Manueline architecture.

Much of Lagos was razed in the 1755 earthquake, at which time it lost its position as the capital of the Algarve. Today only ruins remain of its former walls of fortification. However, traces of the old are still to be discovered on the back streets. On Rua Silva Lopes, just off the waterfront, sits the 18th-century **Igreja de Santo António** (Church of St. Anthony). Decorating the altar are some of Portugal's most notable rococo gilt carvings. Begun in the 17th century, they were damaged in the earthquake, but subsequently restored. What you see today represents the work of many artisans—at times, each of them apparently pursuing a different theme.

Attached to the church is the **Museu Municipal Dr. José Formosinho** (tel. 082/623-01), containing replicas of the fret-cut chimneys of the Algarve, three-dimensional cork carvings, 16th-century vestments, ceramics, 17th-century embroidery, ecclesiastical sculpture, a painting gallery, weapons, minerals, and a numismatic collection. An oddity is a sort of believe-it-or-not section, displaying among other things an eight-legged calf. In the archeological wing are Neolithic artifacts, along with Roman mosaics found at Boca do Rio near Budens, fragments of statuary and columns, and other remains of antiquity from excavations along the Algarve. Charging an admission of 80$ (55¢), the museum is open daily except Monday and holidays from 9:30 a.m. to 12:30 p.m. and 2 to 5 p.m.

The old **Customs House** on Praça Infante Dom Henriques stands as a painful reminder of the Age of Exploration. The arcaded slave market, the only one of its kind in Europe, looks peaceful today, but under its four Romanesque arches captives taken from their homelands were sold to the highest bidder. The house opens onto a peaceful square, dominated by a statue of Henry the Navigator.

The Algarve's most westerly golf course is signposted left off EN125 at Odéaxere. Five of this course's 18 holes are on sand dunes bordering the beach. The address is **Clube de Golfe de Palmares,** Companhia de Empreendimentos Turisticos de Lagos, Monte Palmares, Meia Praia (tel. 082/629-61).

Lagos is 21 miles east of Sagres, 164 miles south of Lisbon, and 49 miles west of Faro. To reach it by rail from Lisbon, take the ferryboat at Praça do Comércio across the Tagus to Barreiro. There, connections to Lagos can be made on the Southern Line Railway.

WHERE TO STAY

A 20th-century castle, **Hotel de Lagos,** 1 Rua Nova da Aldeia, 8600 Lagos (tel. 082/620-11), has its own ramparts and moats (a heated swimming pool and a paddling pool). This first-class hotel is spread out over three acres of hilltop overlooking Lagos, so no matter which room you're assigned, you'll have a view, even if it's one opening upon a sun-trap courtyard with semitropical greenery. The main room has a hacienda atmosphere, with a background of bone-white plaster walls, enlivened by sunny colors. Guests gather here in one of the clusters of soft built-in sofas set on carpets. In a corner logs burn in a fireplace in chilly weather. Excellent meals are served in an expansive harbor-view room, decorated in wood paneling.

A few bedrooms with patios are on the ground level, but most are on the upper six floors, all private baths. The rooms, both single, double, and suites, offer a choice of standard and deluxe. In high season (June through September), the rates are 20,000$ ($130) daily in a twin-bedded room and 16,000$ ($104) in a single. The average bedroom has a background of stark white walls contrasted with warm oriental colors. Most rooms open onto a wedge-shaped balcony where you can eat breakfast. Amenities include game rooms, a restaurant, a poolside bar, two lounge bars, and complete air conditioning.

The Hotel de Lagos also owns Duna Beach Club on Meia Praia Beach, with a heated saltwater swimming pool, a restaurant, a snackbar, and three tennis courts. Guests of the hotel are given a free membership during their stay. A private motor coach makes regularly scheduled trips to the beach club, only five minutes from the hotel. Arrangements can be made for golf at nearby Palmares 18-hole course, where hotel guests get a 20% reduction on green fees; for skindiving and sports fishing in the waters along the coast; for horseback riding through nature's garden; for sailing in the bay; and for international floor shows and gambling in the Algarve's casinos.

Hotel Sa Cristovão, Rossio de São João, 8600 Lagos (tel. 082/630-51), may have been a simple inn at one point, but that is now history. The rather modest beginnings have given way to style. At the edge of town, almost within sight of the harbor, the hotel sits on a busy parkway junction of the coastal highway and the road to Lisbon. There is a solarium. Owned and run by Torralta C.I.F., the first-class hotel is maintained on a personal basis.

The bedrooms are inviting in their uncluttered design. Each room opens onto a private terrace and is priced according to size and placement. The price of a single is 7,000$ ($45.50) daily. Doubles cost 9,000$ ($58.50). A continental breakfast is included in the tariffs.

Opening off the reception are public lounges. The largest uses natural pine slats for the ceiling, cube lighting, and pillars. One part on a lower level makes for intimate seating around a free-standing black fireplace. Before-dinner drinks are available in the cocktail lounge, which opens onto an inner patio with a fountain waterfall. The hotel closes at the end of October and reopens in April.

Hotel da Meia Praia, Meia Praia, 8600 Lagos (tel. 082/620-01), lies 2½ miles northeast of Lagos. This first-class hotel is for those who want sand, sun, and good food rather than an exciting decor. The hotel, containing 66 bedrooms, all with private bath, stands at a point where a hill begins its rise from the sea. Surrounded by private gardens, it fronts railway tracks and a wide sandy beach, four miles long. The guests play tennis on two professional hard courts, linger in the informal garden where white wrought-iron outdoor furniture is scattered under the olive and palm trees, or loll by the large pools, one for adults, another for children. The oceanside bedrooms have balconies with partitions for sunbathing. The furnishings in the rooms are uncluttered, functional, and modern. The most expensive rooms have sea views; the medium-priced rooms, a sea view and one balcony; and the cheapest rooms have no balconies and overlook the hills. In high season, singles aren't available except at the double rate, 14,000$ ($91) daily for two persons; however, in spring and autumn singles cost 5,500$ ($35.75), and doubles go for 8,500$ ($55.25). Across the entire all-glass front of the hotel are the dining room, lounge, and cocktail bar. The establishment is run by the Torralta group and is open from April to October.

Hotel Riomar, 83 Rua Cándido dos Reis, 8600 Lagos (tel. 082/630-91), is a modern structure in the center of town. It has a pleasant downstairs lounge, a cozy bar, and tasteful decor. In high season, singles rent for 8,000$ ($52) daily and doubles for 10,000$ ($65). The hotel has 40 comfortably furnished bedrooms, each with private bath.

Casa de São Gonçalo da Lagos, 73 Rua Cándido dos Reis, 8600 Lagos (tel. 082/621-71). This pink town villa, with its fancy iron balconies, dates back to the 18th century. At the core of Lagos, close to restaurants and shops, the antique-filled home is almost an undiscovered gem. Most of the public lounges and bedrooms turn, in the Iberian fashion, to the inward peace of a sun-filled patio. Here, surrounded by bougainvillaea climbing up balconies, guests order their breakfast, sitting under a fringed parasol and enjoying the splashing of the fountain. All the furnishings are individualized: delicate hand-embroidered linens, period mahogany tables, silver candlesticks, chests with brass handles, inlaid tip-top tables, fine ornate beds brought from Angola, even crystal chandeliers. In high season, June 1 to September 30, a twin rents for 9,000$ ($58.50) daily, a single for 7,500$ ($48.75). During other months, a twin goes for 7,000$ ($45.50), a single for 5,500$ ($35.75). In the restoration of the house, modern amenities were added, so that each room contains a private bath.

The luxury pension is in a rambling *casa* (house), with various stairways leading to corridors with fine old prints, engravings, and Portuguese ceramic bowls of flowers set on aged hand-carved chests. Guests enjoy get-togethers in the large living room with its comfortable armchairs drawn up around a fireplace. Here, again, the furnishings are personalized, with a preponderance of antiques. Closed from the end of October to April.

WHERE TO DINE

One of the most elaborate and sophisticated menus along the Algarve is offered at **Restaurante Alpendre,** 17 Rua António Barbosa Viana (tel. 627-05). The food is tasty, but portions aren't large. Service tends to be slow, so don't come here if you're rushed. *Gourmet* magazine called the Alpendre "the most celebrated and luxurious restaurant in Lagos." Your afternoon or evening might begin in the downstairs bar where you can have a before-dinner drink, sampling crunchy Algarvian almonds and olives. Later, you can order your meal, selecting from among excellent soups, such as onion au gratin, following with one of the house specialties, such as peppersteak or filets of sole, sautéed in butter, then flambéed with cognac, and served with a sauce of cream, orange and lemon juices, vermouth, and seasonings known only to the chef. Two dessert features are the mixed fruits flambé or crêpes flambés with coffee, both of which are for two persons. Meals are served daily from 12:30 to 3 p.m. and 7 to 11 p.m., costing from 1,800$ ($11.70) to 5,000$ ($32.50), depending on how elaborate your repast is. Reservations are advised.

Restaurante Don Sebastião, 20 Rua 25 de Abril (tel. 627-95), is a rustically decorated tavern, considered among the finest dining choices in Lagos. Run by Portuguese, it offers a varied menu of local specialties, particularly shellfish dishes such as clams and shrimp. Live lobsters are kept on the premises. Often feverish with activity in summer, it features filling and tasty meals at prices ranging from 1,600$ ($10.40) to 3,000$ ($19.50). Meals, including grills, are accompanied by one of the best selections of Portuguese vintage wines in the town. Hours are noon to 3 p.m. and 6:30 to 10 p.m. It is closed on Sunday in winter.

Galeão, 1 Rua de Laranjeira (tel. 639-09), in air-conditioned comfort, offers a wide range of local and continental dishes, and you can "oversee" the action through an exposed kitchen, which gets very busy in season. Meats are savory, and the fish dishes are well prepared and tasty. Count on spending 2,500$ ($16.50) to 3,000$ ($19.50) for a filling repast. Hours are 1 to 3 p.m. and 7 to 10 p.m. It is closed on Sunday.

Pouso do Infante, 11 Rua Alfonso d'Almeida (tel. 628-62), is a pleasant tavern restaurant, with an iron chandelier, walls decorated with local craftwork, and rustic chairs painted green with straw seats. The fare is not experimental in any way, but it's quite tasty. For example, for an appetizer, you're usually faced with such selections as a homemade vegetable soup (generous portions) or a classic Portuguese shrimp cocktail. For a main course, you might order that Portuguese oddity, sole with banana, or veal scaloppine with spaghetti. Also worthy as a main-course choice is chicken curry with rice (not always offered), and my personal favorite, lamb in wine sauce. For dessert, the typical Algarvian selection is a smooth almond cake. Expect to spend 2,500$ ($16.25) to 3,000$ ($19.50). Hours are daily from 12:30 to 3 p.m.

and 7 to 10:30 p.m. Closed from mid-December to mid-January and on Wednesday from October to June.

A Lagosteira, 20 Rua 1 de Maio (tel. 624-86), has long been a mecca for knowledgeable diners in Lagos. Its decor is simple and there's a small bar on one side. On the à la carte menu, the best opener for a big meal is a classic Algarvian fish soup. The most savory opening, however, is clams Lagosteira style. After the fishy beginning, you might happily settle for a sirloin steak grilled over an open fire. Expect to spend 1,800$ ($11.70) to 3,500$ ($22.75) for a meal. The restaurant is open from 12:30 to 3 p.m. and 6:30 to 10:30 p.m.; closed Sunday and the first two weeks in January.

O Trovador, Largo do Convento da Senhora de Gloria (tel. 631-52), is run by Marion (she's from Germany) and Dave (he's English). It's especially nice off-season when comfortable chairs are placed around a log-burning fireplace. But at any time of the year you get a pleasant atmosphere, good service, and good food. The location is up the hill behind the Hotel de Lagos (follow the signs from Rua Vasco da Gama). The cuisine is international. Among the recommended appetizers are homemade chicken liver pâté, an octopus cocktail, a fish pâté with a delicate salmon taste, and escargots bourguignons. Shellfish dishes are prepared in unique Trovador style. Main courses also include Dave's special—a beef casserole cooked in black beer. You might also enjoy Portuguese swordfish. The desserts are all good, but I especially like the homemade cheesecake (not baked) and the coupe Trovador. Expect to spend from 2,000$ ($13). The restaurant is open daily from 7 p.m. to midnight except Sunday and Monday.

Mandarin, at Caliças (tel. 604-24), is good to know about if you're seeking some change-of-pace fare. It is outside Lagos on the road to Meia Praia. In an attractive structure, it is run by helpful people. Parking is available, and from one of the 40 seats in the well-run restaurant you can enjoy panoramic views. There is a bar if you'd like to go early for a drink. Lunch is served by the swimming pool daily in summer from noon to 2:30 p.m., costing from 1,500$ ($9.75). A traditional English roast meal is available on Sunday. Dinner, from 7 to 11 p.m. daily, costs from 2,500$ ($16.25). The specialty is Peking duck with five spices, and some of the ingredients are flown in from Taiwan.

3. Portimão 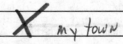 my town

Go here only if you prefer the life of a bustling fishing port and commercial city instead of a hotel perched right on the beach. Ever since the 1930s, Praia da Rocha, two miles away, has snared sun-loving traffic. But the Algarve is so popular in summer that Portimão long ago developed a base of tourists.

The wafting aroma of the noble Portuguese sardine permeates every street and café nook. As a fish-canning center, Portimão leads the Algarve, but it doesn't outpace Setúbal in production. Still, for a change of pace, this town, on an arm of the Arcade River, makes a good stopover center (it also has some fine dining recommendations). Stroll through its gardens, its shops (especially noted for their pottery), drink the wine of the cafés, and roam down to the quays where you will see sardines roasting on braziers. The routine activity of the Algarvians is what gives the town its charm. On its left bank the little whitewashed community of **Ferragudo** is unspoiled, but tame, with a castle.

Between 9:30 and 10:30 a.m. the fishermen can be seen unloading their boats by tossing up wicker baskets full of freshly caught fish. Fish, fruit, and vegetable **markets** are held every morning except Sunday in the market building and open square, closing at 2 p.m. On the first Monday of every month, a day-long, gigantic regional market is held with gypsies selling local artifacts, pottery, wicker, even snake oil.

Boutiques offering the Algarve's best selection of hand-knit sweaters, hand-painted porcelain, and pottery abound.

Many of the buildings in the old quarter of town date back to the mid-18th century when the town was rebuilt after the devastating earthquake of 1755. Roaming the streets, you can peer into delightful hidden courtyards, some with bread ovens built into the three-foot-thick walls, blacksmith stables, tinsmiths, sardine-canning factories where sardines are still cleaned and packed by hand, and carpenters' shops.

Portimão is a perfect escape from the summer rush of visitors (mostly European) in the oceanfront towns, and the room rates are considerably cheaper. A bus runs to the beach at Praia da Roche, mentioned above. Buses or trains leave Portimão for all parts of the Algarve and Portugal. An express bus to Lisbon makes a 4½-hour run.

WHERE TO STAY

In the heart of the old town, **Hotel Globo,** 26 Rua 5 de Outubro, 8500 Portimão (tel. 082/221-51), is an island of contemporary living. A first-class hotel, it is recommended for its clean-cut, well-thought-out design. Snug modern balconies overlook the tile rooftops crusted with moss. In 1967 the owner-manager imported an uninhibited architect to turn his inn into a top-notch hotel. Each of the 71 bedrooms, all with private bath, enjoys good taste in layout and furnishings: matching ebony panels on the wardrobes, built-in headboards, and marble desks. In summer, singles cost 11,000$ ($71.50) daily and doubles 13,000$ ($84.50).

On the ground floor is an uncluttered, attractive lounge with an adjoining lounge and bar. Crowning the top floor is a dining room, the Aquarium, encircled by four glass walls that permit unblocked views of the harbor, ocean, or mountains, its tables set with crystal stemware and flowers. Guests can also enjoy a rooftop cocktail bar and lounge, A1-Kantor.

Albergaría Miradoiro, 13 Rua Machado Santos, 8500 Portimão (tel. 082/230-11), benefits from a charmingly central location, on a quiet square opposite an ornate Manueline church. Its modern façade is banded with concrete balconies. A few of the 26 simple bedrooms contain terraces, and each has a private bath. You're likely to meet an array of European backpackers here, any of whom seem eager to converse and share travelers' stories. With a continental breakfast included, doubles cost from 6,500$ ($42.25) daily, while singles go for 6,000$ ($39). The hotel is open throughout the year, and motorists can usually find a parking space in the square just opposite the hotel.

WHERE TO DINE

One of the oldest restaurants on the Algarve, **The Old Tavern,** 43 Rua Júdice Fialho (tel. 233-25), has a Moorish look, provided by arched corridors and doorways. The restaurant's theme is the Crusades. The menu is of a later era, however, offering such main courses as lamb kidneys in Madeira sauce, marinated wild boar, *cataplana* (a regional specialty of quality clams with pork cooked in white wine), chicken and prawn curry Madras, and Portuguese breast of turkey. If you prefer, you can enjoy fresh lobster, rock lobster, crab, and other seafood which can be chosen from the aquarium in the bar. Dinner costs from 2,500$ ($16.25) and is served daily except Sunday from 6 p.m. to 1 a.m. The bar has been rebuilt with local stone, marble, and clay brick, but it still has an English-pub atmosphere. The owner, Peter Rees, retained the terrazzo floors of the tavern when it was remodeled and redecorated, so that a Portuguese feeling is still here.

Mariners, 28 Rua Santa Isabel (tel. 258-48). Masses of bougainvillaea fill the corners of this restaurant's garden patio. Even without the flowers, you still might be tempted by the vaulted and tile-lined inner room for more formal dining. The owners illuminate much of this place with candlelight, whose glow sparkles on the fine china, good linen, and soothingly repetitive ceiling arches. A relaxing dinner costs from 2,500$ ($16.25) and is likely to include pepper steak, filets of plaice in a mornay sauce, a mixed grill, lasagne, or a hot Indian curry. Lunches, less elaborate and costing from 750$ ($4.90), offer such dishes as beefburgers, and fish and chips, served on the patio or in the bar and dining room upstairs. Hours are daily from noon to 3 p.m. and 7 to 10:30 p.m. *closed*

Dennis Inn & Bar, 10 Rua 5 de Outubro (tel. 242-73), is a home-like conversion of an early-18th-century town villa. For meals daily from 7 p.m. to midnight, homemade chili, shepherd's pie, salads, and meat pies are served in the pub and on the flower-filled garden patio. Charcoal-broiled spareribs, chicken, and giant hamburgers are available in the summer evenings under the stars. Expect to pay from 2,200$ ($14.30) for a meal. The pub comes alive with piano and guitar playing and nightly sing-alongs. It is closed Monday.

Mr. Bojangles Bistro Bar, 1 Rua da Hortinha (tel. 230-42). John is Irish and his business partner, Carolina, is Portuguese. Together they direct one of the neighborhood's most charming bistros. You'll find it behind thick stone walls on a street corner in the old town. There, beneath soaring ceilings criss-crossed with thick and very old beams, you can enjoy such specialties as Manhattan-style clam chowder, cock-a-leekie, homemade garlic bread, entrecôte piri-piri, steak in cognac, and duckling cooked in honey. Many of these dishes are prepared with a dramatic flambé flourish from a rolling cart brought to your table. Full meals begin at 2,200$ ($14.30) to 2,600$ ($16.90). The establishment is open from 7 p.m. to midnight daily except Monday.

Alfredo's, 10 Rua Pe da Cruz (tel. 229-54), is in the old tavern style, on the ground floor of a modern building. Against a backdrop of chalk-white walls, new and old provincial artifacts are combined decoratively. From the dining room, you can see an ornately tiled open kitchen, with a charcoal grill, crocks of lobster, baskets of mushrooms, cabbage, salad greens, even a glass case of fresh fish. You dine on high-back chairs with rush seats, where you can see the carved refectory table laden with cheeses, baskets of fruits, special desserts, and a tall scale. A candle in a brass holder is lit by the waiter, and you make your choice from an à la carte menu. The fish soup, *ameijoas* (clams) à Alfredo's, *pescada* (hake) à marinheira, and tournedos Rossini are recommended. A light and creamy chocolate finishes off a meal nicely at 2,500$ ($16.25) and up. Open daily from noon to 3 p.m. and 7 to 11 p.m.

Lucio's, 10 Tenente Morais Sorães (tel. 242-92), is as simple as can be, but serves the best seafood in town. The rooms command a view of the port and the sea gulls circling the fish boats, even a less romantic gas station. The dining room is small, triangular in shape, with no frills, tiny tables, and tile walls. This is where knowledgeable locals go, too. The kettle of clams resting on your plate as an appetizer will even please an Algarvian fisherman. Lagostas and shrimp are among the most expensive items on the menu, and it's best to inquire the daily price (quotations change constantly, depending on the catch) before ordering. Fresh sardines are grilled to perfection here, and squid holds no terror for the seasoned chef. Your final tab is likely to range from 2,500$ ($16.25). Hours are daily from noon to 3 p.m. and 7 to 11 p.m.

O Bicho Restaurant, 12 Largo Gil Eanes (tel. 229-77), is one of the best places in the Algarve to order cataplana, a typical regional dish consisting of clams, pork, green pepper, tomatoes, and spices, including hot pepper, garlic, and bay leaf. All this is cooked in a special copper pot, also called cataplana, which has a lid that seals the mixture in tightly to steam. Armando Quaresma Rijo, owner and chef at this simple eating place, has made O Bicho popular with locals and discerning tourists. A meal will cost from 1,800$ ($11.70) to 2,500$ ($16.25), served daily from noon to 3 p.m. and 7 to 10 p.m.

Outside of Portimão, one of the best places for dining on both a Portuguese and international cuisine is O Gato, Urbanização da Quintinha, Lote 10-rc, Estrada de Alvor (tel. 276-74). Daily from noon to 3 p.m. and 7 to 11 p.m., the skilled chefs turn out a selection of dishes that are first-rate in both their preparation and choice of

near — take out

ingredients. Its international menu selection is reflected by such classic main dishes as duckling in orange sauce. However, care also goes into regional favorites, including rabbit stew, one of the most savory entrées. A good cataplana is also served, or you may prefer any number of fish and shellfish dishes, along with pepper steak and beef Stroganoff. To begin with, try a refreshing soup such as gazpacho, or razor-thin swordfish which has been smoked and is served with some of the same accompaniments that usually go with caviar. Meals cost from 2,500$ ($16.25) and are served against an attractive backdrop of white walls and mahogany beam trim. If you're feeling expansive, you can end your repast with one of the flambé desserts.

Dining at Porches (Lagoa)

O Leão de Porches (tel. 523-84), in Porches, a small village on the way to Lagoa from Portimão, is a 17th-century farmhouse that has been restored to make a charming restaurant with atmosphere and character. It is owner-operated by Norman L. Fryer, an internationally known restaurateur. This is one of the oldest eating places on the Algarve, and its chef's specialties and quality food make it well known and popular with residents and tourists alike. You can try a wide variety of dishes, including garlic and piri-piri prawns and avocado appetizers. Among main courses are steak à Portuguesa, crispy duck with orange, and a choice of fresh fish. Desserts include almond tart, syllabub, and fresh strawberries with cream. The restaurant is open every night (no lunches), and reservations are advisable. Expect to spend 2,500$ ($16.25) per person, excluding drinks. Hours are 7:15 to 10 p.m. Closed mid-January to the end of February.

4. Sêrra de Monchique

The Monchique range of hills is the Algarve at its cool and verdant height. The rocky peak of the range, some 3,000 feet high, looks down on forested slopes and green valleys, burgeoning with cork-oak, chestnut, pine, and eucalyptus trees, orange groves, Indian corn, heather, mimosa, rosemary, and oleander bushes. Icy water springs from the volcanic rock that makes up the range, flowing down to the towns that lie in its foothills.

The towns of Monchique produce many handcrafts in wood, including chairs, benches, decorated canes, and carved wooden spoons. Other articles made by local artisans are wicker baskets, wool sweaters and stockings, and macramé lace made with linen. A typical industry of the people of the Monchique is the making of charcoal, although this activity is slowly disappearing.

The largest town in the borough is also named **Monchique,** lying on the east side of Mount Fóia, about 16 miles north of Portimão. The town was once engaged in the manufacture of wooden casks and barrels and the making of oakum and rough cloth. The town has a Manueline-style parish church from the 16th century, with an interesting radiated door-facing. Colorful decorated tiles and carved woodwork grace the interior, along with a statue of Our Lady of the Immaculate Conception, an 18th-century work attributed to Machado de Castro. The Convent of Nossa Senhora do Desterro is in ruins, but you can take a look at the curious fountain with decorative tiles and the impressive old magnolia tree in its grounds.

Caldas de Monchique was discovered in Roman days and turned into a spa. The waters, coming from springs in volcanic rock, are still considered good treatment for respiratory disorders, accompanied as they are by the clear air of the highlands.

Nearly eight miles from the town of Monchique, **Alferce,** nestling among trees and mountains, has traces of an ancient fortification. There is also an important handcraft center here. In the opposite direction, west of Monchique about eight miles by the road is **Fóia,** the highest point in the Algarve at almost 3,000 feet. From here you have splendid views of the hills and the sea, seeing all the way to Cape St. Vincent and Sagres on clear days. A TV tower and a restaurant stand on the height.

WHERE TO STAY AND EAT

A small inn in the town of Monchique, **Estalagem Abrigo de Montanha,** 8550 Monchique (tel. 082/921-31) is set amid a botanical garden. With all those camellias, rhododendrons, mimosa, banana palms, and arbutus blooming, plus the tinkling waterfalls, you'd never believe the hot Algarve coast was in the same province. The inn has five double rooms and six suites, each complete with bath. For two persons, the daily rate is 10,000$ ($65) in a room, 12,000$ ($78) in a suite, with a continental breakfast included. On chilly evenings, guests gather before a fireplace in the lounge. In the attractive restaurant, good food is served daily from 12:30 to 3 p.m. and 7:30 to 9:30 p.m. A main meal costs from 1,500$ ($9.75).

---

5. Praia da Rocha

Visited & will AGAIN + TOUR

This creamy yellow beach has long been the most popular seaside resort on the Algarve. The beauty of its rock formations led English voyagers to discover it around 1935. At the outbreak of World War II there were only two small hotels on the Red Coast, interspersed with a few villas, many built by wealthy Portuguese. Nowadays Praia da Rocha is booming, as many have fallen victim to the spell cast by its shoreline and climate.

It is named the Beach of the Rock because of the sculptural formations of the rock. At the end of the mussel-encrusted cliff, where the Arade flows into the sea, the ruins of the **Fort of St. Catarina** lie, the location offering many views of Portimão's satellite, Ferragudo, and of the bay. *FORT*

WHERE TO STAY

Praia da Rocha is endowed with accommodations in all price ranges, the leader of which is the **Algarve Hotel,** Avenida Tomás Cabreira, Praia da Rocha, 8500 Portimão (tel. 082/240-01), which is strictly for those who love glitter and glamour. With a vast staff at one's beck and call, a guest is ensconced in luxury within an elongated block of rooms poised securely on the top ledge of a cliff. On a lower terrace is a huge kidney-shaped heated swimming pool (plus another one for children), with a sundeck cantilevered over still another cliff, projecting above rugged rocks, caves, and a sandy cove.

The main lounge is like a sultan's palace: gold velvet chairs, oriental carpets, brass and teak screens, antique chests, and deep sofas set around a copper-hooded fireplace. The bedrooms have white walls, colored ceilings, intricate tile floors, mirrored entryways, indirect lighting, balconies with garden furniture, and baths with separate showers. Everything is air-conditioned and centrally heated. In April, May, and October, the bed-and-breakfast cost of a single is 14,630$ ($95) daily, rising to 19,250$ ($125) in a double. In June, the rate in a single is 16,940$ ($110), 21,560$ ($140) in a double. From July through September, the rate in a single is 22,330$ ($145) going up to 27,720$ ($180) in a double. You pay another 4,158$ ($27) per person for half board. Costing more, of course, are the Yachting, Oriental, Presidential, and Miradouro suites, each a decorator's tour de force in originality.

In the formal dining room, with its waterside windows, chinoiserie ceilings and pillars, you can order dinner. Two Portuguese chefs, with French backgrounds, provide gourmet meals on the à la carte menu. Buffet luncheons in season are served by the swimming pool. A one-of-a-kind nightclub books top-flight entertainers (even Amália Rodrigues on one occasion), in addition to their regular troupe of folk dancers. The club is like an oriental grotto dug out of a cliff, with three stone walls and a fourth allowing for an oceanic backdrop. Extra services include a sauna, hairdresser, barbershop, manicurist, laundry and dry cleaning, babysitting, boutiques, and complete room service. There's even a social director who plans personalized activities such as fishing parties on the hotel boat (with seafood stews), games of bridge, barbecues on the beach, mini-golf, volleyball, tennis competitions, plus waterskiing and deep-sea fishing.

Tarik Hotel, Praia da Rocha, 8500 Portimão (tel. 082/221-61), is a high-rise resort. A modern four-star hotel and apartment complex, it consists of two adjoining blocks with the same ground floor. As part of the Torralta chain, the hotel allows its guests to use the facilities of the Alvor Tourist Development some three miles away. It attracts sun-seekers, as each room or apartment has a balcony. The hotel is complete with a snackbar and swimming pool. The rooms have contemporary furnishings, strong colors for furniture set against white walls. You can get either a single with sofa bed, a twin-bedded room, a small suite for three or four persons, a studio for two people with a small kitchen, or studio suites for three or four occupants. Rates are based on the season. High season is July through September, mid-season is April, May, and October, and low is November through March. In high season, singles or doubles cost from 8,470$ ($55) daily in a studio. An apartment, suitable for two to three persons, goes for 12,320$ ($80) per day. Children up to 11 get a 50% reduction in season, and a third person (an adult) sharing a room is granted a 20% reduction.

Hotel Júpiter, Avenida Tomás Cabreira, Praia da Rocha, 8500 Portimão (tel. 082/220-41), occupies what might be the most prominent street corner in this bustling summer resort. There's a wrap-around arcade filled with boutiques and a spacious lobby where guests relax, sometimes with drinks, on comfortable couches. The hotel is just across the street from a wide beach, but it has a swimming pool, covered and heated. The Night Star disco provides late-night diversion beneath a metallic ceiling, while a semiformal restaurant, an informal pub, and a cocktail bar offer food and drink. You can enjoy snacks and light lunches at poolside during the summer. The comfortably modern accommodations contain balconies, as well as radio and phone, with views over either the river or the sea. In high season, singles range from 12,500$ ($81.25) daily, and doubles go for 15,000$ ($97.50). Off-season reductions are granted.

Hotel Bela Vista, Avenida Tomás, Praia da Rocha, 8500 Portimão (tel. 082/240-55), is an old mansion built in the Moorish style during the last century by a wealthy family, for use as a summer home. As well as a minaret-type tower that flanks its façade, there's also a statue of the Virgin in ecstasy set into the masonry of one of the building's corners. Since 1934 it's been a special kind of hotel, ideal for those who respond to the architecture of the past. Rated first class, it's set on the oceanside, atop its own palisade, with access to a sandy cove where you can swim. The villa is white, with an ornate tower and terracotta tile roof, a coastal landmark spotted by fishermen bringing in their boats at sundown. It's flanked by the owner's home and a simple cliff-edge annex shaded by palm trees.

The attractive structure and its decorations have been preserved, but plastic furniture has been sneaked into the public lounges. The entry hallway has an art nouveau bronze torchère and a winding staircase, with walls almost covered with 19th-century blue and white tiles depicting allegorical scenes from Portuguese history. Guests enjoy get-togethers around a baronial fireplace with a tile façade. In the high-ceilinged dining hall, meals combine Portuguese cuisine with a continental flair. The 16 bedrooms, all with bath, are priced according to size, plumbing, view, and placement. Those facing the sea, the former master bedrooms, are worth the additional money asked. The main house is preferable to the annex. For a room and continental breakfast in high season, the price is 18,000$ ($117) daily in a single, 20,000$ ($130) in a double. Each room has character, and most of them contain tile dados. Decorations vary from a tile inset shrine of the Virgin Mary to crystal sconces.

Residencial Solar Penquin, Praia da Rocha, 8500 Portimão (tel. 082/243-

visited

08). The foundations of this well-placed hotel were originally those of an ancient Moorish fort. Later, they supported the thick walls of a private house whose red tile roof still juts up near a public park festooned with bougainvillaea and dotted with café tables. As the hotel sits on a cliff jutting out over the sands below, it offers the resort's best view of the beach. Mrs. Dorothy Boulter is the English-born proprietor. With her husband, she occupies an elegantly spacious, somewhat bohemian salon within the hotel, into which guests are sometimes invited for tea. The establishment contains 15 simple bedrooms, each of which is suitable for two people. With a continental breakfast included, these rent for 6,000$ ($39) to 7,000$ ($45.50) daily. The hotel is open March 1 to October 31.

Estalagem Mirasol, Praia da Rocha, 8500 Portimão (tel. 082/240-46). This simple but charming hotel is fronted by a garden rich with flowering vines and shrubs. You'll find it on a street running parallel to the main road beside the beach. It's in a quiet part of the resort, not far from the center. The establishment contains a cool, basement bar and TV room filled with leatherette chairs. The staff is helpful. In winter a fire warms a corner of the dining room. But the rest of the year the windows are thrown open for a view of the surrounding landscape. Singles rent for 6,600$ ($42.90) daily, while doubles cost from 8,000$ ($52). Each of the 23 accommodations comes with private bath, and a continental breakfast is included. Mirasol is closed from November to February.

Residencial Sol, 10 Avenida Tomás Cabreira, Praia da Rocha, 8500 Portimão (tel. 082/240-71). Partly because of its location close to the noisy main drag, the painted concrete façade of this establishment appears somewhat bleak. In this case, however, appearances are deceiving, since the 32 bedrooms offer some of the cleanest and most unpretentiously attractive accommodations in town. Each of the units is designed for two guests, and contains a private bath, phone, radio, and exposed wood. The rooms in back are quieter, but the terrace-dotted front units look across the traffic toward a park filled with bougainvillaea. The breakfast lounge doubles as a TV room. In high season, rear rooms rent for 6,000$ ($39) per night, going up to 6,500$ ($42.25) for a front room with balcony.

WHERE TO DINE

Complete with gilt and crystal, the Titanic, Edificio Colúmbia, Rua Engenheiro Francisco Bivar (tel. 223-71), is the most elegant restaurant in town. It also serves the best food, an array of international specialties, including live shellfish and flambé dishes. In spite of the fact that it is named after the ill-fated luxury liner, it is not on the water, but lies in a modern residential complex. For 2,000$ ($13) to 3,300$ ($21.45), you can dine very well here, ordering such appealing dishes as the fish of the day, pork filet with mushrooms, prawns à la _plancha_ (grilled), and sole Algarve. Service is among the best at the resort. The 100-seat Titanic, which is air-conditioned, sails daily from noon to 2 p.m. and 7 to 11 p.m. It closes from the end of November until the end of December. The kitchen is in open view, and diners should make a reservation, especially in season.

Safari, Rua António Feo (tel. 082/235-40), is a Portuguese-run restaurant with a "taste of Africa" in its cuisine, as its name suggests. Many of its specialties were inspired by the former Portuguese colony of Angola. Built on a cliff overlooking the beach, this third-category restaurant has a glass-enclosed terrace. It is known for its fresh fish and seafood, and many guests in neighboring hotels like to escape the board requirements of their accommodation just to sample one of Safari's good home-cooked meals. The fare includes such delectable dishes as curry Safari, steak Safari, swordfish steak, and shrimp Safari. It's customary to begin your meal with a bowl of savory fish soup. Meals, served from noon to 11 p.m., cost from 2,000$ ($13), and you get good value here.

Bamboo Garden, Avenida Tomás Cabreira, Edificio Lamego (tel. 830-83), which has a classic oriental decor, serves some of the best Chinese food along the coast. In air-conditioned comfort, diners can select from a large menu that includes everything from squid chop suey to prawns with hot sauce. After deciding on a soup or appetizer (try the spring roll), guests can make their selections from various categories, including chicken, beef, duck, squid, and prawns. You might, for example, prefer fried duck with soybean sauce or chicken with almonds from the Algarve. Meals cost from 2,000$ ($13) and are served daily from 12:30 to 3 p.m. and 6 to 11:30 p.m.

6. Praia dos Três Irmãos and Alvor

PRAIA DOS TRÊS IRMÃOS

Went with RAY

Go here for the beach, nine miles of burnished golden sand, broken only by an occasional crag riddled with arched passageways. Just west of the better-known Praia da Rocha, the Beach of the Three Brothers has been discovered by skindivers who explore its undersea grottos and shoreside caves.

Its neighbor is the whitewashed fishing village of **Alvor,** where Portuguese and Moorish arts and traditions have mingled since the Arabs gave up their 500 years of occupation. Alvor was a favorite coastal haunt of King João II. The gambling casino, the **Casino de Alvor** (tel. 231-41), is modest in size compared to the one at Estoril, but it does feature roulette, blackjack, and craps. A restaurant features good food and also offers a floor show at 11 p.m. and 1 a.m. It is open nightly.

Staying in Praia dos Três Irmãos

Alvor Praia, Praia dos Três Irmãos, 8500 Portimão (tel. 082/240-21). "You'll feel like you're loved the moment you walk in the door," said a well-dressed woman visitor from the Midwest. This citadel of hedonism seems to have more joie de vivre than any hotel on the Algarve. Its position is ideal, as are the building, bedrooms, decor, service, and food. On a landscaped crest, the luxury hotel has many of its bedrooms and public rooms exposed to the ocean view, the gardens, and the free-form Olympic-size swimming pool. Gentle walks (or else an elevator) lead down the palisade to the sandy beach and the rugged rocks that rise out of the water.

The accommodations are quite varied, everything from a cowhide-decorated room evoking Arizona's Valley of the Sun, to typical Portuguese accommodations with provincial furnishings. Many of the rooms contain private balconies where guests take breakfast facing the view of the Bay of Lagos.

The rooms contain oversize beds, plenty of clothing space, a long desk-and-chest combination, and well-designed baths with double basins and lots of towels. Singles rent for 19,000$ ($123.50) daily in peak season and doubles for 28,000$ ($182), but reductions are granted otherwise.

The hotel is so self-contained you may never stray from the premises. Inside, a wide, domed airborne staircase leads to a lower level, encircling a Japanese garden and lily pond. The main dining room is on two levels, with three glass walls so that every guest has an ocean view. The Maisonette Grill is considered separately as a restaurant recommendation (see below). Like an exclusive club, the main drinking lounge is equipped with deep leather chairs and decorated with a cubistic modern ceiling. You can get reduced greens fees on a nearby 18-hole golf course. Other sports include horseback riding, waterskiing, and tennis. On the lower level of the hotel are boutiques, a newsstand, hairdressers, and a Finnish sauna.

Delfim Hotel, Praia dos Três Irmãos, 8500 Portimão (tel. 082/271-71). The developers of this hotel chose their site wisely. The Delfim sits near the beach on a scrub-covered hillside whose sands offer a sweeping view of the Algarvian coastline and its dozens of high-rises. With its central tower and its identical wings splayed back like a boomerang in flight, the hotel is one of the most dramatically modern buildings in the region. In spite of its proximity to the beach, many guests prefer the parasol-ringed swimming pool whose circumference encloses a swim-up bar marooned like an island in its midst. Tennis courts are nearby, as well as an assortment of shops, restaurants, and bars. Each of the 325 well-furnished rooms contains a private terrace, bath, radio, and phone. In high season, doubles cost from 17,000$ ($110.50), with singles going for 10,000$ ($65).

Dining in Praia dos Três Irmãos

Maisonette Grill, Hotel Alvor Praia (tel. 240-20), takes its rightful place alongside other distinguished restaurants connected with luxury hotels, such as the Ritz Grill in Lisbon. It is among the smartest places for gourmet cuisine along the Algarve coast. The Grill, in spite of its spaciousness, has an intimate atmosphere, allowing you plenty of time to peruse the à la carte menu. You might begin your meal with vichyssoise. Main courses are likely to include poached turbot with hollandaise and a broiled rib of beef prepared for two persons. The dessert menu has such delicacies as Rothschild soufflé and crêpes suzette. Meals, served nightly from 8 p.m. to midnight, cost from 3,500$ ($22.75).

Restaurante O Búzio, Aldeamento da Prainha (tel. 205-61), stands at the end point of a road that encircles a resort development dotted with private condos and exotic shrubbery. In high season there are so many cars lining the narrow blacktop road that you'd be well advised to park near the resort's entrance, then walk the downhill stretch toward the restaurant.

Lunch and dinner are served in two separate locations. From noon to 3 p.m. daily, lunch is offered on a shaded hillock overlooking one of the best-landscaped pools on the Algarve. Many visitors enjoy the grassy lawns sloping toward the pool so much that they pay an entrance fee and spend the rest of the day beside its waters. If you come only for lunch, there is no entrance fee. For 2,000$ ($13), you can enjoy a light meal, which might include omelets, salads, hamburgers, or fresh fish. The real allure of the place, however, is after dark when dinners are served near the resort's administrative offices. In a room whose blue curtains reflect the color of the shimmering ocean at the bottom of the cliffs, you can enjoy dinner at prices beginning at 2,800$ ($18.20). Reservations are necessary for meals, which might include fish soup, gazpacho, Italian pasta dishes, boiled or grilled fish of the day, peppersteak, and lamb kebabs with saffron-flavored rice. Dinner is every night from 7:30 to 10 p.m. In winter, when it's too cold to eat outside, you can also have lunch in this restaurant. *Ate hore*

During the summer, there is also another restaurant, O Caniço, on the beach, with private access via an elevator cut into the cliff. This one serves mainly grilled fish and salads.

Where Mgt + Jim Live

MONTES DE ALVOR ✗

The first deluxe hotel on the Algarve was the **Penina Golf Hotel,** Montes de Alvor, 8502 Portimão (tel. 082/220-51), between Portimão and Lagos, founded by a group of hotel entrepreneurs. Nowadays, of course, it has much competition from the other luxury choices. Golfing fans remain loyal to the Penina, however, as it is a major sporting mecca. A 36-hole championship golf course was designed by Henry Cotton between the hotel and the sea. Those not sunning themselves by the pool are transported to the hotel beach, with its own snackbar and changing cabins. The ground level of the Penina is devoted to changing rooms, lockers, and a golf school and shops. Other facilities include a sauna, billiard room, a beauty parlor, and a barbershop. Two hard tennis courts are offered. Guests enjoy the Grill Room or the dining room (table d'hôte meals in the latter) for a well-prepared repast, capped by dancing.

Most of the bedrooms contain picture windows and honeycomb balconies providing views of the course and swimming pool or vistas of the Monchique hills. The standard bedrooms are furnished in a pleasant style, combining traditional pieces with Portuguese provincial spool beds. The rooms are spacious enough for off-the-course relaxation, and contain good-size beds and tile baths. In high season, singles rent for 26,950$ ($175) daily, with doubles costing 35,420$ ($230). Meals without wine are another 6,600$ ($40) per person. Reductions are granted off-season.

7. Praia do Carvoeiro

One of the little whitewashed beach fishing villages along the Algarve coast has been turned into an expatriate colony, with many sophisticated Europeans finding it the most ideal place along the coast. It has not been overbuilt (as of yet), and it has a number of excellent restaurants. Accommodations, as of this writing, were still extremely limited, including only one major hotel and time-share units.

Lying about three miles south of the wine-rich town of Lagoa, the sandy beach nestles between two rock masses, creating a solarium. The shadows of the cliffs are cooling, the sea calm. East of the beach on a steep slope is a **belvedere,** dedicated to Our Lady of the Incarnation (*Nossa Senhora da Encarnacão*), from which you have a commanding view of the sea and surrounding cliffs. Not far from the belvedere, you can reach the fascinating **Algar Seco,** a collection of huge reddish stones carved by the sea into interesting shapes and a number of sea caves, often underwater. You go through mazes of rock and down some 134 steps to reach the site. The sea caves can be visited by boat in summer. Ask in the town.

Incidentally, before venturing down to the little commune of Praia do Carvoeiro, you may want to stop off at **Lagoa,** on the main coastal highway. If you announce yourself at the door to the big warehouse here, chances are you'll be allowed to visit the wine cellars.

WHERE TO STAY

A few steps from the sheltered but sandy harbor, **Hotel Dom Sancho,** Praia do Carvoeiro 8400 Faro (tel. 082/573-01), is in a hard-to-miss spot on the main square of the port. If this folkloric village becomes, as its devotees predict, the Portuguese version of St. Tropez, this comfortable hotel will probably be one of its social centers. Its major drawback is that you may not be able to get in, as tour operators have been known to book every room for a whole season. This is a pity for the independent traveler, as the Dom Sancho is the only real hotel in town, although you may find a little guest room or boarding house, perhaps a time-share unit on the hill.

The hotel's thick white walls, angular windows, and flat roof remind visitors of Pueblo Indian dwellings in the American Southwest. The brick-covered courtyard and the vaulted dining room, however, are pure Iberian, as is the polite attention of the well-trained staff. Bedrooms are air-conditioned, containing radios, phones, and unpretentious modern furnishings. Some of the units have private balconies overlooking the port. The 47 rooms rent in high season for 7,800$ ($50.70) to 8,200$ ($53.30) daily in a single, 11,000$ ($71.50) to 12,500$ ($81.25) for double occupancy, with a continental breakfast included.

WHERE TO DINE

A pleasant place to go for dinner is **O Castelo,** Rua do Casino (tel. 572-18). If you're fortunate enough to obtain a table on the outdoor terrace or near one of the establishment's small windows, you'll have a view over the sea. It's actually an Algarve house, whose entrance sits beside the steep road skirting the edge of a harborside cliff. The ambience is relatively sophisticated, and the youthful waiters somehow seem to anticipate your needs. The meals are reasonably priced at 2,800$ ($18.20). Lunch isn't served, but for dinner you might enjoy such specialties as pepper steak, chicken piri-piri, assorted shellfish au gratin, shrimp kebab, and fish cataplana. Dinner is served daily except Sunday from 7 to 10 p.m.

Les Quatre Dauphins, Monte Carvoeiro (tel. 573-15), is the best dining spot in this time-share complex that includes about ten different restaurants, ranging from Fernando Stone Steak, where steaks and shellfish are cooked at your table on a stone, to A Marisqueira, which specializes in seafood. At the "Four Dolphins," you get classic French cuisine, along with an array of international specialties. Whenever possible, fresh produce of the region is used. Meals cost from 3,000$ ($19.50) and are served only from 6:30 p.m. to midnight daily except Thursday. In fair weather, guests prefer to sit at one of the outside tables, where folk dancing is often staged in the square. Otherwise, they retreat inside and enjoy an elegant tavern decor.

THE BAR SCENE

Right in the center of the resort, **Long Bar,** Rua dos Pescadores (tel. 574-35), as its name implies, has the longest bar in town. You might select one of the scattering of outdoor tables, but the heart and soul of the place is visible only from within its British pub-style interior. There, you can order a Sagres beer to accompany a pub lunch or dinner. You might, after a round of drinks or two, decide to order such fare as a baked potato, an omelet, a hamburger, or a sandwich. Meals cost from 1,000$ ($6.50). The bartender specializes in liqueur coffees. Hours are daily from 10 a.m. to 2 a.m.

Smiler's Bar, Rua do Barranco (tel. 573-04). A sampling of the assorted youth of Europe is likely to be crammed between the thick white arches of this bar on a summer night. The place is British owned, and it's the most popular bar in town. Its regulars also claim that it serves the best beer. Hard drinks cost 325$ ($2.10), with beer going for 150$ ($1). Hours are 10 a.m. (sometimes 11 a.m.) to 1 a.m. (or perhaps 2 a.m. if business warrants it).

---

8. Silves

When you pass through the Moorish-inspired entrance of this hillside town, you quickly become aware that Silves is unlike the other towns and villages of the Algarve. It lives in the past, recalling its heyday when it was known as Xelb, the seat of Muslim culture in the south before it fell to the crusaders. Christian warriors and earthquakes have been rough on Silves. But somehow the **Castle of Silves,** crowning the hilltop, has held on, although it's seen better days. Once the blood of the Muslims, staging their last stand in Silves, "flowed like red wine," as one Portuguese historian put it. The cries and screams of women and children resounded over the walls. Nowadays the only sound you're likely to hear is the loud rock music coming from the gatekeeper's house.

The red sandstone castle may date back to the 9th century. From its ramparts you can look down the saffron-mossed tile roofs of the village houses, down the narrow cobbled streets where roosters strut and scrappy dogs sleep peacefully in the doorways. Inside the walls, the government has planted a flower garden, adorning it with golden chrysanthemums and scarlet poinsettias. In the fortress, water rushes through a huge cistern and a deep well made of sandstone. Below are dungeon chambers and labyrinthine tunnels where the last of the Moors hid out before the crusaders found them and sent them to their deaths.

The 13th-century former **Cathedral of Silves** (now a church), down below, was built in the Gothic style. You can wander through its aisles and nave, noting perhaps beauty in their simplicity. Both the chancel and transept date from a later period, having been built in the flamboyant Gothic style. The Christian architects who originally built it may have torn down an old mosque. Many of the tombs contained here are believed to have been the graves of crusaders who took the town in 1244. The Gothic structure is considered one of the most outstanding religious monuments in the Algarve.

Outside the main part of town, near an orange grove (one of the local Silves boys will surely volunteer as your inexpensive guide), a lonely open-air pavilion shelters a 15th-century stone lacework cross. This ecclesiastical artwork is two-faced, depicting a pietà (the face of Christ is destroyed) on one side, the Crucifixion on the other. It has been declared a national monument of incalculable value.

WHERE TO EAT

Silves is most often visited on a day trip from one of the beach towns to the south. For that reason, many visitors find themselves in Silves at lunchtime. Restaurants here are very simple but also very cheap.

One of the best is **Rui,** 27 Rua Comendador Vilarim (tel. 44-26-82), which is known for its shellfish such as lobster and its superb grills. In fact, the owners of this restaurant have their own shellfish nursery. They serve good-tasting meals along with regional wines for 1,800$ ($11.70) and up per person. Rui is the largest restaurant in town, and can take as many as 120 diners on its busiest day. It is open daily from noon to 4 p.m. and 6 to 11 p.m. In winter it is closed on Tuesday.

Ladeira, Ladeira de São Pedro (tel. 44-28-70), is smaller, seating 40 diners. It is also cheaper, charging from 1,700$ ($11.05) for a filling meal. Regional specialties are featured, and the place is known for its "home-cooking." Service is from noon to 3 p.m. and 6 to 10 p.m. It is closed on Sunday.

---

9. Armação de Pêra

Squat fishermen's cottages make up the core of this ancient village. It rests almost at water's edge on a curvy bay that comes near to its Golden Beach, one of the largest along Portugal's southern coast. In the direction of Portimão are rolling low ridges, toward Albufeira's rosy cliffs. Because Armação de Pêra has such a fine beach, it has almost become engulfed in a sea of high-rise buildings, which have virtually eliminated its once rather charming character.

Once Armação de Pêra was utilized by the Phoenicians as a trading post and stopping-off point for cruises around Cape St. Vincent. Near the center of the village is a wide beach where fishing boats are drawn up on the sands when a fish auction (lota) is held.

While at the resort, you may want to walk out to **Nossa Senhora da Rocha** (Our Lady of the Rock), a Romanesque chapel on a 95-foot-high stone that sticks out into the ocean like the prow of a boat. Underneath are the cathedral-size **Sea Grottos** (Furnas). To visit these, you have to call at the Tourist Office, Avenida Marginal (tel. 321-45), and make arrangements to go out in a boat, but they're certainly worth the effort. Unique in the Algarve, the sea caves are entered through a series of arches that frame the sky and ocean from the inside. In their galleries and vaults, where pigeons nest, the splashing and cooing reverberate in the upper stalactite-studded chambers.

The nearest railway station is at the village of Alcantarilha, five miles away.

WHERE TO STAY

A deluxe establishment, **Hotel Viking,** Praia da Senhora da Rocha, 8365 Armação de Pêra (tel. 082/323-36), lies about a mile southwest of the resort, with many signs directing you. It rises in a mass of gray stone and buff-colored concrete between two spits of land jutting into the sea. The hotel has many and diverse amenities, including a replica of a 19th-century café set into the windbreak of a cobblestone courtyard, an English pub, a large cocktail bar leading into an enormous dining room, a TV room filled with card tables, a basement-level disco, and an array of in- and outdoor bars. My favorite place within the grounds is the clifftop pair of swimming pools. There, within a view of the rugged geology marking this region of Portugal, you can stretch out under bamboo parasols, between the shades of large terracotta pots festooned with geraniums and trailing strands of ivy.

Even the geodesic dome of the lobby's skylight illuminates a splashing fountain ringed with glistening slabs of white marble. Each of the comfortably contemporary rooms, 184 in all, contains a private balcony angled toward a view of the sea, and each has a marble-covered bath, wall-to-wall carpeting, a mini-bar, radio, and phone. In high season, doubles rent for 22,400$ ($145.60) daily, with singles going for 14,400$ ($93.60). Reductions are granted otherwise. The Viking also contains tennis courts, puts out lavishly decorated buffets, and has a wide array of "above and below" water sports, as well as a beauty salon, a sauna, massage facilities, and a Jacuzzi.

Vilalara, Praia das Gaivotas, 8365 Armaçao de Pêra (tel. 082/31-23-33), is a luxury apartment complex on a cliffside, with a sandy beach—all in all, a self-contained miniature resort one mile west of Armação de Pêra. International magazines have acclaimed its good taste, which has attracted diplomats, movie stars, members of royalty, as well as business executives. Curving with the contour of the coast, the apartments are built in a serpentine fashion, two floors of one-, two-, and three-bedroom units, each with a private sun-pocket terrace balcony. That balcony is furnished in bamboo and rattan. A long continuous flower box softens the look at the railing. Each apartment is spacious and delightful, with a living room, a fully equipped kitchen, a veranda with a southern view, and each bedroom has its own tile bath. A junior suite without a kitchen but with breakfast included rents for 20,500$ ($133.25) daily, single or double occupancy. A two-bedroom, two-bath apartment with a kitchen but without breakfast included costs four occupants 35,000$ ($227.50) a day. Off-season reductions are granted.

The major dining focus is the Vilalara Restaurant recommended separately. The hotel contains what it calls a club, with dining and wining facilities, as well as tennis courts, three swimming pools (one for children), and a disco. The snack bar/grill restaurant is near the pool. The complex has an indoor-outdoor informality that is casually chic.

Hotel do Garbe, Avenida Marginal, 8365 Armaçao de Pêra (tel. 082/321-87), is a self-contained resort dominating the top of a cliff, with a sandy beach at its feet. Stone steps lead through the terraced palisade to the hotel, built block fashion, its white walls, bedroom balconies, and public terraces shining in the summer sun. The public rooms, on several levels, are modern, but warmed by their colors and natural wood. In the main sitting room, with its open fireplace, furnishings are grouped with an eye to the sea view; likewise, the dining hall turns to the sea. If you're just passing through, you can order a luncheon or dinner for 2,500$ ($16.25).

The bedrooms combine Nordic and Algarvian features. Often a room will have window seats, beds set on pine frames, an occasional white skin throw rug, a red parasol on a private patio, and leather-toned tile floors. Room rates vary according to placement, size, and view, the higher tariffs for one of the luxury or junior suites. The high-season rate for one person is from 7,500$ ($48.75) daily, rising to 19,000$ ($123.50) for two guests. Reductions are granted otherwise. Taxes and service are included in the tariffs.

Hotel do Levante, 8365 Armaçao de Pêra (tel. 082/323-22). Many repeat visitors consider this their favorite hotel on the Algarve. It's contained within a Mediterranean-style villa set on a hill away from the congestion of the resort. From a position near the lobby, visitors have a sweeping view of the sea, the high-rises along the coast, and a pair of swimming pools dug into the shrub-bordered terraces. The hotel opened in 1967. Some of the bedrooms open onto enclosed courtyards, where pines glimmer from festoons of colored lights. Others have a view of the sea, and each contains a radio, phone, and a private balcony or terrace. Perhaps best of all, a formal garden, laid out in a star-shaped pattern, includes the name of the hotel spelled out amid the greenery. A hacienda-like dining room, replete with leather-backed chairs and pure white walls, serves well-prepared meals to a largely English or German clientele. In the peak summer season, singles rent for 12,000$ ($78) daily, and doubles cost from 17,000$ ($110.50), including a continental breakfast.

WHERE TO DINE

It's worth the effort it takes to get to the **Panorama Sol Grill** (tel. 082/31-24-24). You'll find it on a road west of town leading to the Hotel Levante and the Hotel Viking. At first you might think that the only available seating is on the simple benches, under sunscreens that have been set up on the outdoor walled-in terrace. No one will object if you want to sit there. However, you'll be rewarded if you continue to climb past the outdoor grill to the top of the stairs, entering a baronial dining hall. There, within view of a huge stone fireplace, you can eat in more dignified circumstances. The establishment is the creation of a former resident of Castelo Branco, José Gomes, who provides personal attention and service.

Regardless of where you choose to sit, you'll have to give your menu order at the grill, where the day's catch, as well as an array of meats, is laid out in a refrigerated case for your inspection. Average meals cost from 2,500$ ($16.25) and might include silver bass, fresh asparagus, and several preparations of beef, veal, or pork, plus live lobster from the restaurant's aquarium. The establishment is open for lunch from 12:30 to 3 p.m. and dinner from 6:30 to 10 p.m. every day in summer. Between February and the end of April it is closed every Wednesday, and between November and February it is completely closed.

Vilalara, Praia das Gaivotas (tel. 31-23-33), one mile west of Armação de Pêra, was recommended previously as a hotel. In this luxury apartment complex, with its splendid flower gardens, Vilalara also serves some of the finest food on the Algarve. The restaurant is open only for dinner, which is served nightly from 8 to 11 p.m. and costs from 3,000$ ($19.50) to 5,000$ ($32.50), depending on what you order. Service, which is deluxe, is in a restaurant that has a big-windowed panoramic view of the sea and black painted bamboo chairs and black and white decor. The chefs use only top quality ingredients and prepare dishes with flair. These include the freshest of seafood, along with an array of international dishes and Portuguese specialties. An indoor and outdoor grill and its adjacent snack bar are often closed for part of the year, but the restaurant is open all year.

Santola, Largo 25 de Abril (tel. 323-32), has long been established. Its faithful patrons remember Armação de Pêra when it was just a fishing village. At the edge of the beach, "The Crab" specializes in a wide range of dishes, placing the emphasis on seafood. It does excellent charcoal grills and has several continental specialties to tempt diners, who pay from 3,000$ ($19.50) for a good-tasting meal. Service is from noon to 3 p.m. and 6:30 p.m. to midnight (closed Thursday for lunch). From one of its tables you can enjoy a panoramic view. In winter a fireplace adds the proper glow, and all year round the bar is popular.

10. Albufeira

This cliffside fishing village is the St. Tropez of the Algarve. The lazy life, sunshine, beaches, and cheap food make it a haven for young people and artists, although the villagers haven't quite made up their minds as to what they think of the invasion that began in the late 1960s. Some of them, however, open the doors of their cottages to those seeking a place to stay for a few escudos a night. Those without the money often sleep in a tent on the cliff, or under the sky.

The village retains characteristics more readily associated with a North African seaside community. Its streets are steep, the villas drunkenly staggered up and down the hillside. Albufeira rises above a sickle-shaped beach that shines in the bright sunlight. A rocky grottoed bluff separates the strip used by the sunbathers from the working beach, where brightly painted fishing boats are drawn up on the sand. Access to the beach is through a tunneled rock passageway.

In accommodations, the resort is well supplied. The tariffs in many of the establishments are more suited to the middle-class pocketbook than that of the young people who favor the place so much.

WHERE TO STAY

The leading candidate, **Hotel Montechoro,** 8200 Albufeira (tel. 089/526-51), is generally conceded to be the finest hotel in the area for the individual traveler not wanting to stay at the nearby Club Med. However, the Montechoro, looking like a hotel you might encounter in North Africa, lies some two miles northeast of the center of Albufeira. It's a fully equipped resort complex, a four-star hotel with ample facilities such as a pair of swimming pools, professional tennis courts, four squash courts, a sauna, and a gymnasium. You might get lost here, as it contains 362 air-conditioned bedrooms. Rooms are often done in an extremely modern style. The most elegant way of staying here is to book into one of the 48 well-furnished suites. In summer, singles cost from 12,320$ ($80) to 15,400$ ($100) daily and doubles from 13,860$ ($90) to 16,940$ ($110), prices including taxes. The higher rates are imposed from July to September. A four-course meal goes for 3,850$ ($25), and you can dine in either the grill room, within its panoramic view, or the regular restaurant. Lots of regional merchandise is sold at shops within the hotel precincts.

Clube Mediterráneo da Balaia, Praia Maria Luísa, 8200 Albufeira (tel. 089/526-81). Tiers of roughly hewn balconies rise sky high, and the public rooms seem to flow one into another, with connecting passageways. Above the central core, corridors lead to the bedrooms, all of which are uncluttered, with furnishings coordinated in simple textured fabrics. Near the main building are 12 bungalows, each having at least two bedrooms with a kitchenette and private terrace. They are built in rowhouse style. The hotel accepts both individuals and groups. All reservations must be requested through an agency named Lufrantur, 90 Rua da Prata, 1100 Lisboa (tel. 01/87-85-12). Reservations are only accepted for a minimum of a week's stay. There are about nine different rates depending on the time of the year. The tariffs per week range from 80,000$ ($520) to 130,000$ ($845) per person, based on double occupancy and including full board. Add 20% to these tariffs if you desire single occupancy.

The manager has arranged a number of social and sporting activities through the sports shop, from waterskiing to clay pigeon shooting (an 18-hole golf course is nearby). Most guests, however, like to lounge by the heated swimming pool, enjoying a buffet luncheon. The drawing rooms and salons are too numerous to itemize. Also on the premises is a disco, featuring occasional fado and folklore entertainers.

The resort is four miles east of Albufeira on hilly land, encompassing a shoreline of rugged rock formations and a series of coves for surf swimming.

Hotel Sol e Mar, 8200 Albufeira (tel. 089/521-21), has captured the prime position within the village. It deceives you with its two-story entrance on the upper palisade. When you walk across the spacious, sun-filled lounges to the picture windows and look down, it's a six-story drop. Hugging the cliff are bedrooms and a wide stone terrace with garden furniture and parasols. On still a lower level is a sandy beach. There are 74 bedrooms, only six of which are singles. All contain private balconies. The twins have wooden headboards, locally painted seascapes, slimline armchairs, and plenty of wardrobe space. In high summer season, the single or double rate is the same: 14,000$ ($91) daily. However, in off-season, singles rent for 8,000$ ($52) and doubles for 10,000$ ($65). A continental breakfast is included, and a table d'hôte luncheon or dinner is priced at 2,000$ ($13).

Guests are a continental crowd with a sprinkling of Americans. Diners take their meals in a two-level room, opposite a drinking lounge, a room for card players, and a television room. After-dinner concerts are played on the electric organ till long past midnight. During the day, guests take the elevator to the lower sun terrace to find swimming, sunbathing, and the Esplanade Café, designed as a Portuguese tavern with Madeira stools, decorative tiles, and hanging anchors. Every night except Monday, guests dance at the Disco Sol e Mar to the latest records.

Estalagem do Cerro, Rua Samora Barros, 8200 Albufeira (tel. 089/521-63), captures Algarvian charm yet doesn't neglect modern amenities. Its English name is "the Inn of the Craggy Hill" and it is located at the top of a hill overlooking Albufeira's bay, about a 10-minute walk down to the beach. An older, regional style building has been recently renovated, but its character has been maintained. It is joined to a modern structure in a similar Moorish style. The bedrooms have private bath and a veranda overlooking the sea, pool, or garden. Each is tastefully furnished and contains such necessities as a phone. Singles rent for 7,000$ ($45.50) to 9,000$ ($58.50) daily, with doubles costing 8,000$ ($52) to 12,000$ ($78). A panoramic dining room provides good meals for 1,500$ ($9.75). Here you are served both regional dishes and international specialties in air-conditioned comfort. Before or after dinner, guests gather in a comfortable, modernized bar or its patio. On most nights, guests can dance to disco music, but fado and folkloric shows are also presented on some nights. The inn has an outdoor heated swimming pool in a garden setting. Other facilities include a hairdressing salon, sauna, massage facilities, solarium, Jacuzzi, and Turkish bath. There's also a fully equipped gym. The inn is rated four stars, which is the equivalent of a three-star hotel. Its 83 bedrooms are carefully supervised by the Negrão Neto family, who offer an inviting atmosphere.

Mar a Vista, Cêrro da Piedade, 8200 Albufeira (tel. 089/521-54). From the crow's-nest vantage point of this estalagem, you can gaze out over the rooftops of the village below, the beach dotted with bright tents for bathers. The rooftop breakfast room of this first-class inn, decorated in a provincial style with blond paneling, takes advantage of the view. The estalagem is composed of two buildings. The principal structure, covered with climbing plants, has 34 bedrooms, a bar, and the breakfast room. The second building contains four bedrooms. There is a well-cared-for walled garden and plenty of space to park cars. Most of the rooms contain private balconies. The walls are hung with interesting prints; the furnishings, although not sumptuous, are typical and comfortable. In summer, singles rent for 8,000$ ($52) daily, with doubles costing 9,000$ ($58.50). In off-season, singles are 5,000$ ($32.50) and doubles 6,000$ ($39). Closed from November to April.

Hotel Boa-Vista, 6 Rua Samora Barros, 8200 Albufeira (tel. 089/521-75). Built in the Algarvian style, and set high above the sea outside the village center, the "Residence of the Good View" offers two different modes of living: one in its amenity-loaded main building, another in its block of furnished efficiencies across the street. The style, the welcome, the level of taste are set by a private hotel chain called Glitter Hotels. A special feature is a temperature-controlled swimming pool with an encircling moat.

International cuisine is served in the panoramic restaurant/grill bar with a view of the bay. The rooms open onto balconies, from which you can look down upon the white-washed, orange-tile-roofed cottages to the bay below. The private baths are superb, in gray and white with marble. Traditional wickerwork decor is used, with matching carpets and ceramics. For a real bargain, consider the nearby apartments, ideal for the family. Each of the 15 suites contains a kitchen, dining room, lounge, and balcony. Each can accommodate up to four persons and is furnished with twin beds, double settee, sofa, armchairs, refrigerator, stove, and marble-topped sink. Rooms and apartments cost more from June through October, renting for 11,500$ ($74.75) to 13,000$ ($84.50) daily in a single, 13,500$ ($87.75) to 16,000$ ($104) and up in a double, with a continental breakfast included.

Hotel Rocamar, Largo Jacinto d'Ayet, 8200 Albufeira (tel. 089/526-96). Depending on how much wine you've had for lunch, this cubistic hotel might look alternately like an updated version of a Moorish castle, a well-ordered assemblage of building blocks, or the partially excavated side of a stone quarry. It rises seven stories above the tawny-colored cliffs that slope down to one of the most inviting beaches along the Algarve. Many of its windows, and all of its balconies, benefit from the view this provides. The hotel is within walking distance of the attractions of town, yet its more secluded location enables guests to relax within the sun-washed confines of their simple but comfortable bedrooms. An Iberian-style dining room serves conservative but well-prepared meals, and a contemporary bar offers the possibility of a congenial tête-à-tête. In high season, singles cost from 6,500$ ($42.25) daily, while doubles go from 12,000$ ($78), including a continental breakfast.

Villa Recife, 6 Rua Miguel Bombarda, 8200 Albufeira (tel. 089/520-47), is a self-catering hotel entered through a café that fills its front garden. Sometimes a live band entertains here on a wooden platform near an encircling wall. The establishment was originally built as a private home. Today the palms and bougainvillaea that the original owners planted tower over the entranceway, whose walls are covered with blue, white, and yellow azulejos. A cabaña bar dispenses tropical drinks. The hotel has been expanded to include a total of 92 accommodations, about 20 of which are contained within the original villa. The majority, however, are found in a modern rear wing, whose design is invisible from the front garden. There, studio apartments all contain a tiny terrace, oak cabinets, and a kitchenette. Off-season, singles stay here for 4,500$ ($29.25) daily, with doubles costing 5,800$ ($37.70). In high season, the single and double rate is the same: 8,000$ ($52). Four persons can rent an apartment for 7,800$ ($50.70) to 10,000$ ($65) daily, depending on the season.

Hotel da Aldeia, Avenida Dr. Francisco Sa Carneiro, 8200 Albufeira (tel. 089/550-31), is a complete holiday complex, where you have the advantage of an apartment, villa, or hotel room. It's in the holiday village of Areias de São João, near Golden Beach, about a mile from Albufeira. You'll find adequate recreation facilities—a tennis court, mini-golf, two adjoining swimming pools with spacious sun terraces and a snackbar, plus a piano bar and live entertainment weekly. Across the road is a restaurant if you don't want to cook a meal in your own kitchen. The apartments have one and two bedrooms, accommodating a maximum of six guests, and the villas have two to four bedrooms, housing as many as ten guests, although that might be extremely crowded. All units have fully equipped kitchens, and maid service includes dish washing, cleaning, and making of beds. Suites and apartments are handsomely decorated, using strong colors and natural wood furniture with rattan and bamboo. Built-in headboards hold telephones and provide background music and light switches. You have a choice of sea, pool, or mountain view, and you can even have half- or full-board rates if desired. A double room peaks at 8,000$ ($52) daily, and a suite for two costs 9,000$ ($58.50). Each extra bed carries a 1,200$ ($7.80) supplement. A buffet breakfast is included in the rates. Lunch or dinner is 1,500$ ($9.75), or you can ask for full board, available for 2,500$ ($16.25) per person daily in addition to the room prices. Discounts of 20% are granted mid-season and 50% off-season.

Aparthotel Auramar, Praia dos Aveiros, 8200 Albufeira (tel. 089/533-37), at the edge of Albufeira, sits on a low cliff overlooking a sandy beach, like a friendly fortress facing the ocean. Close to the sea cliff is an outstanding recreation area, with the finest swimming pool in the area. There's an informal snackbar, and the main building has a restaurant providing Portuguese and an international cuisine. Essentially an apartment house, the Auramar offers meals as well as a bar lounge. The 282 fine apartments have living-room furnishings in addition to a kitchenette and a terrace for sunbathing. In high season, only double rates are in effect: 16,000$ ($104) daily. In spring and fall, however, singles rent for 8,000$ ($52) daily and doubles for 11,000$ ($71.50). A continental breakfast is included in the daily rates.

Hotel Baltum, Avenida 25 de Abril, 8200 Albufeira (tel. 089/521-06), is a one-minute walk from the main beach strip. The hotel and its nearby annex offer modern accommodations. In the main building, the Baltum rents 53 rooms, each with central heating, private bath, and phone, and some offer a private balcony. Cozy sitting areas—furnished with leather chairs, blond coffee tables, and couches —are available to those willing to spend a few more escudos. In high season, only twins and doubles are rented, costing 6,100$ ($39.65) to 7,100$ ($46.15) daily, with breakfast included. The solarium-terrace with its little bar has music.

The annex, called the **Anexo Baltum,** Rua Cándido dos Reis, 8200 Albufeira (tel. 089/521-07), is in the center of the village, near the Cine Pax. The lobby is dominated by a circular staircase (the walls of which are lined from floor to ceiling with decorative tiles). The rooms here are similar to those at the Hotel Baltum, being even newer, and equipped with showers instead of tubs. You'll have to do your soaking in the Atlantic. Some of the streamlined bedrooms have balconies, and others open onto an uninspired view of the central air shaft. The rates are the same here as at the main hotel.

Apartamentos Albufeira Jardim, Cêrro da Piedade, 8200 Albufeira (tel. 089/520-85), is becoming increasingly popular with visitors who like to stay in one place for a while before resuming their touring. Standing on a hill overlooking the resort, it rents attractively furnished studio apartments that are ideal for families. Units include a fully equipped kitchen. The good news is that you don't have to do your cleaning, as the management provides daily maid service. In high season, a studio rents for 8,500$ ($55.25) daily for two persons, a bedroom and living room suitable for four for 16,500$ ($107.25), and two bedrooms and a living room suitable for six persons for 25,000$ ($162.50). Balconies from the apartments open onto the ocean and a view of Albufeira. As a further enticement, there are two restaurants, two coffee shops, three bars, three tennis courts, and five pools (including two baby pools).

WHERE TO DINE

The pleasant **Restaurante Alfredo,** 9-11 Rua 5 de Outubro (tel. 520-59), serves what are really banquets. Just a minute's stroll from the market square, it is housed in an old building that looks as if it's always been an inn. It's full of atmosphere, with crude wooden tables and chairs just made for leisurely drinking. The second-floor restaurant is a heavily beamed room with a marble slab floor and simple wooden tables. Ceiling fans create a cooling breeze, and a semi-visible kitchen provides all the visual entertainment many diners require. Your meal might include tuna salad, Cataplana clams, and bream or swordfish, as well as tournedos with mushrooms or Portuguese-style steak. The wine of the house, Regengos, is sold by the glass. A meal usually costs around 3,000$ ($19.50). Reservations are required. The restaurant is open daily from noon to 3 p.m. and 6:30 to 11 p.m.

O Montinho, at Montechoro (tel. 539-59), is the finest restaurant in the area, lying two miles northeast of Albufeira. Set on a dusty red-clay plateau, behind the already-recommended Hotel Montechoro, this Portuguese quinta has a red-tile roof and a covering of ivy and oleander, along with white stucco walls. Its terrace design looks almost fortified against the parking lot outside. You get an old Iberian feeling here, with raftered ceilings, carved chairs, and Algarvian accents. A host of international visitors comes here nightly except Sunday for dinner from 7:30 to 11 p.m. The chef's specialties include hot fish and herb pâté with a shellfish sauce, monkfish escalope with "melted" leeks, and duckling confit or else filet of duckling with fruit.

Other dishes are changed regularly to offer novelty to the regular clients. A menu dégustation of four courses costs 2,500$ ($16.25), or else you can order à la carte for 2,500$ ($16.25) to 3,800$ ($24.70).

The Beach Basket (O Cabaz da Praia), 7 Praça Miguel Bombarda (tel. 521-37), near the Sol e Mar Hotel, sits on a colorful little square near the Church of São Sebastian, which is now a museum. The restaurant is owned by David Shean, who came here from England many years ago. In a former fisherman's cottage, he created a restaurant with an inviting ambience and good food. With its large, sheltered terrace, it offers diners a view over the main Albufeira beach. The cuisine is international, with emphasis on French cooking, including such favorites as freshly caught sole, served meunière style, and suprême of chicken topped with a mushroom sauce. All main courses are served with a selection of fresh vegetables. The restaurant is renowned for its Algarve soufflé omelet and lemon meringue pie. Expect to pay 1,800$ ($11.70) for a meal. Hours at this popular restaurant are daily from noon to 2 p.m. and 7 to 10 p.m.

La Cigale, Olhos d'Água (tel. 506-37), stands right on the beach 4½ miles from Albufeira, with a terrace that makes this a romantic choice at night. Here is your cliché of the sunny southern coast of Europe. Fortunately, the food matches the atmosphere, enough so that the place draws a lot of diners who have villas on the Algarve—hence, reservations are important. The wine list is fairly distinguished, in keeping with the impressive food. The management seems to operate everything with amiable efficiency. Expect to spend from 2,000$ ($13). It is open for dinner from 7 to 10:30 p.m. daily.

Café Doris, Areias de Sao Joao (tel. 524-55), is a rotisserie-crêperie and restaurant, German operated, which does some well-prepared specialties in crêpes, home-baked cakes, and ice creams. Ice cream comes in many flavors, including one delectable cup with fresh strawberries at 400$ ($2.60). To begin your meal, a rich-tasting goulash meat soup is always offered. You might follow with the roast pork with onion sauce or a good steak, accompanied by a mixed salad with cream sauce and herbs and lyonnaise potatoes. In addition, Doris has an unusual selection of hot drinks, including coffee Algarve (with Medronho). From October till June, a different special dish is offered every night from 7 to 10 p.m. Expect to spend from 1,500$ ($9.75). You can visit from 10 a.m. to midnight; closed Thursday. Doris runs this pleasant place with her husband, Horst Hewer, and partners Werngard and Manuel Alves.

Fernando, Avenida 25 de Abril, on the main square (tel. 521-16), with a large terrace, temptingly displays low-priced tourist menus. I always go here for the fish of the day, never knowing what I'm going to get. You can always count on a good soup, most often fish based, and, if you're tired of fish, the chef will fix you a simple steak. Desserts aren't special but very fattening. For an average meal, the tab will range from 2,000$ ($13). There's a pleasant indoor dining room as well. Hours are daily from noon to 3 p.m. and 6:30 to 10:30 p.m.

Beefeater Carvery, 87 Rua 5 de Outubro (tel. 543-34), stirs a nostalgia for England. The cook offers three specialties—roast pork, roast turkey, and of course, the classic roast beef. All of these come with a selection of side dishes, with fresh vegetables, potatoes, Yorkshire pudding, apple sauce, cranberry sauce, and *real* gravy. For dessert, try the best apple crumble on the Algarve. Servings are generous. Expect to spend around 2,000$ ($13). The carvery is open daily from 7 to 10 p.m.

A Ruína, Cais Herculano (tel. 520-94), sits right opposite the fish market. From the arcaded dining room, with its long, wooden, candlelit tables, you can peer at the fishermen mending their nets. Another cave-like room has more tables and a bar. The decor is unpretentious, and the seafood is fresh. A bowl of good-tasting soup will get you going, then it's on to one of the fish specialties, perhaps grilled fresh tuna. The fish stew, caldeirada, is the chef's specialty. Desserts tend to run to custard and mousse. A complete meal will come to around 2,000$ ($13) to 3,000$ ($19.50). The restaurant is open daily from noon to 3 p.m. and 6:30 to 10:30 p.m.

Jardim d'Allah (tel. 522-96) stands across the road from the Hotel Sol e Mar. In the old quarter of Albufeira, it is an appealing choice, with occasional live music. Garden tables are placed out in the Moroccan-style courtyard. Inside it has an attractive decor with cathedral-like windows. A family-run place, it offers evening dining that is fairly festive, going for around 2,200$ ($14.30) to 2,800$ ($18.20) and served daily from 7 to 11 p.m. Specialties include sirloin Allah, red mullet meunière, grilled sea bream, fresh tuna steak, and shrimp piri-piri.

O Dias, Praça Miguel Bombarda (tel. 552-46), near the already-recommended Beach Basket, is a Portuguese-run restaurant with good food and reasonable prices, with meals costing from 2,000$ ($13). An outside terrace overlooks the sea, and this is, of course, the most desirable seating. Main dishes include various versions of fresh fish and shellfish, including lobster and squid. The charcoal grills are among the most delectable. The restaurant is open from 12:30 to 2:30 p.m. and 7 to 10:30 p.m. daily except Wednesday.

THE LOCAL PUB

In the center of the village, **Harry's Bar** (tel. 540-90) is on the market square. Sir Harry (Warner) can be distinguished by his beaming smile and RAF moustache. His fashionable bar is a center for any bloke who has abandoned his Cotswold tweeds for the lighter threads of the Algarve. Converts swear that Sir Harry's is their Algarvian "local," and after about a quarter of a century, it has earned the reputation of being the Algarve's most popular international rendezvous. The bar merges the ambience of a black-and-white timbered village pub with the coziness of a Portuguese fisherman's cottage.

Beneath the low natural beams, a comfortable array of Savonarola chairs, crude tables, and wooden settles are found on two levels, divided by wrought-iron railings. The collection of rifles, steins, gleaming copper pots and pans, and earthenware water jugs provides a genuine sense of the past. A bar of herringbone brick and timbers has heel-propping stools, attracting those drawn to the center of the action. Most drinks, such as a rum and coke, go for 350$ ($2.30), and a small beer for 100$ (65¢). Hearty sandwiches and other bar snacks are served as well. It's open daily all year from 10 a.m. to 2 a.m.

A TASTE OF PORT

Devotees of port wine patronize **Caves do Vinho do Porto,** 23 Rua da Liberdade (tel. 532-29), a "cave" with cool rooms arched in brick and its walls of wine bottles quietly "aging." The bar has the finest collection of port wine along the Algarve, and you can make your selection, either by the glass or bottle. Other drinks are available as well. If you're stopping off for an apéritif, ask for a Porto Branco. A glass of port ranges from 180$ ($1.15) for a Tawny to 300$ ($1.95) for a Red Porto. Soothing music enhances the ambience. Hours are daily from 9 a.m. to 2 a.m.

11. Praia de Quarteira

Between Albufeira and Faro, this once-sleepy fishing village used to be known only to a handful of artists who provided amusement for the local fishermen and their varinas. Now with the invasion of outsiders, the traditional way of life has been upset. What was Quarteira has been swallowed up in a sea of high-rise buildings. The big attraction, of course, is one of the longest beaches along the Algarve, filled in summer not only with vacationing Portuguese but with hordes of Europeans who descend on Quarteira, also supplying a much-needed boost to the local economy.

Surprisingly, Praia de Quarteira has very few hotels. Most of its accommodations are apartment blocks that visitors from the north, from the Midlands of England to Frankfurt, book for a week or two for their holiday. I feel the typical North American visitor will find more charm elsewhere. But for those who want to give it a try, here are some recommendations.

Golfers who don't want to pay the high tariffs at Vale do Lobo or Vilamoura (both of which have 18-hole golf courses) can stay inexpensively in Quarteira at one of the accommodations listed below. The above-mentioned courses are only a ten-minute drive away, and Quarteira lies about seven miles from the Faro Airport.

WHERE TO STAY

One of the most popular hostelries in town is **Hotel Dom José,** Avenida Infante de Sagres, 8125 Quarteira (tel. 089/343-10). Travel agents in Britain consider the amenities offered by this three-star hotel to be considerably better than its official status dictates. Consequently, it is (deservedly) often heavily booked even in low season. Its pool is separated from the portside promenade of town by a low wall, behind which a well-developed subculture thrives among the largely British clientele. At its tallest point, the hotel has nine balconied stories. The outlying wings are shorter, of course. The velvet sofas of the public rooms are filled every evening with convivial holiday-makers, enjoying drinks, the live music, and the air-conditioned view of the sea beyond. An aquarium bubbles behind the darkly exotic-looking bar. In another corner of the ground floor, a lattice-covered room contains a widescreen TV and a garden-style list of salad and sandwich treats. There's even a disco, as well as a sea-view restaurant.

Each of the 134 comfortably furnished rooms contains a private bath, phone, and radio. With a continental breakfast included, twins peak at 10,164$ ($66) daily in high season when only doubles are rented. In off-season, a twin goes for 6,776$ ($44) daily, with singles costing 5,236$ ($34).

Atis Hotel, Avenida Paralela a Infante de Sagres, 8125 Quarteira (tel. 089/343-33). The main artery on which this hotel is located is so completely lined with high-rise apartment blocks that comparisons are sometimes made to the canyons of Wall Street. Fortunately, many of its balconied rooms look out over the beach, which is just a short walk away. Horizontal bands of bare concrete curve sinuously around the jutting balconies, many of which are accented with white stripes. A tiny outdoor swimming pool is separated from the sidewalk by a peek-a-boo fence; however, many clients prefer to bathe at the beach instead. There's a snack bar, along with a darkly paneled drinking bar, plus a TV room on the ground floor. The hotel offers 77 rooms, each with bath. In high season, singles rent for 7,600$ ($49.40) daily, with doubles costing 9,600$ ($62.40). There are off-season reductions.

WHERE TO DINE

About two miles from Quarteira on Estrada de Loulé, **Etons** (tel. 353-26) stands in the pines. The menu changes nightly, so what is presented below should only suggest the type of cuisine offered. Usually there's a rich good-tasting soup, or you might begin your meal with smoked swordfish, which looks like smoked salmon but, to me at least, tastes even better. The leg of lamb is often excellent. Expect to pay about 2,000$ ($13). The restaurant serves meals from 7 to 11 p.m. daily.

Restaurante Atlântico, 91 Avenida Infante de Sagres (tel. 351-42). You'll find the protective awning of this portside restaurant on the main promenade of town, sitting near a cluster of other restaurants that look very much alike. The place is crowded and popular (often when the others are empty), and it's patronized by an array of international and often scantily clad diners. The hosts direct a staff of waiters who bring out such specialties as fish soup Algarve style, king prawns Atlântico, pepper steak, clams in their shells, and other regional dishes. Full meals, served daily in summer from noon to 11 p.m., cost from 1,800$ ($11.70). Off-season, it is open only from noon to 3:30 p.m. daily.

Restaurante O Pescador, Largo Cortés Real (tel. 347-55), is an unpretentious restaurant across the parking lot from the fish market, just west of the straw market. Beneath a wooden lattice-accented ceiling, diners enjoy friendly service and impeccably fresh fish and vegetables. A very clean display case contains some of the ingredients that go into the meals. Full dinners, costing from 2,000$ ($13) each, include grilled filet of pork, Portuguese steak, grilled gray mullet, grilled prawns, or fresh hake. Lunch is served daily from 1 to 3 p.m. and dinner from 7 to 10 p.m.

Bonnie's Wine Bar, Avenida Infante de Sagres (tel. 343-12). This outpost of Britain thrives within a cocoon of pine paneling, comfortable banquettes, mugs of beer, and assorted banners from soccer teams. This is more a pub than a wine bar, where the accents are more Cockney than Iberian and where any Anglophile will feel at home. An English breakfast is served every morning for about 500$ ($3.25). On Sunday, a fixed-price meal, with roast beef and traditional English fixings, goes for 1,200$ ($7.80). The rest of the week, you can order such light meals as omelets, a ploughman's lunch, and steak-and-kidney pie for around 1,200$ ($7.80). Wine is sold by the glass or bottle, but many customers prefer to drink beer. Food is served daily from 10:30 a.m. to 4 p.m. and 6:30 p.m. to midnight.

12. Vilamoura

Although the remains of a Roman villa were discovered when builders were working on the marina, the history of this settlement is yet to be written. At a central point on the Algarve coast, only 11 miles from Faro Airport, Vilamoura is an expansive land-development project, the largest private tourist "urbanization" in Europe. Plans call for a city larger than Faro and an interior lake linked with the bay and ocean by two canals. One can sum up the Vilamoura situation by comparing it to the weather of New England: "If you don't like it now, wait a minute!" There is already a 1,000-boat marina for pleasure boats. At the moment it is filled with what are called "holiday villages," along with apartment complexes. Sports get much attention here: two 18-hole golf courses, along with water sports, tennis courts, and a riding center. The yachting set is attracted to the marina, especially in summer, and shops and other tourist facilities, including restaurants and bars, can occupy many a day.

More than 100 hotels are projected, but at the moment you'll have to make do with a more limited selection.

WHERE TO STAY

A five-star choice, **Vilamoura Marinotel,** Vilamoura, 8126 Quarteira Codex (tel. 089/333-10), is considered by some as the finest deluxe hotel on the Algarve. It has some 324 employees for its 389 guest rooms. Operated by a Spanish company, HUSA International Hotels, the Marinotel was a dream long in coming true. Originally launched in 1974, construction was delayed because of the revolution and the tight-money situation, but by spring of 1987, the hotel was officially opened and has proved just as popular with the Portuguese as with international visitors. During the slower winter months it becomes a convention hotel, but in summer is overrun with holiday makers. The hotel mainly employs young Algarvians on its staff.

Rising like a massive pile, the rectangular hotel sits next to the Vilamoura Marina. Each of its attractive and well-furnished bedrooms provides a view, either of the marina or the ocean. A large swimming pool stands between the ocean and the hotel, and there is direct access to the beach. The interior, with lounge space for 500 guests, is decorated with both traditional and modern designs. It is characterized by high ceilings and wide-open staircases, with an effective use made of silver, red, and white. Rooms are well equipped with air conditioning, mini-bar, TV, and private bath, of course. In high season, singles rent for 19,250$ ($125.15) daily and doubles for 25,850$ ($168.05). Off-season reductions are granted, depending on the month. Tariffs include an American buffet breakfast in the main restaurant. More expensive suites are also available.

Its dining facilities (see below) are among the best at Vilamoura. Health-club devotees will find good facilities here, including a Jacuzzi and a sauna. Fado, folk dancing, fashion shows, and occasional barbecues round out the program.

One of the most stylish hostelries at this resort is **Hotel Atlántis Vilamoura,** Vilamoura, 8125 Quarteira (tel. 089/325-35). A Moorish flavor is imparted by the pointed arches accenting the façade. Set away from the congested section of Vilamoura, the style is Iberian contemporary, with gleaming marble, coffered wooden ceilings, and polished mirrors. The sophisticated decor of the bar is dimly lit, with a piano providing evening music. A large, wind-shaded terrace is filled with plants, and a big indoor pool is covered with a dome decorated with bas-reliefs. A coffeeshop remains open throughout the day, while a more formal restaurant caters to a more elegant clientele.

Each of the 302 well-furnished rooms and the eight suites contains a TV, mini-bar, and a sea-view veranda, among the other amenities. In high season, singles rent for 19,600$ ($127.40) daily with doubles costing from 28,000$ ($182). Off-season reductions are granted. Hotel patrons receive a 20% discount at a nearby golf course. A health club is on the premises, as well as three tennis courts and an outdoor pool for bathers wishing to avoid saltwater swimming. A sandy beach lies away from the hotel.

Dom Pedro Golf Hotel, Vilamoura, 8125 Quarteira (tel. 089/354-50), is a large hotel of first-class comfort, right in the tourist complex of Vilamoura. The 261-room center stands near the casino, and there is a choice of three swimming pools, including one for children. The public rooms are sleekly styled, and the private rooms are pleasantly furnished and carpeted, with private terraces. In high season, singles pay 15,000$ ($97.50) daily, with doubles costing 19,000$ ($123.50). Three tennis courts are available, and after a game guests can enjoy a bar overlooking the pool. Other facilities include a sauna, massage, and hairdresser. The staff at the hotel arranges for guests to go deep-sea fishing or riding from its fine stable of horses, as well as reduced greens fees at various golf courses in the Algarve.

Vilamoura Golf Motel, Vilamoura, 8125 Quarteira (tel. 089/323-21), is for golf enthusiasts, among others. It is located on a Frank Pennink championship golf course surrounded by pine trees. Only minutes from the ocean and a marina, it enjoys a tranquil setting that forms part of the biggest tourist complex on the Algarve. Operated by Sointal Casinos do Algarve, it offers 52 well-furnished bedrooms and suites, each with private terrace and tile bath. In high season, the single rate is 7,300$ ($47.45) daily, with twins renting for 10,150$ ($66) to 11,600$ ($75.40). The hotel has many facilities including a large patio with two swimming pools. The complex is designed in a typical modern Algarvian style, with much use made of local materials including dark woods, polished tiles, and Portuguese mosaics. Guests heavily patronize the nearby diversions, including an 18-hole golf course (6,877 yards), tennis courts, and the casino.

Estalagem da Cegonha, Centro Hípico de Vilamoura, Vilamoura, 8125 Quarteira (tel. 089/343-77), stands at Poço de Boliqueime, Vilamoura, about 4½ miles from the golf course, casino, marina, and beach, on the national road between Portimão and Faro. The ancient inn lies in a peaceful setting, adjoining the riding stables (which charge reasonable rates, incidentally). There are only ten rooms, but they are large and cozily decorated, each containing a private bath. In high season, singles rent for 7,600$ ($49.40) daily, doubles for 8,300$ ($53.95). The decoration is in a típico style. The chef at the inn has won an award for regional food. Before or after dinner, you can enjoy drinks in one of the comfortable bars. A horse-jumping contest is held every year in September.

WHERE TO DINE

A shopping and dining complex, the Centro Comércial da Marinha, across from the marina, is filled with restaurants, many of dubious quality. Nevertheless, many are popular more for their colorful location than for their cuisine. The best food is consistently served at the already-recommended **Vilamoura Marinotel** (tel. 333-10). The most exclusive—and most expensive—dining spot here is the Sirius Grill on the main floor. It is separated from a chic rendezvous center, the Bar Castor, by a grand piano on a dais. Live music filters into both areas. This drinking and dining establishment is the most elegant in Vilamoura. The bar—stylish, modern, and monochromatic—offers a large variety of drinks and is open daily from 11 a.m. to 11 p.m.

Overlooking the marina, the Sirius Grill is high-ceilinged, with a sophisticated, unfussy decor. The chefs prepare a splendid cuisine, and the service is formal. You might begin with assorted smoked fish and follow with one of the seafood specialties such as lobster cassolete, turbot in seafood sauce, sea bass flambé with fennel, or stuffed trout. Meat dishes use only the finest cuts, as reflected by the T-bone steak or the tournedos stuffed with shrimps and scallops and served with a béarnaise sauce. Meals cost 4,000$ ($26) and up and are served nightly from 7 to 11:30 p.m.

The food is also excellently prepared in the large, airy Aries dining room, also at the Vilamoura Marinotel. This dining room is built on two levels and opens onto the swimming pool and ocean. Lavishly decorated with tiles, it is elegantly appointed, with one of the finest young staffs on the Algarve. A set menu for 3,600$ ($23.40) changes daily, selections can be made from an à la carte list. Traditional dishes and Iberian regional specialties are the main fare. Specific dishes are likely to include chicken breast Oscar, roast pork with garlic, or grilled swordfish, preceded by one of the soups or appetizers. Hours are daily from 12:30 to 2:30 p.m. and 7:30 to 10 p.m.

AFTER DARK

Close to the Vilamoura Golf Club is the **Vilamoura Casino** (tel. 329-19), one of the finest, featuring a gambling salon with roulette, blackjack, French banque, and baccarat. A separate salon is devoted to slot machines. There is a 250-seat supper club, with a floor show at 10:45 p.m. nightly. Admission to the slot machines and main gambling room is 100$ (65¢). The casino is open from 4 p.m. to 3 a.m. every day of the year. Tourists must present their passports.

Skipper's Disco Club, Loja 38, Centro Comércial da Marinha (tel. 342-51), in a restaurant and shopping complex close to the marina, is the most popular stopover on the nighttime rounds. Guests drink at street level at the vaguely nautical bar before descending to dance in the basement to the latest in recorded music. The entrance fee is 1,000$ ($6.50). Hours are from 10 p.m. to 5 a.m. nightly. You can also order snacks such as beefburgers and sandwiches. The club is owned by Barbara and Jack Parkinson, who stopped off here as they were sailing around the world and fell in love with the place.

They also operate the best-known bar in the area, a short walk from Skipper's. It's called **Wellies,** Centro Comércial da Marinha (tel. 341-50), overlooking some 1,000 yachts in the harbor, which put in here from all over the world. A favorite of the yachting set, it also attracts an international nonboating crowd, who enjoy draft beer and live music nightly from 7:30 p.m. to 1 a.m. A Portuguese brandy costs 150$ ($1), and a draft beer goes for 200$ ($1.30).

Next door to the bar is **Restaurant Wellies,** Centro Comércial da Marinha (tel. 341-50), which is open from 10 a.m. to 11 p.m. Also overlooking the marina, it starts its day by offering a traditional English breakfast, then continues with a selection of international favorites, including steak-and-kidney pie, chicken piri-piri (very hot), along with burgers (in fact, it's sometimes known as the Hamburger House). You can dine inside or out on the terrace, paying from 1,500$ ($9.75) for a meal.

---

13. Vale do Lobo

The name Valley of the Wolf suggests some forlorn spot, set amid bleak terrain. Hardly likely! The *Vale,* west of Faro, about a 20-minute drive from the airport, is the site of a golf course designed by Henry Cotton, the British champion. Some of the holes are played by the sea, resulting in many an anxious moment when a shot may hook out over the water a precarious distance from the green. Another nine-hole course and a nine-hole par-three course, a putting green, and driving range have been installed.

Reached through fig orchards, cork forests, and a valley of tufted pines, the seaside strongly evokes Carmel, California. Pale golden cliffs jut out over sandy beaches that stretch brilliantly in the distance until they disappear into a faint haze.

A DELUXE GOLF HOTEL

A citadel of ostentatious living, **Hotel Dona Filipa,** Vale de Lobo, Almansil, 8106 Loulé (tel. 089/941-41), has such touches as gold-painted palms holding up the ceiling. The grounds are impressive, embracing 450 acres of rugged coastline with steep cliffs, inlets, and sandy bays. The exterior of the hotel is comparatively uninspired, but a greater dimension was brought to the interior by Duarte Pinto Coelho. Green silk banquettes, marble fireplaces, Portuguese ceramic lamps, old prints over baroque-style love seats—the flair is lush. Aside from a Chinese room for card playing, the most popular meeting point is the Gothic Bar, with its cathedral-like stools, wooden decorations, and matching floor and upholstery fabric in tile patterns.

There are 135 air-conditioned rooms—all with bath, most with balcony. In summer, a single rents for 26,950$ ($175) daily, rising to 35,420$ ($230) in a double. Off-season, singles cost 22,330$ ($145) and doubles 29,260$ ($190). A meal in the restaurant averages around 6,930$ ($45). All prices include service and taxes. Greens fees at the Vale do Lobo championship 27-hole golf course are reduced for hotel guests. Dining is formal and gracious, with a knowledgeable maître d'hôtel and wine steward guiding you on your selections. At the beach is a disco, where international records are played for dancing (occasionally, folk artists and fadistas perform).

A RESORT CENTER

A pocket of posh living is **Quinta do Lago,** Almansil, 8100 Loulé (tel. 089/967-85), near Almansil, ten miles west of Faro, a sprawling 1,600-acre estate that sells private plots within it. The hotel is an investment of Saudi Arabian Prince Faisal, but he has wisely turned over management to the Venice-Simplon Orient Express staff, which is also a hotel chain. The resort offers a riding center, one of the best in southern Europe; a 27-hole golf course, designed by American course architect William F. Mitchell, and recognized among the top six in Europe; tennis courts; the Patio Club, the Algarve's sophisticated disco; the luxurious Quinta Park Country Club Apartments, overlooking the seawater lake and provided with modern comforts. You can also make arrangements to stay there. The quinta offers 141 bedrooms and nine suites. In high season, singles rent for 26,000$ ($169) to 28,000$ ($182) daily, and doubles for 34,000$ ($221) to 36,000$ ($234). Studios for two cost 40,000$ ($260). These rates are in effect from July to September; after that, reductions are granted.

The Pergola Restaurant is for those who prefer an informal grill room. It overlooks a swimming pool for both children and adults. There's a modern clubhouse with a restaurant and bar close to the golf driving range and overlooking the Bermuda green of the B1 fairway. The Beach Pavilion (at the beach, of course) offers a menu of snacks, light meals, and drinks. A specialty restaurant serves Italian cuisine, and the Navegador Restaurant offers a varied menu, including several traditional Portuguese dishes.

An excellent dining choice nearby, which is not part of Quinta do Logo management, is **Shepherds Casa Velha** (tel. 943-57), which is open for dinner nightly, except Monday, from 7 to 10:30 p.m. Full meals cost from 4,000$ ($26) to 5,000$ ($32.50). The restaurant is renowned for its fine food and impeccable service. Chateaubriand for two persons, a rack or saddle of lamb persillé (also for two persons), délices of sole, sea bass Quinta do Lago, fishermen's soup, and smoked swordfish with horseradish sauce are recommended. The dessert specialty is crêpes. Dinners are eaten to the sound of piano and guitar music.

14. Faro

Flowers brought in from the countryside are plentiful. In the blue lagoon sailing enthusiasts glide by. A typical old quarter flanks the ruined ramparts that proved all too vulnerable in the past. At the yacht harbor starlings and sparrows flutter nervously, while children run noisily to the pastry shops to buy stuffed figs and almond cakes. Beyond the waterfront lie the tree-studded avenues and cobbled alleyways of the city.

Once loved by the Romans and later by the Moors, Faro is the capital of the Algarve. Sit at a café sampling the wine and you'll watch yesterday and today pass by. An old man walks ahead, pulling a donkey on which a parasol-shaded girl in a white dress is sitting. Brushing past is a German student in shorts, tanned golden by the sun. Faro is a hodgepodge of life and activity: it's been rumbled, sacked, and "quaked" by everybody from Mother Nature to the Earl of Essex (Elizabeth's favorite).

Since Afonso III drove out the Moors for the last time in 1266, Faro has been Portuguese. On its outskirts an international jet airport brings in thousands of visitors every summer. The airport has done more than anything else to speed tourism not only to Faro but to the Algarve in general, as jet planes make it possible to reach Faro from Lisbon in 30 minutes.

The most bizarre attraction is the *Capela d'Ossos* (Chapel of Bones), entered from the rear of the **Igreja de Nossa Senhora do Monte do Carmo do Faro,** via a courtyard. Erected in the 19th century, this chapel is completely lined with the skulls and bones of human skeletons, an extraordinarily ossicular rococo. In all, it's estimated there are 1,245 human skulls. Hours are 9:30 a.m. to 12:30 p.m. and 3 to 5 p.m. daily.

The church, built in 1713, contains a gilded baroque altar. Likewise, its façade is baroque, with a bell tower rising from each side. Topping the belfries are gilded mosque-like cupolas, connected by a balustraded railing. The windows of the upper levels are latticed and framed with gold; statues stand in each of the niches on either side of the main portal.

Other religious monuments include the old Sé (cathedral), built in the Gothic and Renaissance styles (originally a Muslim mosque stood on this site); the **Church of St. Francis,** with panels of glazed earthenware tiles in milk white and Dutch blue, depicting the life of the patron saint; and the **Convent of Our Lady of the Assumption,** declared a national monument and noted for its Renaissance portal and cloister.

But most visitors don't come to Faro to look at churches, regardless how interesting they are. Rather, they take the harbor ferry to the wide, white sandy beaches called the **Praia de Faro,** on an islet. The ride is available only in summer. The beach is also connected to the mainland by bridge, a distance of about 3½ miles from the town center. Once there, you can waterski and fish or just rent a deckchair and umbrella and lounge in the sun.

WHERE TO STAY

Dominating the harbor like a fortress is the **Eva,** Avenida da República, 8000 Faro (tel. 089/240-54), a modern, eight-floor hotel occupying an entire side of the yacht-clogged harbor, providing direct sea views from most of the bedrooms. Bedrooms are air-conditioned, furnished in a restrained style, and have private tile baths. In high season, double rooms rent for 10,500$ ($68.25) to 13,800$ ($89.70) daily. There are no singles. The better rooms open onto the water. The Eva's best feature is a penthouse restaurant and rooftop swimming pool, supported on 16 posts, with sun terraces and a bar. Dancing is offered at the hotel's disco five nights a week. Other facilities include a snackbar, three cocktail bars, a hairdresser, and a boutique.

Hotel Faro, Praça D. Francisco Gomes, 8002 Faro Codex (tel. 089/220-76), is a first-class B hotel with 52 rooms (eight with shower) opening right onto the bustling harbor, a prime position. The furnishings in the rooms are comfortable but uninspired, and many contain balconies opening right onto the square which tends to be noisy until late at night. In high season, singles rent for 6,500$ ($42.25) daily, with doubles costing 7,600$ ($49.40) to 10,100$ ($65.65). Taxes are included. The least expensive rooms contain a shower bath. The suites have a small sitting room with a bed sofa, suitable for a third person. In a light and spacious room, the restaurant serves French and Portuguese dishes complemented by a well-coordinated wine list. The bar provides drinks, which you can order from the mezzanine while surveying the scene below.

Casa de Lumena, 27 Praça Alexandre Herculano, 8000 Faro (tel. 089/80-19-90), was once the town house of a reigning sardine family of Faro, but now it's an English-run pensão with telephones in the rooms, central heating, and a bar, the Grapevine, where the international community often meets at lunchtime. It sits on a square shaded by jacaranda trees. Built at the edge of the sidewalk with wrought-iron gratings at its windows, the Lumena offers renovated and upgraded accommodations, all with private baths. The rooms are of different shapes and furnished in part with pieces inherited with the casa. Throughout are antiques, carved chests, satinwood tables, painted dressers, and armoires. A double room for two people with a continental breakfast costs about 6,000$ ($39) daily. The restaurant is open for lunch and in the evening, charging from 1,800$ ($11.70) for a meal.

Hotel Albacor, 25 Rua Brites Almeida, 8000 Faro (tel. 089/220-93). A few of the rooms in this well-located hotel contain small balconies. All of them have a tile bath, phone, and a comfortably unpretentious decor that is spotlessly clean. This is a good choice for a budget hotel, and because of that, is likely to be full of a loyal repeat clientele unless you make reservations in advance in high season. There's a bar on the ground floor, plus an elevator. The English-speaking staff is most helpful. Doubles cost from 6,000$ ($39) daily, while singles go for 5,800$ ($37.70), with a continental breakfast included.

WHERE TO DINE

The leading restaurant in town is **Restaurante Cidade Velha,** 19 Rua Domingos Guieiro (tel. 271-45). It used to be one of the best-located private homes in Faro. Today it serves as the very charming culinary hideaway of José Dias and his Finnish wife, Miriam. You'll find it in back of the cathedral, behind thick stone walls built at least 250 years ago. You'll be invited to enjoy an apéritif in the tiny bar near the entrance. There, a disconnected iron stove—perhaps a memento of Miriam's homeland—adds a decorative accent.

Your meal will be served in one of a pair of rooms, each with a vaulted brick ceiling. Reservations, which are important, can either be phoned in or left in person early in the day with one of the vested waiters. Full meals, priced at 2,500$ ($16.25) and up, might include crab cakes or smoked swordfish with horseradish sauce, followed with roast rack of lamb with rosemary and mint sauce or roast duck with an apricot sauce. Lunch is served from 12:30 to 2 p.m., Monday to Friday, and dinner from 7:30 to 11:30 p.m., Monday to Saturday. Closed Sunday.

Restaurant Lady Susan, 28 Rua 1 de Dezembro (tel. 288-57). Blue and white tiles cover the façade of this storefront-like restaurant in a quiet part of town. Inside, the style is like that of an elegant but undersized tavern. The establishment is the private and well-crafted domain of Robert and Susan Eustáce, who take personal—and justified—pride in all that happens here. You can leave your menu choices to Robert. These may include fish of the day, a pepper steak in a creamy sauce, shrimp Algarve style, sole in white wine, seafood Wellington, and an array of flambé specialties. You can enjoy a light meal at the bar. However, if you opt for the full culinary experience, count on spending from 2,500$ ($16.25). Reservations are strongly suggested. The restaurant is closed Saturday and Sunday. Monday to Friday, meals are served from noon to 2:30 p.m. and 7:30 to 10:30 p.m.

Café Chelsea, 28 Rua de Francisco Gomes (tel. 284-59). On a stone-paved street thronged with pedestrians, this restaurant offers a well-prepared cuisine. You can select a table in the open air or between the colorful tile walls of the ground-floor interior. Diners, however, looking for a different kind of atmosphere will press on to the upper-level dining room, where the style is art nouveau, with a decor that includes varied stripes of blue and white tiles, touches of scarlet, bentwood chairs and tables, a prominent bar, and big windows looking out over the street. Full meals in any of the restaurant's seating areas cost from 2,200$ ($14.30) each. Menu specialties include Portuguese beefsteak, pork filet, Chelsea hamburgers, Spanish omelets, an array of pasta dishes, and Indian curried prawns, plus an array of salads. The establishment is open for both lunch and dinner from noon to 11 p.m. daily.

Dois Irmãos, 18 Largo do Terreiro do Bispo (tel. 233-37), is a popular Portuguese bistro, founded in 1925, with a no-nonsense atmosphere. Yet it has its devotees. The menu is as modest as the establishment and its prices, but you get a good choice of fresh fish and shellfish dishes. Ignore the paper napkins and concentrate on the fine kettle of fish placed before you. Clams in a savory sauce is a favorite, and sole is regularly featured. But, of course, everything depends on the catch of the day. Service is slow and amiable, and no one seems in a hurry. For a seafood dinner, your bill is likely to run from 1,500$ ($9.75). Open daily from 10 a.m. to 11 p.m.

FARO AFTER DARK

The most popular disco in town, **Sheherazade,** Hotel Eva, Avenida da República (tel. 240-54), is just off the lobby of the leading hotel in Faro. It is open every weekday night from 9 p.m. to 2 a.m. Saturday and Sunday, it's usually packed with young people who mingle with tourists. Guests can also enjoy the afternoon tea dances from 4 to 7 p.m. The disco opens later, at 10 p.m., staying open until 2 a.m., for another round of electronic boogie. There is regional folk dancing every Thursday night, followed by a program of typical Portuguese fado and guitars on Friday night.

STAYING AT SANTA BÁRBARA DE NEXE

The only *Relais & Châteax* member in Portugal, **Hotel La Réserve,** Santa Barbara de Nexe, 8000 Faro (tel. 089/904-74), is near a hamlet about seven miles from Faro. It offers luxury accommodations in a modern and elegant country-estate atmosphere. The hotel has two swimming pools and a tennis court. It lies in its own six-acre parkland. All of the 20 handsome suites have a southern sea view and private terrace, radio, TV, mini-bar, direct-dial phone, and kitchenette. A studio apartment rents for 17,280$ ($112.30) daily for one person in high season, and two people pay 23,760$ ($154.45). Charges for a deluxe apartment are 19,440$ ($126.35) for a single, 25,920$ ($168.50) for a double. Rates are reduced off-season. All tariffs include breakfast, the service charge, and taxes. The hotel has a snackbar, two bars for drinks, and an international restaurant.

Restaurant La Réserve (tel. 902-34), in a building adjacent to the hotel structure, is operated by the same winning U.S./Swiss alliance as the hotel—Victor and Katja Fuchs. It is the finest dining room in the Algarve and among the best you are likely to encounter in Portugal. Their dinners are carefully presented, and they care about the freshness of their meats, fish, and produce. A specialty is smoked swordfish, which is as fine as any served at Lisbon's more famous Avis. Along with this dish, served in razor-thin slices, it is customary to drink a glass of chilled vodka. Try also the oriental shrimp served on a bed of rice with a fried banana. A succulent local duckling, crisp on the outside and tender inside, makes a good main course. The duck is served with potato croquettes and red cabbage. La Réserve also features a special six-course menu dégustation, composed of favorite specialties that the chef has created over the years.

The best Portuguese wines are on the wine list, including the well-known *vinho verde* (green wine) of the north. Expect to spend from 5,000$ ($32.50) per person for a meal, which you can be sure will be worth it. The restaurant is open from 7 to 11 p.m. daily except Tuesday. It's important to call for reservations. Each guest gets personal service at this fine restaurant.

15. Loulé

Loulé, 9½ miles north of Faro, is a market town in the heart of the chimney district of the Algarve. If you ever thought that chimneys couldn't excite you, you haven't seen the ones here. From many of the houses and cottages, these fret-cut plaster towers rise. You may even see one on the house of a very discriminating dog! They resemble fine lacework or filigree in stone; others are as delicately contrived as forms of snow crystals blown against glass.

Loulé and villages around it are among areas of the Algarve known for their handcrafts, producing work in palm fronds and esparto, such as handbags, baskets, mats, and hats. Loulé crafts workers also make copper articles, candles, bright-colored harnesses, delicate wrought-iron pieces, clogs, cloth shoes and slippers, tinware, and pottery. Products are displayed in workshops at the foot of the walls of an old fortress and in other showrooms. The medieval castle is in the center of town.

Of special interest is the celebration of Carnival in Loulé, which outdoes its neighbors in its spectacular display of floats, with costumed people dancing in the streets. Another interesting event is the *romaria*, which takes place on April 15 or the nearest Sunday thereto. The statue of *Mão Soberana* (literally Sovereign Mother) is carried through the town from the **Chapel of Nossa Senhora da Piedade**, a little more than a mile from the town center. The Renaissance chapel site provides a good view over the surrounding region and the sea.

In Loulé, you may want to visit the Gothic-style **Parish Church**, which was given to the town in the latter 13th century, and the **Church of the Misericórdia**, looking like a wedding cake, especially its Manueline entrance. The town also contains the remains of a fortress-castle that Afonso III captured from the Moors.

FOOD AND LODGING

Very few people come to Loulé seeking accommodations, as there are no recommendable hotels. Most visitors come just for the day, and those people will usually be searching for a restaurant, of which Loulé has a number of fine establishments.

However, for those who want a room, there is the **Pensão Residencial Iberica**, 157 Avenida Marçal Pacheco, 8100 Loulé (tel. 089/620-27), which is simplicity and modesty itself. However, ever since it was mentioned in the *New York Times,* visitors from northeast America have shown up at its door. Double rooms cost 5,000$ ($32.50) daily, and singles go for 4,000$ ($26). A continental breakfast is served.

For meals, you can go to **O Avenida,** 13 Avenida José da Costa Mealha (tel. 621-06), which is on the main street of Loulé. It is one of the finer restaurants along the Algarve. The restaurant is attractively decorated in tavern style. It serves daily except Sunday from noon to 3 p.m. and 7 to 10 p.m. In air-conditioned comfort, you can enjoy an apéritif at its bar before being shown to a table. Its specialty is shellfish cooked cataplana style. Meals cost from 2,000$ ($13). Occasional live entertainment is featured. Closed Sunday and for most of November.

Outside of town, about 2½ miles along the road to Faro (EN-125-4) is the **Outside In,** Sítio de Valados (tel. 904-43), a converted country house with panoramic views of 15½ miles of coastline. The French chef and the owner, also a chef, prepare the most savory and freshest viands in the entire area. Knowing vacationers come here nightly, as the fame of its *cozinha francesa* (French cuisine) has spread to the up-market beach resorts. Specialties include langoustines au gratin, sole Veronique, and fantail of duck, along with la tulip aux trois sorbets. The place has an enormous wine cellar. Expect to pay from 3,500$ ($22.75) to 4,500$ ($29.25) for a meal. Food is served from 7:30 to 10 p.m. daily except Monday. Outside In has recently received several international awards.

16. São Brás de Alportel

Traveling north from Faro for 12½ miles, you'll pass through groves of figs, almonds, and oranges, through pine woods where resin collects in wooden cups on the tree trunks. At the end of the run, you'll come upon isolated São Brás de Alportel, one of the most charming and least-known spots on the Algarve.

Far from the crowded beaches, it attracts those wanting pure air, peace, and quiet—a bucolic setting filled with flowers pushing through nutmeg-colored soil. Northeast of Loulé, this whitewashed, tile-roofed town rarely gets lively except on market days. Like its neighbor, Faro, it is noted for its perforated plaster chimneys. Lying at the foot of the Sêrra do Caldeirão, the whole area has been called one vast garden.

FOOD AND LODGING

A change of pace from the seaside accommodations is offered at **Pousada de São Brás,** Estrada de Lisboa, N2, 8150 São Brás de Alportel (tel. 089/423-05). The government-owned inn is a hilltop villa, with fret-cut limestone chimneys and a crow's-nest view of the surrounding sêrras. It's approached through a fig orchard in which stones have been painted with welcomes in many languages.

Many visitors arrive just for lunch or dinner (served daily from 12:30 to 2:30 p.m. and 7:30 to 9:30 p.m.), returning to the coastline by night, but a knowing few remain for the evening. In the dining room, rustic mountain tavern chairs and tables rest on hand-woven rugs. The soft sofa before the wood-burning fireplace is a perfect place for lingering over a cup of coffee. The 2,500$ ($16.25) table d'hôte dinner offers soup, a fish course, a meat dish, vegetables, and dessert. The cuisine is plain, but good. After dinner you may want to retire to the beamed-ceilinged sitting room to watch the embers of the evening's fire die down. Then trundle upstairs, past the large ornamented tasseled donkey collar for a night's sleep in cozy beds in a room cooled by highland breezes. The bedrooms contain private baths. Singles rent for 11,500$ ($74.75) daily and doubles for 12,500$ ($81.25).

17. Estói and Milreu

A little village some six miles northeast of Faro, **Estói** is still mainly unspoiled by throngs of tourists. Those who come here are objects of some interest, stared at by old women sheltered behind the curtains of their little houses. Begging children are likely to follow sightseers around. Sometimes you may even see women washing their clothing in a public trough. Garden walls are decaying here and the cottages worn by time and the weather.

The principal sight in Estói is the Palácio do Visconde de Estói, with a baroque, salmon-pink façade. Built in the late 18th century for Francisco José de Moura Coutinho, and rescued from near ruin by José Francisco da Silva between 1893 and 1909, today it could use a massive infusion of cash. A palm-lined walk leads to terraced gardens set with orange trees along the balusters. Statues, busts, vases, and ornamental lakes adorn the terraces; azulejos and Roman mosaics adorn the gardens. Stairways, fountains, and belvederes rise beside cypresses, magnolia trees, patches of lavender, and climbing roses. This has been called a "cross between Versailles and the water gardens of the Villa d'Este near Rome."

The villa is not open to the public, but the grounds can be visited. To enter, ring a bell at the iron gates outside the palm-lined walk. A caretaker will guide you to the gardens. There is no entrance fee, but the caretaker should be tipped.

About half a mile west of Estói is **Milreu**, which was the Roman town of Ossonoba in the 1st century A.D. Two broken capitals and some fluted columns stand on ground blanketed by buttercups. In classical times the Roman soldiers, seeing the gardens of the Algarve in the spring, decided that a Temple of Venus was in order here, and you see its remains. Around the temple, ruins of baths and houses have been uncovered, with mosaics of interest. Little excavation has been done, however. There is no admission charge, no guard, just a lonely field where once a thriving spa existed.

18. Olhão

Olhão has been called a living re-creation of a Georges Braque collage. This is the famous cubist town of the Algarve, so long beloved by painters. In its heart, white blocks stacked one upon the other, with flat red-tile roofs and exterior stairways on the stark walls, evoke the aura of the casbahs of North African cities.

But let us not paint too romantic a portrait. Many readers have found it disappointing. J. L. Busey writes: "It turned out to be dirty, dusty, very poverty-stricken in appearance, and almost entirely without any eating facilities." Another reader, Mrs. Jules Berman of Kensington, Maryland, writes: "Olhão has almost disappeared before the onslaught of modern commercialism. Apartments have almost obliterated this famous cubist town. Yes, we finally found some fishermen on the beach!"

I totally agree with these assessments. If you do go there, I hope you'll be able to attend the fish market near the waterfront when a *lota* (auction) is under way. Olhão is also known for its bullfights of the sea, in which fishermen wrestle with struggling tuna trapped in nets and headed for the smelly warehouses along the harbor.

For the best view, climb Cabeça Hill, its grottos punctured with stalagmites and stalactites, or perhaps St. Michael's Mount, offering a panorama of the Casbah-like

Barreta. Finally, for what is perhaps one of the most idyllic beaches on the Algarve, take a ten-minute motorboat ride to the **Ilha de Armona,** a nautical mile away. Olhão is 6½ miles west of Faro.

WHERE TO EAT

Restaurants tend to be very simple but they are reasonably priced, and nearly all of them feature fresh fish.

Escondidinho, R.J.P. Leonardo (tel. 726-74), also attracts those who are devotees of Portuguese home-cooking. Stick to the fish dishes and, chances are, your bill will rarely run more than 2,000$ ($13). It is open daily except Sunday from noon to 3 p.m. and 7 to 9 p.m.

19. Tavira

An Algarvian gem, sleepy Tavira sits like a town of the past century. It's approached through green fields studded with almond and carob trees, the latter producing a dry pod of hard seeds in sweet pulp (eaten by both people and animals). Sometimes called the Venice of the Algarve, Tavira lies on the banks of the Ségua and Gilão Rivers, which meet under a seven-arched Roman bridge. In the town square, palms and pepper trees rustle amid the cool arches of the arcade.

A tunny fishing center, Tavira is cut off from the sea by an elongated spit of sand, the **Ilha de Tavira,** which begins west of Cacela and runs all the way past the fishing village of Fuzeta. On this sandbar, reached by motorboat, are two beaches: the **Praia de Tavira** and the **Praia de Fuzeta.** Others prefer to go to the beach at the tiny village of **Santa Luzia,** about two miles from the heart of town.

Tavira is festive looking with floridly decorated chimneys topping many of the houses, some of which are graced with emerald-green tiles and wrought-iron balconies capped by finials. Many doorways are adorned with fretwork. The liveliest action, however, centers on the fruit and vegetable market on the river esplanade. The town lies about 19 miles east of Faro.

FOOD AND LODGING

A choice place to stay is **Eurotel,** Quinta das Oliveiras, 8800 Tavira (tel. 081/220-41). The grounds of this sprawling white-walled hotel are incorporated into one of the Algarve's many residential vacation developments. Visitors will find two tennis courts and a full array of water sports. Set on the edge of the sea, on a flat terrain dotted with trees, the hotel's concrete wings, with their arches, Iberian balconies, and wooden balustrades, are visible from far away. The establishment includes two bars, a snackbar, and a restaurant. Much of the social life here revolves around one of the two swimming pools. Well-furnished singles peak at 6,000$ ($39) daily, with twins going for 8,000$ ($52) in summer, and all tariffs include a continental breakfast. The hotel lies midway between Tavira and Cabanas Beach, about 1¼ miles from each.

The English Rose, 14 Avenida Don Matheus Teixeira d'Azevedo (tel. 222-47), is the finest dining choice within the town. It not only has the most beautiful name of any restaurant in the vicinity, it dispenses a continental cuisine with flair and style. The staff serves food daily from 11:30 a.m. to 2 p.m. and 7:30 to 10:30 p.m. A three-course lunch at 1,200$ ($7.80) is one of the best values around. For dinner, you are likely to spend from 1,800$ ($11.70) up. In the tavern and carvery, bar snacks are also offered.

Restaurante Imperial, 22 Rua José Pires Padinha (tel. 223-06), is a small, air-conditioned eating place off the main square, where you can order regional food, including sarrabulho de marisco, arroz de marisco, porco à camponesa, frango na caçarola, mariscos sempre frescos, and other Portuguese dishes, accompanied by vegetables, and good local wines. One of my favorite meals here centers around pork and clams with french fries, topped off with a rich egg and almond dessert. Meals cost from 1,500$ ($9.75) per person, including wine. Food is served daily from noon to 3 p.m. and 7 to 10 p.m.

DINING AT MANTA ROTA

One of my favorite dining choices in the area is **The Stable,** Praia da Manta Rota (tel. 952-46), set at the edge of a wide stretch of sand dotted with sunbathers, clumps of seaweed, and dozens of beach umbrellas. Many visitors welcome the opportunity to escape into the shade of the beamed-ceilinged interior, where thick timbers alternate, Algarve style, with rows of bamboo. The staff here is genuinely charming, handling everyday requests with aplomb. Full meals are priced at 2,200$ ($14.30) and include such specialties as fried clams with garlic, beefsteak Portuguese style, crab and lobster from an aquarium, and Alentejo tomato soup. The restaurant serves daily from noon to 3 p.m. and 7 to 10 p.m.

---

20. Monte Gordo

Monte Gordo is the last in a long line of Algarvian resorts, lying as it does directly west of the frontier town of Vila Real de Santo António at the mouth of the Guardiana River. Its wide beach, one of the finest along the southern coast of Portugal, is backed by lowlands studded with pines.

Sadly, this was once a sleepy little fishing village. But nowadays the varinas urge their sons to work in the hotels instead of the sea, fishing for tips instead of tunny. Monte Gordo has succumbed to the high rises, often attracting wealthy Spaniards from across the border. One reader described it as a "compact version of Ocean City, Maryland." Nevertheless, it has many good hotels, and a number of Europeans use it as their place in the Algarvian sun.

WHERE TO STAY

Monte Gordo is well supplied with hotels.

Hotel Alcazar, Rua de Ceuta, Monte Gordo, 8900 Vila Real de Santo António (tel. 081/421-84), is owned by casino interests and has seen some wear in its day. Yet many critics consider it the best hotel in town. Its palm-fringed façade alternates rust-colored brick with curved expanses of white balconies. A free-form pool is built on terraces into the retaining walls that shelter it from the wind and extend the hot-weather season late into the autumn. The interior design is a vaguely Arab-style series of repetitive arches and vaults crafted from distressed concrete. The resulting niches offer dozens of intimate cave-like retreats, which at night sparkle from the pinpoint lighting of table lamps handcrafted from sheets of perforated copper. Each of the 95 bedrooms contains its own soundproof terrace, a private bath, phone, radio, and air conditioning. Depending on the season, singles range from 6,500$ ($42.25) to 9,750$ ($63.40) daily, and doubles cost 9,000$ ($58.50) to 14,000$ ($91), including a continental breakfast.

There's a disco in the basement for nighttime roving. One of the sunken living rooms off the main lobby shows recently released video movies. Near the bar, live music ushers in the night from 6 p.m. to midnight. One of the hotel's most alluring spots is under the soaring ceiling of the in-house restaurant, where formal meals are served by a polite staff in a modern setting. The hotel isn't located on the beach, but the sea is within walking distance.

Hotel Vasco da Gama, Avenida Infante Dom Henriques, Monte Gordo, 8900

Vila Real de Santo António (tel. 081/443-21). Its entrepreneurs know what their northern guests seek—lots of sunbathing and swimming. Although it enjoys a position on a long, wide, sandy beach, it also offers an Olympic swimming pool with high-dive board, and nearly an acre of flagstoned sun terrace. Inside is a sky-high oceanfront dining room, with additional tables on the mezzanine, plus several well-furnished lounges with many groupings of chairs. Other conveniences include two drinking bars, and a boîte where it's possible to dance to records or combos several nights a week. While the hotel is geared to large groups, individual guests are welcomed as well. In high season, singles rent for 9,150$ ($59.50) daily and doubles for 10,900$ ($70.85), with off-season reductions. All the rooms are furnished conservatively. Glass doors open onto balconies, and the baths are tiled.

Hotel dos Navegadores, Monte Gordo, 8900 Vila Real de Santo António (tel. 081/424-90). The sign in front of this large hotel is so discreet you might mistake the building for an apartment house. The establishment is popular with vacationing Portuguese and British families, who congregate under the dome covering the atrium's swimming pool, a short distance from the reception desk. In some ways the hotel evokes a Caribbean retreat. You'll find an open bar willing to serve you a fruit-laden drink, along with an array of semitropical plants scattered throughout the wide expanses of the clean and functional public rooms. About three-quarters of the 346 bedrooms have a private balcony. Each room has a private bath. In high season, singles rent for 8,000$ ($52) daily and doubles for 11,200$ ($72.80). The beach is only five minutes away by foot. There's an array of boutiques in a corridor near the swimming pool, along with a hairdresser. There's a children's center to amuse children between the ages of 3 and 12. The hotel will also procure babysitters in the evening if you request it.

Casablanca Inn, Monte Gordo, 8900 Vila Real de Santo António (tel. 081/424-44). It is not directly on the beach, but its frontage on a flower-dotted downtown park makes up for it. Owner Carlos Fernandes and his family designed it to look a lot like something you might find in a wealthy part of Morocco. There's a lush flower garden in front, a series of arched and recessed balconies, and a format similar to one that a modern Humphrey Bogart might have built in an updated version of *Casablanca*—in fact the lobby-level bar is called Rick's and is covered with movie photos of Hollywood's most romantic couple. The 42 bedrooms each contain a terrace, a private bath, a radio, and phone. At night the bar is popular with younger people, especially on Wednesday when live fado music begins at 10:30 p.m. You can enjoy the bar's café terrace for simple lunches every day from 11 a.m. to 2 p.m. and for drinks in the evening between 5:30 p.m. and 1 a.m. Live organ music is part of the weekly entertainment. Depending on the season, and with a continental breakfast included, singles range from 4,000$ ($26) to 6,500$ ($42.25) daily, while doubles cost 6,000$ ($39) to 9,000$ ($58.50). The beach is about a ten-minute stroll away.

Pensão Residência Catavento, Rua Projectada, Monte Gordo, 8900 Vila Real de Santo António (tel. 081/424-28), is the best bargain in Monte Gordo, rated by the government as a luxury boarding house. This Inn of the Weathervane is owned by a company that maintains a simplicity and cleanliness that have won them many repeat customers. Their rooms are so pristine they're almost monastic. In high season, singles cost 5,500$ ($35.75) daily, and doubles go for 7,000$ ($45.50). Tariffs include a continental breakfast. Closed October to May.

Albergaría Monte Gordo, Monte Gordo, 8900 Vila Real de Santo António (tel. 081/421-24), is a modern, streamlined building, open to sea and sky, emulating pueblo architecture. It is across the road from an immense sweep of beach, clean and colorful with the local fishing boats. Each room has a private bathroom, and a double with terrace and sea view costs 4,800$ ($21.20) daily in summer, 3,000$ ($19.50) in winter. A continental breakfast is included. The atmosphere is informal, the staff helpful. Many speak English. Sylvia de Almeida, who manages the inn, has added a decorative touch to the public rooms with her fabric and needlework hangings. There is a lively bar and a good restaurant, known for its soups and local fish dishes. Nonresidents may enjoy its sea-view location and fine service. The peaceful winter atmosphere makes this a place ideal for writers, painters, or people looking for the simple life.

WHERE TO DINE

A place I especially like is the **Copacabana,** 13 Avenida Infante Dom Enrique (tel. 424-64). Because of its oriental roof and its vivid pink bougainvillaea, this indoor/outdoor restaurant looks almost like a piece of Macão-made porcelain. Its entrance is flanked with a pair of feathery pine trees, which give a sparse shade to a few of the tables set out in the courtyard. Under an oriental arcade, you can watch the chefs working in the heat of an exposed grill. Many patrons prefer to sit outdoors within view of the sea, which lies just across the street. Others retreat to the interior, which is walled in wood. You can order such specialties as fondue of fish for two, grilled chicken, steak Diane, grilled suckling pig, bread-and-egg soup, or swordfish Copacabana, as well as grilled kid and even chili-burgers if that is your desire. Full meals cost from 2,500$ ($16.25) and are served at lunch from noon to 3 p.m. and at dinner from 7 to 10 p.m. seven days a week.

---

21. Vila Real de Santo António

Twenty years after the Marquês de Pombal rebuilt Lisbon, which had been destroyed in the great earthquake of 1755, he sent architects and builders to Vila Real de Santo António where they reestablished the frontier town on the bank opposite Spain. It took only five months to build the town. Pombal's motivation was jealousy of Spain. Much has changed, of course, although the Praça de Pombal remains. An obelisk stands in the center of the square, which is paved with inlays of black and white tiles radiating like rays of the sun, and filled with orange trees. Separated from its Iberian neighbor by the Guadiana River, Vila Real de Santo António offers a car-ferry between Portugal and Ayamonte, Spain.

A long esplanade, the Avenida da República, lines the river, and from its northern extremity you can view the Spanish town across the way. Gaily painted horse-drawn carriages take you sightseeing past the shipyards, the lighthouse, or to the bullfights in July and August.

A short drive north on the road to Mertola takes you to the gull-gray castle-fortress of **Castro Marim.** This formidable structure is a legacy of the old border wars between Spain and Portugal. The ramparts and walls watch Spain across the river. Afonso III, who expelled the Moors from this region, founded the original fortress, which was razed by the 1755 earthquake. Inside the walls are the ruins of the Church of São Tiago, dedicated to St. James.

FOOD AND LODGING

The best accommodation in town is **Hotel Apolo,** Avenida dos Bombeiros Portugueses, 8900 Vila Real de Santo António (tel. 081/444-48), on the western edge of town as you enter Vila Real from Monte Gordo or Faro. Near the beach and the river, it attracts vacationers as well as travelers who don't want to cross the Spanish border at night. The hotel is attractive inside, with a spacious marble-floored lobby leading into a large and tastefully congenial bar scattered with comfortable sofas and flooded with sunlight. Each of the 42 simply furnished bedrooms has a private balcony and bath. With a continental breakfast included, singles rent for 7,500$ ($48.75) daily, and doubles cost from 8,000$ ($52).

Edmundo, 55 Avenida da República (tel. 446-89), has long been known in the Algarve, attracting Spaniards from across the river who often visit just for the day "for a glimpse of Portugal." One of the most popular restaurants in Vila Real, it overlooks the river and Spain across the water, a view you will enjoy if you get a sidewalk table. The people who run this place are friendly, and they are proud of their repertoire of local cuisine, especially fresh fish. You might begin with a shrimp cocktail, then follow with fried sole, crayfish, or sautéed red mullet. You can also order meat dishes, such as lamb cutlets and veal filet. Count on spending 2,300$ ($14.95) to 3,000$ ($19.50). Hours are daily from noon to 3 p.m. and 7 to 10 p.m.

ALENTEJO AND RIBATEJO

The adjoining provinces of Alentejo and Ribatejo are the heartland of Portugal. But while Ribatejo is a land of bull-breeding pastures, Alentejo is characterized as a plain of fire and ice.

Ribatejo is the country of the river, where the Tagus, coming from Spain, overflows its banks in winter. It is famed for blue grass, Arabian horses, and black bulls. The most striking feature, however, is a human one: the *campinos,* the sturdy horsemen of the region in their stocking caps. Theirs is the job of harnessing the Arabian pride of their horses and searching out the intangible quality of bravery in the bulls. Whether visiting the château of the Templars, rising in the middle of the Tagus at Almourol, or attending an exciting *festa brava,* when the hooves of horses and the rumble of bulls reverberate in the streets of Vila Franca de Xira, you'll marvel at the passion of the people of Ribatejo. Their fadistas have long been noted for intensity.

The cork-producing plains of Alentejo (literally, beyond the Tagus) compose the largest province in Portugal—so large, in fact, that the government has divided it into Alto Alentejo in the north (capital: Évora), and Baixo Alentejo in the south (capital: Beja). Even today it's difficult to reach. Take the Ponte 25 de Abril across the Tagus via Setúbal, or go all the way north to Vila Franca de Xira, then head east.

In Alentejo the locals have insulated themselves in whitewashed houses with tiny windows that keep in heat in the cold winters, coolness during the scorching summers. The least populated of Portuguese provinces, Alentejo possesses seemingly endless fields of wheat, and is the world's largest producer of cork (the trees can be stripped only once in nine years).

In winter the men are a dramatic sight in their characteristic capes, which are long brown coats with two short tiered capes, often adorned with a red fox collar. The women are even more colorful, especially when they are working in the rice paddies or wheatfields. Their skirts and patterned undergarments are short so they can wade barefooted into the paddies. Over a knitted cowl, with a "peek through" for their eyes, is a brimmed felt hat usually studded with flowers.

From our last stopover in the Algarve, we head north once again, approaching the cities of the plains.

1. Beja

The capital of Baixo Alentejo, founded by Julius Caesar and once known as Pax Julia, rises like a pyramid above the surrounding fields of swaying wheat, only 116 miles from Lisbon.

The fame of Beja rests on what many authorities believe to be a literary hoax. In the mid-17th century, in the Convent of Conceição, a young nun named Soror Mariana Alcoforado is said to have fallen in love with a French military officer, identified as the chevalier de Chamily. He was believed to have seduced her, then to have left Beja never to return again.

The girl's outpouring of grief and anguish found literary release in the *Five Love Letters of a Portuguese Nun*. Published in Paris in 1669, they created a sensation and have remained an epistolary classic of self-revelation and remorse ever since. In 1926, F. C. Green wrote "Who Was the Author of the *Lettres Portugaises*?" claiming that their true writer was the Comte de Guilleragues. However, a modern Portuguese study has submitted evidence that the *Lettres Portugaises* were in fact written by the nun, Sister Alcoforado.

The mid-15th-century convent has been turned into a **Regional Museum,** the Museu Rainha D. Leonor (tel. 233-51), at the Largo da Conceição. It houses a varied assortment of artworks, artifacts, and historical curios, including Roman axes, sarcophagi, Roman amphorae, statuary of Florentine marble, Chinese porcelains from 1541, paintings of Saints Jerome, Augustine, and Bartholomew assigned to Ribera, delicate silverwork, vestments, and dummies dressed in regional Alentejo costumes, 17th-century Spanish and 15th-, 16th-, 17th-, and 18th-century Portuguese paintings.

One of its most unusual exhibits is a grille through which the nun and the Frenchman were supposed to have exchanged intimacies. Also displayed are copies of early editions of the literary classic, even an engraving of the count, revealing him to be chubby cheeked.

The walls, especially those of the cloister, are profusely decorated with antique tiles, some blue and white, others emerald green. There are sacred relics as well, along with elaborate candelabra, and a gilded baroque altar with marble inlay work in pink, black, gold, and gray.

In summer the museum is open from 9:30 a.m. to 1 p.m. and 2:30 to 5:45 p.m. daily except Monday. Winter hours are 9:30 a.m. to 1 p.m. and 2:30 to 5 p.m. except Monday. The regular admission is 25$ (15¢).

Crowning the town is **Castelo de Beja,** which King Dinis built in the early 14th century on the ruins of a Roman fortress. Although some of its turreted walls have been restored, the defensive towers are gone, save for a long marble keep. Traditionally the final stronghold in the castle's fortifications, the old keep appears to be battling the weather and gold fungi. The walls are grown over with ivy, the last encroachment upon its former glory. From the keep, you can enjoy a view of the provincial capital and the outlying fields. The castle opens onto the Largo Dr. Lima Faleiro.

WHERE TO STAY

Many visitors consider the **Residencial Cristina,** 71 Rua de Mértola, 7800 Beja (tel. 084/230-35), to be the best place to stay in Beja. A friendly management rents 31 simply furnished rooms, making the Cristina the largest hostelry in town. Everything is immaculately kept, and the price is very low: from 3,200$ ($20.80) daily in a single, rising to 4,200$ ($27.30) in a double. A continental breakfast, included in the tariff, is the only meal served.

Santa Bárbara, 56 Rua de Mértola, 7800 Beja (tel. 084/220-28), is a little oasis in a town that has few suitable accommodations. The residência is a bandbox building, shiny clean and well kept. It's all small scale, with only a whisper of a reception lobby and elevator. There are two street-level salons, each partially covered with elegant blue and yellow tiles. The 26 compact rooms are adequate, with carpeting, good beds, tile baths with showers, and central heating in the winter. The cost of staying here is low: 3,000$ ($19.50) daily for one person, 4,200$ ($27.30) for two. No meals are served except a continental breakfast, which is included in the price.

WHERE TO DINE

Beja is rather lacking in first- or even second-class restaurants. However, at the **Luís da Rocha,** 63 Rua Capitão João Francisco de Sousa (tel. 231-79), on the same street as the Tourist Office, you can sit downstairs in the café where the whole town seems to congregate for coffee and pastries, or go upstairs where a spacious neon-lit dining room features a complete menu for 1,500$ ($9.75). You might begin with one of the cream soups, prepared fresh daily, then follow with boiled or fried fish or else pork with clams in the Alentejo style. Hours are daily from noon to 3:30 p.m. and 7 to 10 p.m.

---

2. Serpa

Still languishing in the Middle Ages, Serpa is a walled town with defensive towers. Its origins go back to 1295 when it was incorporated into the kingdom of Portugal after having belonged to the Infante of Serpa, Dom Fernando, brother of Dom Sancho II. Overlooking the vast Alentejo plain, Serpa is a town of narrow streets and latticed windows, famous for the cheese that bears its name, as well as for pork sausage and sweets. Silvery olive trees surround the approaches to the town, and the whiteness of the buildings contrasts with the red-brown of the plains. The wild beauty of the River Guadiana, endless fields of grain, and cork-oak groves mark the landscape. In the town, you can see unique painted furniture, an archeological museum, and several ancient churches.

Serpa lies only 20 miles west of Vila Verde de Ficalho (the Spanish frontier). To the east at a distance of 18½ miles stands Beja. Today Serpa has become a stopping-off place for lunch or just a rest stop for travelers on the way to and from Spain, and many motorists like to spend the night here at the hilltop pousada.

FOOD AND LODGING

A government-owned tourist inn, **Pousada de São Gens,** Alto de São Gens, Serpa 7830 Beja (tel. 084/903-27), is set at the crown of the hill of São Gens, in keeping with the Portuguese love of vistas. On clear nights guests can see all the way to Spain. Although a long way from the Algarve, the architecture is Moorish inspired, almost a pueblo villa with white walls easily seen as you ascend the winding road past olive trees. The pousada is family run and has a home-like atmosphere. All the 18 bedrooms have a private bath, tiled in aqua and white. The furnishings are modern, making use of bold colors. Depending on the season, doubles cost 6,700$ ($43.55) to 9,800$ ($63.70) daily, and singles run 5,500$ ($35.75) to 8,700$ ($56.55). A continental breakfast is included in all the tariffs.

In winter dinner is served in a salon with a coved ceiling; in the warmer months the wide veranda is also used by diners. A Portuguese cuisine is offered, with many dishes of the region featured. A complete meal, including soup, a fish course with potatoes, a meat dish with vegetables, and dessert, goes for 2,300$ ($14.95) to 2,500$ ($16.25). Food is served from 12:30 to 2:30 p.m. and 7:30 to 9:30 p.m. Before dinner, you can have a drink in the gold-and-white bar or in one of the stark-white living rooms.

3. Monsaraz

The old fortified town of Monsaraz lies 32 miles to the east of Évora on the way to Spain. It's a village of antique whitewashed houses, with cobbled lanes and many reminders of the Moors who held out here until they were conquered in 1166. Some of the women still wear the traditional garb: men's hats on their shawl-covered heads and men's pants under their skirts. This was obviously done as a protection against the sun. The town overlooks the Guadiana Valley, forming the border between Spain and Portugal.

Still walled, Monsaraz can easily be visited in an afternoon from Évora. As you stroll its streets, look for the original coats-of-arms on the 17th- and 18th-century houses. As you scale the ramparts, you'll have a view over what looks like a cross between a bull ring and a Greek theater. The highlight of the town is a visit along the main street, **Rua Direita,** which has the most distinguished architecture, along with wrought-iron grilles, balconies, and outside staircases. The former **Tribunal** is noted for its fresco depicting "true" and "false" justice, and the town has a church with a 16th-century marble tomb along with a more recent pillory nearby (it dates from the 1700s). Opposite the parish church is the 16th-century **Misericord Hospital,** with a lovely assembly hall on the second floor. King Dinis in the 1200s rebuilt the town **castle,** which saw later fortified additions in the 17th century.

FOOD AND LODGING

If you'd like to dine or stay over in the town, your choice is **Estalagem de Monsaraz,** Largo de São Bartolomeu, 7200 Reguengos de Monsaraz (tel. 066/551-12). Overlooking the valley, this antiques-filled inn is most often visited by "day trippers" for lunch. There, in the heat of the afternoon, they enjoy the gardens and scented arbors. Under a beamed ceiling, guests might begin with a robust vegetable soup or Chaves ham. For a main course, they can select sole meunière or acorn-sweetened pork with a savory baby-clam sauce. You might skip the regular desserts and opt instead for one of the fresh fruits of the region. Its melons have been compared to "the taste of Château d'Yquem," and its oranges have been called "candy sweet." Meals cost from 1,200$ ($7.80) and are best sampled with local Borges branco.

For those wishing to stop over, the estalagem offers six tiny but attractively decorated bedrooms, each with striped rugs and hand-painted headboards. A double room rents for 3,500$ ($22.75) nightly, a single for 1,900$ ($12.35).

4. Évora

The capital of Alto Alentejo is a historical curio. Considering its size and location, it is something of an architectural phenomenon, its builders freely adapting whatever they desired from mudéjar to Manueline, from Roman to rococo. Évora lives up to its reputation as the Museum City. As it lies only 96 miles from Lisbon, it is often visited on a day trip from the capital, but that's a long trek.

Nearly every street in Évora is filled with 16th- and 17th-century houses, many with tile patios. Cobblestones, labyrinthine streets, arcades, squares with bubbling fountains, whitewashed houses, a profuse display of Moorish-inspired arches characterize the town, all of which used to be enclosed behind medieval walls.

Many conquerors have passed through, and several have left architectural remains. To the Romans at the time of Julius Caesar, Évora was known as Liberalitas Julia. Perhaps its heyday was in the 16th century, during the reign of João III, when it became the Montmartre of Portugal, and avant-garde artists congregated under the aegis of royalty. Included among them were the playwright Gil Vicente.

Évora today is a sleepy provincial capital, perhaps self-consciously aware of its monuments. One local historian actually recommended to an American couple that they must see at least 59 monuments. Rest assured that you can capture the essence by seeing only a fraction of that number.

THE SIGHTS

The major monument in Évora is the **Temple of Diana**, in the Praça do Giraldo, directly in front of the government-owned pousada. Dating from either the 1st or 2nd century A.D., it is a light, graceful structure, with 14 granite Corinthian columns topped by marble capitals. Of course, no one can prove that it was actually dedicated to the goddess, but it is a good guess. Incidentally, the temple withstood the earthquake of 1755, and there is evidence that it was once used as a slaughterhouse. Don't fail to walk through the garden for a view of the Roman aqueduct and the surrounding countryside.

A short stroll leads to the **Sé (cathedral).** Bulky and heavy, the mother church of Évora was built in the Roman-Gothic style between 1186 and 1204, although notably restored and redesigned over the centuries. The stone façade is flanked by two square towers, both topped by cones, one surrounded by satellite spires. The interior consists of a nave and two aisles. The main altar, from the 18th century, is the finest in town, made of marble in tones of pink, black, and white.

At the sculptured work *The Lady of Mothers,* young women pray for fertility. A French couple, whose marriage had produced no children, prayed here and the wife found herself pregnant by the time she returned to Paris. The next year the couple returned to Évora, bringing their new child.

The museum, charging an admission of 100$ (65¢), is open from 9 a.m. to noon and 2 to 5 p.m., except Monday. It houses treasures from the church, the most notable of which is a 13th-century Virgin carved out of ivory (it opens to reveal a collection of scenes from her life). A reliquary is studded with 1,426 precious stones, including sapphires, rubies, diamonds, and emeralds. The most valuable item is a piece of wood said to have come from the True Cross.

In the 14th-century cloister, the medallions of the Apostles include the Star of David, incongruous in a Catholic church. A cross in the ceiling, called the Key of the Cloister, marks the last stone to be set into place.

The **Royal Church of St. Francis** is visited by those wanting to see its ghoulish **Chapel of Bones** (Casa dos Ossos). The chancel walls and central pillars are lined with human skulls and other parts of skeletons. Alternate legends have it that the bones came either from soldiers who died in a big battle, or from plague victims. Over the door is the sign: "Our bones who stay here are waiting for yours!" The stone chapel dates from the 16th century. The church was built in the Gothic style with Manueline influences between 1460 and 1510. Admission is 25$ (15¢). Hours are 9 a.m. to 1 p.m. and 2:30 to 6 p.m. Monday to Saturday, from 10 to 11:30 a.m. and 2:30 to 6 p.m. Sunday.

The **Church of Our Lady of Grace** (Igreja Nossa Senhora de Graça) is visited chiefly for its baroque façade, with huge classical nudes over the pillars. Above each group of lazing stone giants is a sphere with a flame atop. These pieces of sculpture are often compared to works by Michelangelo. The church was built in Évora's heyday in the reign of João III. The central window shaft is flanked by columns and large stone rosettes, the lower level supported by ponderous neoclassic columns.

You may want to visit the **Ancient University** (Universidade de Évora). In 1559, as a result of the cultural flowering of Évora, a university was constructed and placed under the tutelage of the Jesuits. It flourished until the Jesuit-hating Marquês de Pombal closed it in the 18th century. The baroque structure is double tiered and built around a large quadrangle. The arches are supported by marble pillars, the interior ceilings constructed with Brazilwood. The inner courtyard is lined with blue and white tiles. Other azulejo representations, depicting women, wild animals, angels, cherubs, and costumed men contrast with the austere elegance of the classrooms and the elongated refectory. The compound is no longer used as a university, although pupils (the equivalent of high-school students in America) attend class here. It is open (but ask permission first) from 9 a.m. to 12:30 p.m. and 2 to 5 p.m. Monday to Friday.

Facing the Temple of Diana is the **Church of St. John the Evangelist.** Next door to the government-owned pousada, this private Gothic-mudéjar church is connected to the palace built by the dukes of Cadaval. However, it is open to the public —in fact, it is one of the gems of Évora, although seemingly little visited. It contains a collection of azulejos from the 18th century. A guide will show you a macabre sight: an old cistern filled with neatly stacked bones removed from tombs. In the sacristy of the chapel are some paintings, including a ghastly rendition of Africans slaughtering a Christian missionary. A curiosity is a painting of a pope that not only has moving eyes, but moving feet. In addition, you can see part of the wall that once completely encircled Évora.

Museum of Ancient Art (Museu de Évora), Largo Conde de Vila Flor (tel. 226-04), is in the 16th- and 17th-century episcopal palace. Roman, medieval, Manueline, and Luso-Moorish sculptures are displayed on the ground floor. Here you'll see a remnant of a vestal virgin in marble, a 14th-century marble *Annunciation,* and a Holy Trinity in Ança stone, dating from the 1500s. On the floor above, of major interest is a 16th-century Flemish-school polyptych depicting the life of the Virgin, panels of an altarpiece, also from the Flemish school, on the subject of Christ's Passion, and pictures by Portuguese artists of the 16th and 17th centuries. The museum is open from 10 a.m. to 12:30 p.m. and 2 to 5 p.m. daily except Monday. Admission is 200$ ($1).

WHERE TO STAY

One of the finest government-owned tourist inns in Portugal is **Pousada dos Lóios,** Largo Conde de Vila Flor, 7000 Évora (tel. 066/240-51). It occupies Lóios Monastery, built in 1485 on the site of the old Évora Castle which was destroyed during a riot in 1384. A powerful noble, Don Rodrigo Afonso de Melo, founded the monastery and carried two baskets of soil and the first stone for the foundation ceremony on his back. Kings João II, IV, and V used to visit the monastery. The chapter room, with doorways in Moorish-Portuguese style, dating from the beginning of the 16th century, was the place where the official Inquisition reports were kept. After the 1755 earthquake, extensive work was done to repair and preserve the structure. Through the years it was used as a telegraph station, a primary school, an army barracks, and offices. The opening of the pousada in 1965 made possible the architectural restoration of the monastery. Its position in the museum-like center of Évora is prime, between the cathedral and the ghost-like Roman Temple of Diana.

There's a salon in white and gold (a one-time private chapel), with an ornate Pompeian-style decor and frescoes. It's decorated with antique furnishings, hand-woven draperies, crystal chandeliers and sconces, and painted medallion portraits. There are 31 double rooms and one suite, now unrecognizably luxurious when compared to the quarters of old. All have private bath and central heating. They're furnished in a traditional provincial style, with a blending of antique reproductions. Double rooms cost 17,600$ ($114.40) daily, and singles go for 15,000$ ($97.50). Taxes, service, and a continental breakfast are included in this tariff. Ask for a room in the interior.

Even if you're not bedding down for the night, like a pilgrim of old, you should at least stop for a regional meal of Alto Alentejo. In winter, meals are served in the main dining hall, with its heavy chandeliers. But in fair weather most guests dine in and around the cloister, at tables set under the Manueline fan-vaulted ceiling and an ornate Moorish doorway leading to the Chapter House. You pay 3,100$ ($20.15) for a complete luncheon or dinner. For this, you get a basket of freshly baked bread and butter, a bowl of hot soup, followed by a fish dish, such as sole prepared in a herb-flavored tomato sauce and accompanied by mashed potatoes. For your main course, try the acorn-sweetened pork cooked with clams in the manner of Alentejo. For dessert, a trolley of assorted pastries is wheeled by. Food is served daily from 12:30 to 2:30 p.m. and 7:30 to 9:30 p.m.

Hotel Planicie, 40 Rua Miguel Bombarda, 7000 Évora (tel. 240-26). Its symmetry, its stone window frames, and its severe façade make it resemble an old Tuscan villa. Inside, a tasteful modernization added hundreds of slabs of glistening marble but retained many of the best features of its original construction. Especially appealing is the vaulted brick ceiling of the basement bar. A member of the Best Western reservation system, the hotel contains 33 bedrooms, each of which has a private bath, heating, TV, a phone. With breakfast included, singles cost 6,600$ ($42.90) daily, doubles 7,700$ ($50.05), and triples 9,700$ ($63.40). Well-prepared meals, each costing from 1,800$ ($11.70), are served in the street-level dining room daily from noon to 3 p.m. and 7 to 10 p.m. daily.

Albergaría Vitoria, Rua Diana de Lis, 7000 Évora (tel. 066/271-74). Set inconveniently near the beltway surrounding the old city, this modern concrete-walled hotel juts above a dusty neighborhood of villas. Its location is on the southeastern edge of the city, about a mile from the cathedral, but it could be a handy address in summer when all the central hotels are full. Built in 1985, it contains 45 doubles but only three singles, each with balcony, private bath, phone, radio, and air conditioning. Singles with breakfast included rent for 7,200$ ($46.80) daily and doubles for 8,200$ ($53.30). Only breakfast is served in the dining room, but the Vitoria has a bar on the premises.

Residencial Riviera, 49 Rua 5 de Outubro, 7000 Évora (tel. 066/233-04), was built beside the cobblestones of what is said to be the most charming street in town, about two blocks downhill from the cathedral. Originally designed as a private villa, it has retained many handcrafted details from the original building, including stone window frames, ornate iron balustrades, and the blue and yellow tiles of its foyer. Each of its 22 comfortable bedrooms contains a bath, TV, and phone, and comes with a continental breakfast included in the price. Singles rent for 5,000$ ($32.50) daily, and doubles cost 9,000$ ($58.50).

Farther away, **Santa Clara,** 19 Travessa da Milheira, 7000 Évora (tel. 066/241-41), is another good bet, especially if your requirements are simple. Near the city car park, it is within walking distance of the major sightseeing attractions of Évora. The management rents 29 well-kept bedrooms at modest prices, ranging from 4,500$ ($29.25) in a single and from 6,000$ ($39) in a double. The hotel has a good restaurant, serving regional specialties and local wines, with meals priced from 1,500$ ($9.75).

O Eborense, 1 Largo da Misericórdia, 7000 Évora (tel. 066/220-31), is a delightful guesthouse with a touch of grandeur in the form of a stone staircase leading up to an entrance lined with plants and decorated with tiles. Your hosts are Mr. and Mrs. Serrabulho, who have recently improved the building, making the bedrooms more comfortable but keeping the original and antique atmosphere. They offer 29 rooms, all in the main building, all clean, traditional, and quite pleasant. Singles range from 5,000$ ($32.50) daily, and doubles from 7,000$ ($45.50). A continental breakfast is included. You can sit on the terrace nursing a drink and peering through the cloister-like, mullioned veranda. An adjoining rooftop garden-café attracts sunworshipers.

WHERE TO DINE

The most atmospheric restaurant in Évora is the **Cozinha de St. Humberto,** 39 Rua da Moeda (tel. 242-51). Hidden away in a narrow side street leading down from the Praça do Giraldo, it is rustically decorated with old pots, blunderbusses, standing lamps, a grandfather clock, and kettles hanging from the ceiling. Carnations stand on each table, and you sit in rush chairs or on divan-settees. In warm weather, you can enjoy a gazpacho alentejana, followed by fried fish with tomato and garlic or pork Évora style (a real meal in itself), topped off by regional cheese. A bottle of Borba wine is a good companion with most meals. A complete meal costs 1,400$ ($9.10) to 2,200$ ($14.30). Food is served daily from noon to 3:30 p.m. and 7 to 10:30 p.m. The restaurant is closed from mid-February to early March.

Fialho, 14 Travessa Mascarenhas (tel. 230-79), is considered the most traditional restaurant at Évora. Its entrance is unprepossessing, but the interior warms considerably. The decoration is in the style of a Portuguese tavern, and the cookery is regional. You get good shellfish dishes along with such fare as pork with baby clams in a savory sauce. In season you might also be able to order partridge. Seating 80 patrons, the restaurant is air-conditioned and serves meals from noon to midnight (closed Monday). The cost ranges from 1,800$ ($11.70) to 2,800$ ($18.20). The restaurant is likely to be closed for most of September.

Guião, 81 Rua da República (tel. 224-27), is a regional tavern that appears on most lists as one of the best three or four restaurants of Évora. It lies a short distance off the main square, the Praça do Giraldo. Dining is on two levels. The decor is filled with Portuguese charm, including a beamed ceiling and antique blue and white tiles. Family run, it offers local wines and specialties. Meals—hearty and robust fare—are most filling, costing from 1,800$ ($11.70). A typical bill of fare includes grilled squid, grilled fish, swordfish steak, and clams with pork in the Alentejo style. At certain times of the year the kitchen prepares partridge. Hours are daily from noon to 3:30 p.m. and 7 to 10 p.m.

5. Vila Viçosa

This borough was the near-private dominion of the dukes of Bragança, the last royal rulers of Portugal. Thirty-four miles northeast of Évora, Vila Viçosa has been a ducal seat since 1442. But what cast it into worldwide prominence was when one of its members journeyed to Lisbon in 1640 to be declared the head of a new royal dynasty. Ruling as João IV, he freed Portugal from 60 years of Spanish domination.

Ironically, one of the last of the Bragança kings, Carlos I, spent his last night dining under his favored antler chandeliers before making the journey to Lisbon. His staff, lined up at the Terreiro do Paço, waved him and his older son good-bye. But when they arrived at another Terreiro do Paço (this one in Lisbon), the reception was less friendly. Both died by an assassin's bullets.

The **Paço Ducal de Vila Viçosa** (tel. 986-59) remains as a memorial to the Braganças. You'll see pictures of the last king, Manuel II, who fled with his mother, Amélia, into exile in 1910. The uniforms of Carlos I are here as well. Perhaps the most remarkable personal exhibit is a gallery of Carlos's (known as the painter king) paintings and watercolors. As one critic put it, he was a better artist than a king.

The inside of the palace and its furnishings are a collage of faded mementos, foreign art influences, and nostalgic specters of a once-royal life. As with a fine tapestry, separating the diverse treasures is difficult. They include a frescoed Salon of Hercules, tapestries based on Rubens's cartoons, 16th-century Persian carpets, 17th-century armor, an oratory with grotesque motifs, a Medusa chamber, Louis XVI furnishings, a 17th-century Holy Cross with 6,500 precious stones (rubies, diamonds, pearls, and emeralds), hand-carved armoires, a chapel faced with pink marble, a sword and shield collection (even spears from Angola), and cloisters dating from the early 16th century. The kitchen is filled with copper pots and utensils used by the royal family (a spit for roasting the big game Carlos I was fond of hunting), and a Coach Museum, containing some 80 carriages, from the 18th, 19th, and 20th centuries, with equipment, and a sedan chair. After your visit, you can stroll through the Garden of the Duchesses.

In the archives you can see the bequest of Manuel II: his priceless library of printed books from the 15th and 16th centuries, including editions of *Os Lusíadas* by Luís de Camões. The music archives contain what remains from the Schola Cantorum instituted by the dukes in the 17th, 18th, and 19th centuries. The palace is open daily, charging an admission of 300$ ($1.95). Hours in winter are 9:30 a.m. to 1 p.m. and 2 to 5 p.m., in summer to 6 p.m.; closed Monday and holidays.

Today the white town of Vila Viçosa rests unchanged in the midst of the olive-green carpeted marble hills which are spotted with orange trees. The town is guarded by a walled castle (tel. 981-28) dating from the 14th century, with a quartet of tall towers and crenellated walls. It is a natural extension of the museum in the palace. There is also an archeological museum with artifacts from Paleolithic, Neolithic, Iron Age, and Roman civilizations found around Vila Viçosa. Admission to the castle is 100$ (65¢). There are 22 churches in Vila Viçosa, many almost casually containing treasures, but only the most dedicated of visitors seek them out.

WHERE TO STAY

A 16th-century palace, **Casa dos Arcos,** 16 Praça Martim Afonso de Sousa, Vila Viçosa, 7000 Évora (tel. 066/425-18), has Renaissance lines and balcony windows. Lying only a two-minute walk from the palace, and located behind an aristocratically severe façade, it overlooks a cobblestone square. There is a quiet neighborhood feeling to the place. The wall decorations are neoclassic, and there is a family oratory adorned with canvas paintings and frescos. Pillars of white stone support the graceful arcade outside and decorate a small indoor courtyard. You can have a comfortable and relaxed stay here. A single with bath costs 6,000$ ($39) daily for bed and a continental breakfast; a double with bath goes for 7,000$ ($45.50). The proprietor is Maria Jardim Hintze Ribeiro.

WHERE TO DINE

Near the football field, **Ouro Branco,** 43 Campo da Restauração (tel. 985-56), has a warm and cozy ambience. You get good Portuguese local fare. Occasionally some of the coffee- and brandy-drinking Alentejo "cowboys" show up. Even though inland, the restaurant is known as a *marisqueira,* which in Portuguese designates a place where fresh shellfish is available. The regional fare is savory. Your meal might begin with a bowl of soup made from a rich stock of turnips, greens, and red beans, and follow with garlic-flavored pork. Seating 80, with a bar, the restaurant serves from noon to 4 p.m. and 6:30 to 11 p.m. daily except Monday. Meals cost 2,000$ ($13) and up.

6. Borba

The town that marble built, Borba lies only 2½ miles from Vila Viçosa. On the way there you'll pass quarries filled with black, white, and multicolored deposits. In the village, marble is king. Along the streets many cottages have door trimmings and facings of marble, and the women get down on their hands and knees to scrub their doorways, a source of special pride to them.

On **Rua S. Bartolomeu** sits a church, also dedicated to S. Bartolomeu. It contains a groined ceiling; walls lined with azulejos in blue, white, and gold; and an altar in black and white marble. The richly decorated ceiling is painted with four major medallions, one depicting decapitation. As Portuguese churches go, this one isn't remarkable. What is remarkable, however, are eight nearby antique shops (amazing for such a small town), which are filled with interesting buys. Borba is also a big wine center, and you may want to sample the local brew at a café (or perhaps at the pousada at Elvas).

On the outskirts is a remarkable sight, **Museu de Cristo,** on the main road to Estremoz at Vila Lobos. It lies almost 2 miles from Borba and 5½ miles from Estremoz. The entrance is inauspicious, on a farm by the side of the road. In front is an antique shop filled with a hodgepodge of wares, including many pieces from Alentejo. In the rear, the museum is the most intimate and personal one in Portugal. It's owned by the Lôbo family.

Started more than four decades ago, the collection includes 3,000 crucifixes. One would suspect that this figure will change, as the Museum of Christ is still making acquisitions. The late founding father of the family started collecting primitive crucifixes from the country people, bartering his excess farm produce, picking up more figures in his travels to North Africa, Angola, and Spain.

The present collection spans about 13 centuries, 42 countries, and countless artistic traditions. Some of the figures were hollowed out to hide money in the 16th century. One of the finest is from 18th-century Florence, showing a skull and crossbones at the bottom. In the other rooms of the museum are regional artifacts and furnishings. The museum may be viewed from 8 a.m. to 10 p.m. in summer (till 6 p.m. in winter). You should make a contribution.

FOOD AND LODGING

In Borba, the best kitchen is the **Restaurant Lisbeto,** 31 Rua Mateus Pais, Borba, 7000 Évora (tel. 066/943-32). Don't expect grandeur or culinary finesse. What you get is a warm welcome from members of the António Ganito family, along with solidly filling regional fare. You pass through a long and narrow anteroom, whose wood-trimmed walls are warmed by a tiny pot-bellied stove. Gregarious diners request a stand-up apéritif at the bar before heading into the tiled blue-and-white dining room, where imprints of horseshoes fill in the spaces of the otherwise unadorned plaster. Full meals are served daily from noon to 4 p.m. and 7:30 to 10 p.m., costing from 1,600$ ($10.40). Menu choices are recited orally, and are likely to include codfish Lisbeto style, sopa alentejano, and loin of pork. A trio of simple bedrooms, each with private bath, is also rented out if you'd like to spend the night in Borba. The rate ranges from 1,500$ ($9.75) to 2,200$ ($14.30) daily, either single or double occupancy.

7. Estremoz

Rising from the Alentejo plain like a pyramid of salt set to dry in the sun, fortified Estremoz is in the center of the marble-quarry region of Alentejo, 108 miles east of Lisbon and 28½ miles from Évora. Cottages and mansions alike utilize the abundant marble in making windows and apertures or in fashioning balustrades and banisters.

THE SIGHTS

From the ramparts of its **castle**, dating from the 13th-century reign of King Dinis, the plains of Alentejo are spread before you. Although one 75-year-old British lady is reported to have walked it, it's best to drive your car to the top of the Upper Town, bringing it to a stop on the Largo de Dom Dinis. The stones of the castle, the cradle of the town's past, were decaying so badly that the city fathers pressed for its restoration in 1970.

The large imposing keep, attached to a palace, dominates the central plaza. Dinis's saintly wife, Isabella, died in the castle. Isabella was unofficially proclaimed a saint by her local followers, even in life however, one of her detractors wrote, "Poor Dinis!" Also opening onto the marble- and stone-paved largo are two modest chapels and a church. As in medieval days, soldiers still walk the ramparts, guarding the fortress.

With enough promenading Portuguese soldiers to man a garrison, the open quadrangle in the center of the Lower Town is called the **Rossio de Marquês de Pombal.** The **Town Hall,** with its twin bell towers, opens onto this square, and the walls of its grand stairway are lined with antique azulejos in blue and white, depicting hunting, pastoral, and historical scenes.

The **Estremoz Potteries** turn out the traditional earthenware of the region. It is famous for *moringues,* wide- or narrow-mouthed jars with two spouts and one handle. A type associated with royalty, called "kings' jugs," is decorated with marble inlays. Primitive figurines of religious and lay characters are interesting, as well as those of animals.

The **Rural Museum,** 62b on the main square (tel. 225-38), has displays showing the life of people of the Alentejo through models and crafts. It is open for guided tours from 10 a.m. to 1 p.m. and 3 to 6 p.m. (to 5:30 p.m. in winter) daily except Monday. Admission is 50$ (35¢).

The **Chapel of the Queen Saint** has walls decorated with blue azulejos showing scenes in the life of Isabella of Aragon, wife of King Dinis, called the Queen Saint. See especially the Miracle of the Roses portrayal. Ask at the Rural Museum or the pousada about visiting the chapel.

In the **Church of St. Mary,** dating from the 16th century, you'll see pictures by Portuguese primitive painters. The church formed part of the ancient fortress.

Another church worth a stop is about a mile south of the town on the road to Bencatel, the **Church of Our Lady of the Martyrs** (Nossa Senhora dos Mártires), with beautiful azulejos and an entrance marked by a Manueline arch. Dating from 1844, the church has a nave chevet after the French Gothic style of architecture.

WHERE TO STAY

The best of the government-owned tourist inns is the **Pousada da Rainha Santa Isabel,** Largo de Dom Dinis, 7100 Estremoz (tel. 068/226-18). Within the old castle dominating the town, and overlooking the battlements and the Estremoz plain, it is a deluxe establishment, with gold leaf, marble, velvet, and satin mingling with antiques in the bedrooms and corridors. Before his departure for India, Vasco da Gama was received by Dom Manuel in the salon of this castle. In 1698 a terrible explosion followed by fire destroyed the royal residence, but ostentatious alterations were carried out. It became an armory and later was adapted to serve as a barracks, and then an industrial school, but its transformation into a castle-pousada has restored it as a historical monument. In perfect style, comfort is provided within the framework of history. Therefore, don't be surprised that prices differ from those of the less regal pousadas.

There are three suites and 20 bedrooms, all with bath. Singles, including service charges, cost 14,900$ ($96.85) daily, with twins and the double going for 16,600$ ($107.90). The vaulted dining room is cavernous but elegant. The menu is both international and regional. Try, for example, braised duck with olive sauce, or perhaps partridge stuffed with vegetables. If featured, you might want to be daring and order the grilled wild boar with a hot pepper sauce. A meal costs 2,200$ ($14.30) to 3,000$ ($19.50). Food is served daily from 12:30 to 3 p.m. and 7:30 to 10 p.m.

Residência Carvalho, 27 Largo da República, 7100 Estremoz (tel. 068/227-12), is clean, simple, and inexpensive, just what you may be looking for in an emergency. Depending on the plumbing, singles range from 1,400$ ($9.10) to 1,800$ ($11.70) daily, with doubles costing 2,300$ ($14.95) to 3,200$ ($20.80). A continental breakfast, the only meal served, is included. The Carvalho is a possible stop in case the pousada is full and you're tired, two likely possibilities.

WHERE TO DINE

Good food in a pleasant ambience is offered at **Aguîas d'Ouro,** 27 Rossio do Marquês de Pombal (tel. 221-96). The Golden Eagles faces the largest square in Estremoz, its mosaic and marble balconied façade suggesting a doge's palace. On the second floor are several connecting dining rooms with rough white plaster walls under ceramic brick ceilings; heavy sumptuous black leather armchairs and white-draped tables. The meal begins with a dish of homemade pâté with rye bread. À la carte dishes only are offered, including a large bowl of spinach and bean soup with crispy croutons floating on top. Main dishes include stuffed partridge and pork and clams. The chocolate mousse is the featured dessert. A complete meal costs from 1,800$ ($11.70). It is open daily from noon to 3 p.m. and 7 to 10 p.m.

8. Elvas

This city of the plums, known for its crenellated fortifications, is less than seven miles from Badajoz, Spain. The walled town is characterized by narrow cobblestone streets (pedestrians have to duck into doorways to allow automobiles to inch by), and is surely an anachronism, so tenaciously does it hold on to its monuments and history. The town was held by the Moors until 1226. It later was frequently assaulted and besieged by Spanish troops, being defeated in the War of the Oranges in 1801, which was ended by a peace treaty signed at Badajoz. Elvas remained part of Portugal, but its neighbor, Olivença, became Spanish. The Elvas ramparts are an outstanding example of 17th-century fortifications. There are fortified gates, curtain walls, moats, and bastions, with sloping banks (glacis) around them.

Lining the steep hilly streets are tightly packed gold- and oyster-colored cottages topped by tile roofs. Many of the doors leading to the houses are only five feet high. In the tiny windows are numerous canary cages and flowering geraniums. Water is transported to Elvas by the four-tier **Amoreira Aqueduct,** built between 1498 and 1622, coming from about five miles southwest of the town.

In the Praça Dom Sancho II (honoring the king who reconstructed the town) stands the **Sé (cathedral),** forbidding and fortress-like. Under a cone-shaped dome, it is decorated with gargoyles, turrets, and a florid Manueline portal. The cathedral opens onto a black-and-white-diamonded square. A short walk up the hill to the right of the cathedral leads to the **Largo Santa Clara,** a small plaza on which was erected an odd Manueline pillory, with four wrought-iron dragon heads.

On the south side of Largo Santa Clara is the **Church of Our Lady of Consolation** (Igreja Nossa Senhora de Consolação), an octagonal, 16th-century Renaissance building with a cupola lined with 17th-century azulejos.

The **castle** built by the Moors and strengthened by the Christian rulers in the 14th and 16th centuries, is open from 9:30 a.m. to 12:30 p.m. and 2:30 to 7 p.m. daily except Thursday (closes at 5:30 p.m. from October 10 to April 30). From the top of the castle's ramparts, you have a panoramic view of the town and its fortifications, as well as the surrounding country.

WHERE TO STAY

A major link in the government-inn circuit is the **Pousada de Santa Luzia,** Avenida de Badajoz, 7350 Elvas (tel. 068/621-94), a hacienda-style building just outside the city walls at the edge of a busy highway (Estrada N4). It was built some 50 years ago as a private hotel, lying about a five-minute walk east of the center of town. The bone-white stucco villa faces the fortifications. The entire ground floor is devoted to a living room, an L-shaped dining salon, and a bar—all opening through thick arches onto a Moorish courtyard with fountain, lily pond, and orange trees.

There are some bedrooms on the upper floor, but you can also stay in the nearby annex, a villa with a two-story entrance hall and an ornate staircase. The hotel offers only 16 bedrooms, so getting in here without a reservation could be difficult. Singles peak at 11,300$ ($73.45) daily and doubles at 12,500$ ($81.25). Meals cost from 2,700$ ($17.55) and are served daily from noon to 4 p.m. and 8 to 10 p.m. The menu is extensive. Noteworthy are the fish dishes, including grilled red mullet and natural oysters. The restaurant in the pousada is reputed to be the finest in the area.

Since the pousada is likely to be full, you might try instead **Estalagem Dom Sancho II,** 20 Praça da República, 7350 Elvas (tel. 068/626-84), which sits proudly on the main square of Elvas. The location is perfect for walking around the village. Some of the rooms open onto the old square, and from your window you can look down upon the former town hall and, to the north, the old cathedral. However, one of the rooms in the rear would be much quieter. The hotel is furnished in period pieces, offering 26 small but still quite adequate units. A double costs 6,700$ ($43.55) daily, and singles go for 5,200$ ($33.80), these tariffs including a continental breakfast. The hotel offers an excellent dining room that serves Portuguese specialties every day; a complete meal costs from 1,800$ ($11.70) per person.

In terms of general amenities, the best selection—certainly the largest in town —is **Dom Luís,** Avenida de Badajoz (along the N4), 7350 Elvas (tel. 068/627-56), which is a well-run hotel with 61 rooms furnished in a modern style. Prices are reasonable too, ranging from 6,500$ ($42.25) per day in a single to 8,000$ ($52) in a double. The hotel also has a good restaurant, serving regional wines and local dishes, with prices beginning at 1,800$ ($11.70). Seating 130, the restaurant is air-conditioned in summer. Meals are served daily from 12:30 to 2:30 p.m. and 7:30 to 10 p.m.

WHERE TO DINE

Many guests will want to take their meals at the pousada, previously recommended. However, a more adventurous choice is the **Estalagem Don Quixote,** Rte. N4, Pedras Negras (tel. 620-14), about two miles west of Elvas. This isolated compound is the end point for many a gastronomic pilgrimage in the area. The place is especially busy on weekends, when it adopts a holiday feeling, with lots of convivial chatter and a kind of frenzied table service. You can order a drink in the leather-upholstered English-style bar near the entrance. The sprawling and sunny dining room greets newcomers with the sight of rows of fresh fish arranged on ice behind glass cases. Amid an Iberian traditional decor you can order full meals costing 1,500$ ($9.75), served daily from noon to 3 p.m. and 7 to 10:30 p.m. Specialties include shellfish rice, grilled sole, grilled swordfish, roast pork, beefsteak alentejano, and at least five different kinds of shellfish.

Restaurante O Estribo, 33 Rua da Cadeia (tel. 629-83), on the square, is a pleasant place to eat, offering good, filling Portuguese meals at reasonable prices. You can feast on fish dishes, lamb, or a tasty goatmeat stew after starting with a soup such as gazpacho (in deference to neighboring Spain) or an appetizer. The fruits served here are excellent conclusions to your meal, as is the regional cheese. Expect to spend from 1,800$ ($11.70) for a satisfactory meal, served daily from noon to 4 p.m. and 7 to 10 p.m. The restaurant is clean, and the staff provides good service.

9. Arraiolos

This small village has been famous since the 13th century for its carpets. Early designs were imitations of Persian designs, but were soon developed and expanded by the craftspeople until the 18th century, when the creative impulse seemed to cease. The present rugs follow the old designs religiously. They are made of heavy wool (the yarns tinted by natural dyes), are handmade, and often contain elaborate needlework. Many of the most elegant are displayed at the Museum of Antique Art in Lisbon. Even if you can't stop off at Arraiolos, you may want to see a wide-ranging display for sale at the **Casa Quintão,** 30 Rua Ivens in Lisbon (tel. 36-58-37).

In Arraiolos, **Tapêtes de Arraiolos Condestável** (tel. 422-19) is open from 9 a.m. to 1 p.m. and 2 to 7 p.m. daily except Sunday. You can visit the workshop Monday to Friday from 8 a.m. to noon and 1 to 6 p.m. This shop has a branch in Évora.

WHERE TO EAT

This rug town has never been known for its restaurants. However, if you are a collector and are passing through on a shopping trip, you might try **Arca de Noé,** 23 Rua St. Condestável (tel. 424-27). This place, patronized almost exclusively by locals, is inexpensive in price, with meals costing from 1,800$ ($11.70). For that, you get regional cookery and wines, served daily except Tuesday from noon to 10 p.m. Typical dishes include a hearty vegetable soup, the inevitable salt cod, and fried fish of the day.

10. Portalegre

Portalegre is more than 13 miles from the border post at Marvão, providing motorists with the shortest route between Lisbon and Madrid. Three miles away lies the mountain of São Mamede. The town, a center for cork production, is filled with baroque mansions, particularly on Rua 19 de Junho. In the 16th century it was known for its tapestries. Silk mills were started in Portalegre in the late 17th century.

Manufactura de Tapeçarias de Portalegre (Tapestry Workshops), Parque da Corredoura (tel. 232-83), in the old Jesuit monastery, can be visited daily except Sunday from 9:30 to 11:30 a.m. and 2:30 to 5:30 p.m. Go up the stairs from the ground floor and ring the bell at the left-hand door. Visitors are taken through the weaving room with its hand-looms, studios where designs are worked out, and the display room.

The **cathedral** has a fine altarpiece in one of its chapels. The sacristy walls are covered with azulejos. The interior of the building, from the 16th century, is behind an 18th-century façade with wrought-iron balconies, granite pilasters, and marble columns at the door.

José Régio Museum, near Praça da Republica (tel. 236-25), has collections of folk and religious art of the region, including 300 crucifixes. Antique pottery and statuettes of St. Anthony are included in the collection, along with wrought iron and forged iron pieces. Many regional artifacts, such as powder horns, are also exhibited. Guided tours, costing 50$ (35¢), are conducted from 9:30 a.m. to 12:30 p.m. and 2 to 6 p.m. except on Monday.

Museu Municipal de Portalegre (tel. 216-16), Portalegre's Municipal Museum, near the cathedral in the former seminary, is open from 10 a.m. to 12:30 p.m. and 2 to 5:30 p.m. daily. Here you can see treasures of sacred art including a gilded wooden Spanish pietà from the late 15th century, a polychrome terracotta altarpiece and gold and silver church plate from the 16th century, as well as a number of other examples of ecclesiastical art. Arraiolos carpets from the 17th and 18th centuries are on exhibit, plus antique furniture, pottery, and porcelain. Admission is 50$ (35¢). Close to the museum is the **Yellow Palace** with delicate wrought-iron grillwork.

FOOD AND LODGING

The best place to stay in Portalegre is the **Hotel D. João III,** Avenida de Liberdade, 7300 Portalegre (tel. 045/211-93). A modern hotel, its decor includes wide use of native materials, including stone. The 60 bedrooms all have private baths, phones, and balconies, some looking out onto a town park. A single rents for 5,000$ ($32.50) daily and a double for 7,500$ ($48.75). The hotel has a swimming pool (in use from May to October), a bar, and elevators. The dining room on the top floor has a panoramic view of the town and the amphitheater of hills in the distance. Meals cost 2,000$ ($13) and up. The hotel dining room, in fact, is one of the most reliable choices for dining in the area, and you can do so daily from 12:30 to 3 p.m. and 7:30 to 10 p.m.

Alpendre, 21 Rua 31 de Janeiro (tel. 216-11), is among the best of the local eateries, with a modern decor. It dispenses a typical Portuguese cuisine (try the pork with clams), along with a good selection of wines. Nearly 100 patrons can be accommodated, enjoying air conditioning in summer and a fireplace in winter. Meals, costing from 2,000$ ($13), are served daily except Monday from noon to midnight.

Another suitable candidate is the **Quinta da Saúde,** Sêrra de Portalegre (tel. 223-24), which also offers regional specialties, national dishes, and good wines. Try for a table with a panoramic view. Meals, costing from 2,000$ ($13), are served daily from noon to 11 p.m. The restaurant is located less than two miles from the center of town.

---

11. Marvão

This ancient walled hill town, lying close to Castelo de Vide, is well preserved and is visited chiefly for its spectacular views. Just under four miles from the Spanish frontier, the once-fortified medieval stronghold retains a rich flavor of the Middle Ages. Those with limited time who can explore only one border town in Portugal should make it this one. It's that panoramic.

You get to Marvão by following a road around the promontory on which the little town was built, past the Church of Our Lady of the Star, the curtain walls, watchtowers, and parapets. Arcaded passageways, balconied houses with wrought-iron grillwork and Manueline windows, and a number of churches can be seen along the hilly streets.

The castle, built in the 13th century, stands at the western part of the rocky promontory. You can walk along the parapet, taking in a panoramic view of the surrounding country, all the way to the Spanish mountains in the east, as well as a vast sweep of Portuguese mountain ranges.

The population of Marvão is small. If you arrive in the afternoon, you may think you're in a ghost town. Most of the inhabitants are working in the fields outside the walls.

FOOD AND LODGING

There is really only one recommendable choice. It's **Pousada de Santa Maria de Marvão,** Marvão, 7330 Portalegre (tel. 045/932-01), which stands in the upper levels of the town sandwiched between two impossibly narrow cobblestone streets. With a total of 13 bedrooms, it is a small pousada, but one of the most charming and interesting in Portugal. It was created when the Portuguese government combined three antique houses into one graceful unit, staffing it with competent employees, and adding rows of panoramic windows to encompass one of the most breathtaking views in Iberia.

The establishment's social center lies within the combined living and dining room, where a cozy and intimate bar, a tile-surrounded hearth, deep, comfortable sofas, and carefully decorated tables create an undeniable charm. Service is from 12:30 to 3 p.m. and 7:30 to 10 p.m. daily, with meals costing from 2,200$ ($14.30) to 2,500$ ($16.25). Typical menu choices include grilled prawns piri-piri, partridge, scampi, or clams Alentejo. Each of the well-furnished bedrooms contains a phone and private bath, and many open onto views. Singles rent for 11,300$ ($73.45) daily and doubles for 12,500$ ($81.25).

---

12. Castelo de Vide

At an altitude of 1,800 feet, this spa town lies at the foot of a castle. Nature has endowed Castelo de Vide with therapeutic waters. Inside its walls stand whitewashed houses, some on squares little changed since the 15th and 16th centuries. A view of pine woods, chestnuts, and oak trees gives the town a resort atmosphere. Cromlechs in the area testify to the ancient origin of the town. It was conquered by the Romans in A.D. 44 and destroyed by Vandals in 411.

Praça Dom Pedro V is the main square, on which stands the Church of Santa Maria, the late-17th-century town hall, the Santo Amaro Hospital of the same era, and a handsome 18th-century mansion.

The **castle** was built outside the walls. A 12th-century round tower leads to the keep, damaged in the early 18th century by an explosion. You can get a view of the town from a room with a Gothic cupola. The castle has played a part in the history of Castelo de Vide for a long time. It was rebuilt by the Arabs in 1299. At this fortress the contract for marriage of King Dinis to Dona Isabella of Aragón was signed.

The **Judiaria,** or Jewish Quarter, is a sector of narrow alleyways and small houses, with the richest collection of ogival doors in Portugal. This quarter also abounds with cats. A medieval synagogue has been restored. Below the Jewish Quarter is an attractive little square with a baroque fountain.

FOOD AND LODGING

Castelo de Vide has a number of modest but acceptable lodgings if you're planning to stay overnight here.

At the **Hotel Sol e Sêrra,** 7320 Castelo de Vide (tel. 045/913-01), the building's modern lines contrast with the antique architecture of the town surrounding it. It lies near the center within a white stucco façade pierced with evenly spaced rows of recessed loggias like the kind you find on the Mediterranean. Built in 1983, the hotel contains 50 reasonably comfortable bedrooms. Each of these offers a private bath, radio, and phone, and many also open onto private balconies. Singles rent for 4,500$ ($29.25) daily, with doubles going for 7,000$ ($45.50). A fixed-price meal in the dining room goes for 1,500$ ($9.75).

Estalagem Jardim and **Estalagem S. Paulo,** 6 Rua Sequeiro Sameiro, 7320 Castelo de Vide (tel. 045/912-17), combine to offer the visitor a total of 40 simply furnished but clean bedrooms. The rates, which include a continental breakfast, are 4,000$ ($26) daily in a single, 5,000$ ($32.50) in a double. The estalagem complex also has one of the best restaurants in town, charging from 2,000$ ($13) for a regional meal with wine. Food is served daily from 12:30 to 2:30 p.m. and 7:30 to 9:30 p.m. Guests can swim in the pool or play squash on the courts of the complex.

Dom Pedro V, Praça Dom Pedro V (tel. 912-36). It is generally conceded that this restaurant, outside the hotels, is the best independent eatery in town. In air-conditioned comfort, some 80 guests can select from a varied menu of regional dishes with good and inexpensively priced wines. Meals cost from 2,000$ ($13). Service is daily except Monday from 12:30 to 3:30 p.m. and 7:30 to 10:30 p.m. The restaurant also has a bar and disco.

13. Abrantes

After passing a dramatic view of the Tagus at Rodão, you arrive at Abrantes in central Portugal. The location is 88 miles from Lisbon, and 38 miles from Santarém. A town of whitewashed stone, it lies on the bank of the Tagus. The river must be crossed again to gain entrance to the town. Here, you see the ruins of a Roman bridge extending into the water.

High on a hill, the old **fortress** was rebuilt during the reign of King Dinis. It was already dilapidated by the beginning of the 19th century. To reach the fortifications, you must go through a labryinth of narrow streets. Once at its belvedere, a panoramic view of the valley, mountains, and foothills unfolds.

There's a small **museum** in the Church of Santa Maria, already ancient when it was rebuilt in the 15th century. Here you can see a 15th-century statue of the Virgin and Child on the high altar. Of some interest is the 16th-century carving in stone of the Trinity. The museum is open from 10 a.m. to 12:30 p.m. and 2 to 5 p.m. daily except Monday and holidays. No admission is charged.

FOOD AND LODGING

Standing on a plateau above the town, **Hotel de Turismo,** Largo de Santo António, 2200 Abrantes (tel. 041/212-61), overlooks the town on one side and the castle and mountains on the other. It's a pink-stucco concrete building, somewhat resembling an elementary school. A total of 40 comfortable bedrooms is offered, each with private bath. Singles rent for 5,500$ ($37.75) daily and doubles for 6,500$ ($42.25). The dining room is panoramic, serving from 12:30 to 3 p.m. and 7:30 to 10 p.m. Typical dishes served here are gazpacho, cannelloni Piedmont, and Portuguese loin of pork, perhaps a mixed grill on a brochette. A complete meal is offered for 1,800$ ($11.70) to 2,200$ ($14.30). An Olympic-size swimming pool belonging to the town is near the hotel.

Pelicano, Rua Nossa Senhora Conceição (tel. 223-17), is one of the best bets for good and low-cost regional cookery. Seating nearly 50 diners, it serves daily except Thursday from noon to 3 p.m. and 7 to 10:30 p.m. In air-conditioned comfort but fairly modest decor guests can enjoy meals for 1,500$ ($9.75). Service is polite and efficient.

Cristina, Rio de Moinhos (tel. 041/981-77), is one of the largest restaurants in town, offering service to more than 200 diners if need be. It is open daily from noon to 3 p.m. and 7 to 10:30 p.m. (closed Monday). Meals cost from 1,500$ ($9.75) to 1,800$ ($11.70) and include a fine array of fresh fish and meat dishes and good regional wines.

14. Tomar

Divided by the Nabão River, historic Tomar lies 85 miles from Lisbon, 40 miles from Santarém. Tomar was integrally bound to the fate of the notorious quasi-religious order of the Knights Templar. In the 12th century these powerful and wealthy monks established the beginnings of the **Convento de Cristo** (Convent of

Christ) (tel. 334-81) on a tree-studded hill overlooking the town. Originally a monastery, it evolved into a kind of grand headquarters for the Templars. These knights, who swore a vow of chastity, had fought ferociously at Santarém against the Moors. As a result of their growing military might, they built a massive walled castle at Tomar in 1160. The ruins, especially the walls, can be seen today.

By 1314 the pope was urged to suppress their power, as they had made many enemies, and their great riches were coveted by others. King Dinis allowed them to regroup their forces under the new aegis of the Order of Christ. Henry the Navigator became the most famous of the grand masters, using much of their money to subsidize his explorations.

From its inception the monastery underwent five centuries of inspired builders, including Manuel I (the Fortunate). It also saw its destroyers, notably the overzealous troops of Napoleon in 1810 who turned it into a barracks. What remains on the top of the hill, however, is one of Portugal's most brilliant architectural accomplishments.

The portal of the Templars Church is in the Manueline style, depicting everything from leaves to chubby cherubs. Inside, you enter an octagonal church with eight columns, said to have been modeled after the Temple of the Holy Sepulchre at Jerusalem. The effect is like a mosque, linking Christian with Muslim culture, as in Córdoba's Mezquita. Howard La Fay called it "a muted echo of Byzantium in scarlet and dull gold." The damage done by the French troops is much in evidence. On the other side, the church is in the Manueline style with rosettes. Throughout you'll see the insignia of the Templars.

The monastery embraces eight cloisters in a variety of styles. The most notable one, a two-tiered structure built in 1557 by Diogo de Torralva, exhibits perfect symmetry, the almost severe academic use of the classical form that distinguishes the Palladian school. A guide will also take you on a brief tour of a dormitory where the monks lived in cells.

The monastery possesses some of the greatest Manueline stonework. An example is the grotesque west window of the Chapter House. At first, you may be confused by the forms emanating from the window; but a closer inspection reveals a meticulous symbolic and literal depiction of Portugal's sea lore and power. Knots and ropes, mariners and the tools of their craft, silken sails wafting in stone, re-created coral seascapes, all delicately interwoven in this chef d'oeuvre of the whole movement.

The monastery is open from 9:30 a.m. to 12:30 p.m. and 2 to 6 p.m. (to 5 p.m. off-season). Admission is 100$ (65¢).

Tomar has many other sights of interest. On the way up the hill, you can stop off at the **Chapel of Our Lady of Conception,** crowned by small cupolas and jutting out over the town. Reached via an avenue of trees, it was built in the Renaissance style in the mid-16th century, and its interior is a forest of white Corinthian pillars.

In the heart of town, the **Church of St. John the Baptist** opens onto the Praça da República, built by Manuel I, with black and white diamond mosaics. Dating from the 15th century, the church contains a white-and-gold baroque altar (a chapel to the right is faced with antique tiles). In and around the church are the narrow cobblestone streets of Tomar, where shops sell dried codfish, and wrought-iron balconies are hung with bird cages and flower pots.

FOOD AND LODGING

The modern four-story 84-room **Hotel dos Templários,** 2300 Tomar (tel. 049/321-21) seems incongruously placed in such a small town. Pooling their know-how, in 1967 five local businessmen created this five-floor structure set on the banks of the river. Facilities include wide sun terraces, a riverside swimming pool fed by a fountain, a tennis court, even a greenhouse.

The interior is spacious, including the lounges. There is a terrace-view dining room. The bedrooms are suitable, containing private baths, plus air conditioning and heating. In high season (April 1 to October 31) doubles rent for as little as 9,000$ ($58.50) daily. Singles go for 6,300$ ($40.95). Children up to 8 years old are accommodated in their parents' room for half price. Most guests have breakfast either in their room or in a sunny salon overlooking the river. In the evening they gather around the huge living room fireplace for drinks. If you're passing through, you can stop in for a table d'hôte luncheon or dinner for 2,000$ ($13) and up. Hours are daily from 1 to 2:30 p.m. and 8 to 9:30 p.m.

Hotel Residencial Trovador, Rua Dr. Joaquim Ribeiro, 2300 Tomar (tel. 049/315-67). Only an inspection of its bedrooms will reveal the high value of a stopover here. Each is outfitted with conservatively patterned wallpaper, a tile bath, TV, phone, and lots of well-scrubbed comfort. With a continental breakfast included, singles cost 6,000$ ($39) daily and doubles from 7,000$ ($45.50) to 8,000$ ($52). One room suitable for up to five occupants rents for 10,500$ ($68.25). Built in 1982 by the polite family who still own it today, the hotel contains 30 bedrooms, a basement bar with disco music, and a breakfast-only policy that most visitors find appealing. The location is near the commercial center of town in a neighborhood of apartment buildings.

Bella Vista, corner Rua Marquês de Pombal and Rua Ronte do Choupo (tel. 328-70), is, as its name indicates, a restaurant with a pretty view of the town and a small canal. You can dine outside, under a bower, or in rustic dining rooms decorated with plates, flowers, plants, and racks to hang your hat on. Meals are simple but plentiful, the prices low. Usually the cook makes a fresh pot of vegetable soup every day. For your main course, the fare includes fried trout or sole, always pork chops with potatoes. About the only exotic item you'll find is chicken curry with rice. Round off your meal with some of the local cheese. Everybody who dines here always orders a carafe of the local wine. Count on spending from 2,000$ ($13) for your meal. Hours are noon to 3 p.m. and 7 to 9:30 p.m.; closed Tuesday and in November.

In the Environs

Pousada de São Pedro, Castelo de Bode, 2300 Tomar (tel. 049/381-59). When it was built in the 1950s, it was used to house teams of engineers working on the nearby dam at Castelo de Bode. After the dam was completed in 1970, the government converted it into one of the country's most unusual pousadas. From the flagstone-covered terrace in back you get a closeup view of Portugal's version of Hoover Dam. It curves gracefully against a wall of water, upon which local residents sail, swim, and sun themselves.

The pousada has a scattering of Portuguese antiques, some of them ecclesiastical, in its stone-trimmed hallways. These corridors lead to 16 unpretentious bedrooms, each with private bath. They cost 9,800$ ($63.70) daily in a double, 8,700$ ($56.55) in a single, with a continental breakfast included. The public rooms are more alluring than the bedrooms. The breeze-filled bar near the terrace is decorated a lot like an elegant private living room, with well-upholstered sofas and a fireplace. The pousada serves some of the best food in the area, both international and regional specialties, with meals costing from 2,300$ ($14.95). Hours of service are daily from 12:30 to 2:30 p.m. and 7:30 to 9:30 p.m. The pousada is between Tomar and Constância. The exact location is nine miles southeast of Tomar.

Estalagem Vale da Ursa, 6100 Cernache do Bonjardim (tel. 074/675-11), lies 20 miles from the town of Tomar, 35 miles from the shrine of Fátima, and 100 miles north of Lisbon. Situated near the bridge, over the lake, Castelo do Bode, the hotel is a tranquil choice, where you can use such facilities as a swimming pool and tennis courts and also fish from the lake's edge. It offers 12 pleasantly furnished bedrooms, each with bath and private terrace overlooking the lake. Singles rent for 4,200$ ($27.30) to 5,500$ ($35.75) daily, depending on the season, and doubles for 5,200$ ($33.80) to 8,200$ ($53.30). The kitchen offers an international as well as a regional cuisine, with meals costing from 1,500$ ($9.75).

15. Santarém

The Portuguese use the words "noble" or "Gothic" in describing this town, 49 miles north of Lisbon. The garrison here, set on a spur of land overlooking the river, has always been a key fortification. Afonso Henriques, the country's first king, drove out the Moors in 1147, and ordered the construction of the Cistercian monastery at Alcobaça to commemorate that feat.

Santarém still overlooks the low-lying lands devoted to cattle, vineyards, olive groves, even corn. It seems as if the whole of Ribatejo is spread out before one's eyes from the vantage point of the **Portas do Sol** (the Gates of the Sun), a park of tile fountains, flowering plants and bushes, statuary, red benches, and globe lamps. At times the river is so shallow that sandy islets appear; at other moments, it overflows its banks. The gardens are reached by heading out the Avenida 5 de Outubro.

One of the main squares is **Praça de Sá da Bandeira,** lying right off the Garden of the Republic. Opening onto the largo is the **College of the Patriarchal See,** whose multiwindowed, niched, and statuary-studded façade takes up an entire side of the plaza. Inside, the main altar is decorated with marble and alabaster inlays, and flanked by four serpentine columns. Alabaster statues of saints, azulejos, and a baroque trompe l'oeil ceiling add to the lushness. Across the way from the seminary (entrance at the end of the Rua Cidade da Covilha) sits the octagonal, domed **Chapel of Our Lady of Pity,** whose neoclassic style is enhanced by trompe l'oeil paintings.

One of the town's most interesting churches, **São João de Alporão,** right off the Rua São Martinho, en route to the Portas do Sol, has been converted into an **Archeological Museum.** Built in the Romanesque-Gothic style, probably in the 12th century, it is graced with a rose window and multiple-arched doorway. Inside is the elaborate tomb of Dom Duarte de Menezes, built by his wife after he died at the hands of the Moors. So badly mutilated was the body that the remains consisted of a lone tooth. The collection of Roman sarcophagi is more interesting. The museum is open from 10 a.m. to noon and 2 to 5 p.m. daily except Monday.

Nearby, the Gothic **Church of Graça,** dating from 1380, has a rose window carved from a single stone. At the corner of Calçada da Graça and the Rua Vila de Belmonte, it has been completely restored and contains some carved tombs, and an architecture characterized by simple arches.

FOOD AND LODGING

Rated second class, **Hotel Abidis,** 4 Rua Fuilherme de Azevedo, 2000 Santarém (tel. 043/220-17), is a place at which to order meals or enjoy a night's sleep. Although the reception area is small, the bedrooms are personalized, with old-style furnishings and matching fabrics at the windows, on the beds, and at the dressing tables. Rates depend on the plumbing and the season: singles cost 2,000$ ($13) to 3,400$ ($22.10) daily, and doubles go for 3,400$ ($22.10) to 5,650$ ($36.75).

The dining room is decorated in the Ribatejo tavern style. Noted for its attentive service and fine cuisine, it offers a table d'hôte luncheon or dinner for 2,500$ ($16.25) and up. A typical meal is likely to include a bowl of onion soup, followed by turbot cooked with pimiento rice, a main course of roast kid, a carafe of good wine, cheese, and fresh fruit. The setting is very attractive: a blue and white tile dado, ox-yoke chandeliers, and provincial chairs.

You might also seek accommodations at the **Victoria,** 21 Rua 2 Visconde de Santarém, 2000 Santarém (tel. 043/225-73), which has more than a dozen simply furnished rooms rented at modest prices: 4,000$ ($26) daily in a single and 5,000$ ($32.50) in a double. The Victoria doesn't have a restaurant, but a continental breakfast is included in the tariffs.

Portas do Sol, Jardim das Portas do Sol (tel. 295-20), offers the most scenic location in a garden. Try for a terrace table opening onto a panoramic view. One of the best restaurants in Santarém, it serves meals, costing from 2,000$ ($13), from 12:30 to 3 p.m. and 7:30 to 10 p.m. It is closed on Sunday night and all day Monday. Good regional cookery and wines are offered and the place is fairly intimate, holding only about three dozen diners.

---

16. Vila Franca de Xira

Vila Franca de Xira is the Pamplona of Portugal. Twice a year the frenzied community ordeal of the *festa brava,* the running of the bulls, is staged. The Red Waistcoat is held the first week of July, and the Annual Fair the first week of October. Bullfights are also held at these events. In the countryside around Vila Franca, 20 miles north of Lisbon, are pasturelands that are breeding grounds for the black bulls. There's a modern speedway to take you there.

At the festivals, a herd of black bulls, fresh and primed for the rings of Lisbon or Cascais, are let loose in the main street of town. With the smaller side streets heavily barricaded, the *corrida* is ready to begin. When the *campinos* (Ribatejo cowboys with their traditional stocking caps) first turn the bulls loose in the streets, the animals appear bewildered and confused.

The crowds hoot and holler, trying to make the massive bulls break rank. When one inevitably does, melees and frantic dashes follow, with occasional displays on the part of some young aspirant matador of virtuosity with the cape. The cape, incidentally, is likely to be an old piece of sack cloth or a quilt. The bulls are rarely intimidated by those who taunt them. Many a hopeful matador has been pulled by his arms to the safety of a spectator-filled wrought-iron balcony. Numerous injuries result, and the hospital staff is reinforced by recruits from Lisbon.

Attacked by many who consider it barbaric, the pagan custom is still well-preserved on the streets of Vila Franca de Xira on at least two occasions of the year.

The **Museu Etnografico de Vila Franca de Xira** (Ethnographic Museum of the Arenas) has some sculptures and pictures pertaining to the local region and to the art of bullfighting, as well as traditional 19th-century costumes of cattle breeders, fishermen, and peasants. It's open daily except Monday and holidays from 10 a.m. to 12:30 p.m. and 2 to 6 p.m.

Two miles north, along a road called António Lucio Baptista that passes under the motorway, watch for **Monte Gordo Belvedere** (Miradouro), up a hill between two windmills. From that spot, you have a panoramic view of hills, vineyards, quintas, and the plain of Ribatejo.

FOOD AND LODGING

The most desirable place to stay is the **Quinta São Jorge,** Estrada de Monte Gordo, 2600 Vila Franca de Xira (tel. 063/221-43), just over a mile from Vila Franca de Xira. The road leading to this enclosed quinta will take you around some hairpin turns and over tortuous dirt roads. Finally you'll arrive in front of a forbidding-looking iron gate. Behind this lies a sprawling compound of impressively proportioned buildings, some of them pink, others buff in color. They look as if they might have served as anything from a monastery to a prosperous but now attractively faded seat of a large Portuguese country estate. Unless the gate is open, you'll have to ring a hand-pulled bell to alert the staff to your arrival. Guests enjoy use of the quinta's luxurious living rooms. There are four double rooms and three singles, each with private bath. Doubles rent for 10,000$ ($65) daily, and singles go for 6,000$ ($39). Residents of the quinta can order dinner, costing from 1,500$ ($9.75) per person. There is a swimming pool, plus a riding ring.

In town, the best restaurant is **O Redondel,** Praça de Touros (tel. 229-73), along the Estrada de Lisbon (the road to Lisbon). At the bullring, it is filled to over-flowing on the days of a fight, but otherwise it's more subdued. The cookery is regional, and it's washed down with plenty of local wines. There's a bar, and some 70 patrons can enjoy the air conditioning. The restaurant serves daily except Monday from noon to 3 p.m. and 7 to 10 p.m., with meals costing 1,500$ ($9.75) and up. The staff takes a vacation for part of August.

COIMBRA AND THE BEIRAS

Fortress towns and feudal castles . . . undulating plains . . . steep wine-producing slopes . . . the mountain blocks of Estrêla . . . pine woods and sand dunes . . . golden beaches . . . Roman ruins . . . a former royal forest . . . salt marshes . . . spas with curative springs . . . poplar-lined river banks . . . and water wheels sending rainbow-hued spray into the air.

To many observers, the three provinces of the Beiras, encompassing the university city of **Coimbra,** are the quintessence of Portugal. *Beira* is a Portuguese word meaning edge or border. The trio of provinces includes **Beira Litoral** (coastal), **Beira Baixa** (low), and **Beira Alta** (high).

Embraced in the region is the **Sêrra da Estrêla,** Portugal's highest land mass and haven for skiers in winter, cool retreat in summer. The Mondego River, the main stream of the region, is navigable, and the only major artery in Portugal that has its source within the boundaries of the country.

The granite soil produced by the great range of sêrras blankets the rocky slopes of the Dão and Mondego River valleys and is responsible for the wine of the region: the ruby red or lemon-colored Dão.

The Beiras are a subtle land, a sort of Portugal in miniature.

---

1. Leiria

About 20 miles from Alcobaça, on the road to Coimbra, the town of Leiria rests on the banks of the Liz and spreads casually over the surrounding hills. From any point you can see the great **Castle of Leiria** (Castelo de Leiria), once occupied by Dinis, the poet king, and his wife, called Saint Isabella. Tower-topped and imposing still, it has been extensively restored.

The castle church, as well as the palace, is pure Gothic. From an arched balcony, the city and its surroundings can be viewed. The castle lies on the summit of a volcanic outcrop. It was practically inaccessible to invaders. The Moors had their defense redoubt on this hill while they were taking possession of the major part of the Iberian Peninsula. The fortress was first taken for Portugal by its first king, Afonso Henriques, in the 12th century, and was twice recovered by him after the Moors had retaken it, the last recovery being definitive.

To reach the castle, you may take either a car or a bus, right to the front door. On the way to the castle, you might also visit **St. Peter's Church,** dating from the 12th century. The fortress is open from 9 a.m. to 7 p.m. April to October. During other months it's open from 9 a.m. to 6 p.m. Admission is 40$ (25¢).

Around Leiria is one of the oldest state forests in the world. In about 1300 Dinis began the systematic planting of the **Pinhal do Rei,** with trees brought from the Landes area in France. He hoped to curb the spread of sand dunes, which ocean gusts were extending deep into the heartland. The forest, still maintained today, provided timber used to build the caravels to explore the Sea of Darkness.

Many motorists find Leiria a convenient stopping point for the night.

WHERE TO STAY

An 11-story, well-styled hostelry, **Hotel Eurosol,** Rua D. José Alves Correia da Silva, 2400 Leiria (tel. 044/241-01), competes in position with the stone castle crowning the opposite hill. All 92 bedrooms offer views, and rank successfully with any first-class hotel in the north. They are smartly simple, making use of built-in headboards and wardrobe walls of wood paneling. All of them contain private baths in tile. In a single room, the half-board rate is 7,200$ ($46.80) daily; in a double, 11,600$ ($75.40). Taxes and service are included.

The hotel is the social hub of Leiria, attracting business people to its rooftop lounge bar and dining room. Individual lunches or dinners cost 1,800$ ($11.70) on the four-course table d'hôte. Lighter meals are offered in an adjoining snackbar. The restaurant entrance lounge is decorated with a contemporary wall hanging, depicting the story of the building of the castle. Time your visit to enjoy a dip in the open-air swimming pool, with its tile terrace. There's a lower-level boîte for after-dinner diversions.

Residencial São Francisco, 26 Rua São Francisco, 2400 Leiria (tel. 044/251-42), lies on the top floor of a ten-story building in the center of town, a short walk from the river. Some of the bedrooms offer pleasant views of Leiria. Each is furnished with private bath, radio, phone, patterned wallpaper, and a collection of leatherette furniture. The 18 well-maintained bedrooms rent for 5,500$ ($35.75) daily in a single, rising to 7,000$ ($45.50) in a double. A cubbyhole bar in one of the public rooms serves drinks; but no meals, other than the continental breakfast included in the rates, are served.

Ramalhete Residencial, 30 Rua Dr. Correia Mateus, 2400 Leiria (tel. 044/268-22). Whoever decorated this pleasant hotel did so with a sense of hospitality and good taste. Many guests claim that their favorite retreat within the establishment is inside the wood-paneled bar, where subtle lighting from downward-directed wall sconces give an added coziness to the comfortable leather-covered chairs and partially mirrored ceiling. A reading room, with an occasionally used card table, provides a cozy environment for reading or quiet conversation. The 28 comfortable bedrooms each contain a private bath, TV, and simple furnishings. Singles cost from 4,200$ ($27.30) daily, and doubles pay 5,200$ ($33.80), including a continental breakfast. No other meals are served at this second-floor inn.

Hotel São Luis, Rua Henrique Sommer, 2400 Leiria (tel. 044/250-41), is one of the best budget accommodations in Leiria. Ranked only two stars by the government, it is one of the newest hotels in town, and it's spotlessly maintained. Some of the accommodations are quite spacious, with a private bath and balcony. You don't get a lot of frills here, but you do get comfort and convenience along with a good price: 3,500$ ($22.75) in a single, 4,750$ ($30.90) in a double. A good breakfast, including ham and fresh fruit along with juice and freshly baked bread, is included in the tariffs quoted. Breakfast, incidentally, is the only meal served.

WHERE TO DINE

Considered the best independent restaurant in Leiria, the **Reis,** 17 Rua Wenceslau de Morais (tel. 248-34), is a fairly large place, seating 120, with faithful devotees who like both its food and its inexpensive prices. The chef specializes in grills, along with good regional fare such as hearty soups, fresh fish from the sea, and meats. Meals, costing from 1,800$ ($11.70), are served daily from noon to 3 p.m. and 7 to 10 p.m. In winter, a fireplace makes the Reis more inviting. It is closed on Saturday and holidays.

2. São Pedro de Moel

If you care to relax before plunging into the Coimbra heartlands, São Pedro de Moel is an undiscovered place. The bracing Atlantic breezes pervade the little village, perched on a cliff above the water. New villas have sprung up, yet the old quarter retains it cobblestoned streets.

The scattered rocks offshore create controlled beach conditions, rolling breakers and rippling surf. The beaches are white and sandy, running up to the village's gray-walled ramparts. Paths border the cliffside, leading to the coastal lighthouse and a panoramic view. Centuries ago this was a small natural seaport, set between King Dinis's verdant pine forest and the Atlantic. Today fishermen and divers find ideal conditions here, with a variety of fish to be caught.

The emerging resort is 14 miles west of Leiria and can be reached via a six-mile drive toward the sea from the glass-manufacturing center at Marinha Grande. Along the way you'll pass donkeys laden with twigs, the scent of pine mingling with salt air.

FOOD AND LODGING

On a palisade above the beach at the residential edge of the village, **Hotel Mar e Sol,** Avenida Sa Melo, São Pedro de Moel, 2430 Marinha Grande (tel. 044/591-82), is a stark-white, three-story, modern hostelry. Its vantage point gives about half of its 42 bedrooms views overlooking the ocean. It's for sun-and-sea addicts only, as there are no extravagant lounge facilities and only a minimum-size dining room. The compact bedrooms, all with private bath, are simply furnished with a mixture of contemporary and traditional pieces. The cost for two people is 7,000$ ($45.50) daily. Singles pay from 6,000$ ($39). This second-class hotel is immaculate and comfortable.

Hotel de São Pedro, Rua Adolfo Leitao, São Pedro de Moel, 2430 Marinha Grande (tel. 044/591-20), is another desirable place to stay. It is larger than the Mar e Sol, containing a total of 53 simply but comfortably furnished bedrooms. Singles rent for 6,000$ ($39) daily, while doubles cost 7,500$ ($48.75). The modern hotel has provided private baths for all its rooms. You can also visit just for a meal, paying from 1,800$ ($11.70). The hotel is located between the ocean and the pine woods named after King Dinis.

O Pai dos Frangos, Praia Velha, 2430 Marinha Grande (tel. 044/591-58), does more than provide chicken on its menu, as its name suggests. Open all year, it is a good selection for cozinha Portuguesa. The chef does many savory fish dishes, none more notable than arroz de marisco (shellfish rice) and a bubbling caldeirada. Meals cost from 1,800$ ($11.70) to 2,000$ ($13), including wine of the region and are served daily except Monday from noon to 10 p.m. The restaurant is large, seating 200 patrons, who enjoy the panoramic ocean view.

3. Figueira da Foz

Old villas on the sea compete with apartment houses. On the north side at the Beach of Brightness, Portuguese families frolic, the wealthier ones hitting the gambling casino at night. Back in the Old Town fishermen dry cod in the sun. Others make their living by reclaiming salt from the marshes, and having their wives scoop it up and carry it back to town in wicker baskets on their heads.

At the mouth of the Mondego River, Figueira da Foz literally means Fig Tree at the Mouth of the River. How it got that name is long forgotten. North of Cascais and Estoril, Fig Tree is the best-known and oldest resort along the Atlantic coastline of Iberia. Aside from its climate (city fathers claim that the sun shines 2,772 hours annually), the most outstanding feature is the town's golden sandy beach, stretching for more than two miles.

Those who don't like the beach can swim in a pool sandwiched between the Grande Hotel da Figueira and the Estalagem da Piscina-Praia on the main esplanade. Should the beach crowds get you down, you can always go for a trek into the **Sêrra da Boa Viagem,** a range of hills whose summit is a favorite vantage point for photographers and sightseers.

Most visitors don't come to Figueira to look at museums, but there is one exceptional one, the **Casa do Paço,** 4 Largo Prof. Vitor Guerra (tel. 221-59), the head office of the Associação Comercial e Industrial, a one-minute walk from the post office and esplanade. It contains one of the world's greatest collections of Delft tiles, numbering almost 7,000 and most often depicting warriors with gaudy plumage (some blowing trumpets). The puce and blue tiles are detailed and subtly executed. The casa was the palace of Conde Bispo de Coimbra, D. João de Melo, who came here in the last century when Figueira was frequented by royalty, like San Sebastian in Spain. The tiles may be viewed from 9:30 a.m. to 12:30 p.m. and 2 to 5 p.m. daily (no admission is charged).

Bullfights are popular in season. The old-style bullring operates from mid-July to September.

Grand Casino Peninsular, 54 Rua Bernardo Lopes (tel. 220-41). It is open from 3 p.m. to 3 a.m. daily from May to October, featuring shows, dancing, a nightclub, and, of course, gambling salons. Admission to the games rooms is 800$ ($5.20), and a passport is required.

Just two miles north of Figueira, bypassed by new construction and sitting placidly on a ridge near the sea, is **Buarcos,** a fishing village far removed from casinos and beaches. From the central square to the stone sea walls, it is pure and unspoiled.

Cod dries in wire racks in the sun, streets faintly move with activity, and native women with loaded baskets on their heads, arms akimbo, look out with bright eyes from under dark scarfs.

Figueira lies 80 miles south of Porto, 125 miles north of Lisbon, and 25 miles west of Coimbra. It is well supplied with accommodations.

WHERE TO STAY

The leading choice is **Grande Hotel da Figueira,** Avenida 25 de Abril, 3080 Figueira da Foz (tel. 033/221-46), lying on the seafront promenade overlooking the ocean. Just walk across the esplanade and you have a clean sandy beach at your disposal. Or, as a guest of the hotel, you have free entrance to the adjoining Olympic-size saltwater swimming pool. The interior of the hotel is a world of marble and glass, more like a big city hotel than a resort accommodation. A few of the rooms on the sea have glass-enclosed balconies. Most rooms have open balconies. In all, 91 bedrooms are rented, each with private bath, TV, radio, and phone. In high season, two persons pay from 10,600$ ($68.90) to 12,000$ ($78) daily, with singles costing from 7,000$ ($45.50) to 7,650$ ($49.75). Other facilities include an à la carte restaurant, a piano bar, and a table games room. The hotel is open all year.

Hotel Internacional, 20 Avenida da Liberdade, 3080 Figueira da Foz (tel. 033/220-41), lies on a quiet street bordered by trees in the vicinity of the beach and near the Casino and shopping area. This three-star hotel with 50 well-furnished bedrooms offers a clean and contemporary kind of comfort to both business people and vacationers alike. In high season, singles rent for 5,500$ ($35.75) to 8,000$ ($52) daily, with doubles costing 7,500$ ($48.75) to 8,500$ ($55.25). There's a swimming pool nearby for guests who prefer not to go to the beach. The hotel receives guests all year.

Aparthotel Atlantico, Avenida 25 de Abril, 3080 Figueira da Foz (tel. 033/240-45), is a tower-like structure rising aside the Grande Hotel, with panoramic views over the ocean, the River Mondego, and the beach. Seventy fully equipped apartments are rented, each with living room, bedroom, full bath, kitchenette, phone, and radio. In high season, two persons in an apartment pay from 7,500$ ($48.75) to 8,200$ ($53.30) daily. Two to four guests can rent an apartment on a daily basis for 7,700$ ($50.05) to 12,000$ ($78). Guests often book in here for a week, shopping for provisions in the nearby supermarket and walking across the busy street to the wide sandy beach. Guests are admitted free to the Olympic-sized swimming pool nearby.

Estalagem da Piscina, 7 Rua Santa Catarina, 3080 Figueira da Foz (tel. 033/224-20). This "inn of the swimming pool" is a bargain for the resort. An intimate and small hotel, it offers 20 comfortable bedrooms, each with private bath and balcony opening onto the swimming pool and sea. The swimming pool area includes a restaurant and snack bar. In high season, doubles range from 8,250$ ($53.65) to 9,200$ ($59.80) daily. The inn is open only from May to October.

Costa de Prata, 1 Esplanada Silva Guimarães, 3080 Figueira da Foz (tel. 033/266-10), is a pleasant 71-room hotel built on a piazza that was terraced above the traffic-clogged beachside road running through town. Its peaceful but central location is one of its strongest points. It rises seven stories above the concrete in a series of beige and white balconies. There's no restaurant, but good drinks are served in the wood-paneled lobby bar. The well-furnished bedrooms each contain a private bath, costing from 7,500$ ($48.75) daily in a double and from 6,000$ ($39) in a single, with a continental breakfast included.

WHERE TO DINE

People come to the **Restaurante Tubarão,** Avenida 25 de Abril (tel. 234-45), for the food, not the decor. You dine in a large room filled with cloth-covered tables and cooled by revolving ceiling fans. There is a sweeping view of the beach across the esplanade. Some of the tables spill onto the sidewalk, yet because of pedestrian traffic there they are often empty. A café in an adjoining room serves drinks throughout the day and night. A battery of hurried waiters will serve you full meals, costing from 1,800$ ($11.70). Specialties include gambas à la plancha (grilled shrimp), grilled codfish, shellfish-flavored rice, seafood soup, and a variety of crab, lobster, and shrimp, priced by weight. Hours are daily from noon to 4 p.m. and 7 to 11 p.m.

Restaurante Julio, 30 Rua Dr. Francisco Dinis (tel. 279-92). The unprepossessing building that contains this establishment lies in the old part of town, away from the beach. However, it is still eagerly sought out by many visitors because of its reputation for serving some of the best and most reasonably priced viands in the resort. Full meals cost from 1,800$ ($11.70) and might include stuffed squid, cod casserole, stuffed veal, tripe with beans, rabbit, and young goatmeat. Open daily from noon to 3 p.m. and 7 to 10 p.m.

FOOD AND LODGING IN BUARCOS

A *restaurant avec chambres,* **Restaurante-Pensão Teimoso,** Estrada do Cabo Mondego, 3080 Figueira da Foz (tel. 033/227-85), is a regional fish restaurant right on the shore, with a wing of modern rooms reserved for overnight guests. The *Teimoso* (a Portuguese word meaning stubborn or mulish) is family operated. This place started many years ago with a simple waterfront restaurant. As business grew, the owner added more rooms. He attracts visitors and locals alike who know of his bountiful meals: his shellfish soup, regional dishes such as fresh bass baked in a tomato sauce, roast kid, and suckling pig. Clams are served in a savory broth, and the roast veal is reliable. Desserts are not spectacular. Expect to spend from 1,500$ ($9.75) to 1,800$ ($11.70). The decor of the dining room is barren, but the room has a fine view of the water. Food is served daily from noon to 3:30 p.m. and 7:30 to 10:30 p.m.

There are 14 rooms, all with private bath. Tariffs for doubles range from 3,000$ ($19.50) to 4,000$ ($26) daily. Some of the newer rooms, prettily decorated and equipped with private sun terraces overlooking the ocean, may go a little higher. It's hard to get in from July through September, so make reservations.

More charming, and a half mile closer to town, is the **Tamargueira,** Estrada do Cabo Mondego, Buarcos, 3080 Figueira da Foz (tel. 033/225-14), where you dine in an oval-shaped room with chandeliers made of ships' steering wheels. There's a fireplace at one end of the room, and the walls are decorated with typical plates and fishermen's nets. In good weather you can sit on the spacious terrace, from which you have a view of the sea. Menu specialties are caldeirada a mista a pescador, arroz de mariscos (rice with shellfish), costela à Tamargueira, feijoada à Beirão. You can finish with a mousse or custard. Expect to pay from 1,800$ ($11.70) to 2,500$ ($16.25) for a meal, which can be served anytime from 8 a.m. to 1 a.m. daily. There are also 20 rooms available, furnished in simple New England style, all with baths. Doubles cost 7,500$ ($48.75) daily, and singles go for 7,000$ ($45.50).

MONTEMOR-O-VELHO

Between Figueira da Foz and Coimbra, overlooking the fertile Mondego River valley, is the historic village of Montemor the Old. Dating from the 8th century, the ruins of the **Castle of Montemor-o-Velho** (tel. 683-80), built by the Moors, crown the hilltop. The main road runs scenically past villas, shrines, high walls, and churches. Narrow cobblestone streets will lead you to the restored walls and ramparts, from which there is a fine vista of the valley.

The castle became a royal palace under Sancho I in the 12th century, and stood until it was destroyed by the French during the first invasion by Napoleon. It witnessed many moments in Portuguese history—perhaps the most infamous being when Afonso IV sanctioned (according to historian Pero Coelho) the plot to kill Inês de Castro, mistress of the king's son. The castle is a moving medieval setting, especially when sparrows play in the air over its time-worn stones. It is open for visitors from 10 a.m. to 12:30 p.m. and 2 to 5 p.m. daily except Monday. Admission is free.

---

4. Coimbra

Black-caped students strumming guitars and singing a serenade of their own fado hilario on narrow cobblestone streets . . . tattered hems of fraying gowns that speak of heartbreak (some say conquest) . . . colored ribbons flying from the black student garb, signifying a young man's destined profession (for example, violet for pharmacy) . . . and a stream that "flows with the blood of the tortured Inês de Castro," who was crowned queen of Portugal after her death. Coimbra, the most romantic city in Portugal, was the inspiration for the popular song, "April in Portugal." On the weather-washed right bank of the muddy Mondego, Coimbra is also the educational center of the country, its university having been founded at Lisbon in 1290.

The students of Coimbra band together in republics, usually renting cramped buildings in the old quarter, some up many flights of winding stairs. The republic isn't very democratic, run as it is on a strict seniority basis. A typical evening's bill of fare in a republic is likely to include grilled sardines, bread, and a glass of wine.

An invitation to one of these student dormitories will give you an insight into Coimbra rarely experienced by the foreign visitor. If you get an invitation, I hope the evening will be capped by the students presenting you with a fado concert. To show your gratitude, if you should happen onto an invitation, cigarettes are much appreciated.

HOTELS

Unfortunately, Coimbra is far better supplied with attractions than it is with hotels and restaurants. But there are the following recommendations.

Don Luís, Quinta da Verzea, 3000 Coimbra (tel. 039/84-15-10). Built in 1989, this is the newest and most stylish hotel in the Coimbra area. About half a mile south of the city, it lies on the road heading toward Lisbon. It has a pleasing modern design, brown marble floors, a restaurant, and 100 bedrooms. Each of these contains a private bath, phone, mini-bar, and TV. Classified as a three-star hotel, it contains amenities that might conceivably justify a four-star rating. In high season, singles cost 8,500$ ($55.25) daily, doubles 9,500$ ($61.75), and triples 11,500$ ($74.75).

Hotel Bragança, 10 Largo das Ameias, 3000 Coimbra (tel. 039/221-71), is a bandbox five-floor hotel, built next door to the railway station. Primarily catering to business people, it does a thriving trade in the summer season. A few of its bedrooms open onto balconies overlooking the main road. All of the 83 units contain private baths; the furnishings are utilitarian. The rooms vary in plumbing, size, and placement. Two persons pay 6,500$ ($42.25) daily. Singles are priced at 5,000$ ($32.50). A continental breakfast is included.

Hotel Oslo, 25 Avenida Fernão de Magalhães, 3000 Coimbra (tel. 039/290-71), lies on one of the busiest streets of town, and offers 33 comfortably modern accommodations. The design, as its name suggests, is a somewhat chilly form of Scandinavian modern. The unpretentious contemporary bedrooms offer safe overnight accommodations (if you're a light sleeper, ask for a room in the rear). Doubles cost from 7,000$ ($45.50) daily and singles go for 6,000$ ($39), including a continental breakfast. There's a bar and restaurant on the fourth floor.

Pensão Residencial Alentejana, 1 Rua Dr. Henriques Seco, 3000 Coimbra (tel. 039/259-24), is one of the best pensions in this university city. All its 14 accommodations are with private bath, and some are furnished with antiques. This boarding house is located in a reconstructed old villa, near Praça da República in the center of Coimbra. The accommodations are on the second and third floors. On the first or ground floor is a store. Serving breakfast only, the Alentejana charges 3,500$ ($22.75) daily in a single and 4,000$ ($26) in a double.

Domus, 62 Rua Adelino Veiga, 3000 Coimbra (tel. 039/285-84), lies above an appliance store on a narrow commercial street near the train station. Its façade is covered with machine-made golden-brown tiles, and its rectangular windows are trimmed with slabs of marble. The reception desk is at the top of a flight of stairs, one floor above ground level. The staff will check you into one of the 15 usually large and clean rooms. Many of them are filled with contrasting patterns of carpeting and wallpaper, creating a functional but cozy family atmosphere. A stereo system plays in the TV lounge, which also doubles as the breakfast room. With a continental breakfast included, singles rent for 3,500$ ($22.75) daily, and doubles go for 4,200$ ($27.30). Each accommodation has a small private bath.

Residencial Larbelo, 33 Largo de Portagem, 3000 Coimbra (tel. 039/290-92). The lime-green, heavily ornamented façade sits on a statue-centered square just to the side of the river in the heart of town, near the tourist office. In the narrow reception area, a polite receptionist (who might speak very little English) will check you into a relatively clean and simple bedroom. With a continental breakfast included, doubles cost 3,500$ ($22.75) daily, and singles go for 3,300$ ($21.45).

Hotel Internacional, 4 Avenida Emidio Navarro, 3000 Coimbra (tel. 039/255-03), is clean and very simple. It's unabashedly Portuguese in its mentality and decor. A few steps from the train station, it occupies a once-grand 19th-century building whose interior has, over the years, been updated. The insignificant lobby is staffed by members of the family who own the property. English is definitely not their second tongue. After registering, you climb a steep series of staircases to rooms that are often tiny. The furniture is vintage 1920s and no unit has a private bath. But what a welcome relief to find any room in hotel-scarce Coimbra. Singles cost from 1,500$ ($9.75) daily, doubles go for 2,600$ ($16.90), and triples peak at 3,000$ ($19.50).

WHERE TO DINE

Considered the best restaurant in Coimbra, **Piscinas,** Rua Dom Manuel (tel. 71-70-13), is hard to reach, lying on the eastern side of town in a sports complex. It's best to go there by taxi. On the second floor, the air-conditioned restaurant, seating 230 patrons, opens onto a panoramic view. Parking is easily available. Service is from noon to 3 p.m. and 7 to 10 p.m. daily except Monday. Meals cost 1,800$ ($11.70) and up. Both Portuguese and continental specialties are served. You might begin with shellfish soup or escargots, then follow with one of the main-dish specialties, including beef Piscinas, grilled sole, pepper steak, pork piri-piri, or fondue bourguignonne. To finish your repast, why not an Irish coffee? Piano music is played at night.

Dom Pedro, 58 Avenida Emidio Navarro (tel. 291-08), stands across the street from the bank of the river, near a congested part of town. After negotiating a vaulted hallway, you'll find yourself in an attractive room whose tables are grouped around a splashing fountain. Above the fountain, a high ceiling is supported by four thick columns connected to one another by a series of arches. This, plus the random tile patterns of birds, animals, and flowers, contribute to an Iberian ambience. In winter a corner fireplace throws off some welcome heat. In summer the thick walls and terracotta floor provide a kind of air conditioning. Full meals, costing from 1,800$ ($11.70) to 2,500$ ($16.25), might include such specialties as codfish Dom Pedro, trout meunière, pepper steak, and pork cutlet milanese. Hours are noon to 3:30 p.m. and 7 to 10:30 p.m. daily except Monday.

O Alfredo, 32 Rua João das Regras (tel. 232-88), lies on the less populated side of the river on the street that funnels into the Santa Clara bridge. This unobtrusive pink-fronted restaurant looks more like a snackbar than a formal dining establishment. The ambience is pleasant, albeit simple. Full meals, costing 1,800$ ($11.70) to 2,500$ ($16.25), might include pork in the style of Alentejo, rice with shrimp, an array of shellfish, Portuguese-style stew, several types of clam dishes, grilled steak, and regional varieties of fish and meat. Hours are daily from noon to 3 p.m. and 7 to 10 p.m.

Pinto d'Ouro (Golden Chicken), 68 Avenida João das Regras (tel. 250-08), is one of my favorite dining rooms in the district. A bar serving snacks is alluring. The little tables in the nook adjoining the dining room are preferred. A good dish is clams in a wine garlic sauce. On one recent occasion I began a fine regional repast with caldo verde, followed by a large portion of roast *cabrito* (goat) with french fries, rice, and salad, concluding with a huge amount of vine-ripened strawberries sprinkled with sugar, as well as coffee. Vinho verde accompanied the meal, and, as an added surprise, I enjoyed fresh goat cheese as an appetizer. Service was fast, and the entire bill came to only 1,800$ ($11.70). Hours are daily from noon to 4 p.m. and 6:30 to 11 p.m.

Café Nicola, 35 Rua Ferreira Borges (tel. 220-61), is a plain but modern little second-floor restaurant over an old-fashioned delicatessen and pastry shop. It's spartan inside, even the flowers are usually wilted, but tradition is to be respected. Students gather here for strong coffee. The window tables provide box seats for looking at the teeming street. The food is good but plain, and the platters of fish or meat are usually large enough to be shared by two. The cuisine, as might be expected, is regional. A nourishing bowl of the soup of the day begins most meals. After that you can order filet of fish, roast chicken, chicken cutlets, or veal croquettes. Open daily for lunch from 12:30 to 3 p.m. and for dinner from 7:30 to 9:30 p.m., the establishment charges from 2,500$ ($16.25) to 2,800$ ($18.20) for a full meal. Closed Sunday.

Democratica, 7 Travessa do Rua Nova (tel. 237-84), is a stark budget restaurant popular with students and travelers on a shoestring budget. This place couldn't be simpler, with a little dining room, tiles on the walls, and the kitchen in the back. The servings are large. The soup has the hearty flavor of the fertile fields of central and north Portugal (it's usually a caldo verde). Most likely the fish will be hake, and it's often served with greens and potatoes. A typical dessert would be rice pudding. Everybody orders a carafe of the local wine, and the final tab is around 1,500$ ($9.75). It opens at 9:30 a.m. but starts serving lunch at 11:30 a.m., lasting until 3 p.m. Dinner is from 7 to 10 p.m. Closed Sunday.

A LANDMARK COFFEEHOUSE

The most famous coffeehouse in Coimbra, perhaps in the north of Portugal, is **Café Santa Cruz,** Praça 8 de Maio (tel. 336-17). It's in a former auxiliary chapel of the cathedral, and has a high ceiling supported by flamboyant stone ribbing and vaulting of fitted stone. There's a paneled waiters' station with a marble top handsome enough to serve as an altar in its own right. Now a favorite gathering place in Coimbra, day or night, it has a casual mood. Cigarette butts are tossed on the floor. Scores of students and professors come here to read the daily newspapers. There's no bar to stand at, so everyone takes a seat at one of the hexagonal marble-topped tables, sitting on an intricately tooled leather chair. If you order cognac, the shot will overflow the rim of the glass. But most patrons ask for a big glass of coffee with milk, costing 60$ ($3.90) at a table. In winter, the café is open from 7 a.m. to 11 p.m.; in summer, hours are 7 a.m. to 2 a.m. Closed Sunday.

WALKING AROUND COIMBRA

Coimbra's charms and mysteries unfold as you walk up Rua F. Borges passing under the Gothic **Arch of Almedina,** with its coat-of-arms. From that point, you can continue up the steep street, past antique shops, to the old quarter.

The focal point for most pilgrims, of course, is the **University of Coimbra,** established in the town in 1537 on orders from João III. Among its alumni are Luís Vas de Camões (the country's greatest poet, author of the national epic, *Os Lusíadas*); St. Anthony of Padua (also the patron saint of Lisbon); even the late Dr. Salazar, once a professor of economics.

If you'll ignore the cold statuary and architecture on the Largo de Dom Dinis, you can pass under the 17th-century **Porta Pérrea** into the inner core of the academy. The steps on the right will take you along a cloistered arcade, **Via Latina,** to the **Sala dos Capelos,** the site of graduation ceremonies. You enter into a world with a twisted rope ceiling, a portrait gallery of Portuguese kings, walls of red damask, and the inevitable azulejos. Afterward you can visit the **University Chapel,** decorated with an 18th-century organ, 16th-century candelabra, a painted ceiling, 17th-century tiles, and a fine Manueline portal.

Of course, the architectural gem of the entire town is the baroque **University Library** (*Biblioteca-Geral da Universidade*) next door, with its chinoiserie motifs and elaborate decoration. Established between 1716 and 1723 and donated by João V, it shelters more than a million volumes. The interior is composed of a trio of high-ceilinged salons walled by two-story tiers of lacquer-decorated bookshelves. The pale jade and sedate lemon marble inlaid floors complement the jeweled gold and emerald of the profuse gilt. The library tables are ebony and lustrous rosewood, imported from the former colonies in India and Brazil. Three-dimensional ceilings and the zooming telescopic effect of the room structure focus on the large portrait of João V, set against a backdrop of imitation curtains in wood. The side galleries, with their walls of valuable books in law, theology, and humanities of the 16th to the 18th century, the supporting pillars, the intricate impedimenta—all are dazzling, even noble. You may want to save the library for last; after viewing this masterpiece, other sights pale by comparison. Admission free, it is open from 9 a.m. to 5:30 p.m. Closed Sunday.

To wind down after leaving the library, walk to the end of the belvedere for a panoramic view of the river—equal to scenes on the Rhine—and the rooftops of the old quarter. On the square stand a statue of João III and the famous curfew-signaling clock of Coimbra, known as "cabra," meaning goat.

A short walk from the university square leads you to **Machado de Castro National Museum,** Largo Dr. José Rodrigues (tel. 237-27). Named after the greatest Portuguese sculptor of the 18th century, this museum is one of the finest in the north. Built over a Roman building as the Paço Episcopal in 1592, it houses a collection of ecclesiastical sculpture, especially polychrome, much of which dates from the 14th to the 18th centuries. The other exhibits include vestments, a relic of Saint Isabella, paintings, antiques, coaches, silver chalices, old jewelry, embroideries, retables, and 16th-century ceramic representations of the Apostles and Christ. The museum is open from 10 a.m. to 1 p.m. and 2 to 5 p.m., charging an admission of 150$ ($1). Closed Monday.

Across the way is the **New Cathedral (Sé Nova),** with its 17th century coldly neoclassic interior. More interesting is the **Old Cathedral (Sé Velha).** At Largo da Sé Velha, the cathedral founded in 1170 enjoys associations with Saint Anthony of Padua. Crenellated and staunch as a fortress, it is entered by passing under a Romanesque portal. Usually a student is there, willing to show you (for a tip, of course) the precincts, including the restored cloister. The pride of this monument is the gilded Flemish retable over the main altar, with a crucifix on the top. To the left of the altar is a 16th-century chapel designed by a French artist, and containing the tomb of one of the bishops of Coimbra.

Reached by going up Rua Visconde da Luz, the **Santa Cruz Church** is a former monastery, founded in the late 12th century when Afonso Henriques, Portugal's first king, ruled. However, its original Romanesque style gave way to Manueline restorers in 1507. The much popularized "Romeo and Juliet" story of Portugal, involving Pedro the Cruel and Inês de Castro reached its climax in this church. It was here that Pedro forced his courtiers to pay homage to her royal corpse and kiss her hand.

The lower part of the walls inside are decorated with azulejos. Groined in the profuse Manueline manner, the interior houses the Gothic sarcophagi of Afonso Henriques, his feet resting on a lion, and that of his son, Sancho I. The pulpit nearby is one of the achievements of the Renaissance in Portugal, carved by João de Ruão in the 16th century. The choir stalls preserve, in carved configurations, the symbolism, mythology, and historical import of Portuguese exploration. With its twisted columns and 13th-century tombs, the two-tiered Gothic-Manueline cloister is impressive.

The façade makes Santa Cruz one of the finest monuments in the land. Decorated like an architectural birthday cake, it is topped with finials and crosses, its portal top-heavy with a baroque porch, an unusual blending of styles. It's overadorned, but fascinating.

ACROSS THE MANDEGO

On the left bank lie four of the most interesting and least visited attractions of Coimbra. On the silt-laden banks of the Mondego stand the gutted, flooded, and crumbling remains of **Santa Clara-a-Velha,** a Gothic convent built in the 14th century. This church once housed the body of Coimbra's patron saint, Isabella, although her remains were transferred to the New Convent higher up on the hill. Rising out of the inrushing river, the Roman arches are reflected in the canals, evoking a Venetian scene. You can walk through the upper part only, as the river has already reclaimed the floor. The former convent is reached by crossing the Santa Clara Bridge, and turning left down the cobblestone street (Rua de Baixo).

Commanding a view of right-bank Coimbra, the **Convent of Santa Clara-a-Nova** provides a setting for the tomb of St. Isabella. Built during the reign of João IV, the convent is an incongruous blend of church and military garrison.

The church is noted for a rich baroque interior and Renaissance cloister. In the rear, behind a grille, is the tomb of the saint (usually closed except on special occasions). When her body was removed in 1677, her remains are said to have been well preserved, even though she died in 1336. Instead of regal robes, she preferred to be buried in the simplest habit of the order of the Poor Clares. At the main altar is the silver tomb (a sacristan will light it for you), which the ecclesiastical hierarchy considered more appropriate after her canonization.

At least for youngsters, the main attraction of Coimbra is **Portugal dos Pequenitos** (tel. 039/81-30-21). Called Portugal for the Little Ones, it is reached by crossing Ponte de Santa Clara and heading out Rua António Agusto Gonsalves. It's a mélange of miniature houses from every province of Portugal, including Madeira and the Azores, even the distant foreign settlements of Timor and Macau. It gives one the impression of a Gulliver strolling across a Lilliputian world. The recreations include palaces, an Indian temple, a Brazilian pavilion (with photos of gauchos), a windmill, a castle, and the 16th-century House of Diamonds from Lisbon. From April to September, hours are daily from 9 a.m. to 7 p.m.; otherwise, from 9 a.m. to 5:30 p.m. Entrance is 150$ ($1).

Farther up the road is the final attraction, the **Quinta das Lagrimas** (the Garden of Tears; tel. 039/232-52). In "sweet Mondego's solitary groves," in the words of Camões, lived Inês de Castro, mistress of Pedro, and their three illegitimate children. Although they are the property of the Osório Cabral family since the 18th century, the gardens are visited by romantics from many countries. You can't go inside the house, but you can wander through the greenery to the spring fountain, known as the Fonte dos Amores. It was at the quinta on Camões' "black night obscure" that the Spanish beauty was set upon by assassins hired by her lover's father. Pedro returned, finding her in a pool of blood, her throat slit.

So classic and enduring a Portuguese love story is it that who would want to suggest that it wasn't true, or that the murder didn't happen at the Garden of Tears? You can visit from 9 a.m. to 7 p.m. daily at no charge.

5. Mealhada

The little hamlet of Mealhada, almost 12 miles north of Coimbra, is devoted to selling roast suckling pig. The town lies off the main road. The porcine pièce de résistance appears on menus in Portuguese as *leitão assado*.

SAMPLING ROAST SUCKLING PIG

Restaurants specializing in the tasty pork dish line the highway, and everyone seems to go to **Pedro dos Leitões,** EN 1 (tel. 220-62), for reasons I don't fully understand. I can't detect the difference between the suckling pig served here from that at other establishments. However, tradition prevails. Pedro dos Leitões is usually mobbed on a summer day—even if you arrive before noon (which is considered early for Portugal). The place seats 220 patrons from noon to 3 p.m. and 7 to 10 p.m., and it's open all year except on Monday.

The name of the restaurant means "Pete of the Suckling Pigs." The decor is simple, and the service frantic and rushed. Suckling pig is priced by the kilo. If you don't want the house specialty, you can order such dishes as grilled sole or veal scallops with madeira sauce. Enjoy your meal, which will cost from 2,000$ ($13), with the local sparkling wine, like a champagne, called Bomfinal. The pigs are spit-roasted over coals, and you can watch the cooking process if you wish.

WHERE TO STAY

For accommodations, I recommend **Quinta dos Três Piñheiros,** 3050 Mealhada (tel. 031/223-91). This property once contained only a farmhouse and a few outbuildings. Today it has grown into a rambling string of motel-like accommodations, as well as what has become the most famous disco in the entire region. You won't lack for entertainment if you check in here. The disco opens every night at 8. Its urban decor includes the kind of accessories you'd expect to find in New York or Paris, including clouds of vapor, wrap-around sounds, and what has been labeled the most sophisticated light show of any disco in Portugal.

The in-house dining room sits in what used to be the estate's wine press. Today, with the stone of its original walls exposed, the building serves well-prepared regional specialties, including roast suckling pig, shellfish rice, blanquette of veal, and a wide array of fresh fish. Full meals begin at 1,800$ ($11.70) and are served daily from noon to 4 p.m. and 7 to 10:30 p.m. The motel also has 53 well-furnished rooms. With a continental breakfast included, singles go for 5,000$ ($32.50) daily, and doubles cost from 6,500$ ($42.25).

6. Conimbriga

One of the great Roman archeological finds of Europe, the village of Conimbriga lies less than ten miles southwest of Coimbra. Conimbriga, the site of a Celtic settlement established in the Iron Age, was occupied by the Romans in the late 1st century. Since then and up to the 5th century A.D., the town knew a peaceful life. The site lies near a Roman camp, but the town never served as a military outpost, although it was on a Roman road connecting Lisbon (Roman Olissipo) and Braga (Roman Braccaria). Visitors walk from a small **museum** (Museu Monográfico) along the Roman road to enter the ruins. The museum contains artifacts from the ruins, including a bust of Augustus Caesar that originally stood in the Augustan temple of the town.

Roman mosaics in almost perfect condition have been unearthed in diggings in the area. The designs are triangular, octagonal, and circular—executed in blood-red, mustard, gray, sienna, and yellow. Motifs include beasts from North Africa and delicately wrought hunting scenes. Mosaics displaying mythological themes can be seen in one of the houses. Subjects include Perseus slaying the Medusa and the Minotaur of Crete in his labyrinth.

The diggings display to good advantage the complex functional apparatus of Roman ingenuity. Columns form peristyles around reflecting pools, and the remains of fountains stand in courtyards. There are ruins of temples, a forum, patrician houses, water conduits and drains. Feeding the public and private baths of the town were special heating and steam installations with elaborate piping systems. Conimbriga even had its own aqueduct.

The **House of Cantaber** is a large residence, in the remains of which the life of the Romans in Conimbriga can be traced. The house was occupied until the family of Cantaber was seized by invaders, who also effectively put an end to the town in the middle of the 5th century.

Another point of interest is the **House of the Fountains,** constructed before the 4th century, when it was partially destroyed by the building of the town wall. Much of the house has been excavated, and visitors can see remains of early Roman architecture as it was carried out in the provinces. Visits are possible from June 1 to September 30 from 10 a.m. to 1 p.m. and 2 to 6 p.m. daily. In off-season, it is open from 10 a.m. to 1 p.m. and 2 to 5 p.m. Closed Monday. Admission is 300$ ($1.95) in summer, 200$ ($1.30) in winter. For information, call 941-77). If you don't have a car, you can reach the site by taking a bus from Coimbra to Condeixa. The bus, Avíc Mondego, leaves Coimbra at 9:30 a.m. and 1:30 p.m., returning at 1:50 and 6:10 p.m. Conimbriga lies about a mile away, reached either by walking (through an olive grove) or by hiring a taxi in the village.

---

7. Buçaco

The rich, tranquil beauty of the forests of Buçaco, 17½ miles from Coimbra, were initially discovered by a humble order of barefoot Carmelites, following the dictates of seclusion prescribed by their founder. In 1628 they founded a monastery at Buçaco, and built it with materials from the surrounding hills. Around the forest they erected a wall to further isolate themselves and to keep women out.

These barefoot friars had a special love for plants and trees, and each year they cultivated the natural foliage and planted specimens sent them from distant orders. Buçaco had always been a riot of growth: ferns, pines, cork, eucalyptus, and pink and blue clusters of hydrangea. But the friars introduced such exotic additions as the monkey puzzle, a tall Chilean pine with branches so convoluted it confuses monkeys that climb in it. The pride of the forest, however, remains its stately cypresses and cedars.

Such was the beauty of the preserve that a papal bull, issued in 1643, threatened excommunication to anyone who destroyed a tree. Even though the monastery was abolished in 1834, the forest has been preserved. Filled with natural spring waters, the earth bubbles with many cool fountains, the best known of which is **Fonte Fria** (cold fountain).

The forest of Buçaco was the battleground where Wellington defeated the Napoleonic legions under Marshal André Masséna. The Iron Duke slept in a simple cloister cell right after the battle. A small **Museum of the Peninsular War** reconstructs much of the drama of this turning point in the Napoleonic invasion of Iberia.

It's about a half mile from the hotel. The very slim museum collection consists of engravings plus a few guns.

In the beginning of the 20th century, a great deal of the Carmelite monastery was torn down to make way for the royal hunting lodge and palace hotel of Carlos I and his wife, Queen Amélia. He hardly had time to enjoy it, as he was assassinated in 1908. Luigi Manini, an Italian architect, masterminded this neo-Manueline structure of parapets, buttresses, armillary spheres, galleries with flamboyant arches, towers, and turrets. After the fall of the Braganças, wealthy tourists took their afternoon tea by the pools underneath the trellis hung with blossoming wisteria.

One of the best ways to savor Buçaco is to make the 1,800-foot ride to **Cruz Alta** (high cross) by car through forests, past hermitages. At the summit is a view considered by many to be the best in Portugal.

LIFE IN AN OLD PALACE

Guests can stay in elegant surroundings at the **Palace Hotel do Buçaco,** Mata do Buçaco, Buçaco, 3050 Mealhada (tel. 031/931-01). "Good-bye forever," Queen Amélia said on her last visit to Buçaco in 1945. The government had permitted her a sentimental journey (in a limousine with ladies-in-waiting) to visit all the places where she had spent her reigning years before her flight to England in 1910. The palace is an architectural fantasy. The designer borrowed heavily from everywhere: the Jerónimos Monastery at Belém, the Doge's Palace at Venice, the Graustark Castles of Bavaria. One of the most resplendently grandiose palaces in Europe, it is set in the center of a 250-acre forest. The structure is still intact and impressive, especially its grand staircase with ornate marble balustrades, 15-foot-wide bronze torchères, and walls of frescoes, some painted by Carlos. There are several drawing rooms and salons, a potpourri of architectural whims.

In 1910, the Swiss head of the kitchen, the king's cook, persuaded the government to let him run the palace as a hotel. There are 60 bedrooms, of which the most spectacular is the Queen's Suite, which has its own private parlor, dressing room, sumptuous marble bath, and even a private dining room. In some cases the baths were once the adjoining rooms for a valet or maid. Doubles with breakfast included range in price from 13,000$ ($84.50) to 20,000$ ($130) daily, with singles going for 11,000$ ($71.50) to 14,000$ ($91).

The dining room is a theatrical success, the tables set with fine stemware and silver. Of note is the wooden Gothic ceiling and the view through two 20-foot-wide arched windows onto the gardens and the encircling neo-Manueline terrace. Even if you're not staying here, you should stop in for lunch or dinner, costing 3,000$ ($19.50) for a table d'hôte. A typical repast: first, gnocchi, followed by sea bass with vegetables. For a third course, perhaps filet of veal, tender and sweet, will be served with a rosette of potatoes, topped by dessert, an assortment of cheese and crackers, and the fresh fruit of the season. In the cellars below, the palace stores more than 100,000 bottles of its own wine, both red and white. It is open all year.

8. Luso

Luso is a little spa town 19½ miles from Coimbra on the northwestern side of the Buçaco mountain, boasting a mild climate and thermal waters for both drinking and bathing. The radioactive and hypotonic water, low in mineral content, is said to have great efficacy in the treatment of kidney ailments, alimentary complaints, and circulatory problems, as well as allergies of the respiratory tract or of the skin.

Besides the health-giving aspects of the spa, it is also a resort area, sharing many of its facilities with Buçaco, just two miles away. During the spa season, festivities and sports events are held at the casino, nightclub, and tennis courts, as well as on the lake and at the two swimming pools, one of which is heated. Thermal spa enthusiasts flock here generally from June 1 through October, some arriving on the main-line *Sud-Express* (Lisbon-Paris).

FOOD AND LODGING

With a backdrop of rolling forests, **Grande Hotel das Termas,** Rua dos Banhos, Luso, 3050 Mealhada (tel. 031/934-50), nestles in a valley in the midst of abundant foliage. It is a sprawling establishment adjacent to the spa, offering roomy bedchambers, each with private bath and phone. Habitués praise its thermal spa fa-cilities. The emphasis is on good health. You can swim in a 150-foot Olympic-size pool, lounge and sunbathe on the surrounding grassy terrace, or relax under the weeping willows and bougainvillaea arbor. There are hard tennis courts, mini-golf, and, at night, a boîte for dancing.

The accommodations are comfortable in well-proportioned bedrooms, with matching furnishings. Some of the rooms open onto private terraces, with views of the tree-covered valley. The bed-and-breakfast rate in a double room is from 9,240$ ($60) daily; in a single, from 7,700$ ($50). Lunch or dinner is an extra 2,310$ ($15). The meals are large (the cuisine is both regional and international), and they are served in a mural-decorated dining room. Try a bottle of full-bodied Messias red wine from nearby Mealhada.

Hotel Eden, Rua Emidio Navarro, Luso, 3050 Mealhada (tel. 031/931-71). At last Luso has a modern hotel. This attractive 56-bedroom hotel opened in 1983. The tone is set by the modern lobby with its Picasso-style mural covering one of the walls. It was the work of a Portuguese artist, Jorge do Açor. The Eden stands on a hill above the flowering central garden near what used to be the town's belle époque casino. The bedrooms are pleasantly and comfortably furnished, containing private baths and balconies. Singles in high season cost 6,000$ ($39) daily, with doubles renting for 7,500$ ($48.75), with a continental breakfast included. The hotel also has a restaurant, serving good food and wine, a complete meal costing from 1,200$ ($7.80).

Restaurant O Cesteiro, Rua Dr. Lúcio Pais Abranches (tel. 933-60), is an un-pretentious restaurant on the road leading outside of town in the direction of Mealhada. It occupies a spacious room whose façade is covered with a simple sign and plain brown tiles. Inside is a popular bar that does a brisk business with local artisans and farmers. Full meals are served at lunch from noon to 2:45 p.m. and dinner from 7 to 9:45 p.m. every day of the week except Wednesday. The price for a full meal is 1,500$ ($9.75), and the fare is likely to include duck stew, roast goat, pimiento-flavored pork, and an array of fish dishes, including cod.

---

9. Curía

Forming a well-known tourist triangle with Luso, 7 miles away, and Buçaco, 16 miles, is Curía, in the foothills of the Sêrra de Estrêla. Its spa has long been a draw to people seeking the curative properties of medicinal waters in a secluded spot. Among its recreation facilities, there are tennis courts, swimming pools, roller-skating rinks, boating on the lake, cinemas, and tea houses. Curía has its own railway station. The season for taking the waters here—calcium sulfated, slightly saline, so-dium and magnesium bicarbonated—is from April 1 to October 30, although June 1 sees the beginning of the largest influx of visitors.

In the Bairrada wine-growing district, Curía offers the fine wines of the region as well as such famous local cuisine as roast suckling pig, roast kid, and sweets.

FOOD AND LODGING

Receiving guests since 1926, **Palace Hotel de Curía,** Curía, 3780 Anadia (tel. 031/521-31) is still an elegant accommodation. As you drive past the town's tourist office, you can catch a glimpse of this hotel's façade through a protective grouping of shrubbery. Four female faces, almost outlandishly oversized, gaze enigmatically over the gardens and parasols of the front garden. Their presence, along with the thousands of pounds of stone ornamentation, imply life on a grand scale.

Between the twin towers of the hotel's Italianate façade are sandwiched 120 bedrooms, many of them quite spacious and each with private bath. The hotel is open only between April 1 and October 30. With a continental breakfast included, singles are priced from 6,500$ ($42.25) to 12,000$ ($81.25) daily and doubles from 7,000$ ($45.50) to 13,000$ ($84.50).

There's a rectangular swimming pool on the grounds, as well as tennis courts. Horseback riding can also be arranged. Perhaps best of all, the hotel seems to exude a benign air of self-confidence, based on its having served as a temporary retreat for dozens of prestigious cosmopolites over the decades.

Hotel das Termas, Curia, 3780 Anadia (tel. 031/521-85), is approached via a curving dirt road leading through a park-like setting with lacy shade trees—quiet and secluded. Open all year, it offers facilities for health and relaxation, including a free-form swimming pool encircled with orange trees and umbrella tables. In the park a rustic wooden bridge leads over a lake to walks and the tennis courts. The lounge is relaxed and casual, furnished with provincial pieces and hand-loomed rugs. The dining hall, with its parquet floors and brick fireplace is like a tavern, especially when filled with guests who aren't hesitant to chat from table to table. Even the bedrooms have a homelike feeling; with lots of floral chintz, wooden beds, and walls of wardrobe space. Most of the 36 rooms contain private baths. Rates range from 7,500$ ($48.75) daily in a single, from 10,500$ ($68.25) in a double. One commentator likened the Hotel das Termas to the Raffles Hotel in Singapore a few decades ago, with its British colonial atmosphere, along with lots of brass and wicker.

Pensão Lourenço, Curia, 3780 Anadia (tel. 031/522-14). Throughout the spa, a series of signs points motorists to this simple inn, which you'll eventually find in a tree-lined hollow away from the center of the town. It occupies a pair of buildings set on either side of a narrow road, almost forming its own miniature village. One of the buildings operates a ground-floor café whose tables and whose patrons sometimes spill over into the road. Most of the clients are elderly, many of them pensioners who come to Curía season after season. They form a closely knit community of shared interests and needs. The pension is open only between June and September. Rooms with baths cost 2,500$ ($16.25) daily in a single, 3,500$ ($22.75) in a double.

---

10. Aveiro

The town on the lagoon, Aveiro is crisscrossed by myriad canals, spanned by low-arched bridges. At the mouth of the Vouga River, it is cut off from the sea by a long sand bar protecting clusters of islets. The architecture is almost Flemish, a good foil for a setting of low willow-reed flatlands, salt marshes, spray-misted dunes, and rice paddies.

On the lagoon, brightly painted swan-necked boats traverse the waters. Called *barcos moliceiros,* these flat-bottomed vessels hold fishermen who harvest seaweed used for fertilizer. They are ever on the lookout for eels, a specialty of the region, which they catch in the shoals studded with lotus and water lilies. Outside the town are extensive salt pits, lined with pyramids, fog-white in color.

The surrounding lagoons and many secret pools dotting the landscape make a boat excursion, which is reminiscent of a trip into bayou country. Inquire at the **Tourist Office,** Praça da República (tel. 236-80). The town is quite congested, and many readers have expressed their disappointment upon visiting here, citing the incessant whine of the Vespa, as well as the relatively stagnant canal water, which is foul smelling. Others, however, find it worth the journey.

The **Convent of Jesus,** at Praça do Milenário, is hailed as the finest example of the baroque style in Portugal. At the convent, the Infanta Santa Joana, sister of João II and daughter of Afonso V, took the veil in 1472. Her tomb, an inlaid rectangle of marble quarried in Italy, attracts many pilgrims. Its pale delicate pinks and roses lend it the air of a cherub-topped confection.

The convent, owned by the state and now the **Aveiro Museum** (tel. 232-97), displays a lock of the saint's hair, her belt and rosary, and a complete pictorial study of her life. A portrait of her, painted in intonaco, is exceptional. But what characterizes the convent is its carved giltwork, lustrous in the chapel, despite the dust.

In this setting is an assortment of 15th-century paintings, royal portraits of Carlos I and Manuel II (the last two Bragança kings), antique ceramics, and 16th-, 17th-, and 18th-century sculptures. There are also some well-preserved 18th- and 19th-century coaches and carriages. After viewing all this, you can walk through the cloisters with their Doric columns. The museum is open from 10 a.m. to 12:30 p.m. and 2 to 5 p.m., charging 150$ ($1) Closed Monday.

On the same square is the 15th-century **Church of St. Domingos,** with its blue and gold altarpieces and egg-shaped windows flanking the upper part of the nave. The façade, in the Gothic-Manueline style, is decorated with four flame finials. To the right (facing) is a bell tower. There are other churches as well, especially the **Chapel of Senhor Jesus das Barrocas,** built in the shape of an octagon in 1722.

Aviero is less than 35 miles from Coimbra, 41½ miles from Porto.

After a meal of stewed eels and a bottle of the hearty Bairrada wine, you might wish to explore some of the settlements along the lagoon, specifically **Ilhavo,** three miles south of Aveiro. Here you can stop off at the **Municipal Museum of Ilhavo,** 13 Rua Serpa Pinto (tel. 32-17-97), an unpretentious gallery that offers an insight into the lives of people who live with the sea. Inside you can see seascape paintings, boating paraphernalia, fishing equipment, ship models, and other exhibits. Hours are 9 a.m. to 12:30 p.m. and 2 to 5:30 p.m. except Sunday and Tuesday when it opens at 2, closing at 5:30 p.m. Admission is free.

From Ilhavo, drive along an avenue of olive trees to **Vista Alegre,** the village of the Vista Alegre porcelain works. Founded in 1824, the establishment is noted for its delicate decorated china. To visit it on a tree-shaded square, you must write in advance to the director of the factory at Lugar da Vista Alegre, 3830 Ilhavo (tel. 034/32-23-65).

WHERE TO STAY

The newest and best place in town is **Hotel Afonso V,** 65 Rua Dr. Manuel das Neves, 3800 Aveiro (tel. 034/251-91). A recent enlargement and renovation turned its original core into a glossy contemporary structure. If you're driving, you'll find small but well-placed signs directing you to the establishment. It stands in a residential neighborhood lined with trees. The façade is lined with small sea-green tiles. Inside, the lobby is a marble-floored haven operating from 10 p.m. to 4 a.m. The hotel has a disco and an English-style pub, as well as an adjacent pair of restaurants (see my dining recommendations for Aveiro). With a continental breakfast included, well-furnished singles rent for 5,900$ ($38.35) to 6,350$ ($41.30), and doubles cost 6,800$ ($44.20) to 7,450$ ($48.45).

Hotel Imperial, Rua Dr. Nascimento Leitão, 3800 Aveiro (tel. 034/221-41), attracts the youth of the community who gravitate to the lower lounge social center for drinks and TV, or to the open and airy dining room with its two glass walls. They look forward to their Sunday dates here—the 1,900$ ($12.35) dinners or the drinks on the open terrace. Many of the bedrooms and each of the lounges overlook the Ria de Aveiro and the garden of the Aveiro Museum, the old convent described earlier. All the rooms contain private bath, satellite TV, and direct-dial phone, as well as individually controlled central heating. A double costs from 7,400$ ($48.10) daily, and a single rents for 6,400$ ($41.60). The furnishings are contemporary, with many built-in features, and the color schemes are soothing. A few suites are available; they include a living room and a twin-bedded chamber with bath.

Arcada Hotel, 4 Rua Viana do Castelo, 3800 Aveiro (tel. 034/230-01), enjoys an enviable position in the center of Aveiro, with a view of the river traffic in the canal out front. In the summer, from your bedroom window you can see the white pyramids of drying salt on the flats. The hotel has been modernized, but the classic façade of beige and white has remained. Many of the rooms open onto balconies, and the rooftop is decorated with ornate finials. The hotel occupies the second, third, and fourth floors of the old building. There are 52 bedrooms, each with bath, phone, TV, and central heating. Doubles rent for 6,000$ ($39) daily, and singles go for 5,000$ ($32.50). A continental breakfast, included in the rates, is the only meal served.

Paloma Blanca, 23 Rua Luís Gomes de Carvalho, 3800 Aveiro (tel. 034/225-29). The design of what used to be an aristocratic private villa is Moorish. An iron fence encloses the three-sided courtyard in front, where a splashing fountain is surrounded by mature trees, trailing vines, and hand-painted gold and white tiles. The best rooms look out over the third-floor loggia onto a goldfish-filled basin in the garden. You'll find this well-preserved house—known in Portuguese as an *antiga moradia senhorial*—on a busy downtown street leading into the city from Porto. Well-furnished and often old-fashioned singles rent for 4,800$ ($31.20) daily, and doubles go for 6,500$ ($42.25).

WHERE TO DINE

The position of **A Cozinha do Rei,** Hotel Afonso V, 65 Rua Dr. Manuel des Neves (tel. 268-02), in the newest hotel in the city, adds to its appeal. You'll face a choice as you enter. On the right is an informal snackbar/luncheonette arrangement. Meals in the snackbar, costing from 1,800$ ($11.70), might include cream of seafood soup, a range of omelets, squid, beefsteak Henri IV, veal cutlets with cream, and several kinds of grilled fish. A refrigerated case near the bar displays the day's catch of fresh fish and shellfish. Across the hallway, on the left as you enter, a more formal restaurant dispenses top-notch meals at 2,800$ ($18.20) and up in a modernized and sun-washed elaboration of a grand restaurant. Service is among the best in town. Open daily from noon to midnight.

Restaurante Centenário, 9 Largo do Mercado (tel. 227-98), stands at the side of Aveiro's version of Les Halles. From the restaurant's front door, you can see the teeming covered market, whose laborers often stream up to the elongated bar after their early-morning unloadings of fresh produce. Most visitors, however, will gravitate to a napery-covered table for a well-prepared lunch or dinner. The modern, high-ceilinged room contains lots of well-polished wood and has a large window opening onto the street. A less-often-used name for the restaurant is "A Casa da Sopa do Mar." As anyone can guess, that shellfish-laden soup is the house specialty. In addition to a steaming bowlful, you can also order grilled pork or veal, fried or grilled sole, codfish "brasa," and an array of other specials. Full meals begin at a reasonable 1,500$ ($9.75). Hours are daily from 9 a.m. to midnight.

Galo d'Ouro, 2 Travessa do Mercado (tel. 234-56), also stands in the vicinity of the covered market, just off a sidewalk with the most amusing cobblestone patterns in town. You step down into a high-ceilinged modern room, darkly illuminated with a cubbyhole bar serving drinks throughout the afternoon. A handful of tables, covered with clean white napery, is available for full meals, costing from 1,800$ ($11.70). Main dishes include fried eels, grilled sole, and grilled whiting, and you might finish off with the cheese of the country or pineapple in port wine. The wine of the house is inexpensive and flavorful, and the chef's specialty is beef Gala d'Ouro. The restaurant serves from noon to 5 p.m. and 7 p.m. to midnight daily except Thursday.

AN INN BETWEEN THE SEA AND THE LAGOON

The government operates a pousada in the area, lying about 18½ miles from Aveiro. It's the **Pousada da Ria,** Bico do Muranzel, 3870 Torreira-Murtosa (tel. 034/483-32), which stands on a promontory surrounded on three sides by water. Between the sea and the lagoon, it is a contemporary building where the architect made much use of glass, with rows of balconies on its second floor. You can reach it by going by boat from Aveiro (passengers only) or else by taking a long drive via Murtosa and Torreira until you reach this sandy spit. Along the way, you pass Phoenician-style boats in the harbor, sand dunes, and pine trees, not to mention a lot of trucks.

At the pousada, a waterside terrace opens onto views of fishing craft. The inn is popular with holiday-seeking Portuguese families who often book all its 19 bedrooms, which rent for 11,300$ ($73.45) daily in a single, 12,500$ ($81.25) in a double. The rooms are compact, furnished with built-in pieces. If you're stopping for a meal, the cost is from 2,500$ ($16.25). The chef's specialty is *caldeirada à ria,* a savory fish stew. A sunny Sunday is likely to be bedlam; otherwise, it's a peaceful haven.

FOOD AND LODGING AT CACIA

Set beside the highway, **Hotel João Padeiro,** Cacia, 3800 Aveiro (tel. 034/91-13-26), is a sienna-colored building concealing an elegant accommodation. It used to be an unpretentious village café until the Simões family transformed it more than a decade ago. It can serve as an elegantly perfect weekend retreat. You enter a velvet-covered reception area filled with family antiques. A polite staff member will usher you via elevator to the brick-vaulted upstairs hallways and then to your room. Each unit is different, usually containing some form of antique four-poster bed. Most of the beds are cornered with spindle-turned posts, and flanked with elaborately crafted headboards. Each room contains a tastefully modern bath, exuberantly flowered wallpaper, and a coved ceiling, as well as a hand-crocheted bedspread. With a continental breakfast included, singles rent for 5,100 ($33.15) daily, while doubles cost from 6,600$ ($42.90). Some suites go for 7,700$ ($50.05) for two people.

The true flavor of the establishment, however, isn't appreciated until dinnertime. You might enjoy an apéritif in the Iberian-style bar, where well-rubbed leather covers the walls and where the ceiling is carefully crafted. In cold weather, a sweeping expanse of flagstones, fashioned into a curved fireplace, warms a distant corner of the restaurant. Meals are served in a blue-and-white dining room, with massive Portuguese chests, leather-upholstered chairs, and fresh flowers. The paintings ringing the walls of the room are the work of a well-known Portuguese artist, João de Sousa Araujo.

Meals from a distinguished menu are priced from 3,000$ ($19.50). Specialties are likely to include a shellfish omelet, house-style filet of sole, goat cooked in wine, fried eels, and lobster curry, finished off with a walnut tart. The restaurant is open daily for lunch from 12:30 to 3 p.m. and for dinner from 7:30 to 10 p.m. Closed Christmas.

Cacia is about 4½ miles from Aveiro.

AN INN IN THE VOUGA VALLEY

On a rise above the Vouga River stands the **Pousada de Santo António,** Mourisca de Vouga, 3750 Agueda (tel. 034/52-12-30), a large villa in a fine location near the main Lisbon–Porto highway. The meadowlands and river valley are lush, filling the dining and living-room windows with the picture postcard colors. Large natural flagstones make up the front courtyard, ushering you into a renovated villa decorated like a warm provincial inn. All 13 rooms have their own bath and contain striped rugs and floral bedspreads. High headboards on the country-style beds and patterned stone floors give an air of simple comfort. Rates are 11,300$ ($73.45) daily for a single, 12,500$ ($81.25) for a double.

Meals are served daily from 12:30 to 3 p.m. and 7:30 to 10 p.m. At dinner, whether you begin with a caldeirada or caldo verde, be sure to request, if available, the veal or bacalhau codfish, followed by the fruits of the valley. A meal costs from 2,250$ ($14.65) to 2,500$ ($16.25). A continental breakfast is included in the price of the room. A swimming pool is an inviting attraction for guests.

The pousada is about 157 miles north of Lisbon, 30 miles from Coimbra, and 48 miles from Porto. Caramulo and Talhada's mountains are in the background.

11. Caramulo

Set against a background of mimosa and heather-laden mountains, this tiny resort is a gem and a good vantage point for going to see striking views of the surrounding country. About two miles north from town, at the end of a dirt road to the left, is a watchtower from which a panoramic view of the **Sêrra do Caramulo** unfolds.

From the tip of this mountain, about 4½ miles from town at Caramulhino, you can see a breathtaking sweep that includes the Lapa, the Estrêla, the Lousa and Buçaco ranges, and the Sêrras da Gralheira and do Montemura, as well as the coastal plain. To reach the best viewing place on the 3,500-foot-high peak, take Avenue Abel de Lacerda from Caramulo west to the N230-3 road and then go about half a mile on foot.

Another panoramic vista spreads out from the summit of **Cabeço da Neve,** off the same road taken to go to Caramulinho.

The Museum of Art of Caramulo (tel. 862-70) houses at least 60 veteran and vintage cars, including a 1905 four-cylinder Dedion-Bouton, a 1909 Fiat, an 1898 Hurtu, a 1904 Minerva, a 1913 Gregoire, a 1911 Rolls-Royce, and a 1902 Darracq. These antique cars are restored to perfect condition. A few early bicycles, one dating back to 1865, and motorcycles are also exhibited. In addition to the ground-floor car display area, workshop, and library, there is an upper gallery where more vehicles are exhibited. Access to this is gained by a wide staircase at one end of the balustrade formed of crankshafts and camshafts from vintage engines. The museum also contains Portuguese and foreign paintings, sculpture, designs, engravings, the art of the goldsmith, ceramics, antique furniture, and tapestries. Admission is 300$ ($1.95), and hours are daily from 10 a.m. to 6 p.m.

These attractions are 50 miles north of Coimbra, midway between Aveiro and Viseu.

For accommodations Caramulo has an inn.

FOOD AND LODGING

High as an eagle's nest, **Pousada de S. Jerónimo,** 3475 Caramulo (tel. 032/ 862-91) is near the crest of a mountain ridge. Its panoramic view is comparable to sights encountered in Switzerland and Austria. The inn is like a spread-out chalet, with an esthetically pleasing design. You ascend to the reception, living, and dining rooms, with one salon flowing into another. In winter guests sit by the copper-hooded fireplace. Beyond the wooden grille is a pleasant dining room, the window wall providing views of the hills. Dinner is candlelit, and guests sit on hand-carved provincial chairs sampling the country-style cooking. If you're just dropping in, a table d'hôte luncheon or dinner goes for 2,500$ ($16.25) and up. Food is served from 12:30 to 3 p.m. and 7:30 to 10 p.m. daily.

The six double rooms are small but attractive, all with private bath. Portuguese antiques and reproductions are used—ornate iron headboards, a slab of wood as a console. Wide windows open onto vista-scanning private balconies. The cost for a double with shower is 9,800$ ($63.70) daily, and a single goes for 8,700$ ($56.55). The pousada has a private park, a swimming pool, and a playground. If you enjoy fishing, the Rivers Agueda and the Criz provide trout and *achigas,* a local barbel. From here, you can follow the Besteiros valley and from its Varandahs, 48 miles along, you can see the impressive Estrêla Mountains.

A POUSADA ON THE COIMBRA-GUARDA HIGHWAY

On a well-traveled road, the best place to stop for food and lodging is **Pousada de Santa Bárbara,** Póvoa das Quartas, 3400 Oliveira do Hospital (tel. 038/522-52). Not luxurious, it is suitable for those seeking a mountain spot. There are only 16 double rooms, but each comes equipped with a bath and phone. One person is charged 11,300$ ($73.45) daily for a room with a continental breakfast, and two people pay 12,500$ ($81.25). Don't be put off by the unimpressive façade. No bedroom in the pousada faces the road. It is very well designed, with a fantastic view of the valley from all the units, lounges, and restaurant.

If you're driving and would like to stop by for lunch or dinner, a set meal in the provincial dining room costs 2,200$ ($14.30) to 2,500$ ($16.25). Food is served daily from 12:30 to 3 p.m. and 7:30 to 10 p.m. The pousada has one of the best chefs in Portugal. Even the set menu offers a large choice of dishes. My American-style chicken would never have been recognized by an American, but it was superb nonetheless. The trout, however, is the pièce de résistance. Grilled with mushrooms, it's served with the backbone removed and a slice of cured ham. The sweet regional tarte evokes a Sintra cheesecake, but with "lashings" of honey and almonds.

Oliveira do Hospital belonged to the 12th-century hospitaler religious Order of St. John of Jerusalem. You can visit **Ferreira Chapel,** part of the mother church, and there are traces of an ancient **Roman village** less than two miles away. Farther south you come across **Lourosa,** whose parish church dates back to 912. It is the only one in the country in the mozarab style. About 12 miles from Póvoa das Quartas, in the village of **Avo,** is the mother church, a pillory, and the ruins of a castle whose handsome façade is almost intact.

The River Alva has a plentiful supply of fish and eels.

STAYING IN CANAS DE SENHORIM

The hotel at Urgeiriça is set amid the forested countryside near Canas de Senhorim, and is connected with all the major cities of Portugal by fine highways. The hotel lies about 25 miles from the Estrêla Mountains, popular with winter sports enthusiasts, and is 186 miles north of Lisbon, 102 miles from Porto, just 50 miles northeast of Coimbra, and 16 miles from the country town of Viseu.

Hotel Urgeiriça, Urgeiriça, Canas de Senhorim, 3500 Viseu (tel. 032/672-67). Its baronial granite walls, worthy of a grandee, were erected in 1939 by an English entrepreneur who had just made a fortune mining uranium in the nearby hills. Six years later, realizing the site's potential, he transformed his house into a hotel. It quickly became known as a stylish place to visit, and in time it lured such luminaries as Queen Elizabeth and Sir Anthony Eden. Nowadays, you'll find a less stylish version of its glamorous era, where bartenders still wear uniforms and bow ties, and bowls of flowers are picked hours before in the sprawling gardens.

Even if it's only for a meal, you should consider it for a stopover. The bread is baked on the premises, some of the wine comes from nearby vineyards, and formal service is the norm in a vast and impressive dining room lined with five palace-size portraits of British kings. Meals cost from 1,500$ ($9.75) per person and are served daily from 12:30 to 2:30 p.m. and 7:30 to 9:30 p.m. A bar whose leather decor and carved oak would be suitable for a private club in London allows guests the pleasure of relaxing before fireplaces of chiselled granite, watching pine roots slowly dissolve into ash. More athletic guests are drawn to the tennis court and the swimming pool.

One of the most amazing aspects of this hotel is the large number of Georgian antiques filling each of the 53 bedrooms. Their sheer quantities, coupled with high ceilings and English accessories, create very much the feeling of a wealthy private house where someone is just about to ring the bell to announce supper. The hotel charges 6,500$ ($42.25) daily in a double room, 5,500$ ($35.75) in a single.

---

12. Viseu

The capital of Beira Alta province, Viseu is a quiet country town. But it is also a city of art treasures, palaces, and churches. Its local hero is an ancient Lusitanian rebel leader, Viriato. At the entrance of Viseu is the **Cova de Viriato,** where the rebel, a combination Spartacus and Robin Hood, made his camp and plotted the moves that turned back the Roman tide.

Some of the country's most gifted artisans ply their timeless trade in and around Viseu. Where racks creak and looms hum, the busy weaver women create the unique quilts and carpets of Vil de Moinhos. Local artisans of Molelos produce the region's provincial pottery, and women with nimble fingers embroider feather-fine, light bone lace.

There is much to see and explore at random in Viseu: the cubistic network of tiled overlapping rooftops and entwining narrow alleyways and the encroaching macadam streets. However, if your time is limited, head at once to the **Ardo da Sé,** one of the most harmonious squares in Portugal, often referred to as the showplace of Viseu. There you'll find the town's three leading buildings: a cathedral, a museum, and a church.

The severe Renaissance façade of the **Viseu Cathedral (Sé)** evokes a fortress. Two lofty bell towers, unadorned stone up to the balustraded summit with crowning cupolas, can be seen from almost any point in or approaching the town. The second-story windows in the façade, two rectangular and one oval, are latticed and symmetrically surrounded by niches containing religious statuary.

On your right, you will first find the two-story Renaissance cloister adorned with classic pillars and arcades faced with azulejos. The interior of the sé is basically Gothic, but is infused with Manueline and baroque decorations. Plain, slender Romanesque columns line the nave, supporting the vaulted Manueline ceiling with its nautically roped groining. The basic color scheme inside plays brilliant gilding against muted gold stone. However, the full emphasis is centered on the Roman arched chancel, climaxed by an elegantly carved retable above the main altar. The chancel makes ingenious use of color counterpoint, with copper, green gold, and brownish-yellow complementing the gilt work. The ceiling is continued in the sacristy.

Next door to the cathedral is the **Museum of Grão Vasco** (tel. 262-49), named after the 16th-century painter, also known as Vasco Fernandes. The major works of this Portuguese master are displayed here, especially *La Pontecôte,* with the lance-like tongues of fire hurtling toward the saints, some devout, others apathetic.

Besides the works of this fine Portuguese primitive and his followers, the museum has a moving and tender *St. Raphael* by the outstanding 18th-century sculptor Machado de Castro. Enameled reliquaries, Byzantine artifacts, liturgical apparel, a Manueline monstrance dating from 1533, and a chalice with vermeil pendants from

1626 are a few of the items on view. The museum is open from 10 a.m. to 12:30 p.m. and 2 to 5 p.m. daily except Sunday. Admission is 150$ ($1).

Across the square from the cathedral is the palatial **Misericórdia Church** from the 18th century. Its pristine façade contrasts with the cathedral's baroque granite decorations, spirals, large windows and portal frames, balustrades, and matching towers.

WHERE TO STAY

In the heart of town, **Grão Vasco,** Rua Gaspar Barreiros, 3500 Viseu (tel. 032/235-11), surrounded by gardens and parks, is built motel fashion, with the bedroom balconies overlooking the swimming pool. After days of driving in the hotel-lean environs, it's a pleasure to check into this establishment. Popular with business people, it also attracts tourists, especially in the summer months. The decor is colorful and contemporary. The bedrooms are usually large, utilizing Portuguese traditional furnishings. The price for a double starts at 7,000$ ($45.50) daily. For a single, the rate is 6,100$ ($39.65). The dining room has a baronial stone fireplace, plus good cuisine, with many international dishes. If you're just dropping in you can sample an à la carte luncheon or dinner for 1,600$ ($10.40) to 2,200$ ($14.30).

Hotel Avenida, 1 Avenida Alberto Sandaio, 3500 Viseu (tel. 032/234-32), is a personalized small hotel right off the Rossio, the main plaza of town. Inside, it is the domain of the personable Mário Abrantes da Motto Veiga, who has combined his collection of antiques from Africa and China with pieces of fine old Portuguese furniture. He's created an inviting aura, bound to attract admirers of his eclectic taste. Each of the bedrooms varies in size, character, and price; and most of the 40 rooms have private shower or bath. The nightly rate is 3,500$ ($22.75) for one person, 5,000$ ($32.50) for two. There's a nice room (210B) with a high coved bed and an old refectory table and chair, which includes an adjoining chamber with a wooden spindle bed and a marble-topped chest that is like a nun's retreat. Meals in the plain, family-style dining room are well prepared and generous. They cost from 1,500$ ($9.75).

WHERE TO DINE

Outside of the hotels, **Coritço,** 47 Rua Augusto Hilário (tel. 238-53), is usually the first name mentioned when you ask a discerning local for a good independent eatery. This is the type of place the Portuguese call *típico,* meaning it is decorated in a typical local style and serves good regional cookery. You can dine in one of several rooms any day but Wednesday, from noon to 2:30 p.m. and 7 to 11 p.m. Meals are reasonable in price, costing from 2,000$ ($13).

You might also try **Trave Negra,** 40 Rua do Loureiros (tel. 032/261-38), which features the local cookery of the region, and does so daily except Thursday, from noon to 3 p.m. and 7 to 10:30 p.m. The cost is from 2,000$ ($13) for a well-prepared meal. The regional wines are good too. Before dinner you might drop into the bar for an apéritif.

---

13. Sêrra da Estrêla

From January to May, the great granite Sêrra da Estrêla is the winter sports center of Portugal. In summer, campers, trout fishermen, and mountain climbers dominate. Once almost completely isolated from the rest of the country, the major points of interest in the Sêrra da Estrêla are now linked by roads.

The land is also the home of the Cão de Sena, or "dog of the mountain." The area is a major sheep-raising district as well and is infested with wild animals, especially packs of wolves. Reader A. Wayne Magnitzky writes: "The throats of the sheep dogs are protected from the teeth of wolves by an iron collar with long sharp spikes.

Imagine the wolf's surprise when he attempts to throttle the dog and ends up with a long spike through his mouth!" The dogs survive by sucking ewes' milk.

One major auto route is from Covilhá to Seia via **Torre,** the latter the highest point in Portugal, at an altitude of 6,500 feet. From its summit, a panoramic view unfolds.

Covilhá is on the southern flank of the Sêrra, near the Zêzere Valley. A town of steep and narrow streets, it is known for its Monument to Our Lady of the Conception, a 25-foot statue of the Virgin Mary carved out of granite. Steps also carved out of granite lead to the statue. The sculptor was killed near this spot in a car accident, shortly after completing his work. The town is at its liveliest from June 22 to 25 when people from the neighboring hills come in for the Fair of Sãotiago, and sell handcrafts.

Covilhá used to be known as the "dormitory" for the **Penhas da Saúde** sports area, at 4,500 feet above sea level.

FOOD AND LODGING AT MANTEIGAS

Instead of continuing to Seia, an alternate route is to go along the Rio Zêzere to **Manteigas,** a little town with several balconied 17th-century houses. It lies between mountain ranges. The town of Manteigas is known to have been the last refuge of the primitive fighting groups of the Herminíos Mountains. King Sancho I gave the town a charter in 1178, ratified by King Emanuel I in 1514. From there you can take an excursion to the **Poço do Inferno,** or Hell's Mouth. This is a gorge with waterfalls. The distance from Manteigas along an unsurfaced and narrow road is about four miles.

Hotel Manteigas, Caldas de Manteigas, 6260 Manteigas (tel. 075/471-14), about 1¼ miles from the town of Manteigas, is in the Estrêla Mountains. Its 26 well-furnished rooms have been restored and redecorated, and there is a lounge for the guests. Singles rent for 7,500$ ($48.75) daily, and doubles go for 8,500$ ($55.25). Meals in the large, pleasant dining room consist of wholesome food, including the famous Sêrra da Estrêla mountain cheese, and cost from 1,600$ ($10.40).

About 8½ miles from Manteigas, the government runs the **Pousada de São Lourenço,** Estrada de Gouveia, 6260 Manteigas (tel. 075/981-50), which stands at a height of 4,900 feet above sea level on a mountainside and offers a panoramic view. Only 12 double rooms with bath are available, renting for 9,500$ ($61.75) daily. A single person in one of the rooms pays 8,000$ ($52). The comfort at this rustic pousada, surrounded by pine-studded mountains and a serene valley, is outstanding, and the country food is good. You have a selection of regional dishes, including the delectable Sêrra cheese and Zimbro brandy. A complete meal costs from 2,500$ ($16.25). The pousada lies about 56 miles from the Spanish border, 2 miles from Penhas Douradas.

From the pousada, you can visit such places as Penhas de Saúde, Torre, Piornos, Covão, Pedras da Marreca, and Portas dos Herminíos, as well as the beautiful mountain lakes.

14. Castelo Branco

The capital of Beira Baixa, Castelo Branco lies near the Spanish frontier, a distance of 157 miles from Lisbon. The city is beautiful and often filled with flowers. Shoppers may want to acquire some of the multicolored embroidery done by the women of the town. Some of the designs haven't been changed since the 17th century. Today the economy of Castelo Branco is based on production of cork, cheese, olive oil, and honey.

The **gardens of the former Bishop's Palace** (Jardim do Antigo Paço Episcopal), established in the 17th century, are well kept and formal, with banks of flowers, clipped box hedges, a statue-bedecked staircase, and numerous pools and fountains. The baroque statues in the garden are mostly life-size, depicting signs of the zodiac, the Apostles, and Portuguese royalty. You can visit the gardens daily from dawn to dusk, except that there is no entrance from noon to 1 p.m.

Tavares Proença Regional Museum, in the old Bishop's Palace (tel. 242-77), has displays of coins, earthenware, archeological discoveries, arms and armor, and Roman artifacts on the ground floor. As you ascend the staircase, look at the 16th-century Flemish tapestry depicting the biblical story of Lot. Upstairs are more tapestries, as well as paintings by 16th-century Portuguese artists, a 17th-century cupboard carved by skilled Portuguese craftsmen and other old furniture of the country, plus traditional embroidered bedspreads of the town. A room on this floor is devoted to modern art, and you can see a weaver's loom. Hours are Monday to Tuesday from 9 a.m. to 12:30 p.m., Wednesday, Thursday, and Friday, from 2 to 5:30 p.m., and Saturday and Sunday from 10 to 11:30 a.m. and 2 to 5:30 p.m. Admission is 200$ ($1.30).

From the gardens of the old Bishop's Palace, you can go under an arcaded staircase along Rua de Frei Bartolomeu da Costa to see the carved **Cross of St. John,** standing over a crown of seaweed on a twisted base from the 16th century.

The ruins of a Moorish **castle,** rebuilt in the time of King Dinis, are reached by going to the Church of St. Mary of the Castle. From here you can take the stairs up to Miradoura de São Gens, a landscaped lookout that provides a view of the countryside dotted with olive trees and of the town.

The town takes about an hour to explore. Most motorists seem to stop just for a look at the gardens.

FOOD AND LODGING

One of the best places to stay—out of an admittedly modest lot—is **Residencial Arraiana,** 18 Avenida 1 de Maio, 6000 Castelo Branco (tel. 072/216-34), which rents out 30 simply furnished but comfortable bedrooms, charging from 5,500$ ($35.75) daily in a double and from 4,000$ ($26) in a single. The hotel doesn't have a restaurant, but a continental breakfast is included in the tariff.

Another possibility for an overnight stopover is **Caravela,** 24 Rua do Saibreiro, 6000 Castelo Branco (tel. 072/239-39), which is modesty itself but clean and neat. The hotel offers 12 rooms with bath and 14 without bath. Bathless singles rent for only 1,000$ ($6.50) daily, and bathless doubles go for 2,800$ ($18.20). With bath, singles cost 3,000$ ($19.50) daily, and doubles are priced at 3,500$ ($22.75).

Restaurants are not outstanding, but most of them offer good value. All of them are inexpensive.

Try **Arcádia,** 13 Sidónio País Ave. (tel. 219-33), for a good and filling meal of regional cookery. Meals cost from 1,500$ ($9.75) and are served daily except Wednesday from noon to 3:30 p.m. and 7 to 11:30 p.m.

Another possibility is **Ti Lourdes,** Estrada Montalvão (tel. 210-06), which has many regional specialties, along with good and inexpensively priced wines. Seating 100 patrons, it also features fresh shellfish. It serves from 11:30 a.m. to midnight daily except Saturday. Meals cost 1,800$ ($11.70) and up. In winter a fireplace provides a warming glow.

---

15. Guarda

Between Porto and Salamanca, a university city in Spain, Guarda is the highest town in Portugal. Built at an altitude of some 3,400 feet, it is some two-thirds of a mile above sea level, in the eastern foothills of the Sêrra da Estrêla. In the Beira Alta, it stands 28 miles from Vilar Formoso, 136 miles from Porto, and 212 miles from Lisbon.

Because of its commanding position, the site of Guarda has been occupied since prehistoric days and is thought to have been an outpost of the Roman legions under Julius Caesar. The Visigoths used it as a fortress, which fell to the Moors. They were in turn ousted by the Christians, and Guarda was a stronghold of the Portuguese even up to the early 19th-century French invasion, when it lost its role as guardian of the Beira Alta. Today it is a pleasant summer resort.

Founded in the latter part of the 14th century, its **Sé (cathedral)** deserves some of your time. Originally the architects planned to build it in the Gothic style. However, by its completion in the mid-16th century, Renaissance, even Manueline, stylistic changes appeared in the plans. Two different styles can be seen in the façade facing north. Inside you'll find a Renaissance altarpiece, a fine Gothic tomb, a "Last Supper" altarpiece, and even more interesting is to take the stairs at the corner of the south transept. These will lead you to the rooftop of the cathedral where you'll have an excellent view of not only Guarda but the Sêrra da Estrêla.

Other sights include the **Ferreiros Tower,** an 18th-century **Misericórdia Church,** and from many vista points **views** of the Mondego and Zêzere Valleys below. There are also many ancient churches and old houses, some dating from the 16th century. You'll see many of these around Praça Luís de Camões (Cathedral Square).

FOOD AND LODGING

A first-class choice, **Hotel de Turismo,** Avenida Coronel Orlindo de Carvalho, 6301 Guarda (tel. 071/222-06), is centrally located in a traditional building. Rooms are well furnished and comfortable. Singles rent for 6,800$ ($44.20) daily, going up to 10,500$ ($68.25) in a double. Children traveling with their parents can be housed in the same room at reduced rates. Most guests prefer to stay here on the full-board plan, which carries a supplement of 3,000$ ($19.50) per person. A good Portuguese and international cuisine is featured.

Residência Filipe, 9 Rua Vasco da Gama, 6300 Guarda (tel. 071/226-58), is the second-best hotel in Guarda, standing in the heart of town a block from the central square and the cathedral, almost opposite the Ferreiros Tower. The 37 rooms are simply furnished but adequate, and you'll be served by an accommodating staff. A double with a private shower costs 7,000$ ($45.50) daily, and singles go for 4,000$ ($26). There is a dining room, serving good meals for 1,800$ ($11.70) and up.

Not counting the hotels, the best restaurant in town is outside the city. It's **O Telheiro,** EN 16 (tel. 213-56). Seating some 115 diners, the restaurant is air-conditioned and opens onto a panoramic vista. Good regional cookery and wines are served here at prices beginning at 2,200$ ($14.30). Service is daily from noon to 3 p.m. and 7:30 to 10:30 p.m.

Try also the more central **Fragata,** 17 Rua 31 de Janeiro (tel. 224-93), which has fine Portuguese cookery and inexpensively priced wines. Meals begin at a modest 1,500$ ($9.75) and go up from there. The waiters are polite and helpful. Go daily from 11 a.m. to 3 p.m. and 6 to 10 p.m. There is also a bar.

THE FORTIFIED TOWNS OF THE EAST

Near the Spanish border in the Beira Alta, a string of small towns were fortified throughout the centuries, with Guarda as the main fortress. These medieval guardians of the border area still stand, the remains of their castles and walls still visible. Starting at the farthest northeastern point of the fortifications from Guarda and proceeding clockwise around the leading fortress, they are:

Castelo Melhor, 45 miles northeast of Guarda, is near the confluence of the Douro and Coa Rivers. The little village, built onto a rocky promontory, has a well-preserved medieval wall with round towers. Olive trees surround the village.

Castelo Rodrigo, 35½ miles to Guarda's northeast, was a place of importance in the Middle Ages but has become just a pleasant, once-fortified hamlet.

Almeida stands on a hill 37 miles northeast of Guarda, about 6 miles from the Spanish border. Worth seeing are the double fortifications and other protective devices, including arched gateways and bridges leading into the town. The town has some tile-covered mansions.

It is here that the government decided to open one of its "frontier" pousadas, the **Pousada Senhora das Neves**, 6350 Almeida (tel. 071/542-90). An attractive, handsomely decorated place, it offers a total of 21 well-furnished bedrooms.

Highest rates are charged in the summer months when a single rents for 11,300$ ($73.45) daily and a double for 12,500$ ($81.25). The pousada also has a good restaurant and bar serving some of the finest meals in the area, with luncheons or dinners priced from 2,500$ ($16.25).

About 30½ miles east of the main guardian town is **Castelo Bom,** dating from the time of King Dinis I. There isn't much left of the early Middle Ages fortress, but the village still clusters around the hill which was once a stronghold. One ruined tower and a Gothic gate still stand. The Coa River runs past.

Quite near Castelo Bom is **Castelo Mendo,** 32 miles almost due east from Guarda on a craggy little hill. An interesting pillory is here, in front of a 17th-century church. The loftiest punishment cage in the province (23 feet up), it stands atop an octagon-shaped pillar. Fragments of a Gothic wall and some Renaissance structures still stand. Little remains of the castle but portions of a keep and a chapel. From the top of the hill on which the castle stood, you can look out over the Coa River valley.

The little town of **Sabugal,** 21 miles to the southeast of Guarda, is on a hill where the town grew up around the castle. The town belonged to Spain until the late 13th century. It was a part of the dowry of Isabella of Aragon when she became the bride of King Dinis I of Portugal. The castle can be visited by asking for the key at the town hall (Camera Municipal).

Sortelha, 27 miles south of Guarda, was a 12th-century fortress with a village within the fortified wall. It stands on a promontory that overlooks the valley of the Upper Zêzere River. You enter the old town by one of the big Gothic gates in the fortified wall. The houses climbing up the rise to the headland are built of granite.

Belmonte is a little town 17 miles south of Guarda standing on a spur of a foothill of the Sêrra da Estrêla, still proudly showing the square towers of the keep of its ancient fortress a long way off. The castle was built by King Dinis I. You can walk around the perimeter. The castle is open daily from 8 a.m. to noon and 1 to 5 p.m.

The man who discovered Brazil, navigator Pedro Álvares Cabral, was born in Belmonte and is honored by a statue standing on the main street. The town also has a parish church, Igreja de São Tiago, which can be visited from 8 a.m. to 6 p.m. It contains the tombs of Cabral and his mother, as well as a 13th-century pietá, carved out of one block of stone. Some mementos of the Roman days are in the church, and there is a Roman tower, **Centum Cellas,** about 2½ miles north of Belmonte.

About 30 miles due west of Guarda is **Linhares,** on a road that ends with a winding rough stretch. Built on a high bluff in the reign of King Dinis I, the outer walls of the castle and two towers still stand. The castle site overlooks the upper valley of the Mondego River.

Celerico da Beira, which lies 17½ miles to the northwest of the main guardian city, is on a hilly outcrop at the end of the Sêrra da Estrêla, where the castle ruins stand at the top.

On a plateau of the Sérra da Estrêla, 30 miles north of Guarda, is **Trancoso,** with the ramparts of its fortress still standing. There is a 9th-century wall that was rebuilt and its fortifications strengthened over the centuries. This is where King Dinis and Isabella of Aragon (the Queen Saint) were married in 1282. An old pillory stands in the middle of the town.

Marialva, 40 miles north of Guarda, has remains of a castle built in 1200. You can see a keep and a tower still standing in the ruined walls, with remnants of the old village here and there.

Last of the fortified towns that can be visited today is **Penedona,** 44 miles directly north of Guarda, on a craggy hill. The castle fortress beside which the town grew up can be visited by going up a set of steps and through the ramparts. Ask at the house on the left at the bottom of the steps. From the parapets of the castle, you can see the rugged plain leading to Trás-os-Montes.

PORTO AND ITS ENVIRONS

Portugal's second city, Porto, is the home of port wine, traditionally drunk in tulip-shaped glasses. The grapes that produce the wine come from the vineyards along the arid slopes of the Douro River Valley, many miles inland. At harvest time in autumn, the hills echo with the trilling of flutes, the cadence of drums.

The wine is brought to lodges at **Vila Nora de Gaia,** across the river from Porto, where it is blended, aged, and processed. In the past it was transported on flat-bottomed boats called *barcos rabelos.* With their long trailing rudders and sails flapping in the breeze, these boats with tails skirted down the Douro like swallows. Nowadays they have virtually given way to the train or even the unglamorous truck.

PORTO

Porto not only gave its name to the port wine, but to the whole country, the name deriving from the old settlement of Portus Cale. The Douro, from Rio do Ouro or river of gold, has always been the source of Porto's life blood. It enjoys many sunny days, yet at times Porto has been called a gray city of mist and rain.

It's set on a rocky gorge that the Douro cut out of a great stone mass. Ann Bridge wrote, "The whole thing looks like a singularly dangerous spider's web flung across space." Porto's most interesting quarter is the **Alfândega.** Here the steep narrow streets, hardly big enough for a car to pass through, and the balconied houses evoke Lisbon's Alfama, though the quarter has its own distinctive character. The Alfândega preserves the timeless color of many of the old buildings and cobbled ruas lining the riverbank.

Many write off Porto as an industrial city with some spectacular bridges, but that assessment is unfair. The provincial capital and university seat has its own artistic treasures, as we will see.

1. Orientation

Porto (Oporto in English) stretches along the last three miles of the River Douro on its right bank and is the hub of a communication network in north Portugal. At a distance of some 175 miles north of Lisbon, Porto is easily reached by train from the capital. Of course, the quickest and easiest method of getting there is by airplane. TAP, the Portuguese airline, provides quick connection between the two cities, and there are daily flights all year.

The **airport** of Pedras Rubras lies some nine miles from Porto. A taxi, the most convenient transport, from the airport into the center of Porto costs from 1,500$ ($9.75) to 1,800$ ($11.70). There is also good bus service into the center of the city from the airport. The no. 56 bus runs from Praça de Lisboa. For information about TAP at the airport, call 02/948-21-44. The main office of TAP is at 105 Praça Mousinho de Albuquerque (tel. 02/69-98-41) in Porto.

There are three main **railway stations** in Porto. They include São Bento Station (tel. 02/227-22) in the center of the city, lying only a block from the Praça da Liberdade. This station has trains serving the Douro Valley, along with destinations in the north, including Viana de Castelo and Braga. To the west of the center, but connected to São Bento by rail service, Campanhã Station is one of the most important. It serves the south of Portugal, including Lisbon, as well as international routes. For information, phone 01/56-41-41. Less important, Trindade Station (tel. 02/25-224) handles traffic in the immediate environs of Porto, including to the beach resort of Póvoa do Varzim and to the historic old city of Guimarães (refer to the Minho district in the next chapter).

It is also possible to come from Lisbon by **bus** (there are at least eight departures from Lisbon). Arriving passengers are deposited at the bus depot at 366 Rua Alexandre Herculano (tel. 02/269-54). Service is provided by the national bus company, Rodoviária Nacional.

Regardless of your method of transport, you will need to acquaint yourself with the geography of this rather complicated city. Its bridges, as mentioned, are famous. Connecting the right bank to the port wine center of Vila Nova de Gaia and the lands south is the **Maria Pía Bridge,** an architectural feat of Eiffel (yes, the same man who designed the Eiffel Tower in Paris). Another much-needed bridge spanning the Douro is the **Dom Luís I Bridge.** An iron bridge of two roadways, it was completed in 1886 by Seyrig, the Belgian engineer inspired by Eiffel. Another bridge, **Arrábida Bridge,** which opened in 1963, is bright and contemporary. Totally Portuguese in concept and execution, it is one of the largest single-span reinforced-concrete arches in Europe, representing the work of Edgar Cardoso.

The heart of Porto is **Avenida dos Aliados,** a wide paseo with a parklike center where families used to go for a stroll. It is bounded on the south by the **Praça General Humberto Delgado.** Two major shopping streets of Porto lie on either side of the Praça da Libereade: **Rua Clérigos** and **Rua 31 de Janeiro.** Rua Clérigos leads to the landmark Torre dos Clérigos, which to some is the symbol of Porto.

PRACTICAL FACTS

Some data applicable mainly to Porto and its environs may be of help during your visit.

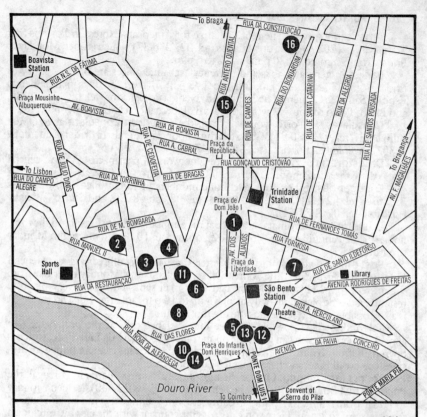

PORTO

```
0      ft    984
0      m     300
```

KEY TO SIGHTS:

1. Town Hall
2. Soares dos Reis National Museum
3. Santo António Hospital
4. Churches of Carmo and Carmelites
5. Cathedral (Sé)
6. Torre dos Clérigos
7. Church of Santo Ildefonso
8. Church of São Bento da Vitória
9. Stock Exchange
10. Basilica and Museum of St. Francis
11. University
12. Church of Santa Clara
13. Casa Museu de Guerra Junqueiro
14. Jardim do Infante Dom Henrique
15. Church of N.S. de Lapa
16. Church of the Immaculate Conception

American Express: The representative for American Express in Porto is Star Travel Service, 202 Avenida dos Aliados (tel. 02/236-37), which is open Monday to Friday from 9 a.m. to 12:30 p.m. and 2 to 6 p.m.

Banks: In general, banks and currency-exchange offices are open Monday to Friday from 8:30 to 11:45 a.m. and 1 to 2:45 p.m. Two central ones include Banco Espirito Santo & Comércial de Lisboa, 45 Avenida dos Aliados (tel. 02/32-00-31), and Banco Pinto & Sotto Mayor, 26 Praça da Liberdade (tel. 02/32-15-56).

Consulates: In Porto, you will reach the **American Consulate** at 826 Rua Júlio Dinis (tel. 02/630-94). Go to the third floor. There is also a **British Consulate** at 3072 Avenida da Boavista (tel. 02/68-47-89).

Drugstores: Porto is well serviced by a network of pharmacies. A most central one is the Farmacia Central do Porto, 203 31 de Janeiro (tel. 02/216-84).

Emergencies: Emergency telephone numbers include **police** (tel. 02/268-21), **fire** (tel. 02/48-41-21), **Red Cross** (tel. 02/66-68-72), and **Santo António Hospital** (tel. 02/273-54).

Laundry: A laundromat is available at the Shopping Center Brasilia on the third floor. It's the Penguin (tel. 02/69-50-32), open from 10 a.m. to midnight, Monday to Saturday.

Post office: If you want to mail a letter, the main post office is at Praça General Humberto Delgado, near the Tourist Office. It sells stamps Monday to Friday from 9 a.m. to 7 p.m. However, if you had your mail sent general delivery or poste restante, it can be picked up daily from 8 a.m. to 10 p.m. at Largo 1 de Dezembro. It is also possible to send telegrams during those hours.

Telephone: It is possible to place long-distance calls at the post office (see above). Otherwise, you can go to the phone office at 62 Praça da Liberdade, which is open daily from 8 a.m. to 11:30 p.m. By placing your calls at these public institutions you avoid hotel surcharges, which can be steep.

Tourist information: One of the most helpful tourist boards in Portugal, the **Porto Tourist Board,** 25 Rua Clube Fenianos (tel. 02/31-27-40), is open Monday to Friday from 9 a.m. to 7 p.m., on Saturday from 9 a.m. to 4 p.m., and on Sunday from 10 a.m. to 1 p.m. Here you can acquaint yourself with the city by watching a film, *Letter from Oporto,* during operating hours of the office without making previous arrangements.

Transportation: Porto is well serviced by a network of **buses, trolley buses,** and **trams,** with tickets costing from 95$ (60¢). However, it is cheaper to purchase a Turístico Pass, entitling you to four days of transportation, if you plan to do extensive touring in the Porto area. The cost is 850$ ($5.55). They can be bought at various tobacco shops and kiosks around town. **Taxis** are available day and night. Call 02/488-06 for radio taxis or hail one on the street or at a taxi stand.

---

2. The Hotels

There has long been a lack of top-rated accommodations in this capital of the north. Some so-called first-class hotels could only be recommended in the direst of emergencies. However, in recent years the outlook has brightened considerably. With the addition of several new first-class hotels, and the restoration of some interesting older properties, Porto now provides the most interesting selection of superior accommodations north of Lisbon.

THE TOP HOTELS

The most traditional, and usually the first, choice of visitors to Porto is the plushly furnished **Hotel Infante de Sagres,** 62 Praça de Lencastre, 4000 Porto (tel. 02/281-01). Its richness in handcrafted ornamentation convinces most visitors that it dates from the 19th century. Actually it was constructed in 1951 by a wealthy textile manufacturer. Its imposing mass of carved paneling, stained glass, and wrought iron was assembled solely to house the businessman's powerful clients during their trips to Porto. The most beautiful mantelpiece found in any hotel sits beneath the circular balcony ventilating the upstairs music room. The fireplace was designed and carved by one of the hotel's former night porters in his spare time over a period of years.

Its rosters are filled with the names of rich and famous clients who once settled themselves into one of the upholstered armchairs in the antique-laden lobbies. They include Princess Anne and Prince Philip, the president of Portugal, along with many of his cabinet ministers, the governor of São Paulo, and everybody from the president of Zaire to delegations from the People's Republic of China. Today many of the establishment's original employees continue to staff the hotel, including its charming and conscientious manager, Fernando de Sousa. The 84-room hotel maintains one of the highest ratios of employees to guests (1.3 employees per room) of any hotel in Porto and offers excellent service. In fact, the staff of this palace seems to have developed strong feelings of loyalty.

The management has thoughtfully created a parasol- and plant-dotted sun terrace within a central courtyard for warm-weather enjoyment. Bedrooms contain large marble-covered baths, color TVs, mini-bars, and elegantly conservative furniture. Year-round rates for the standard rooms are 17,000 ($110.50) to 18,500$ ($120.25) daily in a single, 19,500$ ($126.75) to 21,000$ ($136.50) in a double. All tariffs include a continental breakfast. The hotel's high-ceilinged dining room serves formal breakfasts, lunches, and dinners in an old-world format. In addition, room service is available 24 hours a day.

Parking is possible in front of the hotel's pink-walled façade. It sits immediately to the side of a monumental square flanked by the Town Hall and Porto's showplace, Avenida dos Aliados.

Porto Sheraton, 1269 Avenida da Boavista, 4100 Porto (tel. 02/66-88-22). Opened with a flourish in 1986, this is now considered the most stylish and desirable modern hotel in Porto. It rises across the street from its most noteworthy competitor, the Meridien, above the apartments and private villas of the Boavista section, a short distance from the commercial center of the city. Set back from a busy street and ringed with parking, it was designed with discreet bands of differently hued stone and impressive rows of bronze-colored glass to reflect the glare of the Portuguese sunlight. Inside, a battalion of leather chairs is clustered within earshot of a bandstand and a bar, out of which emerge upbeat music and convivial chatter, respectively. The hotel contains a heated swimming pool, a squash court, a health club, an elegant restaurant, and 253 air-conditioned bedrooms. Each of these offers a hairdryer, a mini-bar, radio, TV with video movies, and phone. Depending on the accommodation, singles range from 18,000$ ($117) to 22,000$ ($143) daily, and doubles from 20,000$ ($130) to 24,000$ ($156).

Le Meridien, 1466 Avenida da Boavista, 4100 Porto (tel. 02/66-89-63). One of the most dramatically modern hotels in town is fronted with three vertical rows of bay windows stretching to the top of its skyscraping concrete shell. You'll pass beneath a jutting five-sided entrance portico before finding yourself inside this hotel, owned by Air France and designed especially to make French-speaking business travelers and vacationers feel at home. Dozens of plants are reflected in the mirrors, which seem to enlarge the marble- and chrome-covered lobby. The musician performing in the modern lobby-level bar might be accompanied by a synthesizer, making the ambience there smooth and mellow. There's a health club on the third floor, plus a terrace restaurant (covered separately in my dining recommendations). A basement-level disco is open every night from 10:30 p.m. to 4 a.m., except on Sunday.

Opened in 1984, the hotel provides 232 well-furnished bedrooms, each with TV, a mini-bar, in-house video movies, private bath, and phone. Singles cost from 21,000$ ($136.50) to 27,000$ ($175.50) daily, and doubles go for 24,000$

($156) to 30,000$ ($195), including a continental breakfast, taxes, and service. The hotel stands about two miles from the heart of the city, an inexpensive taxi ride.

Hotel Ipanema, 156 Rua Campo Alegre, 4100 Porto (tel. 02/66-80-61), is one of the best four-star hotels in Portugal, having opened its doors in 1984. A sleek modern structure, it has become a feature of the city's skyline. Its elongated rows of smoked glass are visible from the highway stretching toward Lisbon. In fact, one of the establishment's best points is that it's easy to find. Just exit the highway from Lisbon at the signs indicating the direction of Porto, and you'll find it on a cobblestone-covered road leading to the center of town, about a mile away. Inside, an attractive and dimly lit bar looks over a plant-filled atrium. The marble-walled lobby contains an unusual collection of Brazilian sculpture, perhaps to honor the namesake of the hotel. Meals in the Restaurant Rios are especially popular on Sunday, when a buffet is served. Each of the handsomely furnished bedrooms is accented with cedar and has views over Porto, along with a radio, a tile bath, and TV. Singles range from 18,600$ ($120.90) daily and doubles from 19,000$ ($123.50), including a continental breakfast. Car parking is available on the premises.

Porto-Atlântico Hotel, 61 Rua Afonso Lopes Vieria, 4100 Porto (tel. 02/69-49-41), is the residential facility of a complex built on the outskirts of Porto, containing a cinema, gymnasium, inside/outside swimming pool, and a sauna, among other amenities. The hotel has 58 carpeted bedrooms, with balconies and all the conveniences of a five-star hostelry. Singles range in price from 15,500$ ($100.75) to 16,500$ ($107.25) daily, and doubles go for 16,500$ ($107.25) to 17,500$ ($113.75). On the premises is a fine restaurant, Foco (see my dining recommendations). Service here is efficient and polite. The warmly paneled bar has comfortable low-slung leather chairs, and there's an outdoor terrace.

THE MEDIUM-PRICED RANGE

Even though it was conceived for commercial travelers, **Dom Henrique,** 179 Rua Guedes de Azevedo, 4000 Porto (tel. 02/257-55), is equally accommodating to tourists. In the city center, this hotel, which was recently restored, rises 18 floors and offers 112 rooms, of which 21 are executive suites. There's even a presidential suite. Each well-furnished accommodation is equipped with color TV, video, radio, refrigerated bar, direct-dial phone, and hairdryer. The charges are 13,500$ ($87.75) daily in a single, rising to 15,000$ ($97.50) in a double. Spectacular views can be seen through the hotel's 17th floor bar, Anrrique, and 18th floor restaurant and grill, O Nave. Food is served daily from 12:30 to 2 p.m. and 7:30 to 10 p.m., with meals costing from 2,200$ ($14.30). On the ground floor, clients can order light meals at the coffee shop, Tabula, which is open daily from 7 a.m. to 2 a.m.

Hotel Castor, 685 Rua Alegria, 4000 Porto (tel. 02/57-00-14). Built in the late 1960s, this white-walled hotel lies within a relatively quiet neighborhood in a section of town rarely visited by tourists. Known for its pleasant staff and its scattering of antiques, the hotel boasts a comfortably contemporary interior where two stylish restaurants do a respectable business in their own right. One is an Italian-style trattoria, offering pizzas on its bill of fare along with other specialties. My favorite corner of the hotel is Beaver's Disco, where a large-screen TV shows transmissions from throughout Europe. The format is that of a stylish pub (music is played only on weekends). Each of the conservatively decorated bedrooms contains a private bath, TV, radio, phone, and mini-bar. With breakfast included, singles cost 9,500$ ($61.75) daily, doubles 11,000$ ($71.50), and triples 13,600$ ($88.40).

Albergaría Miradouro, 598 Rua da Alegria, 4000 Porto (tel. 02/57-07-17), is like an eagle's nest, a slim 13-floor baby skyscraper built atop a hill outside the main part of the city. The Miradouro offers vista-scanning rooms (you can watch ships laden with port making their way to the open sea). The small-scale public rooms are tasteful. The lower bar is decorated with wall tiles from Japan and Portugal. Two plush elevators whisk you to an upper bar, with walls opening onto a view. The more expensive corner rooms are preferred, of course. In these, two walls have built-in wardrobes and chests (with a built-in pair of beds); the walls are all glass. In all the rooms you'll find a vestibule, luggage storage, a valet stand, desks, and sitting room. There are 30 rooms, all with private bath. One person pays from 6,000$ ($39) daily, and two persons are charged 7,000$ ($45.50). A continental breakfast only is served. The facilities include a subterranean garage.

Hotel São João, 120 Rua do Bonjardim, 4000 Porto (tel. 02/216-62), is in a class by itself: the only hotel-residência of its type to be rated deluxe by the government. Such a designation shows what deep imprint human warmth can make upon a limited framework, especially when the owners have good taste, a certain flair, plus a concern for the welfare of their guests. Accomplishing this is the Baldaque family, who own the top floor of a modern building right in the heart of Porto.

You ascend in an elevator. The living room is inviting with its fireplace nook, deep sofa, and antiques, such as a grandfather clock. The main corridor leading to the bedrooms is like an art gallery, with old tapestries, high-back 18th-century chairs, engravings, and large copper bowls of flowers. The bedrooms—only 14 in all, each a double—combine modern with traditional furnishings, reserving a section for a sitting area. Every room contains its own pink and white marble bath. One person pays 9,500$ ($61.75) daily, and two are charged 12,000$ ($78), including a continental breakfast.

Grande Hotel da Batalha, 116 Praça da Batakham, 4000 Porto (tel. 02/205-71), is highly favored by international buyers of port wine. A substantial business person's hotel, it has comfortable rooms and an excellent restaurant where one can order Portuguese specialties. Each of the 142 bedrooms has a radio, phone, and tile bath. A single rents for 8,500$ ($55.25) daily and a double for 10,000$ ($65). The bedrooms have a lighter decorative treatment than the public rooms, yet the lounge, the bar, and the restaurant are quite adequate. The hotel is in the center of the city.

Albergaría de São José, 172 Rua de Alegria, 4000 Porto (tel. 02/38-02-61), is a modern, corner, first-class inn, with all the facilities you'll need for a pleasant stay in Porto. While the lobby, the lounge, and the regional drinking bar are furnished in a contemporary idiom, the bedrooms have antique furnishings that connect you with regional Portugal. The carved mahogany beds are old world in their elegance. Each room has selected music, phones, and a tile bath. A single costs 6,000$ ($39) daily, a double costs 8,100$ ($52.65). There's a private hotel garage.

Grande Hotel do Porto, 197 Rua Santa Catarina, 4000 Porto (tel. 02/281-76), right in the heart of the town, offers comparatively moderate rates. It has been given a facelift, and contains 100 bedrooms, each with bath, central heating, and air conditioning. Best of all are the brightly painted rooms, all modern, with many built-in tables. A single rents for 8,000$ ($52) daily. Doubles are priced at 8,800$ ($57.20). A continental breakfast is included. Many Portuguese families are attracted to this hotel, drawn by its near grandeur. Along the main-corridor lounge, with its row of marble pillars and crystal chandeliers, are small lounges; at one end is a bar. There's a fine old-world dining room with six chandeliers and ornate curtains.

Hotel do Imperio, 130 Praça da Batalha, 4000 Porto (tel. 02/268-61), is a modern 100-room hotel, close to the railway station in the heart of the city. It's rather well designed and attractive for a railway-station hotel, with a streamlined interior decor. Bedrooms are well thought out, tasteful, with color-harmonized schemes. Units come with wall globe lights, bedside tables, phones, central heating, and private tile baths. The cost of a single is 6,500$ ($42.25) daily, and a double runs 8,000$ ($52), including breakfast. Children up to 8 years are granted a 50% reduction.

THE BUDGET RANGE

You can have a pleasant stay at the **Castelo de Santa Catarina,** 1347 Rua de Santa Catarina, 4000 Porto (tel. 02/49-55-99). In the 1920s a Brazilian military officer returned to his native Porto determined to create the most flamboyant residence in town. Drawing upon the resources of his influential family, who manufactured ceramic tiles, he created a sprawling compound of greenhouses, terraced gardens, a chapel, and a sumptuous main house. To encircle them, he added a semicircular crescent of servants' quarters. Today the tile-covered exterior walls almost give an encapsulated history of Portugal. What used to be one of the residential showplaces of Porto is behind a high wall in a commercial neighborhood about a mile from the center where the owner has arranged 25 rentable bedrooms.

After ringing the bell, you'll be ushered down a labyrinthine series of halls and narrow stairways. To get to your room, you'll pass through lushly opulent but disorganized sitting rooms and ballrooms, illuminated with crystal chandeliers. Each of the small bedrooms contains a set of carved antique furniture, often of rosewood. The plumbing fixtures are designed with a florid, appealing art nouveau flair. Doubles rent for 7,500$ ($48.75) daily, and singles cost 4,750$ ($30.90), with a continental breakfast included. Go here for an insight into another era, and don't expect the services of a hotel.

Pensão Residencial Rex, 117 Praça da República, 4000 Porto (tel. 02/245-48). The façade of this establishment fits in gracefully with its location on one of the most beautiful squares of Porto. Its design is a classicized derivation of art nouveau, replete with sea-green tiles, cast-iron embellishments, and Roman-style window treatments. The semi-majestic marble staircase leading into the reception area from the street is lined with richly colored paneling that looks as if it had just been oiled. The lobby and each of the 21 bedrooms is crowned with an ornately molded plaster ceiling embellished with painted highlights, and much of the furniture is antique. The bathrooms, however, have been modernized. With a continental breakfast included, a double or a single rents for 5,000$ ($32.50) daily. There's a tiny bar in the TV lounge at the back of the ground floor, but no restaurant. The iron gates enclosing an adjacent driveway swing open on request to allow you to park a car.

Albergaría Girassol, 133 Rua Sá da Bandeira, 4000 Porto (tel. 02/218-91), is a modest little upper-floor inn. The hotel offers 18 nicely designed and furnished rooms with private bath. Each bed has a built-in headboard. Rooms at the rear are quieter. Including continental breakfast, a single rents for 5,000$ ($32.50) daily and a double for 5,500$ ($35.75). There's a small TV lounge with soft leather chairs, all tasteful and cozy. You can have your morning meal in a little breakfast room.

Hotel Peninsular, 21 Rua Sá da Bandeira, 4000 Porto (tel. 02/230-12). The only reminder of this building's original purpose as an outbuilding to a nearby church is a lobby mural crafted from blue and white tiles, showing a coronation. Today the building is an unpretentiously pleasant hotel, outfitted with 50 simple and low-cost bedrooms. It stands near the train station of St. Bento in the heart of the city. There's a restaurant one floor above the street, which is accessible via a darkly stained stairway near the reception desk. The belle époque façade is marked with an incongruous neon sign. Bedrooms, all but six with private bath, rent for 5,000$ ($32.50) daily in a single, 6,300$ ($40.95) in a double, and include a continental breakfast.

3. Where to Dine

When Prince Henry the Navigator was rounding up the cattle in the Douro Valley for his men aboard the legendary caravels, he shipped out the juicy steaks and left the tripe behind. Faced with the tripe, the denizens of Porto responded bravely and began inventing recipes for it. To this day they carry the appellation of tripe eaters, and it has become their favorite local dish. To sample the most characteristic specialty of Porto, you can order *tripas à moda do Porto* (tripe stewed with spicy sausage and string beans). Of course, the city offers other viands, and quite good ones at that.

Restaurante Foco, Hotel Porto-Atlântico, 86 Rua Afonso Lopes Vieira (tel.

66-72-48). The entrance to this attractive restaurant outside town is adjacent to the already-recommended hotel that houses it. It's worth the excursion by taxi from the center, partially because of its unobtrusive and polite but very thorough service. You'll find the establishment within a quadrangle created by a complex of residential apartment buildings, a few minutes' drive past Le Meridien Hotel. Before dinner, you can enjoy a drink in one of the low-slung leather chairs in a tiny corner of the restaurant. You'll then be ushered past a screen of plants to a chair in the luxuriously modern dining room. From the windows you'll have a view of the swimming pool. Meals are priced from 4,000$ ($26) and might include trout Transmontana style, grilled squid on a skewer, pork chunks Minho style, roasted kid, smoked salmon, and a daily specialty of the chef. Food is served daily from 12:30 to 3 p.m. and 7 to 11 p.m.

Restaurante Escondidinho, 144 Rua de Passos Manuel (tel. 210-79), is a regional tavern, popular with the leading port wine merchants and the English. The name means hidden or masked. The entrance alone is a clue, a façade in burnt-orange tile framing an arch leading to the L-shaped dining room. Inside is a world of time-blackened beams and timbers, a corner baronial stone fireplace, and carved wooden shelf brackets holding a collection of antique Portuguese ceramics. The chairs, with their intricate carving and brass studs, are just right for a cardinal, or at least a friar. The waiters are old world, yet proud of the prevailing informality. They feel free to speak their minds, candidly telling you the day's best dishes. Take their word.

The shellfish soup and the charcoaled sardines are always reliable. The chef's special dishes include hake in madeira sauce and a chateaubriand for two. Desserts include a kirsch omelet or an orange pudding. An average meal will cost from 4,500$ ($29.25), served from noon to 3 p.m. and 7 to 10 p.m. Telephone for reservations. Closed Sunday.

Mesa Antiga, 208 Rua de St. Ildefonso (tel. 264-32). Its impeccably crafted blue and white tiles combine with its gnarled ceiling beams for a hint of the dignified severity of old Portugal. Above well-ordered rows of dining tables, brass trumpeters rise from the curves of brass chandeliers. The food served here, everything home-made, is among the best regional cuisine in Porto. Conjured from a tiny kitchen by members of the owner's family, platters emerge steaming hot. Full meals cost from 2,500$ ($16.25) and are served from noon to midnight. Specialties include a delectable version of grilled sole served with a fresh and aromatic green sauce, squid on a spit, and an array of daily specials. The most typical dish is tripe prepared in the old-fashioned method of Porto. The restaurant is on a crowded and narrow street in the commercial center.

Portucale Restaurante, 598 Rua da Alegria (tel. 278-61), perches on the roof-top of the Albergaria Miradouro. Seemingly the highest point in town, outside the heart of the city, it offers wide views of the river, the boats, and rooftops. Two elevators zip you to the 13th floor, from which you ascend to the dining room via a spiral staircase, crossing a tiny lily and fish pond. Despite the infinity of the panoramic sweep, the restaurant is fairly intimate, with tables set with fine silver, china, and flowers. There's an appetizing pastry cart.

The hand-woven hanging is by Camarinha, the artist who designed the à la carte menu. Specialties of the house include *bacalhau* (dried codfish) a marinheiro, *cabrito à serrana* (kid in wine sauce), smoked swordfish, lomos do pescado, steak flambé, rice, and mushrooms, and homemade cakes. For a complete dinner, the costs range from 2,800$ ($18.20) to 5,500$ ($35.75). Open daily from 12:30 to 3 p.m. and 7:30 to 10 p.m.

Les Terrasses, Le Meridien, 1466 Avenida da Boavista (tel. 02/66-89-63), advertises itself as a restaurant and brasserie, but its uniformed maître d'hôtel and its plush gardenlike decor give it the aura of a formal dining room. Off the lobby of this hotel owned by Air France, it lies nearly three miles from the city center. The restaurant is open daily for both lunch and dinner. A wooden terrace, covered with lace-like cast-iron garden furniture, offers the option of dining under the trees outside. Most guests, however, prefer the air-conditioned interior because of the noise of passing traffic. Tables are separated into semiprivate alcoves. Menu specialties reflect a strong French influence, with the addition of many Portuguese regional dishes as well. The wine steward will be pleased to suggest a reasonably priced vintage of Portuguese wine to accompany your meal, which might cost as much as 6,000$ ($39). Reservations are a good idea. Hours are daily from 12:30 to 3 p.m. and 7:30 to 11 p.m.

Restaurante Chinês, 38 Avenida Vimara Peres (tel. 289-15), is Porto's leading Chinese restaurant. Housed in a modern building at the entrance to Dom Luís I Bridge, it is an incongruous combination of the new and the old. Setting the mood are traditional Chinese lanterns and a dragon mural. It is a spacious two-level dining room. For your appetizer you might select from such choices as egg flower soup, fried wonton, or even fried almonds. Main courses include prawns with curry, sweet-and-sour fish, and breast of chicken with pineapple. For dessert, there are many appetizing selections, including bananas with honey. A dinner begins at 2,000$ ($13). Food is served from 12:30 to 2:30 p.m. and 7:30 to 10:30 p.m.

Aquário Marisqueiro, 179 Rua Rodrigues Sampaio (tel. 222-31), is one of the finest seafood restaurants in Porto—actually two, connected by a central kitchen. Its location is within sight of the City Hall, and close to either of two leading hotels: the Infante de Sagres and the Hotel São João. Marine fare reigns supreme at this "aquarium." Soup made by boiling the shells of mariscos is a good beginner. Main fish orders include cod, of course. An excellent fish dish is clams in the Spanish style, but the house specialty is an açorda (a type of bread panada) of shellfish. The prices of these two dishes vary according to the season. Sole is your safest bet, and trout with ham is even more interesting. A typical dinner here will cost 1,800$ ($11.70) to 2,800$ ($18.20). Hours are 11:30 a.m. to 11 p.m. daily except Sunday.

Restaurant Orfeu, 928 Rua de Júlio Dinis (tel. 643-22). Don't confuse this completely competent restaurant with the shabby café and snackbar that occupies its street level. Descend stone stairs to reach the basement-level restaurant, which is especially popular with Porto's business community. Once seated at one of the roomy tables, a battalion of polite waiters will take your order. You can select from such dishes as leg of lamb, chateaubriand, perhaps partridge or hare. Calves' kidneys are prepared with a madeira sauce and, for dessert, you might like the bananas with cognac. Meals cost from 2,000$ ($13). Hours are from 8 a.m. to midnight daily. The restaurant is air-conditioned.

Restaurant Tripeiro, 195 Rua Passos Manuel (tel. 258-86). This restaurant's textured stucco walls and elaborately crafted wooden ceiling offer a cool and dark retreat from the glaring sunlight outside. A group of efficient waiters serves full meals priced from 2,000$ ($13) apiece. You can enjoy *vinho verde* (green wine), which is ideal with the specialty of the chef, *tripas* (tripe) à moda do Porto, in honor of the namesake of the restaurant. In addition, you might order several different preparations of codfish or any of several beef or shellfish dishes (the latter priced by the kilo). Meals are served from noon to 3 p.m. and 7 to 10:30 p.m. Closed Sunday.

Garrafão, 53 Rua António Nobre, Leça da Palmeira (tel. 995-17-35), a traditional restaurant in the suburbs, overlooks the Praia Boa Nova. Attractively situated, with a pleasant decor, it seats about 100 and serves mainly seafood. The prices of the seafood specialties vary according to the season. The Garrafão is known also for its wine cellar, containing a large selection of the best Portuguese wines. À la carte specialties feature a shrimp omelet, shellfish soup, grilled sole, veal dishes, and caramel custard. The tab is likely to run 1,800$ ($11.70) to 4,000$ ($26) for a complete meal. The restaurant has a pleasant dining room with windows over the beach. It is open from noon to 5 p.m. and 7 p.m. to midnight daily except Sunday.

Taverna do Bebobos, 21-25 Cais da Ribeira (tel. 31-35-65), is perhaps the oldest (founded 1876) and smallest restaurant in Porto, directly on the riverside dock. Women sell fish on the quay, and overhead, fluttering from wrought-iron balconies, are lines of laundry. Inside, the ground floor has a service bar with every sort of knickknack on its little tables. A narrow open staircase leads to an intimate dining room upstairs with a corner stone fireplace, a coved ceiling, an iron scale filled with sprouting onions, a five-foot-high coffee mill, brass and copper pans, ships' lanterns, and a flamboyantly painted pottery crèche. On the tables are hunks of dark, crusty "mother earth" bread, and the portions are large enough to be shared. To begin your meal, you might order a hearty bowl of caldo verde or a plate of grilled sardines. For a main course, I'd suggest either trout with ham, regional codfish, or pork prepared in the Alentejana style (that is, with a savory clam sauce). A fruit salad finishes the meal nicely. Count on spending 1,800$ ($11.70) to 3,000$ ($19.50) for a complete meal, plus the cost of your wine. Because of the small number of tables, it's necessary to have your hotel call and make a reservation for you. The place is open from noon to 2:30 p.m. and 7 to 9:30 p.m. daily except Sunday.

A Brasileira, 116 Rua do Bonjardim (tel. 271-46), is an art deco coffee-house, the virtual social center of Porto, plus a first-class restaurant and a bustling snackbar. In the restaurant part of the complex you can order cream of shellfish soup followed by such main dishes as roast chicken, grilled trout, or veal liver, topped off by chocolate mousse. An average meal costs 1,800$ ($11.70) to 2,000$ ($13). Hours are daily from noon to 3 p.m. and 7 to 10:30 p.m.

Abadia, 22 Rua do Ateneu Comércial do Porto (tel. 287-57), stands on a short street with a patio entrance. It has an open dining mezzanine. The cook specializes in fresh fish dishes, such as codfish Abadia and codfish Gomes de Sá. He also offers other dishes such as tripe stew Porto and fried pork. Soups are hearty and full of flavor. Count on spending 1,200$ ($7.80). Large and clean, the restaurant serves daily from noon to 10 p.m.

---

4. What to See and Do

Exploring the sights of Porto requires some probing. But your discoveries will compensate for the effort. The Tourist Office suggests that one needs at least three days to explore Porto, but most foreign visitors don't spend that much time here. For those on a rushed schedule, the most famous sightseeing attractions include a visit to a wine lodge at Vila Nova de Gaia; the panoramic view from the Torre dos Clérigos, with its view of the Douro; a visit to the Sé (cathedral); a stroll through the most important museum, Soares dos Reis National; a walk through Ribeira, the old quarter, with its little alleyways leading to the harbor (best seen on market days); and if time remains, a visit to the Gothic church of St. Francis, with its stunning baroque interior.

THE CATHEDRAL DISTRICT

At the Terreiro de Sé, the **Sé (cathedral)** has grown and changed with the city —that is, until about the 18th century. Originally founded by a medieval queen and designed in a foreboding, basically Romanesque style, it is now a monument to changing architectural tastes. Part of the twin towers, the rose window, the naves, and the vestry are all elements of the original 13th-century structure. However, the austere Gothic cloister was added at the end of the 14th century and was later decorated with azulejos depicting events from the Song of Solomon. Opening off the cloister is the Chapel of St. Vincent, built in the closing years of the 16th century.

The main chapel was erected in the 17th century, and in 1736 the baroque architect Nicolo Nasoni of Italy added the north façade and its attractive loggia. The monumental altar is flanked by twisted columns, the nave by fading frescoes. In the small baroque Chapel of the Holy Sacrament (to the left of the main altar) is an altarpiece fashioned entirely of silver, the work so elaborate that the whole piece gives the illusion of constant movement.

Outside on the Cathedral Square is a Manueline-style pillory and a statue of Vimara Peres, the warrior of Afonso III of León, who captured ancient Portucale in 868. To the side, also on the same square, is the 18th-century **Archbishop's Palace,** sequestered for municipal offices. Noted for its granite-cased doors and windows, it also contains an exceptional stairway inside.

In back of the cathedral is one of the most charming típico streets of Porto: **Rua da Dom Hugo.** Along its route, you'll pass the **Chapel of Our Lady of Truths.** It's invariably closed, but you can peek through the grillwork at the gilded rococo altar, with a statue of the Virgin at the center.

Down the same street, you'll reach **Casa Museu de Guerra Junqueiro** (tel. 31-36-44). This famous Portuguese poet lived between 1850 and 1923. The house was built by the Italian architect Nicolo Nasoni (1691–1773). Each room is arranged to preserve the private art collection and memorabilia of Guerra Junqueiro.

The collection includes Georgian and Portuguese silver, Flemish chests, Italian, oriental, Spanish, and Portuguese ceramics, and ecclesiastical wood and stone carvings. Joining the many examples of religious sculpture are an Italian Renaissance desk, metal plates said to have been made in Nürnberg, a 16th-century Brussels tapestry, as well as interesting Portuguese furniture. Hours are from 10 a.m. to 12:30 p.m. and 2 to 5:30 p.m. Monday to Saturday, from 2 to 6 p.m. Sunday. Admission is 50$ (35¢), except on Saturday and Sunday when it is free.

In the same district, you can cross the busy artery, Avenida Dom Afonso Henriques, and head down Rua Saraiva de Carvalho until you reach Largo de 1 de Dezembro and—

The **Church of Santa Clara.** First completed in 1416, the interior was transformed by the impassioned artists of the 17th century, masters of woodwork and gilding. The number of man-hours invested is staggering to contemplate. There is hardly a square inch that isn't covered with angels, saints, cherubs, patterned designs, and great knobbed bosses in an architectural scramble of rococo and baroque, one of the most exceptional examples in Portugal. The clerestory windows permit the sunlight to flood in, making a golden crown of the upper regions. The façade is squat and plain, however.

If the keeper of the keys takes a liking to you, he'll take you on a behind-the-scenes tour of the precincts. In the Tribute Room, for example, you'll see a devil carved on the choir stalls. Throughout the tour you will see a hodgepodge of many bad, fading paintings, some not even hung—just propped casually in the corner. But it's intriguing to see what lies beyond all the glitter and glamour out front.

Sights Near the Cathedral

Passing alongside the water, you can look for a front row of buildings on **Rua Nova da Alfândega.** Underneath these structures is an arcade that is a continuous row of Romanesque arches. Perhaps they faced the waterfront until the street was built at a high level like a dike.

Up from this major artery is one of the most colorful sectors of Porto. If time allows, wander through some of the stepped back streets. In other places, the area might be called a slum or ghetto, but in Porto, the district has such style— vegetable-and meat-stuffed arcaded markets, churches, museums, monuments, even such elegant buildings as the Stock Exchange and the British Factory—that it retains a certain punch.

A good point to begin your exploration is on the main **Praça do Infante Dom Henriques,** named after the Porto-born Henry the Navigator, who launched Portugal on its Age of Discovery. At this square you can visit the big covered food market, where tripe is sold in great quantities.

Facing the square (entrance on Rua da Bolsa) is the **Stock Exchange,** housed in the imposing 19th-century Palácio da Bolsa. It is known for its Moorish Hall, a much-modified pastiche resembling a room in the Alhambra at Granada. The walls, ceiling, and balcony are a gilded mass of patterns and geometrical configurations.

The pastel-blue column bases glow in sunlight filtered through intricately latticed octagonal skylights and floral side windows. Guided tours are conducted daily except Saturday and Sunday from 9 a.m. to 1 p.m. and 1:30 to 5 p.m. in summer (off-season, from 9 a.m. to noon and 2 to 5 p.m.).

Basilica of St. Francis, reached by steps up from the waterfront and opening onto Rua da San Francisco, was built in the Gothic style between 1383 and 1410. But in the 17th and 18th centuries it underwent extensive rococo dressing. The vault pillars and columns are lined with gilded woodwork: cherubs, garlands of roses, cornucopia of fruit, and frenzied animals, entwined and dripping with gold. Many of the wide-ribbed Gothic arches are made of marble resembling the Italian forest-green serpentine variety. The marble almost seems to fade and blend with the gray granite columns and floors.

The Romanesque rosette dominates the façade, whose square portal is flanked by double twisted columns. Above the columns, a profusely ornamented niche contains a simple white statue of the patron saint. In the rose window, 12 mullions emanate from the central circle in apostolic symbolism, ending in a swag-like stone fringe. The steps seem to spill out into the square fan-like along the base of the curved walls.

Next door you can visit the **Museum of St. Francis** (tel. 264-93). The sacristan estimates that 30,000 human skulls have been interred in the cellars. Even though he may be exaggerating, this dank building was once the burial ground for rich or poor. Nowadays it is a catacomb unique in Portugal.

A section of it looks like an antique shop. There are paintings too, one of St. Francis of Assisi worshiping Christ on the Cross. Oddities include some of the first paper money printed in Portugal and an 18th-century ambulance that was really a sedan chair. The Sala de Sessoes adds a note of unexpected elegance. Built in the rich baroque style, it is now a meeting hall with a Louis XIV table and João V chairs. Wherever you go in the room, the painted eyes of framed bishops follow you, watching like Big Brother. The museum is open June 1 to September 30 daily from 9 a.m. to noon and 2 to 6 p.m. Off-season, it keeps the same hours. However, on Saturday and Sunday it doesn't open until 10 a.m. The admission is 200$ ($1.30).

Also reached by steps up from the water is one of the city's leading museums, sheltered on a típico square and rarely visited. Culture seekers are usually beset with escudo-hungry children who live in the jumble of dwellings nearby.

Museum of Ethnography and History of Douro Litoral, Largo S. João Novo (tel. 220-10), celebrates the arts, handcrafts, and culture of the Douro River valley. It's a rustic potpourri of spinning wheels, looms, and animal and fish traps nostalgically evoking the simple lifestyle of the peasant. Roman coins and other artifacts remind one that legions from far afield once marched in and settled on the banks of the river.

Earthenware jugs from Vita-da-Feira, gold filigree work, a bas-relief of a provincial cottage, and a three-faced Christ are among the exhibits, along with primitive puppets, provincial bedrooms, ceramics, dolls in regional costume, ship models, decorative ox yokes, weathervanes, cannon balls, spears, antique sarcophagi, even a wine press. Any or all of the above may be viewed from 10 a.m. to noon and 2 to 5 p.m. daily, except Sunday and Monday. Admission is free.

THE TOP MUSEUM

Created in 1833 by order of the king, Dom Pedro IV, **Soares dos Reis National Museum,** Rua de Dom Manuel II (tel. 271-10), was called the Museu Portugal when it was opened to the public in 1840. One hundred years later it was declared a National Museum and was dedicated to Soares dos Reis (1847–1889), the noted sculptor from Porto, and the name was changed. *Desterrado* and *Flor Agreste* are remarkable sculptures by this artist, but good portraits and allegorical figures can also be seen in the same gallery.

In the foreign painters collection, you'll find Dutch, Flemish, Italian, and

French works, including two François Clouets (1522–1572) portraits and landscapes by Jean Pillement (1727–1808). The most representative and unified display is that of the Portuguese 19th-century painters, particularly from the Porto School. Henrique Pousão (1859–1887) and Silva Porto (1850–1893) are represented by fine naturalistic work.

Also displayed in the museum are decorative arts, including ceramics, glassware, gold and silver work, furniture, and other objects.

The museum is open daily, except Monday, from 10 a.m. to 5 p.m., charging an admission of 150$ ($1), except on entrance-free Sunday.

WHERE PORT IS KING

Across the river from Porto, in **Vila Nova de Gaia,** are the port wine lodges. Like the sherry makers at Jerez de la Frontera, Spain, these establishments are hospitable, inviting guests to tour their precincts.

The largest of these lodges, **Real Vinícola** (tel. 30-54-62), is a prime example of the art of wine making. It is here that the blending, aging, and selection processes take place. Dating from 1889, the warehouses contain specially treated oaken vats. The wine is bolstered with brandies and vintage wines to maintain its character. The vast cellars, dark, cool, and moist, are the resting place for port that ranges in age from 5 to 70 years. However, the oldest bottle in the company's museum is dated 1765. In one tunnel section alone there are four million bottles of Portuguese sparkling wines.

If you wish to learn the intricacies of production and development of port wine, from tasting to decanting, arrive and announce yourself. You'll be guided through the cask- and vat-lined cellars and tunnels. At the company tavern, you can purchase fine wine packed in wicker baskets. Hours are 9 a.m. to noon and 2 to 5 p.m. Monday to Friday.

You can also visit many other port wine centers. One of the most famous is **Porto Sandeman,** 3 Largo Miguel Bombarda (tel. 39-21-31). Hours are from 9:30 a.m. to 12:30 p.m. and 2 to 5 p.m. Monday to Friday from October 1 to March 31, and from 9:30 a.m. to 5 p.m. daily from April 1 to September 30.

OTHER SIGHTS

There are many other monuments and sights worth exploring in Porto, especially the 18th-century **Torre dos Clérigos** (tel. 217-29), the landmark tower of the city, rising to a height of nearly 250 feet. The tallest tower in Portugal, it was designed by an Italian named Nicolo Nasoni. From its summit there's a view of the Douro River, the valley gorge, and the far reaches of the city. The tower can be visited from 10:30 a.m. to noon and 3:30 (3 p.m. on Sunday) to 5 p.m. daily except Wednesday. Entrance is 25$ (15¢).

PORTO AFTER DARK

There's no better way to begin your evening in Porto than by paying a visit to the **Solar do Vinho do Porto,** housed in the building of the Romantic Museum of Quinta da Macieirinha at 220 Rua de Entre Quintas (tel. 69-77-93). This is maintained by the Port Wine Institute, a government body that controls the quality of the wine and authorizes its export. At the address given, visitors can taste the different types of port from 10 a.m. to 11:30 p.m. Monday to Friday and from 11 a.m. to 10:30 p.m. Saturday. Closed Sunday. In this old building, you will also have a view of the Douro.

The real fado is in Lisbon, but Porto does offer a club or two where you can hear these typical songs and listen to guitar music. **Mal Cozinhado,** 13 Rua do Outeirinho (tel. 38-13-19), a "casa de fado," is the best. It's a safe bet, as the music is excellent. The so-called Bad Kitchen also serves food, but in case its name frightens you away you can visit for drinks only. A minimum of 2,500$ ($16.25) is imposed, but it can be spent on drinks. Meals cost from 4,000$ ($26) to 5,000$ ($32.50). Hours are nightly from 8:30 p.m. to 3 a.m. It is located near the river.

While in Porto, you shouldn't miss having coffee in one of the oldtime "Brazilian" cafés. My favorite is the **Majestic Café,** 112 Rua de Santa Catarina (tel. 238-87), one of those ornate places where burghers and poets congregated. The wood-and-mirror decor, jasper pillars, and sculpted cherubs over pilasters evoke the craftsmanship of another era. Rows of leather-backed banquettes line both sides of the oblong room, in front of which two rows of round-top tables stand. In the rear is a small garden and a counter where coffee is prepared in the old way. A coffee with milk is served in a large glass placed within a bronze holder, so you won't burn your fingers. The café was opened in 1922 and is still going strong. You can enjoy the best port wine and also order beefsteak and light meals, costing from 1,200$ ($7.80). It is open daily except Sunday from 8 a.m. to 9:30 p.m.

Member's Restaurant, Twin's Disco, 1000 Rua do Passeio Alegre (tel. 68-57-40), are found in one of the most fashionable parts of Porto, the Foz. The restaurant is chic and sophisticated, perhaps more so than any other spot in town. After a satisfying meal, you can enjoy action in the disco club, contained in the same three-story building near the beach at the mouth of the Douro. Reservations are recommended for dinner on the top floor, which serves nightly except Sunday from 8 p.m. to 3:30 a.m., full meals costing from 2,000$ ($13). Specialties include crabmeat crêpes, fresh fish, and an array of grilled meats prepared in both classic and modern ways. One floor above the restaurant is a pub where an open fireplace and a piano player compete for attention. Alluring and sedate, the pub is open daily from 8 p.m. to 4 a.m. On the street level, the disco is open nightly from 10 p.m. to 4 a.m. Entrance to its black-and-white precincts costs 1,000$ ($6.50) for nonmembers. One drink is included in the price. All three floors of this establishment are closed in August.

Romanoff, Shopping Center Brasilia, 113 Praça Mousinho Albuquerque (tel. 69-22-25), is the most interesting and best-decorated bar and pool hall in Porto. It's on the street level of the city's biggest shopping center, behind speakeasy doors and stained-glass windows. Inside, a team of designers created a reassuring world of burnished gilt, bevelled mirrors, bronze replicas of fleet-footed Mercuries, and art nouveau flourishes. Waiters in pink shirts and bow ties serve beer for 250$ ($1.65), rent pool cues by the hour, and tend to the wide-angled video screen where late releases from Europe and America add a postmodern electronic note. It's open daily from 2 p.m. to 2 a.m.

Drinks (Chequers) Pub, Fifth Floor, Shopping Center Brasilia, 113 Praça Mousinho Albuquerque (tel. 69-73-25), is another watering spot within this massive shopping center. It opens at 1 p.m. but isn't dependent on the whims of shoppers, as it remains open until 2 a.m., long after the last shopper has retreated. The decor is warmly upholstered and modern, and the place is popular with young people, who order beer at 200$ ($1.30).

SHOPPING

For information about what to buy in Porto, refer to "Shopping in Portugal," chapter VII.

BEACHING IT

A long, busy beach at **Matosinhos,** five miles north of Porto, draws large crowds in good weather. The bustling little fishing town lies at the mouth of the River Leça. It is reached by following Avenida da Boavista out of the city. Separated by rocky crags are the beaches of Matosinhos, Leça (which also has swimming pools), Cabo do Mundo, Paraíso, and Angeiras.

In the town, you can visit the **Church of Bom Jesus of Matosinhos,** whose major treasure is an ancient wooden statue of Christ at the end of the high altar. The statue has made the church a place of annual pilgrimages. The 18th-century church has coats-of-arms, pinnacles, and torches on the exterior. Note the woodcarvings in the chancel and the coffered ceiling.

---

5. Espinho

A popular place on the Costa Verde is Espinho, 12 miles south of Porto. This modern beach resort offers many activities and is drawing larger crowds of vacationers each year. The town has a range of shops and restaurants, hotels and campsites in the pine woods near the sandy beach. Sports enthusiasts will find tennis courts, a bullfighting ring, and an 18-hole golf course.

The big gray **casino** at Espinho (tel. 72-02-38), open all year, has a restaurant and nightclub in addition to the gaming tables. Here you can play roulette, French banque, baccarat, and slot machines. International cabaret is offered in the nightclub.

Water sports available here include sailing and rowing on the Paramos Lagoon and surfing in the Atlantic. Cabañas line part of the beach, and there are swimming pools in the Solar Atlântico recreation complex overlooking the ocean.

FOOD AND LODGING

The best place to stay in Espinho is the **Hotel Praiagolfe,** Rua 6, 4500 Espinho (tel. 02/72-06-30), a totally renovated accommodation offering many modern comforts. It overlooks the sea, and the railway station is about 165 feet away. Each of its 139 bedrooms has a private bath, TV, and direct-dial phone. In high season, doubles rent for 12,000$ ($78.00) daily, and singles go for 10,000$ ($65), with a continental breakfast included. A fixed-price lunch or dinner costs from 1,800$ ($11.70). The hotel offers an indoor swimming pool, a squash court, and a health club, as well as a disco. Tennis courts and golf courses are nearby. In summer, the establishment is almost continuously booked, so making advance reservations is imperative.

On the Outskirts

Hotel Solverde/Granja, Praia da Granja, 4400 Vila Nova de Gaia (tel. 02/72-61-11), is one of the most luxurious hotels in the north of Portugal. Opened in 1989, it stands on the beach of Granja, about 10 miles north of Porto and less than a mile south of Espinho. It is about 20 miles from the Porto airport. There are 177 well-furnished bedrooms, including five suites. The tariffs are among the lowest in Portugal for a five-star hotel. In high season, singles range from 13,000$ ($84.50) to 15,500$ ($100.75) daily, with doubles costing 15,000$ ($97.50) to 17,500$ ($113.75). Facilities include a grill and a restaurant, a coffee shop, several bars, a disco, a health club, and three swimming pools with salt water (one of them indoors), four tennis courts, and a heliport.

EXPLORING THE COAST

An underrated stretch of coastal resorts and fishing villages lies between Porto and the southern reaches of the Minho district. The Atlantic waters, however, are likely to be on the chilly side, even in July and August. The communities along this northern highway of the sun are patronized mainly by the Portuguese. In recent years, these resorts have grown tremendously. They are, however, known more to European vacationers than to Americans (the latter still prefer the Algarve).

6. Vila do Conde

Lying at the mouth of the River Ave, the little town of Vila do Conde—its fortress-guarded sandy beaches, rocky reefs, and charm—has been discovered by summer vacationers. Along the wharfs you may still see piles of rough, hand-hewn timbers used in the building of the sardine fleet, for shipbuilding is a traditional industry of the town, and a few wooden-hulled vessels are still made, some for the local fishing fleet and others for use on the cod banks of Newfoundland.

The women of the town have long engaged in the making of lace using a shuttle, a craft handed down from generation to generation. So revered is this activity that a festival, the Feast of St. John, celebrates it with processions by the lacemakers, called *rendilheiras,* together with the *mordomas,* the women who manage the cottage-industry homes, the latter wearing magnificent chains and other ornaments of gold. During the third week in June the lacemakers parade through the narrow, 16th-century streets of the town. Visitors are welcomed at the lacemaking school on Rua do Lidador, **Escola de Rendas.**

The famous hand-knit and embroidered fishermen's sweaters are also made here. The making of sweets, (there is a famous confectionery from convent recipes) is another occupation in the town, providing part of the rich local cuisine.

The **Convent of St. Clare** (Mosteiro de Santa Clara), a large, squat structure sitting fortress-like on a hill, was founded in the 14th century. In the upper rooms you can see relics and paintings garnered through the centuries by the Poor Clares. The building is now a charity home. Simplicity and opulence play against each other in a combination of Gothic and Romanesque styles in the structure. The plain altar of its church offers contrast to the gilded stalls behind the communion grilles and the ornately decorated ceilings. A side chapel contains 14th-century sarcophagi. One is the elaborately carved tomb of Don Afonso Sanche, founder of the convent, the feet of his effigy resting on a lion. The tomb of his wife, Dona Teresa Martins, topped by a figure dressed in the habit of a Franciscan Tertiary nun, and those of two of their children are also here.

The present monastery was built in the 1700s, accompanied by construction of a 999-arch aqueduct bringing water from Póvoa do Varzim, close by. Part of the water conduit is still visible.

The **Parish Church** (Igreja Matriz), dating from the 16th century, and a pillory can also be seen.

Just 17 miles from Porto, Vila do Conde is served by a modern highway.

FOOD AND LODGING

A superior inn, **Estalagem do Brasão,** Avenida Coronel Alberto Graça, 4480 Vila do Conde (tel. 052/640-16), is styled more like a gracious pousada. Located in the center of the village, it's worth considering if only for its lofty dining room. The bedrooms are compact, of contemporary design, with tile baths. Rooms have twin beds with built-in headboards, and comfortable, stylish armchairs, a TV, and a bar. The cost, including a continental breakfast, is 3,000$ ($19.50) to 5,000$ ($32.50) daily in a single, 4,000$ ($26) to 5,500$ ($35.75) in a double. A set lunch or dinner goes for 1,800$ ($11.70). The chef turns out three specialties on the à la carte menu —codfish Brasão, beef Brasão, and omelet Brasão. There's a combination bar and disco, plus a private parking lot.

There are a number of beachfront restaurants, of which **Pioneiro,** Avenida Manuel Barros (tel. 63-29-12), is not only one of the best, but one of the largest. Offering a panoramic view of the water, it can seat up to 265 patrons. Along the esplanade, it specializes in the cookery of the region and fresh shellfish. Meals cost 1,800$ ($11.70) and up, and hours are noon to 3 p.m. and 7 to 11 p.m. It is closed on Monday.

7. Póvoa do Varzim

In the big bustling cafés of this town, beneath ornate roofs and gables, skimpily clad tourists idyllically take their afternoon glass of port wine (some have several). Seemingly unaware of them, the *pescadores* (fishermen) of the town go on with their work. Franz Villier wrote: "Here the boat-owners are kings, and morality reigns. Drunkards and debauchees may not aspire to the honour of fishing, unless it happens that the owner is one himself."

The southern part of the town is occupied by the fishing industry, which has remained the major economic support of the town, despite its emergence as a seaside resort. Daily (except Saturday, Sunday, and holidays), the auction of the fishermen's catch is fascinating to watch, the women selling what their men have brought in. Along the beach in the fishermen's quarter, huge piles of seaweed, drying for use as fertilizer, look like little round thatched huts.

Póvoa de Varzim has developed into a leading resort on the Costa Verde. Its broad, sandy north beaches are dotted with white canvas tents known as *toldo,* suspended on two poles. Other entertainment amenities include an Olympic swimming pool, tennis courts, a roller-skating rink, and a gambling casino.

The **casino,** which has a restaurant offering international cuisine, is open all year from 3 p.m. to 3 a.m. Games people play are roulette, French banque, and slot machines. Nightly cabaret with a floor show is presented.

Of interest in the immediate countryside are the "sunken gardens" that farmers have established among the sand dunes. They dug deep into the sand to find moisture for their crops, planting grape vines in the sand heaps above to keep them from sliding down. From these vines, they get a good crop of wine grapes each year, and in the gardens at the bottom they produce many types of vegetables growing right out of the unfriendly sand.

WHERE TO STAY

The most desirable accommodation in town is **Vermar Hotel,** Avenida dos Banhos, 4491 Póvoa do Varzim (tel. 052/68-34-01), a high-rise hotel with 208 well-furnished bedrooms. In fact, this is among the leading hotels of Portugal. The service, for example, is among the finest I've encountered in the north. Once you're inside, the heat, noise, and the traffic of this bustling resort seem far away. The hotel is about half a mile from the town center, standing back from a road flanking the shoreline.

A stylish and spacious series of ground-floor public rooms contain unusual ceramic murals, several pieces of sculpture ringed with plants, a bar, and a modern dining room. The comfortably low-slung chairs of one of the reading areas looks out over the hotel's pair of curved swimming pools and the nearby tennis courts. There's even an occasional Portuguese antique scattered amid the greenery and the brown marble of the interior. Facilities include a sauna, a disco, and a children's playground. Each of the bedrooms contains a sun terrace, private bath, and radio. Depending on the accommodations, in high season singles cost 11,600$ ($75.40) daily, and doubles go for 12,650$ ($82.25). Substantial low-season reductions are granted.

In the Environs

Estalagem Santo André, Aver-o-Mar, 4490 Póvoa de Varzim (tel. 052/68-18-81). Set at the edge of the sea, amid a flat alluvial landscape that evokes Holland, this angular hacienda-style beach hotel draws a largely Portuguese clientele, especially in summer. Many visitors prefer its isolation and its position among the dunes to the more congested neighborhood of Varzim, whose high-rise buildings are visible across the landscape.

The inn's public rooms are the kind of airy, sophisticated places where open hearths blend well with modern paintings. The elegant restaurant sports a formally dressed staff, windows on three sides, and a view of the sand and the Atlantic. Built in the mid-1970s, the hotel contains 50 bedrooms, each with private bath, color TV, and piped-in music. Each also overlooks the sea and has a private balcony. Suitable for one or two occupants, rooms range from 9,250$ ($60.15) to 10,500$ ($68.25) daily, depending on the season, with breakfast included. If you just want to stop in for a well-prepared meal, averaging 2,500$ ($16.25), you can do so. Hours are daily from 12:30 to 2:30 p.m. and 7:30 to 9:30 p.m. throughout the year.

WHERE TO DINE
Everybody's favorite restaurant seems to be **Casa dos Frangos II,** Rte. N13 (tel. 68-15-22), in spite of its location just north of Póvoa de Varzim on the route to Viana do Castelo. An often very, very busy establishment, it is known for its fish stew, a savory kettle of Neptune's delights. Other regional specialties are served as well, and you can enjoy them in air conditioning from noon to 11 p.m. Meals cost 1,500$ ($9.75) to 2,500$ ($16.25). The restaurant is closed on Monday.

If you want something more central, try **Enseada,** Passeio Alegre (tel. 68-44-34), which is on the beach in the vicinity of the casino. Many residents from Porto come here in summer (it seats some 400 diners), enjoying grills and typical regional fare, including baked codfish, rabbit, fish filets with rice, and beef dishes, at reasonable prices. The classic soup, of course, is caldo verde. Meals cost from 1,800$ ($11.70). Hours are daily from 8 a.m. to midnight.

SHOPPING
In the Tourist Office, 160 Avenida Mouzinho de Albuquerque (tel. 62-46-09), you can see a display of local costumes, including the famous fishermen's sweaters, made in neighboring Vila do Conde, as well as rag cloaks and rugs. These items are available at shops in the town.

Ourivesaria Gomes, Rua da Junqueira (tel. 62-46-38), is sought out by Portuguese people from all over the country. A 100-foot-long counter gleams with a display of silverware, and you can watch the smiths at work at their benches.

Lindomar, 24 Rua dos Cafés (tel. 62-06-06), sells pottery, fishermen's sweaters, and filigree work, as well as souvenir items.

To see, and perhaps purchase to take home, something from one of the country's largest collections of wines, liquors, and liqueurs, go to **Garrafeira do Alberto,** Estrada Nacional, no. 13 (tel. 68-26-66), which is open from 10 a.m. to noon and 2:30 to 8 p.m.

---

8. Ofir and Fão

Once through the pine forests of **Ofir,** 29 miles from Porto, you gaze down on a long white sandy spit dotted with wind-swept dunes and suffused with the sharp cries of seagulls. Imagine a pure unspoiled Cape Cod. The beach is dramatic any time of the year, but exceptional during the summer months. Ofir is considered by many as the best beach resort between Porto and Viana do Castelo. The White Horse Rocks, according to legend, were formed when fiery steeds from the royal stock of King Solomon were wrecked upon the beach.

While the hotels of Ofir offer guests every convenience in a secluded setting, the nearest shops and more local color are found one to two miles inland on an estuary of the Cávado River at **Fão,** which dates back to Roman times. Framed by mountain ridges in the background and a river valley, the village is the sleepy destination of all visitors to Ofir. The *sargaceiros* (literally, gatherers of sargasso), with their stout fustian tunics, rake the offshore breakers for the seaweed used in making fertilizer. On the quays you can lunch on sardines off the smoking braziers. At the end of the day you can soothe your overdose of sunshine with a mellow glass of port wine.

The accommodations in these two towns are among the best along the coast north of Porto.

STAYING IN OFIR

In its own way, **Hotel de Ofir,** Avenida Raul de Sousa Martins, Praia de Ofir, 4740 Fão (tel. 053/96-13-83), competes with the resort developments on the Algarve. It's a resort unto itself, with a vast playground terrace, two swimming pools (one for children), two tennis courts, and a flagstone terrace bordering soft green lawns. The hotel has a disco and a bowling alley as well.

The hotel is divided into three sections. The older central core contains bedrooms furnished in the traditional Portuguese fashion, with reproductions of regional furniture; the adjoining wings are modern. One section is quite luxurious, built motel style right along the dunes, with a row of white tents and a pure sandy beach in full view of the second-floor bedroom balconies. There are rather well-styled public rooms for the evening's activities, but the principal focus is on the wide oceanfront terrace, where guests sunbathe and order refreshments under umbrellas. A dining room with comfortable armchairs opens onto the sea. The bedrooms have a well-conceived sense of style with substantial pieces of furniture placed against pleasantly colored backgrounds. Singles peak at 8,000$ ($52) daily and doubles at 12,000$ ($78).

Estalagem Parque do Rio, Ofir, 4740 Esposende (tel. 053/96-15-21) is a modern first-class inn on the Cávado River in a pine-covered garden, five minutes from the main beach. It has two excellent garden swimming pools with surrounding lawns. The resort, planned for those who stay for more than one day, offers a full social life. The atmosphere is like that in a skiing lodge and includes a natural stone fireplace. In the beamed dining room, a snug wood-paneled bar is set against a stone wall, and you'll find several lounges for get-togethers. Each bedroom is well-conceived, having a tile bath, a private balcony, a telephone, and central heating. For half board, the rate ranges from 6,500$ ($42.25) to 7,250$ ($47.15) daily in a single, 10,000$ ($65) to 12,300$ ($79.95) for two persons sharing a room.

THE MINHO DISTRICT

Corn Granaries on granite stilts . . . heather-covered hills . . . fishing villages . . . poplar-shaded river valleys . . . terraces scaling slopes . . . ramparts guarding against long-dead enemies . . . *sargaceiros* in fustian tunics raking for seaweed . . . and heavily laden vines at grape harvest.

The Minho occupies the most northwestern corner of Portugal, and is almost a land unto itself. The district begins some 25 miles north of Porto, stretching to the frontier of Galicia in northwestern Spain. In fact, the Minhotons and the Galicians share many common characteristics.

Granite plateaus undulate across the countryside, broken by the green valleys of the Minho, Ave, Cávado, and Lima Rivers. Bountiful granite quarries stand agape amid the hills. From the great church façades in Braga and Guimarães to the humblest of village cottages, this material has been employed for centuries. Green pasturelands contrast sharply with forests filled with cedars and chestnuts.

The small size of the district and the proximity of one town to another makes hamlet-hopping easy. Even the biggest towns—**Viana do Castelo, Guimarães,** and **Braga**—are provincial. You can sometimes see wooden carts in the streets drawn by pairs of dappled and chocolate-brown oxen. These noble beasts have become subjects for the regional pottery and ceramics for which the Minho, and especially Viana do Castelo, are known.

Religious *festas* are excuses for bringing the hard-working people out into the streets for days of merry-making and celebrations including folk songs, dances, and, of course, displays of traditional costumes. The young girls and women often wear woolen skirts and gaily decorated aprons in floral or geometric designs. Their bodices are pinned with golden filigree and draped with layers of heart- or cross-shaped pendants.

Historically, the Minho was the spawning ground of Portuguese independence. It was from here that Afonso Henriques, the first king, made his plans to capture the south from the Moors. Battlemented castles along the frontier attest to the former hostilities with Spain, and fortresses, ruined sentinels that once protected the river accesses to the heartland, still stand above the coastal villages.

1. Guimarães

The cradle of Portugal, Guimarães suffers from a benign malady which the French call "embarras de richesses." At the foot of a range of sêrras, this first capital of Portugal has successfully preserved a medieval atmosphere in its core.

AROUND THE TOWN

Dominating the skyline is the 10th-century **Castle of Guimarães,** where Afonso Henriques, Portugal's first king, was born sometime between 1094 and 1111 (historians disagree). The castle dates from 996. High-pitched crenels top the strategically placed square towers and the looming keep, said to have been the birthplace of Afonso. The view is magnificent. With the church bells ringing in the distance, and roosters crowing early in the morning, the setting seems straight out of the Middle Ages.

Almost in the shadow of the castle is the 12th-century **St. Michael of the Castle,** a squat, rectangular Romanesque church where the liberator was baptized. Nearby is a heroic statue of the mustachioed Afonso, his head helmeted, his figure clad in a suit of armor, sword and shield in hand.

From the keep of the castle you can see the four-winged **Palace of the Dukes of Bragança.** Constructed in the 15th century, it has been heavily restored. Many critics have dismissed the rebuilt structure with contempt. However, if you're not a purist, you may find a guided tour interesting. Perched on the slope of a hill, the palace possesses a varied assortment of treasures, including a number of portraits such as Catherine of Bragança, who married Charles II of England, the merrie monarch and lover of Nell Gwyn. There are copies of the large Pastrana tapestries depicting scenes from the Portuguese wars in North Africa, scabbards and helmets in the armor room, antiques, Persian hangings, Indian urns, ceramics, and Chinese porcelains. The chapel opens onto the throne chairs of the duke and duchess. Nearby are the double-tiered cloisters. From June 1 to September 30 hours are daily from 9 a.m. to 6 p.m., costing 300$ ($1.95). Off-season hours are from 10 a.m. to 5:30 p.m. with a 200$ ($1.30) admission charged.

By far the most dramatic interior of any church in town belongs to **São Francisco,** on Largo de São Francisco. Entered through a Gothic portal, the spacious interior is faced with Delft-blue and white azulejos. Some of the color tones seem to bathe the whole interior in moonlight. In the transept to the right of the main altar is a minature re-creation of the living room of a church prelate. With meticulous detail, from the burgundy-colored cardinal's chapeau resting on a wall sconce, to the minature dog and cat. On the second altar on the right is a polychrome tree of life, representing 12 crowned kings and the Virgin, her hands clasped, her feet resting upon the heads of three cherubs. The palace next door, with its embellished tile façade, may be visited by appointment only (tel. 41-22-28).

If you'd like to step into the Middle Ages for an hour or two, take a stroll down **Rua de Santa Maria,** which has remained essentially unchanged, except nowadays you're likely to hear some blaring music, in English no less. Proud town houses, once the residence of the nobility, stand beside humble dwellings. The hand-carved balconies, aged by the years, are most often garnished with iron lanterns, not to mention laundry.

At the end you'll come upon a charming square in the heart of the old town,

Largo da Oliveira (Olive Tree Square). Seek out an odd chapelette in front of a church. Composed of four ogival arches, it is said to mark the spot where in the 6th century Wamba was asked to give up the simple toil of working his fields to become the king of the Goths. Thrusting his olive stick into the tilled soil, he declared he would accept only if his stick sprouted leaves. So it did, and he did—or that was the tale told.

The church, called the **Collegiate Church of the Olive Tree** (Igreja Nossa Senhora da Oliveira), was originally a 10th-century temple erected by Mumadona, a Galician countess. It has changed with the centuries: Romanesque giving way to Gothic, and then to more sterile neoclassicism.

In the Romanesque cloister and in the buildings of the old monastery of the church is the **Museum of Alberto Sampaio.** Besides a large silver collection, it displays the tunic worn by João I at the battle of Aljubarrota that decided Portugal's fate. In addition, there are priestly garments, paintings, ceramics, and medieval sculpture. A fresco illustrates a gloating Salome, rapturous over the severed head of John the Baptist. In one of the rooms, there are pieces from a baroque chapel with enormous wood-carved angels bearing torches. The museum is open from 10 a.m. to 1 p.m. and 2 to 5:30 p.m. except on Monday and holidays. Admission is 200$ ($1.30).

Martins Sarmento Museum (tel. 41-59-69), situated partially in the Church of St. Dominic's (São Domingos) Gothic cloister, has on display artifacts from the prehistoric (Bronze Age to Iron Age) settlements at Sabroso and Briteiros, excavated by the archeologist for whom the museum was named. Hours are 10 a.m. to noon and 2 to 5 p.m.; closed Monday. Admission is 100$ (65¢).

Guimarães is about 30 miles from Porto and 43 miles from Viana do Castelo.

WHERE TO STAY

Its foundations date from the 12th century, but **Pousada de Santa Marinha da Costa,** Estrada de Penha, 4800 Guimarães (tel. 053/41-84-53), in its restored version, is arguably the most impressive pousada in Portugal. It was originally built in 1154 as an Augustinian convent by the mother of Afonso Henriques. The baroque façade was added in the 18th century when the soaring interior hallways and spurting fountains were installed as crowning touches. The lushly ornate Manueline church that occupies part of the building still offers mass on Sunday, but the sprawling ex-convent was never outfitted as stylishly as you'll see it today. The property lies at the end of a winding road about a mile and a quarter north of the center of town. Signs indicate the direction. You park in the hilltop courtyard outside the main entrance.

You'd be well advised to explore both the upper hallways and gardens. One of my favorite rooms is a large, beautifully furnished salon. A sunken bar, ringed with blue and yellow tiles, serves drinks near the anteroom of the vaulted dining room. At the end of one of the soaring hallways, a fountain bubbles beneath an intricate wooden ceiling, surrounded by an open arcade that encompasses a view of the faraway mountains.

Bedrooms are a pleasing blend of old stonework, modern plasterwork, plush accessories, efficient baths, and a scattering of Portuguese lithographs. With a continental breakfast included, the 51 rooms rent for 14,600$ ($94.90) daily in a single, going up to 16,600$ ($107.90) in a double. Meals, served in the dining room, cost 2,500$ ($16.25) to 2,800$ ($18.20). Hours are daily from 12:30 to 2:30 p.m. and 7:30 to 9:30 p.m.

Pousada de Santa Maria de Oliveira, Largo de Oliveira, 4800 Guimarães (tel. 053/41-21-57), is now the second pousada in town, quite different in ambience from the previously recommended hotel. It was created when a handful of very old town houses were combined into a single rambling hotel. Many of their original features have been preserved. The street that contains the pousada is so narrow that you'll have to park somewhere within a well-marked lot about 100 feet from the front entrance. It still has a loyal clientele who value its location on one of the most beautiful medieval squares of Portugal, as well as its distinctive country-inn flavor. This establishment exudes a cozy kind of intimate warmth. The feeling is heightened by the wooden ceilings, tavern bar, and the fireplace inside the warmly decorated restaurant, whose windows look out over the square.

The views from the comfortably efficient bedrooms usually look out past spindle-turned balustrades over the stone-trimmed city around it. With a continental breakfast included, singles cost from 11,300$ ($73.45) daily, while doubles go for 12,500$ ($81.25). Fixed-price meals in the dining room, served from 12:30 to 2:30 p.m. and 7:30 to 9:30 p.m., cost 2,500$ ($16.25). Specialties include a special beef à la pousada, fondue for two persons, and flambé versions of beef and veal.

Fundador Dom Pedro Hotel, 740 Avenida Dom Afonso Henriques, 4800 Guimarães (tel. 053/41-37-81), stands in the center of the city, offering 63 comfortable rooms and nine suites, each equipped with phone, private bar, piped-in music, and a mini-bar. The Dom Pedro, along with the previous recommendations, makes a night in Guimarães a lot more palatable than in days of yore. The hotel isn't necessarily great on style, but it's modern, functional, well kept, and, as a further compensation, offers fine service. Two elevators take you to the rooms, which cost from 9,500$ ($61.75) daily in a double, from 9,000$ ($58.50) in a single. The hotel, inaugurated in 1980, has a penthouse bar with snacks, and there's private parking.

WHERE TO DINE

Many people think **Virabar,** Largo 28 de Maio (tel. 41-41-16), is the best restaurant outside the pousadas. It is certainly one of the most pleasant in town, seating 70 diners in air-conditioned comfort. Alternatively, it warms them with a fireplace in winter. A good local cuisine is served, costing from 2,000$ ($13) to 2,800$ ($18.20). Hours are daily from noon to 3 p.m. and 7 to 10 p.m.

Nicolino, 106 Largo Toural (tel. 41-20-83), is patronized heavily by locals who enjoy its good fish and meat dishes. Service is efficient, and meals cost 1,500$ ($9.75) to 1,800$ ($11.70). Food is dispensed from noon to 3 p.m. and 7 to 11 p.m. daily.

Mirapenha, Estrada Fafe (tel. 41-15-32), is a typical restaurant just outside the town, a reasonably priced taxi ride's distance. Fine local food is served, an average meal costing from 1,400$ ($9.10) to 1,800$ ($11.70). Hours are daily from 12:30 to 2:30 p.m. and 8 to 9:30 p.m.

QUINTAS IN THE ENVIRONS

If you plan to spend a few days exploring the Minho, you may want to anchor in at one of the following quintas, which are among the best accommodations in the area. In restored manors, you can live with Portuguese aristocracy in a style far more luxurious than the usual hotels.

Casa do Ribeiro, 4800 Guimarães (tel. 053/41-08-81), lies near Guimarães on the road to Pevidem in the village of São Cristóvão do Selho. It is a noble house, whose ancient walls contain valuable details and traces of the elegant and grand style of life that prevailed there. That alone justifies a visit. D. Maria do Carmo Ferraz Pinto rents four doubles and one single, which share sitting rooms and a dining room. Four rooms contain bath and one does not. Charges are 7900$ ($51.35) daily in a single, 8,200$ ($53.30) in a double. Guests are welcomed from March to November, and pleasant gardens and a farm surrounded by woods are part of the property.

Paço de São Cipriano, Taboadelo, 4800 Guimarães (tel. 053/48-13-37), is tucked away on the outskirts of Guimarães. It is known for its dignified aristocratic architecture and its beautiful gardens. João Santiago de Sottomayor has five handsomely furnished rooms with private bath for rent. The charge for a single occupant is 8,500$ ($55.25) daily, with two persons paying 10,250$ ($66.65).

2. Braga

Nearly everywhere you look in Braga there's a church, a palace, a garden, or a fountain. Known to the Romans as Bracara Augusta, it also resounded to the footsteps of other conquerors—the Suevi, the Visigoths, and the Moors. For centuries it has been an archepiscopal see and a pilgrimage site (the Visigoths are said to have renounced their heresies here). Braga is 31 miles from Porto.

AROUND THE TOWN

Inside the town, interest focuses on the **Sé,** the **Cathedral of Braga.** It was built in the 12th century by Count Henry of Burgundy and Dona Teresa. Following his demise, she was chased out of town because of an illicit love affair; but in death Henry and Teresa were reunited in their tombs in the Chapel of Kings.

The Sé didn't escape subsequent decorative and architectural styles. The north triple-arched façade is austere and dominating, with a large stone-laced Roman arch flanked by two smaller Gothic ones. What appear to be the skeletons of cupolas top the façade's dual bell towers, which flank a lofty rooftop niche containing a larger-than-life statue of the Virgin and Child. Under a carved baldachin in the apse is a statue of "Our Lady of the Milk"—that is, the Virgin breast-feeding the infant Jesus Christ. The statue is in the Manueline style—but somehow pious, restrained.

Once inside the structure, you'll believe you've entered one of the darkest citadels of Christendom. However, if you can see them, the interior decorations are profuse, particularly a pair of huge 18th-century organs gilded with baroque decorations. In the 1330 Capela da Gloría is the sarcophagus of Archbishop Dom Gonçalo Pereira, with an unctuous expression on his face, carved by order of the prelate himself.

For 100$ (65¢), you can visit the **Treasury of the Cathedral** and the **Museum of Sacred Art,** an upstairs repository of Braga's most precious works of art. Included are elaborately carved choir stalls from the 18th century, embroidered vestments from the 16th through the 18th centuries, a 14th-century statue of the Virgin and a Gothic chalice from the same period, plus the custódia of Dom Gaspar de Bragança. This treasury house may be visited daily from 8:30 a.m. to 6:30 p.m. in summer, from 8:30 a.m. to 12:30 p.m. and 1:30 to 5:30 p.m. in winter. In the cloister is a pietà, reflecting human grief.

Biscainhos Museum, Rua dos Biscainhos (tel. 276-45), is in Biscainhos Palace, a building from the 17th and 18th centuries that for about 300 years has been the house of a noble family. The original gardens, including the baroque ornamental garden, an orchard, and a kitchen garden are still there. The museum, whose interior has painted and ornamented ceilings and walls with panels of figurative and neoclassic tiles, offers an example of an 18th-century Portuguese aristocratic home. Its exhibition rooms contain collections of Portuguese furniture and pottery, glassware, silverware, textiles and Portuguese, oriental, and Dutch Delft porcelain. The museum is open from 10 a.m. to 12:15 p.m. and 2 to 5:15 p.m. except Monday and holidays. Admission is 150$ ($1).

Three miles southeast of Braga is the nationally renowned **Bom Jesus do Monte.** The hilltop pilgrimage site is reached via foot, funicular, or a tree-lined roadway. A double baroque granite staircase dating from the 18th century may look exhausting; but if it's any consolation, pilgrims often climb it on their knees.

Less elaborate than the stairway of Remédios at Lamego, the stairs at Bom Jesus (Good Jesus) are nevertheless equally impressive. On the numerous landings are gardens, grottos, small chapels, sculptures, and allegorical stone figures set in fountains.

Designed by Carlos Amarante in 1811, the hilltop **Chapel of the Miracles** contains many reminders, even anatomical re-creations, of the diseased and sick who have claimed cures. In foggy weather the mountain is enshrouded in mist, but on most days you can walk along the mosaic sidewalks and belvederes, past white and black swans, and view the provincial capital at every turn.

WHERE TO STAY IN BRAGA

The best hotel in town, **Hotel Turismo Dom Pedro,** Praçeta João XXI, Avenida da Liberdade, 4700 Braga (tel. 053/270-91), is in a 1950s-era 11-story building fronted with flowering gardens and a parking lot. As you face the sprawling building, you'll find its entrance beneath an arcade that also shelters some cafés. Inside, all is air-conditioned calm and comfort. The two-story lobby is set below a spacious lounge bar and restaurant, where you can enjoy a drink and a meal in a warmly burnished wood-paneled ambience. Each of the comfortable bedrooms contains a spacious balcony, whose walls are covered with blue and white tiles. There's a rooftop swimming pool and a snackbar on the eighth floor for residents. The 132 bedrooms rent for 7,000$ ($45.50) daily in a single, rising to 9,000$ ($58.50) in a double.

The hotel stands on a busy corner of traffic arteries, just outside the most densely populated section of Braga.

Hotel João XXI, 849 Avenida João XXI, 4700 Braga (tel. 053/221-46), is a good stopover hotel in its bracket (second class). On a tree-shaded avenue leading to Bom Jesus do Monte, it stands opposite the leading first-class hotel of Braga. The entry to this modern little six-floor hotel is a salute to the 19th century. The tiny street-floor reception room is decorated à la Louis XVI. The social center of the hotel is the living room-lounge with well-selected furnishings featuring an open fireplace for the nippy months. At the restaurant on the sixth floor you can order breakfast or an evening meal. The latter costs from 1,250$ ($8.15) per person. The bedrooms are in a warm modern decor, furnished with semi-traditional pieces, with the accent on neatness and efficiency. Each of the 28 rooms has its own private bath, the singles have double beds, and you get either a shower or tub as you require. The price, including a continental breakfast, for a single is 3,500$ ($22.75) daily, and a double costs 4,500$ ($29.25).

Hotel Francfort, 7 Avenida Central, 4700 Braga (tel. 053/226-48). It's the kind of hotel where you might share the hallway, and possibly the bathroom at the end of the corridor, with a research group from England. The hotel is characterized by its century-old landmark façade, covered with scarlet tiles. It sits across a busy street from one of the flowering gardens of Braga. None of the staff is likely to speak English. The simply furnished bedrooms are one of the bargains of the town. The hotel rents 18 rooms, of which 15 are bathless. All those with bath are doubles. Singles range from 2,000$ ($13) nightly, with doubles going for 3,000$ ($19.50) to 4,200$ ($27.30). There's a simple restaurant in a room adjacent to the ground-floor lobby.

WHERE TO STAY AT BOM JESUS DO MONTE

Many visitors to Braga prefer to stay high on the hill overlooking the city at the sanctuary of Bom Jesus do Monte. If you're interested in views and don't mind mingling with a lot of pilgrims, then you might want to do the same. The views at night are among the most exciting in the north of Portugal.

Hotel do Elevador, Bom Jesus Do Monte, 4700 Braga (tel. 053/250-11), is not unlike a private hillside villa—furnished in a plush manner with antiques, paintings, and objets d'art—except for the 25 bedrooms, which have contemporary appointments. Every bedroom has a private bath, central heating, and phone. The price for one person is 4,500$ ($29.25) to 8,000$ ($52) daily, 5,400$ ($35.10) to 9,000$ ($58.50) in a double, including a continental breakfast, the rate depending on the season. At your table with a view, the price of a complete luncheon or dinner is around 1,800$ ($11.70).

Hotel do Parque, Bom Jesus do Monte, 4700 Braga (tel. 053/220-48), is a turn-of-the-century villa that reopened in 1987 as one of the best hotels in the Braga area. Furnished in a high standard traditional style, it offers 49 bedrooms. Each is well-furnished and equipped with all the modern amenities, including a private bath, TV and radio, as well as air conditioning. Singles rent for 8,000$ ($52) daily, with doubles costing 9,000$ ($58.50). Set on elegantly maintained grounds, the hotel serves only breakfast, but lunch or dinner can be ordered at the previously recommended Hotel do Elevador, which is under the same ownership. Guests enjoy drinks in the hotel bar or else relax in a spacious sitting room with an open fireplace.

Sul Americano, Bom Jesus do Monte, 4700 Braga (tel. 053/225-15), on a plaza overlooking the church and valley, is like a country inn, ideal for pilgrims who want a basic budget hotel. It is a three-story villa adorned with blue and white tiles resting under a red-tile roof. The entry is small, the dining room has a few token antiques, and bedrooms are simplicity itself. Some are twin-bedded with private bath. The cost in a double, depending on the plumbing, ranges from 3,500$ ($22.75) to 4,200$ ($27.30) daily for two persons. Singles pay 2,800$ ($18.20) to 3,200$ ($20.80).

WHERE TO DINE

An old stone structure, **O Inácio,** 4 Campo das Hortas (tel. 223-35), has rugged walls and hand-hewn beams. In the cold-weather months a fire burns in an open hearth. The decor is rustic, with regional pottery and oxen yokes. Your host will often advise about his specialties of the day. Usually these are bacalhau (codfish) à Inácio, papas de sarrabulho (a regional stew), and bife na cacarola. Roast kid is also featured occasionally. Most fish dishes (and they're fresh) are good alternative choices. The dessert surprise is a rum omelet soufflé. Count on spending 1,800$ ($11.70) to 2,500$ ($16.25). The owner has a well-stocked wine cellar, and in my opinion, serves the best cuisine in Braga. Hours are noon to 3 p.m. and 7:30 to 10 p.m.; closed Monday and the first week in October.

Another good possibility for dining, **Conde Dom Henrique,** 17 Rua Forno (tel. 287-03), has long attracted local residents with its blend of regional fare and good wine. The prices also have something to do with its popularity: from 1,400$ ($9.10) to 2,200$ ($14.30) for a good-tasting meal. Hours are daily except Wednesday from noon to 2 p.m. and 7:30 to 9:30 p.m.

City-Rio, Lugar da Estrada-Ferreiros (tel. 252-41), is a large restaurant, seating some 250 patrons, that offers not only Portuguese but Brazilian specialties. It charges 1,800$ ($11.70) and up for a fine meal with an excellent selection of wine. It also keeps long hours: from 11 a.m. to midnight, daily except Thursday. Parking is available.

Helvética, Quinta do Casal-Penoucos (tel. 716-42), on the outskirts, is another good bet for change-of-pace fare. It offers not only Portuguese regional dishes, but French cuisine as well. Seating some three dozen diners in air-conditioned comfort, it serves daily from noon to 3 p.m. and 7 to 10 p.m. Meals cost 2,000$ ($13) and up.

Marisqueira, 1 Rua Castelo (tel. 221-52), as its name suggests, serves some of the best—and freshest—shellfish dishes in Braga. A local favorite, it charges from 2,200$ ($14.30) for a fish dinner, unless you order lobster or shrimp. Meals are served daily from noon to 3 p.m. and 7 to 10 p.m.

LUXURY IN THE ENVIRONS

The most romantic accommodation is in the environs. At Frades, near Póvoa de Lanhoso, to the east of Braga, the **Casa de Requeixo,** Póvoa de Lanhoso (tel. 053/93-11-12), is an elegant and massive stone mansion of the 16th and 17th centuries. From a base here, you can explore the area by taking one of several itineraries in either the Minho or the National Park of Peneda-Gêres. Dr. Manuel Artur Norton has four beautifully furnished rooms with a private bath, large living room, a dining room, and a kitchen. Charges are 8,000$ ($52) daily in a double, 7,000$ ($45.50) in a single. The quinta combines the best qualities of the past with modern-day comfort, and offers both in a bucolic setting.

---

3. Barcelos

Fourteen miles west of Braga, Barcelos is a sprawling river town, resting on a plateau ringed by green hills. Wrought-iron street lanterns glimmer late in the evening long after the market in the open square of **Campo da República** has closed down. Barcelos does not feature any single major attraction, only itself, taken as a whole, with its ensemble of sights and curiosities, and that is more than enough.

Market day, on Thursday, in the fountain-centered Campo da República, almost 450 yards square, is a major event. You can purchase such local handcrafted items as rugs, dyed pillows stuffed with chicken feathers, Portuguese chandeliers, crochet work, local pottery, and, of course, the Barcelos cockerels. These hand-painted earthenware cocks are the most characteristic souvenirs of Portugal and often seem a symbol of the country. The worship of the Barcelos Rooster derives from a legend concerning a Gallego sentenced to hang, despite his protestations of innocence. In a last-hour appeal to the judge (who was having dinner at the time), the condemned man made a bold statement: If his manifestation of innocence were true, the roasted rooster resting on the magistrate's plate would get up and crow. Suddenly, a gloriously scarlet-plumed cockerel rose from the plate, crowing loud and long. The man was acquitted, of course.

AROUND THE TOWN

Opening onto the tree-studded main square are some of the finest buildings in Barcelos. The **Igreja do Terço** from the 18th century resembles a palace more than a church, with a central niche façade topped by finials and a cross. The interior tilework around the baroque altar depicts scenes of monks at labor and a moving rendition of the Last Supper. Also fronting the campo, with its fountain, is the **Hospital da Misericórdia,** a long formal building of the 17th century, behind a spiked fence, taking up almost half a side of the square.

Of more interest, however, is the small octagonal **Temple of Senhor da Cruz,** with a cupola faced with tiles. An upper balustrade, punctuated by large stone finials and a latticed round window about the square portal, provide contrast to the austerity of the walls. The interior is more sumptuous, with crystal, marble, and gilt.

Overlooking the swirling Cávado River are the ruins of the **Palace of the Braganças,** dating from 1786. The original palace site, as well as the town of Barcelos itself, was bestowed on Nuño Álvares by João I as a gift in gratitude for his bravery in the 1385 battle at Aljubarrota.

On the façade is a representation of the palace, re-created in splendor. You can wander through the ruins, which have been turned into an archeological museum, left relatively unguarded and filled with sarcophagi, heralded shields, and an 18th-century tile fountain. A museum of ceramics underneath the palace encapsulates the evolution of that handcraft (look for the blood-red ceramic oxen, with their lyre-shaped horns).

The shadow from the high palace chimney stretches across the old pillory in the courtyard below. The structure even exceeds in height the bell tower of the adjoining **Igreja Matriz.** Fronting the river, this Gothic church contains a baroque altar and an interior whose sides are faced with multicolored tiles. The altar is an array of cherubs, grapes, gold leaf, and birds.

WHERE TO STAY

Not only is the **Albergaría Condes de Barcelos,** Avenida Alcaides de Faria, 4750 Barcelos (tel. 053/820-61), the one really good hotel in Barcelos, but it has a delightful pousada style with furnishings made by local artisans. Beds are intricately carved. The 30-bedroom inn, a part of a three-story complex, stands mostly on thick pillars, in the Corbusier manner, and has an inner courtyard. The hotel is just a little way from the center of town, within walking distance of the artisan sales museum. Natural wood paneling is used generously in the dining room, the main lounge, and the bar-lounge. The cost for a double is 6,800$ ($44.20) daily, and singles run 4,900$ ($31.85).

Arantes Residencial, 34 Avenida da Liberdade, 4750 Barcelos (tel. 053/81-13-26), is one of the largest boarding houses in town. It offers comfortable rooms for 2,500$ ($16.25) daily in a single, 4,200$ ($27.30) in a double, with a continental breakfast included.

Residencial Dom Nuno, 1 Transversal Avenida Dom Nuno Álvares Pereira, 4750 Barcelos (tel. 053/81-50-84), is preferred by many visitors over the Albergaría Condes de Barcelos. The Dom Nuno is on a quieter street, about halfway between the tourist zone of the village and the Condes de Barcelos. Rooms are attractively furnished, and everything has a bright, modern look. The rate, with a continental breakfast included, is 4,500$ ($29.25) daily in a double and from 4,200$ ($27.30) in the one single. This is one of the friendliest little inns you are likely to find in this part of Portugal.

WHERE TO DINE

One of my favorites has long been **Dom António,** 87 Rua Dom António Barroso (tel. 81-22-85). On a pedestrian street in the heart of town, it occupies the ground floor of a town house. Regional food and wine are dispensed here throughout the day from 11:30 a.m. to 11 p.m. Meals cost from 1,800$ ($11.70).

Arantes Restaurant, 33 Avenida da Liberdade (tel. 81-16-45), is one of the largest restaurants in town. It too offers Portuguese cookery, with many regional dishes, serving complete meals for 1,800$ ($11.70). Hours are daily from noon to 3 p.m. and 7 to 10 p.m.

SHOPPING

For information about what to buy in Barcelos, refer to "Shopping in Portugal," chapter VII.

---

4. Esposende

Esposende is a beach-resort town between Viana do Castelo, 12½ miles, and Porto, 30 miles to the south. The pines and sand dunes are swept by the Atlantic breezes, and cows graze in nearby pastures. The surrounding countryside is no longer as unspoiled as it used to be, although you'll still see an occasional ox cart in the street. The area has been extensively developed, and there's a wide new road running along the seafront. Men and women in fustian clothes and broad-brimmed hats work the vineyards in the foothills. The beach is large and fine, lining both sides of the Cávado estuary. Small fishing vessels plod up the river carrying anglers to the bass upstream. Recent archeological diggings have revealed the remains of a Roman city and necropolis, but that doesn't seem to have disturbed Esposende in the least.

FOOD AND LODGING

A semi-modern hotel on the river, **Hotel Suave Mar,** Avenida Eng. Arantes e Oliveira, 4740 Esposende (tel. 053/96-14-45), attracts budgeteers who don't want to pay for the superior first-class accommodations at neighboring Ofir and Fão. The lodgings are pleasant and comfortable, and the place has 68 bedrooms. Singles rent for 7,000$ ($45.50) daily, and doubles go for 8,000$ ($52). Most guests, however, prefer to stay here on full-board terms, paying from 7,200$ ($46.80) to 9,700$

($63.05) per person daily. It's also possible to visit just for a meal, costing from 1,800$ ($11.70). One reader found the barbecued chicken "the best I've tasted in Portugal." The Suave Mar is open all year, although you may have the place to yourself off-season.

Nélia Hotel, Avenida Valentin Ribeiro, 4740 Esposende (tel. 053/96-12-44), is an inn in the center of the resort. The interior has a regional style. The bedrooms have wall dressing tables and mirrors, plus hand-carved wooden beds with interwoven leather headboards. Doubles cost 7,500$ ($48.75) daily, and singles go for 8,500 ($55.25).

Estalagem Zende, Rte. N13, 4740 Esposende (tel. 053/96-18-85), is rated by the government as a luxury inn. It lies on the main road to Viana do Castelo, right outside Esposende. Some 14 well-maintained bedrooms are rented, each with private bath and phone. In winter they are centrally heated. The charge is from 7,000$ ($45.50) daily in a double room, 5,500$ ($35.75) in a single. The inn has a good restaurant and cocktail bar, and it serves some of the best food in Esposende. A meal costs from 1,800$ ($11.70) and up. In winter, a fire blazes on the hearth. Food is served daily from 12:30 to 3 p.m. and 7:30 to 10 p.m.

Martins dos Frangos, R.S. Januário (tel. 96-18-65), is among the best of the independents, and it's reasonable in price, charging from 1,800$ ($11.70) for a complete meal. It's one of the biggest restaurants in the area, seating some 375 diners. It also keeps long hours: from 11 a.m. to 11 p.m. The location is on the road between Porto and Viana do Castelo. You'll spot it after the bridge over the Cálvado River.

---

5. Viana do Castelo

Viana do Castelo sits complacently between an estuary of the Lima River and a base of rolling hills. The Princess of the Lima, as she is called, is northern Portugal's city of folklore. The setting is enhanced by an occasional ox cart with wooden wheels clacking along the stone streets. Some of the boatmen of the city, their faces weatherbeaten, can be seen near the waterfront, offering to sell visitors a slow cruise along the riverbanks.

But for the best view, scale the **Monte de Santa Luzia,** reached by a funicular ride or, if you have a car, along a twisting road. From the Hotel de Santa Luzia at the summit, a great view unfolds, including Eiffel's bridge spanning the Lima.

Viana do Castelo is noted for its pottery and regional handcrafts (many can be purchased in the Friday market). It is even better known for its regional dress, best seen at the annual festa (the Friday, Saturday, and Sunday nearest to August 20) of Nossa Senhora de Agonia (Our Lady of Agony) when the women wear bright, strident colors of oranges, scarlets, and Prussian blue, with their layers of golden necklaces with heart- and cross-shaped pendants.

AROUND THE TOWN

The center of town is **Praça da República,** one of the handsomest squares in Portugal. At its heart is the much-photographed **Chafariz Fountain,** constructed in the 16th century, with water spewing from the mouths of its figures. The most impressive building on the square is the **Misericórdia,** a dour, squat, three-story structure, unique in the country. The lower level is an arcade composed of five austere Roman arches, whereas the two upper levels are ponderous Renaissance balconies. All are crowned by a rooftop crucifix. The four supporting pillars of each level are primitive caryatid-like figures between which are interspersed bright-red geraniums in flower boxes. Adjoining the Charity Hospital is a church fronting Rua da Bandeira. Inside is a combination of pictorial tiles made in 1714, ornate baroque altars, a painted ceiling, and wood carvings.

The other building dominating the praça is the old **Town Hall,** constructed over an arcade made up of three wide and low Gothic arches. The Tourist Office occupies the headquarters upstairs at Avenida Candido dos Reis (tel. 226-20). The crenel-topped façade displays a royal coat-of-arms and wrought-iron balcony windows above each arch. Originally the Paços do Concelho, it was constructed during the reign of Manuel I and completed under João III. From the small sidewalk tables and chairs, you can observe the square's activities and sample pastries such as torta de Viana.

Igreja Matriz, down Rua Cabral at Largo do Instituto Histórico do Minho, was begun by João I in 1285 and completed in 1433. Dominated by a large Gothic arched portal, the façade is flanked by two battlemented towers. The interior archway is carved with granite figures, acanthus leaves, and simplistic statuary with moonshaped faces. The inside is cold but with an excellent trompe l'oeil ceiling.

Viana do Castelo, only 44 miles north of Porto, is possible either as an overnight stopover or as the goal of a one-day trip. The beaches are large and sandy, guarded by an age-old fortress standing at the river's mouth.

WHERE TO STAY

Some 3½ miles from the center, **Hotel Santa Luzia,** Santa Luzia, 4900 Viana do Castelo (tel. 058/221-92), sits on a wooded hillside high above the most congested part of the city. It stands just behind the illuminated dome of the Basilica de Santa Luzia, which was constructed in the neo-Byzantine style. Built in 1895, the hotel has neoclassical details and granite balconies, giving it the appearance of a royal palace, especially when it is floodlit at night. To reach it, you have to negotiate winding cobblestone roads, which, because of their curves, take motorists through a forest. Once at the summit, the view over the city and the river is the best in the region.

In 1986 the hotel was completely renovated, an art deco sheen added to the high-ceilinged public rooms. It has long expanses of glistening marble, stylish accessories from the Jazz Age, a comfortable bar and restaurant, and 47 spacious and comfortably furnished bedrooms arranged along both sides of enormous and echoing hallways. Each room contains a private bath and phone. Singles rent for 10,000$ ($65) daily, and doubles go for 11,500$ ($74.75), with breakfast included. Fixed-price meals in the dining room begin at 3,000$ ($19.50) and are served daily from 12:30 to 3 p.m. and 7:30 to 10 p.m. There's an outdoor swimming pool sunk into one of the hotel's gardens.

Hotel Afonso III, 494 Avenida Dom Afonso III, 4900 Viana do Castelo (tel. 058/241-23), is a first-class hotel, which opened in 1971. Offering eight floors of comfort, it contains 89 accommodations, each with its own bath. More than half are graced with a private balcony as well. The attractively furnished rooms rent for 9,000$ ($58.50) daily for one person, increasing to 12,000$ ($78) for two, including breakfast. Dinner costs from 2,000$ ($13). The contemporary decor consists mainly of black and white marble, with a lobby sheathed with nautically inspired designs crafted from richly grained hardwood. The overall tone is both simple and sophisticated. A restaurant on the seventh floor provides a panoramic view over the Lima River. Other facilities include a convention hall, a boîte, and swimming pools. Bar facilities are available.

Hotel do Parque, Praça da Galiza, 4900 Viana do Castelo (tel. 058/241-51), is a 120-bedroom four-star hotel at the base of the bridge crossing the Lima River on the edge of town. It has a motel/mini-resort flavor, its lounges overlooking an outdoor swimming pool with grass terrace. On its rooftop is a panoramic restaurant, serving regional and international dishes, and adjoining it is a solarium with a refreshment area. Intermixed with the main-floor lounge is an interior winter garden. The lounges have soft leather armchairs. For evening entertainment there is a disco-boîte. Bedrooms are quite contemporary, with plenty of built-in furnishings, tile baths, heating, phone, piped-in music, and balconies. Singles cost 10,750$ ($69.90) daily, and doubles go for 12,750$ ($82.90), with breakfast included.

Hotel Viana Sol, Largo Vasco da Gama, 4900 Viana do Castelo (tel. 058/263-23). Set behind a dignified granite and stucco façade, near a commemorative column and fountain in the center of town, this well-designed hotel opened in 1986. In contrast to its elegantly severe exterior, its spacious public rooms were stylishly sheathed with layers of glistening white marble, capped with a mirrored ceiling, and illuminated with a three-tiered atrium lit with a skylight and filled with plants. A lobby bar lies within earshot of a pagoda-shaped fountain and is ringed with a scarlet-and-black decor. Each of the well-furnished bedrooms, 65 in all, contains a private bath, TV, and phone. Singles cost 8,500$ ($55.25) daily, and doubles go for 11,000$ ($71.50). A continental breakfast is included. There's a restaurant on the premises, plus a swimming pool, health club, tennis courts, and squash courts.

Hotel Aliança, Avenida dos Combatentes da Grande Guerra, 4900 Viana do Castelo (tel. 058/230-01), was originally built in the 18th century, but its façade was restored in 1962, leaving a streamlined stucco sheathing with granite window trim. It sits on the corner of the town's main street at the edge of the river, within sight of the loading derricks and cranes. This is by no means a stylish or upscale hotel, but its slightly dowdy charm and the sincere concern of the Portuguese family who run it more than compensate. Each of the 30 rooms is likely to have a high ceiling, slightly frayed furniture, and a blandly old-fashioned color scheme, along with accessories from the 1930s. About half the units contain a private bath. Doubles cost 6,900$ ($44.85) daily, including a continental breakfast. Singles rent for 3,500$ ($22.75).

Residencial Viana Mar, 215 Avenida dos Combatentes da Grande Guerra, 4900 Viana do Castelo (tel. 058/230-54), is on the main commercial thoroughfare of town behind a granite façade whose severity is relieved by colorful awnings. Inside, near the nondescript reception area, lies a sunken bar. About half of the 36 simple bedrooms contain a private bath, and each is filled with basic furnishings. Bathless singles rent for 2,500$ ($16.25) daily, and doubles cost 3,000$ ($19.50) to 3,800$ ($24.70), with a continental breakfast included. A few of the hotel's rooms are contained in two nearby annexes.

WHERE TO DINE

Like a country house in the center of town, **Os 3 Potes,** 7-9 Beco dos Fornos (tel. 234-32), off Praça da República, was an old bakery before its conversion into one of the best regional restaurants in Viana do Castelo. From Praça da República, head down Rua de Sacadura Cabral (the restaurant is somewhat hard to find, but worth the search). The atmosphere is rustic, and on Friday and Saturday from June to September folk dancing is offered. The food is good too, but you should have your hotel call in advance to make a reservation. I'd suggest caldo verde to begin, followed by such good-tasting main dishes as codfish 3 Potes, lampreys (eels), or fondue bourguignonne. I always skip dessert, settling for the Irish coffee instead. Expect to spend 1,500$ ($9.75) to 2,200$ ($14.30), plus the cost of your wine. The restaurant serves food from noon to 3:30 p.m. and 7 p.m. to midnight Tuesday to Sunday; closed Monday.

Hotel do Parque Restaurant, Parque da Galiza (tel. 241-51). In addition to offering a good selection of well-prepared food, this panoramic restaurant in a previously recommended hotel offers a sweeping view of the River Lima and the famous bridge designed by Gustav Eiffel. The restaurant sits on the topmost floor of this hotel, reached via an elevator from the lobby. Amid a modern decor of turquoise and white, you can enjoy full meals costing from 2,800$ ($18.20) and served daily from 12:30 to 2:30 p.m. and 7:30 to 9:30 p.m. The bill of fare includes cream soups, pork piri-piri, pepper steak, and grilled turbot.

Alambique, 86 Rua Manuel Espregueira (tel. 238-94). You enter this typical Portuguese restaurant through a large wine vat. Inside you'll find many of the specialties for which the cooks of northern Portugal are known, including codfish Antiga Viana, *churrasco de porco* (pork), *cabrito* (goat), tripe Porto style, and lampreys bordelaise. One of the chef's most memorable dishes is *feijuada à transmontana*, a bean-and-meat stew. For a beginning, you can order either sopa alentejana or sopa do mar. A complete meal costs 3,000$ ($19.50) to 4,000$ ($26) and is served from noon to 3 p.m. and 7 to 10 p.m.

Dolce Vita, 44 Rua Poço (tel. 248-60), as its name suggests, is an Italian eatery and pizzeria. The food is good here, and reasonable in price: meals cost from 1,500$ ($9.75). Service is from noon to 3 p.m. and 7 to 10 p.m. daily except Monday. The pizzas are considered the best in town, and you might try some concoctions unfamiliar to you, including one made with bacalhau (codfish). You can also order some good pastas, such as lasagne Dolce Vita. Among more familiar Italian specialties are beef pizzaiola, veal cutlet bolognese, and risotto piemontese.

Túnel, 3 Rua dos Manjovos (tel. 221-88), has an excellent regional cuisine. It lies right off Avenida des Combatantes de Grande Guerra. At certain times you can order quail or roast kid. The fish dishes are usually the best, however. You might begin with a rich-tasting vegetable soup, made with fresh vegetables from the field. Count on spending 1,500$ ($9.75) or more. The dining room is on the second floor. You pass through a simple snackbar at ground level. Hours are daily from noon to 2 p.m. and 7 to 10 p.m.

QUINTAS IN THE ENVIRONS

The most romantic way to stay in and around Viana do Castelo is not at one of the hotels recommended above, but at one of the antique quintas in the environs. In restored manor houses you can stay with the Portuguese aristocracy. You can make reservations through **Delegação de Turismo de Ponte de Lima,** TURIHAB— Associação Turismo de Habitação, Praça da República, 4990 Ponte de Lima (tel. 058/94-23-35). Payment is made by check sent directly to the owners, with 50% prepayment required when your reservation is made. A minimum stay of three nights is required, and bookings must be made at least three days before your planned arrival. The environs of Viana do Castelo have some of the most elaborate and stylized quintas and manor houses in all of Portugal. A random sampling of the best ones include the following:

Solar de Cortegaça, Subportela, 4900 Viana do Castelo (tel. 058/97-16-39), lies in the parish of Subportela on the left bank of the Lima River near the road connection (EN 203) between Viana do Castelo and Ponte de Lima. Recently restored, it has much modern comfort, but its architectural characteristics have been preserved. The house dates back four centuries. D. Maria Filomena de Abreu Coutinho rents three double rooms with private bath, charging 5,000$ ($32.50) daily for a single, 8,000$ ($52) for a double. There are several sitting and dining rooms, as well as a garden.

Casa de Requeijo, Arcos de Valdevez (tel. 058/652-72), is a 17th-century house standing behind a crenellated wall typical of the 18th century. It overlooks the River Vez, where you can go boating or canoeing. Catherine and Alberto Alves Pereira rent out two apartments and eight double rooms with private baths. In the main building, guests can use the sitting room with TV, video, bar, and piano, or play cards in the living room. Ping-pong and tennis can be played in the garden, and there's a terrace with a barbecue.

At Meadela, just outside Viana do Castelo on the road to Ponte de Lima, **Casa do Ameal,** Rua do Meal, 4900 Viana do Castelo (tel. 058/224-03) is the domain of Mrs. Maria Elisa Vilhena. The property has a long aristocratic heritage, and is almost a small museum of valuable costumes collected by the family over the generations. The casa offers two double rooms and four apartments. Doubles are bathless, but the apartments contain facilities. Rates are 8,000$ ($52) daily in a double, and 10,500$ ($68.25) in an apartment for four persons. Guests are free to enjoy the gardens and grounds.

Paço d'Anha, Anha, 4900 Viana do Castelo (tel. 058/32-24-59), has centuries of tradition. A fine example of Portuguese aristocratic architecture, it is in a beautiful setting near the Atlantic coast, with pine woods, lawns, and vineyards where the fine and fruity Paço d'Anha Vinho Verde white wine is produced. In the annexes next to the main building there are four apartments, each with two double beds, a bath, a sitting room with a fireplace, and a kitchen. The price of one of the apartments is 13,000$ ($84.50) daily for four persons in high season or 11,500$ ($74.75) in low season. Guests can use the facilities available at the farm, including a tennis court. They can take walks in the surrounding gardens and woods and visit the manor and cellars that date from the 17th century. There's always a supply of wood available for the fireplaces.

---

6. Ponte de Lima

Upriver 12 miles from Viana do Castelo is Ponte de Lima, which is exactly what one hopes a Portuguese village will be like. The drive along the north side of the river takes you through grape arbors, pastoral villages, and forests of cedar, pine, and chestnut. Red-cheeked peasants stand silhouetted against moss-green stone walls or cease their toil in the cabbage fields to watch you pass. A modern bridge and motorway lead into the town from upriver, although the original bridge here was built by the Romans.

The town, founded on the site of a Celtic settlement, was developed by the Romans, who named it Forum Limicorum. It was important to them for both river trade and river defense, and the town was enclosed with thick stone walls, guarding the bridge across the Lima. Part of the Roman bridge is still in use, together with its buttressed extension, made under King Dom Pedro in 1355 because of changes in the river's course. Sometimes you'll see women wringing out their clothes along the banks of the river. At certain times of the year the Lima is likely to be dry, but when it is full, anglers often catch trout in its waters.

The Roman wall has been partially destroyed to make room for roads, but you can walk along the top of what's left. An 18th-century fountain graces the town's main square, and houses of that era are still occupied. Ruins of ramparts from the Middle Ages and a solitary keep can be seen, opposite the old bridge.

Go up the stone steps of the keep to visit the **Biblioteca Public Municipal,** founded in the early 18th century. Here archives are rich in historic documents of the town.

Two churches at right angles to one another, **São Francisco** and **Santo António,** have been secularized and now contain museum treasures and artwork, especially handsome woodcarving. Of particular interest in São Francisco is a strange image of St. George astride a saddle on a wooden trestle. The museum is open daily except Tuesday from 10 a.m. to noon and 2 to 5:30 p.m.

The fame of the Ponte de Lima **market** is known throughout Portugal. In a riverside setting, it takes place on alternate Mondays. The sellers show up in colorful regional costumes. On the north side of the bridge is the cattle market where oxen and steers are sold. A little bag nestling between the horns of the animals contains a "magic potion" said to ward off the evil eye. Below the bridge is a place reserved for eating such al fresco delights as roast sardines accompanied by glasses of vinho verde. Taking the riverside walk, you can survey the stalls of various craftspeople, including cobblers, carpenters, and goldsmiths.

STAYING AT QUINTAS, FARMS, AND MANORS

In recent years Ponte de Lima has opened a collection of beautiful properties, including manor houses and farms, that makes staying in this northern area reason enough to visit. For information on properties in and around Ponte de Lima, get in touch with **Delegacão de Turismo de Ponte de Lima** at the address given above, under "Quintas in the Environs."

Casa de Sabadão, 4990 Ponte de Lima (tel. 058/94-19-63) lies in the hamlet of Sabadão, in the suburbs of Ponte de Lima. The area is known for its gentle landscape and peaceful atmosphere. This special quinta offers three well-furnished double rooms, each with a private bath. Everything is in good taste, and tourists enjoy the comfort and hospitality. They also share use of the living room and dining room. Rates for two persons range from 7,000$ ($45.50) to 8,200$ ($53.30) daily, depending on the season. D. Maria Eulália Abreu Lima e Fonseca is the hostess.

Casa de Outeiro, Arcozelo, 4990 Ponte de Lima (tel. 058/94-12-06), is a large farm, an 18th-century quinta that provides one of the coziest and most comfortable country homes in the area. Dr. João Gomes de Abreu Lima rents two doubles with bath and one bathless double, with facilities nearby. The rate for two persons is 8,200$ ($53.30) nightly. Sitting rooms, a dining room, and a large kitchen are provided for use of guests. The location is on the outskirts of Ponte de Lima.

Also a lovely farm near Ponte de Lima, the **Casa de Antepaço,** 4990 Ponte de Lima (tel. 058/94-17-02) is owned by Dr. Francisco de Abreu Lima. It is a beautifully restored stone house that has been modernized with all up-to-date conveniences. The hospitable doctor rents out four double rooms, each with private bath, charging 8,200$ ($53.30) nightly for two persons. Guests have use of a living room with a fireplace, a library, and a kitchen. There is an attractive terrace and a garden opening onto a view of the Lima River.

Casa de Abades, São Martinho da Gândara, 4990 Ponte de Lima (tel. 058/94-16-27), is a lovely manor house in a thickly wooded area, most suitable for an idyllic retreat. Mrs. Maria Madalena Graça rents a private apartment with one double and two single bedrooms, a sitting room, and a small kitchenette. Four persons can stay here at a cost of 1,900$ ($70.85) per night.

Casa das Torres, Facha, 4990 Ponte de Lima (tel. 058/94-13-69), run by Manuel Correia Malheiros, is a majestic house, an example of the aristocratic architecture that existed at the time of Dom João V. It overlooks the countryside, and is an ideal location for the gentle life. There is a double room with private bath in the main building, priced at 8,200$ ($53.50) per night, and an annex has an apartment with two double rooms and a private bath, as well as a sitting room and kitchenette, costing four persons 10,900$ ($70.85) daily. The estate also has lovely gardens and, as another lure, a swimming pool.

Casa do Barreiro, Gemieira, 4990 Ponte de Lima (tel. 058/94-19-73). Gaspar Malheiro has adapted this manor house to accommodate paying guests in luxurious style. The casa offers seven double rooms (five with bath and two without). The charge is 8,200$ ($53.30) daily. The place is lavishly decorated with antiques and set in a farming area.

WHERE TO DINE

A good local independent eatery is **Encanada,** Praça Municipal (tel. 94-11-89). Opening onto an esplanade, it offers some 140 diners a panoramic view of this beautiful countryside. Meals cost from 1,800$ ($11.70) and are served daily from noon to 3 p.m. and 7 to 10 p.m., except Thursday night. Good regional fare and wines are featured.

Gaio, Rua Agostinho J. Taveira (tel. 94-12-51), also has its devotees. Even larger, it serves a bountiful cuisine, much of it coming from the garden-rich district of the Minho. Meals, costing only 1,500$ ($9.75), are served from noon to 3 p.m. and 7 to 10 p.m. It is closed on Wednesday.

7. Valença do Minho

The walled battlements of Valença do Minho, 33 miles northeast of Viana do Castelo, stand today as a reminder of ancient hostilities between Portugal and Spain.

In fact, when Afonso III ruled Portugal, the forces of Castile and León besieged and destroyed much of Valença do Minho.

A narrow covered gateway across a moat takes you into the center of this walled village of cobblestone streets, ancient stone houses, pots of geraniums, wrought-iron balconies, and old street lanterns. Incorporated into the 13th-century fortress, a government-owned pousada opens onto a belvedere, from which you can enjoy one of the finest views in the Minho. The old cannons are still mounted, no longer seriously, looking down on the **International Bridge** across the Minho to Spain.

On the other side of the river is the Spanish town of **Tuy,** once a blood enemy, and now a sister-town to Valença do Minho. Tuy is noted for its narrow, steep streets and walls erected on top of ancient Roman fortifications. The battlemented turrets and towers of the cathedral-fortress have stood guard on the frontier since 1170.

While in Valença do Minho, you may get hooked on the local specialty, lampreys (eels). Order them fresh from the river, served in a spicy pepper sauce.

FOOD AND LODGING

An attractive, comfortable place to stay is the **Pousada de São Teotónio,** 4930 Valença do Minho (tel. 051/222-52). The Portuguese government tried to outshine its rival counterpart across the border, a Spanish parador. Although lodged among some of Portugal's most unspoiled antiquities, the pousada is contemporary in concept. It's built villa-fashion on several levels, with an entrance portico connecting the main building with an annex. Most of the lounges and bedrooms not only have a view of the river and Tuy, but also open onto a courtyard with a lawn and reflecting pool.

The public rooms are spacious, flowing one into another, containing wooden ceilings, tile floors, and various retreat nooks. The lounge has a wide stone fireplace, a 15-foot plank coffee table, and hand-loomed rugs. Many of the bedrooms have balconies, and 14 of the 16 rooms are equipped with private bath. Single rooms range in price from 12,300$ ($79.95) daily; doubles, 13,500$ ($87.75). If you stop only for a meal (and many do), the cost ranges from 1,950$ ($12.70) to 2,700$ ($17.55) for a five-course table d'hôte luncheon or dinner. The helpings are bountiful and the dishes good, if you like regional cooking. The wooden-ceiling dining room takes full advantage of the view of the river and Spain.

Outside of the pousada, your best bet for a good meal is **Arcádia,** Tuido (tel. 233-46), which does good grills—both fish and meat—along with many regional specialties. It also has a good wine cellar. Meals cost from 1,500$ ($9.75), and service is daily except Thursday from noon to 4 p.m. and 7 to 11 p.m. You can enjoy an apéritif in the bar before being shown to your table. In winter the place is warmed by a fireplace.

---

8. Pousada-Hopping in Minho

Many visitors consider pousada-hopping the most rewarding way of exploring Portugal. Every government-owned inn lies in a characteristic region, as well as a special scenic spot. (The first *pousada,* a place to rest, was founded in the 12th century, offering pilgrims a roof, a bed, and a candle. That hospitality today includes all the amenities of modern comfort.) Pousadas in this northern region of Portugal include the following:

Pousada de São Bento, Caniçada do Minho, 4850 Vieira do Minho (tel. 053/571-90) overlooks the winding road that runs between Caldeirinhas and Pontes do Rio Caldo. The pousada was originally built as the opulent private villa of an engineer who supervised the construction of a nearby dam. It was later enlarged. Undeniably romantic, it has stone walls and smallish windows that remind some guests of an alpine chalet, except for the masses of vines trailing across its façade.

Inside, a cathedral ceiling is supported by decoratively massive wooden trusses, creating a kind of canopy over a pair of granite fireplaces.

This small pousada, has 18 bedrooms, each with bath. Singles rent for 11,300$ ($73.45) daily, and doubles go for 12,500$ ($81.25). Meals, served from 12:30 to 2:30 p.m. and 7:30 to 9:30 p.m., cost 2,500$ ($16.25). A magnet with guests is the swimming pool. The landscape is so beautiful, however, that you may prefer to make the pousada a base from which to explore. This area abounds in luxuriant vegetation and rippling waterfalls, and there's lots of game in the wooded areas. The park of Peneda-Gerês and the ancient stone cloisters of Santa Maria do Bouro and Our Lady of Abadia are easy sightseeing targets. The pousada, on the Braga-Gerês highway, is 16 miles from Vieria do Minho at Caniçada do Minho and about 18½ miles east of Braga.

Pousada de Dom Diniz, Praça da Liberdade, 4920 Vila Nova de Cerveira (tel. 051/956-01), lies within the remains of an ancient fortress, in the northwestern town of Vila Nova de Cerveira, close to the Minho River and the Spanish border. The history of this government-run hotel goes back to 1321 when Dom Denis granted the castle its charter. Parts of the original interior of the castle have been incorporated into the pousada, whose rooms are in seven buildings, all within crenellated ramparts entered through a massive arched gate reached by going up the hill from the main square of the village, site of the reception area. It contains 26 rooms and three suites; 11 of the units have private patios. Some of the rooms look out over the cobblestone streets of the village. The accommodations are pleasantly decorated with reproductions of old Minho furniture. You can take your apéritif on the stone terrace with a view of the countryside. The rates range from 16,600$ ($107.90) daily for a double with a continental breakfast, from 14,900$ ($96.85) for a single. A three-course dinner of regional specialties costs 2,500$ ($16.25) to 3,200$ ($20.80). Food is served daily from 12:30 to 3 p.m. and 7:30 to 9:30 p.m. The pousada has a bar and a disco.

TRÁS-OS-MONTES

The far northeastern province of Portugal is a wild, rugged land—Trás-os-Montes, a name meaning "beyond the mountains." Extending from south of the Upper Douro at Lamego, the province stretches north to Spain. Vila Real is its capital. The high plateau, lying between the mountain ranges of Marão and Gerês, is broken up by rocky crests as well as deep valleys where most of the population lives, usually in houses constructed from shale or granite. Much of the plateau is arid land, but swift rivers and their tributaries supply ample water for the use of the people, and some of the valleys have fertile farmland. The Tâmega River Valley is known for the thermal springs found there as far back as Roman days.

This land is rich in history and tradition, offering the visitor a new world to discover, from pre-Roman castles to prehistoric dolmens and cromlechs to pillories and interesting old churches. The inhabitants of this region are of Celtic descent, and most speak a dialect of Galician.

You can reach Trás-os-Montes by train from Porto to Régua, not far from Lamego, which serves as a gateway into the province in the Pais do Vinho, where grapes from vineyards on the terraced hills provide the wines that are credited to Porto. Lamego is actually in the province of Beira Alta. You can drive through this land of splendid savagery, but don't expect superhighways.

1. Amarante

The little town of Amarante is not actually in Trás-os-Montes, but lies along the border of that province. It serves as a good gateway to this little-known and underexplored region. The town lies north of the Upper Douro Valley on the

Tâmega River as it flows southward to join the Douro east of Porto, which is 40 miles from Amarante. Amarante is 30 miles west of Vila Real, the capital of Trás-os-Montes.

From the Ponte de Amarante, built over the Tâmega in 1790, you can see wooden balconies that extend out over the river, with willow trees drooping on the banks—a lovely and romantic setting. At the entrance to the bridge sits the former **Convent of St. Gonçalo** with a tile-faced dome.

Inside is a theatrical welter of baroque decoration. The altarpiece is a cherubic romp, with silver-haired cherubs frolicking all over the columns and ceiling. The pillars on each side of the altar are festooned with wreaths and bouquets of flowers, and the supporting columns have bazarre hermaphroditic figures costumed in black, gold, and scarlet. Notable is the baroque organ, held up by a gilded merman.

The convent contains the tomb of St. Gonçalo, the patron saint of marriages and unmarried women. His feast day is on the first weekend of June, and it is the custom for unmarried women and bachelors to exchange cakes baked in the shape of phalluses on that day. It seems that the vestige of a pagan fertility rite has survived, or else St. Gonçalo himself is having a final chuckle.

A POUSADA

On a remote mountain pass, **Pousada de São Gonçalo,** Sêrra do Marão, 4600 Amarante (tel. 055/46-11-23), 16 miles from Amarante along Rte. N15, is almost snowbound in winter, but a sun trap in summer. A modern version of a roadside inn, it is a retreat. The approach, between Amarante and Vila Real, is forlorn, with no signs of life. The place is called Bela Vista, near the Alto de Espinho. Pine woods grow for miles around in every direction.

The pousada is furnished in the regional style, more like a hilltop home than an inn. Antique console tables, high wooden chests, tile floors, country-style armchairs, an open fireplace, and statuary add to that effect. Only 15 rooms with bath are available, so it's wise to make reservations. The rooms are furnished with a few antiques interspersed with passable reproductions. A single rents for 8,500$ ($55.25) daily and a double for 9,500$ ($61.75).

Meals are hearty and filling. A complete table d'hôte lunch or dinner costs from 2,000$ ($13) to 2,600$ ($16.90) and includes homemade bread and a ceramic pitcher of wine. You may want to try cabbage soup, trout stuffed with smoked ham, or kid stew serrana style, or roasted until it's brown and crispy. Desserts are the special pride of the cook: perhaps you'll receive a creamy layer cake studded with almonds that looks just like a porcupine. Food is served daily from 12:30 to 3 p.m. and 7:30 to 9:30 p.m.

FOOD AND LODGING IN TOWN

If the pousada is full, or if you'd prefer to stay in Amarante, the best choice is the **Hotel Navarras,** Rua António Carneiro, 4600 Amarante (tel. 055/42-40-36). Rooms are usually available here throughout the year, except at the time of the feast of St. Gonçalo. The hotel rents 61 comfortably furnished rooms, which for the most part are large, well kept, and furnished in a contemporary style. The single rate is 7,000$ ($45.50) daily, rising to 8,350$ ($54.30) in a double. Many of the bedrooms also open onto a terrace. There is also a most welcome swimming pool. Breakfast, included in the rates, is the only meal served.

Within the town, the best food is obtained at **Zé da Calçada,** Rua 31 de Janeiro (tel. 42-20-23). In fact, many discerning local patrons prefer this 60-seat place to the cookery at the pousada. A four-star restaurant, Zé da Calçada offers good home-cooking and specialties from various regions of Portugal. Naturally, it has a superb collection of the best wines of this vineyard-rich part of Portugal. Meals cost from 2,500$ ($16.25) and are served daily from noon to 3:30 p.m. and 5 to 10 p.m. The decoration is in the regional style, and there is a pleasant terrace in summer, a fire-place in winter.

2. Lamego

This old bishopric on the wooded slopes of Mount Penude is a good example of baroque harmony. Many of its public and private buildings (even the town cinema) show this unifying style, an example of community planning rarely achieved. The main square has a public garden and adjoins a leisurely, tree-lined esplanade, where the denizens of Lamego promenade in the evenings. Behind the statue of Bishop Dom Miguel is his former palace, converted into a museum displaying sculpture and French tapestries.

AROUND THE TOWN

Across the way is the **Cathedral of Lamego (Sé)**, originally built in the Romanesque style, then overlaid with Gothic and baroque ornamentation. The ceilings are frescoed, but in dire need of repair. Adjoining is a Renaissance cloister, with a chapel containing a large baroque altar. A second chapel contains pictorial tiles illustrating a touching scene of children bathing in a tub.

Crowning a forested sêrra, overlooking Lamego, is the well-known 18th-century mecca of **Nossa Senhora dos Remédios** (Our Lady of the Cures). Leading to it is an elegant baroque stairway, the Spanish Steps of Lamego, broken by nine fountain-centered and profusely decorated landings. The faithful scale the steps on their knees, as they do on Rome's Scala Santa (Holy Steps).

The granite balustrade is topped with various resplendent finials and statues in Roman battle dress, vases and urns, spheres and niches, plus some saccharine pictorial tiles. The fountains are interesting; one is decorated with four grotesques, each spouting water from its mouth.

The ruins of a 12th-century fortified castle stand on a hill opposite the one occupied by the sanctuary.

Museu de Lamego fills more than 30 rooms of the old Bishop's Palace. Of special note are five paintings on wood from the early 16th century, from the altarpiece of the cathedral, and the Brussels tapestries, also from the 16th century. You'll see lots of reminders of the baroque period in the museum, including two chapels of gilded, carved wood upstairs and examples of ecclesiastical sculpture from the Middle Ages to the 17th century, plus a baroque chapel, on the ground floor. Chinese porcelains and paintings on silk, azulejos, pottery, furniture, paintings, sculpture, and gold and silver religious objects are also displayed. The museum has guided tours from 10 a.m. to 12:30 p.m. and 2 to 5 p.m. daily except Monday. Admission is 200$ ($1.30); free on Sunday.

You can visit the **Chapel of the Exile** (Igreja do Desterro) by asking for the key at 126 Rua Cardoso Avelino, right across the street. The 1640 chapel has 17th-century azulejos and 18th-century carved, gilded wood. The ceiling, with paintings of the life of Christ, is particularly noteworthy.

FOOD AND LODGING

Near the commercial outskirts of the town, **Albergaría do Cerrado,** Lugar do Cerrado, Lamego, 5100 Viseu (tel. 054/631-64), lies behind a yellow balconied façade. By almost anyone's standards, this is considered the most up-to-date and comfortable hotel in town. It is certainly the most convenient and the best accessorized, but not necessarily the most charming. Popular with business travelers, it contains 30 bedrooms, each outfitted with a predictable international style, including a private bath, balcony, and piped-in music. With a continental breakfast included, singles cost 7,000$ ($45.50) daily; doubles 8,500$ ($55.27).

Hotel Parque, Santuario de Nossa Senhora dos Remédios, 5100 Lamego (tel. 054/621-05). Its severe dignity and pristine façade hint at its origins early in the 20th century as the monastery connected to the Church of Nossa Senhora dos Remédios, a few steps away. In the late 1960s it was converted into a 36-room hotel, each of whose units was renovated in 1984. No other hotel in Lamego affords visitors such a desirable location, next to one of the finest baroque ensembles in north Portugal. If you select this hotel, allow enough time for a leisurely promenade down the lushly ornate stairs leading to the center of town, 15 pedestrian minutes away. The experience is well worth the effort.

Each room at the hotel contains a private bath and phone, and comes with a continental breakfast included in the price. Singles cost 5,250$ ($34.15) daily, and doubles go for 6,000$ ($39). Don't overlook the Parque's dining room as a luncheon or dinner possibility. Meals, costing from 1,800$ ($11.70), are served daily from 12:30 to 2 p.m. and 7:30 to 9:30 p.m.

Outside the hotels, Lamego has several places at which you can eat. One of the most convenient, because of its hours, is **Welwitschia,** Rua Columela (tel. 632-53). Good regional cookery is the feature here, and the chef is rightly proud of his fresh shellfish, which he prepares in many different ways. You can patronize either the restaurant, ordering full-course meals, or else use Welwitschia as a snackbar. Charging from 1,800$ ($11.70) for a meal, it serves daily from noon to 1 a.m.

Turisêrra, Sêrra Meadas (tel. 633-80), is the choice if you want not only more elaborate cooking but a panoramic view. Local food and regional specialties from throughout Portugal are served here daily except Monday from noon to 3 p.m. and 7 to 10 p.m. Meals cost from 1,800$ ($11.70) and up.

3. Vila Real

The capital of Trás-os-Montes is a lively little town 70 miles from Porto, built on a hilly plateau in the foothills of the Sêrra do Marão. Some parts of the town are linked with others by bridges across the ravines. Gorges cut by the Corgo and Cabril Rivers, which flow together here, can be seen from a terrace high above, where a castle once stood. The lookout is reached in a direct line from the cemetery. From this vicinity, you can also see houses overhanging the ravine of the Corgo.

The **Cathedral (Sé) of São Domingos** is in the main square. The Gothic building has a high altar with gold reredos.

St. Peter's Church (Igreja São Pedro), just off the main street of the town, Avenida Carvalho Araujo, has a handsome ceiling of high relief, carved, gilded paneling, plus a chancel lined with colorful azulejos.

The **House of Diogo Cão,** 19 Avenida Carvalho Araujo, is reputedly the birthplace of the navigator who discovered the Congo River in Africa in 1482. The exterior of the house was altered and is now in the 16th-century Italian Renaissance style.

The **Town Hall** (Câmera Municipal; tel. 228-19), also on the main street, has an Italian Renaissance-style stone staircase. In front stands a lantern pillory.

If you happen to be in the area toward the end of June, you may get to purchase some of the fine black pottery of the region, which is sold at St. Peter's Fair.

For information about Vila Real and the surrounding country, stop at the **Tourist Center** (Turismo), 69 Avenida Carvalho Araujo (tel. 228-19), which is in an interesting old building.

FOOD AND LODGING

The best place to stay is a four-star hotel, **Albergaría Cabanelas,** Rua Dom Pedro de Castro, 5000 Vila Real (tel. 059/231-53). It is a modern hotel, with a desirable "heart of town" location, and it has an elevator as well as a polite staff. The two dozen rooms of the inn are simply furnished but comfortable, all well maintained.

Singles cost 3,500$ ($22.75) daily and doubles 5,500$ ($35.75). You can also enjoy a meal based on regional cuisine (see below).

Its chief competitor is the even more modern **Hotel Miracorgo,** Avenida 1° de Maio, 5000 Vila Real (tel. 059/250-01), in a commercial section of the city. A tall, somewhat impersonal structure, this hotel offers a total of 76 single and double bedrooms that are air-conditioned. Singles rent for 8,200$ ($53.30) daily, and doubles cost 11,200$ ($72.80). Breakfast is the only meal served. Rooms are color coordinated and simply furnished in a modern idiom. On the premises is a well-stocked bar along with an indoor swimming pool and a health club. Many of the upper rooms open onto panoramic views.

Restaurante O Espadeiro, Avenida Almeida Lucena (tel. 223-02), is the finest independent restaurant in town. In business since 1969, it adopted the tradename O Espadeiro (the swordsman) after a brave transmontano warrior, Lourenço Viegas. You climb a flight of stairs to this modern, well-decorated restaurant, which has a large sunny terrace and a bar, opening onto a good view. Its chefs are proud of their region and its foodstuffs. They feature such fare as bundles of stewed tripe, roast kid from the oven, and a delectable grilled trout stuffed with a Parma-style ham. However, many diners come here just to sample that local version of a great Brazilian dish, *feijoada à transmontana,* a savory, well-seasoned and spiced stew with beans and various types of meats. Meals cost from 11,800$ ($11.70) and are served daily from noon to 3 p.m. and 7 to 11:30 p.m.

An alternative choice in a previously recommended hotel is **Cabanelas,** Rua Dom Pedro de Castro (tel. 231-53), which has good food and wine, and dispenses both with good service. Meals, costing from 2,000$ ($13) to 2,300$ ($14.95), are served daily from noon to 3 p.m. and 7:30 to 10 p.m. Provincial cookery is the style here, and you get a good selection of meat and fresh fish. You can sample such dishes as grilled pork, grilled shrimp, or a well-flavored fish stew, perhaps beginning with a caldo verde. The dining room lies one floor above street level. Parking is available.

MATEUS

About two miles east of Vila Real, on the road to Sabrosa, is the village of Mateus where the quinta of the Conde de Vila Real is centered. The grapes of the original Mateus rosé wine were grown in the vineyards here.

Mateus solar (manor house) dates from the early 18th century. Although the façade looks like the picture on the Mateus rosé bottles, the house, a creation of the architect Nicolau Nasoni, is better than the picture. The solar now belongs to a cultural organization, the Foundation of the Casa de Mateus, internationally known for its activity in the fields of music and plastic arts, plus international seminars. In summer, hours are from 9 a.m. to 1 p.m. and 2 to 6 p.m. daily except Sunday. In winter tours are given daily except Sunday from 9 a.m. to noon and 1 to 4 p.m. A guided tour of the farm costs 250$ ($1.65), but you must pay 350$ ($2.30) to see both the farm and the palace. The gardens are among the most beautiful of Europe. For more information, write Mateus Solar, Mateus, 5000 Vila Real.

4. Alijó

The village dates back to the year 1226, and those who it seek out 27 miles from Vila Real and 97 from Porto, will be rewarded. It has a heritage rich in pre-Roman fortifications and antiquities. In its midst is a giant plane tree, planted in 1856, whose trunk measures almost 20 feet in circumference.

In the heart of the Douro wine-producing region of Portugal, Alijó is a pleasant stop for the visitor in search of rural charm and a delightful sampling of regional Portuguese food and wine.

Within the town, **Pousada do Barão de Forrester,** Rua José Rufino, 5070

Alijó (tel. 059/952-15), will give you a taste of Trasmontanian hospitality. It's a very pleasant pousada with only 11 bedrooms, all with bath, along with comfortable lounges and a wood-beamed restaurant with two terraces (one closed in, the other open). There are two bars, and if you're here on a cold wintry day, the cozy fireplace is a welcome sight. The inn is decorated in regional style, and in keeping with the character of the area there is a vineyard as well as a garden, a swimming pool (one of the bars is beside it), and a tennis court. The rates at the pousada run from 9,800$ ($63.70) daily in a double, from 8,700$ ($56.55) in a single, with a continental breakfast included. A three-course country dinner can be enjoyed for 2,400$ ($26). Food is served daily from noon to 3 p.m. and 7:30 to 9:30 p.m.

The pousada is dedicated to a Scotsman, Joseph James Forrester, who first opened the Douro River to navigation, and was given the title of "Barão" or baron by Fernando II in recognition of his contribution to the wine trade.

5. Vidago and Pedras Salgadas

Lying in the heart of the northwest section of Trás-os-Montes are two little spa towns—Vidago, 27 miles from Vila Real, and Pedras Salgadas, 19 miles from the capital of the province. The valley, 1,000 to 2,000 feet above sea level, in which they are situated, is a favorite vacation spot for the Portuguese that became popular in the country's days of empire. Today the spa region has a mild climate with many sunny days, and many recreational facilities are offered in both places.

Vidago, as a hot-spring resort, offers a modern swimming pool with a bar, two clay tennis courts, a mountain golf course with nine holes and pro golf instruction, horseback riding, gambling, discos, boating on a large lake, a children's playground, and a beach about three miles away on the Tâmega River, where food and drink are available. There is a large park where visitors can stroll along paths shaded by tall trees.

It's a short drive from Vidago to Pedras Salgadas. Along the way you might like to turn off to see a Roman road and bridge and the tiny mill for grinding corn.

At Pedras Salgadas, you can take the waters of the spa at the springhouses or just go to look at these ornate facilities with their doors and windows of intricate wrought iron. The little spa town has discos, a casino, and swimming, plus tennis courts, mini-golf, horseback riding, boating, and amusements for children. Many of the Portuguese who come here for holidays like to camp out. Hiking in the surrounding country is a popular pursuit, and you can even head for the Minheu Mountain, a high day's climb, if you wish.

Restoration is being carried out on turn-of-the-century hotels in the spa region, which is gaining in popularity with many European tourists in addition to the Portuguese.

FOOD AND LODGING

My favorite in the area is the **Palace Hotel,** Vidago, 5455 Pedras Salgadas (tel. 076/973-56), in the heart of this little spa village. Built in the grand manner in 1910, this sprawling pink-and-white hotel is one of Portugal's most vivid architectural symbols of the belle epoque. Set within acres of gardens and forest, it opens all its soaring public rooms in summer, when Iberian breezes carry scents of flowers past one of the most elegant horseshoe-shaped staircases in the north. In winter, only the modern granite-sided annex, known as the Estalagem, is open, with a bar and Wolf's Restaurant, considered the best in the area, serving daily in both summer and winter from 12:30 to 2 p.m. and 7:30 to 9 p.m., and offering meals costing from 2,500$ ($16.25). In summer, the main hotel is open, as well as all the annexes and the Edwardian-era main dining room.

Depending on the season and the accommodation, and with half board included, singles cost 5,600$ ($36.40) to 12,500$ ($81.25) daily, and doubles go for 7,100$ ($46.15) to 16,000$ ($104). The rooms in the modern inn are more expensive and considered more desirable, but tradition-minded guests may prefer the more vintage accommodations. As in any turn-of-the-century hotel, the quality, size, and exposure of the bedrooms will vary greatly. Some are outfitted in a very grand manner, with lots of room, whereas others are smaller and simpler in amenities. Around the hotel are tennis courts, swimming, golf, lake volleyball courts, a disco, and spa baths in a private park.

Besides at the major hotel, you can find simple food and good regional wines at **Bringelas,** 2 Estrada Nacional (tel. 972-31), in Vidago. This no-frills place is patronized by locals who come here for the home-cooking, and features such traditional dishes as codfish, roast veal, and tripe in port wine. Charging from 1,500$ ($9.75) for a complete meal, it serves daily from noon to 3 p.m. and 7:30 to 10 p.m. Outside of town, the restaurant lies on the road to Pedras Salgadas. In summer, tables are placed outside, offering a view over the valley.

In Pedras Salgadas, the best place to dine is a large restaurant, **São Martinho** (tel. 442-78), which is capable of seating as many as 400 diners. Charging from 1,400$ ($9.10) for a simple meal, it serves daily from noon to 3:30 p.m. and 7 to 9:30 p.m. Good provincial cookery is featured, along with plenty of wine. Parking is available, and in winter a fireplace burns brightly.

---

6. Chaves

A quiet spa town today, Chaves, on the banks of the Tâmega River, was known to the Romans as Aquae Flaviae. The thermal springs brought the place to prominence, and it became an important stop on the route from Astorga in what is now Spain to Braga in Portugal. Trajan fortified the town and had a handsome 16-arch bridge built across the river. Chaves takes its name from the fact that it was the key (*chave*) or gateway to northern Portugal, lying only about 7 miles from the Spanish border and 40 miles from Vila Real.

AROUND THE TOWN

The town was under Moorish control for a few centuries and was refortified after being liberated by the Christian forces. The new defenses were set up to discourage inroads by the Spanish. The castle, built by King Dinis, was the home of the first duke of Bragança, an illegitimate son of King João I. All that remains is the keep and the outer wall, with towers. **A Military Museum,** occupying four stories of the keep, displays ancient arms and armor, guns and uniforms from World War I, and mementos of Portuguese wars. If you are hardy enough to climb the 120 steps to the top, you can look out over the town and the farms of the fertile valley below. Guided tours of the Military Museum may be taken on a combination ticket with admission to the—

Flaviense Region Museum (Museu de Região Flaviense; tel. 219-65) is in the palace of the dukes of Bragança, next to the Castle of Muralha on Largo de Camões. The castle keep is a military section, with displays dating from the time of King João I to the present. The dukes' palace includes archeology, epigraphy, heraldry, numismatics, painting, ethnography, and other sciences. The museum is open from 10 a.m. to noon and 2 to 6 p.m. daily except Monday. Admission is 30$ (20¢).

The **Church of the Misericord,** at right angles to the parish church on Praça de Camões, is a baroque building with balconies and salomonic (twisted) columns. Inside are huge panels of blue and white azulejos showing New Testament scenes, a gilded altarpiece of wood, and 18th-century ceiling paintings. In front of the parish church is a Manueline-type pillory.

From the ancient bridge, gardens run down to the river. The bridge no longer has all its arches and parapets, but at its south end are milestones with Roman carvings.

WHERE TO STAY

Accommodations tend to be limited and simple here. The best of the lot is **Hotel Trajano,** Travessa Cândido dos Reis, 5400 Chaves (tel. 076/224-15). Clean, contemporary, and accented with such accessories as Roman breastplates and wall-mounted chariots pulled by gryphons, this pleasant hotel is on a narrow cul-de-sac in the commercial center of town. The comfortably high-ceilinged public rooms are filled with exposed bricks and clusters of sofas. Its basement contains a separately recommended restaurant (described below). Each of its 39 bedrooms has high Iberian headboards, a private bath, and a phone. Singles cost 4,800$ ($31.20) daily, and doubles go for 5,800$ ($37.70), with a continental breakfast included.

Hotel de Chaves, 25 Rua 25 de Abril, 5400 Chaves (tel. 076/211-18). Its antiquated interior and its lack of dining facilities earn it only one star from the Portuguese government. But anyone yearning for a taste of old-fashioned grandeur might find this an ideal stopover. It lies in the center behind a solid stone façade that looks vaguely fortified. Inside, a high series of ceilings, a creaky wrought-iron elevator, wide upper hallways, and vintage furniture might qualify it as a movie set. The hotel was built around 1920 by members of the Alves family, and neither the owners nor the furnishings have changed much since. You'll be greeted by a staff who speak very little English, then shown to one of the 36 bedrooms, each of which has a divergent array of plumbing. Depending on the facilities, singles range from 2,100$ ($13.65) daily and doubles from 3,000$ ($19.50) to 4,200$ ($27.30). Shared bathroom facilities are found in each of the hallways, and a continental breakfast is included in the price.

WHERE TO DINE

The independent restaurants within the town center are a lackluster lot. The best food is obtained at the previously recommended **Hotel Trajano,** Travessa Cândido dos Reis (tel. 224-15). In the basement of this hotel, the restaurant offers attentive service, a fine cuisine, and a high-ceilinged decor of decorative arches and thick brick stucco. Lunch is daily from 12:30 to 3 p.m. and dinner from 7:30 to 10 p.m. Full meals, cost from 1,800$ ($11.70). Offerings include the predictable range of Portuguese specialties, as well as stewed codfish, filet of veal, and shrimp omelets.

Arado, Ribeira do Pinheiro (tel. 219-96), seems to be heavily preferred by discerning locals. However, it is suitable only for motorists, as it lies about five miles outside of Chaves on the road to Mirandelo. It's a former private villa transformed into a small-scale restaurant, and is known for its regional cookery and wines. The staff is helpful, and they serve daily from noon to 3 p.m. and 7 to 10 p.m. Meals cost from 2,000$ ($13). While dining, guests enjoy a panoramic vista. In winter a fireplace adds an extra glow.

---

7. Bragança

The medieval town of Bragança (Braganza, in English), which became a duchy in the middle of the 14th century, was under the aegis of the House of Bragança, ruling house of Portugal from 1640 until its overthrow early in this century. During those years the heir to the throne of Portugal bore the title of duke of Bragança. The old town on a hilltop is surrounded by a long, fortified wall. It overlooks the modern town in the northeastern reaches of the country on a rise of ground in the Sêrra da Nogueira, some 2,000 feet above sea level. Bragança lies about 86 miles from Vila Real.

AROUND THE TOWN

In the lower town, the **cathedral (Sé),** originally the Church of São João da Baptista, is not up to the standard of many of the cathedrals of Portugal, but there are nine churches in Bragança, so you may find one you like. For instance, the **Church of Santa Maria do Castelo,** beside the Town Hall in the old town, is outstanding for its painted ceiling, depicting the Assumption of the Virgin in many colors. Salomonic (twisted) columns frame the front door.

The oldest **Town Hall** (Domus Municipalis) in Portugal is beside St. Mary's Church. Ask for the key at 40 Rua Dom Fernão o Bravo da Cidadela-Bragança to enter this massive pentagonal structure built over a cistern. The interior is a cavernous room lit by little round arches.

In a small public garden in the citadel stands a Gothic **pillory.** The medieval shaft has been driven through the stone effigy of a boar, which has a depression carved in its snout. The boar is believed to date from the Iron Age, and it is possible that it was used in some ancient pagan rituals.

The **Church of Santa Clara,** renovated in 1764, can be visited, as well as the ancient **Bishop's Palace** (now Baçal's rustic museum) and the 13th-century **Church of St. Vincent.**

To visit the **citadel,** you go through the St. Vincent Square and climb upward. Cars must be left outside the ramparts.

FOOD AND LODGING

A government-owned inn to the southeast of the town, **Pousada da São Bartolomeu,** Estrada de Turismo, 5300 Bragança (tel. 073/224-93), is about a half-hour drive from the Spanish frontier town of Quintanilha. The pousada is on the slope of the hill of São Bartolomeu. The 16 rooms have balconies and private baths, and are furnished in attractive, comfortable style. The room rate for two persons is 9,800$ ($63.70) daily; for a single, 8,700$ ($56.55). A stay here will provide you with a pleasant atmosphere. Built in 1959, the pousada is attractively decorated in part with regional artifacts. The view from its premises at night is the most spectacular in Bragança, taking in the crenellated fortifications of the old city. Drinks are served in a large, masculine lounge ringed with hewn stone and richly textured paneling, within sight of a fireplace alcove dotted with bronze pots. The food served here is the best in Bragança; both regional and international dishes are offered. Meals cost from 2,000$ ($13) to 2,300$ ($14.95) and are served daily from 12:30 to 3 p.m. and 7:30 to 10 p.m.

Hotel Bragança, Avenida Doutor Francisco de Sá Carneiro, 5300 Bragança (tel. 073/225-78), is the leading modern hotel in the town. A boxy, concrete structure, it stands in a commercial center and is popular with traveling business people. However, it comes in handy in summer when the pousada is full. Boldly designed with big windows and loggias, it offers 42 reasonably comfortable rooms. The rate in a single is 7,000$ ($45.50) daily, rising to 8,500$ ($55.25) in a double. The hotel also has a suitable restaurant, serving meals, either lunch or dinner, for 1,500$ ($9.75).

The best choice for economy is **Albergaría Santa Isabel,** 67 Rua Alexandre Herculano, 5300 Bragança (tel. 073/224-27). It's a small-scale hotel set among a handful of stores and businesses in the center of town. The 14 well-scrubbed but simple bedrooms lie behind the blue and white tiles of the modern façade. Each unit contains a private bath and phone, renting for 4,200$ ($27.30) daily in a single, 5,000$ ($32.50) in a double, with a continental breakfast included. In the basement is a breakfast room and bar. Guests who want to watch TV head for one of the leather-upholstered couches in a room near the street-level reception desk.

Outside the hotel dining rooms, the best restaurant is **Plantório,** Estrada Cantarias (tel. 224-26). Offering some 150 diners a panoramic view, it dispenses regional cookery with politeness from noon to 2:30 p.m. and 7 to 9:30 p.m. daily. The wine list is fairly extensive and reasonable in price. Try either the meat or fish dishes, which are well prepared. Meals cost 1,800$ ($11.70) and up.

Another interesting choice is **Arca de Noé,** Avenida do Savor (tel. 227-59), which is the best-known wine cellar in Bragança. It has a varied menu of good dishes, and of course, the stock of wine is superb. Meals, costing from 1,800$ ($11.70), are served daily except Friday from noon to 3 p.m. and 7 to 11 p.m. The restaurant has a bar and a fireplace.

8. Miranda do Douro

The town, 63 miles from Bragança, is perched on a high upland above the Valley of the Douro, which separates Portugal from Spain at this point. A medieval castle once stood guard over the entrance to the town, but only the ruins of the once-proud fortress remain. The people of this old town speak their own dialect, called *Mirandes,* which sounds like a form of Low Latin.

Old customs are still followed here, one of the most interesting being the Pauliteiros Dance, performed on most holidays and always on Santa Bárbara's feast day, the third Sunday in August. The men of the area, wearing white flannel kilts, colorfully embroidered black shirts, and flower-bedecked black hats with red ribbons, perform a dance that consists of striking the *paulitos* (sticks) to a rhythmic beat. This dance is similar to the pyrrhic dance of the ancient Greeks, which was brought to Rome by Julius Caesar. Other festivals and dances are São Martinho's festival of the flowers, the pingacho dance, and the galandum dance.

The former **cathedral (Sé),** a granite Renaissance building, contains some fine gilded woodcarved altarpieces. The choir stalls, also of gilded wood, have backdrops of landscape paintings. Don't miss the little statue of the baby Jesus wearing a top hat. It stands in a glass case in the south transept. From the cathedral terrace you can see the ruins of the cloister of the Bishop's Palace and the Douro flowing far below. You can visit the old cathedral from 8 a.m. to 12:30 p.m. and 2 to 6 p.m. daily except Monday.

An interesting excursion from the town is to the **Miranda do Douro dam,** two miles away along a narrow highway. This is the first of a series of five dams on the section of the river between Spain and Portugal providing electrical power. The power station can be visited. Even if you don't want to go inside the station, the sight of this multi-buttressed dam in a rocky ravine is stunning.

FOOD AND LODGING

If you'd like to stay in the area, **Pousada da Santa Catarina,** 5210 Miranda do Douro (tel. 073/422-55), overlooks the great dam. In this scenic spot, the government-owned inn rents out 12 pleasantly furnished double rooms, all with private bath. A party of two is charged 6,500$ ($42.25) daily in winter and 9,500$ ($61.75) in summer. A single person pays 5,000$ ($32.50) in winter, 8,500$ ($55.25) in summer. A complete lunch of dinner costs 2,600$ ($16.90).

Most guests dine at the pousada. But if you'd like to seek out independent eateries, give **Boteco,** Largo D. João III (tel. 421-50), a try. It has good food and is most reasonable in price, charging from 1,200$ ($7.80) for a meal. Food is served daily from noon to 2 p.m. and 7 to 9 p.m. Private parking is available.

Another suitable choice is **Planalto,** Rua 1 de Maio (tel. 073/423-62), which features regional cookery with meals costing from 1,500$ ($9.75). It is closed on Monday. Hours are 12:30 to 2 p.m. and 8 to 10 p.m. Parking is also available. The staff is most helpful, but I hope you'll know some Portuguese menu terms.

At the same address, the owner of the restaurant runs a pension, also called **Planalto,** Rua 1 de Maio, 5210 Miranda do Douro (tel. 073/422-71). Simply furnished rooms, 42 in all, are rented for 1,800$ ($11.70) daily in a single, 3,200$ ($20.80) in a double.

MADEIRA

The island of Madeira, 530 miles southwest of Portugal, is the mountain peak of a volcanic mass. Its craggy spires and seacoast precipices of umber-dark basalt end with a sheer drop into the blue water. The surrounding sea is so deep that large sperm whales often come near the shore.

The summit of the undersea mountain is found at Madeira's center where the **Pico Ruivo,** often snow-capped, rises to an altitude of 6,105 feet above sea level. From that point project the rocky ribs and ravines of the island, running to the coast. If you stand upon the sea-swept balcony of **Cabo Girão,** one of the world's highest ocean cliffs (1,933 feet above the sea), you'll understand the Eden-like quality of Madeira. Camões called it "at the end of the world."

Madeira, now an autonomous archipelago, is only 35 miles in length, about 13 in breadth at its widest point. It contains nearly 100 miles of coastline, but no beaches. In its volcanic soil, plants and flowers blaze like the Tahitian palette of Gauguin. From jacaranda and masses of bougainvillaea, to orchids and geraniums, whortleberry to prickly pear, poinsettias, cannas, frangipani, birds of paradise, and wisteria, the land is a botanical garden. Custard apples, avocados, mangos, and bananas grow profusely. Fragrances such as vanilla and wild fennel intermingle with sea breezes and pervade the ravines, sweeping down the rocky headlands.

Claimed by the British as a sentimental dominion, Madeira has been popular with them ever since. The post-Victorians arrived, the women in wide-brimmed hats to protect them from the sun. Now that has changed: They make their way here specifically to enjoy the sun. Legend has it that two English lovers discovered the island about half a century before its known date of exploration. Supposedly Robert Machim and Anna d'Arfet, fleeing England, were swept off their course by a tempest and deposited on the eastern coast.

In 1419, João Gonçalves Zarco and Tristão Vaz Teixeira, captains under Henry the Navigator, discovered Madeira while exploring the African coastline, some 350 miles away. As it was densely covered with impenetrable virgin forests, they named it Madeira, meaning wood. Soon it was set afire to clear it for habitation. The holocaust is said to have lasted seven years until all but a small northern section was reduced to ashes.

The hillsides are so richly cultivated today one would never know there had ever been a fire. Many of the groves and vineyards, protected by buffers of sugarcane, grow on stone-wall ledges, which almost spill into the sea. The farmers plant so close to the cliff's edge that they must have at least a dash of goat's blood in them. The terraced mountain slopes are irrigated by a complex network of levadas (or water channels). It is estimated that there are some 1,330 miles of these levadas, and that includes about 25 miles of tunnels. These levadas were originally constructed by slaves and convicts. Built of stone, they are most often one to two feet wide and deep. Water from mountain springs is carried in them.

The climate of Madeira is mild, the mean temperature averaging about 61° Fahrenheit in winter, about 70° Fahrenheit in summer.

MADEIRA: Mean Temperatures Year Round (in °Fahrenheit)

January/March	66.9°
April/June	71.2°
July/September	76.8°
October/December	70.3°

About 25 miles to the northeast, **Porto Santo** is the only other inhabited island in the Madeira archipelago. *Réalités* called it "another world, arid, desolate and waterless." Unlike Madeira, Porto Santo contains beaches, but is not yet developed for mass tourism. It is previewed at the end of this chapter.

GETTING THERE FROM LISBON

The quickest and most convenient way to reach Madeira from Lisbon is on a TAP flight (the trip takes one hour and 30 minutes). The plane stops at the Madeira Airport, then goes on to Porto Santo. However, if you're booking a TAP flight from, say, New York to Lisbon, you can have the side trip to Madeira included at no extra cost, providing you have a regular—that is, not an excursion—ticket.

In addition, TAP has a weekly direct flight between Faro in the Algarve and Funchal, an extension of its Frankfurt–Faro service.

1. Settling into Funchal

The capital of Madeira, Funchal, is the focal point of the entire island and the springboard for outlying villages. When Zarco landed in 1419, the sweet odor of fennel led him to name it after the aromatic herb, called *funcho* in Portuguese. Today the southern coast city of hillside-shelved villas and narrow winding streets is the garden spot of the island. Its numerous estates, including the former residence of the discoverer Zarco, the Quinta das Cruzes, are among the most exotic in Europe.

With a population of 100,000, Funchal has a long street running along the waterfront called **Avenida do Mar.** This often traffic-clogged artery runs in an east-west direction. North of this wide boulevard is **Avenida Arriaga,** which is considered the "main street" of Funchal. At the eastern end of this thoroughfare is the

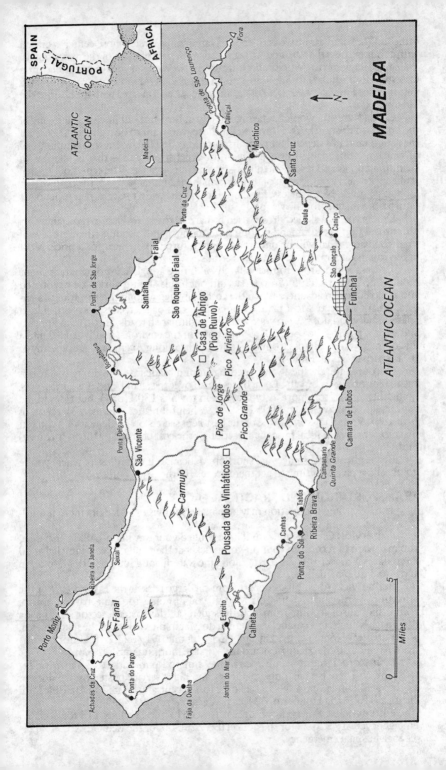

cathedral (Sé), and at the western end is a large traffic circle whose center is graced with a fountain. As the Avenida Arriaga heads west, site of most of the major hotels, it changes its name to **Avenida do Infante.** However, as it moves east it becomes known as **Rua Aljube.** Running in a north-south direction, the other most important street of Funchal, **Avenida Zarco,** links the waterfront area with the heart of the old city.

Chances are you won't be staying directly in the heart of Funchal, but in one of the hotels on the outskirts. However, for those who want to be right in the heart of the action (and not dependent on transportation), I will have a few suggestions, all of which are reasonable in price. The most expensive hotels—that is, those with swimming pools and resort amenities—are on the outskirts. The center of Funchal is filled with heavy traffic most of the day, which means that hotels in the center often tend to be noisy. Nevertheless, for shopping and the widest selection of restaurants Funchal is a magnet for the visitor.

Unless you're a skilled driver, used to narrow roads, reckless drivers, and hairpin turns, I don't recommend renting a car on the island, although there are several local companies that will be only too happy to furnish you a car for a price. Most hotels can make arrangements for **car rentals.**

The less adventurous tourist will rely on hiring a **taxi.** The going rate is about 8,000$ ($52) to 10,000$ ($65) a day, although this should always be negotiated and agreed upon in advance. When the cost is divided among three or four passengers, it isn't so steep. Most taxis are often Peugeots or Mercedes, so you'll ride in relative safety and not have to cope with the nightmarish roads. If you're in Funchal and want a taxi to take you back to your hotel in the environs, you'll usually find a line of them waiting across from the Tourist Office along Avenida Arriaga. Many of the taxi drivers speak English.

Of course, the cheapest way of getting around Madeira—providing you're not rushed for time—is by **bus.** Local buses go all over the island, and it is a most economical means of transport. A typical fare in town is 130$ (85¢), but rides in the countryside can cost up to 500$ ($3.25). A helpful reader, Herman Marcuse, of Arlington, Virginia, wrote: "One of the best-kept secrets on Madeira is that you can make excursions on local buses at a fraction of the cost charged by the tour companies."

Remember that distances are short on Madeira, but regardless of where you're going, allow plenty of time to get there because of the road conditions.

TRANSPORTATION AND PRACTICAL FACTS

The following information may help make your visit to Madeira more rewarding.

Air service: Chances are, you'll have winged your way in on **TAP.** In that case, you may want to reconfirm your on-going ticket at the main office in Funchal at 10 Avenida do Mar (tel. 091/301-51), along the waterfront. Hours are 9 a.m. to noon and 2 to 5:30 p.m. daily.

Bus service: Most buses depart from the large park at the eastern part of the waterfront-bordering Avenida do Mar. If you're going to Camacha or Camico, you'll find buses leaving from a little square at the eastern sector of Rua da Alfandega, which runs parallel to Avenida do Mar in the vicinity of the marketplace.

Buses leave for the **airport** at Santa Cruz (phone 091/522-73 for information) from Avenida do Mar daily from around 7 in the morning until 11 p.m.

Drugstore: Drugstores are open from 9 a.m. to 1 p.m. and 3 to 7 p.m. Monday to Saturday. There is a rotating emergency and night service posted on the door of all chemists. Sunday has a special schedule too. A centrally located and reliable local chemist is Farmácia Honorato, 62 Rua da Carreira (tel. 091/232-97).

Emergencies: Emergency numbers to keep in mind include 115 for, well, an emergency; 091/220-22 for the police; 091/200-00 for the Red Cross; 091/421-11 for a hospital emergency.

Laundry: A good laundromat in Funchal is **Lavandaria Donini,** Rua das Pretas (tel. 091/244-06). Any clothing can be laundered or dry cleaned here within one or two days. It is open Monday to Friday 9 a.m. to 7 p.m.

Post office: If you've had your mail sent *poste restante* (general delivery), you can pick it up at the **Funchal Post Office,** Avenida Zarco (tel. 091/321-31), but you should bring your passport to identify yourself. You can also place long-distance phone calls here, which will help you avoid steep hotel surcharges. It's also possible to send telegrams. The office is open Monday to Friday from 9 a.m. to 6 p.m. and on Saturday from 9 a.m. to 12:30 p.m.

Shops and official buildings: Most shops are open from 9 a.m. to 1 p.m. and 3 to 7 p.m. Monday to Friday; from 9 a.m. to 1 p.m. on Saturday; usually closed Sunday. Municipal buildings are open from 9 a.m. to 12:30 p.m. and 2 to 5:30 p.m. Monday to Friday.

For specific **shopping** suggestions, including the best place to purchase Madeira embroidery, refer to chapter VII, "Shopping in Portugal."

Tourist information: An English-speaking staff runs the desk at the **Madeira Tourist Office,** 18 Avenida Arriaga (tel. 091/256-68). Hours are Monday to Saturday from 9 a.m. to 7 p.m. and on Sunday from 9 a.m. to 1 p.m. Here you'll be given a map of the island, and the staff will also, if asked, make suggestions about the best ways to explore their beautiful island. You can also inquire about ferry connections to the neighboring island of Porto Santo.

---

2. Where to Stay

In summer, when every other European resort on the water socks you with its highest tariffs, Madeira used to experience its "low season." And not because of bad weather, although August is still not the most desirable month to visit because of the *capacete,* a shroud of mist that often envelopes the island.

Summer was traditionally considered the low season because the early British visitors, the first tourists really, set a pattern of mass descent in winter, thereby crowding the hotels and inflating its tariffs.

That long-ago pattern, however, seems to have broken, and Madeira now experiences more of an all-year-round popularity. In fact it's become hard to get an airplane seat there in the peak summer months without reservations made way in advance.

The hotels of Madeira, among the best in all of Portugal, range from some of the finest deluxe citadels in Europe to attractively priced and old-fashioned "quintas" for budgeteers. Many of the best hotels, as mentioned, are on the outskirts of Funchal.

ONE OF EUROPE'S GREAT RESORT HOTELS

The legendary place to stay in Funchal is **Reid's Hotel,** 139 Estrada Monumental, 9000 Funchal, Madeira (tel. 091/230-01). Its position is smashing, along the coastal road at the edge of Funchal, on its own 11 acres of multiterraced gardens all the way down the hillside to the rocky shores. Midway down are two saltwater swimming pools thrust out onto a cliff edge, the pair joined by a bridge and fountain. On a still-lower terrace is yet another pool (reached by an elevator) built onto a ledge of rocks. You feel you're swimming in the ocean. The English who frequent the hotel in large numbers (famous guest of the past: Sir Winston Churchill) spend their days strolling along the scented walks lined with blue and pink hydrangeas, hedges of geraniums, gardenias, banana trees, ferns, and white yuccas.

The public rooms and a wing added in 1968 are all tastefully and successfully combined. The main drawing rooms are refreshingly decorated in the colors of the sea with country estate furnishings in either tropical prints or soft solid colors. Afternoon tea is served at the Tea Terrace with a magnificent view of the gardens and Funchal Bay. Lunch is offered in the Garden Restaurant overlooking the pools or at the poolside buffet. The two-level main dining room is classically dignified with Wedgwood paneling and ceiling, plus the inevitable and very English silver trolley holding roast beef. Reid's Grill, on the sixth floor in the garden wing, is recommended separately in the restaurant section.

Of the 165 air-conditioned rooms with radio and TV in the suites, all but 15 face the ocean, and all have private bath. The spacious rooms are conservative in the finest sense, with well-chosen pieces, plenty of storage space, sitting areas, and desks. The baths have marble or tile walls and floors. In winter, singles range from 23,100$ ($150) to 26,180$ ($170) daily, with doubles going for 32,340$ ($210) to 35,420$ ($230). In summer and fall, prices are 17,710$ ($115) to 20,020$ ($130) daily in a single, 25,410$ ($165) to 29,260$ ($190) in a double. The supplement for half board is from 5,390$ ($35) per person daily.

It's hard to be lured away from Reid's garden park, but tennis courts are at your disposal. The hotel is owned by the Blandy family of wine and shipping fame.

THE UPPER BRACKET

The latest addition to the luxury hotels of Funchal is the **Casino Park Hotel,** Avenida do Infante, 9000 Funchal, Madeira (tel. 091/331-11). Just a seven-minute walk from the center of town, the hotel is nestled in a subtropical garden overlooking the harbor. Designed by architect Oscar Niemeyer, the creator of Brasilia, the main building is low (only five stories) and undulating, as if poised for flight from its position on the cliff above the deep waters. The complex is made up of the hotel and conference center and a separate casino. Every conceivable convenience and luxury is available within the Casino Park, including shopping facilities, tennis courts, swimming pools, saunas, billiards, and a health club. Special facilities, including a shallow swimming pool, are provided for the children. You can even arrange fishing, sailing, and golf excursions through the hotel. Variety in dining is also thoughtfully provided, from the luxurious and spacious dining room overlooking the port and town of Funchal, or the international Grill Room with its extensive wine cellar, to the simpler Coffee Shop adjacent to the swimming pool for a refreshing snack after a swim.

The 400 fully air-conditioned rooms each have their own balconies offering superb views of the harbor and town. Each room also has its own private bath, phone, and radio. The rooms are tastefully coordinated with bright, sunny colors that seem to bring the radiance of the island and the sea indoors. A single costs from 16,000$ ($104) daily, and a twin-bedded room goes for 22,000$ ($143), both with a buffet breakfast included. There are two comfortable lounge areas on each floor.

Madeira Palácio, Estrada Monumental, 9000 Funchal, Madeira (tel. 091/300-01), is a luxurious hotel of 260 well-appointed rooms and 18 suites on the seaside route to Camara de Lobos, about two miles from the center of Funchal. The hotel is perched on a cliff over the sea. From here, Madeira's famous high cliff, Cabo Girão, can be seen looming in the distance. Each room is complete with private bath, mini-bar, direct-dial phone, radio, color TV with video systems, and a balcony. The tariff depends on the location. Rooms opening onto the mountains are less expensive than those facing the sea. Rates in a double range from 18,000$ ($117) to 23,000$ ($149.50) daily, from 15,000$ ($97.50) to 18,000$ ($117) in a single. Suites are more expensive, of course.

The star-shaped hotel is most contemporary, with three wings. The public salons and guest rooms are colorfully coordinated, and local woods, native construction materials, and Madeiran fabrics have been used judiciously. During the day guests enjoy a heated swimming pool, an outdoor snack bar, tennis courts in the gardens, and a shopping arcade complete with a hairdresser and a sauna, even table tennis. Visitors may select the hotel's restaurant with its menu of both local and international dishes, or they may prefer the specialties of the à la carte Grill Room. Later, entertainment is provided in the disco. Occasional folk dances are staged here as well.

Hotel Savoy, Avenida do Infante, 9006 Funchal, Madeira (tel. 091/220-31), is one of the leading five-star hotels not only of Madeira but of Portugal. Long known for style and elegance, it stands at the edge of Funchal. Its origins go back to the turn of the century when it was started by a Swiss-trained hotelier, and over the years, like Topsy, it just grew and grew. Today it has a total of 370 rooms, including a dozen suites, with private baths and balconies. Faced with escalating popularity, each generation of management has brought enlargements and improvements. In a twin, the cost ranges from 16,170$ ($105) to 20,020$ ($130) daily, and singles go for 10,780$ ($70) to 14,630$ ($95), including a buffet breakfast.

The hotel is superbly situated, opening onto the ocean and the Bay of Funchal. With its vast public facilities, it captures a peculiar kind of Madeira dolce vita. For your before-dinner libations you have a choice of two bars. There are several restaurants from which to choose, or you can have lunch by the pools. Restaurants include the Bellevue, the Bakkhos Wine/Snack Bar, the Alameda Coffee shop, and the Neptunus by the pool. For more deluxe dining, there is the elegantly decorated Fleur-de-Lys, a grill room with belle époque trappings. This room, closed Sunday, has a panoramic view.

During the day, you can reach two sea water swimming pools (one heated) by elevator. There are also tennis courts, plus a host of other facilities, including a health center, mini-golf, a shopping arcade, hairdressers for both men and women, and the Galaxia nightclub on the top floor, with a panoramic sweep.

Madeira-Sheraton, Largo António Nobre, 9007 Funchal, Madeira (tel. 091/ 310-31), is a luxurious, 17-story, high-rise structure near the Casino with direct access to the sea. The 369-room hotel offers three swimming pools, a restaurant for 300 persons, plus an English pub, a specialty grill, and a disco. The hotel has some amusing eccentricities of design—two trapezium-shaped elevators that transport guests down to their rooms from the reception area. All the accommodations, many furnished in a provincial style, are air-conditioned with private balconies, showers, radios, direct-dial phones, and TV sets in the suites. A single ranges from 14,200$ ($92.30) to 18,000$ ($117) daily, and doubles go for 21,500$ ($139.75) to 29,500$ ($191.75). The least expensive rates are for the standard mountain view, the more expensive for deluxe rooms with a sea view. The rates quoted include service, taxes, and breakfast. The hotel lies on a promontory overlooking Funchal Bay in the fashionable Vale-Verde Garden district, next to the century-old landmark, Reid's. Its oceanfront exposure to the south offers dawn to dusk sunlight on all pool terraces and seaside guestroom balconies and patios.

Hotel Vila Ramos, 7 Azinhaga da Casa Branca, 9000 Funchal, Madeira (tel. 091/311-81), built in the mid-1970s and surrounded by sloping banana groves, lies on the western outskirts of Funchal. Rated four stars, it is known for its attractive swimming pool and its conservative decor. It contains such amenities as an English-style reading room, a duet of restaurants, an outdoor gazebo-shaped bar, an attentive staff, and a balconied façade composed of brown tile and pink-painted concrete. Each of the rooms has a private bath, phone, balcony, and radio. Singles range from 8,000$ ($52) daily and doubles from 10,000$ ($65) to 11,000$ ($71.50).

THE MIDDLE BRACKET

Standing on a hillside above the town, **Hotel São João,** 74 Rua das Maravilhas, 9000 Funchal, Madeira (tel. 091/461-11), is a modern four-star hotel with a total of 208 well-furnished bedrooms and suites. Each of the rooms is equipped with private bath, air conditioning, phone, and a private terrace. The hotel charges from 7,500$ ($48.75) daily in a single, 12,300$ ($79.95) in a double, including a continental breakfast. You can quench your thirst at one of the three well-decorated bars or assuage your hunger at either the self-service snackbar at poolside or the restaurant, both of which serve good food and wine. During the day, guests have the use of an outdoor swimming pool, and the hotel also has several planned activities, bringing in folkloric shows and bands for dancing. A courtesy bus makes frequent runs into Funchal.

Hotel Raga, 302 Estrada Monumental, 9000 Funchal, Madeira (tel. 091/330-01). Only its windows face onto the sea and the traffic artery of the Estrada Monumental, about a half mile west of the center of town. Its lobby is reached via a winding and hilly road stretching through a neighborhood of multistoried modern buildings. It was originally designed as an apartment building, which explains its large rooms, big closets, and kitchenettes (however, you can use only the refrigerators, not the stoves). Each of the 158 bedrooms has a tile bath, a wedge-shaped balcony, a phone, and in most cases, a sofa that can be converted into an extra bed. Singles cost 6,700$ ($43.55) daily, and doubles go for 10,800$ ($70.20), with a continental breakfast included. The hotel contains a pair of restaurants, a snackbar, a hairdresser, a basement nightclub with an organist, a TV lounge, and a many-sided swimming pool sunk into the slope of the terraces overlooking the ocean.

Hotel Alto Lido, 316 Estrada Monumental, 9000 Funchal, Madeira (tel. 091/291-97), on the road at the western end of the environs of Funchal, has staggered concrete balconies and a riot of lushly planted vines, aloe plants, and bougainvillaea. Its verdant screening helps to create one of the most appealing façades in Madeira. Built in 1983, the hotel has a swimming pool, a restaurant, two bars, and a much-needed parking garage, along with 118 comfortably furnished bedrooms. Each of these units has a TV, private bath, phone, and balcony. Prices quoted to you in the marble-sheathed lobby, including a continental breakfast, are 8,000$ ($52) daily in a single, 11,000$ ($71.50) in a double.

Quinta do Sol, 6 Rua Dr. Pita, 9000 Funchal, Madeira (tel. 091/641-51) a four-star hotel, is among the best in its category in Madeira. Occupying an attractive setting, it offers a total of 114 well-furnished bedrooms, plus about half a dozen suites. Each comes with a private bath and air conditioning, and some have their own balconies. The charge is from 8,500$ ($55.25) to 10,750$ ($69.90) daily in a single and 11,000$ ($71.50) to 15,500$ ($100.75) in a double, with a buffet breakfast included. Many guests prefer to stay here on full-board terms, which begin at 12,500$ ($81.25) per person daily in one of the standard accommodations. The hotel has a number of public facilities that make it resort worthy, including a swimming pool, well-decorated lounges, a rooftop solarium, and a bar and restaurant offering good food and wine.

Hotel Orquidea, 71 Rua dos Netos, 9000 Funchal, Madeira (tel. 091/260-91). "The Orchid" blooms right in Funchal. A first-class hotel, it offers 70 small but comfortable bedrooms, each with private bath and phone. Most of the accommodations open onto their own terraces. Inside, the atmosphere is sleek modern, with polished marble surfaces. For a room with a buffet breakfast, one person in high season pays 5,000$ ($32.50) to 5,800$ ($37.70) daily, that fee increasing to 5,500$ ($35.75) to 7,000$ ($45.50) for two, taxes included. The best feature of the hotel is its rooftop terrace, with a panoramic view of the town and port.

Hotel Santa Isabel, Avenida do Infante, 9006 Funchal, Madeira (tel. 091/231-11), is adjacent to Hotel Savoy and under the same management. It is an excellent small hotel with a homelike feeling and a well-deserved reputation for service and comfort. In the center of the deluxe hotel belt, it has a rooftop terrace, snackbar, swimming pool, cocktail bar, well-appointed lounge overlooking the gardens, solarium, and use of the numerous facilities of the Hotel Savoy. The 69 bedrooms all have freshly maintained tile baths, phones, and radios. There are two grades of accommodations, ranging from the more expensive ones facing the sea to the cheaper units opening onto a garden and a mountain view. Bed-and-breakfast in a twin costs from 10,780$ ($70) to 13,860$ ($90) daily, and a single rents for 7,700$ ($50) to 9,240$ ($60). Meals are taken in the Savoy dining room.

Hotel do Carmo, 10 Travessa do Rego, 9000 Funchal, Madeira (tel. 091/290-

01), provides modern accommodations right in the center of Funchal. It is erected in a cellular honeycomb fashion, each bedroom opening onto its own private balcony. While there is no surrounding garden, guests gather during the day for dips in the L-shaped rooftop swimming pool from which there is a good view of the harbor. Created by the Fernandes family, it was designed for guests who have limited purses and want to be near the bazaars in the heart of the city's life. The bedrooms are simple, with contemporary furnishings, and tile bathrooms. For a room and a continental breakfast, one person pays 4,620$ ($30) (U.S.) daily; two people, 5,540$ ($36). Meals are served in a spacious dining room, decorated with a green harlequin tile floor. A little lounge opens onto an inner patio.

Girassol, 256 Estrada Monumental, 9000 Funchal, Madeira (tel. 091/310-51), built in 1972, is a 132-room hotel offering immaculate accommodations at reasonable tariffs. It's on the outskirts of Funchal, overlooking the Tourist Club, where guests are allowed access to the sea at a small charge. Every one of its accommodations has a sunny balcony, half overlooking the mountains, the rest viewing the sea. Each chamber also comes complete with private bath, including a shower, plus a radio and a phone. Most double rooms are, in fact, suites, consisting of bedroom, bathroom, small sitting room, and veranda. The room decor is bright and cheerful. Two people can stay here at a cost of 10,500$ ($68.25) daily. Singles go for 6,500$ ($42.25), and all tariffs include taxes and service. Two swimming pools are available, one for children. Guests can also catch the sun on the 12th-floor solarium. On the street level is a bar and social lounge; even a hairdressing salon. Ballroom dancing and floor shows are offered in the disco, and there's a tea lounge on the second floor. Two other special features are an entrance courtyard with a series of interconnected angular reflecting pools and a dining room with sea views.

THE BUDGET RANGE

A gracious old manor house, **Quinta da Penha de França,** 2 Rua da Penha de França, 9000 Funchal, Madeira (tel. 091/290-87), has been turned into a guesthouse. Like a family home, the quinta is chock full of antiques, paintings, and silver. Near the Savoy, it stands in its own garden right on a ledge almost hanging over the harbor. It's a short walk to the center of the bazaars and is opposite an ancient chapel. The four-story antiga casa is bone white with dark-green shutters, plus small-panel windows overlooking the ocean. Across the front terrace is a good-size swimming pool with white iron garden chairs arranged for lazy lounging. Set on the hillside in the midst of poinsettias, bamboo, sugarcane, and coffee plants is a wine lodge and stone washhouse now converted into guest rooms. Twin-bedded rooms with bath go for 13,000$ ($84.50), including a continental breakfast.

Hotel Windsor, 4A Rua das Hortas, 9000 Funchal, Madeira (tel. 091/330-83), opened with fanfare in 1987, is one of the most stylish hotels in Funchal. Rated four stars, it has a marble-sheathed lobby laden with plants, wicker chairs, and art deco accessories. The hotel was constructed in two separate buildings, connected by an aerial passageway stretching above a sun-flooded enclosed courtyard. There is also a café and bar designed like a Jazz Age nightclub a few paces from the reception desk. The parking garage is almost a necessity in this crowded commercial neighborhood. Also popular is a cramped but convivial rooftop swimming pool with an outdoor bar. Because of its enclosure by the buildings in the town center, few of the 67 bedrooms have any kind of view. But each is nicely decorated, with wall-to-wall carpeting, phone, and private bath. With a continental breakfast included, singles cost from 4,500$ ($29.25) daily, and doubles rent for 6,300$ ($40.95).

Residencial Santa Clara, 16B Calçada do Pico, 9000 Funchal, Madeira (tel. 091/241-94), in the upper reaches of Funchal, is a breakfast-only hotel reached via the narrow winding streets of an old-fashioned residential section. Behind an iron gate, at the end of a narrow driveway bordered with fragrant vines and flaming hibiscus, lies the kind of villa many visitors dream of owning for themselves. Prefaced with a gracefully curved double staircase, the villa was built in 1926 by a wealthy

Portuguese family in a lushly ornate art nouveau style. Inside, floors crafted from Brazilian hardwoods compete for attention with trompe l'oeil ceilings and a scattering of antiques. The hotel contains 22 rooms, each of which offers a widely different set of facilities. Singles cost from 4,500$ ($29.25) daily and doubles from 6,000$ ($39). Its only drawback is its popularity, which might make getting a room difficult without an advance reservation.

Hotel Madeira, 21 Rua Ivens, 9009 Funchal Codex, Madeira (tel. 091/300-71), is in the center of Funchal behind the park and in the quietest part of the town. The rooms are clean and comfortable, and there is a rooftop swimming pool with a solarium area, where the bar and snack services never give you a chance to be thirsty. It has the most extraordinary panoramic view of the town, mountains, and sea. The hotel rents a total of 30 bedrooms, each with a private bath, costing 6,500$ ($42.25) daily in a double, 6,000$ ($39) in a single, including a continental breakfast. Rooms are arranged around a plant-filled atrium. One of the nicest aspects of this hotel, built in 1971, is the sheltered miradores attached to each of the accommodations.

Residencial Greco, 16 Rua do Carmo, 9000 Funchal, Madeira (tel. 091/300-81), in one of Funchal's concrete towers, offers 28 slightly frayed but comfortable bedrooms, scattered over four floors of the building. Prices quoted in the narrow reception vestibule, with a continental breakfast included, range from 3,500$ ($22.75) to 3,900$ ($25.35) daily in a single, 4,800$ ($21.20) to 5,400$ ($35.10) in a double. Each accommodation has a balcony, private bath, phone, and relatively large dimensions. The best units are quiet because of their exposure to the sprawl of Funchal's residential sections and the faraway sea.

Albergaría Catedral, 13 Rua do Aljube, 9000 Funchal, Madeira (tel. 091/300-91), for its price bracket, is a good choice if you want to be in the center of town. Don't judge it by its dark and narrow entrance, lying across the street from the cathedral. Climb a flight of stairs to a slickly "moderno" reception area, where you'll be assigned one of the establishment's 25 comfortable bedrooms. They occupy four floors of a five-story building, and the quieter ones in the rear, unfortunately, don't have much of a view. In front, many of the units have balconies open to the street noise. Each room has a phone and private bath. With a continental breakfast included, doubles cost 4,500$ ($29.25) daily, and singles rent for 4,000$ ($26). The sunniest and most pleasant rooms lie on the two uppermost floors.

Quinta Lembranca, 159 Estrada Monumental, 9000 Funchal, Madeira (tel. 091/626-84). Translated from the Portuguese, its name means "villa of memories," and memories are what most visitors retain after a stay here. It combines a country-style quiet with an ideal location a few paces from the world-famous Reid's Hotel, about half a mile west of the commercial center of Funchal. From the dizzying traffic of the Estrada Monumental, you'll walk down a long, sloping driveway whose cobblestones are shaded with a canopy of vines. Amid clusters of yellow-flowered hibiscus lies a 50-year-old villa, raised on concrete piers above the nearby sea. You're welcomed by the gracious owner, Senhor Figueira. The place contains five bedrooms to rent, each with private bath, lots of space, and conservative furnishings. With a continental breakfast included, singles rent for 6,000$ ($39) daily and doubles for 7,000$ ($45.50). You should write well in advance for a reservation.

Pensão Santos, 200 Estrada Monumental, 9000 Funchal, Madeira (tel. 091/208-82), standing a few inches from the edge of a busy street, a half mile west of the center of Funchal and a few paces from Reid's Hotel, rises proudly in faded but aristocratic neoclassical splendor. It was built in 1925 as a private house, but was converted into a budget-conscious pension 11 years later. Its proprietors are the sprightly and kind-hearted Ricardo Santos and his wife. The place contains 18 rooms to rent, each of which has a labyrinthine floor plan, with doors and passageways that may be opened or closed depending on the space a client requests. The rooms are furnished with an eclectic mix. The atmospheric dowdiness merely adds to the charm, and a slightly overgrown garden beckons to any visitor. With a continental breakfast included, singles range from 5,000$ ($32.50) daily and doubles from 7,000$ ($45.50).

MACHICO

At Machico on the east coast where the Portuguese first landed, you'll find more hotels. This part of land-scarce Madeira is being rapidly developed. Scores of tiny vacation villas climb the hillside. In the complex is a yacht club, plus an elegant bridge club. Machico is about 5 minutes from the airport, but a good 30-minute run along a twisting road to Funchal.

The best hotel here is **Hotel Dom Pedro Baía,** Estrada de São Roque, 9200 Machico, Madeira (tel. 091/96-27-51), a modern structure that boasts sea views, private baths, and phones for every room. The sparsely furnished rooms are well kept, comfortable, and tastefully appointed. On the bed-and-breakfast plan, the single rate is 7,700$ ($50) daily, that tariff rising to 10,000$ ($65) for two. An extra meal is 2,156$ ($14). Good food is served in the Panoramic Restaurant. A bar, a heated saltwater swimming pool, sun terraces, a beach, even a disco, make this a nice choice.

3. Where to Dine

Many of the major hotels require full or half board in high season; but perhaps you'll be able to sneak away for a regional meal at one of the recommendations listed below. The list begins, however, with the pick of the hotel restaurants, which are all in the grill rooms, the specialty restaurants, of the three leading five-star hotels of Madeira.

THE UPPER BRACKET

Try to dine at least once at **Reid's Grill,** Reid's Hotel, 139 Estrada Monumental (tel. 230-01), generally conceded to be the island's finest restaurant. On the sixth-floor of the hotel's garden wing, diners have musical entertainment by a pianist. Both guests and the local gentry consider it the perfect place to celebrate a new amour or console oneself after the loss of an old love. True to English tradition, clients in winter often still dress for dinner, the women perhaps in silk, the men sedate in black tie.

The chef offers a wide variety of French specialties and also some typical Portuguese dishes. For your palatable preliminaries, you can try everything from Portuguese soup to the chef's own smoked fish. Particular favorites are the caldeirada, a fish stew, and lobster (grilled or poached). To top your repast, you can select from the dessert trolley or ask for a hot soufflé, preferably made of passion fruit or strawberries. A meal here will cost you an average of 6,000$ ($39). Dinner, the only meal served, is offered daily from 7:30 to 11 p.m.

Another elegant choice for dining, the **Vigia Grill Room** of the Casino Park Hotel, Avenida do Infante (tel. 331-11), is superb. The grill is housed in a large, modern dark-bronze room, opening onto an outdoor terrace. Pin lighting and candles, along with an impeccably polite staff, add to this glamorous ambience. Not only do you receive well-prepared food and immaculate service, but the view of Funchal at night is enthralling. For 6,000$ ($39) to 7,000$ ($45.50), a diner can enjoy a cocktail before dinner, then perhaps the shrimp flambé, prepared right in front of you. This is one of the chef's many specialties, including not only the shrimps, but mushrooms, onions, brandy, wine, and a tomato sauce. It comes with a fresh vegetable such as peas and carrots. Main courses include chateaubriand (for two), piccata of pork, and duck with orange sauce. If you're not flambéd out, you can order for dessert a crêpe suzette flamed in brandy. Go only for dinner, from 7:30 to 11 nightly.

Fleur-dy-Lys, Hotel Savoy, Avenida do Infante (tel. 220-31). Its most devoted admirers claim that this restaurant serves the finest food in Madeira. It is certainly one of the most panoramic spots for dining, opening onto the twinkling lights of Funchal. Decorated vaguely in a belle époque style, it has an eclectic decor with antique reproductions and oriental carpets. Guests can observe the activity in an open-grill kitchen covered with pewter facsimiles of the establishment's namesake. Only dinner is served, and it's offered nightly from 7 to 11:30 p.m. Reservations are important, and even with one you sometimes have to wait a long time. Meals cost from 4,000$ ($26) and are likely to include an array of well-prepared international dishes such as grilled salmon steak, lobster mornay, spring lamb cutlets, beef Stroganoff, and duckling in orange sauce.

THE MEDIUM-PRICED RANGE

Right on the waterfront is **Restaurante Caravela,** 15-17 Avenida do Mar (tel. 284-64), a modern dining spot. You can dine on a glass-enclosed terrace with an open fireplace or else in the inner room where you sit in wicker chairs. Reached by elevator, the top-floor restaurant gives guests a view of the cruise ships arriving and departing. You can order both lunch and dinner, as well as afternoon tea with open-faced Danish smørrebröd sandwiches. Perhaps the finest regional dish is *espetada,* skewered meat flavored with garlic and bay leaves, and served only on special request. Unpretentious and proud of the native Portuguese dishes, the restaurant features Caravela fish, but also turns out international dishes, such as châteaubriand flambé. Meals begin at 1,500$ ($9.75), going up to 2,500$ ($16.25), to which you must add the cost of your wine. The restaurant is open seven days a week, with lunch served from noon to 3 p.m.; dinner, from 6:30 to 10 p.m.

Golfinho, 21 Largo do Corpo Santo (tel. 267-74), lies in the eastern section of town, near the waterfront, in the midst of the largest cluster of restaurants in Funchal. Even without a reservation, you can always manage to get a table at one of these establishments because there are so many of them.

The rich and warm-textured decor of the Golfinho cost its owners a fortune. Virtually every corner of its compact but well-decorated interior is covered with an eye-catching array of burnished pieces that make for a visual feast. After the waiter seats you on one of the scallop-backed Portuguese chairs, you order some of the best fresh fish and shellfish served in Madeira. You might, for example, begin with smoked swordfish and then follow with either grilled steak or lobster. However, fresh lobster should be ordered in advance; likewise, that savory kettle of fish, caldeirada, as preparation takes about three hours. A more typical fish, and one famous in Madeira for its taste, is espada. The bulbous eyes and fearsome teeth of this fish belie its tasty flesh. Sometimes espada is served with a fresh banana. Meals cost from 3,200$ ($20.80) at the Golfinho, which is open from noon to 3 p.m. and 7 to 11 p.m. daily except Sunday.

Restaurant Romana, 15 Largo do Corpo Santo (tel. 289-56), under French management, is one of the leading restaurants of Madeira. The service is excellent. Customers have included the king and queen of Sweden, the queen mother of Denmark, Amalia Rodriguez, and the prince of Monaco. Comfortable and decorated in a rustic style, the Romana, is considered a top rendezvous spot in town for both residents and visitors. Alain Glacet, the owner, oversees a kitchen that is based on fresh fish and top quality meats, served in both Madeira Island and international style. You can eat a full course lunch for $10 (U.S.) or an à la carte dinner for about $16. Open all year, daily from 11 a.m. to 10:30 p.m. Reservations for dinner are recommended. The Romana will send a free minibus to pick you up.

Kon-Tiki, 9 Rua do Favila (tel. 647-37), offers some of the best food on the island in a location near the Hotel Sheraton. The building is part of an old-fashioned quinta. You're welcomed by Walter and Gunnel Andresen, who speak English. You will be shown to a table either in their intimate restaurant (some of the paintings are by Gunnel) or on a glassed-in terrace overlooking a well-tended garden. From noon to 10:30 p.m. daily except Monday you can enjoy such dishes as warm home-smoked fresh mackerel, chicken with curry, or goulash soup. You can cook your own filet steak on a sizzling hot beefstone imported from Finland, or order a pepper steak, perhaps espada flambé with prawns. Everything seems to be good, especially the fresh fruit flambés to finish off a meal. Meals cost from 5,000$ ($32.50).

Casa da Carochinha (Lady Bird), 2-A Rua de São Francisco (tel. 236-95), is a favorite retreat, known especially to the British visitors and expatriates who are so fond of Madeira. The restaurant faces the Centenary Gardens, near the Tourist Office. The casa abounds in Edwardian English charm and serves a refined continental cuisine. This is perhaps the only place in Madeira where the chef does not use garlic. Specialties include coq au vin, beef Stroganoff, roast beef with Yorkshire pudding, and duck with orange sauce. Meals begin at 2,200$ ($14.30), and each guest enjoys a complimentary glass of madeira with the food. A flag of his or her country is also placed on the spotless white Nottingham lace tablecloth. The casa is open daily except Sunday for lunch, served from noon to 2 p.m., and for dinner, 7 to 10 p.m. It is also possible to visit for afternoon tea from 3:30 to 5:30 p.m.

Casa dos Reis, 103 Rua Imperatriz D. Amélia (tel. 251-82), in an appealing neighborhood just downhill from the Hotel Sheraton, is elegant and tranquil, with polished mahogany armchairs, brass chandeliers, and the aura of an aristocratic private club. The establishment serves meals daily from noon to 3 p.m. and 7 to 11 p.m. Avoid the snackbar one flight above street level and head for a table in the more formal dining room. Full meals cost from 2,900$ ($18.85) and include the chef's special fish soup, grilled scabbard fish, chateaubriand, chicken curry, shellfish stew, and fried squid in garlic.

THE BUDGET RANGE

In the center of town, **O Patio Jardim Tropicale**, 21 Avenida Zarco (tel. 273-76), is totally concealed within the inner courtyard of a complex of commercial buildings. Its entrance near a newspaper kiosk is easy to overlook because of its narrow width and insufficient lighting. Once inside, however, you'll enter a welcome refuge from the noise and traffic outside. You can sip coffee at one of the iron tables in the atrium, but many of the local shopkeepers head every day for the pleasant restaurant. One of the best lunchtime bargains in Funchal is a heaping platter of the dish of the day, usually roast chicken or stewed codfish with onions. Full meals cost from 1,500$ ($9.75), and might include house-style beef or squid, followed by pineapple flambé. The well-scrubbed wooden tables fill up from noon to 10 p.m. daily except Sunday.

Restaurant Estrelicia, Hotel Madeira, 21 Rua Ivens (tel. 300-71), is on a platform above the lobby, within earshot of a fountain. It has a modern, no-frills decor. If you'd like some light, cool fare instead of the heavy Portuguese cuisine, I'd suggest a luncheon there. It's a welcome change to have a light cold meat and salad lunch, one that's tasty, nicely served, and in a clean restaurant with several amenities, including, on occasion, orchids placed on the tables. Most meals cost from 1,500$ ($9.75) and are likely to feature cold roast beef (or ham) with a fresh green salad, fish and chips, or else a tuna-fish salad platter. You can also order more substantial fare at night, including tournedos and pork cutlets. Hours are daily from 12:30 to 2:30 p.m. and 7:30 to 9:30 p.m.

Dos Combatentes, 1 Rua Ivens (tel. 213-88), is a good choice for regional food, a favorite of Funchal's colony of doctors and lawyers. At the top of the Municipal Gardens, this simple Portuguese restaurant serves well-prepared dishes, including rabbit stew, roast chicken, stewed squid, and codfish. The Portuguese eat a lot, so the portions are ample, and two vegetables and a green salad come with the main dish if required. Desserts are likely to be simple, including caramel custard and chocolate mousse or fresh fruit, and most dinners begin with a bowl of the soup of the day. A dinner is likely to cost around 1,500$ ($9.75). The waiters are efficient, and hours are daily from noon to 3 p.m. and 7 to 10 p.m.

Pensão Restaurante Universal, 4 Rua de João Tavira (tel. 206-18), stands in the center of town, one minute from the cathedral. Three restaurants are in an old house, said to be the first hotel in Madeira. Various steaks are charcoal grilled for you, and you can also order such fare as scabbard fish prepared five different ways and roast chicken Mexican style. The cook also prepares a filet espada. Expect to spend from 1,500$ ($9.75) for a complete meal. One of the restaurants is open daily from 8 a.m. to 10 p.m., serving meals and snacks all day. The other two operate only from noon to 3 p.m. and 6 to 10 p.m. The same menu is served in all three restaurants.

The popular **Bakkhos Wine Bar,** Rua Imperatriz D. Amélia (tel. 220-31), owned and operated by the Hotel Savoy, lies at the rear entrance to that hotel. You'll dine amid Moroccan lattices at smallish tables serviced by English-speaking waiters in red coats. The place is open daily from 11 a.m. to 11 p.m., serving full meals from 1,800$ ($11.70). The menu lists "typical dishes of the islands," including tuna steaks, stewed octopus, Portuguese-style liver, and wine by the carafe. Another offering is pasta, such as lasagne, spaghetti, or fettuccine, as well as salads or sandwiches, if you're dining light.

O Espadarte, 5 Estrada da Boa Nova (tel. 280-65), is an uncluttered and unpretentious restaurant in a low-slung concrete building perched between a steep road and the mountains, about a mile east of Funchal on the road to the airport. It's owned and operated by a team of Portuguese entrepreneurs who have spent time in many other parts of the world. Guests dine at long trestle tables. Specialties include grilled trout or espada, pepper steak, beef on a skewer, grilled pork cutlets, and Portuguese sardines. In honor of their namesake, which means swordfish, the restaurant does its own smoked swordfish, which is the most delectable appetizer you can order. Some nights are devoted to folklore and fado. Open daily except Monday from noon to 3 p.m. and 7 to 11 p.m., the establishment serves full meals, priced from 1,800$ ($11.70).

Gavinas, Rua do Gorgulho (tel. 269-08), is reached by heading out the Estrada Monumental to the Lido. Once this was only a little garage-like cottage, drawing the "slumming" chic of Madeira. But its popularity grew until its owners tore down the old shack and reconstructed a modern restaurant. The fish is as fresh as one can imagine. No fancy sauces, no elaborate service—just hearty sea fare is still the rule of the kitchen. Perhaps you'll be there the day when a savory caldeirada (fish stew) has just been prepared. Most guests, however, gravitate to one of the fresh grilled fish platters. The price of a meal (including a salad and bread) begins at 1,500$ ($9.75), plus the cost of your beer or wine. Gavinas is open daily from noon to midnight.

A good place to have lunch, **Escola de Hotelaria e Turismo da Madeira** (Madeira Hotel and Tourism School), Quinta Magnólia, 10 Rua Dr. Pita (tel. 640-13), is in a charming old estate overlooking the bay. The daily menu offers a choice of specially prepared dishes for each course. The bar opens at 12:30 p.m., with cocktails made by advanced students, who are attentive to the desires of the patrons. Lunch is served promptly at 1 p.m., Monday to Friday, accompanied by wine and coffee. A four-course lunch costs from 1,600$ ($10.40). It is necessary to reserve a table by telephoning in advance.

TEA AND PASTRIES

An old-fashioned tea and pastry shop as well as a restaurant, **Casa Minas Gerais** (The Corner Shop), Avenida do Infante (tel. 233-81), has been around for some 50 years. At its central serving bar, waiters make pots of tea and coffee or else pour madeira wine. Before sitting at one of the little tables, clients pick out a pastry. A pot of tea for two costs 180$ ($1.15). One section of the establishment is a restaurant, serving meals for 1,500$ ($9.75), including such fare as spaghetti bolognese, mixed grill, grilled chicken, and fish soup. Hours are 9 a.m. to 11 p.m. daily. The tall ceiling is supported by painted columns capped with vine motifs. The Corner Shop opens onto a circular fountain and the busy boulevard.

4. The Sights

Funchal is the center of Madeira's wine industry. Grapes have grown in the region since the early 15th century when Henry the Navigator introduced vines and sugarcane to the slopes. In Funchal, the must (fresh wine) from the black and white grapes is used to make Bual, Sercial, and Malmsey. It's cultivated for its bittersweet tang (women used to scent their handkerchiefs with it). The wine growers still transport the foot-pressed must in goatskin bottles over the rough terrain by *borracheiros*. Naturally, it undergoes extensive pasteurization in its refinement and blending.

Madeira Wine Company, 28 Avenida Arriaga (tel. 201-21), next to the Tourist Office offers samples from its diverse stock. Inside this former convent, dating from 1790, are murals depicting the wine pressing (by foot) and harvesting processes, which proceed according to traditions established hundreds of years ago. You can savor the slightly burnt sweetness in a setting of old barrels, wine kegs, and time-mellowed chairs and tables made from aged wine kegs. Incidentally, Napoleon passed this way on his journey into exile on St. Helena in 1815. Bottles from a vintage year were given to him, but death came before the former emperor could sample them.

Of the churches of Funchal, the most intriguing is the rustic 15th-century **Sé (cathedral),** with its Moorish carved cedar ceiling, stone floors, Gothic arches, stained-glass windows, and baroque altars.

Just down the street from the Cruzes Museum is the baroque **Convent of Santa Clara,** Calçada de Santa Clara, with walled tiles, a painted wooden ceiling, and the tomb of Zarco, the discoverer of Madeira. The church is said to have been built by the granddaughter of Zarco the year Columbus discovered America.

Museu da Quinta das Cruzes, 1 Calçada do Pico (tel. 223-82), is the ancient residence of Madeira's discoverer, João Gonçalves Zarco. The surrounding park is of botanical interest and contains an orchid collection of note. The museum houses many fine examples of English furniture and China trade porcelains brought to Madeira by expatriate Englishmen during the 18th century, rare Indo-Portuguese cabinets, and the unique chests, native to Madeira, fashioned from *caixas de açúcar* (sugar boxes, which date from the 17th century). Also worth noting is a superb collection of antique Portuguese silver. The museum is open daily except Sunday from 10 a.m. to noon and 2 to 6 p.m., and charges 100$ (65¢).

The land and aquatic animal life of the archipelago is represented at the **City Museum and Aquarium,** 31 Rua da Mouraria (tel. 297-61). Moray eels, eagle rays, scorpion fish, sea cucumbers, sea zephyrs, sharp-nosed puffers, and loggerhead turtles, as well as many of the beautifully plumed birds seen around Madeira, are represented here. Monday to Friday, the museum and aquarium are open from 10 a.m. to 8 p.m. On Saturday and Sunday hours are noon to 6 p.m. Closed Monday. Admission is 50$ (35¢); free to children under 12.

The **Municipal Square** is a study in light and dark, its plaza paved with hundreds of black and white lava half moons. The whitewashed buildings surrounding it have black stone trim and ochre-colored tile roofs. In all, it's an atmosphere of stately beauty.

You can also visit a **lota** (fish auction) and many bazaars selling local handcrafts. At the lota, seafood is auctioned off to housewives and restaurant owners. Horse mackerel, grouper, mullet, tunny (sometimes weighing hundreds of pounds), freshwater eels, even a slab of barracuda, will find its way to the stalls.

In the bazaars you can purchase needlepoint tapestries, Madeira wines, laces, embroidery on Swiss organdy or Irish linen, plus all sorts of local crafts such as goat-skin boots or Camacha basketry of water willows. The **City Market**, at the Praça do Comércio on Saturday, is a study in color, offering everything from yams to paw-paws.

Jardim Botanico lies about 2½ miles from Funchal on the road to Camacha. It is said to be one of the best botanical gardens in Iberia, with faraway views of the bay. It is open daily from 9 a.m. to 6 p.m., charging an admission of 250$ ($1.65). For more information, phone 360-37.

The most exciting (and most crowded) time to visit Funchal is during the **End of the Year Festival,** December 30 to January 1. Fireworks light up the Bay of Fun-chal, the mountains in the background forming an amphitheater. Floodlit cruise ships anchor in the harbor to the delight of passengers who revel until dawn.

---

5. The Sporting Life

The pleasant climate of Madeira invites visitors to enjoy outdoor activities, even if they consist mainly of strolling through the city of Funchal and along park path-ways and country lanes. Time was when the visiting Victorians (some of the men looking like Mr. Pickwick) were carried around the islands in hammocks slung on poles and supported by two husky bearers. Nowadays this form of transport is a nos-talgic memory. As one official put it: "The Communists objected to it. They consid-er it a form of slavery." A more popular means of transport in Funchal is to hire a bullock-pulled, wheel-less sledge on the Avenida do Mar, near the pier.

By far the most famous rides, however, are . . .

THE TOBOGGAN RIDES

Descents are made by toboggan from Monte, about four miles from Funchal. You ascend by taxi, about a 20-minute trip costing 900$ ($5.85) one way. Before you begin your descent, you can visit the **Church of Nossa Senhora do Monte**, which contains the iron tomb of the last of the Hapsburgs, the Emperor Charles who died in Madeira in 1922 of pneumonia. From a belvedere nearby, you can look down on the whole of Funchal: the narrow streets, the plazas, and especially the *cais*, that long docking pier set in deep-blue mirror-like water.

The toboggan is a wide wicker basket with wooden runners. The baskets were the main means of transport in Monte from 1849 to 1942. The nearly two-mile ride takes ten minutes. As it rushes down the slippery smooth cobblestones, it is directed and sometimes propelled by two expert, straw-hatted guides who yaw the ropes like nimble-footed seamen. You may need to fortify yourself with a glass or two of ma-deira wine before taking the plunge. From Monte to Funchal the ride costs 1,400$ ($9.10) per person. You can also take the toboggan ride from **Terreiro da Luta** to Funchal for 2,300$ ($14.95). At Terreiro da Luta, at a height of 2,875 feet, you'll enjoy another splendid view of Funchal. Here also are monuments to Zarco and Our Lady of Peace.

SWIMMING

Since Madeira doesn't have beaches, guests use one of the swimming pools, most often provided by a hotel. However, if your hotel doesn't have one, you can use the facilities of the **Lido Swimming Pool Complex** (Complexo Balnear do Lido), which has an Olympic-size pool, plus a spacious pool for children as well. It is open in summer daily from 8 a.m. to 7 p.m. (in the off-season from 9 a.m. to 6 p.m.). Adults pay 170$ ($1.10) and children, 80$ (50¢) to use the pool. A special ticket, costing 80$ (50¢), is sold to visitors who want to use the upper deck only. You can rent sunbeds and umbrellas for 160$ ($1.05) each.

The complex is equipped with several facilities, including a café, a restaurant, an ice-cream parlor, bars, and a water-sports headquarters. To reach it, head out the Estrada Monumental from Funchal, turning onto the Rua do Gorgulho (the turnoff is marked).

GOLF

In the northeastern part of Madeira, in the hamlet of Santo da Sêrra, is the Madeira golf course (tel. 551-39). This golf course, at more than 2,000 feet above sea level, enjoys an attractive setting in a forested area with mimosa and eucalyptus. It opened as a nine-hole course, but there was an almost immediate demand to extend it to 18 holes. In the clubhouse is a changing room, as well as a lounge area and bar. Clubs can be rented, and local caddies are available.

TENNIS

Most of the first-class and deluxe establishments have their own courts. If you're in a hotel without a court, you can often obtain permission to play at a major hotel if you make a reservation (you'll be charged a small fee, of course). Naturally, guests of the hotel get priority.

HORSEBACK RIDING

For equestrians, the **Centro de Hipismo da Madeira,** Caminho dos Pretos (tel. 249-82), arranges this increasingly popular activity. Vacationers go riding every day from 9:30 a.m. to 5 p.m. except Saturday and Sunday.

WATER SPORTS

The activities desks of several of the major hotels, including the Savoy and Reid's, will arrange these activities for you, even if you're not a guest of the establishment. Naturally, you must pay for whatever services you book. Waterskiing can be arranged, as can windsurfing and boat rentals. Sailing dinghies can also be rented. If you want to go snorkeling or scuba-diving, check with the Inter Atlas Hotel, Garajau-Caniço (tel. 93-24-21).

DEEP-SEA FISHING

This is a popular sport in Madeira. The catch is mainly longtail tuna, blue marlin, swordfish, and several varieties of shark, along with other denizens of the deep. Boats can generally be rented for moderate costs. The Tourist Office will supply you with up-to-date information about boat rentals and the latest rates.

6. Funchal After Dark

Casino Park Complex (tel. 252-28), open daily from 8 p.m. to 3 a.m., is the glittering target for most visitors to the island. On its own grounds in the center of town, it is just minutes from most of the big hotels. "Indoor sports" include roulette, chemin de fer, French banque, craps, blackjack, and slot machines for the "Dixie cup" crowd. Designed by Oscar Niemeyer, the architect of Brasilia, the complex features a 400-room, five-star deluxe hotel (the Casino Park), plus a nightclub and cabaret with international entertainment. At the restaurant continental and Portuguese specialties are served.

Admission to the Casino is easy for foreign tourists, who take along their passports or some other identification card. The entrance fee to the game room is 350$ ($2.30). The nightclub, Zodiaco, has a show at 12:30 a.m., imposing a cover charge of 600$ ($3.90), with drinks costing from 400$ ($2.60). Or else you can patronize the Cabaret, which has dinner from 8 p.m., dancing from 9:30 p.m. Dinner costs 6,000$ ($39) to 7,000$ ($45.50), but if you visit just for the show, the cover charge is 750$ ($4.90). There's a floor show at 10:45 p.m.

The Prince Albert, Rua da Imperatriz D. Amélia (tel. 317-93), is a Victorian pub in Madeira, complete with cut plush velvet walls, tufted banquettes, and English pub memorabilia. You're greeted with a "Good evening, sir." Next to the Savoy, the pub serves oversize mugs of beer and a cross sampling of all the accents of England. Drinks are offered at the curved bar or at one of the tables under Edwardian fringed lamps. The establishment is open daily from 11 a.m. to 2 a.m.

O Farol Disco Club, Madeira-Sheraton, Largo António Nobre (tel. 310-31), considered the best, most interesting, and safest disco on the island, lies in a circular outbuilding near the lagoon-shaped swimming pool of this five-star hotel already recommended. To reach it, most visitors pass through the hotel lobby, descending open-toed flights of stairs and passing through the hotel gardens. The disco offers current music, rows of curved windows overlooking the sea, and several tiers of curved platforms whose visual focus is the dance floor. Visitors pay 1,000$ ($6.50) at the door, which builds up a drink credit. Scotch and soda costs 400$ ($2.60). The music lasts every night except Sunday from 10 p.m. to 3 a.m.

Joe's Bar (tel. 290-87) stands on the grounds of the previously recommended Quinta da Penha de França, on the Rua da Penha de França. It is decorated in a turn-of-the-century style. Hours are daily from 12:30 p.m. to 2 a.m.

---

7. Excursions in Madeira

To explore and savor Madeira, the adventurous visitor with endless time will go on foot across some of the trails. Hand-hewn stones and gravel-sided embankments lead one (but definitely not the queasy) along precipitous ledges, down into lush ravines, across flowering meadows. These dizzying paths are found everywhere from the hillsides of the wine-rich region of Estreito de Câmara de Lobos to the wickerwork center of Camacha. A much easier way to go, of course, is on an organized tour, or to use the local buses, although you may prefer to risk the hazardous driving on hairpin curves.

Heading west from Funchal, you'll pass banana groves almost spilling into the sea, women doing their laundry on rocks, and homes so tiny they're almost like dollhouses. Less than six miles away lies the coastal village of **Câmara de Lobos** (Room of the Wolves), the subject of several paintings by Sir Winston Churchill. A sheltered and tranquil shell-shaped cove, it is set amid rocks and towering cliffs, with hill-climbing cottages, terraces, and date palms. In the late afternoon naked youngsters loll and play in the cove, alongside the bobbing fishing boats in such colors as sunflower gold, kelly green, and marine blue.

The road north from the village through the vineyards leads to **Estreito de Câmara de Lobos,** the heart of the wine-growing region that produces madeira. The men who cultivate the ribbon-like terraces can be seen laboring in the fields, wearing brown stocking caps with tasseled tops. Along the way you'll spot women sitting on mossy stone steps, doing Madeira embroidery. At times clouds move in over the mountaintops obscuring the view, then pass off toward the sea or tumble down a hillside.

Scaling a hill studded with pine and eucalyptus, you'll reach **Cabo Girão,** the oceanside cliff mentioned in the introduction. Considered the second-loftiest promontory in Europe, a belvedere overlooks the sea and the saffron-colored rocks below. Close by, you can see how the land is cultivated in Madeira, one terrace seemingly no larger than a small throw rug. (Incidentally, the blondes you see in and around here aren't peroxided. Rather, the straw-colored hair was inherited from early Flemish settlers sent to the island.)

Try to return to Funchal by veering off the coastal road, past São Martinho to the belvedere at **Pico dos Barcelos.** In one of the most idyllic spots on the island, you can see the ocean, the mountains, orange and banana groves, bougainvillaea, poinsettias, and the capital. Whether it's roosters crowing, babies crying in faraway huts, or goats bleating, the sound carries for miles.

By heading north from Funchal, you can visit some of the most outstanding spots in the heart of the island. Going first through Santo António, you'll eventually reach **Curral das Freiras,** a petite village huddled around an old monastery at the bottom of an extinct volcanic crater. The site, whose name means Corral of the Nuns, was originally a secluded convent that protected the good sisters from sea-weary, woman-hungry mariners and pirates.

If you go north in a different direction, one of the goals is **Santana.** Many visitors have described it as something out of Disney's *Fantasia.* Picture an alpine setting, complete with waterfalls, cobblestone streets, green meadows sprinkled with multicolored blossoms, thatched cottages, swarms of roses, and plunging ravines. Of it, novelist Paul Bowles once wrote: "It is as if a 19th-century painter with a taste for the baroque had invented a countryside to suit his own personal fantasy. It is the sort of picture that used to adorn the grocer's calendar."

Southwest of the village is **Queimadas,** the site of a 3,000-foot-high rest house. From here, many people make the three-hour trek to the apex of **Pico Ruivo** (Purple Peak), referred to earlier as the highest point on the island, 6,105 feet above sea level.

In the east, about 18 miles from Funchal (a short drive from the airport) is historic **Machico,** with its much-visited **Church of Senhor dos Milagres,** dating from the mid-15th century. According to legend, the church was built over the tombs of the two star-crossed English lovers, Robert Machim and Anna d'Arfet. Try to view the village from the belvedere of **Camõe Pequeno.** In the vicinity is a grotto 300 feet long, said to be the deepest in Madeira.

On the way back from Machico, you can detour inland to **Camacha,** perched in a setting of flowers and orchards. It's the island center of the wickerwork industry. You can buy here (although the stores in Funchal are heavily supplied), or just watch chairs and other items being made by the local crafts people.

ORGANIZED TOURS

Those who stay only in Funchal miss what the island is about. If you don't care to venture into the mountains in your own automobile, then take one of the many excursions to different sections of the island. The tours reach virtually every accessible point in Madeira from Porto Moniz to Câmara de Lobos, and many of the excursions are terminated in Monte where you can finish with a toboggan ride into Funchal. Various tours leave every day; the major jaunt to Porto Moniz and Cabo Girão costs 4,500$ ($29.25), including lunch. A half-day volcano and toboggan tour costs 2,500$ ($16.25). One of the more interesting tours is a visit to the wicker works at Camacha, among other attractions costing 2,750$ ($17.90).

Madeira possesses a number of travel agencies, including Wagons-Lits Cook. If you go to any of them, you can receive detailed information about the island tours available. Not all are by motorcoach; some are by boat. You can also pick up information at the **Official Tourist Bureau,** 18 Avenida Arriaga (tel. 290-57).

---

8. Dining Around the Island

While exploring Madeira, you may want to arrange luncheon stopovers at one of the following recommendations:

The government-owned **Pousada dos Vinháticos,** Sêrra de Agua, 9350 Ribeira Brava (tel. 091/95-23-44), is near the top of a pass on the winding road to São Vincente. Guests can visit just for a meal or else spend the night. The pousada, a tavern-style building with a brick terrace, is built of solid stone. Visitors can absorb the unmarred mountain views from the terrace. The cooking is regional, and complete meals, served daily from noon to 3 p.m. and 7 to 9:30 p.m., cost 1,800$

($11.50). Most of the bedrooms are in Portuguese modern, although a few accommodations contain antiques. All have private baths and good views and are kept immaculate. The price of a double room is 7,500$ ($48.75) daily, and a single is 6,500$ ($42.25), including a continental breakfast.

Áquàrio, Seixal (tel. 641-96), is a waterfront fish restaurant too often ignored by visitors who flock to the dining spots of Porto Moniz, where they have to fight for a seat. Clients at Áquàrio enjoy some of the tastiest cooking on the island. The kitchen turns out simple fare, but its cooking often outdistances the table d'hôte menus served in the deluxe hotels. Everything is prepared fresh. The proprietor oversees every serving by the waitresses. To begin with, one gets a heaping basket of homemade bread and a carafe of the local wine. I recommend the grilled fish of the day, served with three vegetables. Soups are hearty, the helpings generous. The price of a meal ranges from 2,000$ ($13). The decor is nautical, the walls decorated with objects rescued from the sea. On sale are handmade straw and reed baskets. Lunch only is offered, and you can arrive daily from noon to 3:30 p.m.

A Cabana, Beira da Quinta São Jorge (tel. 572-91), is a colony of circular cottages with central roofs, arranged at the edge of a cliff on the northern coast of Madeira. True to the architecture of the region, the roofs are thatched. The furnishings are crude but attractive. A much larger circular thatched hut with an open beamed ceiling provides good-tasting lunches, served daily from noon to 3 p.m., costing 2,000$ ($13). Many of the dishes are cooked on a large open semicircular charcoal fireplace. Specialties include beef grilled on a spit, roast chicken, roast cod, panada, and bolos do caco, a typical bread.

Jardim do Sol, Livremento, Caniço, on the coast highway east of Funchal (tel. 93-21-23). This roadside inn is like a hunting lodge, with knotty-pine walls, a mezzanine, rattan chairs, and two walls of glass with a view of the sea through tall pines. The owner has installed framed murals of the local fishermen, a bamboo bar, and window boxes overflowing with marigolds. The proprietor caters not only to the residents of Funchal, but to the cruise ships that tie up in port.

A 2,000$ ($13) table d'hôte luncheon or dinner is offered. You'll be given a first course, usually a big bowl of good-tasting soup, followed by a fish dish such as filet of scabbard, then a meat course, a dessert, and finally fresh fruit. Lunch is daily from noon to 4 p.m.; dinner, from 7 to 10 p.m.

A Seta, 80 Estrada do Livramento, Monte (tel. 203-06), is for regional cuisine supreme. The mountainside restaurant is a tavern where you can order inexpensive and tasty meals. The decor is rustic, with a burnt-wood trim, walls covered with pine cones, and crude natural pine tables. An inner dining room adjoins an open kitchen, with a charcoal spit and oven, ideal for those who want to watch the action.

First of all, a plate of coarse brown homemade bread still warm from the oven is put at your place. Above each table is a hook to which is attached a long skewer of charcoal-broiled meat. You slip off chunks while mopping up the juices with your crusty bread. There are three specialties: beef, chicken, and grilled dry codfish. Seasoned with olive oil, herbs, garlic, and bay leaves, these concoctions are called *espetadas*. Fried potatoes are always done well here (ask for some hot sauce). For a fine repast, count on spending around 2,000$ ($13). Hours are noon to 3 p.m. and 6 to 9 p.m. daily except Wednesday.

9. Porto Santo

Another island of the little Madeira group is Porto Santo, some 24 miles to the northeast of the main land mass and very different from that island. It is only nine miles long and three miles wide, yet it boasts a four-mile strip of fine, sandy beach along the southern shore. The island is not as hilly as Madeira: its highest elevation is about 1,670 feet above sea level, at **Pico do Facho.**

This island was the first on which the discoverers of Madeira, João Gonçalves Zarco and Tristão Vaz Teixiera, landed in 1418. These captains, serving Prince Henry the Navigator, took refuge here when a storm blew them off course, and named it Porto Santo (Holy Port) to express gratitude for their survival. It was not until 1419 that they were in condition to sail on and make the landfall at Madeira. Henry gave Teixiera and Zarco authority to run Madeira, but he placed Porto Santo in the hands of Bartolomeu Perestrello, who made his mark on the island. At least, he is reported to have brought in rabbits as a future food source, but instead, it is said, they ate everything in sight, laying waste to the vegetation already there and not helping future crops much.

Christopher Columbus slept here. He married Isobel Moniz, the daughter of Perestrello, before going on to Funchal to prepare for his planned sea exploration. The house in which he is claimed to have lived is in an alley back of the little white church in the town of **Villa Baleira,** which is also called Porto Santo.

The island gets very dry in summer, which makes it popular with beach-goers but not very good for crops. Produced in winter, the foodstuffs grown on Porto Santo include grain, tomatoes, figs, and melons, as well as grapes from which a sweet white wine is made. Islanders who don't farm go fishing. The low hills are crowned here with a few remaining unusual windmills.

The water of Porto Santo is supposed to have therapeutic values, which have made it a popular drink not only on the island but also in Madeira and Portugal. The water-bottling plants, fish canneries, and a lime kiln are industries of Porto Santo.

The little town with two names lies beneath **Pico do Castelo,** a height on which stands a ruined 16th-century castle built for defense. For a long time Madeira let Porto Santo shift for itself in this regard, and it fell prey to pirates now and then.

Try to go to the **Fountain in the Sands** (Fonte da Areia), near cliffs above a rocky coast. Here local women wash their clothes in the water flowing out.

Good points from which to get views of the island and its surroundings are **Portela** and **Castelo Peak** (Pico do Castelo). **Ponta da Calheta** is another sight provided by nature, on the south of the island. This point looks to Baixo Islet across a reef-strewn channel constantly pounded by the sea. Black basalt rocks dot the beach.

Independencia sails from Funchal to Porto Santo daily, if the weather is good. The round-trip fare is about 4,000$ ($26), and the trip takes 1½ hours each way. Some hotels or quintas will pack a picnic lunch, which guests can enjoy on the beach. The boat leaves in the early morning, returning in the late afternoon, and giving passengers at least four hours on the Porto Santo beach. The ride is often rough, and many passengers get sick from motion sickness, so be duly warned. For about the same price, you can fly over in the morning on a TAP flight, catching a Funchal-bound plane in Porto Santo in the early evening. In summer, at least six flights are operated daily.

FOOD AND LODGING

The four-star, first-class **Hotel Porto Santo,** Campo de Baixo, 9400 Porto Santo (tel. 091/98-22-72) has only two floors. It was constructed a little more than a mile from Vila Baleira at Suloeste, in a garden setting bordering directly on the large (four-mile-long) beach of gold-colored sand. The Porto Santo offers 93 well-furnished double rooms, including four suites, each with a private bath, phone, and a terrace overlooking the bay. For your room and a continental breakfast, rates are 8,800$ ($57.20) daily in a single, 13,500$ ($87.75) in a double room.

The hotel also has a large restaurant serving a bountiful lunch or dinner for 2,500$ ($16.25). The main lounge has been attractively furnished, and mercifully, air-conditioned. It leads to the main terrace and garden, where there is an open bar. After the hot sun retires a bit, the tennis courts are popular. A swimming pool has been built for guests, and windsurfing is also available.

Hotel Praia Dourada, Rue Dr. Pedro Lomelino, 9400 Porto Santo (tel. 091/

98-23-15), is the leading hotel at Vila Baleira (not that there's much competition). Rooms, each with private bath, are simply furnished but clean. Some three dozen accommodations are rented to both tourists and persons who have business on the island. Charges range from 5,800$ ($37.70) daily in a single to 7,500$ ($48.75) in a double, including a continental breakfast.

Pensão Central, Rua Abel Magna Vasconcelos, 9400 Porto Santo (tel. 091/ 98-22-26), is modesty itself, but clean and immaculate. Also in the capital, Vila Baleira, the pension is among the least expensive places to stay on the island. It rents a dozen bedrooms, each with private bath. Charges range from 3,500$ ($22.75) daily in a single, and from 4,000$ ($26) in a double. The little inn is homelike, its owners welcoming. They offer guests the use of a bar, sun terrace, and restaurant.

Nearly all guests in Porto Santo dine at one of the hotels previously recommended. However, there are some very simple local eateries.

Arsenios, Avenida Dr. Manuel Pestana Gunior (tel. 98-23-48), is perhaps *numero uno* in Porto Santo. It was patterned after a restaurant owned by the same entrepreneur in Funchal, and its Madeira success formula was imported to nearby Porto Santo. It is said to produce the best paella in town. Full meals, including many fresh fish dishes (which depend on the catch of the day), cost from 2,500$ ($16.25). Hours are daily from noon to 11 p.m. The restaurant is located in town on the main road opposite the sea. It is housed in a modern building with large panoramic windows.

Marqués, Rua Maximiliano de Sousa Max (tel. 98-23-19), is another good restaurant, lying in a modern building near the center of town. It serves many varieties of grilled fish and seems to take pride in the offerings of its kitchen. Hours are from noon to 11 p.m. daily, and meals cost from 2,200$ ($14.30).

Por-do-Sol, Sítio da Calheta (tel. 98-23-80), lies on the western tip of the island. Installed in a prefabricated house, it is simply decorated and stays open without interruption daily from 9:30 a.m. to midnight. Three food specialties include espetada (meat on a spit), caldeirada (fish stew made with several kinds of fish), and grilled fish (whatever the catch turned up that day). A meal costs from 1,500$ ($9.75).

Toca do Pescador (tel. 98-21-42) stands almost next to the just-recommended Por-do-Sol. It's the same type of house with the same decor. An unpretentious place, it is open daily from 9:30 a.m. to midnight, serving complete meals for 1,500$ ($9.75). Its kitchen turns out grilled fish (all kinds), meat on a spit, and grilled chicken.

THE AZORES

The lost paradise . . . legends of enchanted princesses . . . hydrangea-bordered highways . . . lakes at the bottom of extinct volcanic craters . . . natural springs of therapeutic waters . . . windmills clacking . . . oxen plowing the fields like a tableau vivant suspended in time . . . and mist and cloud-shrouded islands.

Those seeking an offbeat holiday in Europe can strike out for the remote Azores. It is an archipelago where the winds of the ocean meet, where the cyclones call on each other. Robin Bryans called the islands a "muted mood, a pianissimo untouched by the strident dissonance of industrial Europe."

When the first explorers directed their ships' prows into the Atlantic, the volcanic slopes of the Azores were the westernmost known points of land. Whether the Vikings, the Genoese, the Phoenicians, or whoever, first put into these lands remains unknown. There are those who believe that the Azores are all that remain of the lost continent of Atlantis.

The archipelago spans a distance of more than 500 miles from the southeastern tip of Santa Maria to the northwestern extremity at Corvo. The main island of **São Miguel** lies about 760 miles west of Portugal (2,110 miles east of New York), making the Azores the most isolated islands in the entire Atlantic.

Completely uninhabited when discovered, the Azores were named by Diogo de Silves (a captain of Henry the Navigator) after the hook-beaked *açor* (compared to both a hawk and an eagle), which sailed on the air currents over the coast. The date: 1427 (give or take a year or two). It wasn't long before settlements sprang up. Besides the Portuguese settlers, many from the north, Flemish immigrants came to the central Azores, where place and family names today show this influence.

Eventually it was learned that the entire island group was actually composed of three distinct mini-archipelagos: the eastern section of **Santa Maria** and **São Miguel;** the central with **Terceira** (scene of bullfighting in the streets), **Graciosa** (about 11 miles in length, known for its Sulfur Cave), cigar-shaped **São Jorge** (Raul Brandao's ethereal island of dust and dream), **Pico** (with a cloud-capped mountain), and **Faial** (vulnerable to earthquakes and known for the eerie crater of the extinct volcano, Caldeira); and the western group made up of **Flores** (Flowers) where vegetation runs riot in a setting of lakes, waterfalls, and valleys, and **Corvo** (the smallest member—everybody knows everybody else—and a visit by a foreigner is an occasion).

The Azores are a study in color. The writer who once made the much-publicized characterization, the "Gray Azores," must have been color blind. Much of the color of the archipelago comes from the flowers that grow rampantly in its volcanic soil: azaleas, camellias, heather, agapanthus, rhododendrons. Although occasionally lashed by violent storms, the enchanted islands enjoy a mild climate: the temperature averages around 58° Fahrenheit in winter, only 75° Fahrenheit in summer.

Its rugged people who daily contend with the elements of nature are hospitable to strangers, even though one might have expected such isolated islanders to be insular. Coming back from a walk in the São Miguel hills, two American visitors were stopped by a boy riding a mule. Under a straw hat with a hoe slung over his shoulder, the boy smiled as he bid them *Bom Noite*. The word YALE was written across his sweatshirt. Learning that he spoke a bit of English, the visitors inquired about the letters. It seemed that his uncle had attended Yale. "Do you know him?" the boy asked. "He now lives in Boston."

Every man, woman, and child in the island chain seemingly has relatives living in the United States. Many settled in New Bedford, Massachusetts (of *Moby-Dick* fame), during the whaling heyday of that port, taking jobs as sailors, fishermen, whalers, and caulkers. Many of the immigrants returned to the Azores, however, after earning their fortunes across the sea.

GETTING THERE

At any **TAP** office or at your local travel agent, you can learn the times and frequency of flights to the Azores. If you hold a round-trip ticket from New York to Lisbon, you are allowed to stop free in the Azores, if you make arrangements when you purchase your ticket. The free stopover, however, may not be valid on special excursion tickets.

TAP flies a scheduled service between Logan Airport in Boston and Lisbon, going via Terceira. In off-season there is one flight a week in each direction, increasing to two flights per week in each direction after March 30.

Most flights leaving the Azores for Lisbon depart from San Miguel's airport near Ponta Delgada. This creates confusion for some North American travelers who, coming from Boston, have the intention of exploring one or two of the islands before continuing their trip to the mainland of Portugal. The plane from Boston lands on Terceira, but because of airline schedules, the only convenient departure for Lisbon is from a neighboring island, San Miguel.

You can travel by boat between the two islands, but even the local residents find this both inconvenient and uncomfortable. Far more practical would be to fly.

Service within the Azores is operated by **SATA (Serviço Açoreano de Transportes Aéreos).** Reservations and information about SATA can be made from anywhere in North America by calling the nearest TAP office (or their toll-free number 800/221-7370). All but the tiny island of Corvo have airports, but planes will sometimes choose not to fly during the worst of Atlantic storms.

SATA, however, is generally efficient and punctual. In fact, since 1984 when SATA upgraded its equipment and increased the number of its flights among the islands, boat transportation has been slowly phased out, except for transport among the islands of the Azorean middle group. Boat schedules vary with the seasons, and the local tourist offices will keep you abreast of last-minute schedules.

Because of their geographical situation, the Azores are a favorite port of call for cruises crossing the Atlantic, including, on occasion, the *QE II*. However, stopovers

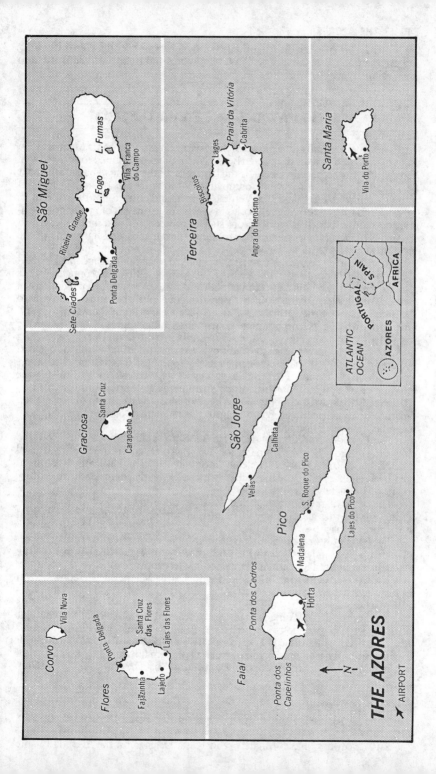

THE AZORES

✈ AIRPORT

←N→

Corvo
Vila Nova

Flores
Ponta Delgada
Fajãzinha
Lajedo
Santa Cruz das Flores
Lajes das Flores

Graciosa
Santa Cruz
Carapacho

São Jorge
Velas
Calheta

Pico
Madalena
S. Roque do Pico
Lajes do Pico

Faial
Ponta dos Cedros
Ponta dos Capelinhos
Horta

São Miguel
L. Fumas
L. Fogo
Ribeira Grande
Vila Franca do Campo
Sete Ciades
Ponta Delgada

Terceira
Biscoitos
Lajes
Praia da Vitória
Cabrita
Angra do Heroísmo

Santa Maria
Vila do Porto

ATLANTIC OCEAN
PORTUGAL
SPAIN
AFRICA
AZORES

are short. Yachts crossing the Atlantic also stop off here frequently. A favorite yacht-ing event among British sailors is the Azab (Azores and back), and the Dutch also hold a similar race.

---

1. São Miguel and Ponta Delgada

The eastern group of the Azores archipelago, consisting of Santa Maria and São Miguel, was the first to be discovered by the Portuguese and claimed for their crown. São Miguel, the second discovery, is the largest of all the islands, measuring about 37 miles long by 9½ miles wide, occupying 290 square miles of land far from its mother country. Also called Ilha Verde (Green Island) because of the color of its pastures and forests, São Miguel glories in vegetation—masses of hydrangeas, azal-eas, and cannas, as well as money crops such as tobacco, tea, and pineapple, grown under glass. Development and stock-breeding have made São Miguel one of the most prosperous islands in the Azores, with a promising economic growth.

Ponta Delgada became the capital and principal town of the island in 1546, hav-ing become well populated in the less than 100 years of settlement. Ponta Delgada is also the seat of the regional government of the Azores. It is a flat, rectangular town about two miles long, lying along the west bank of a lovely bay and conforming to the indentations of the natural coastline. A promenade along the waterfront still lures strollers along its length at night, when the twinkling lights from vessels in the bay add a festive note. The zebra-striped **Avenida Infante Dom Henrique,** circling the waterfront, is the venue for the traditional *passeio,* the leisurely stroll indulged in by parents and their marriageable daughters, by young gallants, visitors, and sailors from ships in the harbor. The promenade area was constructed in the 1860s by the building of a 2,800-foot-long breakwater, making the wide boulevard possible.

In early days, artistic expression in the Azores mainly went into the decoration of churches and chapels and Ponta Delgada has its share of places of worship with magnificent interior decoration.

The **Convent and Chapel of Nossa Senhora da Esperança** dates from the cult of the image of Senhor Santo Cristo, given by Pope Paul III in 1530. The chapel in which the image is kept is completely lined with azulejos. The image is accompa-nied by a reliquary and jewels that have been accumulating since the 17th century and now completely cover the statue.

The walls of the **Church of São José** are lined with blue and white 18th-century glazed tiles alternating with haut-relief carving. A baroque pietà stands in the baptismal chapel.

The **Parish Church of São Sebastião** has a choir in carved cedar and such exot-ic woods as palisander. Built in the 16th century, its façade shows traces of the Manueline style with Renaissance influence in later renovation.

The **Convent of Santo André** houses the **Carlos Machado Museum,** known for historical archives, a library, an art collection, natural history exhibits, ethnologi-cal artifacts, and a collection of toys.

On the outskirts of Ponta Delgada, you can arrange to visit one of the pineapple factories, actually greenhouses, where the fruit is grown under sloping glass roofs that have been whitewashed. The plants are smoked several times during their growth, as this *fumo* method is said to make all of them flower at the same time. For information, check with **Pineapple Plantation,** Rua Dr. Augusto Arruda (tel. 241-26).

TRANSPORTATION

Both **SATA** and **TAP** airlines make flights to the Ponte Delgada Airport (tel. 096/262-61).

SATA's offices on São Miguel are in Ponta Delgada on the Avenida Infante

Dom Henrique (tel. 272-21), and at the airport (Nordela) (tel. 232-61). At Ribeira Grande, the office is at 7 Largo Jardim (tel. 721-47).

TAP's bookings office in Ponta Delgada is on the Avenida Infante Dom Henrique (tel. 262-06). At the airport, call TAP at 246-72.

If you prefer to be an ocean-going visitor to or from the island, get in touch with **Junta Autónoma do Porto de Ponta Delgada,** 1 Rua Teófilo Braga, in Ponta Delgada (tel. 252-21), for information.

Rent-a-car and taxi service are provided by: **Ilha Verde Rent-a-Car,** 19 Praça 5 de Outubro (tel. 252-00); and **Micauto Rent-a-Car,** 109 Avenida Infante Dom Henrique (tel. 243-82). Outside the capital, Micauto has branches at the airport (tel. 243-82), at Ribeira Grande (tel. 721-21), and at Furnas (tel. 542-54).

WHERE TO STAY IN PONTA DELGADA

You can savor the ambience of past centuries at the **Hotel de São Pedro,** Largo Almirante Dunn, 9500 Ponta Delgada, São Miguel, Açores (tel. 096/222-23), while you enjoy the comforts of the 20th. The building was the work of the island's most colorful and legendary figure, Thomas Hickling, who came from Boston on a schooner in 1769. He and his descendants profited from a thriving business growing and exporting oranges to London and St. Petersburg (Leningrad). From their wealth, they built a family homestead with the help of imported craftsmen, and shipped in loads of fine antiques from the continent to furnish it. Their town house, with its Georgian colonial interior, is on the sea, with a high garden wall to provide privacy from the street. Throughout its history it has known many vicissitudes (it was used in World War I as a headquarters for the American navy).

Nowadays one can stay here in comparative luxury for moderate tariffs. Modernization has been carried out effectively.

Because of the noncommercial atmosphere, guests are likely to intermingle freely, and the staff is considerate. The drawing room is formal, with two bronze and crystal chandeliers, a pair of fine 18th-century fruitwood chests, velvet chairs, and a sofa set in front of an Adam-style fireplace. Fresh flowers are everywhere, as important to the character of São Pedro as changing the linen sheets. The drinking lounge seems right from Old Salem, Massachusetts, with its hand-hewn beams and spoke chairs. Drinks are also served on the tiled loggia where you can enjoy the view of the lawn, the water, the stone urns, and the century-old trees. Bedrooms are equipped with traditional pieces, and suites are furnished in the grand manner—one with a huge Napoleonic sleigh bed, another with spindle twin beds. The dining room, scene of many bountiful meals, is recommended separately. Singles range from 6,700$ ($43.55) to 7,900$ ($51.35) daily, with twins and doubles costing 8,250$ ($53.65) to 9,400$ ($61.10). Suites for two persons cost 18,500$ ($120.25).

Hotel Canadiano, 24A Rua do Contado, 9500 Ponta Delgado, São Miguel, Açores (tel. 096/274-21). Built as a hybrid between a hotel and a motel in 1982, it lies on a hillock beside a busy and narrow cobblestone street a brisk walk from the harbor. The hotel has a comfortable and streamlined lobby, a cozy bar (called "The Canuck"), and a snackbar. Its 50 bedrooms lie around a courtyard in back, as well as within a multistory block facing the street. Each unit contains a phone, an intercom, a private bath, and a veranda. With a continental breakfast included, singles cost 5,800$ ($37.70) daily, and doubles go for 6,800$ ($44.20). There's a TV lounge, plus a tennis court on the premises.

Hotel Gaivota Apartamentos, 103 Avenida Marginal, 9500 Ponta Delgado, São Miguel, Açores (tel. 096/232-86). Set on the main seaside promenade, this is one of the few hotels in town offering rooms with private kitchens. Built in the early 1980s, it has a nautically inspired lobby of panels accented with driftwood, an elevator, and a largely European clientele. Each of its 27 units has a phone, a TV, and a pleasant and tasteful collection of Iberian-inspired furnishings. The best accommodations also have a private balcony. Depending on the season and the accommodation, doubles range from 8,000$ ($52) to 9,000$ ($58.50).

Hotel Avenida, Rua Dr. José B.T. Carreiro, 9500 Ponta Delgada, São Miguel, Açores (tel. 096/273-31). The distinctive façade of this six-story hotel has a series of angled windows. It is one of the most modern and up-to-date hotels on the island, rated four stars. In the center of town, it is but a short walk from the beach. Each of its well-decorated and cozy bedrooms, 80 in all, comes with private bath, color TV with in-house video, phone, radio, and central heating. With a continental breakfast included, singles rent for 8,250$ ($53.65) daily, and doubles cost from 9,400$ ($61.60). The comfortable lounges and the attractive bar, with its adjacent restaurant, are fully air-conditioned.

Casa das Palmeiras, 26 Rua Diario dos Açores, 9500 Ponta Delgado, São Miguel, Açores (tel. 096/226-21). The street that contains it is crowded, noisy, and commercial, but once you step inside its walled semitropical garden, all the hubbub will be forgotten. Ringed with gnarled olive trees, this neoclassical villa was once the most prominent building in the neighborhood. Today its high ceilings and slightly tatty walls—envelop a handful of comfortably coordinated bedrooms. Each of these has a refrigerator, phone, and private bath, and several contain some antiques. Depending on the season, and with a continental breakfast included, singles cost 3,500$ ($22.75) to 4,000$ ($26) daily, and doubles rent for 4,000$ ($26) to 5,000$ ($32.50). The building's multicolored central spire, an unusual amalgam of turn-of-the-century styles, can be seen for many blocks.

Residencial América, 58 Rua Manuel Inácio Correia, 9500 Ponta Delgada, São Miguel, Açores (tel. 096/243-51), is one of the best buys for the money on the island. A simple inn, it offers 23 plain but comfortable bedrooms, each well maintained. With a continental breakfast included, singles cost 4,200$ ($27.30) daily, doubles go for 5,400$ ($35.10), and triples for 6,400$ ($41.60). The owners of the inn also have a rent-a-car service.

WHERE TO DINE IN PONTA DELGADA

The best restaurant on the island is in the previously recommended **Hotel de São Pedro,** Largo Almirante Dunn (tel. 222-23). Admiring the architecture and the detailing of this elegant hotel is as much a part of its experience as the cuisine. The dining room, on the second floor, is without equal in charm on the island. A battalion of uniformed waiters give impeccable service. The setting is one of Empire-era chairs, soaring ceilings, and paneling crafted from tropical hardwoods. Naturally, there's a view of the water, along with Sheraton-style cupboards. You can order a full lunch or dinner for 1,600$ ($10.40) to 1,900$ ($12.35), depending on whether you prefer one or two courses. Fish and meat, prepared in traditional Portuguese recipes, are the usual fare. Meals are served from 12:30 to 2:30 p.m. and 7 to 9 p.m. daily.

Outside the hotels, one of the best restaurants is incongruously named **London,** 21 Rua Ernesto do Canto (tel. 225-00). Its chef presents a menu with daily specialties that are well prepared and attractively served. The bill of fare is likely to include grilled creatures of the sea, such as swordfish, whitefish, or octopus. You might also order fried pork chops with bacon, perhaps saltimbocca, having begun with a fish soup. Meals cost from 2,000$ ($13) and are offered daily except Sunday from noon to 2:30 p.m. and 7 to 10 p.m. The cozy restaurant, seating more than two dozen patrons, also has a darkly elegant bar. To reach the restaurant, you climb a flight of stone steps from the street below.

Arturu's, 49F Rua João Francisco Cabral (tel. 249-90), is the most elegant and stylish restaurant on the island. It is located in a modern building at the edge of the center of town. In its air-conditioned interior, you can order an array of international dishes and local specialties. Full meals cost from 2,000$ ($13) and are served from noon to 3 p.m. and 7 to 11 p.m. daily except Monday.

Coliseu, Avenida Roberto Ivens (tel. 271-20), has some of the best Portuguese regional cooking on the island. It has a large, airy, and white-walled interior, with paper table coverings. In all, it's clean, respectable, and a neighborhood institution.

Waiters are helpful, and the kitchen is "on exhibit." The fresh fish is invariably recommended. Try the grilled squid or baked octopus. Meals, costing from 1,800$ ($11.70), are served from noon to 3 p.m. and 6 to 9 p.m. The restaurant, seating 85 patrons, is closed on Tuesday.

Boavista, Rua Ilha de São Miguel (tel. 242-72), is known for having the best shellfish in town, along with a fine selection of country cooking. You can sample a selection of fresh fish dishes costing from 1,800$ ($11.70) for a complete meal. Service is from noon to 2:30 p.m. and 6 to 9 p.m. except on Sunday. The restaurant is just outside the center of town, and is most often reached by taxi.

O Corisco, 28 Rua Manuel da Ponte (tel. 244-44), is one of the best-respected restaurants in the center of Ponta Delgada. It is both a restaurant and a pub, offering regional as well as international cuisine. The chef specializes in shellfish dishes. From noon to 3 p.m. and 6:30 to either 10 or 11 p.m. daily good-tasting meals are served for just 1,500$ ($9.75). No lunch is offered on Sunday or Monday. For a lunch, especially if it's a hot day, you might settle for the tuna salad. However, you can also order more substantial fare, including grilled swordfish, grilled veal, and grilled pork cutlets, followed by coconut pudding or perhaps some cheddar cheese from the Azores.

DINING AROUND THE ISLAND

Don't confine all your dining to Ponta Delgada. There are a number of other excellent restaurants scattered throughout São Miguel. Some, such as those at Furnas, will be previewed later. But if you have a rented car and would like to do some exploring, here is a suggestion.

The most exciting place is **Casa Velha,** Villa Pann-Pópulo de Cima-Livramento (tel. 316-80). Go for dinner only—it costs 2,500$ ($16.25) and up—and plan to make a night of it. You can arrive early to enjoy the bar, and stay later to dance in the disco. The dinner time, however, is from 7 to 11 nightly, and you should call in advance and reserve a table. The chef does a number of both continental and regional specialties, and the restaurant enjoys a reputation for having the best steaks on the island. In summer diners enjoy the esplanade, but in winter they prefer the glow of a fireplace. The dining room is closed Monday.

AROUND THE ISLAND

There are several points of interest to see on São Miguel, most of them bestowed by nature on the island.

Furnas

Following in the footsteps of rheumatic Victorians who shunned the sea cocktail at Brighton to take the baths at Furnas, you'll arrive at one of the richest spas in Europe. The thermal spa season lasts from July 1 to September 30, but a visit is interesting at any time of the year. The geysers and springs make the valley steamy in the district where sulphur fumes pour forth from craters.

The New Yorker described the springs as a place of "bare black rock, blasted by geysers, hot oozing clay, and sulphur-scented smoke. In a grim-looking cave, water boils furiously, now and then leaping up and spilling over in a smoking stream that runs steeply downhill between lava banks." David Dodge called the waters at the baths "cold, warm, boiling, carbonated, uncarbonated, radioactive, tasty, clear, muddy and as you like it, twenty-two kinds to choose from."

The major attraction is **Terra Nostra Park,** founded in 1770 according to an inscribed boulder, by Thomas Hickling, the American vice-consul discussed earlier in the description of São Pedro in Ponta Delgada. Where Hickling left off, the Marquês da Praia eventually took up. However, the latter's grandson at one point was about to destroy the park; but it was rescued by Vasco Bensuade in 1937. A pavilion was built that same year at Furnas Lake, and two years later a nine-hole championship golf course was opened.

It is a botanical garden, filled with azaleas, ferns, camellias, hydrangeas, pines, japonica, and jacaranda. Plants were brought from China, Japan, South America, Mexico, New Zealand, Asia, even the southern United States. White swans float majestically in the ponds studded with red and white lilies, and in the park is an egg-shaped swimming pool filled with muddy thermal waters. Changing cabins are nearby.

Before you go, you may want to take a trip to **Lake Furnas** for a volcano-cooked luncheon. This type of cuisine can be arranged through the Hotel Terra Nostra at Furnas. The cooking is known as à la caldeira. Everything from pullet to horse mackerel is covered with paper or some other wrapping after being well spiced with aromatic herbs. It then is buried in the hot earth, the way the Haitians roast kid. Sometimes whole chickens and yams are dropped into the simmering pools. On Sunday especially, you see families coming to the lakeside for picnics, washing down their meals with *cheiro,* a regional wine.

For dining or accommodations, try:

Hotel Terra Nostra, 9675 Furnas, São Miguel, Açores (tel. 096/541-33), is difficult to find, and the village's labyrinth of one-way streets makes reaching it a bit of an ordeal. Even when you arrive, the restrained detailing of its art deco façade might easily be overlooked if not for its position opposite a rose garden, the largest botanical garden in the Azores. Within its valleys, you'll find lush and verdant planting, along with a large oval basin designed like a giant reflecting pool, and a stone-sided villa like one of the imperial palaces of Brazil.

The hotel was recently expanded. Spacious rooms are rented, each with private bath, phone, and such art deco touches as curved walls and windows made from glass blocks. Singles rent for 4,500 ($29.25) to 6,500$ ($42.25) daily, and doubles go for 5,000$ ($32.50) to 7,500$ ($48.75), depending on the season. Fixed-price meals in the dining room cost from 1,800$ ($11.70) and are served daily from 12:30 to 3 p.m. and 7 to 9:30 p.m.

Sete Cidades

The Seven Cities, an hourglass-shaped lake, was named after a legend; in fact, it is the subject of many myths. The lake, about eight or nine miles in circumference, the upper part blue, the lower emerald green, was supposedly formed by tears shed over a broken love affair: one by a blue-eyed princess, the other by the shepherd boy she loved who was green-eyed. The appellation of Sete Cidades stems from a legend that claims that this site was actually the center of a powerful empire on the lost continent of Atlantis. You can visit a park near the blue lake, called **Jardim Pitoresco,** and enjoy the wafting aroma of the pittosporum flower. The vegetation on the slopes makes this a lush setting.

Cavalo Branco, 23 Rua do Meio Moio, Santa Bárbara, near Capelas (tel. 983-65). While exploring Sete Cidades, this restaurant provides the most appealing dining choice. The lunch hour is long, stretching from noon to 4 p.m. daily, so it easily fits into a sightseeing agenda. The food is good too, with an array of Portuguese cookery and regional specialties. Care and attention go into the menu planning and the selection of food items. For example, they make their own sausage. The oven is fired by wood, which gives added flavor to the grills. Meals cost from 2,000$ ($13), and the restaurant is closed on Monday. If you're there for dinner, hours are 6:30 to 10 p.m.

Pinhal Da Paz Recreational Reserve

Known also as **Mata das Criações,** Pinhal da Paz, comprising more than 120 acres, provides an unforgettable spectacle of color when the flowers are in bloom. Azaleas form a border along the roads through the reserve. Some of the colorful hedges run for nearly ten miles.

Logoa do Fogo
"Fire Lake" occupies the enormous crater of an extinct volcano in the center of the island. It is surrounded by dense vegetation, some of flowering plants. A nature reserve has been created here to protect the area, which includes the Lombades gorge, covered with luxuriant greenery.

Ilheu de Vila Franço
This islet, just off Vila Franço do Campo on the south coast, is one of the great local attractions. It forms a perfectly circular natural swimming pool in which numerous water sports are pursued. The rocks, worn into strange shapes by sea and wind, include a formation that looks like an ancient man-made column.

A Resort at Lagoa
Caloura Hotel Resort, Agua de Pau, 9560 Lagoa, São Miguel, Açores (tel. 096/932-40). The stone buttresses that lean against the balconied sides of this whitewashed hotel give it the look of a Mayan or Aztec temple. It's on the southern coast of the island, about 11 miles from the airport at Ponta Delgada. The establishment is as close to a full resort as anything you'll find on the island. It's set against a windbreak of grass and shrub-dotted hills, within view of the rocky coastline whose waters lap against tormented rocks. Swimming is possible from a natural swimming pool, a variety of sheltered coves, and the nearby beach at Baixa da Areia.

The comfortably contemporary rooms offer spacious sea-view terraces, good beds, and private bath, costing from 8,000$ ($52) daily in a single and from 9,000$ ($58.50) in a double. The hotel also offers car-rental facilities, an 80-seat panoramic restaurant with a view over the sea, and a bar. Menu specialties in the dining room include both international specialties and regional cookery. Meals cost from 2,000$ ($13).

ISLAND CHURCHES
At Vila França do Campo, capital of the island until 1546, the 15th-century **Parish Church of São Miguel** has a carved and gilded chancel and fine stoups in carved basalt. The campanile on the south side has a large decorated bell, the oldest on the island.

The **Chapel of Nossa Senhora da Paz** stands on a hill of the same name, to the north of Vila França. The steps up to this sanctuary of the Virgin Mary are built in an unusual design.

The town of Ribeira Grande has some interesting architecture in buildings of basalt with original windows and decorations. Its **Church of Nossa Senhora da Estrêla,** consecrated in 1517, contains a chapel decorated with pictures, and a Flemish triptych painted on wood. In the upper choir, see the glass case full of little rice flour and gum arabic figures depicting scenes from the Bible.

FESTIVALS
Religious celebrations play an important part in the lives of Açoreans.

The yearly festival honoring the image of **Senhor Santo Cristo,** the possession of the Church and Convent of Esperança in Ponta Delgada, takes place on the fifth Sunday after Easter with a procession through the streets of the capital, which have been carpeted with flowers, particularly azaleas. Lights in the buildings and trees, and carried by participants, make this a sparkling occasion, expressing the religious devotion of the people.

From April to June, the **Festival of the Holy Ghost,** one of the most traditional in the whole archipelago, is held. The celebrations at the village of Rabo de Peixe, on the north coast, are arguably the most colorful, with decorated carts and oxen.

An event on the first Sunday after Easter is the procession of **Senhor dos Enfermos** (Our Lord of the Sick). This is held at many places on São Miguel and other islands, but one of the most impressive observances is the one at Furnas.

As Cavalhadas is a colorful folk event taking place annually at Ribeira Seca (Ribeira Grande) in the north. On June 29, observed as a municipal holiday, the people go on pilgrimage honoring St. Peter, patron saint of the town.

Two other religious celebrations of importance take place on varying dates, which you can check when you arrive on the island. The **procession of St. Michael,** at Vila França do Campo on the south coast, is a curious relic of medieval society, with representations of the various categories of workers around their patron saints. Another celebration is that of **Os Romeiros** (the Pilgrims). Dating back to the 16th century, this event takes place during Lent. À vow is made by men, who go on foot around the island for eight days, praying at all the churches that have an altar to the Blessed Virgin.

SHOPPING

You should make at least one shopping expedition in Ponta Delgada, where you're likely to find bargains galore. You may want to browse through a basket bazaar, with not only a wide selection of baskets, but also wicker and willow chairs, handbags, even some articles made from the pith of a fig tree. Handcrafts produced on São Miguel are simple, made from the material at hand on the island. You'll see flowers fashioned from fish scales, feathers, paper, and cloth; hand-painted pottery; mats made of cornhusks; embroidered linen; hand-woven rugs and bedspreads.

Shops are open Monday to Friday from 9 a.m. to 12:30 p.m. and 2 to 6:30 p.m.

Casa Regional da Ilha Verde (the Regional House of the Green Island), 6 Rua do Aljube (tel. 237-00), is one of the island's better-stocked stores, specializing in embroidered goods. The lacy tablecloths, lace gloves, and bed linens are made in private homes by women throughout the Azores. Other types of goods are pottery, woodcarvings, and wickerware.

Capote e Capelo (named for the traditional form of dress from the 18th century), 20 Rua Dr. Gil Mont'alverne Sequeira (tel. 255-25), has a good selection of souvenir items, regional articles, embroidery, pottery, wickerwork, regional wines and liqueurs, and tobacco products, some from the island's own tobaccos.

Radiante has a variety of products in a number of shops, ranging from jewelry to ceramics to items of decorative arts. Ourivesaria Radiante, 46-48 Rua Machado Santos (tel. 242-74), offers gold, silver, jewelry, watches, and filigree work. The other four Radiante ships offer decorative arts items and artistic and regional ceramics. They are at 51 Rua Machado Santos (tel. 242-74), 27 Rua Manuel Inácio Correia (tel. 251-97), 3 Rua Bruno Tavares Carreiro (tel. 238-97), and 13 Rua São João (tel. 246-06).

Miranda & Ca., Lda., 57 Rua Machado Santos (tel. 263-98), has a good selection of gold, crystal, silver, watches, and other jewelry.

---

2. Santa Maria

Historians consider this little easternmost island of the Azores to be the first of the archipelago discovered by the Portuguese, sometime between 1427 and 1432. Santa Maria's settlement rapidly followed discovery, and the first municipality of the Azores was created here by 1472. In 1493, on the way home from the discovery of America, Columbus moored the *Niña* off Santa Maria to let some of his men go ashore near the village of Anjos to fulfill a vow made on the high seas that they would hear mass on the first land reached where there was a church dedicated to the Virgin Mary.

Santa Maria is unique in the archipelago in having fossils and other formations of sedimentary origin in its soil. Its countryside is varied, from a hilly section in the northeast to the flat portion in the south. The island is only 6 miles wide and 11 miles long, but it is fairly heavily populated. In the settlement period, people came mainly from the provinces of Alentejo and Beira in Portugal, and many of the customs of those regions persist, although time and distance have brought alterations.

Handcrafts of the island consist of articles made to fill everyday needs, including woolen and patchwork quilts and coverlets; linen cloth; work done in wood, leather, straw, and wicker; iron tools; and various kinds of decorative work. Interesting items of homespun clothing are sweaters of coarse wool, embroidered linen shirts, embroidered women's jackets, and suits of estamin. Folk music heard here had its origins on the mainland, although permutations are evident in the songs, dances, and musical instruments. The small, island-made guitars (*violas*) are prevalent.

The principal town of the island is **Vila do Porto,** which has two churches of interest. The **Parish Church,** built in the 19th century over a 15th-century ruin, has the Chapel of Santa Catarina, with a Manueline ceiling, as the sole remaining portion of the original structure. The **Convent of São Francisco** was founded in 1607 and destroyed by pirates nine years later. It was rebuilt in the 18th century and enlarged in the 19th. Of special interest are the chapels with fine reredos in carved work and valuable glazed tiles.

Anjos Chapel, on the north coast, is probably the oldest house of worship in the archipelago. It has work in precious whitewood, fine glazed tiles, and a remarkable 15th-century triptych.

In the village of **Santo Espírito** in the interior of the island is an **Ethnology Museum** housed in a rural building. Also in the village is the **Parish Church of Nossa Senhora da Purificação,** a 16th-century building with a baroque façade of island stone, added in the 18th century. Tradition says the church stands on the first spot where mass was celebrated in the Azores. In and around Santo Espírito, you pass some of the characteristic Azorean windmills with their white sails mellowed to a honey color, clacking in the Atlantic winds.

Other churches of interest are found throughout the little island, especially at Pedras de São Pedro, not far from Vila do Porto.

The highest point on the island, **Pico Alto,** about 1,950 feet above sea level, is a fine spot for a panoramic view of the island and the sea. The coastline is indented all around, with headlands and inlets providing sites for water sports.

Air transport to Santa Maria is provided by SATA (tel. 824-97). The huge, little-used airport near Vila do Porto (tel. 821-37) was built by the U.S. Air Force in 1944 and later accommodated international flights. These, however, have mostly been transferred to Terceira and São Miguel.

For information regarding boat travel to and from the island, get in touch with **Junta Autónoma do Porto de Ponta Delgada** in Vila do Porto (tel. 822-82).

FOOD AND LODGING

There's little to choose from. **Aeroporto Hotel,** Estrada do Aeroporto, 9580 Vila do Porto, Santa Maria, Açores (tel. 096/822-11), is barely adequate as a hotel, but on this island you take what's available. In the closing months of World War II, this site was an Officers Club for the American Air Base of Santa Maria. With the opening of the airport to international jet travel, it was remade into a hotel, rated second class by the government, to provide stopover accommodations, bungalow style.

The living room has fireplaces, a high beamed ceiling, and groups of furniture set for conversation and beverages. There's a bar and a spacious dining room in the Terminal Building providing a hearty and very simple Azorean cuisine. Geared to passengers making the transition between the Old and New Worlds, the Aeroporto Hotel contains 47 rooms with private bath. A double goes from 5,000$ ($32.50) to 6,000$ ($39) daily, and singles cost 5,000$ ($32.50) to 5,400$ ($35.10).

3. Terceira

The third-largest island in the Azores archipelago, and the third to be discovered in the 15th century, is fittingly named Terceira (pronounced Ter-*say*-ra), the Portuguese word for—you guessed it—third. Some 18 miles long and 11 miles wide, the island is the largest of the central group of the Azores, with development leading to a constantly increasing population. The presence here of an international airport, at Lajes, has contributed to the island's becoming more and more engaged in tourism as a major economic factor. An 18-hole golf course, bathing installations on beaches or at natural swimming pools, sea fishing and other water-oriented sports, football fields, cinemas, nightclubs, and "rope" and arena bullfights draw people to Terceira.

AROUND THE ISLAND

Behind the indented coastline is an area dotted with villages and divided into walled fields called *cerrados*. A few miles from the ocean, green pastures contrast with barren lava zones called *mistérios,* and peaks, lakes, and extinct craters attest to the volcanic origin of the Azores. Blossoming shrubs, including the ubiquitous hydrangea, soften the vistas, even in the lava regions of Pico da Bagacina and Pico do Cabrito, where wild cattle are bred. At Boscoitos, on the north coast, you can see unusual volcanic formations together with the noted vineyards in enclosures called *curraletas.*

The principal town of Terceira, **Angra** (now **Angra do Heroísmo),** was the first place in the Azores raised to the status of town, in 1534, the same year it was declared a bishopric by Pope Paul III. (The words "do Heroísmo" were added to honor the bravery of the people in an 1829 struggle that was won by the Royalists of Portugal.) The town was planned in the 16th century, but the outstanding houses were built in the 17th and 18th centuries. The oldest part of the town is considered a regional monument.

Built on the bay (*angra*), the town rises from its center up gentle hills. Damaged by an earthquake in 1980, it is recovering. From the harbor, if you walk along Rua de Lisboa, which runs to Praça da Restauração, you'll see the imposing **Town Hall.** The old white houses, in a style that is typical of Portuguese rural architecture, are distinguished from those on the mainland by the fact that they are required to have sash windows.

The **Castle of São João Baptista,** built by King Philip II of Spain at the time he was also King of Portugal, dominates the town at the foot of Monte Brasil. The main doorway with the royal arms above, an arched bridge, turrets, and a rich interior make this worth seeing. It served at one time as a prison for the notorious sadist, King Afonso VI, and other famous persons have also been incarcerated in it.

Museu de Angra do Heroísmo, Rua João Deus, is housed in the former Convento de São Francisco. It contains collections of weapons, coins and medals, furniture, paintings, musical instruments, ceramics, porcelain, and an interesting ethnology section. It is open Monday to Friday from 9 to 11:30 a.m. and 2 to 5:30 p.m.

Palácio Bettencourt, a 17th-century mansion, is now the home of the District Archives and the Public Library.

Churches of interest in Angra do Heroísmo are the cathedral from the 16th century, with a rich treasury; the Colégio Church (16th and 17th centuries), with its collection of Dutch glazed tiles; the Church of São Francisco where Vasco da Gama buried his brother, Paulo, who had died on a voyage to India; and the Church of São Gonçalo, with its gilt-edged triptych.

Festivals of Terceira are mainly religious, and of special note here is that those dedicated to the Holy Spirit, the most important, continue from Whitsuntide until the end of summer. During this time the residents of the villages contribute offerings that are placed in small, simple structures with elaborate façades, known as *impérios,* looking like little chapels by the roadside. The contributions are then handed out to needy passersby. The festivities end, especially in outlying areas, with rope bullfights in which the bull, held on a rope maneuvered by strong men, is challenged in a run down the village streets.

The largest caldeira in the Azores is on Terceira, **Caldeira de Guilherme Moniz,** with a nine-mile perimeter. In the interior of the island, **Algar do Carvão,** a number of underground grottoes, some more than 300 feet deep, contain striking stalagmites and stalactites.

TRANSPORTATION

Buses take visitors on excursions around the island, where sights at Vila Praia da Vitória, Biscoitos (mentioned above), and Santa Bárbara can be visited. **Empresa de Viação Terceirense, Lda.,** 15 Rua Dr. Sousa Meneses, in Angra do Heroísmo (tel. 095/241-01), arranges these trips.

Car-rental/taxi agencies servicing the island include **AcorAuto Rent-a-Car,** 27B Rua Gervasio Lima, Praia da Vitoria (tel. 095/523-73), where you can arrange to be picked up and delivered back to the Lajes airport.

Ilha 3, 22 Rua Direita (tel. 095/231-15), is another well-known car-rental concern. It requires a minimum rental of one day.

Airlines serving Terceira at the international airport in Lajes, about a 20-minute drive from Angra do Heroísmo, all have offices in the capital. **SATA** has facilities on Rua Dr. Eduardo de Abreu (tel. 095/220-31) in Angra do Heroísmo and at the Lajes airport (tel. 095/520-11).

TAP offices are at 25 Rua Rio de Janeiro (tel. 095/244-89) in Angra do Heroísmo, and at the Lajes airport (tel. 095/521-11).

Information regarding ships taking passengers to and from Terceira is available at **Junta Autónoma do Porto de Angra do Heroísmo,** 115 Rua Lisboa (tel. 01/222-81).

WHERE TO STAY AT ANGRA DO HERÍSMO

A modern hotel in the center of town, **Hotel de Angra,** Praça da Restauração, 9700 Angra do Heroísmo, Terceira, Açores (tel. 095/240-41), built in 1970, is a substantial establishment, set back from a pie-shaped plaza studded with trees. The hotel overlooks a semitropical garden, lying just minutes from the water and the Monte Brasil Park. Not overwhelming in any way, it still has its own dignity and style. The service is good. In all, it sleeps some 172 people in 86 rooms, each of which is well equipped with private bath, phone, and balcony. Singles rent for 7,000$ ($45.50) daily, and doubles cost 8,000$ ($52). The hotel also has a good restaurant with a regional menu, plus other specialties. Meals cost from 1,800$ ($11.70) and are served from noon to 2 p.m. and 7 to 9:30 p.m. The dining room has a panoramic view. In summer, you can overlook the action in the plaza below from an outdoor terrace.

Albergaría Cruzeiro, Praça Dr. Sousa Junior, 9700 Angra do Heroísmo, Terceira, Açores (tel. 095/240-71), in the heart of town, is a most recommendable place to stay if you appreciate up-to-date facilities. All rooms come with private bath, phone, and heating. Singles cost from 5,500$ ($35.75) daily, twins from 6,500$ ($42.25). A continental breakfast and taxes are included. You can also take half or full board. The hall contains wrought-iron furniture and green plants. In addition, there's a restaurant and bar.

Residencial Beira Mar, Esplanda (Rua de São João), 9700 Angra do Heroísmo, Terceira, Açores (tel. 095/251-88). This establishment is best known as a restaurant previewed below. But the staff will also rent you one of its 15 simple but cozy bedrooms upstairs. Each unit contains a private bath, mini-bar, TV, and phone. Depending on the season and the room's exposure, singles rent for 3,000$ ($19.25) to 4,000$ ($26) daily, doubles 4,000$ ($26) to 5,000$ ($32.50), with a continental breakfast included. The location, at the edge of the harbor in the center of the most atmospheric section of town, is ideal.

STAYING AT CABO DA PRAIA

In a setting of natural beauty, **Motel das Nove Ilhas,** Estrada Regional, Cabo da Praia, 9760 Praia da Vitória, Terceira, Açores (tel. 095/531-25), is a holiday house for those seeking a tranquil retreat. A member of the staff of the hotel meets guests at Lajes Airport and provides free transportation to the facilities of Nove Ilhas, about 3½ miles away.

In one of the Nine Islands apartments, clients are near the largest Azorean beach and only two miles from the historic town of Praia da Vitória. The Terceira Island Golf Course is 8½ miles away, and the city of Angra do Heroísmo is 11½ miles away. Each apartment has two bedrooms and a full bath, with tub and shower. A combined living and dining room comes with the apartment, as does an equipped kitchenette, with cutlery, silverware, and dishes. Linens are also provided. One person is charged 3,850$ ($25.05); two persons pay 5,500$ ($35.75); and three persons share a room for 6,300$ ($40.95).

On the precincts are a restaurant, a small market, plus facilities for dry cleaning and laundry. Babysitting can be arranged for parents wanting to be free to tour Terceira.

DINING AROUND THE ISLAND

Most of the restaurants are concentrated at Angra do Heroísmo. However, if you have a car, you can drive along the water and discover other choices.

In Angra do Heroísmo

The best choice is **Marcelino's,** 47 Rue São João (tel. 258-28), an air-conditioned steakhouse with good food and wine. It is widely acclaimed for its Azores beer. Meals, costing 2,000$ ($13) and up, are served daily except Thursday from 12:30 to 3:30 p.m. and 5:30 p.m. to midnight. The chef is adept at preparing meat in almost any style, ranging from pepper steak to Stroganoff. The filet mignon is exceptional, but the chateaubriand (served for two) is perhaps the finest I've had in Portugal. It's especially popular with Americans living on the island. You can also order fish and shellfish dishes. The restaurant is in a second-floor room with a beamed ceiling and heavy pine furniture. There's a bar on the ground level.

Adega Lusitânia, 63 Rua de São Pedro (tel. 223-01), is the place to go if you're seeking some of the best of the regional cuisine of the island. The restaurant is housed in a two-story island villa, with a wrought-iron balcony. It lies about a ten-minute walk from the center. If you're there in hot weather, you can also enjoy some of the best shellfish served on the island. The service is willing and informal. Meals, costing from 1,800$ ($11.70), are served daily except Monday from noon to 3 p.m. and 6 to 10 p.m.

Restaurant Beira Mar, Esplanada (Rua de São João; tel. 251-88), is a lovely restaurant set within a severely dignified villa near the water's edge in the center of town. Large and airy, and staffed with a uniformed battalion of polite waiters, it is ringed with blue and yellow tiles and patronized by colonies of Portuguese families. It's open daily except Monday from noon to 3 p.m. and 6:30 to 10 p.m. Full meals cost from 1,500$ ($9.75) and include a solid array of regional dishes such as hunter's steak and local octopus, along with fresh spider crab and grilled squid. Fresh fish is also available, and international favorites include American-style fried chicken and chateaubriand.

Confiança, 102 Rua Santo Espírito (tel. 232-87), is a place where you can eat informally and inexpensively, paying 1,500$ ($9.75) and up for a good meal served daily from 11 a.m. to 9:30 p.m. Despite the less-than-prepossessing appearance, this restaurant is worthy. This restaurant looks like a narrow storefront from the outside, but inside it is sheathed in tiles. It is very Portuguese in tone, with lots of dark wood. The location is on a side street, a short walk from the Praça Velha. You can enjoy such dishes as caldo verde to begin, followed by fried rabbit, pork Confiança, or grilled red mullet.

Outside Town

Some other good restaurants are found at Praia da Vitória south of the airport, if you like dining with a view of the water and the beach.

Locals tell me that **Churrasqueira Praiense,** Rua Alfândega (tel. 521-59), is the best for fresh shellfish in the summer months. It's popular with U.S. service personnel. Out in the middle of the ocean you expect good fish, and you are served it here. The chef prepares it well, and the portions are large. Meals, costing from 2,000$ ($13), are served daily except Wednesday from 11:30 a.m. to 2:30 p.m. and 5:30 to 9:30 p.m.

There's another good restaurant in the area, **Girassol,** Cabo da Praia (tel. 533-56), which offers a good menu and some fine wine. It's best enjoyed in the summer months because of its esplanade. Meals cost from 2,000$ ($13) and are served daily from noon to 3 p.m. and 5:30 to 11 p.m. Stick to the simplest items, such as fish, and you should find everything pleasing. Service is casual.

---

4. Graciosa

The island acclaimed by its name as "gracious," Graciosa is also known as Ilha Branca (White Island) because of some of its place-names—Pedras Brancas, Sêrra Branca, and Barro Branco. With its low elevation (highest point is Pico Timão at 1,320 feet), this may also be seen as a white island because of surging sea foam and white sandy beaches, which are the backdrop for the white houses that prevail.

The least humid of the Azores, Graciosa occupies a ten- by four-mile chunk of land, northernmost in the central group of the archipelago. The landscape differs from that of most of the other islands, with waving fields of wheat, vineyards, and windmills flapping in the breezes, but there are also volcanic formations worth seeing.

Furna do Enxofre, also called Furna da Caldeira, in the southwest is a lake of warm sulfur water reached by a tunnel between steep rocks. The lake is best seen between 11 a.m. and 2 p.m. when the sun penetrates the narrow mouth at the surface so that you can view the tunnel interior and the lake 330 feet below.

A few miles farther southwest is **Termas do Carapacho,** a spa known for its medicinal waters.

The island's main town is **Santa Cruz da Graciosa,** where you can visit the **Parish Church,** built in the 16th century, with three fine rose windows. See the five 16th-century paintings on wood depicting scenes from the Gospels.

An **Ethnological Museum** displays material on local life, especially the tradition of wine-growing.

Pottery, including bowls, teapots, and mugs, is produced on the island, as are musical instruments. The regional *violas* (small guitars) of Praia, Santa Cruz, and Farol da Ponta da Barca are among island specialties.

SATA provides air service to Graciosa. Offices are at Largo Cons. Jacinto Cândido (tel. 095/724-56) and at the airport (tel. 095/724-58).

WHERE TO STAY

The place to stay on the island is the unassuming three-story hostelry, **Residencial Santa Cruz,** Largo Barão Guadalupe, 9880 Santa Cruz, Graciosa, Açores (tel. 095/723-45). You get good rooms that are clean and well kept, as well as a pleasant reception. Each of the simple rooms contains a bath and a phone. A single costs from 2,500$ ($19.25) daily, and a double goes for 3,800$ ($24.70), with a continental breakfast included. You get a strong dose of local flavor here. The hotel stands in the northeastern corner of the island, the arrival point for most visitors.

5. São Jorge

The long, skinny island of São Jorge—32 miles long by less than 5 miles wide—lies some 40 miles south of Graciosa in the central group of the Azores. Along its length is a range of minor mountains, the highest peak of which is Pico da Esperança, about 3,500 feet above sea level. The plateau of the uplands is used for pastures, and the lower levels are planted in vegetables, vineyards, and orchards. São Jorge is noted for its dairy products; its cheese is internationally known.

The first settlement on the island was at Topo, on the far-southeastern tip, but today the main town is **Vila das Velas,** which is graced by a Parish Church built in 1460, under terms of the will of Prince Henry the Navigator. Its architecture is interesting, as is the fine carved work of its chapels. The Town Hall in Velas was built in the 17th century.

Besides its cheese, São Jorge is known also for the regional coverlets produced as a cottage industry by many of the women of the island, as well as multicolored rugs woven on primitive looms.

Transportation to and from São Jorge is possible by both boat and plane. For information on sea-going service, get in touch with the **Junta Autónoma dos Portos** in Velas (tel. 423-60) and in Calheta (tel. 461-42). In summer, ferryboat service is possible daily, although transportation is curtailed in winter.

Air service is provided by **SATA,** Rua de Santo André, in Velas. Call either the office (tel. 221-45) or the airport (tel. 224-35).

FOOD AND LODGING

In the town of Velas, a suitable bet is **Residencial Neto,** Rua Dr. José Pereira, 9800 Velhas, São Jorge, Açores (tel. 092/424-03). One of the main attractions of this well-maintained inn is its swimming pool, reserved for the use of guests. Each of its spacious and comfortable rooms contains a private bath, as well as a phone, radio, and TV with video. Doubles rent for 3,800$ ($24.70) daily, and singles cost 2,800$ ($18.20), with a continental breakfast and free transportation to and from the airport included. The owners can direct visitors to producers of the world-famous cheese of the island.

Restaurants tend to be very simple on the island, and also very cheap.

One of the best is **Restaurant Velense,** Rua Dr. José Pereira (tel. 421-60), in Velas. You get hearty, well-flavored dishes here, including roast octopus, "kid stew," and fresh clams. Portions are generous, and meals cost from 1,800$ ($11.70). Open daily from 11 a.m. to 10 p.m.

Another possibility is **Restaurante Solmar,** Rua Alm. Cândido Reis (tel. 424-67), which, as its name suggests, specializes in fresh fish. Again, regional cookery is the feature, and it's politely served along with good Portuguese wines—all for a cost of around 1,800$ ($11.70) for a satisfying meal. Hours are daily from 11 a.m. to 2 p.m. and 7 to 11 p.m.

6. Pico

No island of the Azores shows more clearly the volcanic origin of the archipelago than Pico, the Portuguese word for peak, given to the island because of the impressive mountain rising from it to 7,750 feet above sea level. The cloud-shrouded peak, Pico Grande, often snow-capped in winter, can be climbed, but the journey is arduous and only to be made by the stout-hearted and strong-limbed, and with a guide.

The island, today measuring about 29 miles in length and 9 miles in width, and lying 4½ miles from Faial and 11 miles from São Jorge, was rocked by volcanic eruptions in the 18th century. These gave rise to strange stretches of black lava formations, which are known locally as *mistérios*. They provide interesting sights today. Villages are built of the lava material, and the soil with volcanic ash is excellent for the vineyards from which comes much good Azores wine.

Also growing on the island are fruit trees, local cedar, local laurel, and a wealth of flowers. Development of more rugged zones for pastureland bordered by trees has created a delightful countryside with a variety of fauna. Preservation of the natural resources of the island is undertaken through establishment of the Nature Reserve of Pico Island.

Many churches and chapels are scattered throughout the island, ranging from the simple to the grand, and there are also old manor houses, dating from the 17th and 18th centuries, made of basalt with noteworthy ashlar work. A number of religious festivals are held, one of the most interesting being the **Festa dos Baleeiros** (Whalers' Festival), which takes place on the last Sunday in August and is attended by large crowds of islanders and visitors.

Pico produces some of the finest sailors of Portugal. The capital, **Lajes do Pico,** was known as a whaling capital, and the town commemorates it in a **Whalers' Museum** (Museu dos Baleeiros), in the former Casa dos Botes, Rua Capitão-mor Garcia Gonçalves Madruga. Here a unique collection of whalebone and cachalot ivory has been gathered together, along with the various utensils and equipment used in whaling, a whaling boat, and the first motorboat used in this activity. Logbooks of past whaling expeditions have been acquired for the museum.

Near the capital is one of the most interesting of the island's natural formations, the **Furna da Malha,** a 1½-mile natural tunnel formed by sea and volcano action.

In the western coast not far from the little town of Madalena is **Furna de Frei Matias,** one of the most famous caves on the island.

Madalena is the most progressive town on the island, from the modern point of view. Here you can rent a car or take a taxi to explore the surroundings.

SATA provides air service to Madalena. It has offices at Rua Doctor Maria da Gloria Duarte (tel. 924-11) and at the airport (tel. 924-13).

WHERE TO STAY IN MADALENA

A helpful staff welcomes you to **Residencial Pico,** 9950 Madalena, Pico, Açores (tel. 092/922-92). The hotel has 31 simple rooms, each with private bath, TV with video, and phone. Singles staying at this three-star establishment pay 5,500$ ($35.75) daily, with doubles going for 7,000$ ($45.50). A continental breakfast is included in the rates.

The hotel also operates one of the best restaurants on Pico, serving regional specialties. In summer fresh shellfish is abundantly featured, with meals costing 1,800$ ($11.70) and up. Hours are daily from noon to 2:30 p.m. and 7 to 9 p.m. It is closed on Sunday off-season.

FOOD AND LODGING IN LAJES PICO

At the Azores Whaling Center, **Residencial Açor,** 5 Rua D. João Paulino, 9930 Lajes Pico, Pico, Açores (tel. 092/974-38), with views of both sea and mountains from its rooms, offers peace and proximity to the island's nostalgia-laden neighborhoods. The rooms, each with private bath, balcony, and direct-dial phone, are comfortably furnished and reasonably priced: from 2,400$ ($15.60) daily in a single, rising to 2,800$ ($18.20) in a double, with a continental breakfast included.

Restaurante Lagoa (tel. 672-72) is one of the best places to eat on the island, especially in hot weather when you can enjoy the esplanade and the chef's prize collection of shellfish dishes, which he often prepares with savory sauces. Meals cost from 1,800$ ($11.70) and are served daily from noon to 3 p.m. and 6 to 10 p.m. The restaurant is closed on Saturday in winter. All year round good regional cookery, backed up by Portuguese wines, is served to as many as 90 diners.

7. Faial

Shaped roughly like a pentagon, Faial is the most westerly of the central group of islands in the archipelago, and because of its active port, Horta, perhaps the most visited in its group. Faial has had a place in the history of the Azores since its discovery in the middle of the 15th century and its colonization, principally by Flemish people, soon after. Its capital, Horta, was named for the Flemish nobleman, Josse de Hurtere (or Huerta), who led the settlement of the island.

Faial is a place of restful valleys, verdant fields, hydrangea-hedged hillsides; gorgeous camellias are found in the Flemish Valley. Faial and Pico are the chief tourist islands of the Horta district. Many water sports are offered here, including big-game fishing, sailing, rowing, scuba-diving, and windsurfing, as well as swimming. There are also tennis and hiking, in case you're not sea oriented. The island measures about 9 miles across and 13 miles long, so that most of its attractions can be reached easily by walking or short drives. Because of the many hydrangea hedges, Faial is sometimes called the Blue Island.

Horta is attractive, with graceful buildings and a port that draws ships and yachts of many nations, even though it has lost some of its prestige as a naval base attained during World War I and World War II. It was also the center for transatlantic air transport in earlier days when planes crossing the ocean had to have a refueling site.

The port, besides its hustle and bustle as a safe harbor, marina, and fishing scene, has a curious show of fascinating graffiti—the wall of the dock carries hundreds of signatures, dedications, and paintings inscribed here by sailors who have passed through over the years.

Horta has many monuments and churches of interest, as well as museums, which include **Museu da Horta** (Horta Museum), Palácio do Colégio, Largo Duque d'Avila e Bolamo (tel. 233-48), and **Museu de Arte Sacra** (Museum of Sacred Art), at the Church of São Francisco, Rua Consolação Medeiros, remarkable for its collection of religious art as well as work in figwood.

Fort of Santa Cruz dates from the 16th century and has seen history in the making, including attacks by Spanish and British troops, as well as being involved in the Portuguese civil war.

Interesting religious houses include the 17th-century **Parish Church of São Salvador,** with its chapel of São Paulo, known for its two panels of tiles. The **Convent of São Francisco,** built in 1696 on the site of an older structure, has gilt carved work and paintings, but it is probably known for the walls of the chancel lined with azulejos.

In 1957 major volcanic eruptions rocked the northwest coast of the island. **Ponta dos Capelinhos** draws many visitors who come to see the effects of that eruption from the island's westernmost point. The volcano is now classed as dormant, having last acted up in 1973. You can also make an excursion to the **center of the island,** where a volcanic crater is covered inside with vegetation and contains a lake, Cabeço Gordo. This is the highest spot on the island, providing views of Pico and the neighboring islands.

Handcrafts of Faial include embroidery, lace, work in tulle embroidered with straw, wickerwork, and work in figwood.

A major event of the island is **Sea Week,** which starts on the first Sunday in

August. It includes all activities connected with the sea as well as cultural events, and is becoming of international importance.

For car rentals and taxi service at Horta, get in touch with **Auto Turística Faialense,** 1 Caminho do Meio, Praia do Almoxarife (tel. 227-03).

Both **SATA** and **TAP** (Air Portugal) provide air service. The **airport** at Castelo Branco, west of Horta, Aeroportus e Navegação Aérea-ANA E.P., can be reached by phoning 230-81. SATA has offices at Rua Serpa Pinto in Horta (tel. 239-13), and at the airport (tel. 221-11). TAP's office is at 1 Rampa de São Francisco (tel. 226-65).

Information on ships is available from **Junta Autónomo do Porto da Horta,** at the Horta dock (tel. 234-53).

WHERE TO STAY

A five-minute walk from the port, the **Hotel Faial,** Rua Consul Dabney, Angustias, 9900 Horta, Faial, Açores (tel. 092/221-81), is a four-star, first-class hotel, consisting of six buildings like a village in a park. It was originally built as headquarters by Western Union, housing crews working on the laying of the transatlantic cable. The situation is tranquil, as the Fayal is surrounded by gardens offering views onto the sea. The establishment is the major social center for Horta.

The bedrooms are simple but well styled, with modern furnishings. All the units have private bath, TV, and direct-dial phone, and many open onto views of the bay and the inner harbor. Doubles cost 8,500$ ($55.25) daily, and singles rent for 7,500$ ($48.75), with a continental breakfast included in all tariffs. The food, served in a panoramic restaurant overlooking the port, is typical of the region but also has a selection of international dishes. The menu changes daily, with meals costing from 1,800$ ($11.70) if you order the set dinner. Food is served daily from 12:30 to 2 p.m. and 7:30 to 10 p.m. The hotel has a swimming pool, two tennis courts, a disco, a beauty center, and a gift shop.

Estalagem de Santa Cruz, Castelo do Santa Cruz, Rua Vasco da Gama, 9900 Horta, Faial, Açores (tel. 092/226-64). Rated four stars, this inn was built into the foundation of a 16th-century fort at the edge of the harbor overlooking the Marina. Most of what a visitor will see, except for the stone crenellations separating the newest section from the salt-sprayed rocks, is a comfortably contemporary 25-room hotel. The bedrooms usually open through sliding glass doors onto spacious verandas, often shaded from the sun with awnings. Each unit has a well-upholstered set of furniture, with a few wicker pieces thrown in and contains a private bath as well. Singles cost from 7,000$ ($45.50) daily, and doubles go for 8,500$ ($55.25), with a continental breakfast included. There's a small but well-maintained garden on the premises, as well as a bar, a dining room, and a fireplace. Meals, costing from 1,900$ ($12.35), are served daily from 12:30 to 2:30 p.m. and 7:30 to 9:30 p.m. The dining room is severely dignified in the Iberian tradition, with straight-back chairs, white walls, and a big-windowed view of the "fortified" terrace and the sea.

One of the least expensive places to stay on the island is **Pensão-Residencial São Francisco,** 13 Rua Conselheiro Medeiros, Matriz, 9900 Faial, Açores (tel. 092/228-37), a three-star hotel, offering about 30 bedrooms in unpretentiously simple comfort. The management is helpful, and will often give you suggestions about what to see on their island. Singles cost from 3,000$ ($19.50) to 3,500$ ($22.75) daily, while doubles go for 4,200$ ($27.30) to 4,800$ ($31.20), including a continental breakfast.

FOOD AND DRINK

The best place to eat is the **Club Naval de Horta** (tel. 223-31), at the Castelo de Santa Cruz, near the Estalagem de Santa Cruz. It sits in unpretentious simplicity on a stone wharf at the base of the imposing bulk of the former fortress. There's a cramped but convivial one-story building lined with scarred wooden tables, but many guests prefer the shadow of a gnarled plane tree growing stubbornly from the starlit terrace. The best dishes here emerge from the fiery depths of an outdoor grill, whose iron chains and blackened air vents resemble a medieval forge. The Portuguese-English team who run this place offer the best culinary theater in town daily except Monday from 12:30 to 2:30 p.m. and 7 to 9:30 p.m. Even the raw cloves of garlic are chopped on the top of a cross-section of an enormous tree trunk, whose end grains are scrubbed and sanded down at the end of a cooking day. Full meals, which you are likely to consume elbow to elbow with the owners of some of Europe's most glamorous yachts, cost from 1,500$ ($9.75). Specialties include grilled tuna steak, wild rabbit pie, Portuguese-style pork, pot roast, and grilled quail.

Restaurant O Lima, 9 Rua Serpa Pinto (tel. 223-87). Its focus of attention might be on the blaring TV set, but the decor is utterly simple and clean. Still, a drink or a meal here will give you a chance not only to order regional food but to look at local life. The stand-up bar is open daily from 7 a.m. to midnight, and you can eat during those hours. Full meals cost from 1,500$ ($9.75) and might include roast chicken, regional preparations of beef, roast veal, and generous chunks of the deliciously salty island cheddar cheese.

Peter's Café Sport, Rua Tenente Valadim (tel. 223-27). On rainy weekends, it seems as if half the population of the island jams itself between the paneled walls of this watering spot. It's without parallel as the place on the island for yacht owners to mingle with local residents. Scrimshaw is sold from display cases in the walls, and an official-looking exchange office operates out of one of the corners. Naturally, the bar does a brisk business in liquor, snack food, and sandwiches. Famous in yachting circles on either side of the Atlantic, this raffishly unpretentious rendezvous is the domain of José (Peter) Azevedo, a Portuguese-born mariner who worked for many years in the British navy. Unfailingly polite and gentlemanly, Senhor Azevedo has created a legend for himself because of his efforts at keeping visiting sailors and their entourages afloat.

The café opens daily in the early morning, for coffee, eggs, and bacon, but closes its doors from 1 to 4 p.m. The place then reopens, doing a thriving business until at least midnight. Upstairs is a scrimshaw museum. Senhor Azevedo has been collecting the intricately carved pieces of whalebone and walrus tusk for more than 50 years. Today the extraordinary collection comprises more than 2,500 pieces, making it the largest museum of its kind in the world. Pieces range from the religious (you'll see lots of crucifixes) to the profane, but each reflects the hours of isolated tedium of 19th and 20th century sailors far from home with time and a penknife in their hands. The entrance cost is 100$ (65¢), and hours are daily from 9 a.m. to 6 p.m. except for a three-hour break at 1 p.m. Look for the intricately detailed view of the island of Pico as seen from the shoreline of 19th-century Faial, carved into a five-foot section of whale jawbone.

---

8. Flores

The westernmost island of the Azores, and of Europe, is Ilha das Flores, or Island of Flowers, the most beautiful of the archipelago. It has been described as a garden floating on the foam of the sea. Flores and its sister island, Corvo, were the last of the Azores to be discovered by the Portuguese, being claimed for the country in 1452. Early colonization efforts failed, and it was not until 1528 that permanent settlers moved in, many from provinces in the north of Portugal. Fishing is the economic mainstay here.

The island has great natural beauty, with long, dense clumps of hydrangeas climbing over the hills and deep valleys and surrounding the lakes, rocks with grottoes, peaks, and caldeiras, the remains of former volcanoes.

The **grotto at Enxaréus,** between Santa Cruz das Flores, the main village of the island, and **Caveira,** a short distance south along the coast road, is one of the major attractions of Flores. The coast is indented, and the cliffs are spectacular. Waterfalls cascade into the sea at Vale da Fajãzinha, and stone formations, produced by erosion, dot the land. There are seven lakes in the center of the island. The most beautiful, **Lagoa Funda,** is surrounded by sand and sheltered by mountains, with clumps of hydrangeas burgeoning everywhere.

There are a number of churches on Flores, some containing interesting carved work. At **Santa Cruz,** an ethnological museum displays collections of local handcrafts, particularly in ivory objects and lacework. The crafts also include items made of wicker, raffia, seashells, and wood, as well as weaving and work in rushes, based on patterns from the west coast of Africa.

The **Church of São Pedro** in Santa Cruz, built in the 16th century and reno-vated in the 18th, has a notable high altar in carved, gilded, and painted work.

In the parish of Fajãzinha, on the western coast of the island, **Nossa Senhora dos Remédios** is a large house of worship with three naves and an interesting chan-cel. It was built in the late 18th century.

Transportation by air and by boat to and from Flores is possible. The airport at Santa Cruz, **Aeroportos e Navegação Aérea-ANA E.P.** (tel. 092/222-80), ac-commodates small planes. The airline servicing the island is **SATA,** 5 Rua Senador André Freitas (tel. 092/224-25).

FOOD AND LODGING ON FLORES

If you're heading for Flores, you can stay at **Residencia Vila Flores,** Rua Senador Andre Freitas, 9970 Santa Cruz, Flores, Açores (tel. 092/521-90). It is modern, cozy, and unpretentious. There are 38 beds in 17 reasonably comfortable rooms. The building is well insulated against Atlantic gales. Singles pay from 2,500$ ($16.25) nightly, with doubles costing 3,200$ ($20.80). There is a good restaurant one flight above street level.

CORVO

The little sister of Flores, lying about 15 miles to the northeast of the larger of the westernmost part of the archipelago, is Corvo. It got its name from the writings of a Spanish friar who called it "Isla de los Cuervos Marinos," or Island of the Sea Crows. This tiny spot of land, about eight square miles, in the vastness of the Atlan-tic, is rugged, with volcanic peaks and rocks serving as reminders of its origins.

The one village on the island, **Vila Nova do Corvo,** consists of cottages all built in the same style, with whitewashed walls and red tile roofs, laid out in little streets known as *canadas.* From the town, you can see Flores in the distance. Its facilities are very basic and not necessarily recommendable. Hence, it is visited by only the most adventurous of tourists.

A GRAB BAG OF CHARTS

1. MENU TRANSLATIONS
2. A CAPSULE VOCABULARY
3. CURRENCY EXCHANGE

French is still traditionally spoken by guides in provincial museums, but English is increasing in popularity, and is now taught in most schools.

Usually in Lisbon, Estoril, Cascais, Madeira, and on the major coastal resorts of the Algarve, you'll have no problem if you speak only English. However, if you venture inland—to towns of the Alentejo, for example—you may find a few words in the Capsule Vocabulary helpful.

Likewise, menus tend to be bewildering, especially when a chef has named a bean and tripe dish after his favorite aunt. Nevertheless, a basic knowledge of the main dishes in the Portuguese cuisine is essential, especially if you're planning to stay at second-class hotels or eat at local taverns where there's nobody around to translate for you.

1. Menu Translations

SOUPS (SOPAS)

caldo verde potato and cabbage
canja de galinha chicken soup
creme de camarão cream of shrimp
creme de legumes cream of vegetable

sopa à Alentejano Alentejo soup
sopa de cebola onion
sopa de mariscos shellfish
sopa de queijo cheese
sopa de tomate tomato

EGGS (OVOS)

com presunto with ham
cozidos hard boiled
escalfados poached
estrelados fried

mexicos scrambled
omeleta omelet
quentes soft boiled
tortilha Spanish omelet

FISH (PEIXE)

ameijoas clams
atum tuna
bacalhau salted codfish
cherne turbot
camarãos shrimps
eiró eel
lagosta lobster
linguado sole
lulas squid

ostras oysters
peixe espada swordfish
percebes barnacles
pescada hake
robalo bass
salmonete red mullet
santola crab
sardinhas sardines ⌐

SPECIALTIES (ESPECIALIDADES)

bife na frigideira steak with
   mustard sauce
caldeirada fishermen's stew
cozido à portuguêsa Portuguese
   stew

porco Alentejano pork in
   a sauce of tomatoes
   and clams

MEAT (CARNE)

bife steak
borrego lamb
cabrito kid
carneiro mutton
coelho rabbit ⌐
costeletas chops
dobrada tripe
iscas liver

lingua tongue
porco pork
presunto ham
rim kidney
salchichas sausages
vaca beef
vitela veal

POULTRY (AVES)

borracho pigeon
frango chicken
galinha fowl
ganso goose

pato duck
perdiz partridge
peru turkey

VEGETABLES (LEGUMES)

aipo celery
alcachôfra artichoke
arroz rice
azeitonas olives
batatas potatoes
berinjela eggplant
beterrabas beets
cebola onion
feijão bean
nabo turnip

cenouras carrots
cogumelo mushroom
couve-flor cauliflower
couve cabbage
ervilhas peas
espargos asparagus ⌐
espinafres spinach ⌐
favas broad beans
pepino cucumber
tomate tomato

SALAD (SALADA)

agriãos watercress
alface lettuce
salada mista mixed salad

salada verde green salad
Russa Russian

DESSERTS (SOBREMESA)

arroz doce rice pudding —
bolo cake
gelados diversos mixed ice creams
maçã assada baked apple
pastelaria pastry

pêssego Melba peach Melba
pudim flan egg custard
pudim de pão bread pudding
salada de frutas fruit salad
sorvetes sherbets
queijo cheese

FRUITS (FRUTAS)

abacate avocado
alperches apricots
ameixa plum
ananas pineapple
cerajas cherries
figos figs
framboesa raspberry
laranjas oranges
limão lemon
maçãs apples

melancia watermelon
melão melon
morangos strawberries
peras pears
pêssegos peaches
roma pomegranate
tâmara date
toronja grapefruit
uvas grapes

BEVERAGES (BEBIDAS)

água water
água mineral mineral water
café coffee
chá tea
cerveja beer
com gelo with ice
laranjada orangeade

leite milk
sumo de fruta fruit juice
sumo de laranja orange juice
sumo de tomate tomato juice
vinho branco white wine
vinho tinto red wine

CONDIMENTS (CONDIMENTOS)

açúcar sugar
alho garlic
azeite olive oil
caril curry
manteiga butter

mostarda mustard
compota jam
pimenta pepper
sal salt
vinagre vinegar

MISCELLANEOUS

chocolate chocolate
biscoito cracker
gelo ice

gelado ice cream
pão bread
pão torrado toast

COOKING TERMS

assado no forno baked
cozido boiled
estufada braised

frito fried
mal passado rare
bem passado well done

2. A Capsule Vocabulary

Pronounced

Hello	**olá**	oh-lah
How are you?	**como está?**	como esh-tah
Very well	**muito bem**	muy-toh bym
Thank you	**muito obrigado**	muy-toh obree-gah-do
Good-bye	**adeus**	adeush
Please	**faça favor**	fassa fah-vohr
Yes	**sim**	seem
No	**não**	naion
Excuse me	**desculpe-me**	dash-culpa-meh
Give me	**dê-me**	deh-meh
Where is?	**onde fica?**	ondeh feecah
the station	**a estação**	o aish-tassaion
a hotel	**um hotel**	oom hotel
a restaurant	**um restaurante**	om rash-tauranteh
the toilet	**a casa de banho**	ah cahzah de bahnhoo
To the right	**à direita**	aah deeraitah
To the left	**à esquerda**	aah ash-kerdah
Straight ahead	**em frente**	ym fraintah
I would like—	**gostaria de**	goosh-tareeah de
to eat	**comer**	coh-mere
a room	**um quarto**	oom quarr-toh
How much is it?	**quanto custa**	quahnto coosh-tah
The check, please	**à conta se faz, favor**	ah cohnta sa fahsh, fah-vohr
When	**quando**	quandoh
Yesterday	**ontem**	ohntym
Today	**hoje**	hoyhje
Tomorrow	**amanha**	ahmain-hayh
Breakfast	**pequeno almoço**	paikainoh aahlmohssoh
Lunch	**almoço**	aahlmohssoh
Dinner	**jantar**	jain-taah

1	**um** (oom)	14	**catorze** (cahtohrzeh)	40	**quarenta** (quaraintah)
2	**dois** (doysh)	15	**quinze** (keenzeh)	50	**cinquenta** (sseenquaintah)
3	**três** (traishe)	16	**dezasseis** (dehzaissaish)	60	**sessenta** (ssaissaihntah)
4	**quatro** (quaahtroh)	17	**dezassete** (dehrzassaihteh)	70	**setenta** (ssaitaintah)
5	**cinco** (sseencoh)	18	**dezóito** (dehzoytoh)	80	**oitenta** (oyhtaintah)
6	**seis** (ssaish)	19	**dezanove** (dehzanohveh)	90	**noventa** (nohvaintah)
7	**sete** (ssaiteh)	20	**vinte** (veenteh)	100	**cem** (sym)
8	**oito** (oytoh)	30	**trinta** (treehntah)		
9	**nove** (nohveh)				
10	**dez** (daish)				
11	**onze** (onzeh)				
12	**doze** (doze)				
13	**treze** (traihzeh)				

3. Currency Exchange

Escudos	Dollars	Escudos	Dollars
2$	$.01	100$	$ .65
5	.03	150	.98
6	.04	200	1.30
10	.07	300	1.95
15	.10	400	2.60
20	.13	500	3.25
25	.16	600	3.90
30	.20	700	4.55
35	.23	800	5.20
40	.26	900	5.85
45	.29	1,000	6.50
50	.33	2,000	13.00
60	.39	3,000	19.50
75	.49	4,000	26.00

INDEX

Common terms such as **"Church," "Plaza,"** and **"Museum"** (and their Portuguese equivalents) have been transposed if they occur at the beginning of a name. To find such a place or attraction, look under the next significant word (e.g., **"Praça do Comércio"** can be found under **"Comércio, Praça do")**. Attractions named for individuals can be found under the individual's surname.

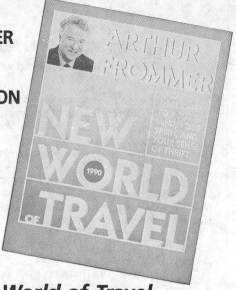

NOW, SAVE MONEY ON ALL YOUR TRAVELS!
Join Frommer's™ Dollarwise® Travel Club

Saving money while traveling is never a simple matter, which is why, over 29 years ago, the **Dollarwise Travel Club** was formed. Actually, the idea came from readers of the Frommer publications who felt that such an organization could bring financial benefits, continuing travel information, and a sense of community to value-conscious travelers all over the world.

In keeping with the money-saving concept, the annual membership fee is low—$18 (U.S. residents) or $20 U.S. (Canadian, Mexican, and other foreign residents)—and is immediately exceeded by the value of your benefits which include:

1. The latest edition of any TWO of the books listed on the following pages.
2. A copy of any one Frommer City Guide.
3. An annual subscription to an 8-page quarterly newspaper, *The Dollarwise Traveler,* which keeps you up-to-date on fast-breaking developments in good-value travel in all parts of the world—bringing you the kind of information you'd have to pay over $35 a year to obtain elsewhere. This consumer-conscious publication also includes the following columns:
   Hospitality Exchange—members all over the world who are willing to provide hospitality to other members as they pass through their home cities.
   Share-a-Trip—requests from members for travel companions who can share costs and help avoid the burdensome single supplement.
   Readers Ask . . . Readers Reply—travel questions from members to which other members reply with authentic firsthand information.
4. Your personal membership card, which entitles you to purchase through the club all Frommer publications for a third to a half off their regular retail prices during the term of your membership.

So why not join this hardy band of international Dollarwise travelers now and participate in its exchange of information and hospitality? Simply send $18 (U.S. residents) or $20 U.S. (Canadian, Mexican, and other foreign residents) along with your name and address to: Frommer's Dollarwise Travel Club, Inc., 15 Columbus Circle, New York, NY 10023. Remember to specify which *two* of the books in section (1) and which *one* in section (2) above you wish to receive in your initial package of member's benefits. Or tear out the next page, check off your choices, and send the page to us with your membership fee.